VINTAGE SPORTS CO

HERITAGE SIGNATURE SPORTS AUCTION

DALLAS, TEXAS | MAY 2-3, 2008 *Featuring: The Stan Finney Collection*

LOT VIEWING

3500 Maple Avenue, 17th Floor
Dallas, Texas 75219
800.872.6467

Thursday, May 1 • 9:00 AM – 5:00 PM CT
Friday, May 2 • 9:00 AM – 5:00 PM CT
by appointment only

FAX BIDDING

Deadline: Friday, May 2 by 12:00 Noon CT
Fax: 214.409.1425

ABSENTEE INTERNET BIDDING

HA.com/Sports • Bid@HA.com
Initial bidding closes at 9:00 PM CT on May 2 for Session I (#9709)
Internet bids close at 10:00 PM CT on May 2 for Session II (#709)

LIVE TELEPHONE BIDDING

Must be arranged before Friday, May 2 by 12:00 Noon CT
Client Service: 866.835.3243

BID LIVE during the Auction on HeritageLive HA.com/Live

AUCTION SESSIONS

3500 Maple Avenue, 17th Floor
Dallas, Texas 75219

Session I: Lots 19001 – 19306
(Mail, Fax, Internet & Phone Extended Bid only) *
Auction #9709
Friday, May 2 • 9:00 PM CT

Session II: Lots 19307 – 19884
(Live Floor, Phone, Mail, Fax, Internet, HeritageLive.com)
Auction #709
Saturday, May 3 • 12:00 Noon CT

Lots are sold at an approximate rate of 100 lots per hour, but it is not uncommon to sell 80-120 lots in any given hour This auction is subject to a 19.5% Buyer's Premium.

LOT PICK UP

Available immediately following Session II
or weekdays 9AM – 5PM, by appointment only.
Contact Client Service at 866.835.3243

AUCTIONEERS

Samuel Foose 11727; Robert Korver 13754; Scott Peterson 13256; Bob Merrill 13408; John Petty 13740; Mike Sadler 16129; Ed Griffith 16343; Andrea Voss 16406; Jacob Walker 16413; Charlie Mead 16418; Eric Thomas 16421.

AUCTION RESULTS

Immediately available at HA.com/Sports

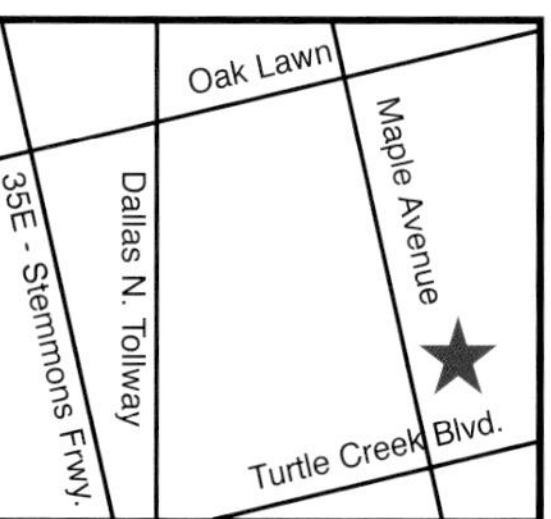

HERITAGE HA.com
Auction Galleries

3500 Maple Avenue, 17th Floor
Dallas, Texas 75219
214.528.3500 • 800.872.6467
214.409.1425 (fax)

irect Client Service Line: Toll-Free 866.835.3243
iew lots online at HA.com/Sports

ıis auction is presented and catalogued by Heritage Auctions, INC.

*This session is presented via catalog and online. Bidding is taken by phone or through our website. There are three phases of bidding during this type of auction:

1) Normal bidding: Bids are taken up until 9 PM CT the night the auction closes.
2) Extended Bidding: On a lot-by-lot basis, individuals that bid on any lots during Normal Bidding may continue to bid on those lots during the next two hours (9 to 11 PM CT).
3) 30 Minute Ending: On a lot-by-lot basis, starting at 11:00 PM CT, any person who has bid on the lot previously may continue to bid on that lot until there are no more bids for 30 minutes.

For example, if you bid on a lot during Normal Bidding, you could participate during Extended Bidding for that lot, but not on lots you did not bid on previously. If a bid was placed at 11:15, the new end time for that lot would become 11:45. If no other bids were placed before 11:45, the lot would close. If you are the high bidder on a lot, changing your bid will not extend the bidding during the 30 Minute Ending phase (only a bid from another bidder will extend bidding).

Cataloged and coordinated by: Stephen Carlisle, Nicholas Hernandez, Lee Iskowitz, Chris Ivy, Mike Provenzale, Jonathan Scheier

Production and Design by: Lisa Fox, Mary Hermann, Kelley Norwine, Michael Puttonen

Catalog and Internet Imaging by: Nick Brotherton, Maribel Cazares, Beatriz Faustino, Andrew Fitzpatrick, Donald Fuller, Kevin Gaddis, Steve Garcia, Patric Glenn, Courts Griner, Haley Hagen, Lindsey Johnson, Lori Mckay, Matt Roppolo, Audra Stroud, Brandon Wade

Operations Support by: James Jackson, Chris Gonzales, Michael Wilson

14719

Steve Ivy
CEO
Co-Chairman
of the Board

Jim Halperin
Co-Chairman
of the Board

Greg Rohan
President

Paul Minshull
Chief Operating Officer

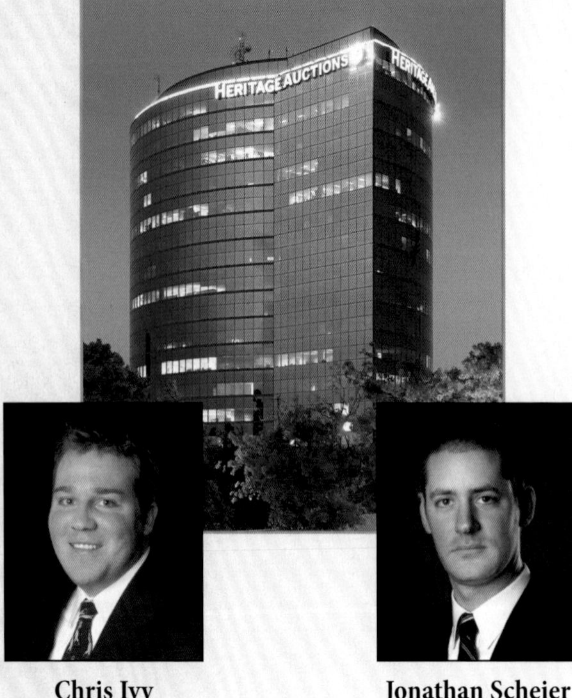

Chris Ivy
Director of
Sports Auctions

Jonathan Scheier
Consignment
Director

Phillip Aman
Consignment
Director

Stephen Carlisle
Consignment
Director

Mike Gutierrez
Consignment
Director

Mark Jordan
Consignment
Director

HERITAGE HA.com
Auction Galleries

3500 Maple Avenue, 17th Floor
Dallas, Texas 75219
214.528.3500 • 800.872.6467 • 214.409.1425 (fax)

Dear Fellow Sports Collector,

It is my great pleasure to welcome the Heritage collecting community to the May 2008 Signature Sports Auction, presented upon the pages that follow. It's hard to believe it's already been six months since our last auction catalog went to print, and now here we are again. The St. Louis Cardinals Hall of Famer Rogers Hornsby once said, "People ask me what I do in winter when there's no baseball. I'll tell you what I do. I stare out the window and wait for spring." It's much the same for us here in Heritage Sports. While the process of building an auction is far more challenging and work-intensive than Hornsby's winters once were, the greatest thrill is seeing the hundreds of pieces within the auction find new homes, and the excitement the pieces bring to those within the Heritage collecting family. It's like Opening Day for the Heritage staff.

And there's plenty to be excited about in the pages that follow, far too much to enumerate in an introductory letter. This auction features what is unquestionably our greatest offering of trading cards to date, highlighted by "The Big Three" rarities of the fabled T206 tobacco card set. Honus Wagner, Eddie Plank and the Sherry Magee error card are each here, establishing this as one of the few auctions in history to feature the trio. The 1869 Peck & Snyder Cincinnati Reds trade card widely considered to be the very first baseball card ever produced, is likewise to be found within, as is the "Arkansas Find" of Mint PM1 pins, each of the nine examples ranking as the finest known in the hobby. Those concentrating on the bubble gum era will find a wide array of high-grade Topps and Bowman sets too.

The memorabilia portion of the auction may be our most balanced to date, with exceptional offerings in game used material and autographs from baseball, football, basketball, hockey and golf. Incredible rookie jerseys, each believed to be the only surviving examples, introduced Hall of Famers "Pistol Pete" Maravich and Albert "Red" Schoendienst to the professional ranks. An incredible 1958 Duke Snider jersey may have been the first worn as a Los Angeles Dodger. Other Hall of Fame gamers once were owned and operated by the likes of Willie Mays, Freddie Lindstrom, Gordie Howe, Bob Gibson, Jim Taylor and Michael Jordan.

Early Philadelphia Athletics star T. Frederick "Topsy" Hartsel provides some fireworks of his own, with his 1910 World Series trophy and game worn jersey consigned to the auction by his family. Another exciting personal collection, likewise making its hobby debut in the pages to follow, is a selection of early Joe Montana material consigned by his first wife Kim. It includes the Hall of Fame quarterback's signed letter of intent to attend Notre Dame, high school game worn artifacts, and handwritten letters discussing everything from their young love to the first days of Notre Dame football practice.

Two incredible collections of autographs represent a significant percentage of those enshrined at Cooperstown, one in government postcard format, and the other comprised of black & white and gold Hall of Fame plaques. The offerings span the spectrum from fan favorites like Ruth and Gehrig to intense rarities like Jesse Burkett and Roderick Wallace. But perhaps the most significant autographed piece in the hobby comes from the pen of the heroic Jackie Robinson, whose perfect blue ink signature closes a letter sent to Giants owner Horace Stoneham announcing his retirement from the game he so fundamentally changed.

Of course, this only scratches the surface of what will surely be remembered as one of the finest auctions of 2008. A large portion of this auction's top trading card offerings derive from the personal collection of Stan Finney, to whom we would like to take this opportunity to offer our most sincere gratitude. Mr. Finney began collecting Topps baseball cards at the age of eight, idolizing Yankees legend Mickey Mantle. As an adult, he was fortunate enough to become a friend of Mantle's, often playing rounds of golf with him at Preston Trails Golf Club, and continuing to collect cards picturing his golfing buddy. I hope that you will enjoy exploring the treasures featured on the pages to follow, and I expect you will find plenty worthy of addition to your personal collection. As always, I close with a note of gratitude to the consignors who have made this auction so unique and intriguing, and to the bidders who will become the proud new owners. Thank you for putting your trust in us, and helping to make Heritage the World's Largest Collectibles Auctioneer.

Sincerely,

Chris Ivy
Director of Sports Auctions

TERMS AND CONDITIONS OF AUCTION

Auctioneer and Auction:

1. This Auction is presented by Heritage Auction Galleries, a d/b/a/ of Heritage Auctions, Inc., or their affiliates Heritage Numismatic Auctions, Inc., or Heritage Vintage Sports Auctions Inc., or Currency Auctions of America, Inc., as identified with the applicable licensing information on the title page of the catalog or on the HA.com Internet site (the "Auctioneer"). The Auction is conducted under these Terms and Conditions of Auction and applicable state and local law. Announcements and corrections from the podium and those made through the Terms and Conditions of Auctions appearing on the Internet at HA.com supersede those in the printed catalog.

Buyer's Premium:

2. On bids placed through Heritage, a Buyer's Premium of fifteen percent (15%) will be added to the successful hammer price bid on lots in Coin and Currency auctions, or nineteen and one-half percent (19.5%) on lots in all other auctions. If your bid is placed through eBay Live, a Buyer's Premium equal to the normal Buyer's Premium plus an additional five percent (5%) of the hammer price will be added to the successful bid up to a maximum Buyer's Premium of Twenty Two and one-half percent (22.5%). There is a minimum Buyer's Premium of $9.00 per lot. In Gallery Auctions (sealed bid auctions of mostly bulk numismatic material), the Buyer's Premium is 19.5%.

Auction Venues:

3. The following Auctions are conducted solely on the Internet: Heritage Weekly Internet Coin, Currency, Comics, and Vintage Movie Poster Auctions; Heritage Monthly Internet Sports and Marketplace Auctions; Final Sessions. Signature Auctions and Grand Format Auctions accept bids on the Internet first, followed by a floor bidding session; bids may be placed prior to the floor bidding session by Internet, telephone, fax, or mail. Heritage Live and eBay Live provide real time bidding options to registered clients.

Bidders:

4. Any person participating or registering for the Auction agrees to be bound by and accepts these Terms and Conditions of Auction ("Bidder(s)").
5. All Bidders must meet Auctioneer's qualifications to bid. Any Bidder who is not a client in good standing of the Auctioneer may be disqualified at Auctioneer's sole option and will not be awarded lots. Such determination may be made by Auctioneer in its sole and unlimited discretion, at any time prior to, during, or even after the close of the Auction. Auctioneer reserves the right to exclude any person it deems in its sole opinion is disruptive to the Auction or is otherwise commercially unsuitable.
6. If an entity places a bid, then the person executing the bid on behalf of the entity agrees to personally guarantee payment for any successful bid.

Credit:

7. Bidders who have not established credit with the Auctioneer must either furnish satisfactory credit information (including two collectibles-related business references) well in advance of the Auction or supply valid credit card information. Bids placed through our Interactive Internet program will only be accepted from pre-registered Bidders; Bidders who are not members of HA.com or affiliates should pre-register at least two business days before the first session to allow adequate time to contact references. Additionally Bidders who have not previously established credit or who wish to bid in excess of their established credit history may be required to provide their social security number or the last four digits thereof to us so a credit check may be performed prior to Auctioneer's acceptance of a bid.

Bidding Options:

8. Bids in Signature Auctions or Grand Format Auctions may be placed as set forth in the printed catalog section entitled "Choose your bidding method." For auctions held solely on the Internet, see the alternatives on HA.com. Review at HA.com/common/howtobid.php.
9. Presentment of Bids: Non-Internet bids (including but not limited to podium, fax, phone and mail bids) are treated similar to floor bids in that they must be on-increment or at a half increment (called a cut bid). Any podium, fax, phone, or mail bids that do not conform to a full or half increment will be rounded up or down to the nearest full or half increment and this revised amount will be considered your high bid.
10. Auctioneer's Execution of Certain Bids. Auctioneer cannot be responsible for your errors in bidding, so carefully check that every bid is entered correctly. When identical mail or FAX bids are submitted, preference is given to the first received. To ensure the greatest accuracy, your written bids should be entered on the standard printed bid sheet and be received at Auctioneer's place of business at least two business days before the Auction start. Auctioneer is not responsible for executing mail bids or FAX bids received on or after the day the first lot is sold, nor Internet bids submitted after the published closing time; nor is Auctioneer responsible for proper execution of bids submitted by telephone, mail, FAX, e-mail, Internet, or in person once the Auction begins. Internet bids may not be withdrawn until your written request is received and acknowledged by Auctioneer (FAX: 214-4438425); such requests must state the reason, and may constitute grounds for withdrawal of bidding privileges. Lots won by mail Bidders will not be delivered at the Auction unless prearranged.
11. Caveat as to Bid Increments. Bid increments (over the current bid level) determine the lowest amount you may bid on a particular lot. Bids greater than one increment over the current bid can be any whole dollar amount. It is possible under several circumstances for winning bids to be between increments, sometimes only $1 above the previous increment. Please see: "How can I lose by less than an increment?" on our website.

The following chart governs current bidding increments.

Current Bid	Bid Increment
<$10	$1
$10 - $29	$2
$30 - $49	$3
$50 - $99	$5
$100 - $199	$10
$200 - $299	$20
$300 - $499	$25
$500 - $999	$50
$1,000 - $1,999	$100
$2,000 - $2,999	$200
$3,000 - $4,999	$250
$5,000 - $9,999	$500
$10,000 - $19,999	$1,000

Current Bid	Bid Increment
$20,000 - $29,999	$2,000
$30,000 - $49,999	$2,500
$50,000 - $99,999	$5,000
$100,000 - $199,999	$10,000
$200,000 - $299,999	$20,000
$300,000 - $499,999	$25,000
$500,000 - $999,999	$50,000
$1,000,000 - $1,999,999	$100,000
$2,000,000 - $2,999,999	$200,000
$3,000,000 - $4,999,999	$250,000
$5,000,000 - $9,999,999	$500,000
>$10,000,000	$1,000,000

12. If Auctioneer calls for a full increment, a floor/phone bidder may request Auctioneer to accept a bid at half of the increment ("Cut Bid") which will be that bidders final bid; if the Auctioneer solicits bids other the expected increment, they will not be considered Cut Bids, and bidders accepting such increments may continue to participate.

Conducting the Auction:

13. Notice of the consignor's liberty to place bids on his lots in the Auction is hereby made in accordance with Article 2 of the Texas Uniform Commercial Code. A "Minimum Bid" is an amount below which the lot will not sell. THE CONSIGNOR OF PROPERTY MAY PLACE WRITTEN "Minimum Bids" ON HIS LOTS IN ADVANCE OF THE AUCTION; ON SUCH LOTS, IF THE HAMMER PRICE DOES NOT MEET THE "Minimum Bid", THE CONSIGNOR MAY PAY A REDUCED COMMISSION ON THOSE LOTS. "Minimum Bids" are generally posted online several days prior to the Auction closing. For any successful bid placed by a consignor on his Property on the Auction floor, or by any means during the live session, or after the "Minimum Bid" for an Auction have been posted, we will require the consignor to pay full Buyer's Premium and Seller's Commissions on such lot.
14. The highest qualified Bidder recognized by the Auctioneer shall be the buyer. In the event of any dispute between any Bidders at an Auction, Auctioneer may at his sole discretion reoffer the lot. Auctioneer's decision and declaration of the winning Bidder shall be final and binding upon all Bidders. Bids properly offered, whether by floor Bidder or other means of bidding, may on occasion be missed or go unrecognized; in such cases, the Auctioneer may declare the recognized bid accepted as the winning bid, regardless of whether a competing bid may have been higher.
15. Auctioneer reserves the right to refuse to honor any bid or to limit the amount of any bid which, in his sole discretion, is not submitted in "Good Faith," or is not supported by satisfactory credit, collectibles references, or otherwise. A bid is considered not made in "Good Faith" when an insolvent or irresponsible person, or a person under the age of eighteen makes it. Regardless of the disclosure of his identity, any bid by a consignor or his agent on a lot consigned by him is deemed to be made in "Good Faith." Any person apparently appearing on the OFAC list is not eligible to bid.
16. Nominal Bids. The Auctioneer in its sole discretion may reject nominal bids, small opening bids, or very nominal advances. If a lot bearing estimates fails to open for 40 –60% of the low estimate, the Auctioneer may pass the item or may place a protective bid on behalf of the consignor.
17. Lots bearing bidding estimates shall open at Auctioneer's discretion (approximately 50% of the low estimate). In the event that no bid meets or exceeds that opening amount, the lot shall pass as unsold.
18. All items are to be purchased per lot as numerically indicated and no lots will be broken. Bids will be accepted in whole dollar amounts only. No "buy" or "unlimited" bids will be accepted. Off-increment bids may be accepted by the Auctioneer at Signature Auctions and Grand Format Auctions. Auctioneer reserves the right to withdraw, prior to the close, any lots from the Auction.
19. Auctioneer reserves the right to rescind the sale in the event of nonpayment, breach of a warranty, disputed ownership, auctioneer's clerical error or omission in exercising bids and reserves, or otherwise. In cases of nonpayment, Auctioneer's election to void a sale does not relieve the Bidder from their obligation to pay Auctioneer its fees (seller's and buyer's premium) and any other damages or expenses pertaining to the lot.
20. Auctioneer occasionally experiences Internet and/or Server service outages during which Bidders cannot participate or place bids. If such outage occurs, we may at our discretion extend bidding for the auction. This policy applies only to widespread outages and not to isolated problems that occur in various parts of the country from time to time. Auctioneer periodically schedules system downtime for maintenance and other purposes, which may be covered by the Outage Policy. Bidders unable to place their Bids through the Internet are directed to bid through Client Services at 1-800-872-6467.
21. The Auctioneer or its affiliates may consign items to be sold in the Auction, and may bid on those lots or any other lots. Auctioneer or affiliates expressly reserve the right to modify any such bids at any time prior to the hammer based upon data made known to the Auctioneer or its affiliates. The Auctioneer may extend advances, guarantees, or loans to certain consignors, and may extend financing or other credits at varying rates to certain Bidders in the auction.
22. The Auctioneer has the right to sell certain unsold items after the close of the Auction. Such lots shall be considered sold during the Auction and all these Terms and Conditions shall apply to such sales including but not limited to the Buyer's Premium, return rights, and disclaimers.

Payment:

23. All sales are strictly for cash in United States dollars. Cash includes: U.S. currency, bank wire, cashier checks, travelers checks, eChecks, and bank money orders, all subject to reporting requirements. Checks may be subject to clearing before delivery of the purchases. Heritage reserves the right to determine if a check constitutes "good funds" when drawn on a U.S. bank for ten days, and thirty days when drawn on an international bank. Credit Card (Visa or Master Card only) and PayPal payments may be accepted up to $10,000 from non-dealers at the sole discretion of the auctioneer, subject to the following limitations: a) sales are only to the cardholder, b) purchases are shipped to the cardholder's registered and verified address, c) Auctioneer may pre-approve the cardholder's credit line, d) a credit card transaction may not be used in conjunction with any other financing or extended terms offered by the Auctioneer, and must transact immediately upon invoice presentation, e) rights of return are governed by these Terms and Conditions, which supersede those conditions promulgated by the card issuer, f) floor Bidders must present their card.
24. Payment is due upon closing of the Auction session, or upon presentment of an invoice. Auctioneer reserves the right to void an invoice if payment in full is not received within 7 days after the close of the Auction. In cases of nonpayment, Auctioneer's election to void a sale does not relieve the Bidder from their obligation to pay Auctioneer its fees (seller's and buyer's premium) on the lot and any other damages pertaining to the lot.
25. Lots delivered in the States of Texas, California, or other states where the Auction may be held, are subject to all applicable state and local taxes, unless appropriate permits are on file with us. Bidder agrees to pay Auctioneer the actual amount of tax due in the event that sales tax is not properly collected due to: 1) an expired, inaccurate, inappropriate tax certificate or declaration, 2) an incorrect interpretation of the applicable statute, 3) or any other reason. The appropriate form or certificate must be on file at and verified by Heritage five days prior to Auction or tax must be paid; only if such form or certificate is received by Heritage within 4 days of the Auction can a tax refund be made. Lots from different Auctions may not be aggregated for sales tax purposes.
26. In the event that a Bidder's payment is dishonored upon presentment(s), Bidder shall pay the maximum statutory processing fee set by applicable state law. If you attempt to pay via eCheck and your financial institution denies this transfer from your bank account, or the payment cannot be completed using the selected funding source, you agree to complete payment using your credit card on file.
27. If any Auction invoice submitted by Auctioneer is not paid in full when due, the unpaid balance will bear interest at the highest rate permitted by law from the date of invoice until paid. If the Auctioneer refers any invoice to an attorney for collection, the buyer agrees to pay attorney's fees, court costs, and other collection costs incurred by Auctioneer. If Auctioneer assigns collection to its in-house legal staff, such attorney's time expended on the matter shall be compensated at a rate comparable to the hourly rate of independent attorneys.

28. In the event a successful Bidder fails to pay all amounts due, Auctioneer reserves the right to resell the merchandise, and such Bidder agrees to pay for the reasonable costs of resale, including a 10% seller's commission, and also to pay any difference between the resale price and the price of the previously successful bid. Auctioneer may sell the merchandise to an under Bidder or at private sale and in such case the Bidder shall be responsible for any deficiency between the original and subsequent sale.
29. Auctioneer reserves the right to require payment in full in good funds before delivery of the merchandise.
30. Auctioneer shall have a lien against the merchandise purchased by the buyer to secure payment of the Auction invoice. Auctioneer is further granted a lien and the right to retain possession of any other property of the buyer then held by the Auctioneer or its affiliates to secure payment of any Auction invoice or any other amounts due the Auctioneer or affiliates from the buyer. With respect to these lien rights, Auctioneer shall have all the rights of a secured creditor under Article 9 of the Texas Uniform Commercial Code, including but not limited to the right of sale. In addition, with respect to payment of the Auction invoice(s), the buyer waives any and all rights of offset he might otherwise have against the Auctioneer and the consignor of the merchandise included on the invoice. If a Bidder owes Auctioneer or its affiliates on any account, Auctioneer and its affiliates shall have the right to offset such unpaid account by any credit balance due Bidder, and it may secure by possessory lien any unpaid amount by any of the Bidder's property in their possession.
31. Title shall not pass to the successful Bidder until all invoices are paid in full. It is the responsibility of the buyer to provide adequate insurance coverage for the items once they have been delivered.

Delivery; Shipping; and Handling Charges:

32. Shipping and handling charges will be added to invoices. Please refer to Auctioneer's website www.HA.com/common/shipping.php for the latest charges or call Auctioneer. Auctioneer is unable to combine purchases from other auctions or affiliates into one package for shipping purposes. Lots won will be shipped in a commercially reasonable time after payment in good funds for the merchandise and the shipping fees is received or credit extended, except when third-party shipment occurs.
33. Successful international Bidders shall provide written shipping instructions, including specified customs declarations, to the Auctioneer for any lots to be delivered outside of the United States. NOTE: Declaration value shall be the item'(s) hammer price together with its buyer's premium and Auctioneer shall use the correct harmonized code for the lot. Domestic Buyers on lots designated for third-party shipment must designate the common carrier, accept risk of loss, and prepay shipping costs.
34. All shipping charges will be borne by the successful Bidder. Any risk of loss during shipment will be borne by the buyer following Auctioneer's delivery to the designated common carrier or third-party shipper, regardless of domestic or foreign shipment.
35. Due to the nature of some items sold, it shall be the responsibility for the successful Bidder to arrange pick-up and shipping through third-parties; as to such items Auctioneer shall have no liability. Failure to pick-up or arrange shipping in a timely fashion (within ten days) shall subject Lots to storage and moving charges, including a $100 administration fee plus $10 daily storage. In the event the Lot is not removed within ninety days, the Lot may be offered for sale to recover any past due storage or moving fees, including a 10% Seller's Fee.
36. The laws of various countries regulate the import or export of certain plant and animal properties, including (but not limited to) items made of (or including) ivory, whalebone, turtleshell, coral, crocodile, or other wildlife. Transport of such lots may require special licenses for export, import, or both. Bidder is responsible for: 1) obtaining all information on such restricted items for both export and import; 2) obtaining all such licenses and/or permits. Delay or failure to obtain any such license or permit does not relieve the buyer of timely compliance with standard payment terms. For further information, please contact Bill Taylor at 800-872-6467 ext. 1280.
37. Any request for shipping verification for undelivered packages must be made within 30 days of shipment by Auctioneer.

Cataloging, Warranties and Disclaimers:

38. NO WARRANTY, WHETHER EXPRESSED OR IMPLIED, IS MADE WITH RESPECT TO ANY DESCRIPTION CONTAINED IN THIS AUCTION OR ANY SECOND OPINE. Any description of the items or second opine contained in this Auction is for the sole purpose of identifying the items for those Bidders who do not have the opportunity to view the lots prior to bidding, and no description of items has been made part of the basis of the bargain or has created any express warranty that the goods would conform to any description made by Auctioneer. Color variations can be expected in any electronic or printed imaging, and are not grounds for the return of any lot.
39. Auctioneer is selling only such right or title to the items being sold as Auctioneer may have by virtue of consignment agreements on the date of auction and disclaims any warranty of title to the Property. Auctioneer disclaims any warranty of merchantability or fitness for any particular purposes. All images, descriptions, sales data, and archival records are the exclusive property of Auctioneer, and may be used by Auctioneer for advertising, promotion, archival records, and any other uses deemed appropriate.
40. Translations of foreign language documents may be provided as a convenience to interested parties. Heritage makes no representation as to the accuracy of those translations and will not be held responsible for errors in bidding arising from inaccuracies in translation.
41. Auctioneer disclaims all liability for damages, consequential or otherwise, arising out of or in connection with the sale of any Property by Auctioneer to Bidder. No third party may rely on any benefit of these Terms and Conditions and any rights, if any, established hereunder are personal to the Bidder and may not be assigned. Any statement made by the Auctioneer is an opinion and does not constitute a warranty or representation. No employee of Auctioneer may alter these Terms and Conditions, and, unless signed by a principal of Auctioneer, any such alteration is null and void.
42. Auctioneer shall not be liable for breakage of glass or damage to frames (patent or latent); such defects, in any event, shall not be a basis for any claim for return or reduction in purchase price.

Release:

43. In consideration of participation in the Auction and the placing of a bid, Bidder expressly releases Auctioneer, its officers, directors and employees, its affiliates, and its outside experts that provide second opines, from any and all claims, cause of action, chose of action, whether at law or equity or any arbitration or mediation rights existing under the rules of any professional society or affiliation based upon the assigned description, or a derivative theory, breach of warranty express or implied, representation or other matter set forth within these Terms and Conditions of Auction or otherwise. In the event of a claim, Bidder agrees that such rights and privileges conferred therein are strictly construed as specifically declared herein; e.g., authenticity, typographical error, etc. and are the exclusive remedy. Bidder, by non-compliance to these express terms of a granted remedy, shall waive any claim against Auctioneer.
44. Notice: Some Property sold by Auctioneer are inherently dangerous e.g. firearms, cannons, and small items that may be swallowed or ingested or may have latent defects all of which may cause harm to a person. Purchaser accepts all risk of loss or damage from its purchase of these items and Auctioneer disclaims any liability whether under contract or tort for damages and losses, direct or inconsequential, and expressly disclaims any warranty as to safety or usage of any lot sold.

Dispute Resolution and Arbitration Provision:

45. By placing a bid or otherwise participating in the auction, Bidder accepts these Terms and Conditions of Auction, and specifically agrees to the alternative dispute resolution provided herein. Arbitration replaces the right to go to court, including the right to a jury trial.
46. Auctioneer in no event shall be responsible for consequential damages, incidental damages, compensatory damages, or other damages arising from the auction of any lot. In the event that Auctioneer cannot deliver the lot or subsequently it is established that the lot lacks title, or other transfer or condition issue is claimed, Auctioneer's liability shall be limited to rescission of sale and refund of purchase price; in no case shall Auctioneer's maximum liability exceed the high bid on that lot, which bid shall be deemed for all purposes the value of the lot. After one year has elapsed, Auctioneer's maximum liability shall be limited to any commissions and fees Auctioneer earned on that lot.
47. In the event of an attribution error, Auctioneer may at its sole discretion, correct the error on the Internet, or, if discovered at a later date, to refund the buyer's purchase price without further obligation.
48. Arbitration Clause: All controversies or claims under this Agreement or arising from or pertaining to: this Agreement or related documents, or to the Properties consigned hereunder, or the enforcement or interpretation hereof of this or any related agreements, or damage to Properties, payment, or any other matter, or because of an alleged breach, default or misrepresentation under the provisions hereof or otherwise, that cannot be settled amicably within one (1) month from the date of notification of either party to the other of such dispute or question, which notice shall specify the details of such dispute or question, shall be settled by final and binding arbitration by one arbitrator appointed by the American Arbitration Association ("AAA"). The arbitration shall be conducted in Dallas, Dallas County, Texas in accordance with the then existing Commercial Arbitration Rules of the AAA. The arbitration shall be brought within two (2) years of the alleged breach, default or misrepresentation or the claim is waived. The prevailing party (a party that is awarded substantial and material relief on its claim or defense) may be awarded its reasonable attorney's fees and costs. Judgment upon the award rendered by the arbitrator may be entered in any court having jurisdiction thereof; provided, however, that the law applicable to any controversy shall be the law of the State of Texas, regardless of its or any other jurisdiction's choice of law principles and under the provisions of the Federal Arbitration Act.
49. No claims of any kind can be considered after the settlements have been made with the consignors. Any dispute after the settlement date is strictly between the Bidder and consignor without involvement or responsibility of the Auctioneer.
50. In consideration of their participation in or application for the Auction, a person or entity (whether the successful Bidder, a Bidder, a purchaser and/or other Auction participant or registrant) agrees that all disputes in any way relating to, arising under, connected with, or incidental to these Terms and Conditions and purchases, or default in payment thereof, shall be arbitrated pursuant to the arbitration provision. In the event that any matter including actions to compel arbitration, construe the agreement, actions in aid or arbitration or otherwise needs to be litigated, such litigation shall be exclusively in the Courts of the State of Texas, in Dallas County, Texas, and if necessary the corresponding appellate courts. The successful Bidder, purchaser, or Auction participant also expressly submits himself to the personal jurisdiction of the State of Texas.
51. These Terms & Conditions provide specific remedies for occurrences in the auction and delivery process. Where such remedies are afforded, they shall be interpreted strictly. Bidder agrees that any claim shall utilize such remedies; Bidder making a claim in excess of those remedies provided in these Terms and Conditions agrees that in no case whatsoever shall Auctioneer's maximum liability exceed the high bid on that lot, which bid shall be deemed for all purposes the value of the lot.

Miscellaneous:

52. Agreements between Bidders and consignors to effectuate a non-sale of an item at Auction, inhibit bidding on a consigned item to enter into a private sale agreement for said item, or to utilize the Auctioneer's Auction to obtain sales for non-selling consigned items subsequent to the Auction, are strictly prohibited. If a subsequent sale of a previously consigned item occurs in violation of this provision, Auctioneer reserves the right to charge Bidder the applicable Buyer's Premium and consignor a Seller's Commission as determined for each auction venue and by the terms of the seller's agreement.
53. Acceptance of these Terms and Conditions qualifies Bidder as a Heritage customer who has consented to be contacted by Heritage in the future. In conformity with "do-not-call" regulations promulgated by the Federal or State regulatory agencies, participation by the Bidder is affirmative consent to being contacted at the phone number shown in his application and this consent shall remain in effect until it is revoked in writing. Heritage may from time to time contact Bidder concerning sale, purchase, and auction opportunities available through Heritage and its affiliates and subsidiaries.
54. Rules of Construction: Auctioneer presents properties in a number of collectible fields. As such, specific venues have promulgated supplemental Terms and Conditions for that venue. Nothing herein shall be construed to waive the general Terms and Conditions of Auction by these additional rules and shall be construed to give force and effect to the rules in their entirety.

State Notices:

Notice as to an Auction in California. Auctioneer has in compliance with Title 2.95 of the California Civil Code as amended October 11, 1993 Sec. 1812.600, posted with the California Secretary of State its bonds for it and its employees, and the auction is being conducted in compliance with Sec. 2338 of the Commercial Code and Sec. 535 of the Penal Code.

Notice as to an Auction in New York City. These Terms and Conditions are designed to conform to the applicable sections of the New York City Department of Consumer Affairs Rules and Regulations as Amended. This is a Public Auction Sale conducted by Auctioneer. The New York City licensed Auctioneers are Kathleen Guzman, No.0762165, and Samuel W. Foose, No.0952360, who will conduct the Auction on behalf of Heritage Auctions, Inc. ("Auctioneer"). All lots are subject to: the consignor's right to bid thereon in accord with these Terms and Conditions of Auction, consignor's option to receive advances on their consignments, and Auctioneer, in its sole discretion, may offer limited extended financing to registered bidders, in accord with Auctioneer's internal credit standards. A registered bidder may inquire whether a lot is subject to an advance or reserve. Auctioneer has made advances to various consignors in this sale.

Notice as to an Auction in Texas. In compliance with TDLR rule 67.100(c)(1), notice is hereby provided that this auction is covered by a Recovery Fund administered by the Texas Department of Licensing and Regulation, P.O. Box 12157, Austin, Texas 78711 (512) 463-6599. Any complaints may be directed to the same address.

Additional Terms & Conditions:
SPORTS COLLECTIBLES AUCTIONS

SPORTS COLLECTIBLES TERM A: Signature Auctions are not on approval. No certified material may be returned because of possible differences of opinion with respect to the grade offered by any third-party organization, dealer, or service. No guarantee of grade is offered for uncertified Property sold and subsequently submitted to a third-party grading service. There are absolutely no exceptions to this policy. Under extremely limited circumstances, (e.g. gross cataloging error) a purchaser, who did not bid from the floor, may request Auctioneer to evaluate voiding a sale; such request must be made in writing detailing the alleged gross error, and submission of the lot to the Auctioneer must be pre-approved by the Auctioneer; A bidder must notify the appropriate department head (check the inside front cover of the catalog or our website for a listing of department heads) in writing of such request within three (3) days of the mail bidder's receipt of the lot. Any lot that is to be evaluated must be in our offices within 30 days after Auction. Grading does not qualify for this evaluation process nor do such complaints constitute a basis to challenge the authenticity of a lot. AFTER THAT 30-DAY PERIOD, NO LOTS MAY BE RETURNED FOR REASONS OTHER THAN AUTHENTICITY. Lots returned must be housed intact in the original holder. No lots purchased by floor Bidders may be returned (including those Bidders acting as agents for others). Late remittance for purchases may be considered just cause to revoke all return privileges.

SPORTS COLLECTIBLES TERM B: Auctions conducted solely on the Internet THREE (3) DAY RETURN POLICY. All lots paid for within seven days of the Internet-only Auction closing are sold with a three (3) day return privilege. You may return lots under the following conditions: Within three days of receipt of the lot, you must first notify Auctioneer by contacting Client Service by phone (1-800-872-6467) or e-mail (Bid@HA.com), and immediately mail the lot(s) fully insured to the attention of Returns, Heritage, 3500 Maple Avenue, 17th Floor, Dallas TX 75219-3941. Lots must be housed intact in their original holder and condition. You are responsible for the insured, safe delivery of any lots. A non-negotiable return fee of 5% of the purchase price ($10 per lot minimum) will be deducted from the refund for each returned lot or billed directly. Postage and handling fees are not refunded. After the three-day period (from receipt), no items may be returned for any reason. Late remittance for purchases revokes all Return privileges.

SPORTS COLLECTIBLES TERM C: Bidders who have inspected the lots prior to any auction will not be granted any return privileges.

SPORTS COLLECTIBLES TERM D: Sportscards sold referencing a third-party grading service are sold "as is" without any express or implied warranty. Certain warranties may be available from the grading services and the Bidder is referred to them for further details: Professional Sports Authenticator (PSA), P.O. Box 6180 Newport Beach, CA 92658; Sportscard Guaranty LLC (SGC) P.O. Box 6919 Parsippany, NJ 07054-6919; Global Authentication (GAI), P.O. Box 57042 Irvine, Ca. 92619; Beckett Grading Service (BGS), 15850 Dallas Parkway, Dallas TX 75248.

SPORTS COLLECTIBLES TERM E: Auctioneer does not warrant authenticity of a sports memorabilia lot when the lot is accompanied by a Certificate of Authenticity, or its equivalent, from an independent third-party authentication provider. Bidder shall solely rely upon warranties of the authentication provider issuing the Certificate or opinion. For information as to such authentication provider's warranties the bidder is directed to: SCD Authentic, 4034 West National Ave., Milwaukee, WI 53215 (800) 345-3168; JO Sports, Inc., P.O. Box 607 Brookhaven, NY 11719 (631) 286-0970; PSA/DNA, 130 Brookshire Lane, Orwigsburg, Pa. 17961; Mike Gutierrez Autographs, 8150 Raintree Drive Suite A, Scottsdale, AZ. 85260; or as otherwise noted on the Certificate.

SPORTS COLLECTIBLES TERM F: Bidders who intend to challenge authenticity or provenance of a lot must notify Auctioneer in writing within thirty (30) days of the Auction's conclusion. In the event Auctioneer cannot deliver the lot or subsequently it is established that the lot lacks title, provenance, authenticity, or other transfer or condition issue is claimed, Auctioneer's liability shall be limited to rescission of sale and refund of purchase price; in no case shall Auctioneer's maximum liability exceed the high bid on that lot, which bid shall be deemed for all purposes the value of the lot. After one year has elapsed, Auctioneer's maximum liability shall be limited to any commissions and fees Auctioneer earned on that lot.

SPORTS COLLECTIBLES TERM G: Auctioneer shall not be liable for any patent or latent defect or controversy pertaining to or arising from any encapsulated collectible. In any such instance, purchaser's remedy, if any, shall be solely against the service certifying the collectible.

SPORTS COLLECTIBLES TERM H: Due to changing grading standards over time, differing interpretations, and to possible mishandling of items by subsequent owners, Auctioneer reserves the right to grade items differently than shown on certificates from any grading service that accompany the items. Auctioneer also reserves the right to grade items differently than the grades shown in the prior catalog should such items be reconsigned to any future auction.

SPORTS COLLECTIBLES TERM I: Although consensus grading is employed by most third-party services, it should be noted as aforesaid that grading is not an exact science. In fact, it is entirely possible that if a lot is broken out of a plastic holder and resubmitted to another grading service or even to the same service, the lot could come back with a different grade assigned.

SPORTS COLLECTIBLES TERM J: Certification does not guarantee protection against the normal risks associated with potentially volatile markets. The degree of liquidity for certified collectibles will vary according to general market conditions and the particular lot involved. For some lots there may be no active market at all at certain points in time.

WIRING INSTRUCTIONS:

Bank Information: JP Morgan Chase Bank, N.A., 270 Park Avenue, New York, NY 10017
Account Name: HERITAGE NUMISMATIC AUCTIONS MASTER ACCOUNT
ABA Number: 021000021
Account Number: 1884827674
Swift Code: CHASUS33

Rev. 2_7_08

Bidding Method for Session 1

Session I: Lots 19001 - 19306
(Internet/Phone Bidding) Auction #9709
Friday, May 2 - 9:00 PM CT

This session is presented via catalog and online. Bidding is taken by phone or through our website. There are three phases of bidding during this type of auction:

1) Normal bidding: Bids are taken up until 9 PM CT the night the auction closes.
2) Extended Bidding: On a lot-by-lot basis, individuals that bid on any lots during Normal Bidding may continue to bid on those lots during the next two hours (9 to 11 PM CT).
3) 30 Minute Ending: On a lot-by-lot basis, starting at 11:00 PM CT, any person who has bid on the lot previously may continue to bid on that lot until there are no more bids for 30 minutes.

For example, if you bid on a lot during Normal Bidding, you could participate during Extended Bidding for that lot, but not on lots you did not bid on previously. If a bid was placed at 11:15, the new end time for that lot would become 11:45. If no other bids were placed before 11:45, the lot would close. If you are the high bidder on a lot, changing your bid will not extend the bidding during the 30 Minute Ending phase (only a bid from another bidder will extend bidding).

Interactive Internet™ Bidding

You can now bid with Heritage's exclusive *Interactive Internet™* program, available only at our web site: HA.com. It's fun, and it's easy!

1. Register online at: **HA.com**
2. View the full-color photography of every single lot in the online catalog!
3. Construct your own personal catalog for preview.
4. View the current opening bids on lots you want; review the prices realized archive.
5. Bid and receive immediate notification if you are the top bidder; later, if someone else bids higher, you will be notified automatically by e-mail.
6. The *Interactive Internet™* program opens the lot on the floor at one increment over the second highest bid. As the high bidder, your secret maximum bid will compete for you during the floor auction, and it is possible that you may be outbid on the floor after Internet bidding closes. Bid early, as the earliest bird wins in the event of a tie bid.
7. After the sale, you will be notified of your success. It's that easy!

Bid Live using *HERITAGE LIVE*

This auction is **"HA.com/Live Enabled"** and has continuous bidding from the time the auction is posted on our site through the live event. **When normal Internet bidding ends, visit HA.com/Live and continue to place Live Proxy bids.** When the item hits the auction block, you can continue to bid live against the floor and other live bidders.

Interactive Internet™ Bidding Instructions

1. Log Onto Website

Log onto **HA.com** and chose the portal you're interested in (i.e., coins, comics, movie posters, fine arts, etc.).

2. Search for Lots

Search or browse for the lot you are interested in. You can do this from the home page, from the Auctions home page, or from the home page for the particular auction in which you wish to participate.

3. Select Lots

Click on the link or the photo icon for the lot you want to bid on.

4. Enter Bid

At the top of the page, next to a small picture of the item, is a box outlining the current bid. Enter the amount of your secret maximum bid in the textbox next to "Secret Maximum Bid." The secret maximum bid is the maximum amount you are willing to pay for the item you are bidding on (for more information about bidding and bid increments, please see the section labeled "Bidding Increments" elsewhere in this catalog). Click on the button marked "Place Absentee Bid." A new area on the same page will open up for you to enter your username (or e-mail address) and password. Enter these, then click "Place Absentee Bid" again.

Current Bid: $0 ($9.00 with Buyer's Premium)
Secret Maximum Bid: (enter whole dollar amounts) $ 50 — $1 or more ($10.00 or more with Buyer's Premium)
Take 6 months to Pay! [Place Absentee Bid]
Buyer's Premium: 15% (minimum $9 per lot) of the successful bid

Current Bid: $0 ($9.00 with Buyer's Premium)
Secret Maximum Bid: (enter whole dollar amounts) $ 50 — $1 or more ($10.00 or more with Buyer's Premium)
Please enter your User Name and Password.
User Name: **Password:**
Keep me signed-in for bidding — Forgot your password?
Take 6 months to Pay! [Place Absentee Bid]
Buyer's Premium: 15% (minimum $9 per lot) of the successful bid

5. Confirm Absentee Bid

You are taken to a page labeled, "Please Confirm Your Bid." This page shows you the name of the item you're bidding on, the current bid, and the maximum bid. When you are satisfied that all the information shown is correct, click on the button labeled, "Confirm Bid."

Please Confirm Your Bid - Auction #374, Lot #16630

Large Size
Fr. TN-12 Hessler X83D $20 March 25, 1815 "Act of February 24, 1815" Treasury Note Very Fine, PC. This India paper plate let...

The Current Bid on this item is: **$550.00** ($632.50 with BP)
Reserve Status: **No Reserve**
Your Maximum Bid is: **$600** ($690.00 with BP)

[Confirm Absentee Bid] [Cancel Absentee Bid]

Before finalizing your bid please read the information below:

Secret Maximum Bid: Our system will place bids on your behalf, using only as much of (but not more than) your secret maximum as is necessary to maintain your high bid position. If another bidder places a higher secret maximum than yours, you will be notified via e-mail that you have been outbid.

This 2005 (CAA) St. Louis, MO (CSNS) Signature Sale is being held in St. Louis, MO on May 5-7, 2005. Online bidding ends at 10:00PM CT the night before the floor session for this lot. Your secret maximum bid will compete for you during the floor auction, and it is possible that you may be outbid on the floor after internet bidding closes. The applicable buyer's premium for this auction is an amount equal to 15% (minimum $9 per lot) of the successful bid. Sales Tax may be charged for this auction if you reside in the following state(s): TX, CA (more info...). Terms and Conditions.

6. Bidding Status Notification

One of two pages is now displayed.

a. If your bid is the current high bid, you will be notified and given additional information as to what might happen to affect your high bidder status over the course of the remainder of the auction. You will also receive a Bid Confirmation notice via email.

Congratulations!

You are the current high bidder on Lot #11042:
Proof Indian Cents - 1865 1C PR 65 Red PCGS. The current Coin Dealer Newsletter (...

Your maximum bid was in the amount of: **$1.00** ($7.00 with BP)
After processing all the open bids for this lot, the current bid price is **$1.00** ($7.00 with BP)
Reserve Status: **Reserve (If Any) Not Posted Yet**

Can I still be outbid?
Yes. You are currently the high bidder, but this does not guarantee that someone else won't outbid you before this auction closes. There are two ways to ***monitor your bid...***

- Use My Bids. You can easily reference every bid you have placed and monitor your bid status on every lot
- Watch your email for outbid notices. When you are outbid, we send you an email to let you know.

b. If your bid is not the current high bid, you will be notified of that fact and given the opportunity to increase your bid.

Your bid is confirmed for Lot #21008, but you have been outbid. A previous bidder placed a maximum bid greater than or equal to yours (tie bids go to the first bidder). (what's a maximum bid?)

CHOOSE YOUR BIDDING METHOD, (CONT'D.)

Mail Bidding at Auction

Mail bidding at auction is fun and easy and only requires a few simple steps.

1. Look through the catalog, and determine the lots of interest.
2. Research their market value by checking price lists and other price guidelines.
3. Fill out your bid sheet, entering your maximum bid on each lot.
4. Verify your bids!
5. Mail Early. Preference is given to the first bids received in case of a tie. When bidding by mail, you frequently purchase items at less than your maximum bid.

Bidding is opened at the published increment above the second highest mail or Internet bid; we act on your behalf as the highest mail bidder. If bidding proceeds, we act as your agent, bidding in increments over the previous bid. This process is continued until you are awarded the lot or you are outbid.

An example of this procedure: You submit a bid of $100, and the second highest mail bid is at $50. Bidding starts at $55 on your behalf. If no other bids are placed, you purchase the lot for $55. If other bids are placed, we bid for you in the posted increments until we reach your maximum bid of $100. If bidding passes your maximum: if you are bidding through the Internet, we will contact you by e-mail; if you bid by mail, we take no other action. Bidding continues until the final bidder wins.

Telephone Bidding

To participate by telephone, please make arrangements by Noon Friday, May 3, with Client Services, Toll Free 866-835-3243.

We strongly recommend that you place preliminary bids by mail, fax, or Internet, even if you intend to participate by telephone. On many occasions this dual approach has helped reduce disappointments due to telephone problems, unexpected travel, late night sessions and time zone differences, etc. We will make sure that you do not bid against yourself.

Mail Bidding Instructions

1. **Name, Address, City, State, Zip**
Your address is needed to mail your purchases. We need your telephone number to communicate any problems or changes that may affect your bids.

2. **References**
If you have not established credit with us from previous auctions, you must send a 25% deposit, or list dealers with whom you have credit established.

3. **Lot Numbers and Bids**
List all lots you desire to purchase. On the reverse are additional columns; you may also use another sheet. Under "Amount" enter the maximum you would pay for that lot (whole dollar amounts only). We will purchase the lot(s) for you as much below your bids as possible.

4. **Total Bid Sheet**
Add up all bids and list that total in the appropriate box.

5. **Sign Your Bid Sheet**
By signing the bid sheet, you have agreed to abide by the Terms of Auction listed in the auction catalog.

MAIL/FAX BID SHEET
Heritage Auction Galleries
1-800-872-6467
HA.com
3500 Maple Avenue, 17th Floor
Dallas, Texas 75219-3941

HERITAGE

NAME William Stark — CUSTOMER # 123456
ADDRESS 4739 - B Bradford Drive — E-MAIL ADDRESS wstark@stark.com
CITY/STATE/ZIP Dallas, TX 75219
DAYTIME PHONE 214-558-8109 — EVENING PHONE 214-528-3500

XYZ Auction Company
ABC Collectibles, Inc.

(Bid in whole dollar amounts only.)

LOT NO.	AMOUNT	LOT NO.	AMOUNT
143	200	3210	325
221	75		
1621	125		
2416	625		
3189	475		

SUBTOTAL 1,825
TOTAL BID 1,825

FAX HOTLINE: 214-443-8425

The official prices realized list that accompanies our auction catalogs is reserved for bidders and consignors only. We are happy to mail one to others upon receipt of $1.00. Written requests should be directed to Customer Service.

6. **Fax Your Bid Sheet**
When time is short submit a Mail Bid Sheet on our exclusive Fax Hotline. There's no faster method to get your bids to us *instantly*. Simply use the **Heritage Fax Hotline number: 214-443-8425.**

When you send us your original after faxing, mark it "Confirmation of Fax" (preferably in red!)

7. **Bidding Increments**
To facilitate bidding, please consult the Bidding Increments chart in the Terms & Conditions.

Steve Ivy - Co-Chairman and CEO

Steve Ivy began collecting and studying rare coins in his youth, and as a teenager in 1963 began advertising coins for sale in national publications. Seven years later, at the age of twenty, he opened Steve Ivy Rare Coins in downtown Dallas, and in 1976, Steve Ivy Numismatic Auctions was incorporated. Steve managed the business as well as serving as chief numismatist, buying and selling hundreds of millions of dollars of coins during the 1970s and early 1980s. In early 1983, James Halperin became a full partner, and the name of the corporation was changed to Heritage Rare Coin Galleries. Steve's primary responsibilities now include management of the marketing and selling efforts of the company, the formation of corporate policy for long-term growth, and corporate relations with financial institutions. He remains intimately involved in numismatics, attending all major national shows. Steve engages in daily discourse with industry leaders on all aspects of the rare coin/currency business, and his views on grading, market trends and hobby developments are respected throughout the industry. He serves on the Board of Directors of the Professional Numismatists Guild (and was immediate past president), is the current Chairman of The Industry Council for Tangible Assets, and is a member of most leading numismatic organizations. Steve's keen appreciation of history is reflected in his active participation in other organizations, including past or present board positions on the Texas Historical Foundation and the Dallas Historical Society (where he also served as Exhibits Chairman). Steve is an avid collector of Texas books, manuscripts, and national currency, and he owns one of the largest and finest collections in private hands. He is also a past Board Chair of Dallas Challenge, and is currently the Finance Chair of the Phoenix House of Texas.

James Halperin - Co-Chairman

Jim Halperin and the traders under his supervision have transacted billions of dollars in rare coin business, and have outsold all other numismatic firms every year for over two decades. Born in Boston in 1952, Jim attended Middlesex School in Concord from 1966 to 1970. At the age of 15, he formed a part-time rare coin business after discovering that he had a knack (along with a nearly photographic memory) for coins. Jim scored a perfect 800 on his math SATs and received early acceptance to Harvard College, but after attending three semesters, he took a permanent leave of absence to pursue his full-time numismatic career. In 1975, Jim personally supervised the protocols for the first mainframe computer system in the numismatic business, which would catapult New England Rare Coin Galleries to the top of the industry in less than four years. In 1983, Jim merged with his friend and former archrival Steve Ivy, whom Jim had long admired. Their partnership has become the world's largest and most successful numismatic company, as well as the third-largest auctioneer in America. Jim remains arguably the best "eye" in the coin business today (he won the professional division of the PCGS World Series of Grading). In the mid-1980s, he authored "How to Grade U.S. Coins" (now posted on the web at www.CoinGrading.com), a highly-acclaimed text upon which the NGC and PCGS grading standards would ultimately be based. Jim is a bit of a Renaissance man, as a well-known futurist, an active collector of EC comics and early 20th-century American art (visit www.jhalpe.com), venture capital investor, philanthropist (he endows a multimillion-dollar health education foundation), and part-time novelist. His first fictional novel, "The Truth Machine," was published in 1996 and became an international science fiction bestseller, and was optioned for movie development by Warner Brothers. Jim's second novel, "The First Immortal," was published in early 1998 and immediately optioned as a Hallmark Hall of Fame television miniseries. Jim is married to Gayle Ziaks, and they have two sons, David and Michael. In 1996, with funding from Jim and Gayle's foundation, Gayle founded Dallas' Dance for the Planet, which has grown to become the largest free dance festival in the world.

Greg Rohan - President

At the age of eight, Greg Rohan started collecting coins as well as buying them for resale to his schoolmates. By 1971, at the age of ten, he was already buying and selling coins from a dealer's table at trade shows in his hometown of Seattle. His business grew rapidly, and by 1985 he had offices in both Seattle and Minneapolis. He joined Heritage in 1987 as Executive Vice-President and Manager of the firm's rare coin business. Today, as an owner and as President of Heritage, his responsibilities include overseeing the firm's private client group and working with top collectors in every field in which Heritage is active. Greg has been involved with many of the rarest items and most important collections handled by the firm, including the purchase and/or sale of the Ed Trompeter Collection (the world's largest numismatic purchase according to the Guinness Book of World Records), the legendary 1894 San Francisco Dime, the 1838 New Orleans Half Dollar, and the 1804 Silver Dollar. During his career, Greg has handled more than $1 billion of rare coins, collectibles and art, and provided expert consultation concerning the authenticity and grade condition of coins for the Professional Coin Grading Service (PCGS). He has provided expert testimony for the United States Attorneys in San Francisco, Dallas, and Philadelphia, and for the Federal Trade Commission (FTC). He has worked with collectors, consignors, and their advisors regarding significant collections of books, manuscripts, comics, currency, jewelry, vintage movie posters, sports and entertainment memorabilia, decorative arts, and fine art. Additionally, Greg is a Sage Society member of the American Numismatic Society, and a member/life member of the PNG, ANA, and most other leading numismatic organizations. Greg is also Chapter Chairman for North Texas of the Young Presidents' Organization (YPO), and is an active supporter of the arts. Greg co-authored "The Collectors Estate Handbook," winner of the NLG's Robert Friedberg Award for numismatic book of the year. Mr. Rohan currently serves on the seven-person Advisory Board to the Federal Reserve Bank of Dallas, in his second appointed term. He and his wife, Lysa, are avid collectors of rare wine, Native American artifacts, and American art.

Paul Minshull - Chief Operating Officer

As Chief Operating Officer, Paul Minshull's managerial responsibilities include integrating sales, personnel, inventory, security and MIS for Heritage. His major accomplishments include overseeing the hardware migration from mainframe to PC, the software migration of all inventory and sales systems, and implementation of a major Internet presence. Heritage's successful employee-suggestion program has generated 200 or more ideas each month since 1995, and has helped increase employee productivity, expand business, and improve employee retention. Paul oversees the company's highly-regarded IT department, and has been the driving force behind Heritage's web development, now a significant portion of Heritage's future plans. As the only numismatic auction house that combines traditional floor bidding with active Internet bidding, the totally interactive system has catapulted Heritage to the top rare coin website (according to Forbes Magazine's "Best of the Web"). Paul was born in Michigan and came to Heritage in 1984 after 12 years as the General Manager of a plastics manufacturing company in Ann Arbor. Since 1987, he has been a general partner in Heritage Capital Properties, Sales Manager, Vice President of Operations, and Chief Operating Officer for all Heritage companies and affiliates since 1996. Paul maintains an active interest in sports and physical fitness, and he and his wife have three children.

Todd Imhof - Vice President
Unlike most professional numismatists, Todd Imhof did not start as a coin collector. Shortly after graduating college in 1987, Todd declined an offer from a prestigious Wall Street bank to join a former high school classmate who was operating a small rare coin company in the Seattle area. The rare coin industry was then undergoing huge changes after the advent of certified grading and growing computer technologies. Being new to the industry, Todd had an easier time than most embracing the new dynamics. He soon discovered a personal passion for rare coins, and for working with high-level collectors. Through his accomplishments, Todd enjoys a reputation envied by the entire numismatic community. During his earlier tenure with Hertzberg Rare Coins, it was named by Inc. magazine as one of the nation's fastest growing private companies 1989-1991. In 1991, Todd co-founded Pinnacle Rarities, Inc., a boutique-styled firm that specialized in servicing the rare coin industry's savviest and most prominent collectors. At 25, he was among the youngest people ever accepted into the Professional Numismatists Guild, and currently serves on its Consumer Protection Committee. In 1992, he was invited to join the Board of Directors for the Industry Council for Tangible Assets, serving as its Chairman 2002-2005. Todd served as Pinnacle's President until his decision to join Heritage in 2006. In the Morse Auction, he became the only person in history to purchase two $1mm+ coins during a single auction session! Todd serves Heritage's Legacy clients, many of whom had previously sought his counsel and found his expertise and integrity to be of great value. Todd really understands what collectors are trying to accomplish, and he has an uncanny ability to identify the perfect coins at the right prices while navigating complex and difficult deals with unsurpassed professionalism.

Chris Ivy - Director of Sports Auctions
Chris has literally grown up in the collectibles business since he began attending shows as a child with his father and working summer jobs at Heritage in every department from shipping to inventory control. At a very young age Chris realized that his true interest was in vintage sports material and he soon began setting up as a dealer at trade shows at the age of twelve. Chris graduated with a BA in History from the University of Texas at Austin and began working at Heritage again in 2001 after serving as a professional grader with Sportscard Guaranty Corporation (SGC) in New Jersey. He was the driving force behind the inception of the Sports auction division in 2003 and today Chris serves as the Director of Sports Auctions for Heritage. In his position, Chris is responsible for the day-to-day operations, combining vision and execution with a balance of business and collecting passion, he works with consignors and recommends the disposition of the collections that come into Heritage in order to maximize each consignor's financial return.

Mike Gutierrez - Consignment Director, Sports
Mike is one of the foremost sports autograph authenticators in the sports memorabilia business and most serious buyers require his approval before purchasing autographs for their personal collections. Mike has over 26 years experience and is one of the few universally respected authorities left standing in a field racked with fraud and forgeries. The industry has been plagued by FBI investigations of fraud and Mike is the single most respected repository of trust in the business. Mike has authenticated some of the finest material in the hobby including the Historic Barry Halper Collection sold through Sotheby's in 1999. Through Butterfield & Butterfield he appraised the Mark McGwire 70th Home Run Baseball for the Fireman's Fund Insurance Company. Additionally, he handled all the memorabilia from The Bruce Lee Estate, The Pete Rozelle Estate, and this last year he appraised Muhammad Ali's Estate of Sports Memorabilia.

Mark Jordan - Consignment Director, Sports
After graduating from Southern Methodist University, Barry relocated to Europe to begin a career in book publishing. He edited "The Encyclopedia Mark has been involved in the sports collectors industry since 1967 when he was a major league bat boy. He was the promoter for the first National Sports Collectors Convention in 1972. He is a nationally known expert in autograph authentication and has appeared on NBC nightly news, The Today show, ESPN, USA Today, The New York Times, Sports Illustrated and other media outlets regarding collectibles. He has been named as one of the 10 most influential persons in the sports autograph industry by Trading Cards Magazine and his showroom was located in the Texas Rangers Ballpark in Arlington for seven years. He graduated from David Lipscomb University in 1976 where he also served as Sports Information Director. He attends many championship events dealing with clients and has been to 18 Super Bowls and 55 World Series games.

Jonathan Scheier - Consignment Director, Sports
Jonathan is a fourth-generation New York Yankees fan who grew up hearing first-hand accounts from his father about Don Larsen's perfect game and Willie Mays' famous catch. For the better part of the past decade, he has made use of this genetic coding and his collegiate background as a Creative Writing major as lead catalog writer for several of the top sports memorabilia auction houses in the industry. Having personally researched and written the catalog copy for tens of millions of dollars of vintage sports memorabilia, Jonathan has earned an education in the hobby that few could match. He has served as a consignment director and as lead cataloger for Heritage Sports Collectibles since the summer of 2004.

Stephen Carlisle - Auction Coordinator / Consignment Director
Stephen started collecting sports cards in the late 1970s and attended shows in the Southern California area (shows that would eventually become the National Sports Collectors Convention several years later). Along with his father, Stephen opened one of Orange County's first full-time sports collectibles stores in 1980. When the store was eventually sold, Stephen continued to sell at shows in southern California and New York until the mid-1990s. Prior to joining Heritage in 2003, Stephen spent several years in the Dominican Republic working with Major League Baseball teams including the Oakland Athletics, the St. Louis Cardinals, the New York Mets and the Boston Red Sox. Stephen holds a BS degree from Ithaca College in New York and enjoys watching sports, as well as spending time with his wife and two daughters.

Norma L. Gonzalez - VP of Operations - Numismatic Auctions
Born in Dallas, Texas, Norma joined the U.S. Navy in August of 1993. During her five-year enlistment, she received her Bachelor's Degree in Resource Management and traveled to Japan, Singapore, Thailand and lived in Cuba for three years. After her enlistment, she moved back to Dallas where her family resides. Norma joined Heritage in 1998; always ready for a challenge, she spent her days at Heritage and her nights pursuing an M. B. A. She was promoted to Vice President in 2003. She currently manages the operations departments, including Coins, Currency, World & Ancient Coins, Sportscards & Memorabilia, Comics, Movie Posters, Pop Culture and Political Memorabilia. Norma enjoys running, biking and spending time with her family. In February 2004 she ran a 26.2-mile marathon in Austin, Texas and later, in March she accomplished a 100-mile bike ride in California.

Kelley Norwine - VP - Marketing
Born and raised in South Carolina, Kelley pursued a double major at Southern Wesleyan University, earning a BA in Music Education and a BS in Business Management. A contestant in the Miss South Carolina pageant, Kelley was later Regional Manager & Director of Training at Bank of Travelers Rest in South Carolina. Relocating to Los Angeles, Kelley became the Regional Manager and Client Services Director for NAS-McCann World Group, an international Advertising & Communications Agency where she was responsible for running one of the largest offices in the country. During her years with NAS Kelley was the recipient of numerous awards including Regional Manager of the Quarter and the NAS Courage and Dedication award. After relocating to Dallas, Kelley took a job as Director of Client Services for TMP/Monster Worldwide and joined Heritage in 2005 as Director of Client Development. She was named VP of Marketing for Heritage in 2007. A cancer survivor, Kelley is an often-requested motivational speaker for the American Cancer Society. In her spare time, she writes music, sings, and plays the piano.

Marti Korver - Manager - Credit/Collections
Marti has been working in numismatics for more than three decades. She was recruited out of the banking profession by Jim Ruddy, and she worked with Paul Rynearson, Karl Stephens, and Judy Cahn on ancients and world coins at Bowers & Ruddy Galleries, in Hollywood, CA. She migrated into the coin auction business, running the bid books for such memorable sales as the Garrett Collection and representing bidders as agent at B&R auctions for 10 years. She also worked as a research assistant for Q. David Bowers for several years. Memorable events included such clients (and friends) as Richard Lobel, John Ford, Harry Bass, and John J. Pittman. She is married to noted professional numismatist and writer, Robert Korver, (who is sometimes seen auctioneering at coin shows) and they migrated to Heritage in Dallas in 1996. She has an RN daughter (who worked her way through college showing lots for Heritage) and a son (who is currently a college student and sometimes a Heritage employee) and a type set of dogs (one black and one white). She currently collects kitschy English teapots and compliments.

SESSION I

PLATINUM LOT INDEX

SESSION II

VINTAGE SPORTS COLLECTIBLES

Internet and Phone Bid Auction #9709 • Session One • Lots 19001-19306
Friday, May 2, 2008 • 9:00 PM CT • Dallas, Texas

A 19.5% Buyer's Premium ($9 Minimum) Will Be Added To All Lots.

Visit HA.com/Sports to view scalable images and bid online.

This session is presented via catalog and online. Bidding is taken by phone or through our website. There are three phases of bidding during this type of auction:

1) Normal bidding: Bids are taken up until 9 PM CT the night the auction closes.
2) Extended Bidding: On a lot-by-lot basis, individuals that bid on any lots during Normal Bidding may continue to bid on those lots during the next two hours (9 to 11 PM CT).
3) 30 Minute Ending: On a lot-by-lot basis, starting at 11:00 PM CT, any person who has bid on the lot previously may continue to bid on that lot until there are no more bids for 30 minutes.

For example, if you bid on a lot during Normal Bidding, you could participate during Extended Bidding for that lot, but not on lots you did not bid on previously. If a bid was placed at 11:15, the new end time for that lot would become 11:45. If no other bids were placed before 11:45, the lot would close. If you are the high bidder on a lot, changing your bid will not extend the bidding during the 30 Minute Ending phase (only a bid from another bidder will extend bidding).

THE BIRTH OF THE HOBBY

19001 **1869 Peck & Snyder Cincinnati Red Stockings Trade Card PSA Authentic.** A fitting opening lot for this May 2008 Signature Sports auction is the artifact widely considered by hobbyists to be the very first baseball card ever produced. Issued just four years after General Lee surrendered his Confederate troops at the Appomattox Courthouse to bring a close to the American Civil War, this trade card began a tradition that now approaches its one hundred fortieth birthday. Even dismissing its status as the first true baseball card, this fantastically scarce relic would rank as one of the greatest treasures of the early game, providing a magnificent team photograph of the "Red Stocking B.B. Club of Cincinnati," the game's first professional team. Second and third from left in the top and bottom rows respectively are George and Harry Wright, the pioneering brothers whose contributions to the development of the sport are far too numerous to recount here. This Hall of Fame pair and eight other members of this historic club are identified by surname and position at the bottom border. The verso features advertising for "The New York City Base Ball and Sportsman's Emporium, one of two known variations of this large format Peck & Snyder. A caricature of a bearded ballplayer assumes the central focus. Minor border trimming must be noted, though this is commonly seen in the few known surviving examples, and the visual effect of this modification is minimal. Otherwise the condition is quite remarkable, with just a half-inch wrinkle at the left border and some very light staining on verso to mention. A rare and exciting opportunity for the advanced collector. **Minimum Bid: $3,750**

19002 1872 CDV (Boston Red Sox) Andy Leonard (George Wright Collection) SGC Authentic. The original pioneering Wright brothers were not Frank and Orville, but George and Harry, who together gave birth to the tradition of professional baseball and are forever immortalized in bronze at Cooperstown. This striking sepia image of the brothers' teammate on the 1872 Boston Red Stockings was removed from George's family album after it was sold several years ago at auction. It remains in the condition it was discovered, a faint oval around the portrait from decades displayed beneath an overlay, and clipped opposing corners. Otherwise the piece remains in fabulous condition with no creasing, tearing or staining. The carte de visite measures 2.5x4.25", and is encapsulated as "Authentic" by SGC, which makes note of its special provenance. **Minimum Bid: $750**

19003 1887 N172 Old Judge Collection (11). Pre-dating the T206 tobacco set by nearly 20 years, the Old Judge set is considered the oldest and largest of all with known variations numbering over 3,500. This terrific group includes **SGC 80 EX/NM 6:** Pete Gillespie; **SGC 60 EX 5:** Henry Boyle (mislabeled by SGC, will be reholdered prior to auction close); **SGC 50 VG/EX 4:** 6 cards - Lave Cross (Louisville), Jim Fogarty, Guy Hecker, Smiling Al Maul, Jocko Milligan (St. Louis AA), George Wood; **SGC 40 VG 3:** Billy Sunday (Chicago); **SGC 20 Fair 1.5:** Tommy McCarthy (HOF) (St. Louis); **SGC 10 Poor 1:** Will Fry. **Minimum Bid: $625**

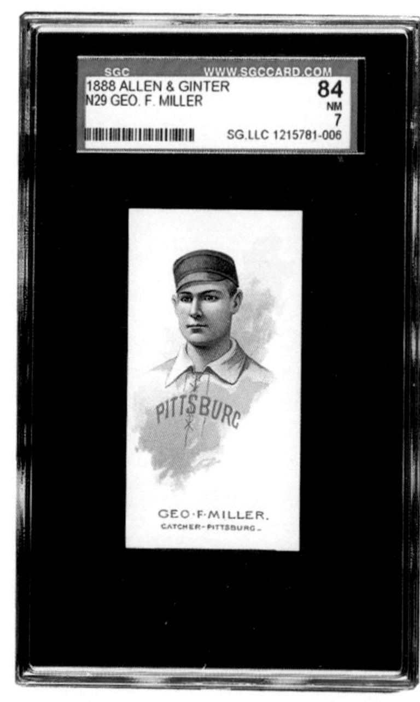

19004 1888 N29 Allen & Ginter George F. Miller SGC 84 NM 7. If you are looking for a compatible match for the Morrell card offered in this auction, then this is it. This card has tremendous eye appeal; from the vibrant colors, to the sharp corners and overall clarity. The surface of the card front appears to have only minor flaws, which do not detract from the overall appeal of this N29 beauty. A stark white color on the front surface, makes the colorful portrait stand out that much more. SGC has graded two examples higher than this fine specimen. **Minimum Bid: $250**

19005 1888 N29 Allen & Ginter John Morrell SGC 84 NM 7. Here is an issue you will not see very often at this high level. This very scarce lithographed artwork depicting John Morrell is a marvel of original detail and preservation. Each aspect of its colorful presentation is crisp and extraordinarily fresh. There are only light touches on the corners, otherwise this card would have commanded a higher grade. SGC has graded only one example at a higher level. This is a very highly quality Near Mint card. **Minimum Bid: $250**

19006 **1904 Allegheny Card Co. Jim Hackett SGC 84 NM 7.** By definition the rarest of all baseball card issues, it is believed that just a single prototype for this boxed card game was ever made, failing to reach production. The set consists of 112 known cards, each featuring only National League players, and cut by hand. The set was discovered in the late 1980's and sold at auction in 1991, and again in 1995, before it was broken up and the cards sold individually. Here we present the one and only example of St. Louis Cardinals first baseman Jim Hackett, rating an impressive NM 7. If you are enamored with "1 of 1" cards, this is clearly the issue for you. **Minimum Bid: $200**

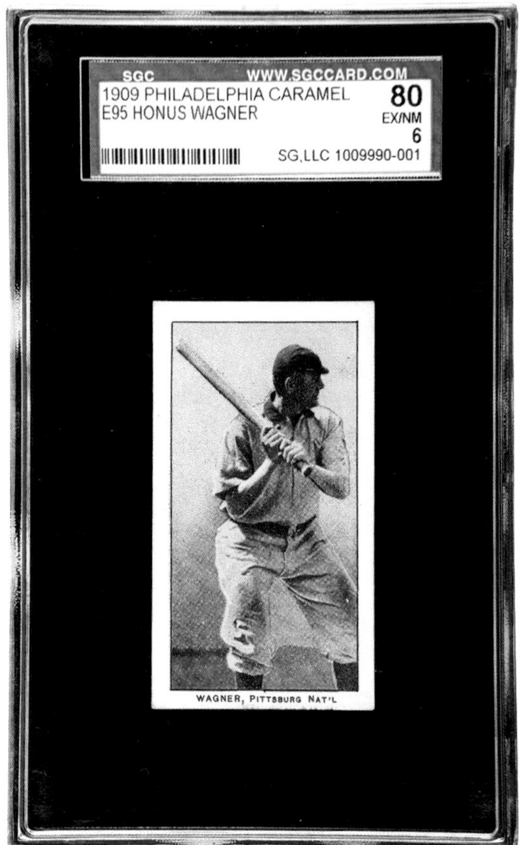

19007 **1909 Philadelphia Caramel E95 Honus Wagner SGC 80 EX/NM 6.** Just twenty-five cards in this tough candy set, but the issue is packed to the gills with the top names of the Dead Ball era, including the likes of Cobb, Crawford, Mathewson, Evers, Plank and Collins. Here we present the card listed first on the checklist back, an honor properly bestowed upon the veteran Pittsburgh Pirates shortstop Honus Wagner. With a design reminiscent of the T206 set, and the same year of issue, this could be considered a very attractive alternative to the six-figure price tag for that other Wagner card. Stunning eye appeal exceeds its already impressive grade. And the SGC population charts find just two examples ever surpassing the representation we present here. **Minimum Bid: $2,000**

19008 **1909 Ramly T204 Walter Johnson SGC 30 Good 2.** Widely considered to be Johnson's rookie, as no other cards dedicated to him predate this issue, this card is likewise the most valuable in the T204 set, which inexplicably fails to include such contemporary legends as Ty Cobb, Cy Young, Christy Mathewson and Napoleon Lajoie. The Ramly set is far more scarce in general than any of the other major tobacco sets issued during the period, and Johnson remains one of its most elusive residents. Though a vertical fold running through Johnson's left ear results in a "Good" grade, one must forgive this flaw in light of the tremendous rarity. Still no shortage of aesthetic appeal here, and certainly no shortage of desirabilty either. **Minimum Bid: $1,250**

19009 **1909-11 T206 Jake Atz SGC 84 NM 7.** Infielder Jake Atz played three game with the Washington Senators in 1902 before finishing his major league career with parts of three season with the Chicago White Sox between 1907 and 1909. The card rates on the upper end of examples from the most popular of the tobacco issues, with centering the only flaw that merits mentioning. **Minimum Bid: $100**

19010 **1909-11 T206 George Brown (Browne), Washington SGC 80 EX/NM 6.** An outfielder, George Brown spent 12 seasons in the big leagues and stole 32 bases during the 1906 season as a member of the New York Giants. Centering and the slightest hint of wear at the corners are the only condition issues of note. **Minimum Bid: $100**

19011 **1909-11 T206 Ty Cobb Portrait Red Background SGC 60 EX 5.** It's a favorite of many collectors of this most beloved of tobacco card issues. The "Georgia Peach" looks so young and innocent, though the blood red background that frames him suggests the fierce, sometimes violent nature that made him the greatest star of the Dead Ball Era. Judged solely on the surface and image itself, there are few specimens that could compete with this one in terms of quality. It is only the typical light corner rounding and all but imperceptible toning to the verso that brings this representation down to earth. A solid purchase for the tobacco card enthusiast. **Minimum Bid: $400**

19012 **1909-11 T206 Jimmy Collins SGC 84 NM 7.** Jimmy Collins was a player-manager for the Minnesota Millers of the American Association in 1909. This followed a Hall of Fame big league career during which he managed the Red Sox to the first modern World Series, defeating the Pirates in 1903. Top to bottom centering is the only noticeable condition flaw for this beautiful representation of the former Boston baseball great. **Minimum Bid: $100**

19013 **1909-11 T206 Ray Demmitt, St. Louis Polar Bear Back SGC 20 Fair 1.5.** One of the true rarities from the T206 set. Demmitt played for the New York Americans in his first season. His second was spent in St. Louis, but for only 10 games. Polar Bear was the only brand to create an "updated" caption placing Demmitt with his second team, the St. Louis' American League franchise. Seldom seen in high grade, this particular card has the typical creasing for a card graded at the FAIR level, but it is well centered and the area around the face remains relatively undisturbed. **Minimum Bid: $300**

19014 **1909-11 T206 Ray Demmitt St. Louis PSA VG-EX 4.** A December 1909 trade of this frankly mediocre outfield talent from the New York Highlanders to the St. Louis Browns has served to give Demmitt a value quite disproportionate to his baseball importance. The updated "St. Louis Americans" caption and "St. L" on his chest make this a rare variation, only offered within packs of "Polar Bear" cigarettes. Only a single example of this ultra-tough card has ever ascended higher on the PSA population charts. An exciting opportunity for the advanced tobacco card collector. **Minimum Bid: $500**

19015 **1909-11 T206 Ted Easterly SGC 84 NM 7.** Ted Easterly, a catcher and outfielder, played for the Cleveland Indians and Chicago White Sox of the American League before finishing his 7-year major league career with a two-year stint as a member of the Federal League's Kansas City Packers club. Top to bottom centering is the only condition flaw of note. **Minimum Bid: $100**

19016 **1909-11 T206 Harry Howell, Portrait SGC 84 NM 7.** Harry Howell enjoyed a thirteen-year career as a big league pitcher at the turn of the century, finishing with a 7-year run as a member of the the St. Louis Browns American League team. Minor wear at the corners is the only condition issue of note. **Minimum Bid: $100**

19017 1909-11 T206 Fielder Jones, Portrait SGC 84 NM 7. Outfielder Fielder Jones played for Brooklyn of the National League and Chicago of the American League before finishing his 15-year major league career with a two-year stint as a member of the Federal League's St. Louis Terriers club. Top to bottom centering is the only condition flaw of note. **Minimum Bid: $100**

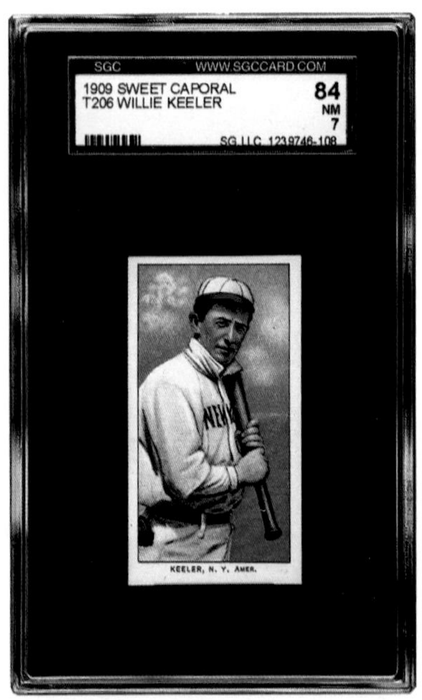

19018 1909-11 T206 Willie Keeler, With Bat SGC 84 NM 7. "Wee Willie" Keeler, who once famously advised, "Hit 'em where they ain't," was one of the game's early great batters. The 5'4" and 140 lb. dynamo practiced what he preached, registering batting averages of .424 in 1897 and .385 in 1898. Keeler was briefly remembered again in 1978 when, in pursuit of Joe DiMaggio's consecutive games hit streak, Pete Rose tied Keeler's NL single season mark of 44 set in 1897. The slightest evidence of wear at the corners is the only condition issue of note. **Minimum Bid: $375**

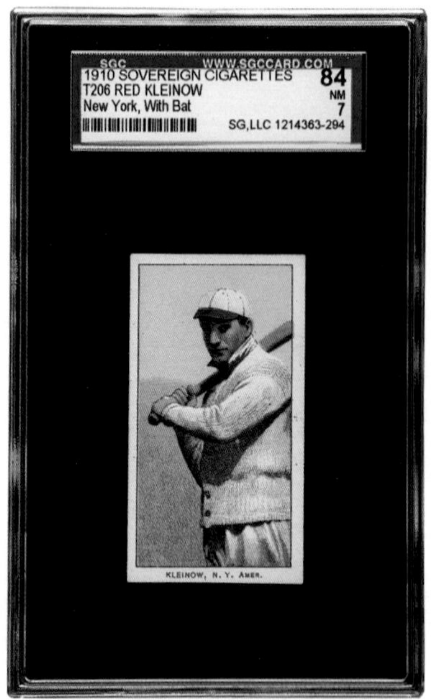

19019 1909-11 T206 Red Kleinow, New York With Bat SGC 84 NM 7. Catcher Red Kleinow applied his trade first with the New York Highlanders and Boston Red Sox of the American League, before wrapping up an 8-season career with one year behind the plate for the senior circuit's Philadelphia Phillies. Minor wear at the corners and a small centering difference are the only condition issue of note. This card is the Sovereign Cigarettes 350 Subjects back variation. **Minimum Bid: $100**

19020 1909-11 T206 Joe Lake, New York SGC 84 NM 7. Joe Lake's 24 complete games in 1910, as a member of St. Louis Browns, were good for seventh place in the American League. That certainly makes it more than a little difficult to compare to our modern day, doesn't it? Minor wear at the corners is the only condition issue apparent. **Minimum Bid: $100**

19021 **1909-11 T206 Sherry Magee (Magie) Error Card SGC 30 Good 2.** To give some idea of the incredible scarcity of this important tobacco card, we'll note that only twenty-five have ever been encapsulated by the SGC grading service, just over four times as many as the six representations of the famed Honus Wagner card, considered one of the rarest pieces of cardboard on earth. Severely abridged print runs are the common thread that causes the skimpiest of supplies of each, as Wagner personally put a stop to his own appearance in the set, and the misspelling of Magee's last name was caught and corrected early in the process. Even the most advanced collections of T206 sets are often short of the coveted "Magie," and so we expect spirited bidding for this nice example. Typical corner rounding is the only noteworthy condition issue, as the surfaces present as well as a card of much loftier rank. **Minimum Bid: $2,000**

19022 **1909-11 T206 Christy Mathewson, Dark Cap SGC 70 EX+ 5.5.** "The Christian Gentleman," Christy Mathewson was a college man who wrote a series of children's books. Mathewson was an upstanding role model at a time when most ballplayers were thought to be hard-living and hard-drinking from the unpolished margins of society. One of the greats to ever grace the mound, Mathewson captured the NL's pitching Triple Crown in 1905 and again in 1908 - leading the circuit in wins, strikeouts and earned run average. The card itself suffers from light touches of wear at the corners, but is still a more than respectable representation for the Hall of Fame pitcher from the induction class of 1936. **Minimum Bid: $300**

19023 **1909-11 T206 Christy Mathewson, Portrait SGC 84 NM 7.** In 1936, Christy Mathewson joined Babe Ruth, Honus Wagner, Ty Cobb and Walter Johnson as the first class of baseball Hall of Famers. A distinction that was well earned, considering his career accomplishments included; leading the league in wins four times, leading the league in strikeouts five times, winning 30 or more games four times, pitching four shutouts and ten complete games in World Series competition and winning 373 regular season contests. Apart from a slight difference in centering from top to bottom, this card displays no obvious conditional flaws to speak of and will provide a top-notch exemplar for any collection of HOF tobacco cards. **Minimum Bid: $500**

19024 **1909-11 T206 Pryor McElveen SGC 84 NM 7.** Pryor McElveen, nicknamed "Humpty" in his day, played three years with Brooklyn National League franchise. Minor wear at the corners is the only obvious condition issue. **Minimum Bid: $100**

19025 **1909-11 T206 Bill O'Hara, St. Louis Polar Bear Back PSA Good 2.** Another one of the rarities from the T-206 set; the Bill O'Hara, St. Louis National League. Similar to Ray Demmitt, he played his 1909 season for the N.Y. Nationals and then was moved to the St. Louis National Franchise. He spent all of 9 games there and never played again in the Majors. This card is also only presented with the Polar Bear back, which usually presents with its typical staining. An overall nice piece, but with a little paper loss on the reverse. **Minimum Bid: $300**

19026 **1909-11 T206 Frank Owen SGC 84 NM 7.** Frank "Yip" Owen began his major league pitching career with the Detroit Tigers in 1901 before moving on to the Chicago White Sox. He earned 20 or more victories with the White Sox in three consecutive seasons spanning from 1904 to 1906. Slight wear at the corners is the only condition issue of note. **Minimum Bid: $100**

GETTYSBURG EDDIE

19027 **1909-11 T206 Eddie Plank SGC 40 VG 3.** Like a schoolboy in fond imitation of his older brother, the T206 Plank hits all the same notes as the fabled Wagner, likewise troubling generations of collectors working to compile a complete set of this most beloved of tobacco issues. Theories for the scarcity of this card paying tribute to Connie Mack's superstar southpaw are identical to the Wagner tales, with aversion to tobacco advertisement and contractual stalemate with the American Tobacco Company the most commonly referenced causes. Recognized baseball card census figures find the populations of these two cards well within striking distance of one another.

Though "Gettysburg Eddie" will probably never dethrone his Pirates contemporary as the key card in the T206 set, the presented example within this auction finds the former in considerably superior condition. Graded VG by the experts at SGC, the proffered Plank exhibits only mild corner rounding to suggest its age, with the face remaining clean and well-placed within its four borders.

Of fourteen examples to have been holstered within an SGC capsule, just four have been deemed superior to this one. With the Plank, the Wagner and the super-tough Magie error card each presented within this auction, one determined collector could clear the three toughest hurdles laid by this classic set in an afternoon, and spend the ensuing months enjoying the slow, steady jog to the finish line. **Minimum Bid: $5,000**

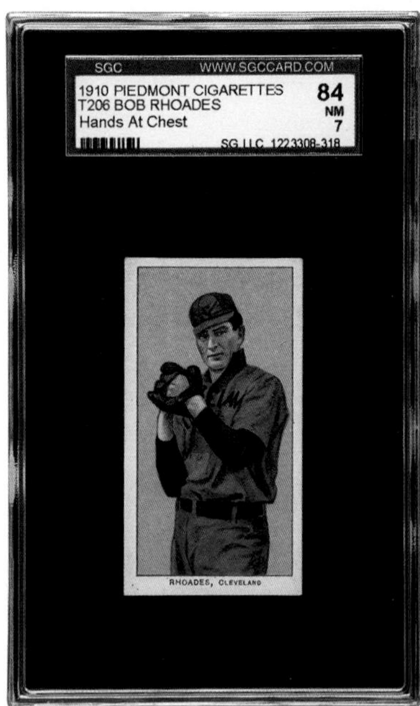

19028 **1909-11 T206 Bob Rhoades (Rhoads), Hands At Chest SGC 84 NM 7.** Barton Emory "Dusty" Rhoads pitched and occasionally played in the outfield for the Cleveland Indians after a brief stay in the National League, first with the Chicago Orphans and later with the St. Louis Cardinals. Minor wear at the corners is the only readily apparent condition issue. **Minimum Bid: $100**

19029 **1909-11 T206 Claude Rossman SGC 84 NM 7.** Claude Rossman was an American League first baseman and outfielder with the Cleveland Naps, Detroit Tigers and St. Louis Browns. He accumulated 33 doubles in 1908, good for second place in the league. A slight difference in centering is the only condition issue of note. **Minimum Bid: $100**

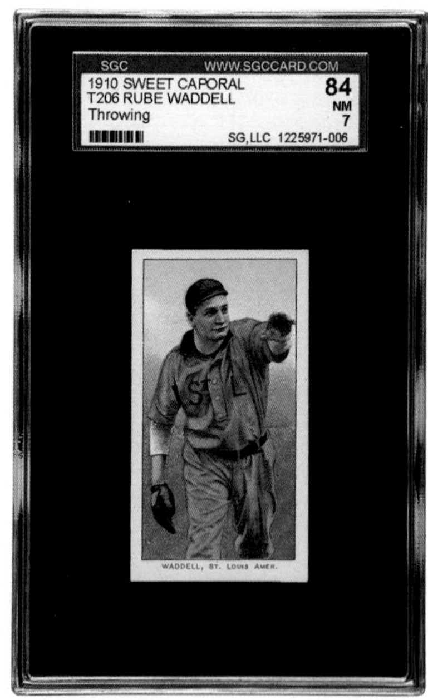

19030 **1909-11 T206 Rube Waddell, Throwing SGC 84 NM 7.** Charles Edward "Rube" Waddell was perhaps the flakiest and most undependable major league star of all time, known to show up drunk for games regularly. His legendary manager Connie Mack once remarked, "The Rube has a two million dollar body and a two cent head." Waddell was inducted into Cooperstown in 1946. The slightest of corner wear and a stray print line are the only condition issues of note for the strong near mint tobacco card. **Minimum Bid: $200**

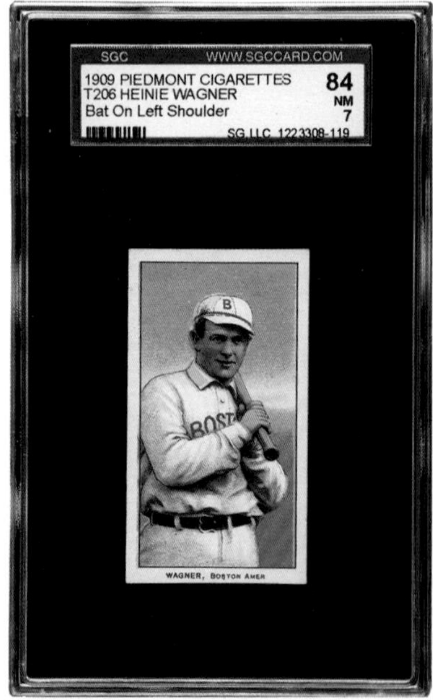

19031 **1909-11 T206 Heinie Wagner, Bat On Left Shoulder SGC 84 NM 7.** This Wagner played 11 seasons for the Boston American League franchise after 17 games with the New York Giants. No slouch, he finished 10th and 12th in AL MVP voting for his 1912 and 1913 campaigns. Minor wear at the corners is the only obvious condition issue. **Minimum Bid: $100**

NO SMOKING

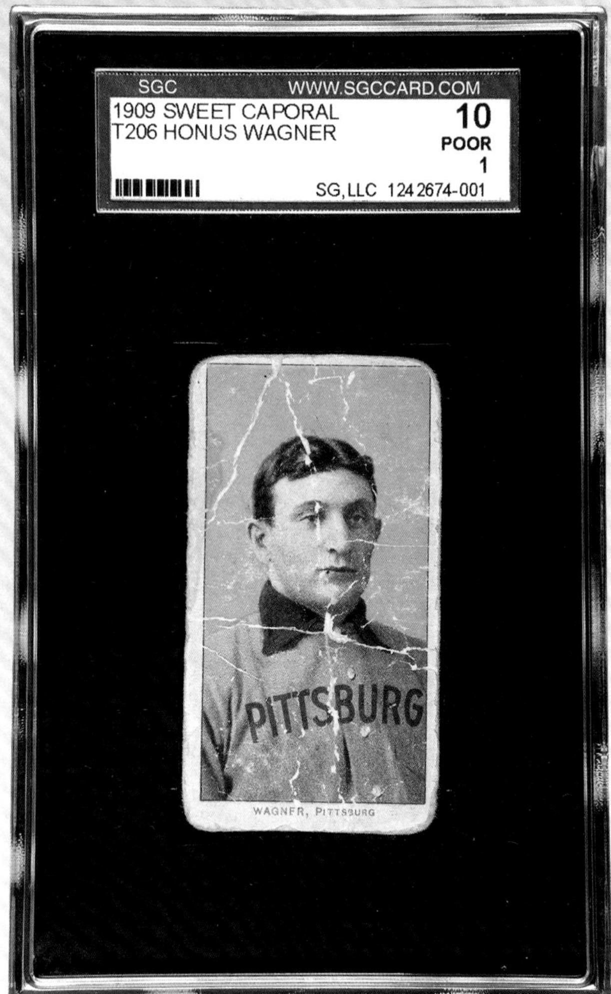

19032 **1909-11 T206 Honus Wagner SGC 10 Poor 1.** "There is something Lincolnesque about him," Pulitzer Prize-winning sports journalist Arthur Daley once wrote, "his rugged homeliness, his simplicity, his integrity, and his true nobility of character." Hall of Fame manager John McGraw considered him the greatest ballplayer of all time, and Ty Cobb recalled him as the one man he couldn't intimidate. Yet despite the universal high praise from friends and foes, and his membership in the 1936 inaugural class of the Baseball Hall of Fame, Honus Wagner is best remembered today as the face on the most valuable and coveted of all baseball cards.

While there is some truth to the argument that Wagner's greatness plays a role in the importance of this ultimate collecting rarity, one must acknowledge that it's a supporting role only. An equal print run to contemporaries like Cobb, Young and Mathewson would almost certainly have found Wagner's value equivalent to those legends' as well. But it was Wagner's refusal of the American Tobacco Company's request for permission to use his image that set him apart and above.

The most popular story to explain this refusal is that Wagner wished to play no role in the promotion of the use of tobacco, though it has been justly stated that he was himself a user, and had appeared in advertisements for many tobacco products previously. Another theory notes Wagner's reputation as a fierce negotiator, arguing that it was nothing more than a case of a failure to agree upon a dollar figure that led the ATC to end production of Wagner's card almost as soon as it started.

This unsolved mystery has only served to further enhance the mystique of the treasure presented here, one of just a few dozen examples of the famed Honus Wagner T206 known to exist. A colorized version of a studio portrait by celebrated early baseball photographer Carl Horner, the unmistakable image on the card face finds the superstar shortstop gazing into the middle distance, set against a backdrop of solid orange. The early spelling of his hometown "Pittsburg" is applied across the chest of his high-collared jersey, and again beside his block lettered surname at the bottom border. The verso provides an advertisement for Sweet Caporal Cigarettes, and the trading cards within, noting "Base Ball Series, 150 Subjects."

Condition is admittedly imperfect, though this is the case for all but a few of the tiny supply of surviving examples. Several creases thread their way through the ancient cardboard, and the passing decades have rounded the corners smooth like water polishing stones in a riverbed. Black fountain pen ink blotches the verso, yet remains mercifully clear of the front. Though the card comes by its Poor rating honestly, it retains a dignified countenance, presenting wonderfully despite its faults.

The opportunity to play a role in the history of a piece such as this is one that should appeal to true collectors of any discipline, not just those with a particular affinity for the sporting world. Stamp collecting has the Inverted Jenny, and comics has Action #1. For baseball card collecting, the T206 Honus Wagner will always hold that special distinction as the ultimate prize, and will establish its owner as one the world's elite hobbyists. **Minimum Bid: $25,000**

19033 **1909-11 T206 Jack Warhop SGC 84 NM 7.** Jack "Chief" Warhop was a regular member of the New York Highlanders and Yankees pitching rotation from 1908 to 1915. He completed 21 of the 23 games he started for the Highlanders in 1909.; Light wear at the corners is the only condition issue of note. **Minimum Bid: $100**

19034 **1909-11 T206 Kaiser Wilhelm, Hands At Chest SGC 84 NM 7.** Kaiser Wilhelm's name is near the top of the list for losses in the NL by a pitcher for the 1904, 1905 and 1908 seasons. However, it should also be noted that he had a fine ERA of 1.87 in 1908 and pitched for particularly weak squads both with the Boston Beaneaters and Brooklyn Superbas. Centering is the only clearly visible condition flaw. **Minimum Bid: $100**

19035 **1909-11 T-206 SGC-Graded Collection with 9 Hall of Famers (111).** Offered is a collection of 111 T-206 cards that includes Hall of Famers and Southern Leaguers with only a small amount of duplication. Highlights include: Graded Cards - **SGC 80 EX/NM 6:** 3 cards w/ Bresnahan (w/Bat), Chance (Portrait Yellow Background) and Grimshaw; **SGC 70 EX+ 5.5:** 4 cards w/ Burns, Camnitz (Hands Above Head), Flick and Liebhardt; **SGC 60 EX 5:** 14 cards w/ Arellanes, Burns, Carey, Cicotte, Devore, Donlan (Seated), Doolan (Fielding), Dougherty (Portrait), Doyle (Portrait), Guiheen, Magee (With Bat), Malarkey, Miller and Quinn; **SGC 50 VG/EX 4:** 44 cards w/ Blackbourne, Brain, Campbell, Crandall (Portrait, With Cap), Doyle (With Bat), Frill, Fromme, Griffith (Batting), Hinchman, Hoffman, Jackson, Jones (Portrait), Keeler (Portrait), Kisinger, Knight (Portrait), Konetchy (Glove Above Head), Kroh, Lavender, Leach (Bending Over), Lentz, Maddox, Manion, Molesworth, Myers (Fielding), Oakes, Pelty (Horizontal Photo), Persons, Powers, Quillen, Rhoades (Hands at Chest), Rudolph, Ryan, Schmidt (Portrait), Schulte (Back View), Aeitz, Seymour (Throwing), Sweeney, Tannehill, Tannehill (L. Tannehill on Front), Tenney, Thielman, Weimer, White (Pitching), Wiltse (Portrait, No Cap); **SGC 40 VG 3:** 23 cards w/ Brown (Chicago), Brown (Portrait), Demmitt (New York), Donlin (Seated), Doolan (Batting), Dougherty (Portrait), Doyle (N.Y. Hands above Head), Elberfeld (Washington, Fielding), Hartsel, Hooker, Knabe, Knight (With Bat), Livingstone, Lord, McBride, O'Brien, Otey, Pickering, Reulbach (Glove Showing), Sheckard (Glove Showing), Sheckard (No Glove Showing), Snodgrass (Catching) and Young (Glove Shows); **SGC 30 GOOD 2:** 1 card, White; **SGC Authentic:** 22 cards w/ Abbaticchio (Brown Sleeves), Abstein, Ames, Bransfield, Carrigan, Chance (Portrait, Yellow Background), Clarke, Cravath, Davis, Downey, Elberfield (Fielding), Groom, Hummel, Jones, McIntyre (Brooklyn), McIntyre (Brooklyn & Chicago), Mullin (With Bat), Needham, Schaefer (Detroit), Stahl, Tannehill (Tannehill on Front) and Violat. **Minimum Bid: $1,000**

THE MONSTER

19036 **1909-11 T206 Near Complete Set (513/521).** Offered is an attractive near set of the popular T206 White Borders. The offered set is consistent all of the way through, sporting superb eye-appeal. A total of 27 cards have been graded by PSA. Highlights include: Graded Cards - **PSA EX 5:** 1 card, Wheat; **PSA VG-EX 4:** 9 cards w/ Brown (Chicago Shirt), Chance/Yellow Portrait, Clarke/Portrait, Collins/Philadelphia, Crawford/Throwing, Huggins/Hands at Mouth, Jennings/One Hand Showing, McGraw/Glove at Hip and Waddell/Throwing; **PSA VG+ 3.5:** 2 cards w/Mathewson/White Cap and McGraw/Finger in Air; **PSA VG 3:** 10 cards w/ Chance/Batting, Chance/Red Portrait, Huggins/Portrait, Johnson/Hands at Chest, Lajoie/Portrait, Mathewson/Dark Cap, Mathewson/Portrait, Speaker, Tinker/Portrait and Young/Portrait Cleveland; **PSA GOOD+ 2.5:** 1 card, Jennings/Both Hands Showing; **PSA GOOD 2:** Brown/Cubs Shirt (MK), Cobb/Green Portrait (MC), Cobb/Red Portrait and Marquard/Follow Through. **Ungraded Cards** - include: Baker (VG), Beckley (VG), Bender/no trees (VG), Bender/trees (GD), Bender/port. (VG/EX), Bresnahan/port. (GD), Bresnahan/bat (trimmed), G. Brown/Wash. (VG), Brown/ port. (GD/VG), Chesbro (GD/VG), Clarke/bat (GD/VG), Cobb/bat off (PR), Cobb/bat on (PR), Collins/Minn. (FR), Crawford/bat (VG), Dahlen/Brooklyn (VG), G, Davis (GD), Duffy (GD), Evers/port. (GD/VG), Evers/"Chi." (GD), Evers/"Cubs" (GD/VG), Flick (VG), Griffith/bat (VG), Griffith/port. (VG), Jennings/port. (GD), Johnson/port. (PR), Joss/hands (GD/VG), Joss/port. (VG), Keeler/port. (VG), Keeler/bat (VG), Kelley (VG/EX), Kleinow/Bost. (trimmed), Lajoie/throw (GD/VG), Lajoie/bat (GD/VG), Lundgren/Chi. (GD/VG), Marquard/hands (trimmed), Marquard/port. (VG), McGinnity (VG), McGraw/no cap (color added), McGraw/cap (GD/VG), Smith/Chic.& Bos. (PR), Tinker/bat off (GD/VG), Tinker/bat on (GD/VG), Tinker/knees (GD/VG), Waddell/port, (GD/VG), Wallace (VG), Walsh (VG), Willis/Pitts. (GD/VG), Willis/bat (VG), Willis/throw (GD), Young/hand (trimmed). Grades 5% EX, 64% VG to VG/EX, 26% FR to GD, 5% trimmed. **Minimum Bid: $5,000**

TOBACCO TREASURES

19037 **1909-1911 T206 White Border Near Set (500/524).** What takes those intrepid few collectors months and years to assemble could be accomplished here with a single bid, as we offer this rare opportunity to acquire a lion's share of the hobby's first great set without the laborious searching. This is a very consistent and exceptionally attractive near complete T206 set that includes 500 of the 524 cards in the set. The condition composite breaks down as follows: 20% EX or better, 53% VG to VG/EX, 20% Poor to Good, 7% Trimmed. A whopping total of 380 cards have been graded by SGC. Included: **SGC 80 EX/MT 6:** 2 cards w/ Ford and Lake; **SGC 70 EX+ 5.5:** 9 cards w/Delehanty, Doolan (catch),Elberfield (port), Fritz, Kleinbow (catch), Merkle (throw), Murphy (bat), Schmidt (throw), and Sullivan; **SGC 60 EX 5:** 90 cards w/ Collins, McGinnity, Wagner (bat on left), and 87 others; **SGC 50 VG/EX 4:** 140 cards w/ Bender (w/trees), Bender (w/no trees), Brown (port), Brown (Chi. on front), Chase (pink), Chase (dark cap), Cicotte, Clarke (bat), Delehanty, Evers (port), Joss (pitch), Joss (port), Keeler (port), Lajoie (port), Marquard (port), Mathewson (white cap), Tinker (bat on shoulder), Tinker (hands on knees), Tinker (port), Waddell (throw), Waddell (port), Wallace (port), Wheat, Willis (throw), Cy Young (glove), and 115 others; **SGC 40 VG 3:** 126 cards w/ Beckley (port), Brown (Cubs), Chase (white cap), Chesbro, Clarke (port), Crawford (bat), Duffy, Evers (bat-Chicago), Griffith (port), Huggins (port), Jennings (one hand), Jennings (both hands), Lajoie (throw), Lajoie (bat), Marquard (follow through), Mathewson (dark cap), McGraw, McGraw (finger), Speaker, Young (bare hand), and 106 others. **SGC 30 Good 2:** 6 cards w/ Baker, Bender (port), Brown, Cobb (bat on shoulder), Cobb (Green), McGraw (port. Cap); **SGC 20 Fair 1.5:** 2 cards w/ Evers (bat and Cubs) and O'Harra (St. Louis Nat'l); **SGC 10 Poor 1:** 1 card w/ Jennings (port. **SGC Authentic:** 4 cards w/ Bresnahan/ bat, Marquard/hips, O'Hara, Young (port) **Ungraded Cards:** 119 cards w/ Bresnahan (port)(trimmed), Chance (throw) (trimmed), Chase (NY Amer)(Vg-Ex), Keeler (NY Amer) (VG), Willis (bat) (Paper loss)and 114 others. A complete listing of each card and grade will be posted with this lot online. **Minimum Bid: $5,000**

19038 **1910 E93 Standard Caramel Co. Ty Cobb SGC 60 EX 5.** The most valuable card in this ultra-tough thirty card candy issue is presented here for the sophisticated collector, one of only two to achieve an EX 60 ranking with just five charting higher. The rare fielding image finds a jacketed Peach rising against a field of orange, a ball locked in his gloved left hand. Centering, color and registration are immaculate, with just the typical corner wear to account for the score as listed. Surfaces are clean and clear. A magnificent specimen dating from the height of Cobb's considerable powers. **Minimum Bid: $1,000**

DUTCH TREAT

19039 **1910 E93 Standard Caramel Honus Wagner PSA NM 7.** Second only to the great Ty Cobb in value within this thirty-card issue, the Old Dutchman shows the fielding form that made him the first shortstop to enter the Baseball Hall of Fame. Colors are so vibrant it's tough to believe that the card will be celebrating its centennial very soon, with the lightest corner touches the only apparent sign of its advanced age. Presented is the only NM 7 on the PSA population charts, with just two ever charting higher. With candy cards establishing themselves as the hottest field in prewar collecting, there's every reason to follow this auction lot carefully. **Minimum Bid: $2,500**

19040 **1910 E96 Philadelphia Caramel Hugh Jennings PSA EX-MT 6.** Perhaps a bit more lipstick and rouge than one might expect from a Hall of Fame manager, but sometimes one must do what it takes to motivate the team. This super-tough candy issue is just for the collector willing to take on a challenge, and the offered example of this Jennings card is the best you'll find, joining two others at the top of the population chart. A wide left border is the main culprit that stops this example from standing alone at the top of the heap, as wear is at a minimum for a card of such advanced age. **Minimum Bid: $300**

19041 **1910-11 T3 Turkey Red Cabinets Christy Mathewson #27 with Checklist Back SGC 50 VG/EX 4.** In an era when baseball was populated by gruff and grizzled gamblers and alcoholics, Matty stood as a symbol of gentlemanly comportment in our national game, a trait that endeared him to the fans of New York City almost as much as did his remarkable talents. Here he looks appropriately serene against a pastel background of green, purple and blue on this most desirable of Dead Ball issues. The standard corner wear forces a technical VG/EX rating, but you'll be hard pressed to find any other that competes with the endless eye appeal of our offering. **Minimum Bid: $1,000**

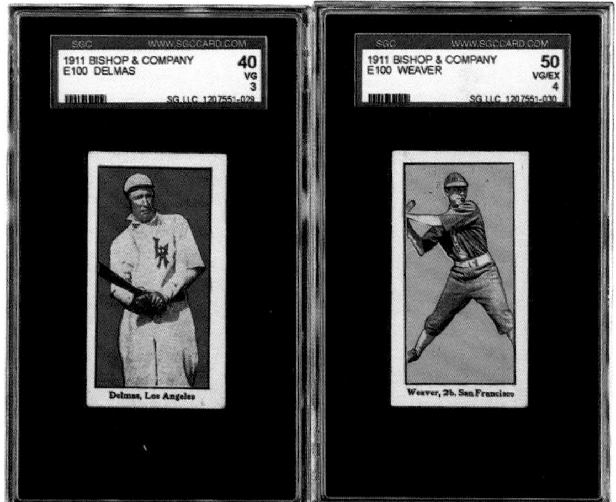

19042 **1911 Bishop & Co. PCL Type 1 (E100) Collection (2).** The cards from this seldom-seen set were issued by the confectioner Bishop & Co. of Los Angeles, which had produced a similar set a year earlier. Both sets showcased star players from the Pacific Coast League. The Buck Weaver card (SGC 50 VG/EX 4) has near perfect centering, tremendous color and rarity. Buck Weaver was one of the most popular "Black Sox" of the 1919 team and his cards have the tendency of selling for more than Hall of Famers of this era, due to his popularity and the lack of cards that are available in the market. The Delmas card (SGC 40 VG 3) presents strong with nice centering, color and rarity. **Minimum Bid: $300**

19043 **1911 E94 Close Candy Ty Cobb PSA EX 5.** Identical in design to the E93 Standard Caramel card likewise presented within this auction, this one provides a green background for the Georgia Peach instead, one of seven color combinations seen within the issue. It's also noteworthy that the Close cards were issued with eleven back variations—ten with overprinting featuring the various candy products marketed by Close, and the eleventh with only the original checklist. Here we encounter that eleventh format. Typical edge wear is the only apparent fault, as the color and registration is wonderful, and even the centering is well within the acceptable range. One of just three Cobbs to rate an EX 5, with only two grading higher. **Minimum Bid: $1,000**

19044 **1911 T201 Mecca Double Folders PSA Graded Complete Set (50).** These cards found in packages of Mecca cigarettes feature one player when the card is open, and another when the set is folded; two players sharing the same pair of legs. The 50-card set contains 100 different players including a number of Hall of Famers. All 50 cards have been graded by PSA with an aggregate SMR value of $. PSA NM 7: Barrett/McGlynn, Chase/Sweeney, Donovan/Stroud (MC), Foster/Ward, Hartzell/Blair, Leach/Gibson, Lobert/Moore; PSA EX/MT 6: Baker/Downie (Downey), Ford/Johnson, Hickman/Hinchman (MC), Killian/Fitzpatrick, Lajoie/Falkenberg, Lush/Hauser, McBride/Elberfeld, McCabe/Starr, Seymour/Dygert, Turner/Stovall, Woodruff/Williams; PSA EX 5: Abstein/Butler, Brown/Hofman, Clarke/Byrne, Collins/Baker, Doyle/Meyers, Evers/Chance, Gaspart/Clarke, Kling/Cole, Lake/Wallace, Liefeld/Simon, Lord/Dougherty, McGinnity/McCarthy, Rucker/Daubert, Speaker/Gardner, Summers/Jennings, Titus/Dooin, Walsh/Payne, Wheat/Bergen, Wiltse/Merkle; PSA VG/EX 4: Cicotte/Thoney, Crawford/Cobb, Huggins/Bresnahan, Lapp/Barry, Matthewson (Mathewson)/Bridwell, Miller/Herzog, Walsh/Payne; PSA VG 3: Bender/Oldring, Downs/Odwell, LaPorte/Stephens, Thomas/Coombs; PSA Good 2: Grant/McLean; PSA PR-FR 1: Johnson/Street, Mattern/Graham.. **Minimum Bid: $1,000**

19045 **1912 T207 Brown Background Louis Lowdermilk PSA VG 3.** With a lifetime pitching record of four victories and five defeats, Lowdermilk is hardly a household name among baseball historians, and seems an unlikely face to appear upon a popular tobacco issue's most valuable card. Severe short-printing has established him as just that, however, and here we present one of just twenty examples ever to find a home in a PSA slab. Rounding of the corners accounts for the grade as listed, but the centering is quite good and the color and surfaces are comparable to those of a much higher grade. Broadleaf back. **Minimum Bid: $500**

19046 **1912 T202 Hassan Triple Folders SGC-Graded Collection (8).** Each card has been graded by SGC. Offered are eight different 1912 Hassan T202, including many Hall of Famers. Highlights of this lot include: **Graded Cards - SGC 80 EX/NM 6:** 2 cards w/#'s 10 Birmingham/Turner *Birmingham's Home Run* and 20 Shean/Chance *Chance Beats Out a Hit*; **SGC 60 EX 5:** 1 card, #14 Oakes/Bresnahan *Catching Him Napping*; **SGC 50 VG/EX 4:** 4 cards w/#'s 3 O'Leary/Cobb *A Desperate Slide For Third,* 16 Foxen/Chance *Chance Beats Out A Hit,* #45 Mathewson/Devlin *Devlin Gets His Man* and 121 McLean/Fromme *Tom Jones At Bat*; SGC 30 GOOD 2: 1 card, #88 Knight/Johnson *Knight Catches A Runner.* **Minimum Bid: $300**

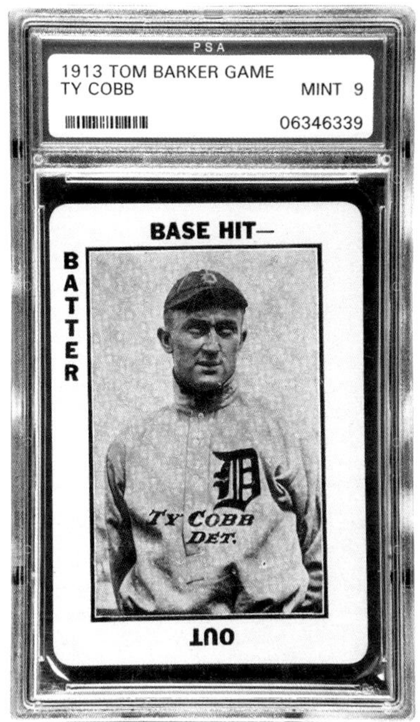

19047 **1913 Tom Barker Game (WG6) Ty Cobb PSA Mint 9.** Ty Cobb, the Southern Baptist slap hitter and master of baseball psychological warfare, is captured on this card displaying his trademark menacing glare at yet another challenger to his baseball supremacy. Nearly identical in format to "The National Game' card set, this issue is distinguished by a different card back. Only two other cards graded by PSA have matched this top mark of Mint 9, with none rating higher. **Minimum Bid: $600**

19048 **1913 T200 Fatima Team Cards Collection (9).** Issued by Ligget & Myers Tobacco Co. in 1913 with Fatima brand cigarettes, the T200 set consists of eight National League and eight American League team cards. Present here are the Chicago Americans, Chicago Nationals, Cincinnati Nationals, (2) Philadelphia Americans, Philadelphia Nationals, St. Louis Nationals, (2) Washington Americans. **Minimum Bid: $650**

19049 1914 B18 Blanket Trio Featuring Joe Jackson, Ty Cobb and Walter Johnson (3). These three, no doubt, would have been the cornerstone pieces of any blanket made from these flannels. All three present EX to EX/MT or better; with Jackson and Johnson being especially nice, retaining all of their original brilliant coloring. **Minimum Bid: $375**

19050 1914 B18 Blankets Collection (80). Commonly sewn together to bed covers or throws, these 5-1/4"-square flannels were issued in 1914 wrapped around several popular brands of tobacco. Different color combinations exist for all 10 teams included in the set. Highlights include Del Baker (brown infield), Frank Chance (green infield), Ty Cobb (white infield), Harry Coveleski (brown infield), Cozy Dolan (purple pennants), Del Gainor (brown infield), Hank Gowdy (brown infield), Earl Hamilton (purple basepaths), Miller Huggins (purple pennants), Ham Hyatt (purple pennants), Walter Johnson (green pennants), Joe Kelley (purple pennants), Rabbit Maranville (white infield), (2) Bill McCallister (purple basepaths, red basepaths), Hub Perdue (brown infield), Del Pratt (purple basepaths), Burt Shotton (red basepaths), (2) Bill Steele (purple pennants, yellow pennants), Casey Stengel (green infield), Jim Viox (purple pennants), Dee Walsh (purple basepaths), Zach Wheat (green infield). Blankets average in condition from VG to EX, several exhibit typical staining associated with the issue. **Minimum Bid: $400**

19051 1916 M101-4 "Everybody's Boys Clothing Department" SGC Graded Collection (19). These black-and-white cards share the format and checklist of the much more common Sporting News M101-4 version and many other regional advertisers. Everybody's is amongst the scarcest advertising backs to be found in this issue and the cards command a premium from type-card and superstar collectors. Includes **SGC 50 VG/EX 4:** 4 cards - #9 J. Franklin Baker, 20 George Burns, 27 Ray Caldwell, 31 Larry Cheney. **SGC 40 VG 3:** 15 cards - #21 Joe Bush, 22 Donie Bush, 23 Art Butler, 24 Bobbie Byrne, 25 Forrest Cady, 26 Jimmy Callahan, 29 George Chalmers, 30 Ray Chapman, 32 Eddie Cicotte, 33 Tom Clarke, 34 Eddie Collins, 36 Charles Comiskey, 39 Harry Coveleskie, 40 Gavvy Cravath, 35 Shauno Collins. **Minimum Bid: $1,000**

19052 **1916 Tango Eggs Buck Weaver (Picture Joe Tinker) NM PSA 7.** The Tango Eggs series was unknown until a discovery of less than 500 cards in 1991. Buck Weaver, one of the infamous "Eight Men Out" from 1919 Chicago Black Sox fame, batted .324 in the Series with no errors committed in the field. While he maintained his innocence, Weaver was banned for having knowledge of the fix and not informing team officials. In a case of mistaken identity, this card actually pictures Joe Tinker - the Hall of Famer of Chicago Cubs fame. **Minimum Bid: $325**

19054 **1915 Cracker Jack Al Bridwell #42 SGC 88 NM/MT 8.** It was Al Bridwell's single against the Chicago Cubs which caused the crucial "Merkle boner" running error that ended up costing the Giants the 1908 pennant. Bridwell ended his playing days in the Federal League as a member of the St. Louis Terriers. With only two examples rated higher by SGC, this card is sure to appeal to the serious Cracker Jack collector. Light touches of wear at the corners are the only noticeable condition issue. **Minimum Bid: $200**

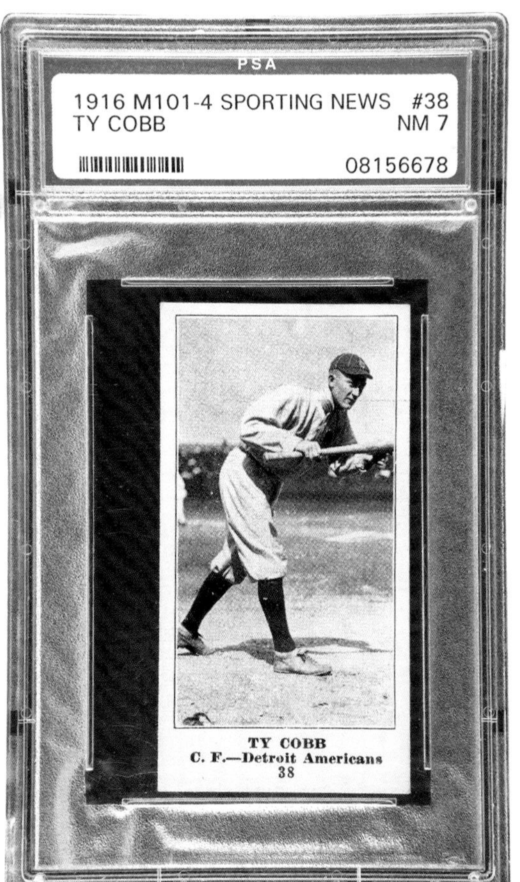

19053 **1916 M101-4 Sporting News Ty Cobb Blank Back #38 PSA NM 7.** Issued the only season of a nine-year stretch in which this first Hall of Famer did not win the American League batting title, this tough blank back version of his coveted *Sporting News* card finds Cobb demonstrating his mastery with the lumber that made him one of just two men in history to reach the magical 4,000 hit mark. Only nine examples of this card have ever been encapsulated by PSA in any grade, and just a single one of them has surpassed this Mint marvel. The lightest of corner touches and a light vertical print line seem to be all that keeps it from sharing the top spot. Certainly one of the toughest Ty Cobb cards in the market today, for the highly sophisticated collector. **Minimum Bid: $,2500**

19055 1915 Cracker Jack Al Bridwell # 42 SGC 96 Mint 9. Al Bridwell played for five teams in his ten seasons and the 1915 season that this Cracker Jack card was issued was his last. This beautiful example is simply unimprovable with perfectly centered borders, a bright, bold registration, and four strong corners. It represents the only example to achieve such lofty mint status in the SGC population reports with none grading higher. **Minimum Bid: $350**

19056 1915 Cracker Jack Charles Comiskey #23 SGC 86 NM+ 7.5. Comiskey's own greed is considered to have been the real motivation for the "Black Sox" selling out to gamblers in 1919. When it was revealed that the players threw the Series for $10,000 because Comiskey had underpaid them for years, his sterling reputation was tarnished. Nonetheless, he was elected to the Hall of Fame in 1939, as an executive. With only one graded higher by SGC, this card is sure to be on the wantlist of more than a few registry collectors. A slight difference in centering from left to right is the only noteworthy condition issue. **Minimum Bid: $350**

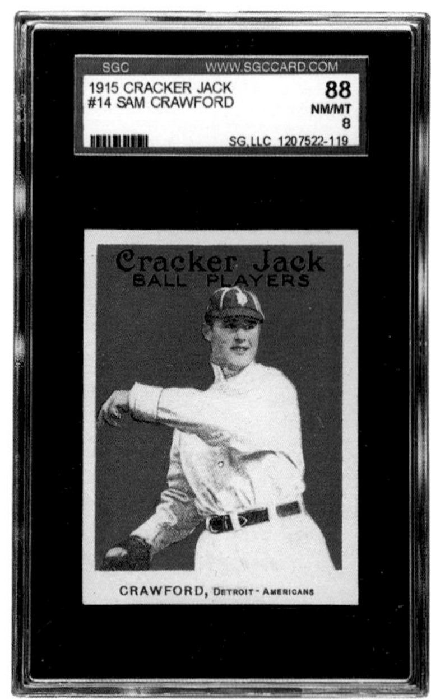

19057 1915 Cracker Jack Sam Crawford #14 SGC 88 NM/MT 8. "Wahoo Sam" Crawford flourished while playing in the shadow of his more famous Hall of Fame teammate Ty Cobb. He fell just short of 3000 hits with 2961 and was inducted into the Hall of Fame in 1957. One of only two of this card to receive the coveted NM/MT 8 designation from SGC, they have graded just one better out of the 19 submitted. The card retains all of its brilliance in color on the front with almost sparkling white borders. A touch of one corner and the slightest discoloration on the card's reverse are all that separate it from blissful perfection. A remarkably strong representation for registry collectors. **Minimum Bid: $400**

19058 1915 Cracker Jack George Mullen #24 SGC 88 NM/MT 8. After a career spent largely with the Detroit Tigers in the American League, George Mullin finished his pitching career in the Federal League with the Indianapolis Hooisers and Newark Pepper. With only one SGC example graded higher, this one is sure to fill someone's wish list. Card features nice centering, strong corners and bold, vivid colors. **Minimum Bid: $200**

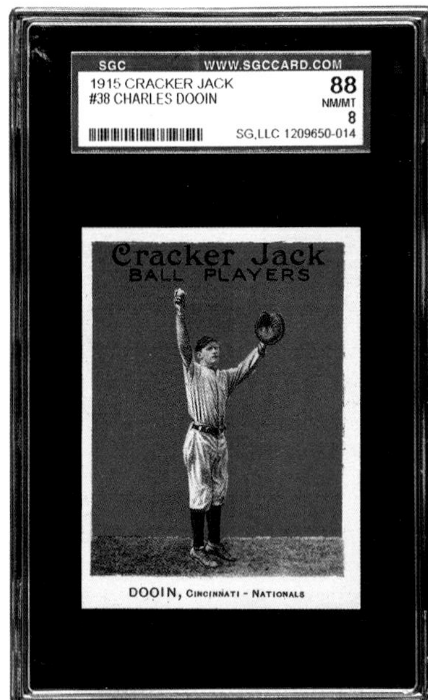

19059 1915 Cracker Jack Charles Dooin #38 SGC 88 NM/MT 8. Despite being listed as a member of the "Cincinnati - Nationals" at the base of this card, it's noteworthy that "Red" only appeared in ten games for the Reds, as the team proved to be just a brief stop-over between the Phillies and the Giants. Of the 18 submitted to SGC, only one has achieved a higher mark than the offered 88 NM/MT 8. Card retains all of its original brilliance, with centering the only flaw holding this one back from a higher grade. **Minimum Bid: $200**

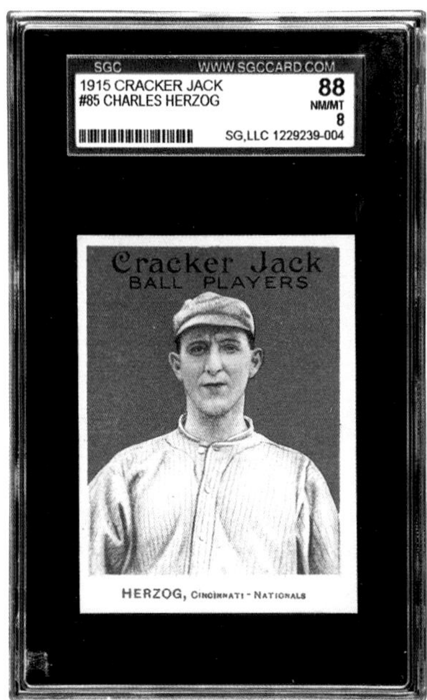

19060 1915 Cracker Jack Charles Herzog #85 SGC 88 NM/MT 8. Charles "Buck" Herzog reached the World Series four times as a member of the New York Giants, finishing on the losing end all four times. Only two of the 17 Herzog cards submitted to SGC have obtained the 88 NM/MT rating (none higher). A definite candidate to fill a lucky collector's registry collection; this card has all the characteristics of a high grade example with vivid colors, borders clean as the driven snow and untouched front and back surfaces. **Minimum Bid: $200**

19061 1915 Cracker Jack Connie Mack #12 PSA NM/MT 8. Over the course of a half century, the Philadelphia Athletics captured five World Series titles under the guidance of Cornelius Alexander McGillicuddy. Connie Mack managed a remarkable 7755 games with the Philadelphia Athletics and Pittsburgh Pirates, finally calling it quits at age 87. Only three of the 64 examples PSA has reviewed have merited a higher grade. The slightest of centering differences and a touch of wear at the corners are the only apparent condition issues. **Minimum Bid: $500**

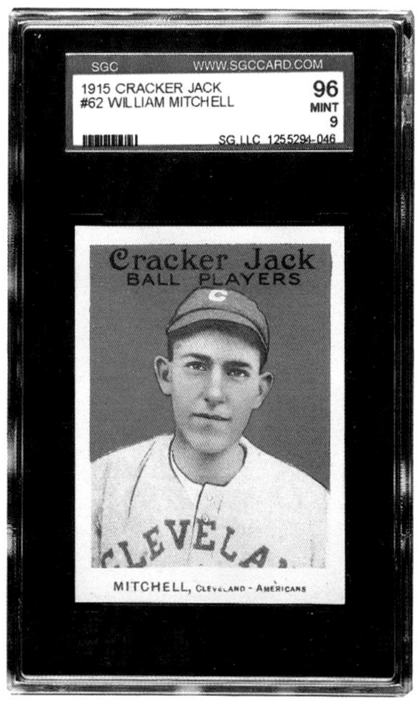

19062 1915 Cracker Jack William Mitchell #62 SGC 96 Mint 9. Cracker Jacks are forever intertwined with the game of baseball and the Cracker Jack issues of the teens still remain some of the most popular in the hobby. This card's intense white borders are notably crisp and each corner has retained its pack fresh strength. This beautiful specimen is the only example to reach Mint 96 status with SGC and only has one equal graded 9 by PSA with none graded higher. **Minimum Bid: $350**

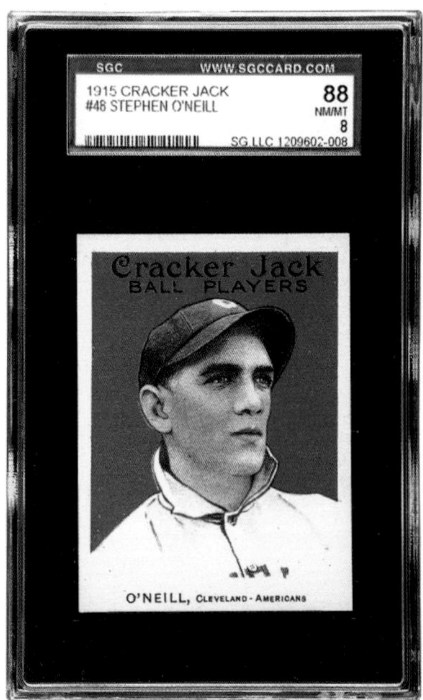

19063 **1915 Cracker Jack Stephen O'Neill #48 SGC 88 NM/MT 8.** Steve O'Neill played in one World Series as a member of the victorious Cleveland Indians in 1920. He would later manage the 1945 Detroit Tigers to another World Series title. Only two other examples of this card have been graded higher by SGC. Card exhibits all of the qualities one would expect from such a high grade specimen; vivid coloring and registration, snow white borders, clean surfaces front and back. The slightest hint of wear at a couple of corners is all that separate this card from absolute perfection. **Minimum Bid: $200**

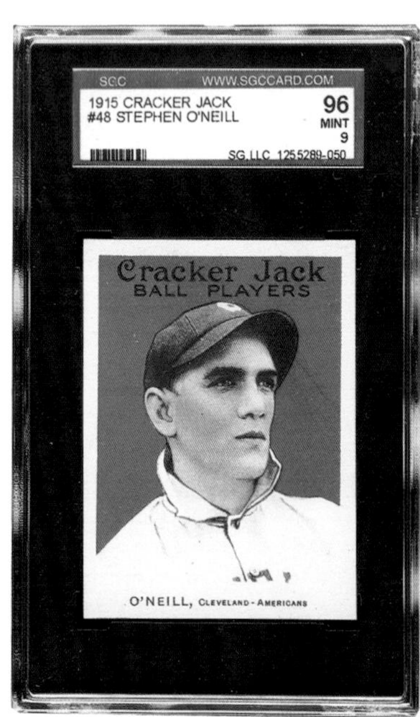

19064 **1915 Cracker Jack Stephen O'Neill #48 SGC 96 Mint 9.** The bright and bold color combined with the flawless printing and four sharp corners make it easy to see why this gorgeous Cracker Jack card was deemed Mint by the graders at SGC. As such, it has the honor of being the only example that has been graded mint by SGC with only one Mint 9 counterpart at PSA and none grading higher. **Minimum Bid: $350**

19065 **1915 Cracker Jack Michael Simon #25 PSA NM-MT 8.** Michael Simon caught seven major league seasons, first with the Pittsburgh Pirates in the National League before finishing in the Federal League with the St. Louis Terriers and Brooklyn Tip-Tops. Of the 50 listed in PSA's population report, only one rates higher; leaving most registry collectors very interested in obtaining the high grade example offered here. Card displays all the necessary attributes to merit such a high mark; four sharp corners, vivid coloring and clear card surfaces. **Minimum Bid: $200**

19066 **1915 Cracker Jack Tris Speaker #65 SGC 84 NM 7.** Among the great hitters of the early 20th century, Tris Speaker must be mentioned in the same conversation alongside Ty Cobb, Joe Jackson, Honus Wagner and Nap Lajoie. During a remarkable 22-year career, Speaker finished with 3514 hits and a lifetime batting average of .345. Only four examples of this card have graded higher of those submitted to SGC. Centering is the only condition issue of note; the card retains bold coloring and displays four strong corners, along with remarkably clean front and back. **Minimum Bid: $300**

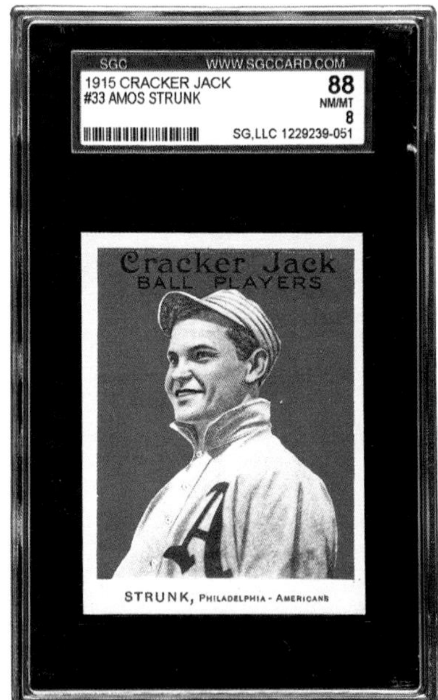

19067 **1915 Cracker Jack Amos Strunk #33 SGC 88 NM-MT 8.** Highly regarded for his defensive skills, Amos Strunk led AL outfielders in fielding percentage five times. Ed Barrow obtained his services trading with Connie Mack before the 1918 World Series. With Strunk patrolling center field, the Red Sox did capture the World Series crown. This is one of five (none higher) of the 17 submitted to SGC to obtain an 88 NM-MT 8 ranking. Centering is the only drawback preventing a more perfect score. **Minimum Bid: $200**

19068 **1915 Cracker Jack Ivy Wingo #130 SGC 88 NM/MT 8.** Ivey Brown Wingo was a catcher with the 1919 Cincinnati Reds team which defeated the infamous Black Sox as part of that year's World Series. Of the 20 examples of this card submitted to SGC, only one has ever obtained a higher grade. A slight difference in centering is the only condition flaw worthy of mention. **Minimum Bid: $200**

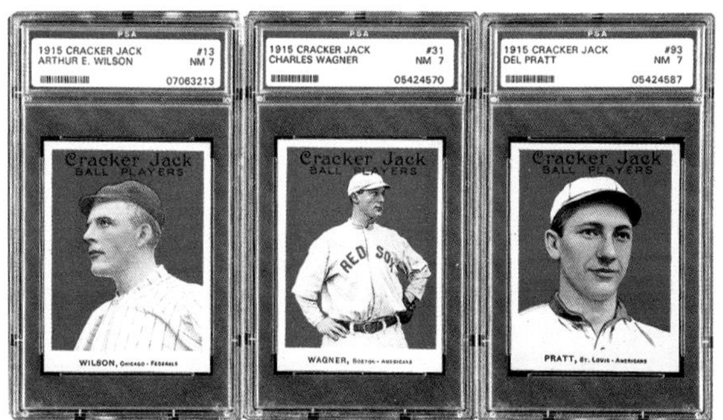

19069 **1915 Cracker Jack Baseball Collection (3).** For those wanting to start a Cracker Jack collection, this group provides a perfect starting point. Cards grade a universal PSA NM 7 and are all three respectable representations. Includes #13 Arthur E. Wilson, 31 Charles Wagner, 93 Del Pratt. **Minimum Bid: $200**

19070 **1915 Cracker Jack Baseball SGC-Graded Collection (14).** Offered is a 14 card collection of SGC-Graded 1915 Cracker Jacks in high grade. Seldom will you see a nice collection of these cards in high grade. All of the examples have been graded SGC 84 NM 7, with the exception of one, which has attained an SGC 86 NM+ 7.5. Highlights include: **Graded - SGC 86 NM+ 7.5:** 1 card, #149 Janvrin; **SGC 84 NM 7:** 11 cards w/#'s 11 Stovall, 45 Luderus, 49 Miller, 56 Milan, 62 Mitchell, 100 Seaton, 102 Fisher, 119 Perring, 134 Marsans, 135 Killifer, 157 Kaiserling, 165 Murphy and 168 Campbell. **Minimum Bid: $500**

19071 **1915 Cracker Jack Baseball SGC-Graded Collection (38).** Presented is a 38 card collection of 1915 Cracker Jacks. This is a nice array of cards from one of the more popular issues, the 1915 Cracker Jack. Some of the lower grade cards present very well on the front, but have some sort of back issues. Highlights include: **Graded: SGC 80 EX/NM 6:** 9 cards w/#'s 5 Miller, 54 O'Toole, 72 Boehling, 96 Becker, 105 Lavender, 106 Birmingham, 108 Magee, 143 Daubert and 147 Magee; **SGC 70 EX+ 5.5:** 1 card, #131 Baumgardner; **SGC 60 EX 5:** 3 cards w/#'s 17 Bresnahan, 51 Rucker and 71 Meyers; **SGC 50 VG/EX 4:** 10 cards w/#'s 64 Archer, 74 Owens, 97 Benton, 104 Saier, 107 Downey, 112 Sweeney, 126 Blair, 127 Schmidt, 129 Caldwell and 174 Veach; **SGC 40 VG 3:** 5 cards w/#'s 27 Carrigan, 70 Clarke, 111 Moran, 125 Niehoff and 153 James; **SGC 30 GOOD 2:** 8 cards w/#'s 4 Doyle, 20 Falkenberg, 23 Comisky, 25 Simon, 45 Luderus, 95 Keating, 142 Packard and 152 McQuillen; **SGC 20 FAIR 1.5:** 2 cards w/#'s 28 Barry and 41. **Minimum Bid: $2,000**

19072 **1921 E121 American Caramel Ty Cobb, Manager on Front Series Of 80 PSA EX-MT 6.** This card is extracted from the scarce American Caramel Series of 80 (E121) set issued in 1921. The baseball careers of Ty Cobb and Babe Ruth overlapped 14 seasons (1914-28), and the older Cobb was reluctant to let go of his supremacy in the game as it transformed from the dead-ball era to the more modern home-run era. Only four PSA examples have been graded at this EX-MT level with only two others attaining higher status. An nicely graded EX-MT card. **Minimum Bid: $300**

19073 **1921 Koester Bread George Ruth SGC 80 EX/NM 6.** The first ever New York City "Subway Series" was the catalyst in giving birth to this exceedingly scarce issue, distributed in October 1921 by New York bakery "E.H. Koester" to celebrate the occasion. The issue made use of the New York Giants and Yankees images from the American Caramel Series of 120 (E121), and added a few more besides. These blank-backed cards are considerably more rare than the E121's, however, and the New York connection makes this Babe Ruth specimen a particular treasure. The fine condition is practically overkill here, with light corner wear the main factor in establishing the EX/MT rating. Only one other example has ever graded higher. **Minimum Bid: $1,500**

19074 **1922 American Caramel Series of 240 (E120) Babe Ruth PSA Poor 1.** Babe Ruth is imaged on this scarce candy card gently holding a baseball, probably just before signing for yet another adoring fan. "The Sultan of Swat" was more often than not a willing signer, despite the enormous volume of requests he must have faced. Ruth single-handedly changed the complexion of the game and helped to transform it with the prodigious long balls which came from his bat. The card has numerous condition issues; a stain on front, crease at the top edge, wear at the corners and signs of removal on the card's reverse. The oval-shaped image of Ruth, much like his influence over the game, remains untouched. **Minimum Bid: $250**

19075 **1922 American Caramel Co. E121 "Babe" Ruth Photo Montage SGC 40 VG 3.** Note the quotation marks around the word "Babe" in our listing title, as it is relevant to the value of the piece. This particularly rare candy card was printed in versions both with and without the punctuation in question, and we offer the scarcer and more desirable variation here. The SGC population charts make no distinction between the four variations of Ruth cards from this issue in their records, but it's still worth noting that only three examples of any style has ever topped this offering. Rounding of corners and a small crease in the bottom left are the only culprits here in regard to condition, leaving the surfaces (and hence the eye appeal) that of a much stronger card. **Minimum Bid: $500**

19076 **1922 Eastern Exhibit Supply Co. Ty Cobb Post Card SGC 84 NM 7.** If you are looking for rarity, along with high grade; you need not look any further. This 1922 Eastern Exhibit Supply Co. card of Ty Cobb supplies all of it. The company, established in 1921, was the major producer of exhibit cards and operated until 1971. This exquisite Ty Cobb is at the top of the grading charts. Of a combined 18 Cobb post cards from this series submitted to SGC and PSA, this is the lone representation (none higher) of a NM 7. The only thing that keep this from grading higher are the light touches on the bottom corners which probably came from the lack of proper storage. A phenomenal card that begs the question; will there be another to ever grade this high or higher. **Minimum Bid: $500**

19077 **1926-1929 Exhibits Babe Ruth Postcard Back-Pose PSA EX 5.** You'll be hard-pressed to find a superior photographic portrait of the game's greatest name than the one utilized here, which finds the Hall of Fame Yankee gripping his trusted Hillerich & Bradsby, his eyes locked upon the viewer's. Only typical edge wear is found to suggest eight decades of life, placing it behind just a single example on the PSA population charts. A rare issue dating from the absolute height of Ruth's powers. **Minimum Bid: $300**

19078 **1932 Zeenut PCL SGC Graded Collection With and Without Coupons (37).** Presented is a collection of 37 1932 Zeenut PCL with Coupons (25) and Without Coupons (12). These are super tough cards to find with the coupons. Although there are not many stars in this series, there are two Oana cards. Highlights include: **Graded Cards - SGC 50 VG/EX 4:** 1 card, Martin; **SGC 40 VG 3:** 3 cards w/ Davis, Ward and Willoughby; **SGC 30 GOOD 2:** 9 cards w/ Cole (WOC), Donovan, Henderson, Martin, Sherlock (WOC), Sulik (2), Thomas (WOC) and Wera; **SGC 20 FAIR 1.5:** 10 cards w/ Campbell, Campbell (WOC), Caveney, Devine, Donovan, Mailho (WOC), Oana, Sankey (WOC), Thomas (WOC) and Walsh (WOC); **SGC 10 POOR 1:** 14 cards w/ Babich, Frazier, Garibaldi, Henderson, Jacobs, Jacobs (WOC), Joiner (WOC), Keesey, Martin (WOC), Oana, Penebsky (2), Pinelli (WOC) and Wera. **Minimum Bid: $500**

19079 **1933-36 Zeenut With Coupon SGC Graded Collection (55).** Every card has been graded by SGC. Offered is a collection of 55 1933-36 Zeenut cards with coupons. There are 40 different players included in this ensemble. Highlights include: **Graded Cards - SGC 60 EX 5:** 3 cards w/ Horne, Kintana and Milho; **SGC 50 VG/EX 4:** 16 cards w/ Backer, Borja, Cox, Donovan, Fitzpatrick, Gibson, Herrmann, Holland, Kampouris, Kintana, Lahman, Palmisano, Pool, Sulik and Woodall (2); **SGC 40 VG 3:** 18 cards w/ Backer, Biongovanni, Deviveiros, Douglas, Eckhardt, Funk, Garibaldi, Glaister, Hafey, Haney, Joiner, Kampouris, Mailho, Mullen, Pillette, Pool, Steinbacker and Woodall; **SGC 30 GOOD 2:** 10 cards w/ Borja, Fitzpatrick (2), Gibson, Hafey, Hartwig, Kelly, Palmisano, Salvo and Stutz; **SGC 20 FAIR 1.5:** 5 cards w/ Coscarart, Glaister, Page, Phebus and Radonitz; **SGC 10 POOR 1:** 3 cards w/ Borja, Quellich and Rhyne. **Minimum Bid: $500**

19080 **1933 R333 DeLong Complete Set (24).** The DeLong Co. of Boston was among the first to sell baseball cards with gum, issuing a set of 24 cards in 1933. This completely graded set includes **SGC 60 EX 5:** #9 Urbanski, 21 Foxx; **PSA EX 5:** #20 Vosmik; **SGC 50 VG/EX 4:** #5 Gehringer, 11 Lindstrom, 13 Maranville, 14 Gomez, 16 Warneke, 18 Dykes, 23 Grove; **SGC 40 VG 3:** #4 Terry, 8 Cuyler, 10 O'Doul, 15 Stephenson, 19 Hafey, 22 Klein; **PSA VG 3:** #6 Cochrane; **GAI VG 3:** #24 Goslin; **SGC 30 Good 2:** #1 McManus, 3 Melillo, 7 Gehrig, 12 Traynor, 17 Martin; **SGC 10 Poor 1:** #2 Simmons. **Minimum Bid: $750**

19082 **1933 Goudey Sport Kings Babe Ruth #2 PSA EX 5.** The title of this Goudey issue sums it up nicely as Ruth is certainly considered to be the king of baseball and he was at the height of his popularity when the issue was released in 1933. This beautiful example was blessed with well centered and even borders on each side as well as strong color and registration from the day it was printed at Goudey. Each of the corners is evenly rounded as this is a very pleasing example of this Sport King in mid grade. **Minimum Bid: $400**

19081 **1933 Sport Kings Gum Ty Cobb #1 PSA EX-MT 6.** Topping even Babe Ruth for the number one spot (the Bambino was card number two), the "Georgia Peach" starts off a set that features the best from Golden Age boxing (Dempsey, Tunney), hockey (Shore, Bailey), football (Grange, Thorpe) and beyond. The mixture of Cobb's star power and his appearance as number one in the set (and, of course, the card's advanced age) make this one of the toughest cards to find in a EX-MT or higher. The only detail that keeps this cards from grading a NM 7 is the centering top-bottom. The picture is as clear as day and the color is second to none. A strong EX-MT card. **Minimum Bid: $300**

19083 **1933 Goudey Sport Kings Carl Hubbell #42 SGC 86 NM+ 7.5** "King Carl" was a deserving inclusion in the Sport Kings issue which included standout athletes from all different sports. He would win the 1933 NL MVP award and lead his New York Giants to World Series glory, going 2-0 and allowing no earned runs in 20 innings work. With only four of the 45 submitted to SGC rating higher, this Sport Kings Carl Hubbell should be in high demand. Centering is the only condition issue worthy of mention. **Minimum Bid: $200**

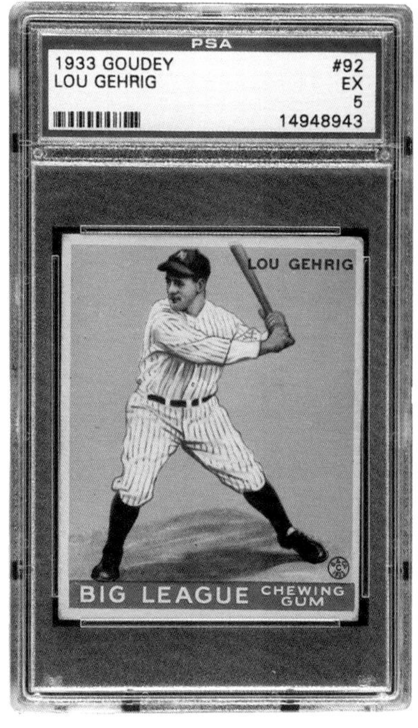

19084 **1933 Goudey Lou Gehrig #92 PSA EX 5.** An affordable piece of one of the game's legendary figures in the prime of his career. Pictured is a ballplayer that had accumulated an astonishing 121 HR's and 509 RBI's over the previous three seasons. This example is in a very respectable excellent condition. A Goudey Gehrig card is a must for any serious vintage baseball card collection. **Minimum Bid: $600**

BEAUTIFUL BABE, PART ONE

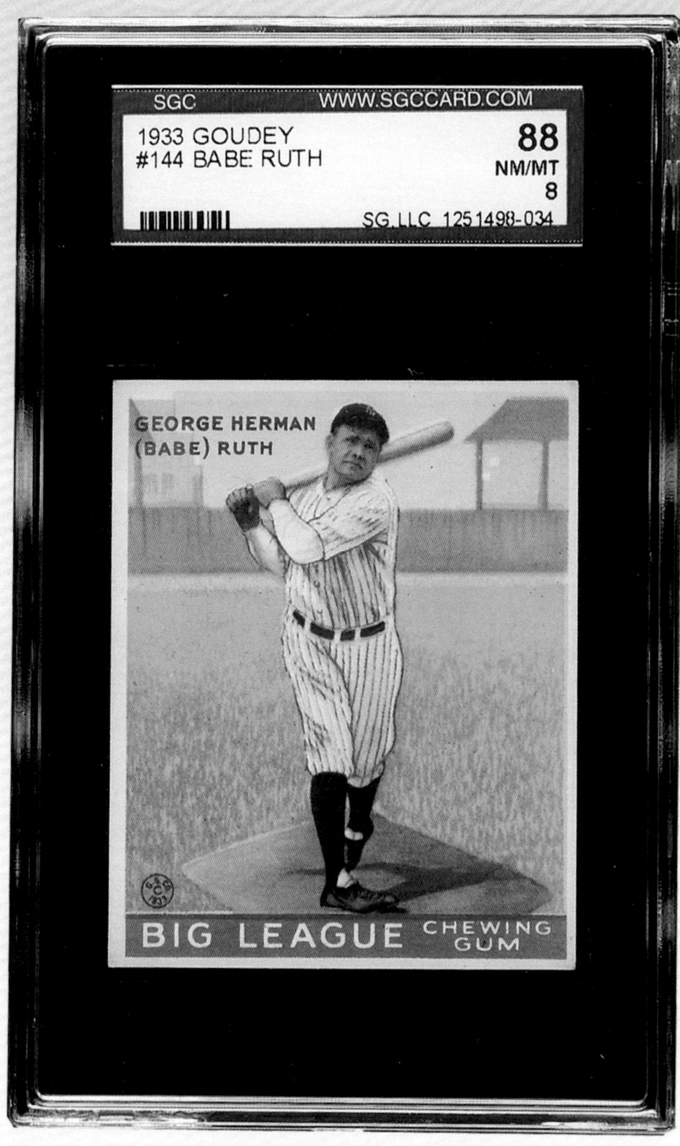

19085 **1933 Goudey Babe Ruth #144 SGC 88 NM/MT 8.** The essence of the Depression-era game, distilled into a single three-inch tall slab of cardboard. The details of the offering are little more than a long list of superlatives, as the set, the player it pictures, and the condition of the card specifically all rank at the pinnacle of the hobby. Joining the 1909-11 T206 and 1952 Topps issues to form the baseball card collecting's "Big Three," the 1933 Goudey set is rightfully considered a consummate masterpiece, with gorgeous portraiture capturing many of the greatest names of the pre-war era. And certainly there was none greater than Babe Ruth, who strikes his classic batting pose here on what may be the set's most recognizable card. Brilliant color and flawless registration brings the Babe to life almost three-quarters of a century after issue, and a stunning absence of wear defies all logic. A minor southern shift in centering and the slightest corner touches are all we can report when pressed to find any variation from utter perfection, and it's little surprise that only two representations have ever risen higher on the SGC population charts. **Minimum Bid: $2,500**

BEAUTIFUL BABE, PART TWO

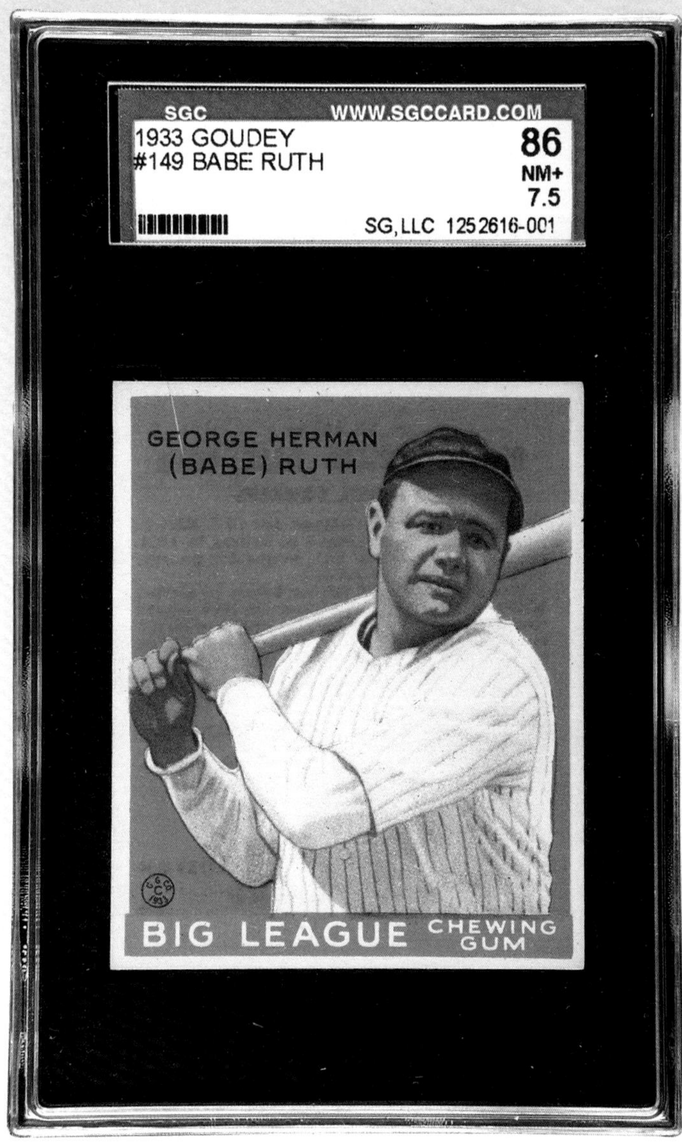

19086 **1933 Goudey Babe Ruth #149 SGC 86 NM+ 7.5.** The first line of his cardback biography summarizes the legendary ballplayer's greatness. "Home run king of the big leagues." As tribute to his sovereignty, Ruth's likeness was featured on four different 1933 Goudey cards. It would be nearly impossible to find a finer specimen, as only one of the 126 reviewed by SGC has received a higher mark. Centering is above the norm; with four strong corners, a clean front and back, and colors that radiate. A few stray printing lines are all that separate this card from even a higher grade. **Minimum Bid: $2,500**

BUBBLE GUM'S BEST

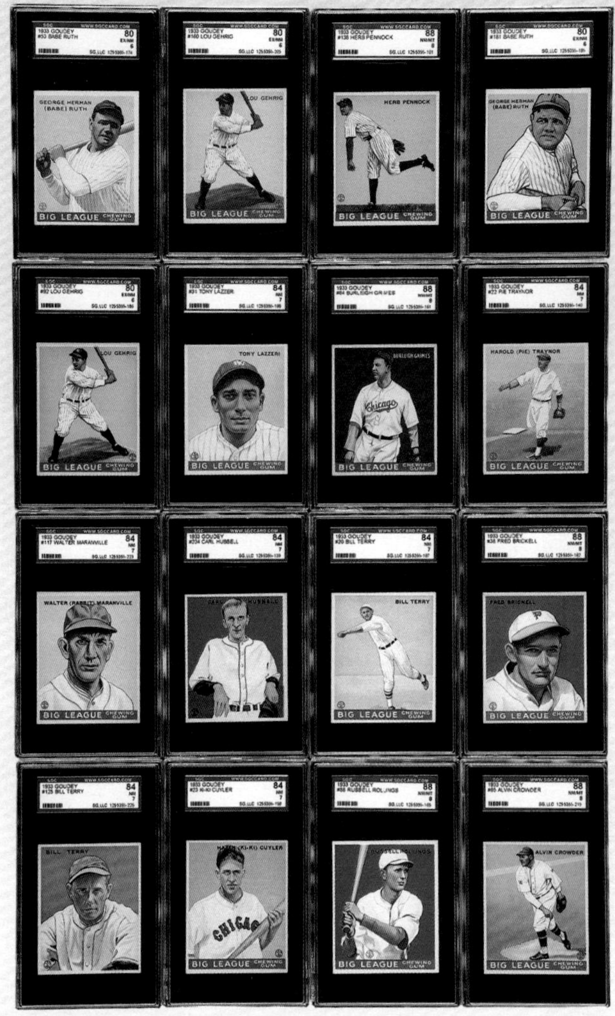

19087 **1933 Goudey Baseball High Grade Near Set (238/239).** The 1933 Goudey baseball set is considered the king of the early gum card issues and it's easy to see why with its tremendous artwork, colors, and multiple Hall of Famers including Ruth, Gehrig, Foxx, Hornsby, Hubbell, Ott. This is an amazingly consistent complete high grade set which is only missing the Babe Ruth #149 card. With over 50% having been graded, that leaves only a little bit of leg work to get the rest of this set done. A total of 126 cards have been graded by SGC with an aggregate SMR value of $55,780. Highlights include: Graded Cards - **SGC 88 NM/MT 8:** 14 cards w/#'s 38, 64 Grimes, 66, 72, 88, 95 Crowder, 129, 138 Pennock, 182, 190, 192, 205, 209 and 238 Critz; **SGC 86 NM+ 7.5:** 11 cards w/#'s 26, 32, 44 Bottomley, 60 Hoyt, 86, 108, 161, 163, 170, 173 and 202 Hartnett; **SGC 84 NM 7:** 49 cards w/#'s 11, 17, 20 Terry, 22 Traynor, 23 Cuyler, 31 Lazzeri, 37, 42 Collins, 51, 61, 63 Cronin, 65, 67, 68, 71, 76 Cochrane, 77, 78, 82, 94, 99, 104, 111, 117 Maranville, 123, 124, 125 Terry, 130 Fitzsimmons, 134 Rice, 137, 145, 146, 152, 157, 162, 165 Sewell, 166, 180, 191, 193, 204, 214, 215, 216 Gomez, 217 Crosetti, 218, 219, 234 Hubbell and 235 Fitzsimmons; **SGC 80 EX/NM 6:** 34 cards w/#'s 1 Bengough, 2 Vance, 5 Herman, 7 Lyons, 9, 10, 13, 34, 46, 53 Ruth, 58 O'Doul, 59, 79 Faber, 80, 83, 85, 89 Speaker, 92 Gehrig, 93, 109 Cronin, 112, 128 Klein, 136, 142, 148, 153, 160 Gehrig, 164 Waner, 181 Ruth, 189 Cronin, 199, 203, 230 Hubbell and 233; **SGC 70 EX+ 5.5:** 5 cards w/#'s 47 Manush, 49 Frisch, 110 Goslin, 119 Hornsby and 223 Dean; SGC 60 EX 5: 8 cards w/#'s 100, 133 Lindstrom, 154 Foxx, 167, 171, 220 Grove, 222 Gehringer and 239; **SGC 50 VG/EX 4:** 4 cards w/#'s 81, 105, 114 and 194 Averill; **SGC 30 GOOD 2:** 1 card, #144 Ruth. Ungraded Cards - include #'s 19 Dickey (GD/VG), 25 Waner (VG), 29 Foxx (trimmed), 35 Simmons (VG/EX), 56 Ruffing (EX), 73 Haines (EX), 74 Rixey (VG/EX), 102 Jackson (GD/VG), 103 Combs (VG), 107 Manush (VG, small), 127 Ott (VG/EX), 147 Durocher (GD/VG), 158 Berg (trimmed), 168 Goslin (trimmed), 187 Manush (EX), 188 Hornsby (EX), 197 Ferrell (VG/EX), 207 Ott (GD), 211 Wilson (EX), 227 Herman (EX), 229 Vaughan (trimmed) and 240 Schumacher (GD/VG). Grades 31% NM to NM/MT, 44% EX to EX/MT, 18% VG to VG/EX, 7% trimmed. **Minimum Bid: $5,000**

19088 **1934 Goudey Baseball PSA-Graded Collection (8).** Presented is a small collection of eight 1934 Goudey cards that have all been graded by PSA, including Hall of Famer Chick Hafey in a PSA NM+ 7.5. All of these cards possess vibrant color, great centering and nice corners. Highlights include: **Graded - PSA NM-MT 8:** 1 card, #45 Melillo; **PSA NM+ 7.5:** 1 card, #34 Hafey; **PSA NM 7:** 4 cards w/#'s 28 Coleman, 31 Jordan, 63 Minter and 64 Grube; **PSA EX 5:** 2 cards w/#'s 22 Vaughn and 29 French. Cumulative SMR value exceeds $1800. **Minimum Bid: $450**

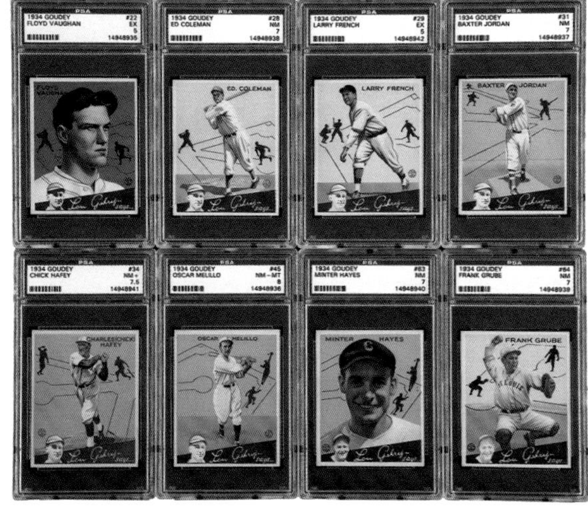

19089 **1934 Canadian Goudey World Wide Gum Uncut Sheet of 72.** Discouraged by taunts that they were behind the times, the Canadian World Wide Gum manufacturers abandoned the design of the 1933 Goudey issue at the midway point, offering the contemporary '34 style from card number forty-nine to ninety-six. And so our neighbors to the north became the beneficiaries of the "Lou Gehrig says..." advice, in both French and English, on the verso, the only way that these cards vary from the American issue. On the face, this incredible sheet is a dead ringer for the 1934 Goudey. And while we'd be thrilled to have just that second forty-eight in a single sheet, this one repeats seventy-three to ninety-six, offering duplicates of every card from John "Blondy" Ryan through John Allen. Happily, this range includes Hall of Famers Hafey, Lombardi, Appling, Earnshaw and Lou Gehrig himself, so that each of these pre-war legends appears twice on the sheet. Lest we forget those who appear only once, we should note that cards forty-nine through seventy-two feature Terry, Grove, Dizzy Dean, Klein, Gehringer, Foxx, Cochrane, Frisch, Paul Waner, Manush, Durocher, Vaughan and Hubbell. That's twenty-three Hall of Fame cards total! A masterful color and paper restoration job has diminished the signs of wear almost to the point of invisibility, but if you look very closely you can spot a seam that runs the length of the second column of cards, and various other scattered wrinkles throughout. But again, like cards one through forty-eight offered in the previous lot, the bright coloring of the cards leaves the impression of a factory-fresh sheet from any reasonable distance. **Minimum Bid: $1,500**

19090 **1934 Goudey Luke Appling #27 PSA NM+ 7.5.** Offered is a very pleasing example of this Goudey issue. Outstanding color retention and the sharp corners are two of the stronger points of the offered Hall of Fame card from the '34 Goudey issue. Notice that the red field that makes up the background remains virtually unmarked. A total of 11 cards have been graded higher than this offering. A very strong NM+ example. **Minimum Bid: $200**

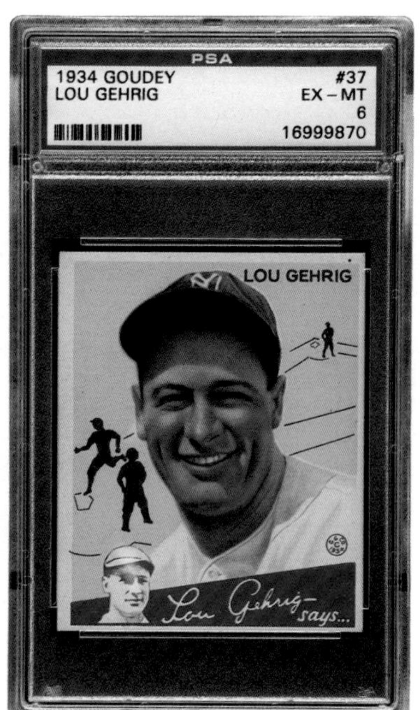

19091 1934 Goudey Lou Gehrig #37 PSA EX-MT 6. Lou Gehrig's portrait graces the front of one of his two 1934 Goudey cards. Gehrig captured the AL's Triple Crown in 1934 with .363-49-165. Top to bottom centering is the only condition issue of note. **Minimum Bid: $500**

19092 1934 Goudey Lou Gehrig #61 PSA EX-MT 6. This is the second of the two Gehrig entries in the 1934 Goudey issue, both of which are considered the tops in the hobby as far as cards from the Iron Horse go. Here we present his #61 card, slabbed by PSA and graded a strong EX-MT exemplar. On the brink of his '34 Triple Crown season, Lou is depicted from the waist up wielding the lumber that would help him attain that goal. A truly pleasing example that many would consider adding to their collection. **Minimum Bid: $600**

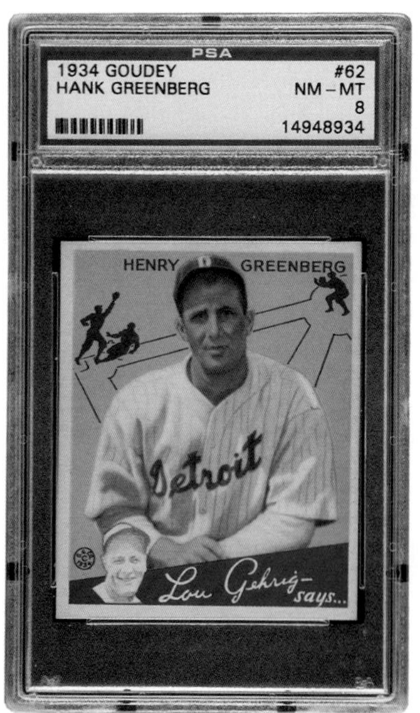

19093 1934 Goudey Hank Greenberg #62 PSA NM-MT 8. With less than a half-dozen copies in the world graded higher, this example ranks close to the top of the plateau. Greenberg broke into the majors in 1930, at just the age of 19 and had a remarkable career that mixed baseball 1930 through 1940 and then the military from 1940 through 1945. He returned to baseball in 1945 and in his first game, picked up right where he left off, with a Home Run. Hank retired in 1947, after playing his last season for the Pirates. He was the first true Jewish superstar to grace the diamond. This is an incredible card from almost every aspect of the card's features including the rich color and clean obverse. The card's borders are suitably bright and its corners are properly formed. This is the must have card for a Tiger Fan or just a Greenberg enthusiast. A strong NM-MT example. **Minimum Bid: $300**

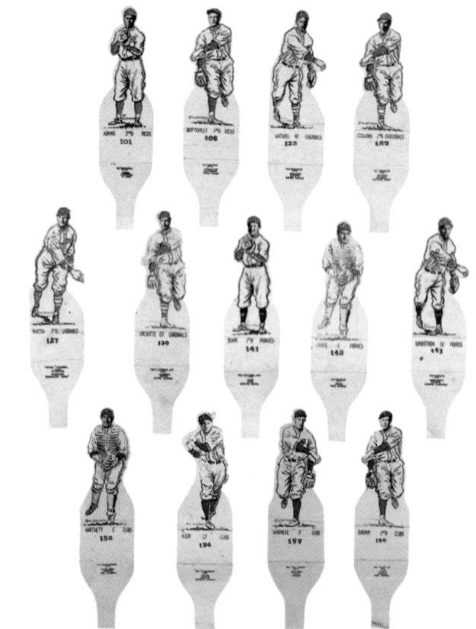

19094 1934 Al Demaree Die-Cuts (R304) Collection (13). Among the rarest 1930s gum cards are those issued by Dietz Gum Co., a Chicago confectioner, in packages of "Ball Players in Action Chewing Gum." The cards, so rare that a complete checklist may never be know, feature photographic portraits of players set upon cartoon bodies drawn by former major league pitcher Al Demaree. Present in the group are Cincinnati Reds - #101 Adams, 108 Bottomley; St. Louis Cardinals - #122 Watkins, 125 Collins, 127 Martin, 130 Orsatti; Pittsburgh Pirates - #141 Suhr, 142 Grace, 143 Lindstrom (uncatalogued); Chicago Cubs - #152 Hartnett, 154 Klein, 157 Warneke (uncatalogued), 160 Grimm. **Minimum Bid: $300**

19095 **1934-36 Batter-Up (R318) Bill Terry #6 PSA NM-MT 8.** Offered is one of the three highest graded examples, with not one having attained a higher grade, of this extremely tough issue to find in high grade. It is not too often you see these cards without the little creasing around the perforations. This is an outstanding specimen with virtually no wear at all, the perforations strongly intact and amazingly sharp corners for an issue that is notorious for corner wear problems. A Very Strong NM-MT example. **Minimum Bid: $200**

19096 **1934-36 Batter-Up (R318) Pie Traynor #14 PSA NM-MT 8.** Offered is one of only two PSA NM-MT examples, with not one having attained a higher grade. It is not too often you see these cards without the little creasing around the perforations. This is an outstanding specimen with virtually no wear at all, the perforations strongly intact and amazingly sharp corners for an issue that is notorious for corner wear problems. **Minimum Bid: $200**

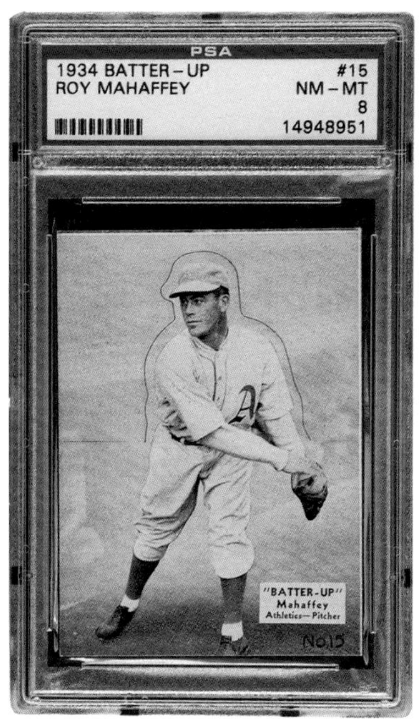

19097 **1934-36 Batter-Up (R318) Roy Mahaffey #15 PSA NM-MT 8.** The presented specimen has only one card that equals this stunning piece. This is a set that is notorious for having many issues; from the centering, to being cut small and creasing at the perforations. This example is not only free of all those issues, but from surface problems as well. You need not look any further if you are looking for a high grade rare example. A Very Strong NM-MT example, especially for the issue. **Minimum Bid: $100**

19098 **1934-36 Batter-Up (R318) Jack Burns #18 PSA NM-MT 8.** Although this example has three others graded at this level, none have received a higher grade. As mentioned in the previous Batter-Up descriptions, these cards usually had many issues, thus rendering them uncapable of receiving high grades. When one finds an example like this, it is hard to pass up. A very strong NM-MT example, especially for the issue. **Minimum Bid: $100**

19099 **1934-36 Batter-Up (R318) PSA-Graded Collection (11).** Provided is a nice collection of 11 1934-36 Batter-Ups, including 7 Hall of Famers, in which every card has been graded by PSA. An extremely tough issue; with its color borders, easy creasing and centering issues. These cards have withstood the test of time and present with bright colors, fairly sharp corners and nice centering. Highlights include - **Graded: PSA NM 7:** 3 cards w/#'s 1 Berger, 2 Brandt and 5 Hubbell; **PSA EX-MT 6:** 6 cards w/#'s 3 Lopez, 7 Martin, 10 Ferrell, 16 Hafey, 22 Rolfe and 31 Grove; **PSA EX 5:** 2 cards w/#'s 23 Gomez and 27 Ott. **Minimum Bid: $500**

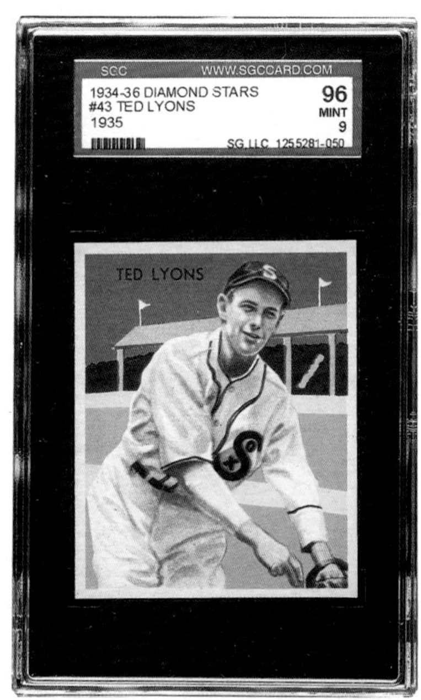

19100 **1935 Diamond Stars Ted Lyons #43 SGC 96 Mint 9.** An art deco style, a hall of fame player, and in mint condition. What else could you ask for? This beauty has it all. With four strong corners, beautiful registration and brightness, it's easy to see why this example is the only one to ever receive a Mint 96 designation from SGC with none ever grading higher. **Minimum Bid: $350**

19101 **1934 Zeenut PCL Joe DiMaggio with Coupon SGC 30 Good 2.** Long before Joe met Marilyn, he carved a path that Ted Williams would later follow; starting his glorious baseball career on the West coast in the Pacific Coast League. Amazingly, as a member of the San Francisco Seals, DiMaggio had a 61-game hitting streak; surpassing even his ML record of 56 straight games with a hit. One of his two cards from the set (the other shows him throwing), both are extremely difficult to find in any condition and it is exceedingly rare to find with the coupon still intact. **Minimum Bid: $600**

19102 **1939 Play Ball Joe DiMaggio #26 SGC 84 NM 7.** Displaying a quality higher than what had been seen previous, the 1939 Play Ball issue by Gum Inc. made use of high quality black-and-white photo and a larger card surface at 2-1/2" x 3-1/8." The DiMaggio card and that of Ted William's rookie are the most sought after from the popular series. Only the centering prevents this example from grading higher; image clarity, corners and card back are impeccable. **Minimum Bid: $300**

19103 **1939-1963 Hall of Fame Plaque Postcards Collection (67).** The first Hall of Fame postcards were issued in two types between 1939-1943. They share an identical format and are differentiated by the typography on back, one set having been issued prior to the Hall of Fame's opening in June, 1939, and a later version issued after that opening. Thirty-four of the thirty-seven issued are present with the following breakdown: Type 1 - G.C. Alexander, Cap Anson, Morgan Bulkeley, Alexander Cartwright, Henry Chadwick, Eddie Collins, Charles Comiskey, Candy Cummings, Buck Ewing, Ban Johnson, Walter Johnson, Willie Keeler, Connie Mack, Christy Mathewson, John McGraw, Charles Radbourne, George Sisler, Al Spalding, Tris Speaker, Honus Wagner, George Wright; Type 2 - Ty Cobb, Lou Gehrig, Napoleon Lajoie, Babe Ruth, Cy Young and 8 Hall of Fame Museum related postcards. From 1944-1952 Albertype was the official producer of the Baseball Hall of Fame's postcards. Twenty-seven of these Type 1 and Type 2 postcards are present including Ty Cobb, Lou Gehrig, Christy Mathewson, Babe Ruth and Honus Wagner. Finally, there are six of the Artvue Hall of Fame postcards produced between 1953-1963 which include Ty Cobb, Hank Greenberg, Carl Hubbell and Mel Ott. Postcards rate a consistent EX/MT or better with very few exceptions. **Minimum Bid: $250**

19104 **1940 Play Ball Jimmie Foxx #133 PSA Good 2, Signed.** The sharpest looking Good 2 card you'll ever see! We assume it's the imperfect centering and light residue on the verso that accounts for the grade, because all four corners are quite sharp and the front surface is clean, providing the perfect home for a 9/10 bold blue ink signature from The Beast himself. A neat relic from the days when Jimmie shared the dugout with a young kid named Ted Williams. **Minimum Bid: $350**

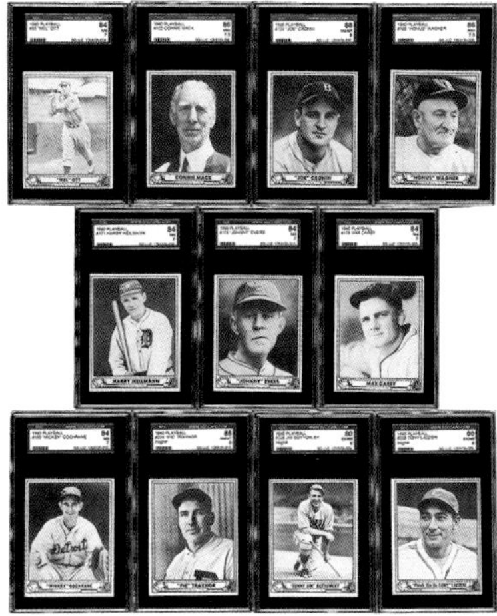

19105 **1940 Play Ball SGC-Graded Collection (11).** High grade examples, all featuring Hall of Fame members and a couple of high-numbered cards to boot. Includes **SGC 88 NM/MT 8:** 2 cards w/#'s 134 Joe Cronin and 224 Pie Traynor; **SGC 86 NM+ 7.5:** 2 cards w/#'s 132 Connie Mack and 168 Honus Wagner; **SGC 84 NM 7:** 5 cards w/#'s 88 Mel Ott, 171 Harry Heilmann, 174 Johnny Evers, 178 Max Carey and 180 Mickey Cochrane; **SGC 80 EX/NM 6:** 2 cards w/#'s 236 Jim Bottomley and 238 Tony Lazzeri. **Minimum Bid: $600**

19106 **1941 Playball "Jimmie" Foxx #13 SGC 86 NM+ 7.5.** In 1940, Foxx surpassed the 500 Home Run plateau and cemented himself as one of the greatest sluggers in the history of the game. Colors and surface present in this example are of top quality and one could argue the grade as being harsh, considering the tremendous centering and overall appearance of this fine NM+ example. One would be hard pressed to find a better example for the grade. Very Strong NM+ card. **Minimum Bid: $250**

19107 **1941 Playball Charley Gehringer #19 SGC 88 NM/MT 8.** Coming off a trip to the 1940 World Series where the Tigers came up one run short in losing to the Cincinnati Reds 2-1 in game 7, Gehringer continued to prove he was worthy of All-Star status. In his 17th year with Detroit, Gehringer hit .313 and scored 108 runs. A lifetime .320 hitter, Gehringer is still considered to be one of the best second basemen of all time. Offered here is a special example of his 1941 Playball issue. This card features vibrant colors and exceptionally sharp corners. Only being a touch off-center prevents this card from grading higher. A very pleasing NM-MT example. **Minimum Bid: $200**

19108 **1941 Playball Red Ruffing #20 SGC 88 NM/MT 8.** This example is one of the highest ever graded by SGC, with only one other receiving a higher mark. Features bold colors and bright white borders. The image of the Yankee Hall of Famer pitcher is free of any surface blemishes. The centering is everything and more than you would expect from a strong NM-MT example. Under totally unforgiving scrutiny, looking for the reason this card isn't in a higher holder, one can barely notice the slightest hints of fuzz at the top right corner on the front and bottom right corner on the back. This card would upgrade virtually any 1941 Playball set! **Minimum Bid: $200**

19109 **1941 Play Ball Joe DiMaggio #71 SGC 88 NM/MT 8.** With eighty-eight submissions to the SGC grading service at the time of this writing, only a single representation of this card dating from the season of DiMaggio's famous fifty-six game hitting streak has topped the offered example. Color and contrast are first rate, with sharp corners and the cleanest of surfaces further establishing the superiority of this tough card. It will be a long wait before a better one comes along. **Minimum Bid: $2,500**

19110 **1941 Play Ball Baseball Near Set (58/72).** Every card has been graded by SGC. Presented is a high grade near set of 1941 Playball baseball, that includes DiMaggio, Williams, Foxx, Greenberg, Reese and much more. While the backs are nearly identical to the previous year's Play Ball issue, the card fronts for the 1941 release are printed in color. This near set includes 58 out of the 72 cards, with the #49-72 cards slightly more difficult than the lower-series cards. A total of 58 cards have been graded by SGC with an aggregate SMR value of $12,430. Highlights include: Graded - **SGC 88 NM/MT 8:** 3 cards w/#'s 3, 24 and 28; **SGC 86 NM+ 7.5:** 2 cards w/#'s 29 and 41; **SGC 84 NM 7:** 17 cards w/#'s 12, 13 Foxx, 18 Greenberg, 20 Ruffing, 21 Keller, 25, 26, 30, 31, 35, 39 Henrich, 41, 44, 46, 60 Klein, 66 and 71 Joe DiMaggio; **SGC 80 EX/NM 6:** 20 cards w/#'s 1 Miller, 2, 4, 5, 7, 9, 11, 15 Cronin, 16, 19 Gehringer, 27, 32, 38, 40, 49, 50, 55, 57, 62 and 70 Dickey; **SGC 70 EX+ 5.5:** 9 cards w/#'s 14 Williams, 34, 37, 45, 47, 52, 54 Reese, 56 Vander Meer and 64 Doerr; **SGC 60 EX 5:** 6 cards w/#'s 10 Vaughn, 51, 63 Dom DiMaggio, 67, 68 and 69; **SGC 50 VG/EX 4:** 1 card, #17. **Minimum Bid: $2,000**

19111 **1948 Bowman Baseball Complete Set (48).** The Bowman company throws its hat into the ring with its premier set, and one of the first baseball card issues in the wake of World War II. There are some great rookie cards including Stan "The Man" Musial, Ralph Kiner, Enos Slaughter, Yogi Berra and more. A total of eighteen cards have been graded by SGC with an aggregate SMR value of $2,205. Highlights include: Graded Cards - **SGC 88 NM/MT 8:** 3 cards w/#'s 10, 16 Lohrke SP and 41; **SGC 86 NM+ 7.5:** 4 cards w/#'s 11, 20 Kerr SP, 45 Sauer and 46; **SGC 84 NM 7:** 6 cards w/#'s 1 Elliott, 3 Kiner, 14 Reynolds, 17 Slaughter, 29 Page SP and 47 Thomson; **SGC 80 EX/NM 6:** 2 cards w/#'s 18 Spahn and 34 Sheldon SP; **SGC 70 EX+ 5.5:** 1 card, #5 Feller; **SGC 60 EX 5:** 2 cards w/#'s 19 Heinrich and 36 Musial. Ungraded Cards - include #'s 4 Mize (VG), 6 Berra (EX), 7 Reiser (EX), 8 Rizzuto (GD), 38 Schoendienst (EX) and 48 Koslo (EX). Grades 25% NM to NM/MT, 69% EX to EX/MT, 6% VG to VG/EX (one lesser). **Minimum Bid: $1,000**

19112 **1948-49 Leaf Jackie Robinson #79 SGC 86 NM+ 7.5.** Jackie Robinson is one of the most significant ballplayers ever to step onto the diamond and his rookie cards are viewed as important cornerstones of any important baseball card collection. It is also a key piece of the intriguing 1948-49 Leaf Gum Co. baseball series which one of the scarcest of all post-war card sets. As PSA NM-MT 8 examples are prohibitively expensive for many enthusiasts, this card will fit well into any high-grade collection. This card is a very solid example. Centering is virtually perfect top-to-bottom and 55/45 towards the right. All four corners are strong but fall just outside NM-MT parameters. **Minimum Bid: $600**

19114 **1949 Bowman Jackie Robinson Rookie #50 SGC 88 NM/MT 8.** Just five examples of this important card have ever graded higher than the specimen we present here, establishing the this offering as one for the collecting elite. This brave barrier buster's portrait is rendered in the boldest of color, and with perfect registration. Centering is very strong, and the edges and corners are remarkably fine. A fitting tribute to the most important figure in professional baseball history. **Minimum Bid: $500**

19113 **1949 Bowman Bob Feller #27 PSA NM-MT 8.** Robert William Andrew Feller came off a farm in Iowa and pitched for the Cleveland Indians at the tender age of 17 in 1936. Amazingly, in August of that first season, Feller struck out fifteen batters in facing the St. Louis Browns. He pitched 18 seasons for the Tribe, despite missing nearly four years to military service. After the attack on Pearl Harbor in 1941, Bob Feller was the first major leaguer to enlist. He was inducted into the Hall of Fame in 1962. This post-war gum card features nice centering, brilliant coloring and a clean back. **Minimum Bid: $100**

19115 **1949 Bowman Satchell Paige #224 SGC 86 NM+ 7.5.** With only nine of this high-numbered rookie card rating higher, this is sure to please the Bowman set or Satchell Paige card collector. The back of his card reads as follows, "One of the most fabulous characters in baseball. Satchell spent many years traveling around the Negro Leagues before being signed to a Cleveland Indian contract. His exact age is not known, but he's been in baseball for years." Funny, this text did not prevent Bowman from including a listed birth date of September 11, 1908 on the same card back. **Minimum Bid: $400**

19116 **1949 Bowman PCL Baseball Completely SGC Graded Near Set (31/36).** A tough minor league near set that will provide a fun challenge for the winning bidder in following the project to its completion. A total of 31 cards have been graded by SGC. Highlights include: **Graded Cards - SGC 88 NM/MT 8:** 5 cards w/#'s 10 Gassaway, 11 Freitas, 13 Jensen, 14 White and 15 Storey; **SGC 86 NM+ 7.5:** 4 cards w/#'s 3 Hodgin, 4 Woods, 19 Holcombe and 20 Ross; **SGC 84 NM 7:** 9 cards w/#'s 5 Rescigno, 6 Grasso, 7 Rucker, 9 Dallessandro, 12 Maltzberger, 16 Lajeski, 17 Glossop, 21 Coscarart and 22 York; **SGC 80 EX/NM 6:** 6 cards w/#'s 1 Anthony, 2 Metkovich, 8 Brewer, 28 Handley, 34 Handley and 35 Seats; **SGC 50 VG/EX 4:** 2 cards w/#'s 18 Raimondi and 33 Tabor; **SGC Authentic A:** 5 cards w/#'s 23 Mooty, 29 Beese, 30 Lazor, 31 Malone and 32 Van Robays. **Minimum Bid: $1,000**

19117 **1950 Bowman Phil Rizzuto #11 PSA NM-MT 8.** The 1950 Major League Player of the Year, Phil Rizzuto played in nine World Series (seven on the winning end) during a 13-season career with the Yankees. The popular shortstop was elected to baseball's Hall of Fame in 1994. This early gum card displays vivid coloring with a clean front and back. **Minimum Bid: $250**

19118 **1950 Bowman Jackie Robinson #22 PSA NM 7.** Jack Roosevelt Robinson broke baseball's "Gentleman's Agreement" in 1947 and earned the NL's ROY award in the process. The back of this card mentions Jackie winning the league's MVP award for his 1949 season, in which he hit a league leading .342 and finished second in the NL with 124 RBIs. This early gum card displays vivid coloring with a clean front and back. Centering and light corner wear are the only conditional flaws that bear mentioning. **Minimum Bid: $250**

19119 **1950 Bowman Yogi Berra #46 PSA NM 7.** Not to be confused with the cartoon character, Lawrence Peter "Yogi" Berra did have his share of hilarious observations on life. Among the more infamous: "It ain't over till it's over." "This is like deja vu all over again." "Nobody goes there anymore; it's too crowded." "Baseball is 90% mental - the other half is physical." "I didn't really say everything I said." This early gum card is a strong specimen, with centering the only obvious conditional flaw. **Minimum Bid: $100**

19120 **1950 Bowman Baseball Roy Campanella #75 PSA NM-MT 8.** Widely considered to have been one of the greatest catchers in the history of the game, Roy Campanella played for the Brooklyn Dodgers and was one of the pioneers in breaking the color barrier in Major League Baseball. Campanella's Hall of Fame career was cut short in 1958 when he was paralyzed in an automobile accident. His card from the popular 1950 Bowman set has been assigned the grade of NM-MT 8; centered even slightly better, it would have merited an even higher mark. **Minimum Bid: $200**

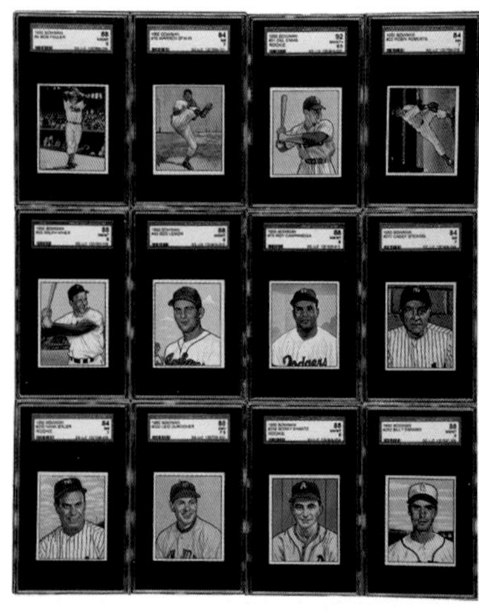

19121 **1950 Bowman Baseball Graded Parital Set (120/252).** A total of 120 different cards including Hall of Famers, minor stars and commons highlight this high grade ensemble. What a great start to completing an SGC graded 1950 Bowman set, with almost 50% having been graded. There are quite a few high ticket cards in this partial graded set including Bob Feller, Roy Campanella, Leo Durocher, Casey Stengel Ralph Kiner, Hank Bauer and much, much more. A total of 120 cards have been graded by SGC with an aggregate SMR value of $10,675. Highlights include: **Graded Cards - SGC 96 MINT 9:** 1 card, #179; **SGC 92 NM/MT+ 8.5:** 8 cards w/#'s 31, 50, 53, 105, 126, 158, 213 and 251; **SGC 88 NM/MT 8:** 32 cards w/#'s 6 Feller, 13, 33 Kiner, 40 Lemon, 47, 49, 61, 68, 75 Campanella, 79, 106, 108. 119, 124, 128, 149, 152, 175, 187, 190, 194, 195, 198, 200, 205, 211, 225, 233, 234 Shantz, 240, 249 and 252; **SGC 86 NM+ 7.5:** 19 cards w/#'s 41, 51, 63 Blackwell, 66, 67, 69, 101, 109, 110, 123, 132 Vernon, 134, 167 Roe, 169, 170, 203, 214, 220 Durocher and 247 Noren; **SGC 84 NM 7:** 51 cards w/#'s 12 Page, 14, 18, 19 Spahn, 20, 27, 32 Roberts, 34, 96, 103, 111, 118, 120, 122, 127, 130, 131, 133, 136, 138 Reynolds, 142, 143, 146, 147, 150, 154, 155, 157, 159, 162, 163, 166, 182, 183, 186, 191, 201, 202, 204, 208, 209, 212, 215 Lopat, 216, 217 Stengel, 219 Bauer, 226, 237, 239, 246 and 248; **SGC 80 EX/NM 6:** 9 cards w/#'s 16, 30, 35 Slaughter, 38, 49, 55, 60, 70 and 115. **Minimum Bid: $500**

19122 **1950-56 Callahan Baseball High Grade Near Set (65/82).** Sold at the Baseball Hall of Fame in Cooperstown and in ballparks around the country, these cards featuring drawings by famed artist Mario DeMarco were produced from 1950 to 1956. B.E. Callahan of Chicago, the publisher of "Who's Who in Baseball," produced the card set. The cards measure 1-3/4" x 2-1/2". Offered is a high-grade partial set (65/82). It is not easy to find these fragile, fifty-eight year-old cards in near mint condition or better. This offering is a great start to gathering a genuine vintage set that contains many of the greatest players in baseball history. Twenty cards have been graded by SGC with an aggregate SMR value of $1292. Highlights include: **Graded Cards - SGC 88 NM/MT 8:** 14 cards w/ Alexander, Brouthers, Cartwright, Chance, Chesboro, Foxx, Gehringer, Heilmann, McCarthy, McGinnity, McGraw, Ott, Radbourne, Young; **SGC 86 NM+ 7.5:** 4 cards w/ Chadwick, Cobb, Grove, Tinker; **SGC 84 NM 7:** 2 cards w/ B.Ruth, Traynor. **Ungraded Cards** - Include D.Dean (EX/MT), Gehrig (EX/MT), Hornsby (NM), W.Johnson (NM), Lajoie (NM), Mathewson (NM), Simmons (EX/MT), Wagner (EX/MT), Waner (NM), Museum Exterior (NM). Grades 70% NM to NM/MT and 30% EX to EX/MT. Seventeen cards are missing (Baker, Barrow, Bender, Chandler, Connolly, Dickey, DiMaggio, Hartnett, Klem, Lyons, Maranville, Schalk, Terry, Vance, Wallace, H.Wright, Museum Interior). **Minimum Bid: $350**

19123 **1950 Philadelphia Phillies Bulletin Pin Ups Set (26).** Two versions of this rare set honoring the National League Champion "Whiz Kids" were issued in late September of that year, the first a newsprint version issued one a day within Philadelphia's The Evening Bulletin, and the second a premium version printed on heavy paper with a semi-gloss finish and blank back. This second, more desirable version was available for a nickel at the newspaper's office or for a dime by mail, and the original mailing envelope that joins this set assures an original ten cent price tag. Some foxing is apparent upon the Dick Whitman and Eddie Sawyer "cards," but otherwise a small degree of border toning is all that prohibits a NRMT rating. A complete and essentially unhandled set, presented for the first time to the collecting hobby. **Minimum Bid: $250**

19124 1951 Bowman Mickey Mantle #253 SGC 80 EX/NM 6. The Mick's first card was almost his last. After struggling in his rookie season to such a degree that he was sent back down to the minors, the young Oklahoman was ready to call it quits. But his father, who had named Mickey after his own baseball hero Mickey Cochrane, wouldn't hear of it. "Just be a little patient," "Mutt" Mantle told him, "Things will get better." And quite clearly they did. So we have Mickey's pop to thank for this card's status as one of the most desirable in post-war collecting, rather than being just a run-of-the-mill high number common. This particular offering represents one of the stronger examples you'll see of this tough, short-printed card; garnering an EX/NM designation from the critical eyes at SGC. **Minimum Bid: $750**

19125 1951 Bowman Mickey Mantle Rookie #253 PSA NM 7. The fabulous portraiture that characterizes the early 1950's Bowman sets joins with the supreme relevance of this iconic star's debut to create one of the most desired and essential cards of the post-war era. The card's appearance in the short-printed high-number series only adds to its scarcity and mystique, with collectors battling fiercely for quality examples such as that which we present here. This issue is known for centering problems and wax stains, but our offering is spared the brunt of such ailments, with the lightest of corner touches all that prevents it from soaring even higher. Only fifty-six unqualified specimens have ever graded higher. **Minimum Bid: $1,500**

19126 1951 Bowman Mickey Mantle #253 SGC 84 NM 7. The Mick's image jumps right out at you and you're hard pressed to find a single print dot on the card. This strong example has four very nice corners, spectacular colors featuring the deepest, boldest blue imaginable on his hat, perfect focus and picture registration with bright, vibrant background coloring. The reverse is virtually flawless with the slightest wax stain to the left of Weight: 175. Here's your rare opportunity to acquire the rookie card of one of baseball's true immortals, Mickey Mantle. Truly important cards like this one never go out of style. Only 15 cards have been graded higher by SGC, which will make this a very highly sought after card. **Minimum Bid: $1,500**

19127 **1951 Bowman Mickey Mantle #253 SGC 92 NM/MT+ 8.5.** Argue all you'd like that the 1952 Topps card is Mickey's true rookie - our calendar tells us that the '51 Bowman was actually the first. We'll also take issue with anybody who claims the Topps rookie is a prettier card, as we're of the opinion that Bowman's designs of the early 1950's represent one of the high water marks in cardboard aesthetics. It surely shows on the flawlessly registered image of the nineteen-year old legend in the making, who stands at batting attention before a cloud-dappled sky on this high-grade rarity. Educated collectors will understand the difficulty in achieving a grade of SGC 92 NM/MT+ 8.5 on any 1951 Bowman, particularly those from the high-number series, which is led off by the Mick. Centering problems abound in this issue, and gum and wax stains are all but epidemic. Our offering is spared the brunt of such ailments, and takes it a step further by sporting four sharp corners and color. Any "flaws" are so minor as to risk overstatement with a mere mention. In short, this one's a real blazer. Of 180 such cards graded by SGC at the time of this writing, the population report tells us that collectors must chase down one of just three cards on earth if they wish to upgrade from an SGC 92 NM/MT+ 8.5. Suffice it to say that finding one of the three cards that top this one will be a difficult ordeal. A tremendous NM/MT+ example of one of the most popular players to ever cross the white base lines. **Minimum Bid: $5,000**

19128 **1952 Bowman Mickey Mantle #101 SGC 88 NM/MT 8 .** The Mick's sophomore season was greeted by what is arguably his most artful baseball card portrait, presented upon the number 101 card in the 1952 Bowman issue. This card has nice centering, clean, crisp white borders and four sharp corners. Surfaces remain clean as a whistle. There have been only four examples that have attained a higher grade than this example. This is a solid NM/MT example, for which one would be hard pressed to find better for the grade. **Minimum Bid: $500**

19129 **1952 Bowman Baseball SGC Graded Partial Set (107/252).** Presented is a high grade 1952 Bowman Baseball partial set that every piece has been graded by SGC, including a plethora of star cards such as Willie Mays, Bob Feller, Yogi Berra, Phil Rizzuto, Casey Stengel and more. A tremendous array of high grade cards all in one ensemble. The 107 SGC graded cards have an aggregate SMR value of $11,290. Highlights include: **Graded Cards - SGC 92 NM/MT+ 8.5:** 25 cards w/#'s 18, 20, 32, 38, 75 Kell, 91, 94 Sewell, 102, 106, 112 Burgess, 124, 144, 148, 153, 172, 182, 184, 189 Piersall, 192, 201, 204 Pafko, 231, 233, 242 and 247; **SGC 88 NM/MT 8:** 35 cards w/#'s 2 Thomson, 16, 24 Furillo, 35, 36, 37 Raschi, 40, 50, 52 Rizzuto, 77, 85, 88, 111, 119, 121, 122, 126, 135, 136, 140, 142 Wynn, 147, 154, 163, 166, 170, 193, 196 Musial, 205, 230, 232 Slaughter, 238, 241, 243 and 249; **SGC 86 NM+ 7.5:** 16 cards w/#'s 1 Berra, 5 Minoso, 7, 8 Reese, 33 McDougald, 64, 67, 68, 70 Erskine, 82, 118, 151, 171, 180, 203 and 221; **SGC 84 NM 7:** 15 cards w/#'s 4 Roberts, 6, 20 Schoendienst, 42, 43 Feller, 71, 90, 105, 176, 179, 181, 191, 217 Stengel, 218 Mays and 225; **SGC 80 EX/NM 6:** 16 cards w/#'s 17 Lopat, 39, 53 Ashburn, 56, 73, 154, 188, 226, 227, 228, 229, 234, 237, 240, 244 Burdette and 245. **Minimum Bid: $1,000**

19130 **1952 Bowman Baseball Complete PSA Graded Set (252).** The 1952 Bowman set features the colorful artwork that the early 1950's Bowman issues were known for and it marks the last time that Bowman produced their popular 2 1/16" x 3 1/8" sized cards. Completely graded set is free any qualifiers that often frustrate the set collector; and with over three-quarters of the cards rating at the EX/MT 6 level or better, a few upgrades are all that is needed to move up the registry rankings. All 252 cards have been graded by PSA with an aggregate SMR value of $10,220. PSA NM/MT 8: #25, 199; PSA NM 7: 48 cards - #3, 7, 13, 17 Lopat, 20, 28, 33 McDougald, 36, 37 Raschi, 42, 45, 70 Erskine, 71, 77, 87, 88, 96 Branca, 99, 102, 103, 121, 122, 124, 126, 134, 143, 145 Mize, 150, 159, 160, 166, 167, 168 Roe, 179, 185, 190, 195, 200, 203, 206, 211, 212, 213, 214, 222, 227, 228, 236; PSA EX/MT 6: 143 cards - #5 Minoso, 6, 8 Reese, 9, 10, 12, 14, 16, 18, 19, 22, 24 Furillo, 27 Garagiola, 29, 31, 32, 34, 38, 39, 40, 44 Campanella, 46, 48, 49, 51, 52 Rizzuto, 53 Ashburn, 54, 55, 56, 57, 58, 59, 60, 61, 63, 65 Bauer, 66, 67, 68, 69, 73, 74, 75 Kell, 76, 78, 79, 82, 83, 84, 85, 86, 89, 90, 91, 92, 93, 94, 95, 97, 98, 101 Mantle, 104, 105 Brown, 106, 108, 110, 112, 114, 115 Doby, 118, 119, 120, 123, 128 Newcombe, 129, 130, 131, 132, 137, 138, 139, 141, 144, 146 Durocher, 147, 148, 149, 151 Rosen, 152, 153, 155, 156 Spahn, 162 Irvin, 163, 164, 165, 169, 170, 171, 173, 174, 175, 176, 177, 180, 181, 182, 184, 186, 187, 189, 191 Friend, 193, 194, 196 Musial, 197, 201, 202, 204, 207, 208, 216, 220, 221, 223, 224, 226, 229, 230, 232 Slaughter, 235, 237 Lollar, 238 McMillan, 239 Mitchell, 241 Parnell, 242, 243, 244 Burdette, 245, 247, 248, 250; PSA EX 5: 53 cards - #1 Berra, 2 Thomson, 4 Roberts, 15, 21 Fox, 23 Lemon, 26, 30 Schoendienst, 35, 41, 47, 50, 62, 72, 80 Hodges, 81, 100, 107, 109, 111, 113, 116 Snider, 117, 125, 127, 133, 135, 136, 140, 142 Wynn, 154, 157, 158 Harris, 161 Jensen, 172, 178, 183, 188, 192, 198, 205, 209, 210, 215, 217 Stengel, 219, 225, 231, 233, 240 Loes, 246, 249 Thompson, 251; PSA VG/EX 4: #11 Kiner, 43 Feller, 218 Mays, 234 Fitzsimmons, 252 Crosetti; PSA Good 2: #64. **Minimum Bid: $2,500**

19131 **1952 Num Num Cleveland Indians Complete Set (20).** Distributed with packages of Num Num potato chips, pretzels and other snack foods, this black-and-white set, like the 1950 issue, was also issued in a slightly different format directly by the team. The Num Num cards have a 1" tab at the bottom which could be redeemed when a complete set was collected, for an autographed baseball. The team-issued version of the cards was printed without the tabs. Also like the 1950 Num Nums, Bob Kennedy's card is unaccountably scarce in the 1952 set. The '52 cards measure 3-1/2" x 5-1/2" including the tab, which has the card number on front, along with redemption details. Highlights include #4 Bob Lemon, 5 Bob Feller (light staining), 6 Early Wynn, 16 Bob Kennedy (no tab), 18 Larry Doby, 20 Al Lopez (VG). Balance of the set retains tabs and averages EX/MT in condition. **Minimum Bid: $500**

19132 **1952 Topps Andy Pafko #1 BVG NM 7.** As the lead card in the landmark 1952 Topps set, it is difficult to find a high grade example. Pafko was traded from the Chicago Cubs to the Brooklyn Dodgers during the 1951 season as part of an eight-player deal between the two clubs. A small adjustment in centering would merit an even higher grade for one of the keys to the 1952 Topps set. **Minimum Bid: $2,000**

19133 **1952 Topps Baseball Joe Page #48 (Sain Bio) SGC 88 NM/MT 8.** One of the true rarities from the landmark 1952 Topps baseball series, this error card features Joe Page on the card front with Johnny Sain's biography on the reverse side. A quick check of both the SGC and PSA population reports shows a combined five cards have achieved this lofty status with none ever grading higher. An important piece of the 1952 Topps registry puzzle indeed. **Minimum Bid: $500**

19134 **1952 Topps Willie Mays #261 SGC 84 NM 7.** A Hall of Fame rookie from one of the hobby's most celebrated sets. While Willie doesn't carry quite the same weight as his fellow newcomer Mickey Mantle among '52 Topps collectors, he is rightfully considered one of the key cards in the set and top examples tend to be fiercely contested at auction. We certainly expect that advanced collectors will give this specimen the attention it deserves, as only six examples have ever charted higher on the SGC population report. Bold colors, strong gloss and an absence of wear accounts for its lofty position. **Minimum Bid: $300**

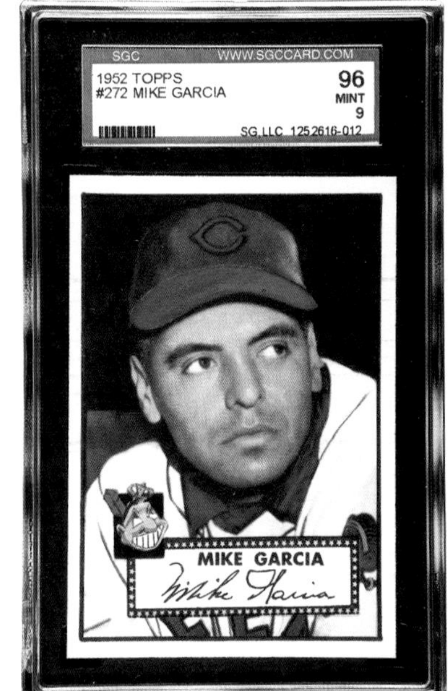

19135 **1952 Topps Baseball Mike Garcia #272 SGC 96 Mint 9.** Another beauty from the ever popular 1952 Topps baseball release. Mike Garcia was a three-time All Star selection with the Cleveland Indians from 1952 to 1954. This is the lone SGC example of this card to achieve this grade with none higher. **Minimum Bid: $250**

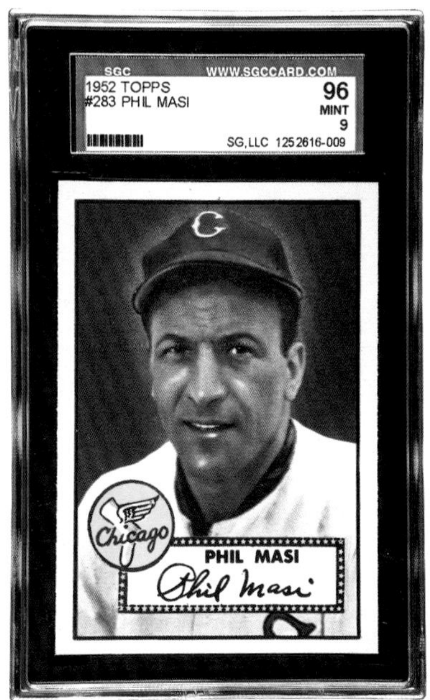

19136 **1952 Topps Baseball Phil Masi #283 SGC 96 Mint 9.** Of the total 8,342 1952 Topps baseball cards submitted to SGC, only 60 have obtained a 96 Mint 9 rating with none higher - less than 1%. This one features Phil Masi as a member of the Chicago White Sox. Masi was a National League All Star selection four straight years between 1945 and 1948. **Minimum Bid: $250**

19137 **1952 Topps Baseball Cliff Fannin #285 SGC 96 Mint 9.** Another in the parade of SGC-graded 96 Mint 9 1952 Topps cards. Cliff Fannin, nicknamed "Mule," was a regular in the St. Louis Browns rotation from 1945 through the 1952 season. This example is the highest rated of the 17 submitted to SGC for grading. **Minimum Bid: $250**

19138 **1952 Topps Baseball Chet Nichols #288 SGC 96 Mint 9.** Of a combined 257 SGC and PSA graded examples, only five 1952 Topps Chet Nichols cards have achieved the coveted Mint 9 designation. Nichols, at the tender age of 20, led the NL in Earned Run Average in 1951 with a sparkling 2.88. He finished runner-up to Willie Mays in the league's ROY balloting, stealing four first place votes along the way. **Minimum Bid: $250**

19139 1952 Topps Baseball Sibby Sisti #293 SGC 96 Mint 9. The only SGC 96 Mint 9 example of the Sisti card; of the 266 submitted to both SGC and PSA, none have ever graded higher. Sisti was the youngest player in the National League, at 18, during the 1939 season. He enjoyed a 13 year career as an infielder with the Boston and later Milwaukee Braves. **Minimum Bid: $250**

19140 1952 Topps Baseball Bob Ross #298 SGC 96 Mint 9. This spectacular specimen from the 1952 Topps baseball release, which ushered in the modern era of sports card collecting, is the only SGC 96 Mint 9 Bob Ross in existence. Ross was signed by the Brooklyn Dodgers as an amateur free agent in 1945 and again in 1949 by the Washington Senators from the Dodgers in the 1949 minor league draft. **Minimum Bid: $250**

19141 1952 Topps Baseball Harry Dorish #303 SGC 96 Mint 9. Another outstanding offering for the 1952 Topps baseball registry collector. Of a combined 244 SGC and PSA graded 1952 Topps cards picturing Harry Dorish, only five have reached Mint 9 status with none ranking higher. Dorish, while pitching for the Chicago White Sox, led the AL in saves in 1952 with 11. **Minimum Bid: $250**

19142 1952 Topps Mickey Mantle Rookie #311 SGC 30 Good 2. The most important and desirable of all post-war trading cards, the Topps Mickey Mantle rookie will remain a dream for many a collector, as the scarcity and demand for the card has driven the price tag well above many a budget. For those intent upon sharing in the joy, but unwilling to part with five figures to do so, we present this rather nice looking example graded "Good" by SGC. The grading points lost upon this coveted rarity relate almost entirely to border issues, with the central focus of the card as fine as those several times the price. From an "eye appeal" standpoint, this will stand as one of the best card bargains of the year. **Minimum Bid: $1,000**

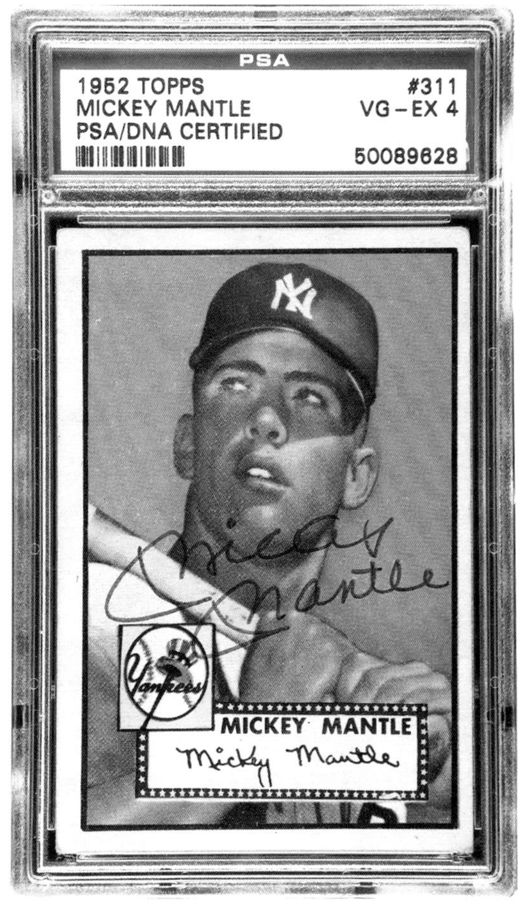

19143 **The Finest Signed 1952 Topps Mickey Mantle #311 PSA VG-EX 4.** The most important and sought after of all post-ward cards is blessed by the hand of the gentleman who established it as such. This coveted rookie from the first great Topps issue finds only typical corner wear and a mild eastward shift in centering to suggest anything other than cardboard perfection, as the color and registration are first rate. Mantle's blue ink signature is likewise unimprovable, helping to establish this offering as one of the most attractive and valuable Mantle signed artifacts in the hobby. **Minimum Bid: $2,500**

19144 **1952 Topps Jackie Robinson #312 SGC 86 NM+ 7.5.** One of the most colorful cards ever in the hobby is presented here in the 1952 Topps Jackie Robinson #312 which has been graded SGC 86 NM+ 7.5. This card presents at the upper echelon of the grade. Near perfect centering, vibrant red color, and overall clarity makes this card a great find. One may search tirelessly for an example of this magnitude, but that search has ended right here. The front has all of the attraction, but the back has perfect centering with no flaws to speak of. A very strong NM+ grade. **Minimum Bid: $600**

19145 **1952 Topps Ed Mathews #407 SGC 70 EX+ 5.5.** Several factors conspire to place the offered cardboard at the top of collectors' want lists. We'll begin with the obvious, noting that this represents the Hall of Fame slugger's rookie offering. The same could be said of the issue itself, the Topps company's famed major debut. Pure happenstance also finds Mathews #407 as the final card in this immensely popular set, making it one of the most problematic in terms of condition. Only thirteen examples have ever topped this one on the SGC population charts, setting supply well below demand for quality specimens. Bid accordingly. **Minimum Bid: $750**

TOPPS OF THE HEAP

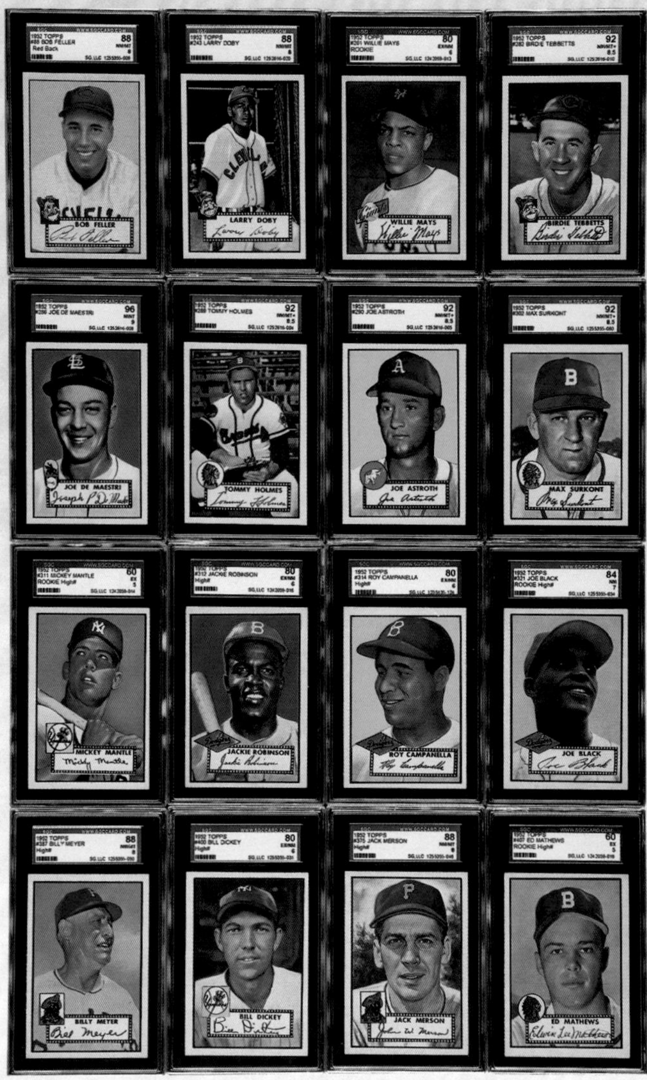

19146 **1952 Topps Baseball Complete Set (407).** The undisputed king of the post-war era, this first great Topps baseball set joins the T206 tobacco issue and the 1933 Goudey set to comprise the hobby's "Big Three." Far from just a coming out party for the industry's most recognizable baseball card purveyor, the 1952 issue holds the most coveted rookie in the game, Mickey Mantle, as well as cards featuring fellow period legends Mays, Mathews, Snider, Campanella and Robinson. Fantastic condition throughout establishes this as one of the finer complete sets to reach the auction block in recent memory. A total of 101 cards have been graded by SGC with an aggregate SMR value of $25,280. Highlights include: **Graded Cards - SGC 96 MINT 9:** 1 card, #286; **SGC 92 NM/MT+ 8.5:** 10 cards w/#'s 264, 281, 282, 285, 289, 290, 291, 292, 302 and 307; **SGC 88 NM/MT 8:** 20 cards w/#'s 55 Boone BB, 84 RB, 88 Feller RB, 144, 154, 243 Doby, 253, 255, 257, 258, 259, 266, 267, 276, 279, 296, 299, 306, 375 and 387 Myers; **SGC 86 NM+ 7.5:** 16 cards w/#'s 86, 98, 105, 125, 225, 228, 252, 263, 265, 268 Lemon, 275, 278, 301, 310, 395 and 402; **SGC 84 NM 7:** 36 cards w/#'s 15 Pesky RB, 32 BB, 41 BB, 82, 97, 107, 114, 118, 184, 195 Minoso, 198, 205, 213, 215 Bauer, 220, 222, 262, 269, 283, 284, 293, 297, 305, 308, 309, 321 Black, 329, 348, 350, 353, 358, 385 Franks, 393, 394 Herman, 401 and 406 Nuxhall; **SGC 80 EX/NM 6:** 16 cards w/#'s 8 BB, 36 Hodges RB, 44 BB, 148, 191 Berra, 234, 261 Mays, 312 Robinson, 313 Thomson, 314 Campanella, 322, 337, 345, 347 Adcock, 360 and 400 Dickey; **SGC 60 EX 5:** 2 cards w/#'s 311 Mantle and 407 Mathews. **Ungraded Cards** - includes #'s 1 Pafko (VG/EX), 2 Runnels (EX), 11 Rizzuto (EX), 20 Loes (VG), 22 DiMaggio (VG/EX), 26 Irvin (EX), 29 Kluszewski (EX), 33 Spahn (VG/EX), 37 Snider (EX), 48 Page (EX/MT), 49 Sain (VG/EX), 59 Roberts (EX), 65 Slaughter (EX), 66 Roe (EX), 67 Reynolds (EX), 91 Schoendienst (EX), 122 Jensen (EX), 129 Mize (VG/EX), 175 Martin (VG/EX), 200 Houk (EX/MT), 216 Ashburn (EX), 227 Garagiola (EX/MT), 246 Kell (EX), 277 Wynn (EX), 315 Durocher (EX), 333 Reese (EX), 372 McDougald (EX), 392 Wilhelm (EX) and 396 Williams (EX). Grades 21% NM to NM/MT, 64% EX to EX/MT, 13% VG to VG/EX. **Minimum Bid: $7,500**

19147 **1953 Bowman Color Baseball Roy Campanella #46 PSA NM-MT 8.** From one of the more popular of the early gum sets, comes this nearly perfect 1953 Bowman Color card depicting HOF catcher Roy Campanella shown with the Brooklyn Dodgers. Prior to the tragic accident which left him paralyzed, Campanella won the National League's MVP award during the 1951, 1953 and 1955 seasons. **Minimum Bid: $200**

19148 **1953 Bowman Color Baseball Complete Set (160).** The first set of contemporary Major League players to feature color photography, this set marks a major milestone in the history of collectible cardboard and remains one of the most popular issues of the post-war era. A total of eighteen cards have been graded by SGC with an aggregate SMR value of $2881. Graded cards - Q #80 Kiner, 81 Slaughter; **SGC 80 EX-NM 6:** #9 Rizzuto, 21 Garagiola; **SGC 70 EX+ 5.5:** #92 Hodges; **SGC 60 EX 5:** #18 Fox, 40 Doby, 114 Feller; **SGC 50 VG-EX 4:** #32 Musial, 44 Bauer/Berra/Mantle, 46 Campanella, 59 Mantle, 97 Mathews, 121 Berra, 153 Ford; **SGC 40 VG 3:** #33 Reese, 117 Snider, 118 Martin. Ungraded cards include #1 Williams (EX/MT), 36 Minoso (EX), 55 Durocher (EX), 62 Kluszewski (VG/EX), 65 Roberts (VG/EX), 84 Bauer (VG/EX), 99 Spahn (GD, red ink on right border of card), 146 Wynn (EX). Grades 71% EX to EX/MT, 29% VG to VG/EX. **Minimum Bid: $1,000**

19149 **1953 Bowman Color Baseball Complete Set (160).** Offered is a solid mid to high grade 1953 Bowman Color Set. The first set of contemporary Major League players to feature color photography, this set marks a major milestone in the history of collectible cardboard and remains one of the most popular issues of the post-war era. A total of 26 cards have been graded by SGC with an aggregate SMR value of $7,670. Highlights include: Graded Cards - **SGC 92 NM/MT+ 8.5:** 2 cards w/#'s 4 and 20; **SGC 88 NM/MT 8:** 11 cards w/#'s 10 Ashburn, 12 Erskine, 23, 25, 41, 75, 80 Kiner, 85, 86, 101 Schoendienst and 102; **SGC 86 NM+ 7.5:** 6 cards w/#'s 11 Shantz, 15, 37, 40 Doby, 73 Pierce and 146 Wynn; **SGC 84 NM 7:** 5 cards w/#'s 32 Musial, 33 Reese, 44 Bauer/Berra/Mantle, 97 Mathews and 99 Spahn; **SGC 80 EX/NM 6:** 2 cards w/#'s 6 and 59 Mantle. Ungraded Cards - include #'s 1 Williams (VG/EX), 9 Rizzuto (EX), 14 Loes (EX), 18 Fox (EX), 21 Garagiola (EX/MT), 24 Jensen (EX), 27 Rashii (EX/MT), 36 Minoso (EX), 46 Campanella (VG/EX), 51 Irvin (EX), 55 Durocher (EX), 57 Burdette (EX), 61 Kell (EX), 62 Kluszewski (EX/MT), 63 McDougald (EX), 65 Roberts (EX), 68 Reynolds (EX/MT), 78 Furillo (EX), 81 Slaughter (EX), 84 Bauer (EX), 92 Hodges (EX), 93 Rizzuto/Martin (EX), 114 Feller (EX/MT), 117 Snider (EX), 118 Martin (EX), 121 Berra (VG/EX), 143 Lopez (EX/MT), 153 Ford (VG/EX), 160 Abrams (VG). Grades 22% NM to NM/MT, 68% EX to EX/MT, 10% VG to VG/EX. **Minimum Bid: $1,500**

19150 1953 Bowman Black and White Baseball Complete Set (64). Similar in all respects to the 1953 Bowman color series; purportedly, the high costs involved in producing the color cards forced Bowman to issue their black and white counterparts. Unlike its counterpart, this set does not contain a lot of star power, but it has a very attractive appeal. A total of 5 cards have been graded by SGC with an aggregate SMR value of $1,150. Highlights include #'s 1 Bell (EX), 15 Mize (VG/EX), 25 Sain (EX), 26 Roe (EX), 27 Lemon (EX), 28 Wilhelm (EX/MT), 33 Kuzava (SGC 92 NM/MT+ 8.5), 35 Wyrosek (SGC 88 NM/MT 8), 36 Piersall (EX), 39 Stengel (SGC 84 NM 7), 41 Ramazotti (SGC 86 NM+ 7.5), 46 Harris (EX/MT), 51 Burdette (EX), 52 Branca (EX) and 54 Miller (SGC 84 NM 7). Grades 11% NM to NM/MT, 89% EX to EX/MT. **Minimum Bid: $300**

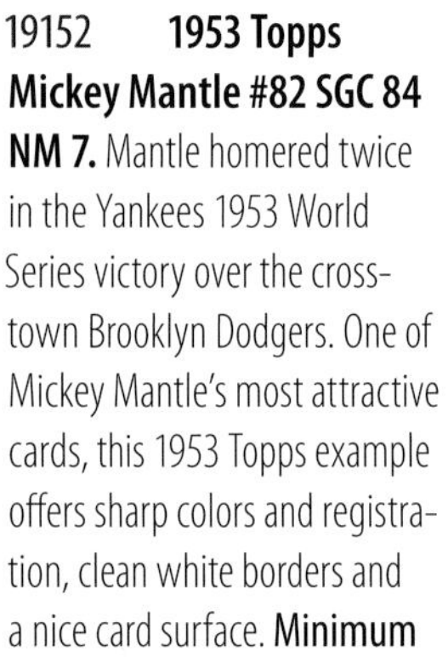

19152 1953 Topps Mickey Mantle #82 SGC 84 NM 7. Mantle homered twice in the Yankees 1953 World Series victory over the cross-town Brooklyn Dodgers. One of Mickey Mantle's most attractive cards, this 1953 Topps example offers sharp colors and registration, clean white borders and a nice card surface. **Minimum Bid: $500**

19151 The Finest Signed 1953 Topps Mickey Mantle #82 PSA VG-EX 4. Fine example of the Mick's sophomore card would alone be reason for celebration, as bright colors and wonderful centering provide the look of a much more expensive grade. But a 10/10 blue ballpoint ink signature from the Commerce Comet vaults this offering into the collecting stratosphere. One of just a small handful of early Mantle Topps cards bearing the Yankee great's signature, this specimen ranks among the strongest. **Minimum Bid: $1,500**

19153 1953 Topps Mickey Mantle #82 SGC 88 NM/MT 8. A timeless card featuring Mantle peering over his left shoulder in the batter's box via the classic Topps original art. This gorgeous specimen is well framed with near perfect 55/45 centering on all borders, four strong corners, and original pack fresh gloss, which leaves us wondering what was holding it back from NM/MT+ status. The reverse is solidly printed and free of stains. A very strong example in Near Mint to Mint condition. **Minimum Bid: $1,500**

19154 **1953 Topps Mickey Mantle #82 SGC 92 NM/MT+ 8.5.** Full bleed color at the lower left corner is the fly in the ointment for most cards from this second great Topps Baseball issue, but this remarkable specimen dodges that pitfall most admirably, providing the look of a card straight out of Eisenhower-era wax. The magic isn't confined solely to that southwest corner though, as a more expansive investigation finds marvelous centering, first-rate color and registration, and corners as sharp as a Mantle line drive. It's no surprise that the featured lot finds itself in the rarest of company, with just three competitors ever charting higher on the SGC population report. **Minimum Bid: $2,500**

19155 **1953 Topps Baseball Phil Rizzuto #114 SGC 92 NM/MT+ 8.5.** The only 92 NM/MT+ 8.5 1953 Topps Phil Rizzuto of the 63 submitted to SGC; displays beautifully, with even centering and bold coloring. Rizzuto, a popular Hall of Fame member from the New York Yankees, was the AL MVP and named the Major League Player of the Year for the 1950 season. **Minimum Bid: $250**

19156 **1953 Topps Baseball Milt Bolling #280 SGC 88 NM/MT 8.** As the last card in the 1953 Topps baseball issue, the Milt Bolling card is extremely difficult to encounter in high grade. Of the 42 Bolling cards submitted to SGC, only four have achieved 88 NM/MT 8 status (none grading higher). Bolling played parts of six seasons in Boston before stops with the Washington Senators and Detroit Tigers. **Minimum Bid: $250**

19157 **1953 Topps Baseball High Grade Complete Set (274).** The second great Topps baseball set was the first ever to include baseball trivia on the backs, a tradition that has continued to this day. But perhaps the greatest baseball trivia question of all might be how a set five and a half decades old could survive in such remarkable condition as the one presented here. This magical offering should thrill even the most discerning of cardboard collectors. A total of 147 cards have been graded by SGC with an aggregate SMR value of $32,472. Highlights include: **Graded Cards - SGC 96 MINT 9:** 10 cards w/#'s 26, 35, 42, 53, 58, 73, 103, 117, 139 and 242; **SGC 92 NM/MT+ 8.5:** 27 cards w/#'s 5, 8, 22, 36, 38, 39, 64, 66 Minoso, 74, 111 Sauer, 113, 118, 124, 127, 133, 134, 148, 167, 206, 208, 212, 214, 233, 235, 239, 240 and 241; **SGC 88 NM/MT 8:** 52 cards w/#'s 3, 6, 10 Burgess SP, 12, 19, 20, 23, 24, 25 Boone, 29, 33, 40, 43 McDougald, 45, 52, 63, 68, 80, 86 Martin, 89, 92, 95, 96, 104 Berra, 108, 110, 114 Rizzuto, 115, 116, 121, 132, 136, 137, 138 Kell, 142, 147 Spahn, 149 DiMaggio, 157, 170, 172, 177, 178, 185, 187, 196, 211, 213, 234, 246 Face, 263 Podres and 278; **SGC 86 NM+ 7.5:** 17 cards w/#'s 54 Feller, 71, 79, 84, 102, 106 SP, 122, 144, 158, 176, 180, 182, 191 Kiner, 229, 248, 273 Haddix and 277; **SGC 84 NM 7:** 29 cards w/#'s 13, 14 Labine, 16, 27 Campanella, 37 Mathews, 55, 61 Wynn SP, 62 Irvin, 77 Mize, 81 Black SP,88, 91, 99, 120, 135 Rosen, 141 Reynolds, 143, 145, 151 Wilhelm, 164, 168, 181, 200, 216, 220 Paige, 224, 232, 254 Roe and 255; **SGC 80 EX/NM 6:** 10 cards w/#'s 1 Robinson, 18, 21, 46, 69, 76 Reese, 82 Mantle, 119 Sain, 186, 226 and 280 Bolling; **SGC 70 EX+ 5.5:** 1 card, #244 Mays. **Ungraded Cards** - include #'s 41 Slaughter (EX/MT), 78 Schoendienst (EX), Kluszewski (EX/MT), 207 Ford (EX), 228 Newhouser (EX), 258 Gilliam (EX/MT) and 264 Woodling (VG/EX). Grades 50% NM to NM/MT, 44% EX to EX/MT, 6% VG to VG/EX. **Minimum Bid: $3,000**

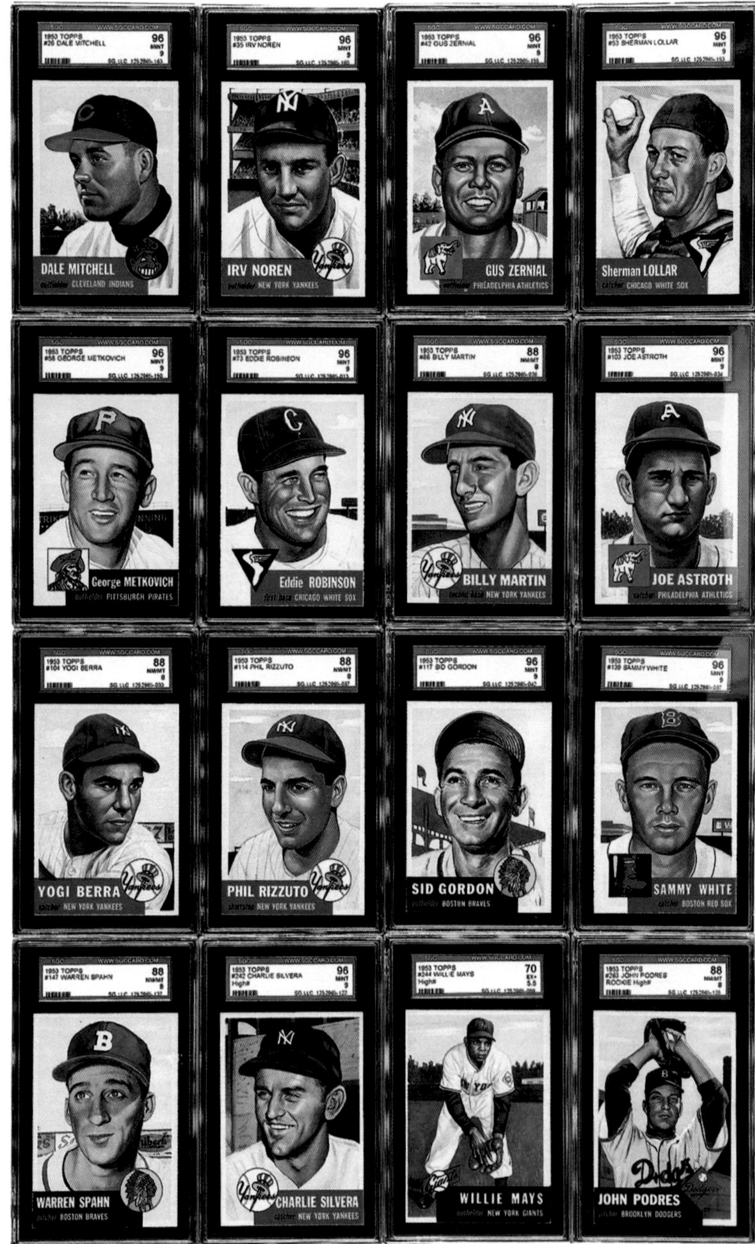

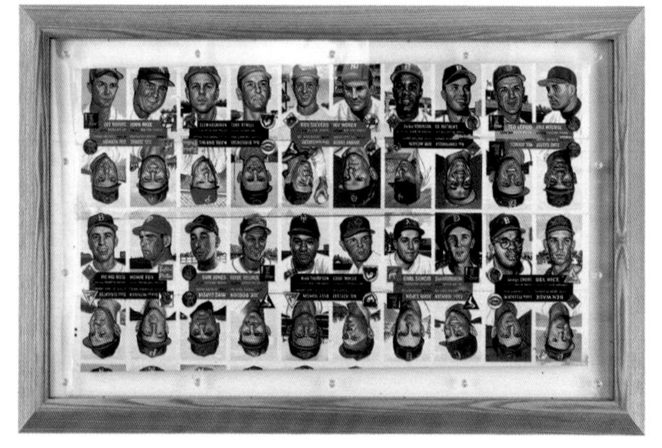

19158 **1953 Topps Baseball Partial Uncut Sheet.** Originally part of an uncut sheet, these four strips of ten cards each form an attractive display. Includes #1 Jackie Robinson, 27 Roy Campanella, 37 Ed Mathews, 41 Enos Slaughter, 76 Pee Wee Reese, 77 Johnny Mize. The strips do suffer from some water damage and paper loss. Also, it should be noted that because of the unusual cut; the cards are not entirely whole without placing strips together. **Minimum Bid: $1,000**

SWEET SHEET

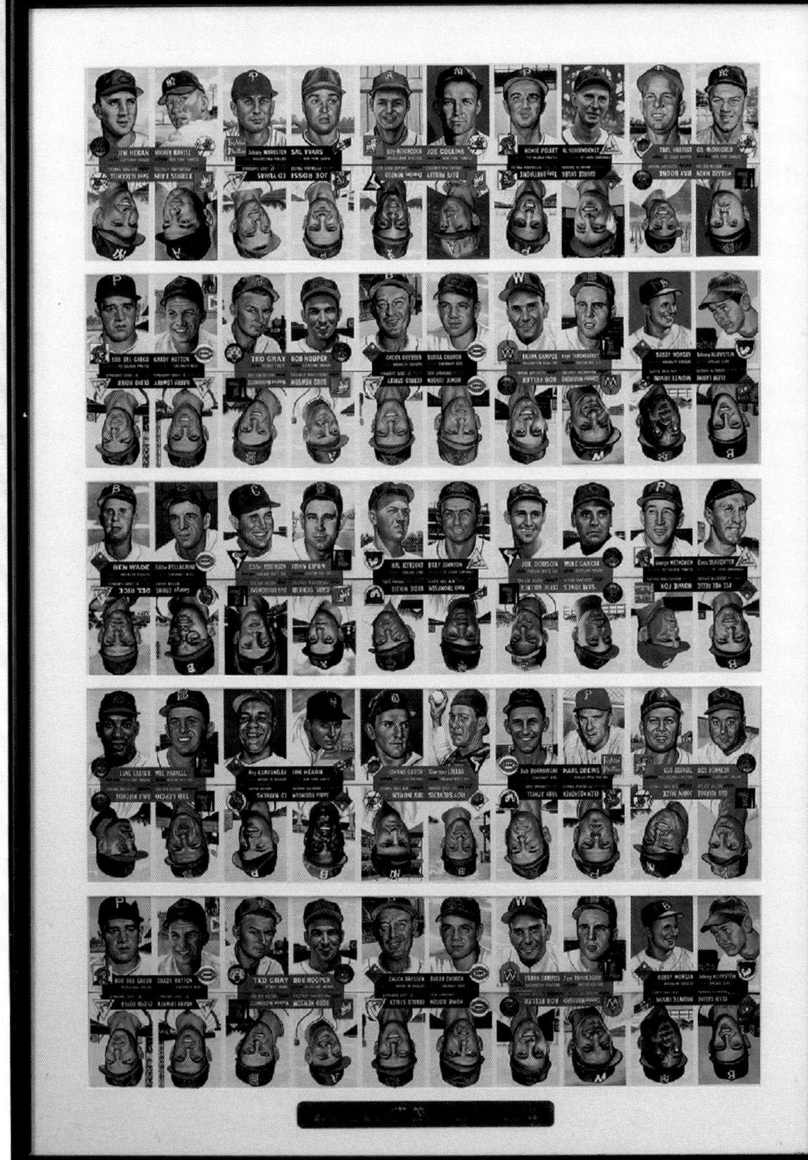

19159 **1953 Topps Baseball Strips Forming a Complete Sheet (10 Strips of 10).** Exceptionally scarce find surfaced almost twenty-five years ago in the warehouse of a carting company hired by Topps to dispose of their salvage in the 1950's. While this company was particularly effective in its work, with not a single uncut sheet from the 1953 set known to the hobby today, somehow these one hundred cards survived in the form of ten horizontally cut strips of ten. A bit of jigsaw puzzle work proved this to be a partially cut complete sheet, providing the collecting community with a singularly unique treasure.

For the cardboard historians among us, the reconstructed sheet acts as a Rosetta Stone of sorts, providing clues as to why some cards from the second great Topps set are relatively easy to locate, and others particularly difficult. Eighty different cards are featured here, numbered from one to eighty-five, with twenty duplicates. We can then assume that the five missing (numbers 10, 44, 61, 72 and 81) were printed at a later date. While cards 1 through 165 are lumped together as to value by most price guides, scarcity among some low numbers, which is explained here, prove this to be an imperfect system.

Having addressed the intriguing Topps forensics, we'll turn our intentions to the specifics of this particular sheet, noting first that the important Jackie Robinson #1, Roy Campanella #27 and Mickey Mantle #82 are present and accounted for, each appearing in spectacular NM/MT condition or better after having been protected by the surrounding cards for decades. Other Hall of Famers appearing at least once: Schoendienst, Feller, Irvin, Mize, Slaughter, Reese and Mathews. While we must stress that Jackie, Campy and Mickey are each blessed by perfectly balanced cuts at top and bottom, in other cases the cuts are too high or low, so as to travel into the boundaries of its upstairs or downstairs neighbors. These imperfect cuts were crucial in piecing the sheet back together, as it made the order of the rows clear. Several cards comprising the rightmost column exhibit a degree of creasing, and Bob Del Greco suffers a bit of paper loss, but the balance is overwhelming fine in light of the aforementioned imperfect cutting of the strips. The cards have been expertly matted and framed to bring out the impressive visuals of a complete sheet, with both front and back available for viewing, and we can assure you that this reconstructed model is as close as you'll ever come to seeing a 1953 Topps sheet in the flesh. **Minimum Bid: $7,500**

19160 **1954 Bowman Baseball Ted Williams #66 PSA NM 7.** One of the more recognizable cards from the hitting great who inspired his share of nicknames including "The Kid," "The Thumper," "The Splendid Splinter," and "Teddy Ballgame." Pulled from the set, likely due to contractual problems, the 1954 Bowman #66 Ted Williams is one of the most sought-after postwar rarities. The Williams card was replaced by Jim Piersall after the initial print run. Slightly off-centered, this example is otherwise beautiful; with sharp corners, a clean back and brilliant coloring. **Minimum Bid: $600**

19161 **1954 Bowman Baseball Whitey Ford #177 SGC 96 Mint 9.** Beautiful representation of the 1954 Bowman #177 Whitey Ford card. Of the 59 examples submitted to SGC, only two others have earned a top grade of 96 Mint 9 with none grading higher. "The Chairman of the Board" had an outstanding ERA of 2.71 in eleven postseasons, helping the Yankees capture six World Series titles. **Minimum Bid: $250**

19162 **1954 Bowman Baseball SGC Graded Partial Set (72/224) .** Every card has been graded by SGC. A total of 72 cards including Hall of Famers, minor stars and commons highlight this high grade ensemble. This is a great start to completing a 1954 Bowman SGC set since more than 30% of the cards have been graded. There are several high ticket cards in this partial set including Willie Mays, Ted Williams, Ernie Banks, Phil Rizzuto, Duke Snider, Billy Martin and much more. A total of 72 cards have been graded by SGC with an aggregate SMR value of $4,329. Highlights include: **Graded Cards - SGC 92 NM/MT+ 8.5:** 3 cards w/#'s 119, 147 and 178; **SGC 88 NM/MT 8:** 26 cards w/#'s 32, 45 Kiner, 51, 52, 56, 59, 63, 70, 72 Yost, 76, 100, 110 Schoendienst, 113 Reynolds, 123, 145 Martin, 151, 159, 165, 166, 170 Snider, 172, 174, 181, 183, 213 and 214; **SGC 86 NM+ 7.5:** 8 cards w/#'s 42, 43, 57 Wilhelm, 88, 142, 188, 209 Woodling and 215; **SGC 84 NM 7:** 17 cards w/#'s 11, 30 Rice, 31 Burgess, 37, 38, 39, 44, 46, 47, 53, 69, 81 Coleman, 83, 86, 97 McDougald, 107, and 132 Feller; **SGC 80 EX/MT 6:** 7 cards w/#'s 1 Rizzuto, 5, 6 Fox, 16, 114, 161 Berra and 190; **SGC 60 EX 5:** 8 cards w/#'s 21, 23 Kuenn, 24, 34, 54, 66 Williams, 71 and 104; **SGC 50 VG/EX 4:** 3 cards w/#'s 77, 89 Mays, and 138 Hodges. **Minimum Bid: $250**

19163 **1954 Bowman Baseball High Grade Complete Set (224)** A colorful set known for its wonderful photography, the 1954 Bowman issue exhibits a classic visual feel representative of the era. A total of 96 cards have been graded by SGC with an aggregate SMR value of $8,365. Highlights include: **Graded Cards - SGC 96 MINT 9:** 16 cards w/#'s 22, 44, 49, 60, 99, 103, 109, 111, 118, 121, 125, 167, 180, 187, 190 and 198; **SGC 92 NM/MT+ 8.5:** 19 cards w/#'s 11, 13, 14, 21 Wertz, 30, 47, 63, 84 Doby, 108, 110 Schoendienst, 126, 127, 148, 150, 152 Vernon, 174, 186, 188 and 197; **SGC 88 NM/MT 8:** 38 cards w/#'s 3, 10 Erskine, 24, 34, 35, 39, 43, 45 Kiner, 46, 62 Slaughter, 69, 70, 76, 77, 78, 81, 82, 83, 92, 94, 98, 120, 132 Feller, 135, 136, 144, 149, 164 Wynn, 168, 176, 177 Ford, 181, 191, 195, 196 Lemon, 200, 205 and 211; **SGC 86 NM+ 7.5:** 11 cards w/#'s 1 Rizzuto, 6 Fox, 31, 32, 52, 59, 71, 87, 165, 189 and 220; **SGC 84 NM 7:** 11 cards w/#'s 26, 51, 58 Reese, 64 Mathews, 73, 89 Mays, 101 Larsen, 113 Reynolds, 130, 145 Martin and 170 Snider; **SGC 70 EX+ 5.5:** 1 card, #65 Mantle. **Ungraded Cards** - includes #'s 15 Ashburn (EX/MT), 38 Minoso (EX/MT), 50 Kell (NM), 57 Wilhelm (EX/MT), 90 Campanella (EX), 95 Roberts (EX), 129 Bauer (EX), 138 Hodges (EX), 161 Berra (EX/MT) and 224 Bruton (EX). Grades 43% NM to NM/MT, 53% EX to EX/MT, 4% VG to VG/EX. **Minimum Bid: $1,500**

19164 **1954 Dan-Dee Potato Chips Bob Feller SGC 88 NM/MT 8.** Bob Feller went 13-3 and bolstered a strong pitching staff that led the Indians to the AL pennant and a World Series appearance in 1954. A review of the SGC population report shows only three 88 NM/MT 8 examples with none graded higher. Issued in bags of potato chips, the cards in this 29-card set are commonly found with grease stains despite their waxed surface. This example is remarkably clean with only a touch of wear at the corners on backside preventing an even higher ranking. **Minimum Bid: $250**

19165 **1954 Dan Dee Potato Chips Near Set (27/29).** One of the more popular of the baseball "regional" issues, these colorful cards are always a conditional challenge due to the waxy surface that was intended to keep the cards protected from the potato chips that they were packaged with. This near set is missing Mickey Mantle and Bob Feller. Fourteen cards have been graded by SGC with an aggregate SMR value of $2150. Highlights include - **Graded Cards: SGC 88 NM/MT 8:** 1 card, Surkont; **SGC 86 NM+ 7.5:** 2 cards w/ Houtteman and Rosen; **SGC 84 NM 7:** 4 cards w/ Cooper, Doby, Gordon and Lopez; **SGC 80 EX/NM 6:** 4 cards w/ Easter, Garcia, Rizzuto and Thomas; **SGC 60 EX 5:** 1 card, Avila; **SGC 50 VG/EX 4:** 2 cards w/ Smith and Wynn. **Ungraded Cards** - Bauer (VG/EX), Friend (EX), Hegan (EX), Hodges (VG), Irvin (VG/EX), Lapalm (VG), Lemon (EX), Mitchell (VG/EX), Roberts (EX), Schoendienst (EX), Snider (VG/EX), Strickland (VG) and Westalke (EX). **Minimum Bid: $500**

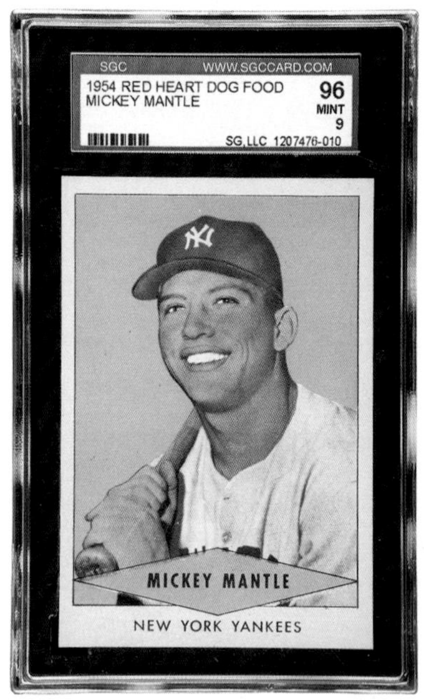

19166 **1954 Red Heart Dog Food Baseball Mickey Mantle SGC 96 Mint 9.** Issued in three 11-card series via a mail-in offer, the Red Heart Dog Food baseball series remains popular for both its player selection and simple design. The most popular card from the set is that of Mickey Mantle; his card featuring him in a casual pose early into his Hall of Fame career with the New York Yankees. Of the 94 submitted to SGC, not one has ever graded higher. The card displays nice centering, four sharp corners, vivid coloring and a clean back. **Minimum Bid: $500**

19167 **1954 Red Heart Complete High Grade Set (33).** Man's best friend and the National Pastime join forces in this set issued with cans of Eisenhower era dog food. A total of 19 cards have been graded by SGC with an aggregate SMR value of $4,685. Highlights include - **Graded Cards - SGC 96 MINT 9:** 1, card Sauer; **SGC 92 NM/MT+ 8.5:** 8 cards w/#'s Cox, Dark, Fain, Kuenn, Lollar, McDougald, Pierce and Slaughter; **SGC 88 NM/MT 8:** 7 cards w/ Ashburn, Bell, Erskine, Gilliam, Mantle, Minoso and Yost; **SGC 86 NM+ 7.5:** 1 card, Martin; **SGC 84 NM 7:** 2 cards Musial and Schoendienst. Ungraded cards include Fox (EX/MT), Kell (NM), Kiner (NM), Kluszewski (NM), Snider (EX) and Spahn (EX). Grades 81% NM to NM/MT, 19% EX to EX/MT. **Minimum Bid: $500**

19168 **1954 Topps Willie Mays #90 SGC 86 NM+ 7.5.** The 1954 baseball season ended with the New York version of the Giants winning the World Series for the last time before heading to California after the 1957 season. Willie Mays was also the NL MVP that season, posting .345-41-110 numbers. Only seven of the 181 submitted to SGC rate higher than this 1954 Topps #90 Willie Mays card. A slight difference in left to right centering is the only condition issue of note. **Minimum Bid: $200**

STILL THE KING

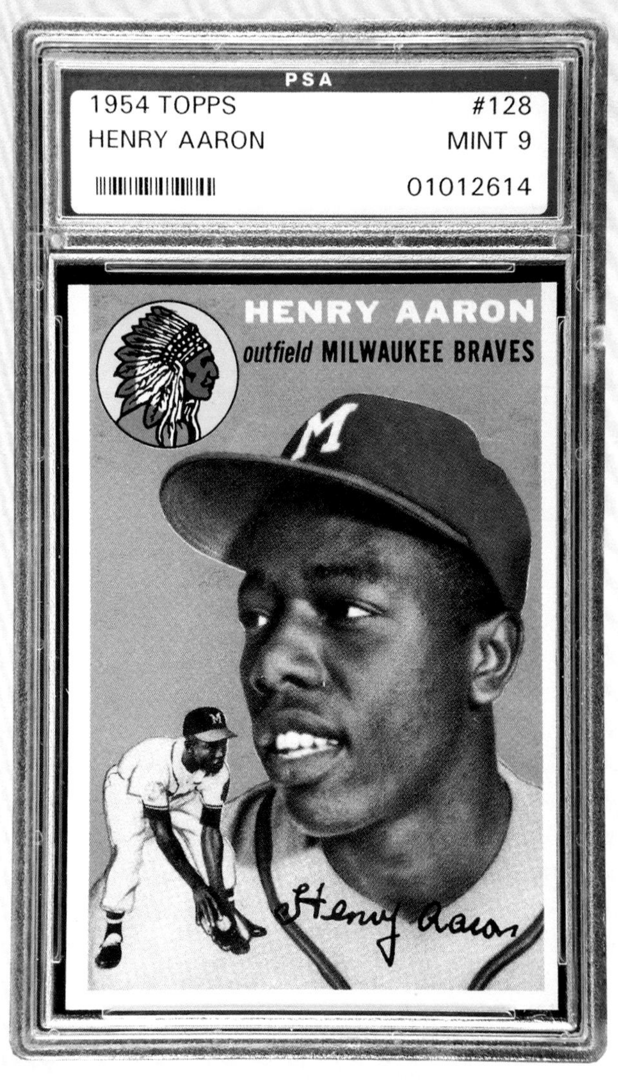

19169 **1954 Topps Hank Aaron Rookie #128 PSA Mint 9.** Certainly one of the hobby's most important post-war cards, a status it will retain even now that Aaron's remarkable 755 career home run total has been surpassed. Though Aaron's own assumption of the home run crown came more than a quarter century after Jackie Robinson broke the color line, Hammerin' Hank was forced to endure everything from racist taunts to death threats as he reeled in the Babe. This exceptional Mint example of his 1954 Topps rookie card is a fitting tribute to the skill and bravery of history's most prolific slugger, remaining to this day entirely unchanged from its emergence from a wax pack over a half century ago. Offering perfect color, registration and centering to go along with its complete absence of wear, it is not surprising that this card finds itself near the top of the record books (much like the man himself) with only two specimens ever grading higher. **Minimum Bid: $2,500**

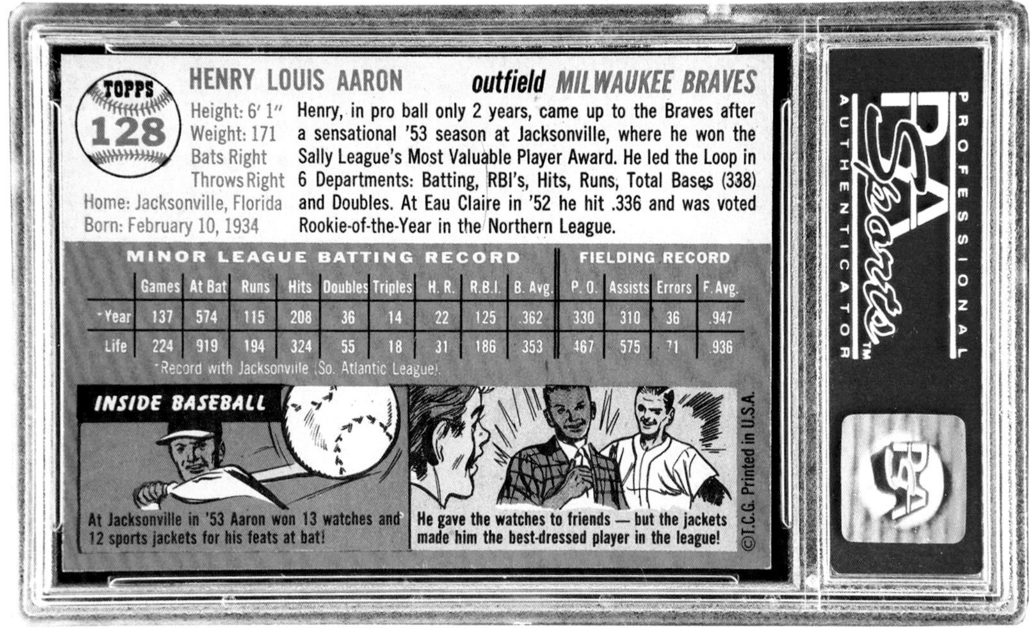

19170 **1954 Topps Al Kaline #201 GAI NM-MT 8.** Like Babe Ruth before him, this Hall of Fame slugger honed his home run skills in the city of Baltimore, Maryland before taking the Big Leagues by storm. This remarkably clean cardboard announced Kaline's arrival to the baseball card collecting world, and boasts fine centering, bright colors and sharp registration. **Minimum Bid: $300**

19171 **1954 Topps Baseball High Grade Complete Set (250).** High-powered rookies have established the 1954 Topps issue as a collector favorite for decades, as legends like Hank Aaron, Al Kaline, Ernie Banks and Tommy Lasorda make their cardboard debuts within. The centering problems that typify the issue are few and far between within this hand-picked set, which finds high grade, low population examples across the spectrum. A total of 124 cards have been graded by SGC (almost 50% of the set) with an aggregate SMR value of $20.479. Highlights include: **Graded Cards - SGC 96 MINT 9:** 9 cards w/#'s 23 Easter, 27, 36 Wilhelm, 56, 61, 69, 73, 131 and 225; **SGC 92 NM/MT+ 8.5:** 19 cards w/#'s 29, 30 Mathews, 33, 45 Ashburn, 46, 55 Cavarretta, 64, 66, 89, 114, 118, 143, 160, 161, 185, 187 Manush, 198, 216 and 232; **SGC 88 NM/MT 8:** 55 cards w/#'s 4 Sauer, 5 Lopat, 11, 14 Roe, 16, 17 Rizzuto, 20 Spahn, 25 Kuenn, 28, 31, 34, 35 Gilliam, 42, 48, 50 Berra, 54 Stephens, 60, 86 Herman, 90 Mays, 93, 97, 116, 129, 138, 139 O'Brien Twins, 144, 148, 150, 151, 154, 156, 157, 166 Podres, 169, 176, 177, 179, 181, 182, 184, 201 Kaline, 204, 205 Sain, 214, 215, 219, 222, 224, 229, 230, 236, 240, 242, 243 and 244; **SGC 86 NM+ 7.5:** 23 cards w/#'s 10 Robinson, 19, 22, 37 Ford, 47, 63, 67, 68, 70, 104, 108, 124, 127, 133, 136, 146, 178, 191, 203, 207, 237, 239 Skowron and 250 Williams; **SGC 84 NM 7:** 12 cards w/#'s 3 Irvin, 6, 13 Martin, 32 Snider, 41, 58, 81, 87 Face, 98 Black, 113, 189 and 226; **SGC 80 EX/NM 6:** 5 cards w/#'s 84, 100, 117, 128 Aaron and 170; **SGC 60 EX 5:** 1 card, #94 Banks. **Ungraded Cards** - include #'s 1 Williams (VG/EX), 7 Kluszewski (NM), 85 Turley (EX/MT), 102 Hodges (EX), 130 Bauer (EX), 132 Lasorda (EX) and 137 Moon (EX/MT). **Grades 61% NM to NM/MT,** 34% EX to EX/MT, 5% VG to VG/EX. **Minimum Bid: $2,500**

19172 **1955 Bowman Hoyt Wilhelm #1 SGC 96 Mint 9 - 1 of 1.** Here we offer a strong Mint example of the always condition sensitive number one card in the 1955 Bowman issue featuring Hall of Fame knuckleballer Hoyt Wilhelm. Wilhelm's image is framed in the classic Bowman television set with perfect centering at 50/50 on all sides. The gloss is dripping off of this beauty and the corners are as sharp as the day it was printed in Philadelphia over five decades ago. This phenomenal example is the only one to ever achieve Mint 9 status from SGC and it has only one counterpart that achieved the same grade from PSA with none ever grading higher. This is a piece that is necessary to start you 1955 Bowman set in style. **Minimum Bid: $500**

19173 **1955 Bowman Mickey Mantle #202 PSA NM 7.** Just as baseball was increasingly being used as a television marketing tool, Bowman decided to capitalize on the nation's growing fascination with the game in the innovative card design they used in 1955. Mickey Mantle and his New York Yankees were one of television's most popular early sporting attractions. This early gum card displays vivid coloring with a clean front and back. **Minimum Bid: $200**

19174 **1955 Bowman Mickey Mantle # 202 SGC 92 NM/MT+ 8.5.** Between the frequent print defects and the dark borders of the 1955 Bowman issue, there are few examples that have survived the fifty three years since they were manufactured in the condition that we offer with this Mantle beauty. The four sharp corners and the original pack fresh gloss stand out when examining this outstanding example. Lastly, the centering perfectly frames the Mick in the classic television design. This is only one of four that have achieved this tough grade from SGC with only one example grading higher. It appears that the original slight rough cut along the top border may be the only thing keeping this phenomenal card from Mint status. **Minimum Bid: $500**

19175 **1955 Bowman Baseball SGC Graded Partial Set (112/320) .** A total of 112 different cards (with an aggregate SMR value of $7,228) including Hall of Famers, minor stars and commons highlight this high grade ensemble. This is a great start to completing an SGC graded 1955 Bowman set, with 35% of the set already graded. There are quite a few high ticket cards in this partial graded set including Phil Rizzuto, Nelson Fox, Whitey Ford, Eddie Mathews, Willie Mays and Ernie Banks. Highlights include: **Graded Cards - SGC 92 NM/MT+ 8.5:** 2 cards w/#'s 12 and 55; **SGC 88 NM/MT 8:** 59 cards w/#'s 7, 10 Rizzuto, 11, 20, 25 Minoso, 26, 49, 54, 57, 58, 59 Ford, 66, 68 Howard, 76, 83, 84, 85, 86, 89 Boudreau, 97 Podres, 98 Gilliam, 99, 100, 103 Mathews, 112, 113, 114, 116, 117, 122, 129, 131, 132 Kuenn, 169 Furillo, 174, 177, 194, 199, 201 Reynolds, 203, 206, 209, 211, 226, 235, 238, 239, 242 Banks, 251, 252, 253, 254, 266, 269, 270, 276, 281, 301 and 313 Donatelli UMP; **SGC 86 NM+ 7.5:** 16 cards w/#'s 60 Slaughter, 67 Larsen, 104, 107, 142, 162, 166, 205, 210, 217, 234, 249, 261, 300, 308 Lopez and 317; **SGC 84 NM 7:** 21 cards w/#'s 9 McDougald, 33 Fox, 41, 70 Burdette, 72, 87, 88, 105, 130 Ashburn, 141, 147, 153, 164, 167, 185, 214, 241, 258, 265 Barlick UMP, 284 and 294; **SGC 80 EX/NM 6:** 5 cards w/#'s 22 Campanella, 134 Feller, 184 Mays, 187 and 246 Bauer; **SGC 70 EX+ 5.5:** 3 cards w/#'s 23 Kaline, 161 and 233; **SGC 60 EX 5:** 5 cards w/#'s 75, 80, 232, 243 and 275; **SGC 50 VG/EX 4:** #278 Neal. **Minimum Bid: $500**

19176 **1955 Bowman Baseball High Grade Complete Set (320).** The popular "television set" presents a significant stumbling block for collectors concentrating on high-grade cards, as the full bleed graphics provide little mercy when it comes to edge and corner wear. This would be Bowman's final baseball set for quite some time. A total of 63 cards have been graded by SGC with an aggregate SMR value of $6,608. Highlights include: **Graded Cards - SGC 96 MINT 9:** 4 cards w/#'s 33 Fox, 139 Bob and Bill Shantz, 215 and 223; **SGC 92 NM/MT+ 8.5:** 15 cards w/#'s 74, 116, 123, 124, 141, 189, 220, 221, 227, 238, 243, 244, 245, 261 and 295; **SGC 88 NM/MT 8:** 34 cards w/#'s 21, 23 Kaline, 27, 29 Schoendienst, 36, 38 Wynn, 67 Larsen, 91, 108, 118, 122, 125, 128, 130 Ashburn, 134 Feller, 146, 159, 165, 166, 191 Lemon, 214, 218, 219, 229, 231, 234, 235, 246 Bauer, 248, 257, 259, 260, 275 and 307; **SGC 86 NM+ 7.5:** 9 cards w/#'s 59 Ford, 68 Howard, 94, 109, 179 Aaron, 190, 212, 242 Banks and 258; **SGC 84 NM 7:** 2 cards w/#'s 105 and 232; **SGC 80 EX/NM 6:** 1 card, #202 Mantle. **Ungraded Cards** - include #'s 1 Wilhelm (EX/MT), 10 Rizzuto (NM), 22 Campanella (EX/MT), 37 Reese (EX), 60 Slaughter (EX/MT), 65 Zimmer (NM), 103 Mathews (EX/MT), 158 Hodges (EX), 168 Berra (EX), 171 Roberts (NM), 184 Mays (trimmed), 197 Kiner (EX/MT), 265 Barlick (EX), 267 Honochick (EX/MT), 303 Conlan (NM), 315 Hubbard (NM). **Grades 71% NM to NM/MT,** 24% EX to EX/MT, 5% measure short. **Minimum Bid: $1,000**

19177 **1955 Topps Double Headers PSA-Graded Near Set (62/66).** This set is a throwback to the 1911 T201 Mecca Double Folders. Offered is a nearly complete set of 1955 Topps Double Headers issue, missing only card #'s 25-26, 111-112, 127-128 and 129-130, with every card graded by PSA. These cards are not easy to find in high grade due to the poor storage options and the perforations that were easily creased. In total there are 62 cards representing 124 players. Highlights include: **Graded - PSA NM-MT 8:** 8 cards w/#'s 31-32 Pollett/Banks (OC), 37-38 (OC), 57-58, 65-66, 71-72, 81-82, 97-98 (OC) and 131-132 (OC); **PSA NM 7:** 15 cards w/#'s 1-2 Rosen/Diering, 19-20, 39-40, 59-60, 61-62, 73-74, 75-76, 77-78, 79-80, 85-86, 89-90, 93-94 (MC), 95-96, 107-108 (MC) and 117-118; **PSA EX-MT 6:** 17 cards w/#'s 3-4 Irvin/Kemmerer, 5-6, 7-8, 15-16, 17-18, 21-22 (MC), 23-24, 27-28, 35-36, 43-44, 51-52, 63-64, 83-84, 87-88, 107-108, 115-116 and 123-124; **PSA EX 5:** 16 cards w/#'s 9-10, 11-12, 41-42, 53-54, 55-56, 67-68, 91-92, 99-100, 101-102, 103-104, 105-106, 109-110, 113-114, 119-120 and 125-126; **PSA VG-EX 4:** 4 cards w/#'s 13-14, 29-30, 33-34 and 45-46 Kaline/Valentine; **PSA VG 3:** 2 cards w/#'s 49-50 and 121-122 Kluszewski/Owens; **PSA Poor 1:** 2 cards w/#'s 47-48 and 69-70 Williams/Smith. Graded cards have an aggregate SMR value $2,775. **Minimum Bid: $500**

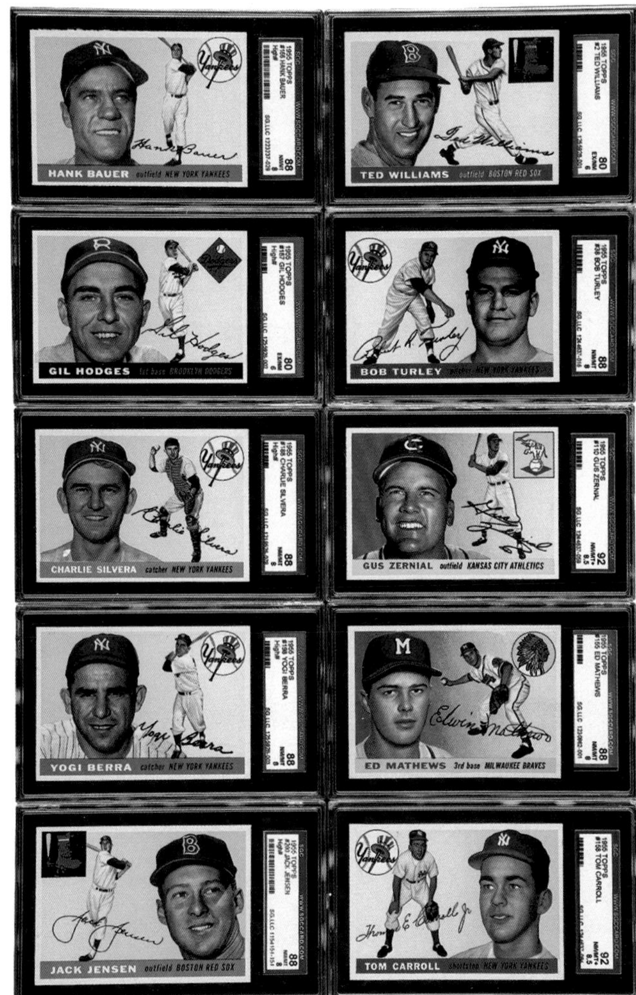

19178 **1955 Topps Baseball Complete Set (206).** The 1955 Topps set with its brand new horizontal design and brilliant colors is one of the most popular sets of the 1950's. This set includes rookie cards of Roberto Clemente, Sandy Koufax and Harmon Killebrew. This set has a total of 47 cards that have been graded by SGC with an aggregate SMR value of $4,770. Highlights include: **Graded Cards - SGC 92 NM/MT+ 8.5:** 2 cards w/#'s 110 and 158; **SGC 88 NM/MT 8:** 20 cards w/#'s 12, 38 Turley, 51, 59, 60, 97, 112, 115, 116, 121, 127, 128, 133, 137, 155 Mathews, 160, 166 Bauer, 188, 198 Berra and 200 Jensen; **SGC 86 NM+ 7.5:** 9 cards w/#'s 21, 43, 52, 93, 129, 140, 148, 156 Black and 171; **SGC 84 NM 7:** 14 cards w/#'s 9, 14, 17, 19, 41, 49, 67, 75 Amoros, 101, 102, 103, 105, 136 and 157; **SGC 80 EX/NM 6:** 2 cards w/#'s 2 Williams and 187 Hodges. **Ungraded Cards** - include #'s 1 Rhodes (VG), 4 Kaline (EX), 28 Banks (EX), 31 Spahn (VG/EX), 47 Aaron (EX), 50 Robinson (EX), 92 Zimmer (EX/MT), 100 Irvin (VG/EX), 120 Kluszewski (EX), 123 Koufax (VG/EX), 124 Killebrew (EX), 125 Boyer (EX), 152 Agganis (EX), 164 Clemente (VG), 189 Rizzuto (VG/EX), 194 Mays (VG/EX), 210 Snider (EX). Grades 26% NM to NM/MT, 62% EX to EX/MT, 12% VG to VG/EX. **Minimum Bid: $1,750**

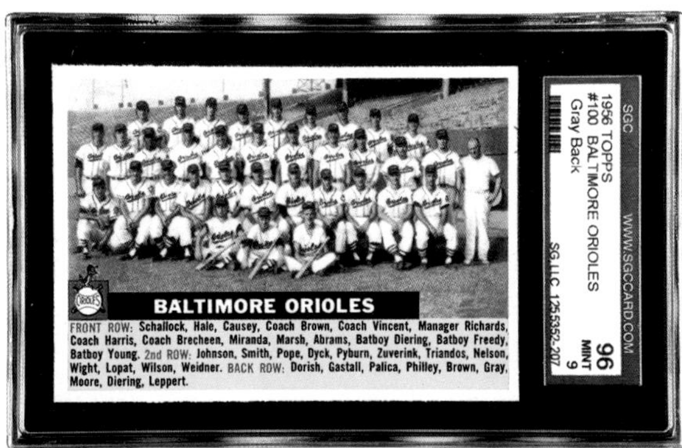

19179 **1956 Topps Baseball Orioles Team #100 SGC 96 Mint 9.** The lone representative with none higher than this 96 Mint 9; the offered 1956 Topps #100 Orioles Team card stands alone in SGC's population report. The Baltimore Orioles should have been so lucky, finishing a distant 6th in the AL race in 1956 with a mark of 69-85. This card is the gray back variation. **Minimum Bid: $100**

19180 **1956 Topps Mickey Mantle #135 PSA EX-MT 6.** Providing an affordable alternative for those wishing to add an attractive card dating to Mantle's Triple Crown season of 1956. Mickey Mantle led the junior circuit in BA, HRs and RBIs with eye-popping .353-52-130 numbers. Nice card with only corner wear detracting from overall appeal. **Minimum Bid: $200**

19181 **1956 Topps Mickey Mantle #135 SGC 84 NM 7.** This bright Topps specimen dated from Mantle's Triple Crown-season features a perfect surface with shimmering gloss and a wholly unimpaired visual presentation. Mild, technically assessed liabilities are restricted to a slightly rightward image alignment and very light touches to the corners. A strong example of one of the most visually appealing cards of the 1950's. **Minimum Bid: $250**

19182 1956 Topps Baseball Mickey Mantle #135 PSA NM-MT 8. Mickey Mantle played 18 seasons with the New York Yankees; none more memorable, with the possible exception of 1961 and the home run chase with Roger Maris, than his 1956 Triple Crown year. This card was released during that fabled 1956 season and has survived the test of time even more than a half decade later. Fine centering, brilliant colors, four sharp corners and a clean back make for a special opportunity to add a fine example of one of the Mick's more popular cards to your collection. **Minimum Bid: $500**

19183 1956 Topps Baseball Mickey Mantle #135 PSA NM-MT+ 8.5. Less than one of every 100 1956 Topps #136 Mickey Mantle cards submitted to PSA has achieved a grade higher than NM/MT 8; marking this as a momentous occasion. One of his most popular cards, it was issued during the season he captured the AL's Triple Crown. He led the league with .352-52-130 numbers, still more than respectable even after the advent of steroids. **Minimum Bid: $750**

19184 1956 Topps Mickey Mantle #135 SGC 92 NM/MT+ 8.5 . When one talks about the all-time greats, Mickey Mantle is right on the tip of our tongue. This card depicts "The Mick" with his big Oklahoma smile, almost as if he knew he would win the triple crown that year and be voted the American League M.V.P. The offered card has near perfect centering, vibrant colors and a clarity that could only be matched with an actual camera. There are not many examples that would merit this lofty grade, but this one has all of the attributes of a Very Strong NM/MT+ grade. **Minimum Bid: $750**

19185 1956 Topps Duke Snider #150 SGC 96 Mint 9. "The Silver Fox" came up on the short end with his Brooklyn Dodgers facing Mickey Mantle's New York Yankees squad in the 1956 Fall Classic. Only two of the 155 1956 Topps #150 Duke Snider cards submitted to SGC have earned the 96 Mint 9 status this one enjoys. Card is virtually flawless; displaying bright colors, beautiful white borders, clean front and back. **Minimum Bid: $200**

19186 1956 Topps Red Schoendienst #165 PSA Mint 9. During a 19-season career, all spent with the St. Louis Cardinals organization, second sacker Red Schoendienst finished in the top 10 in NL MVP voting on four occasions. He was inducted into the Baseball Hall of Fame in 1989. Ten of the 518 examples of this card submitted to PSA have been granted a Mint 9 designation (none higher). **Minimum Bid: $100**

MY FAVORITE SUMMER

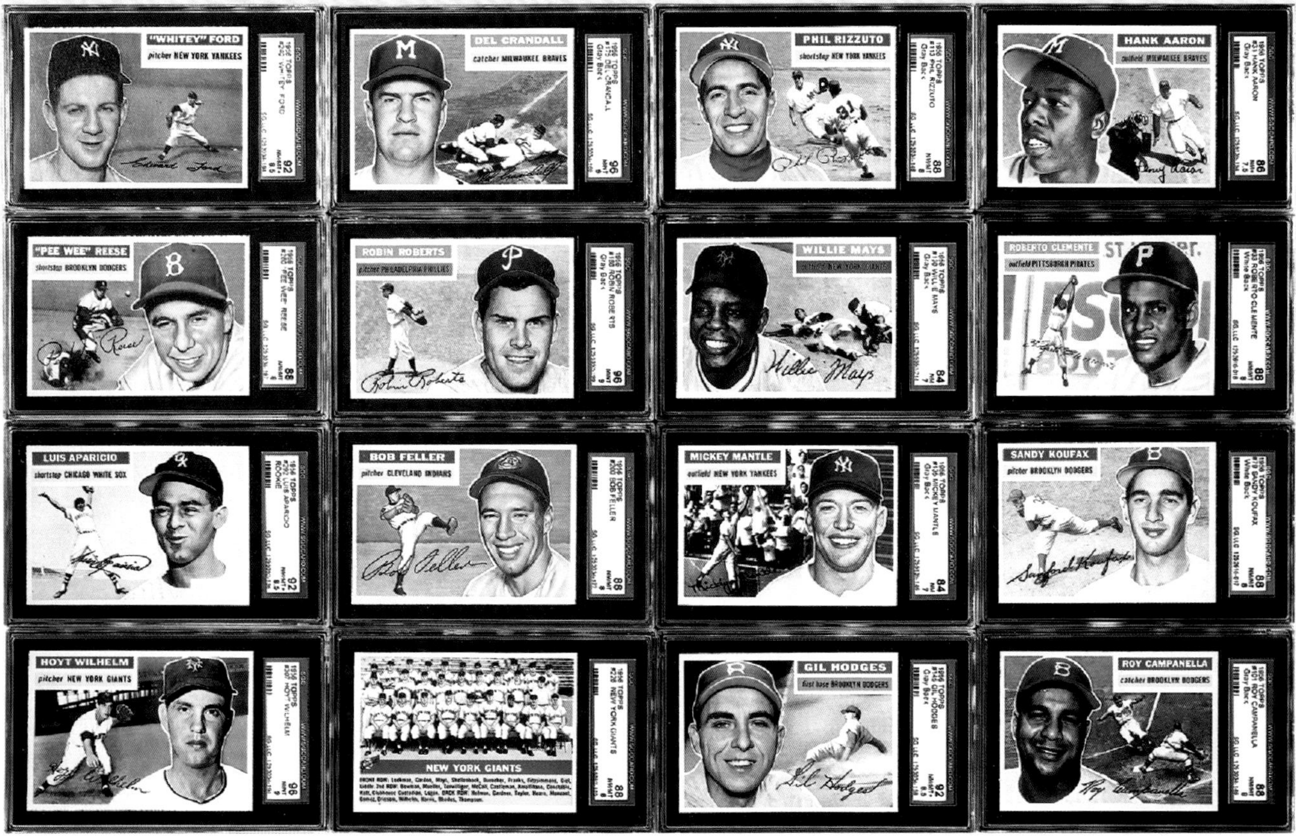

19187 **1956 Topps Baseball High Grade Complete Set (340).** Mickey Mantle called 1956 "My Favorite Summer," a characterization that should surprise few given his Triple Crown heroics and the Yankee World Series victory highlighted by Don Larsen's perfect game. The presented set pays apt tribute to the historic season, with an impressive high-grade theme throughout. A total of 157 cards have been slabbed by SGC, with an aggregate SMR value of $19,225, almost 40% achieving an SGC 88 NM/MT or higher. Highlights include: **Graded Cards - SGC 96 MINT 9:** 26 cards w/#'s 13 Face WB, 28 WB, 48 WB, 49 GB, 56 GB, 89 WB, 96 GB, 127 GB, 137 GB, 142 GB, 147 GB, 154 GB, 156 GB, 157 GB, 175 GB, 180 Roberts GB, 202, 239, 264, 272, 279, 300 Wertz, 307 Wilhelm, 308, 311 and 331; **SGC 92 NM/MT+ 8.5:** 43 cards w/#'s 12 Carey WB, 17 WB, 18 GB, 26 GB, 40 Turley WB, 47 GB, 57 WB, 63 Craig GB, 64 GB, 71 WB, 114 GB, 122 GB, 131 GB, 139 GB, 140 Score GB, 145 Hodges GB, 148 Dark GB, 152 GB, 168 GB, 173 Podres GB, 174, 187 Wynn, 204, 225 McDougald, 228 Vernon, 240 Ford, 242, 246, 266, 288 Cerv, 291, 292 Aparicio, 293, 296, 303, 320, 321, 322, 323, 324, 325, 327 and 332 Larsen; **SGC 88 NM/MT 8:** 61 cards w/#'s 3 WB, 6 WB, 10 Spahn WB, 21 WB, 24 WB, 25 Kluszewski WB, 29 WB, 32 WB, 33 Clemente WB, 34 GB, 39 GB, 44 WB, 45 WB, 46 WB, 51 WB, 54 GB, 78 WB, 79 Koufax WB, 82 WB, 90 Redlegs GB, 95 Brewers GB, 98 GB, 99 Zimmer WB, 101 Campanella GB, 104 Lennon, 111 Red Sox GB, 113 Rizzuto GB, 119 GB, 120 Ashburn GB, 121 Pirates GB, 126 GB, 138 GB, 143 GB, 151 GB, 163 GB, 167 GB, 172 GB, 181 Martin, 184, 189, 193, 194 Irvin, 195 Kell, 198, 199, 200 Feller, 212, 215, 219, 226 Giants, 229, 260 Reese, 263, 280 Gilliam, 281, 283, 286, 287, 298, 304 and 326; **SGC 86 NM+ 7.5:** 12 cards w/#'s 15 Banks GB, 20 Kaline GB, 31 Aaron GB, 41 WB, 72 Phillies GB, 118 Fox GB, 150 Snider GB, 165 Schoendienst GB, 188 White Sox, 190, 191 and 213 Tigers; **SGC 84 NM 7:** 14 cards w/#'s 1 Harridge WB, 5 Williams GB, 30 Robinson WB, 50 WB, 100 Orioles GB, 109 Slaughter GB, 110 Berra GB, 130 Mays GB, 135 Mantle GB, 166 Dodgers GB, 177 Bauer GB, 221, 251 Yankees and CL 2/4; **SGC 80 EX/NM 6:** 1 card, #164 Killebrew. **Ungraded Cards** - include #'s 8 Alston (EX/MT), 61 Skowron (NM), 107 Mathews (EX/MT) and 208 Howard (NM). **Grades 72% NM to NM/MT,** 28% EX to EX/MT (some lesser). **Minimum Bid: $3,500**

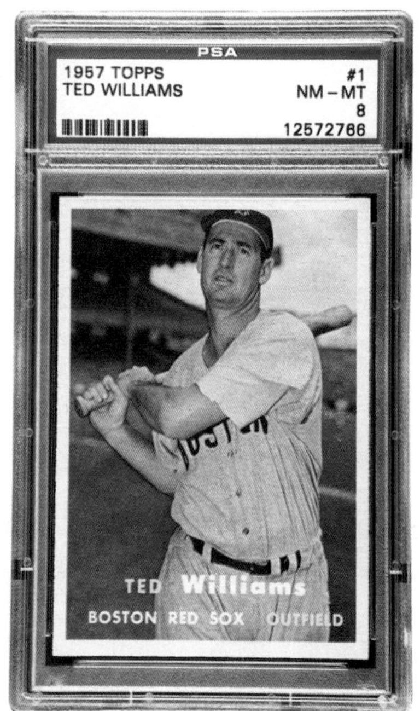

19188 1957 Topps Baseball Ted Williams #1 PSA NM-MT 8. While the appearance as the number one card in a set is intended to be an honor, such a designation in the earlier days of gum card collecting was fraught with peril as the first and last cards in a collected set tended to bear the brunt of the elements. As a result, we find very few examples of the '57 Ted Williams card that can hold a candle to this one, which boasts razor-sharp corners and marvelous gloss to justify its lofty grade. **Minimum Bid: $350**

19189 1957 Topps Mickey Mantle #95 SGC 84 NM 7. The 1957 Topps issue was the first to feature true photography on each card and here we see the Mick in a classic warm up swing pose in his Yankee pinstripes. This issue typically suffers from print defect and registration issues, but that is certainly not the case with this offering as it presents a flawless surface with strong original gloss. Each of the corners has a slight touch, which accounts for the Near mint grade but the aesthetics of this example are very strong. **Minimum Bid: $200**

19190 1957 Topps Baseball Complete Set (407). Presented is a mid to high grade 1957 Topps baseball set. With a very tough mid series and plenty of rookie cards, including Frank Robinson, Brooks Robinson, Jim Bunning, Rocky Colavito and more, makes this set from the 1950's one of the more desirable ones. A total of 33 cards have been graded by SGC. A total of 33 cards have been graded by SGC with an aggregate SMR value of $3,019. Highlights include - **Graded Cards - SGC 92 NM/MT+ 8.5:** 8 cards w/#'s 91, 130 Newcombe, 134, 178, 180, 272, 360 and 374; **SGC 88 NM/MT 8:** 10 cards w/#'s 75, 90 Spahn, 119, 140, 191, 197, 200 McDougald, 261, 367 and 368; **SGC 86 NM+ 7.5:** 6 cards w/#'s 27, 141, 248, 264, 351 and 403; **SGC 84 NM 7:** 7 cards w/#'s 1 Williams, 10 Mays, 20 Aaron, 73, 172, 188 and 302 Koufax; **SGC 80 EX/NM 6:** 2 cards w/#'s 35 Robinson and 400 Dodgers' Sluggers. **Ungraded Cards** - include #'s w/#'s 2 Berra (EX), 7 Aparicio (EX/MT), 15 Roberts (EX/MT), 18 Drysdale (EX/MT), 24 Mazeroski (EX/MT), 25 Ford (EX), 30 Reese (EX),38 Fox (EX), 40 Wynn (NM), 55 Banks (EX), 62 Martin (VG/EX), 70 Ashburn (NM), 76 Clemente (EX/MT), 80 Hodges (EX/MT), 85 Doby (EX/MT), 95 Mantle (VG/EX), 97 Yankees Team (EX/MT), 121 Boyer (EX), 125 Kaline (EX/MT), 165 Kluszewski (EX/MT), 170 Snider (EX/MT), 203 Wilhelm (EX/MT), 210 Campanella (EX/MT), 212 Colavito (EX/MT), 215 Slaughter (EX), 250 Mathews (EX/MT), 277 Podres (EX), 286 Richardson (VG), 312 Kubek (NM), 317 Giants Team (EX), 324 Dodgers Team (EX/MT), 328 Robinson (VG), 338 Bunning (VG/EX) and 407 Yankee Power Hitters (VG/EX). Grades 30% NM to NM/MT, 63% EX to EX/MT, 7% VG to VG/EX. **Minimum Bid: $750**

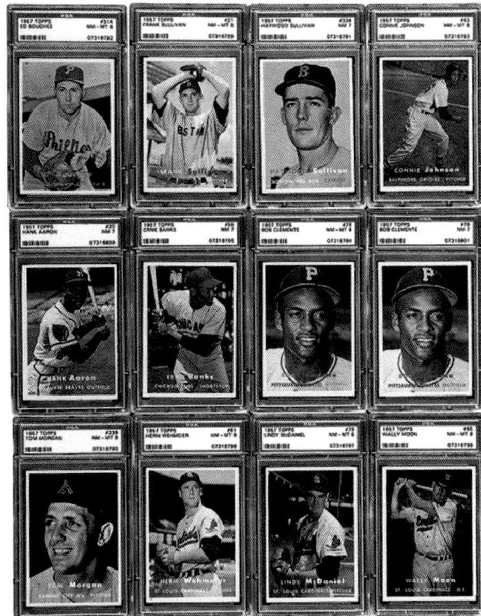

19191 **1957 Topps Baseball Collection (197).** Plenty of stars are included in this collection including Williams, Drysdale, Aaron, Robinson, Clemente and many more. Twelve cards have been graded by PSA with an aggregate SMR value of $1645. Highlights include: **Graded Cards - PSA NM-MT 8:** 8 cards w/#'s 21, 43, 65, 76 Clemente, 79, 81, 239 and 314; **PSA NM 7:** 4 cards w/#'s 20 Aaron, 55 Banks, 76 Clemente and 336. **Ungraded Cards** - include #'s 1 Williams (EX), 7 Aparicio (EX/MT), 10 Mays (VG/EX), 15 Roberts (VG/EX), 18 Drysdale (VG/EX), 20 Aaron (EX), 24 Mazeroski (VG/EX), 30 Reese (EX), 35 Robinson (EX/MT), 38 Fox (EX), 40 Wynn (EX), 55 Banks (EX), 70 Ashburn (GD/VG), 165 Kluszewski (VG/EX), 212 Colavito (FR), 240 Bauer (EX), 272 Shantz (NM), 286 Richardson (FR). Grades 24% NM to NM/MT, 63% EX to EX/MT, 7% VG to VG/EX, 6% lesser. **Minimum Bid: $500**

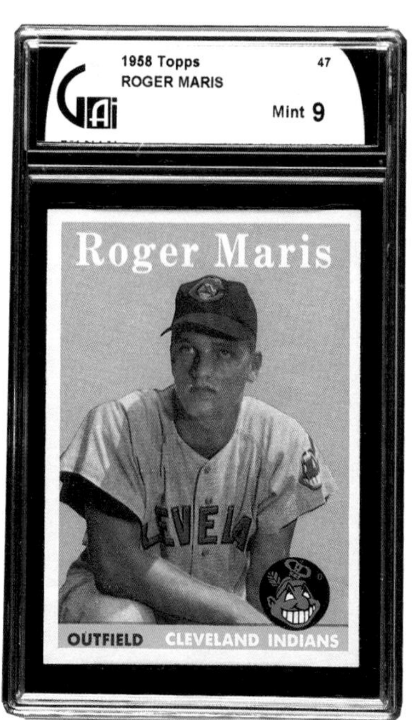

19192 **1958 Topps Roger Maris #47 GAI Mint 9.** This beautiful example of Roger Maris' rookie card features the same bold orange coloring as that of his future teammate, Mickey Mantle's, Topps issue from the same year. It features four strong corners and is free of the typical print defects that are commonly associated with the 1958 Topps issue. It also boasts a well centered and stain free verso making it a quality Mint 9 example for any collection. **Minimum Bid: $750**

19193 **1958 Topps Baseball Mickey Mantle #150 PSA NM 7.** One of the more recognizable images of Mantle from the 1950s Topps series. In this season the Yankees would recapture their magic by squashing the Milwaukee Braves in the Fall classic. This specimen exhibits very sharp corners, a bright background that captures your attention and a sharp, clean image. **Minimum Bid: $200**

19194 **1958 Topps Baseball Mickey Mantle #150 PSA NM-MT 8.** Marvelous photographic portrait of the Mick in his prime makes the '58 Topps card a favorite among collectors, who will certainly be awestruck by the spectacular quality of the offered specimen. Perfect color, gloss and registration give way to terrific centering and sharp corners. **Minimum Bid: $300**

19195 **1958 Topps Mickey Mantle #150 SGC 88 NM/MT 8.** Here we offer a high grade example of Mantle's bold 1958 Topps issue which features a portrait of the Mick after his two consecutive MVP seasons. This specimen is a thoroughly satisfying solution to a perennial condition challenge, in beautiful Near Mint to Mint condition. **Minimum Bid: $300**

19196 **1958 Topps Baseball Complete Set (494).** The 1958 Topps baseball series consists of 494 cards and included "All-Star" cards for the first time. One card (#145) was not issued after Ed Bouchee was suspended from baseball. This issue is noted for bright colors and numerous star cards, including high profile rookies of Maris, Cepeda, and Flood. A total of 46 cards have been graded by SGC with an aggregate SMR value of $3,305. Highlights include: Graded Cards - **SGC 92 NM/MT+ 8.5:** 11 cards w/#'s 117, 127, 149, 202, 210, 211, 234, 252, 279, 330 and 446; **SGC 88 NM/MT 8:** 14 cards w/#'s 65, 112, 120 Podres, 167, 224, 229, 251, 269, 314 Snider/Alston, 315, 336, 364, 407 and 433; **SGC 86 NM+ 7.5:** 7 cards w/#'s 25 Drysdale, 63, 115 Bunning, 152, 160, 162 Hodges and 480 Mathews; **SGC 84 NM 7:** 11 cards w/#'s 5 Mays, 30 Aaron, 47 Maris, 146, 176, 205, 285 Robinson, 301, 370 Berra, 430 and 488 Aaron AS; **SGC 80 EX/NM 6:** 3 cards w/#'s 150 Mantle, 249 and 288 Killebrew. Ungraded Cards - include #'s 1 Williams (GD), 19 Giants (EX), 30 Aaron (VG/EX), 70 Kaline (EX/MT), 85 Aparicio (NM), 88 Snider (EX), 90 Roberts (VG/EX), 100 Wynn (VG/EX), 101 Richardson (EX/MT), 230 Ashburn (EX), 238 Mazeroski (EX), 246 Yankees Team (EX), 270 Spahn (EX), 271 Martin (EX), 307 Robinson (VG), 310 Banks (VG/EX), 320 Ford (EX), 321 Williams/Kluszewski (EX), 343 Cepeda (EX/MT), 351 Braves Fence Busters (EX/MT), 368 Colavito (EX/MT), 375 Reese (EX/MT), 418 Mantle/Aaron (EX), 420 Pinson (VG/EX), 436 Mays/Snider (VG/EX), 440 Mathews (EX), 464 Flood (EX/MT), 476 Musial AS (VG/EX), 482 Banks AS (EX), 484 Robinson AS (VG/EX), 485 Williams AS (EX), 486 Mays AS (VG/EX), 487 Mantle AS (VG/EX) and 494 Spahn AS (EX). Grades 28% NM to NM/MT, 64% EX to EX/MT, 8% VG to VG/EX. **Minimum Bid: $750**

19197 **1958 Topps Baseball Complete Set With 31 Yellow Letters.** The 1958 Topps baseball series consists of 494 cards and included "All-Star" cards for the first time. One card (#145) was not issued after Ed Bouchee was suspended from baseball. This issue is noted for bright colors and numerous star cards, including high profile rookies of Maris, Cepeda, and Flood. A total of 26 cards have been graded by PSA with an aggregate SMR value of $4,610. Included in this set are 31 Yellow Letters, missing #11 Rivera and 79 Williams, for completion. Highlights include: **Graded Cards - PSA NM-MT+ 8.5:** 1 card, #124; **PSA NM-MT 8:** 13 cards w/#'s 20 McDougald Yellow Letter, 30 Aaron (OC), 61 Johnson Yellow Letter, 85 Aparicio (OC) Yellow Letter, 101 Richardson Yellow Letter, 121, 140, 142 Slaughter, 143, 314 Snider/Alston, 425, 477 Skowron AS and 488 Aaron AS; **PSA NM+ 7.5:** 2 cards w/#'s 246 Yankees Team and 351 Braves Fence Busters; **PSA NM 7:** 9 cards w/#'s 52 Clemente Yellow Letter, 88 Snider, 131, 150 Mantle, 285 Robinson, 306, 428 Redlegs Team Alphabetical, 485 Williams AS and 486 Mays AS; **PSA EX 5:** 1 card, #30 Aaron YL. Ungraded Cards - include #'s 1 Williams (VG/EX), 5 Mays (EX), 25 Drysdale (VG/EX), 30 Aaron (EX), 47 Maris (PR), 52 Clemente (VG/EX), 70 Kaline (EX), 85 Aparicio (VG/EX), 90 Roberts (VG/EX), 100 Wynn (EX/MT), 101 Richardson (EX/MT), 115 Bunning (GD/VG), 162 Hodges (EX), 187 Koufax (trimmed), 230 Ashburn (EX/MT), 238 Mazeroski (EX), 270 Spahn (EX), 271 Martin (VG), 288 Killebrew (VG), 307 Robinson (GD), 310 Banks (EX), 320 Ford (VG/EX), 321 Williams/Kluszewski (EX), 343 Cepeda (EX/MT), 368 Colavito (VG/EX), 370 Berra (EX), 375 Reese (EX), 418 Mantle/Aaron (VG/EX), 420 Pinson (VG/EX), 436 Mays/Snider (EX/MT), 440 Mathews (EX), 464 Flood (NM), 476 Musial AS (NM), 480 Mathews AS (VG), 482 Banks AS (EX/MT), 484 Robinson AS (VG/EX), 487 Mantle AS (VG/EX), and 494 Spahn AS (EX). Grades 19% NM to NM/MT, 64% EX to EX/MT, 17% VG to VG/EX. YELLOW LETTERS - (missing 11 Rivera and 79 Williams). Grades 13% NM to NM/MT, 22% EX to EX/MT, 65% VG to VG/EX. **Minimum Bid: $1,750**

19198 **1959 Fleer Ted Williams #68 "Ted Signs For 1959" SGC 92 NM/MT+ 8.5.** Bucky Harris is to blame (or to thank, depending upon your mindset) for the scarcity and corresponding costliness of the number 68 card in this popular set dedicated to the life of the game's greatest hitter. It seems that Fleer had failed to obtain permission for the use of his image, and the card was quickly withdrawn from production. This one managed to escape though, and with flying colors besides. Providing marvelous color and registration to match its sharp corners and strong centering, it ranks behind only six in SGC grading history, one of which is likewise presented within the pages of this auction catalog. **Minimum Bid: $200**

19199 **1959 Fleer Ted Williams # 68 "Ted Signs for 1959" SGC 96 Mint 9.** A mint example of the toughest card from the 1959 Fleer Ted Williams issue, this card is perfect in every respect with four sharp corners, 50/50 centering, and un-improvable focus and print quality. Card number 68 was withdrawn from production because Fleer didn't have permission to use the image of Red Sox General Manager Bucky Harris, who is pictured on this card with Ted as he signs his contract for the 1959 season. Ted was such a tremendous star for card manufacturers that companies annually fought for his contract and Fleer secured his cooperation for its 1959 issue. This represents one of only six examples that have achieved Mint status from SGC with none grading higher. **Minimum Bid: $300**

19200 **1959 Fleer Ted Williams Near Complete Set (79/80).** Each card has been graded by SGC. Offered is the 1959 Fleer Ted Williams Set missing #68 Ted Signs for completion. This set highlights Ted's career from his early days through his retirement. A total of 79 cards have been graded by SGC with an aggregate SMR value of $2,908. Highlights include: **Graded - SGC 96 MINT 9:** 3 cards w/#'s 16, 53 and 78; **SGC 92 NM/MT+ 8.5:** 6 cards w/#'s 12, 22, 41, 43, 61 and 73; **SGC 88 NM/MT 8:** 23 cards w/#'s 10, 14, 17, 19, 20, 21, 23, 25, 27, 30, 32, 46, 48, 51, 55, 62, 67 Williams/Snead, 69, 70 Williams/Thorpe, 72, 76, 77 and 80 Ted's Goals; **SGC 86 NM+ 7.5:** 11 cards w/#'s 1 The Early Years, 7, 15, 18, 33, 42, 44, 64, 65, 71 and 79; SGC 84 NM 7: 9 cards w/#'s 31, 37, 39, 47, 54, 57, 59, 63 All-Star and 74; **SGC 80 EX/NM 6:** 7 cards w/#'s 24, 35, 50, 52, 56, 66 and 75 Ruth/Williams; **SGC 70 EX+ 5.5:** 1 card, #45; **SGC 60 EX 5:** 11 cards w/#'s 2 Williams/Ruth, 3, 4, 6, 8, 29, 36, 38, 40, 49 and 58; **SGC 50 VG/EX 4:** 5 cards w/#'s 5, 11 Williams/Foxx, 13, 34 and 60; **SGC 40 VG 3:** 3 cards w/#'s 9, 26 and 28. **Minimum Bid: $400**

19201 **1959 Fleer Ted Williams High Grade Complete Set (79/80).** The 80-card release from Fleer tells the life story of baseball legend Ted Williams, from early childhood through the 1958 season. Card #68 was withdrawn from the set early in production and is considered scarce. This near set does not contain the #68 Ted Signs card. A total of 25 cards have been graded by SGC with an aggregate SMR value of $3234. Highlights include: **Graded Cards - SGC 96 MINT 9:** 11 cards w/#'s 18, 20, 33, 37, 39 Cronin/Collins/Williams, 50, 52, 65, 67 Williams/Snead, 69 and 74; **SGC 92 NM/MT+ 8.5:** 5 cards w/#'s 7, 24, 31, 35 and 70 Williams/Thorpe; **SGC 88 NM/MT 8:** 8 cards w/#'s 14, 22, 36, 49, 51, 57, 71 and 78; **SGC 84 NM 7:** 1 card, #3. **Ungraded Cards** - include #'s 1 The Early Years (EX), 2 Williams/Ruth (VG/EX), 11 Foxx/Williams (NM), 63 Ted's All-Star (NM), 75 Collins/Ruth/Wiliams (EX/MT), 80 Ted's Goals for 1959 (VG/EX). Grades 70% NM to NM/MT, 25% EX to EX/MT, 5% VG to VG/EX. **Minimum Bid: $500**

19202 **1959 Fleer Ted Williams High Grade Complete Set (80).** The 80-card release from Fleer tells the life story of baseball legend Ted Williams, from early childhood through the 1958 season. Card #68 was withdrawn from the set early in production and is considered scarce. A total of 54 cards have been graded by PSA with an aggregate SMR value of $6,906. Highlights include: **Graded Cards - PSA MINT 9:** 21 cards w/#'s 9 Ted's First Step w/Collins, 24, 26, 34, 35, 37, 40, 41, 42, 44, 49, 50, 54, 55, 56, 57, 58, 62, 65, 69 and 73; **PSA NM-MT+ 8.5:** 4 cards w/#'s 11 Foxx/Williams, 13, 22 and 45; **PSA NM-MT 8:** 25 cards w/#'s 3, 5, 12, 17, 18, 19, 23, 25, 30, 32, 33, 47, 48, 53, 59, 60, 63 Ted's All Star Record, 64, 67 Williams/Snead, 70 Williams/Thorpe, 71, 72, 75 Ruth/Williams, 76 and 77; **PSA NM 7:** 2 cards w/#'s 61 and 68 Ted Signs; **PSA EX-MT 6:** 2 cards w/#'s 2 Williams/Ruth and 79 Where Ted Stands. **Ungraded Cards** - include #'s 1 The Early Years (EX), 39 Collins/Ruth (NM) and 80 Ted's Goals (EX). Grades 90% NM to NM/MT, 10% EX to EX/MT. **Minimum Bid: $750**

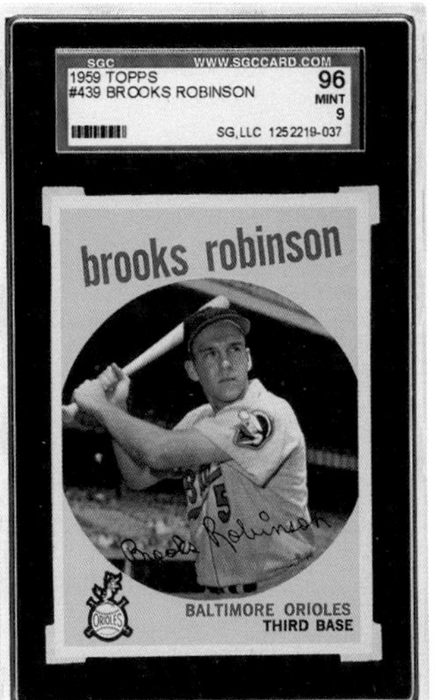

19203 **1959 Topps Brooks Robinson #439 SGC 96 Mint 9.** Brooks Robinson took the 1970 World Series and made it his personal showcase, completing plays at the hot corner that did not seem humanly possible. After he almost singlehandedly won the 1970 World Series for the Orioles, Reds manager Sparky Anderson quipped: "I'm beginning to see Brooks in my sleep. If I dropped this paper plate, he'd pick it up on one hop and throw me out at first." Of the 118 submitted to SGC, this one ranks as the singular best. As the lone SGC 96 Mint 9 example (none graded higher), it should come as no surprise that the card displays all of the characteristics inherent in such a high grade. Beautiful colors, ultra-bright clean borders, four sharp corner and perfect registration are all readily apparent with this card. SGC registry collectors will not want to let this opportunity pass, it may be a long time coming before another of this quality is ever offered. **Minimum Bid: $200**

19204 **1959 Topps Baseball High Grade Complete Set.** This colorful and attractive set features the Bob Gibson rookie card, as well as an abundance of Hall of Famers. In addition to the regular issue of each player, the 1959 collection contains All-Star and Baseball Thrills subsets. Multiple cards of Mantle, Clemente, Mays, Aaron, Kaline and other stars complete the set. A total of 174 cards have been professionally graded (172 by PSA) with an aggregate SMR value of $4,835. An investment-quality set that includes: **Graded Cards - PSA NM-MT 8:** 62 cards w/#'s 29, 64, 67, 75, 86, 110, 123, 124, 128, 132, 137, 140, 141, 142, 146, 161, 162, 184, 192, 193, 196, 210, 211, 214, 215, 216, 219, 228, 243, 249, 252, 253, 257, 265, 272, 274, 276, 279, 290, 292, 294, 306, 314, 316, 321, 337, 338 Anderson, 341, 351, 354, 356, 358, 361, 362, 363, 364, 365, 368, 371, 384, 391, 456; PSA NM-MT 8(MC): 12 cards w/#'s 118, 122, 126, 127, 129, 133, 134, 136, 143, 194, 383, 443; **PSA NM 7:** 98 cards w/#'s 1 Frick, 6, 8, 9, 18, 19, 28, 30 Fox, 31, 47, 55, 56, 59, 61, 65, 66,68, 69, 70, 72, 76, 78, 82-85, 93, 98, 100, 101, 104, 109, 113, 116, 121, 135, 138, 144, 150 Musial, 152, 163 Koufax, 171, 176, 182, 213, 245, 247, 256, 258, 261, 262, 268, 269, 281, 289, 301, 302, 307, 308, 318, 342, 357, 367, 369, 370, 379, 382, 392, 393, 394, 396, 397, 406, 407, 409, 413, 426, 434, 473, 483, 484, 495, 514 Gibson, 515 Killebrew, 517, 519, 534, 541, 548, 551, 556 Fox AS, 558, 560 Aparicio AS, 561 Aaron AS, 563 Mays AS, 564 Mantle AS, 566, 569; **SGC 84 NM 7:** 1 card, #380 Aaron; **GAI NM 7:** 1 card, #62. **Ungraded Cards** - includes #'s 10 Mantle (EX/MT), 20 Snider (EX/MT), 40 Spahn (NM), 50 Mays (EX), 180 Berra (EX/MT), 202 Maris (EX/MT), 260 Wynn (EX/MT), 270 Hodges (EX/MT), 300 Ashburn (VG/EX), 317 NL Hitting Kings (EX/MT), 350 Banks (EX/MT), 352 Roberts (EX/MT), 360 Kaline (EX/MT), 387 Drysdale (EX/MT), 430 Ford (EX/MT), 435 F.Robinson (NM), 439 B.Robinson (EX), 450 Mathews (EX), 461 Mantle HL (VG/EX), 464 Mays HL (EX), 467 Aaron HL (EX), 468 Snider HL (EX), 470 Musial HL (EX), 478 Clemente (EX/MT), 509 Cash (EX/MT), 510 Yankees Team (EX/MT), 543 Corsair Trio (EX), 550 Campanella (EX/MT), 559 Banks AS (EX), 562 Kaline AS (EX/MT), 571 Spahn AS (EX). Grades 45% NM to NM/MT, 55% EX to EX/MT (few lesser). **Minimum Bid: $1,000**

19205 **1959 Topps Baseball High Grade Complete Set (572).** A rookie from the rocket-armed Bob Gibson, a multitude of star cards including Mickey Mantle, Willie Mays, Hank Aaron and Ernie Banks, and the debut of "highlight cards" make the 1959 Topps set an historic one. A total of 68 cards have been graded by SGC with an aggregate SMR value of $4,884. Highlights include: **Graded Cards - SGC 96 MINT 9:** 3 cards w/#'s 32, 138 and 273; **SGC 92 NM/MT+ 8.5:** 9 cards w/#'s 13, 15, 31, 46, 64, 71, 72, 279 and 324; **SGC 88 NM/MT 8:** 33 cards w/#'s 2, 8 Phillies Team, 19, 40 Spahn Born in 1921, 41, 48 Orioles Team, 56, 81, 86, 108, 111, 194, 227, 235, 240 Bauer, 246, 251, 284, 309, 311, 325 Boyer, 360 Kaline, 387 Drysdale, 425, 454, 457 Dodgers Team, 465, 467 Aaron BT, 472, 476, 494, 506 and 527; **SGC 86 NM+ 7.5:** 8 cards w/#'s 69, 98, 180 Berra, 342, 362, 470 Musial BT, 478 Clemente and 563 Mays AS; **SGC 84 NM 7:** 12 cards w/#'s 10 Mantle, 20 Snider, 35 Kluszewski, 60 Turley, 150 Musial, 202 Maris, 212 Aaron/Mathews, 464 Mays BT, 509 Cash, 515 Killebrew, 543 Corsair Trio and 562 Kaline AS; **SGC 80 EX/NM 6:** 3 cards w/#'s 50 Mays, 163 Koufax and 514 Gibson. **Ungraded Cards** - include #'s 102 Alou (EX), 260 Wynn (EX/MT), 270 Hodges (NM), 295 Martin (EX/MT), 300 Ashburn (VG/EX), 317 NL Hitting Kings (EX), 338 Anderson (EX), 350 Banks (EX), 352 Roberts (EX), 380 Aaron (VG/EX), 430 Ford (EX), 435 Robinson (EX/MT), 439 Robinson (EX/MT), 450 Mathews (EX), 461 Mantle HL (EX), 468 Snider HL (NM), 510 Yankees Team (EX/MT), 550 Campanella (EX), 559 Banks AS (EX), 561 Aaron AS (VG/EX), 564 Mantle AS (VG/EX) and 571 Spahn AS (GD). **Grades 31% NM to NM/MT,** 62% EX to EX/MT, 7% VG to VG/EX. **Minimum Bid: $1,000**

19206 **1960 Fleer Baseball High Grade Complete Set (79).** This contains an amazing amount of Hall of Famers. The back of the card give their career highlights and any World Series totals if they played. A total of 21 card have been graded by PSA with an aggregate SMR value of $1,084. Highlights include: **Graded Cards - PSA MINT 9:** 4 cards w/#'s 6 Johnson, 25 Collins, 41 Baker and 73 Giles; **PSA NM-MT+ 8.5:** 1 card, #60; **PSA NM-MT 8:** 14 cards w/#'s 2 Mathewson, 15, 18, 44 Anson, 50 Chance, 56, 58 Gehringer, 61, 62 Wagner, 63, 67 Jennings, 72 Williams, 75 and 79 Kiner; **PSA NM 7:** 2 cards w/#'s 57 and 65. **Ungraded Cards** - include #'s 1 Lajoie (EX/MT), 3 Ruth (EX/MT), 26 Feller (EX), 28 Gehrig (VG/EX), 42 Cobb (NM) and 47 Young (EX). **Grades 51% NM to NM/MT,** 49% EX to EX/MT. **Minimum Bid: $300**

19207 **1960 Leaf Baseball High Grade Complete Set (145).** The complete set of 144, plus the Jim Grant variation card, is offered. This is a very difficult series to complete in top grade due to an extensive and scarce 72-card high number run that comprises half the set. A total of 16 cards have been graded by SGC with an aggregate SMR value of $496. Highlights include: Graded Cards - **SGC 92 NM/MT+ 8.5:** 2 cards w/#'s 18 Gilliam and 137; **SGC 88 NM/MT 8:** 9 cards w/#'s 33, 37 Snider, 42, 46 Boyer, 59, 68, 70, 97 and 110 Averill; **SGC 86 NM+ 7.5:** 2 cards w/#'s 25 Grant, White Cap and 138 Cottier; **SGC 84 NM 7:** 3 cards w/#'s 27 Robinson, 49 Perry and 69 Wilhelm. **Ungraded Cards** - include #'s 1 Aparicio (EX/MT), 6 Alou (NM), 125 Anderson (NM), 128 Cepeda (NM), 141 Flood (NM) and 144 Bunning (EX). **Grades 71% NM to NM/MT,** 29% EX to EX/MT. **Minimum Bid: $500**

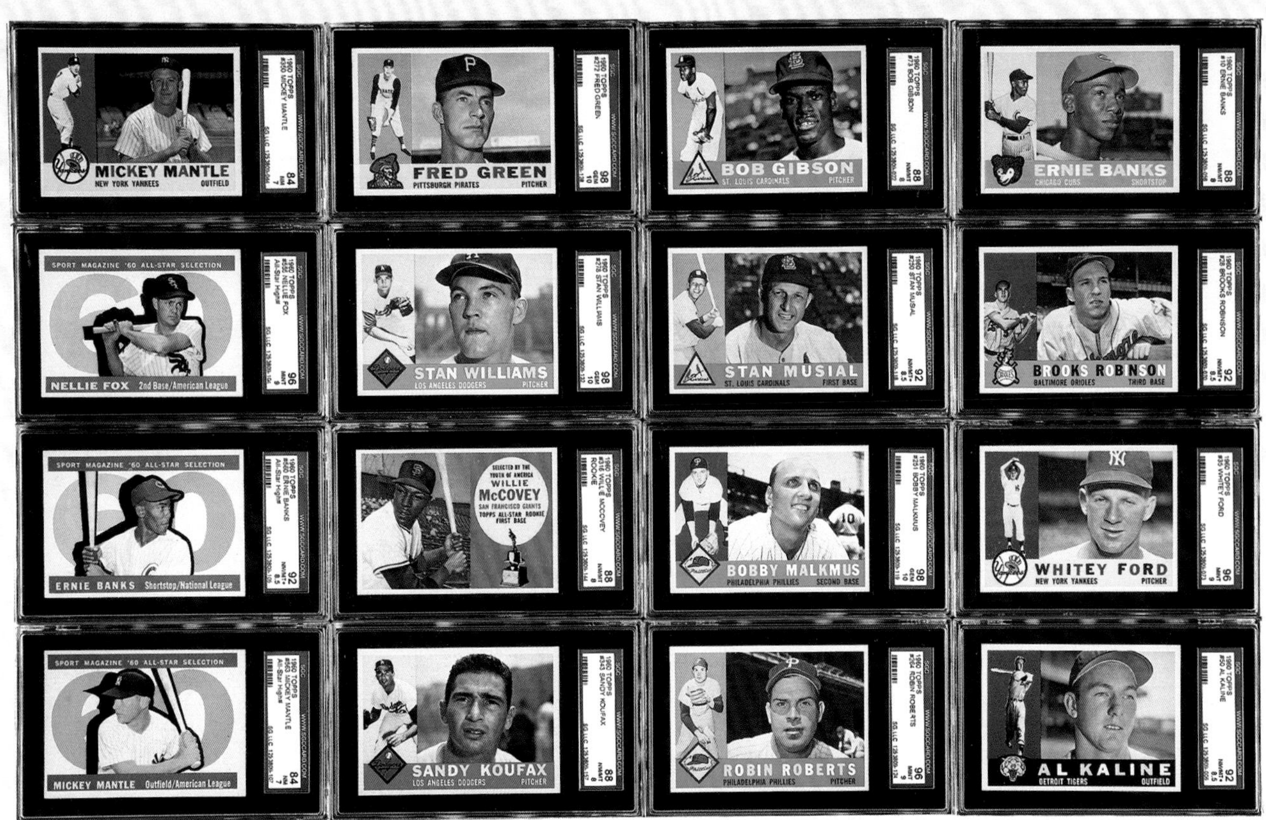

19208 **1960 Topps Baseball High Grade Complete Set (572).** The 1960 Topps issue was the last year that Topps produced a horizontal issue and has always been a collector favorite due to its multiple Hall of famers along with its colorful design. Rookie cards of Carl Yastrzemski, Willie McCovey and Jim Katt highlight the extremely high grade set. Sets like this do not come around to often, especially where more than 28% of the set has already been graded at the NM/MT level or higher, including 3 GEM MINT cards. A total of 176 cards have been graded by SGC with an aggregate SMR in excess of $14,000. Highlights include: **Graded Cards - SGC 98 GEM MINT 10:** 3 cards w/#'s 251, 272 and 278; **SGC 96 MINT 9:** 49 cards w/#'s 11, 22, 23, 32, 35 Ford, 37, 39, 41, 47 Zimmer, 53, 55 Mazeroski, 57, 58, 59, 62, 63, 67, 71, 74, 80, 85, 91, 100 Fox, 103, 104, 108, 234, 243, 245, 252, 260 Colavito/Francona, 262 Bauer, 263, 264 Roberts, 265, 270, 275 Flood, 276, 277, 322, 349, 402, 407, 409, 437, 448 Gentile, 513 Cubs, 521 and 555 Fox AS; **SGC 92 NM/MT+ 8.5:** 55 cards w/#'s 5, 6, 7 Mays/Rigney, 14, 16, 18 Dodgers, 20 Face, 24, 25, 26, 28 Robinson, 29, 34 Anderson, 42, 43 Senators, 45, 46, 49, 50 Kaline, 54, 56, 61, 68, 69, 79, 82, 93, 96 Terry, 106, 121, 239, 240 Aparicio, 242 Cardinals, 250 Musial 258, 259, 261, 279, 286, 311, 312, 314, 330, 382, 393, 410, 429, 436, 457, 458, 487, 504, 533, 540 and 560 Banks AS; **SGC 88 NM/MT 8:** 57 cards w/#'s 10 Banks, 15, 31, 36, 48, 51, 60, 65 Howard, 73 Gibson, 78, 81, 84, 86, 87, 95, 101, 105, 125, 138, 142, 167, 176 Pinson, 205, 207, 241, 246, 247 McDougald, 269, 283, 284, 285, 295 Hodges, 313, 316 McCovey, 332 Yankees, 336, 343 Koufax, 348, 352 Cincy Clouters, 385, 387, 395 Wilhelm, 400 Colavito, 414, 417, 420 Mathews, 425 Podres, 427, 445 Spahn, 474, 484 Pirates, 485 Boyer, 494 Orioles, 496, 511, 520 and 568; **SGC 86 NM+ 7.5:** 3 cards w/#'s 151, 377 Maris and 428; **SGC 84 NM 7:** 8 cards w/#'s 109, 123, 148 Yastrzemski, 160 Mantle/Boyer, 350 Mantle, 553 Skowron AS, 561 Kaline AS and 563 Mantle AS; SGC 80 EX/NM 6: 1 card, #564 Mays AS. **Ungraded Cards** - include #'s 1 Wynn (EX), 136 Kaat (EX), 200 Mays (EX/MT), 210 Killebrew (EX/MT), 300 Aaron (EX), 326 Clemente (VG/EX), 475 Drysdale (EX/MT), 493 Snider (EX/MT), 554 McCovey AS (EX/MT), 558 Mathews AS (EX/MT), 565 Maris AS (EX/MT), 566 Aaron AS (EX), 570 Drysdale AS (EX/MT). **Grades 65% NM to NM/MT,** 30% EX to EX/MT, 5% VG to VG/EX. **Minimum Bid:** $3,500

19209 **1961 Fleer Baseball Greats SGC Graded Collection (15).** Offered are 15 cards from the 1961 Fleer Baseball Greats that have been graded by SGC with an SMR value in excess of $1,200. A series that was difficult to find in high grade due to centering and miscut issues on the reverse. These cards all present at top levels for the grade. Highlights include: **Graded - SGC 98 GEM 10:** 1 card, #115 Jackson; **SGC 96 MINT 9:** 9 cards w/#'s 55 Lombardi, 103 Dugan, 104 Falk, 111 Hadley, 116 Joost, 134 Pipgras, 137 Schumacher, 140 Stephenson and 145 Trosky; **SGC 92 NM/MT+ 8.5:** 5 cards w/#'s 30 Frisch, 43 Hornsby, 67 Newsom, 97 Camilli and 110 Hack. **Minimum Bid: $200**

19210 **1961 Nu-Card Scoops High Grade Complete Set (80).** The Nu-card collection is a collaboration of baseball's most memorable highlights. All cards are presented in an individual newspaper front-page style that makes for a unique and informational baseball set. A total of forty cards have been graded by PSA with an aggregate SMR value in excess of $1,750. (This set is numbered 401 to 480). Highlights include: **Graded Cards - PSA GEM MINT 10:** 3 cards w/#'s 415 Richardson, 420 Banks and 422 Mantle; **PSA MINT 9:** 23 cards w/#'s 402 Spahn, 403 Mazeroski, 406, 407, 410, 416 Maris, 418 Larsen, 419, 421 Musial, 423, 424 Gehrig, 428 Robinson, 433, 437 Reese, 438 DiMaggio, 439 Williams, 449 Killebrew, 451, 455 Ruth, 458 Ott, 466, 468 Colavito and 472 Fox; **PSA NM-MT+ 8.5:** 1 card, #413; **PSA NM-MT 8:** 13 cards w/#'s 408, 434, 444 Roberts, 446, 450 Mantle, 453 Berra, 454, 457 Kluszewski, 462 Aaron, 463 Spahn, 467 DiMaggio, 474 and 479 Hubbell. **Ungraded Cards** - include #'s 404 Mays (NM), 427 Mays (NM), 447 Ruth (EX/MT) and 452 Williams (NM). Grades 76% NM to NM/MT, 24% EX to EX/MT (one lesser). **Minimum Bid: $300**

19211 **1961 Post Cereal Baseball Panels Collection (15).** Two hundred different players are included in this set, but with variations the number of cards exceeds 350. Cards were issued singly and in various panel configurations on the backs of cereal boxes, as well as on thinner stock in 10-card team sheets available from Post via a mail-in offer. Fifteen of the 10-card team sheets are made available here, along with the original mailing envelopes. Includes New York Yankees (#1-9, 12 - Berra, Ford, Maris, Mantle); Chicago White Sox (#19-22, 24-28, 33 - Aparicio, Fox, Wynn, Minoso); Boston Red Sox (#47-54, 124, 56); Cleveland Indians (#142, 58-61, 63-65, 146, 64); Baltimore Orioles (#68-69, 71-77, 80 - Robinson, Wilhelm); Kansas City Athletics (81-90 - Herzog, Bauer); Minnesota Twins (#91-100 - Killebrew) (creased at top and bottom of sheet); Milwaukee Braves (#101-108, 41, 110 - Spahn, Mathews, Aaron); Philadelphia Phillies (#115-123, 55 - Roberts); Pittsburgh Pirates (#125-132, 136,138 - Mazeroski, Clemente); San Francisco Giants (#57, 143-145, 141, 147-150, 152 - Cepeda, Mays, McCovey) (creased at top and bottom of sheet); Los Angeles Dodgers (#156-161, 164, 166-168 - Drysdale, Snider, Hodges); St. Louis Cardinals (#171-180 - Boyer, Flood) (Flood card is creased); Cincinnati Reds (#181-182, 30, 184-190 - Pinson, Robinson, Martin); Chicago Cubs (#191-200 - Banks, Ashburn, Santo) (2nd and 3rd rows including Ashburn are creased) **Minimum Bid: $250**

19212 **1961 Topps Mickey Mantle World Series Game #307 PSA Mint 9.** Long before Reggie Jackson was given the title of "Mr. October," Mickey Mantle was dominating the Fall baseball postseason. In a remarkable 14-year span from 1951 to 1964, Mantle appeared in 12 World Series and produced 18 round trippers with 40 runs batted in, all in just 230 at bats. This Topps special card pays tribute to the postseason star in fine fashion, displaying four sharp corners with clean front and back sides. **Minimum Bid: $200**

19213 **1961 Topps Mickey Mantle #300 SGC 88 NM/MT 8.** This card features the Mick during the 1961 campaign and in the prime of his career when he belted a career high 54 home runs. This pack fresh example is a beautiful memento of that historic season and delivers a fabulous aesthetic with the dark background surrounding his image, and the likeness itself is above reproach. The card's overall appearance is stellar and vibrant, with tremendous color and optimal clarity. **Minimum Bid: $250**

19214 **1961 Topps Baseball Complete Set (587).** Offered is a 1961 Topps Baseball Complete Set in overall solid middle grade. There are many players who have multiple cards attributed to them, including MVP cards, All-Star cards and Highlight cards. A total of 14 cards have been graded by PSA with an aggregate SMR value of $1,910. Highlights include: **Graded Cards - PSA NM-MT+ 8.5:** 1 card, #430 Mazeroski; **PSA NM-MT 8:** 6 cards w/#'s 141 Williams, 200 Spahn, 405 Gehrig HL, 572 Robinson AS, 576 Maris AS and 577 Aaron AS; **PSA NM 7:** 6 cards w/#'s 300 Mantle (OC), 350 Banks, 517 McCovey, 578 Mantle AS, 579 Mays AS and 589 Spahn AS; **PSA EX-MT 6:** 1 card, #150 Mays. **Ungraded Cards** w/#'s 2 Maris (VG/EX), 10 Robinson (EX), 35 Santo (EX), 41 Clemente/Mays LL (VG/EX), 44 Mantle/Maris LL (EX), 80 Killebrew (EX), 120 Mathews (VG/EX), 160 Ford (VG/EX), 207 Dodger Southpaws (VG/EX), 211 Gibson (EX), 228 Yankees Team (EX), 260 Drysdale (EX), 287 Yastrzemski (VG), 290 Musial (EX), 307 Mantle WS (VG/EX), 344 Koufax (VG/EX), 360 Robinson (EX), 371 Skowron SP (EX), 388 Clemente (EX), 401 Ruth HL (VG), 406 Mantle HL (EX/MT), 415 Aaron (VG), 417 Marichal SP (EX), 425 Berra (EX), 429 Kaline (VG/EX), 443 Snider (EX), 455 Wynn (EX), 460 Hodges (EX), 472 Berra MVP (EX), 475 Mantle MVP (EX), 478 Maris MVP (EX/MT), 480 Campanella MVP (EX), 482 Mays MVP (EX), 484 Aaron MVP (EX/MT), 485 Banks MVP (EX), 571 Mazeroski AS (NM), 575 Banks AS (EX), 580 Kaline AS (VG/EX) and 586 Ford AS (VG/EX). Grades 10% NM to NM/MT, 69% EX to EX/MT, 21% VG to VG/EX. **Minimum Bid: $750**

19215 **1961 Topps Baseball Mid to High Grade Complete Set (587).** There are a multitude of star cards in this set, including five Mickey Mantle cards. A total of 55 cards have been graded by PSA with an aggregate SMR value of $4326. Highlights include: Graded Cards - **PSA MINT 9:** 8 cards w/#'s 2 Maris (OC), 18, 49 Drysdale/Koufax LL, 50, 52, 196, 316 and 371 Skowron; **PSA NM-MT+ 8.5:** 4 cards w/#'s 41 Mays/Clemente LL, 285, 363 and 457; **PSA NM-MT 8:** 28 cards w/#'s 42, 43 Banks/Aaron LL, 61, 67, 76, 79, 83, 98 CL, 124, 204, 358, 369, 373 Red Sox, 374, 408 Mathewson HL, 440 Aparicio, 485 Banks MVP, 510, 511, 530, 536, 537, 541, 556, 565 Alou, 568 Skowron AS, 572 Robinson AS and 575 Banks AS; **PSA NM 7:** 15 cards w/#'s 141 Williams, 253, 260 Drysdale, 287 Yastrzemski, 300 Mantle, 311 Ford WS, 443 Snider, 425 Berra, 480 Campanella MVP, 524, 552, 563 Cerv, 570 Fox AS, 578 Mantle AS and 586 Ford AS. **Ungraded Cards** - include #'s 10 Robinson (EX), 35 Santo (EX/MT), 44 Mantle/Maris LL (EX/MT), 80 Killebrew (EX/MT), 120 Mathews (EX/MT), 150 Mays (EX), 160 Ford (EX), 200 Spahn (EX/MT), 207 Dodger Southpaws (EX), 211 Gibson (EX/MT), 228 Yankees Team (VG/EX), 290 Musial (EX/MT), 307 Mantle WS (EX), 344 Koufax (EX/MT), 350 Banks (EX), 360 Robinson (EX), 388 Clemente (EX/MT), 401 Ruth HL (NM), 405 Gehrig HL (EX/MT), 406 Mantle HL (EX), 415 Aaron (EX/MT), 417 Marichal SP (EX/MT), 429 Kaline (EX), 430 Mazeroski SP (EX/MT), 455 Wynn (EX/MT), 460 Hodges (EX), 472 Berra MVP (EX/MT), 475 Mantle MVP (EX/MT), 478 Maris MVP (EX/MT), 482 Mays MVP (EX/MT), 484 Aaron MVP (EX), 517 McCovey (VG/EX), 571 Mazeroski AS (EX), 576 Maris AS (EX/MT), 577 Aaron AS (EX/MT), 579 Mays AS (EX/MT), 580 Kaline AS (EX/MT), 589 Spahn AS (EX). Grades 34% NM to NM/MT, 61% EX to EX/MT, 5% VG to VG/EX. **Minimum Bid: $1,000**

19216 **1962 Salada Plastic Baseball Coin Complete Set (221) Plus Variations (21).** These coins were marketed in both Teas and Pudding mixes. The coins measure 1 3/8" in diameter. This was a difficult set to complete due to the way they were distributed. A total of 17 coins were graded by PSA. Highlights include: **Graded Coins - PSA MINT 9:** 5 coins w/#'s 8 Ford , 18 Kubek, 52 Temple Indians, 97 Wynn, Portrait and 171 Ashburn; **PSA NM-MT 8:** 10 coins w/#'s 33 Berra, 40 Robinson, 71 Aparicio, 79, 109 Koufax, 111 Matthews, 129, 146 Hodges, 173 Cunningham, Cardinals and 198; **PSA NM 7:** 2 coins w/#'s 67 Kaline and 203. **Ungraded Coins** - include #'s 2 Pierce (EX), 4 Brewer (NM), 6 Herbert (NM), 13 Bunning (EX/MT), 23 Maris (EX), 26 Grant (EX/MT), 27 Yastrzemski (EX), 30 Busby (EX/MT), 36 Killebrew (EX), 39 Minoso, White Sox (EX), 39 Minoso Cardinals (EX/MT), 41 Mantle (EX/MT), 60 Wertz (NM), 66 Sievers (EX), 73 Jensen (EX/MT), 79 Keough (NM), 84 Veal (EX), 86 Carey, White Sox (EX/MT), 89 Hansen (EX/MT), 97 Wynn, Pitching (EX), 104 Thomas (NM), 108 Lillis, Cardinals (NM), 116 Bouchee (EX), 121 Kuenn (EX), 142 McCovey (EX), 146 Hodges, Dodgers (EX/MT), 148 Cimoli (VG/EX), 149 Mays (EX), 150 Clemente (EX), 162 Jones (EX), 165 Robinson (VG/EX), 173 Cunningham, White Sox (EX/MT), 177 Banks (EX), 179 Schmidt (NM), 180 Aaron (VG/EX), 207 Williams (EX/MT), 215 Snider (EX/MT). **VARIATIONS** include #'s 7, 24, 34, 39, 51, 52, 68, 86, 91, 97 Wynn, 102, 108, 127 Wills, 129, 135, 146 Hodges, 154, 155, 158, 173, 178. Grades 33% NM to NM/MT, 57% EX to EX/MT, 10% VG to VG/EX. **Minimum Bid: $500**

19217 **1962 Topps Baseball Complete Set (598).** A very tough issue due to the easy chipping on the brown borders, but this presents well above the average. A total of 38 cards have been graded by PSA with an aggregate SMR value of $2,362. Highlights include: Graded Cards - **PSA NM-MT+ 8.5:** 2 cards w/#'s 241 and 546; **PSA NM-MT 8:** 18 cards w/#'s 154, 182, 224, 234 Maris WS, 261, 276, 286, 312 Spahn IA, 313 Maris IA, 334 Red Sox, 357, 370, 469, 563, 577, 591 McDowell, 594 Uecker and 595; **PSA NM 7:** 16 cards w/#'s 5 Koufax, 18 Managers' Dream, 40 Cepeda, 45 Robinson, 199 Perry, 232, 235 Ford WS, 253, 288 Williams, 295, 318 Mantle IA, 340 Drysdale, 498, 527, 544 McCovey and 592 Bouton; **PSA EX-MT 6:** 1 card, #200 Mantle; **PSA EX 5:** 1 card, #10 Clemente. **Ungraded Cards** - include #'s 1 Maris (EX), 25 Banks (EX), 30 Mathews (EX), 50 Musial (EX), 53 Mantle/Maris LL (VG/EX), 60 Koufax/Drysdale LL (EX), 70 Killebrew (EX), 99 Powell (EX/MT), 100 Spahn (VG/EX), 139 Ruth (EX/MT), 140 Gehrig/Ruth (EX/MT), 150 Kaline (EX), 167 McCarver (EX/MT), 218 Torre (EX), 251 Yankees Team (EX/MT), 300 Mays (EX), 310 Ford (EX), 315 Ford IA (EX), 317 Musial IA (EX), 320 Aaron (VG), 350 Robnison (VG/EX), 360 Berra (EX), 387 Brock (EX), 394 Aaron AS (EX/MT), 395 Mays AS (EX), 396 Robinson AS (VG/EX), 401 Maris/Cepeda (VG/EX), 425 Yastrzemski (EX/MT), 471 Mantle AS (EX), 475 Ford AS (EX), 500 Snider (EX), 505 Marichal (EX), 530 Gibson SP (NM), 596 Pepitone (NM), 598 Hickman (EX). Grades 25% NM to NM/MT, 70% EX to EX/MT, 5% VG to VG/EX. **Minimum Bid: $750**

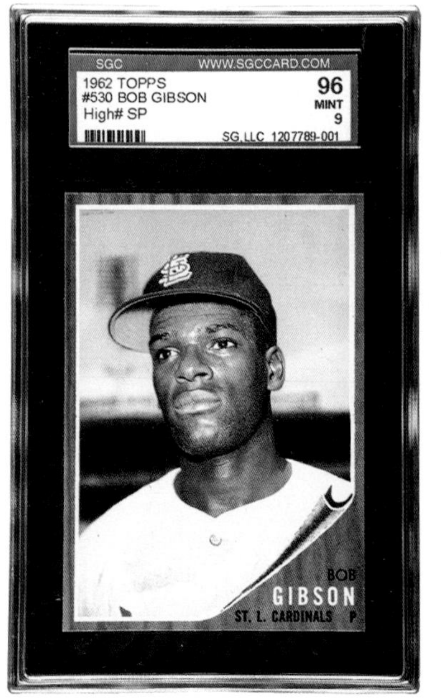

19218 **1962 Topps Bob Gibson #530 SGC 96 Mint 9.** This short-printed high numbered card features one of the more dominant pitchers of any era, 1981 Hall of Fame inductee Bob Gibson of the St. Louis Cardinals. Gibson, an eight-time National League All-Star team selection, was twice elected as World Series MVP and took home two NL Cy Young awards, in addition to being named the league's MVP in 1968. The card itself suffers none of the typical condition issues most of its counterparts from this set so commonly display, due in large part to the distinctive wood grain design so susceptible to chipping. **Minimum Bid: $300**

GOOD WOOD

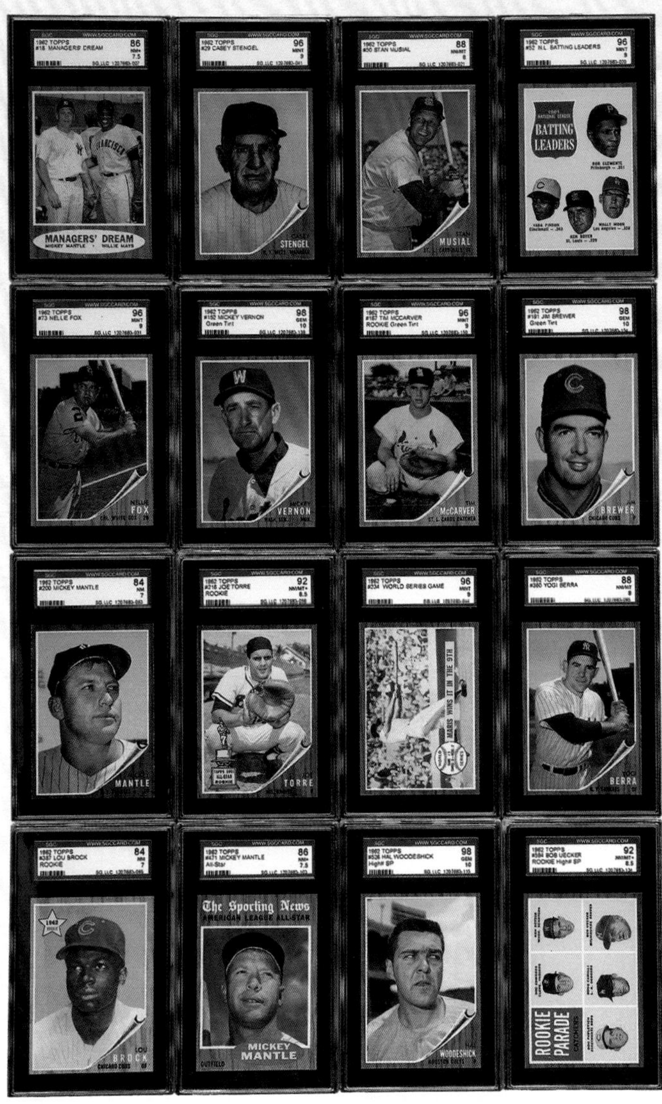

19219 **1962 Topps Baseball High Grade Complete Set (598).** The full-bleed wood grain bordering of this popular set makes it an unforgiving one when it comes to edge and corner wear, making the compilation of a high grade set a noteworthy challenge. The presented set was fashioned from cards pulled directly from a vending case, providing a welcome escape from the typical condition challenges. An amazing 151 cards have been graded by SGC with an aggregate SMR value in excess of $14,000. Highlights include: **Graded Cards - SGC 98 GEM MINT 10:** 3 cards w/#'s 152 Vernon GT, 191 GT and 526 SP; **SGC 96 MINT 9:** 30 cards w/#'s 15, 27, 29 Stengel, 47, 52 Clemente LL, 55, 64, 73 Fox, 107, 126 GT, 127 GT, 164 GT, 167 McCarver GT, 171 GT, 178 GT, 184 GT, 187, 234 Maris WS, 245, 283, 371, 390 Cepeda AS, 397, 454, 555 SP, 558, 562, 573, 578 and 585 SP; **SGC 92 NM/MT+ 8.5:** 36 cards w/#'s 22 CL, 38, 43 Dodgers Team, 58 Spahn LL, 122 GT, 129 Pinstripe Jersey GT, 131 GT, 132 Angels Photo Inset GT, 145 GT, 161 GT, 166 GT, 175 GT, 195 GT, 204, 213 Ashburn, 218 Torre, 220, 228, 239, 253, 263, 264, 344, 345, 376, 377, 380, 403, 421, 529 SP, 537 Indians Team, 554 SP, 569 SP, 577 SP, 586 SP and 594 Uecker SP; **SGC 88 NM/MT 8:** 48 cards w/#'s 9, 32, 39, 41, 50 Musial, 57 Ford LL, 61 Cardinals, 68, 69, 71, 77, 94, 95, 97, 99 Powell, 113 White Sox Team, 140 Gehrig/Ruth, 190 Moon w/Cap, 202, 230, 233, 251 Yankees, 269, 270 and 294 Phillies Team, 302, 333, 334 Red Sox Team, 360 Berra, 381, 386, 399 Spahn AS, 413, 419, 435, 437, 450, 460 Bunning, 485, 488, 524 SP, 539, 540 SP, 550 SP, 552 Cubs Team SP, 579 SP, 580 and 589 Turley; **SGC 86 NM+ 7.5:** 15 cards w/#'s 17, 18 Mantle/Mays, 56 Spahn LL, 67, 90, 121, 323, 396 Robinson AS, 430 Kubek, 471 Mantle AS, 532, 544 McCovey SP, 572 SP, 581 and 591 McDowell SP; **SGC 84 NM 7:** 16 cards w/#'s 70 Killebrew, 84, 147 GT, 199 Perry, 200 Mantle,314, 385 Wynn, 387 Brock, 394 Aaron AS, 395 Mays AS, 398 Drysdale AS, 401 Maris/ Cepeda, 425 Yastrzemski, 461 Hubbs, 549 SP and 584 Twins Team; **SGC 80 EX/NM 6:** 3 cards w/#'s 530 Gibson, 547 and 583. **Ungraded Cards** - include #'s 1 Maris (EX), 5 Koufax (EX/MT), 10 Clemente (EX), 25 Banks (EX), 30 Mathews (NM), 45 Robinson (EX), 53 Mantle/Maris LL (EX/MT), 100 Spahn (EX/MT), 139 Ruth (EX/MT), 150 Kaline (EX/MT), 288 Williams (EX), 300 Mays (EX), 310 Ford (EX/MT), 313 Maris IA (EX), 315 Ford IA (EX/MT), 317 Musial IA (EX/MT), 318 Mantle IA (EX), 320 Aaron (EX/MT), 340 Drysdale (VG), 350 Robinson (EX), 475 Ford AS (EX/MT), 500 Snider (EX), 505 Marichal (NM), 592 Bouton (EX/MT), 596 Pepitone (NM) and 598 Hickman (EX/MT). Grades 61% NM to NM/MT, 39% EX to EX/MT mainly due to centering and not corner wear (some lesser). **Minimum Bid: $2,500**

19220 **1963 Fleer Baseball Complete Set Plus Checklist (67).** Unlike the previous three Fleer issues, this was the first that would include the current players. There are only 66 cards in this set, plus the checklist, because Topps filed a lawsuit against Fleer to stop production. However there is nice array of stars including Roberto Clemente, Sandy Koufax, Bob Gibson, Willie Mays and many others. There are two "short printed" cards, #46 Adcock and the NNO Checklist. A total of 14 cards have been graded by PSA with an aggregate SMR value of $691. Highlights include: **Graded Cards - PSA NM-MT 8:** 1 card, #15 Howser; **PSA NM+ 7.5:** 1 card, #6; **PSA NM 7:** 7 cards w/#'s 16, 35, 40, 46 Adcock, 49, 61 Gibson and 63 White; **PSA EX-MT 6:** 5 cards w/#'s 4 Robinson, 8 Yastrzemski, 18, 41 Drysdale and 42 Koufax. **Ungraded Cards** - include #'s 5 Mays (EX), 32 Santo (EX), 43 Wills (EX), 45 Spahn (EX), 56 Clemente (EX) and Checklist (EX). Grades 14% NM to NM/MT, 81% EX to EX/MT, 5% VG to VG/EX. **Minimum Bid: $250**

19221 **1963 Menko JCM14F Sadaharu Oh #9167 PSA Mint 9.** Sadaharu Oh compiled 868 home runs, 2,170 runs batted and 1,967 runs scored in Japanese major league play. American contemporaries, who competed against Oh in exhibitions, have expressed that Oh would have had little difficulty adjusting to the competition in the United States. This exceptionally rare, 1-3/4" x 2-15/16," card hails from Oh's homeland and is one of probably just a few to have survived. Originally intended as a game piece and not a collectible card, it is quite remarkable that it has survived in this condition. Hand cut to perfection, it displays four sharp corners, exceptional centering and vivid coloring. Only four of this type have been submitted to PSA for grading. **Minimum Bid: $200**

19222 **1963 Topps Mickey Mantle #200 PSA NM+ 7.5.** Coming off his third AL MVP Award that he won in 1962, the Mick was poised to return to the World Series for a fourth consecutive season. This well centered beauty features the Mick in front of the famous Yankee Stadium façade and exhibits four strong corners. **Minimum Bid: $150**

19223 **1963 Topps Mickey Mantle SGC 86 NM+ 7.5.** Offered is a 1963 Topps Mantle with intense, bold colors that delight the senses. This example exhibits very little evidence of wear on the sharp, well-shaped corners. The green caption area is quite clean, and uninterrupted gloss adds to this item's almost uncirculated appearance. The reverse is clean and free of stains. Strong, fully satisfying Near Mint plus condition. **Minimum Bid: $150**

19224 1963 Topps Dodgers Big Three #412 SGC 92 NM/MT+ 8.5. This cardboard gem features the three mid sixties Dodger aces of Koufax, Podres, and Drysdale. It is well centered with 50/50 centering on both the left to right and top to bottom edges with bright, bold original colors as well. A strong example that is just a hair away from Mint status. **Minimum Bid: $150**

19225 1963 Topps Pete Rose Rookie #537 SGC 96 Mint 9. Though the disembodied head design may not win any awards from the judging panel, the magnificent condition of the offered specimen most assuredly will. The full-bleed blue header is merciless when it comes to wear, and a stiff breeze can knock a Rose rookie off the mark in a heartbeat. This Mint example is absent the typical white spots at the edges and corners, and provides marvelous centering and registration besides. When paired with the tremendous historical relevance attached to a card that heralded the arrival of the eventual Hit King, the appeal is as clear as can be. One of just five cards to achieve this lofty mark on the SGC population charts, with none ever ascending higher. **Minimum Bid: $1,000**

19226 1963 Topps Baseball Complete Set (576). A nice rookie crop including the likes of Pete Rose and Willie Stargell, highlight this very colorful ensemble of cards. A total of 34 cards have been professionally graded (34 PSA, 1 SGC and 1 GAI) with an aggregate SMR value of $2458. Highlights include: **Graded Cards - PSA NM-MT+ 8.5:** 1 card, #491; **PSA NM-MT 8:** 18 cards w/#'s 51, 135 Ashburn, 235, 253, 271, 321, 329, 332, 375 Boyer, 380 Banks, 415 Gibson, 425, 440 Marichal, 466 Freehan, 498, 530, 551 and 565; GAI NM+ 7.5: 1 card, #1 Robinson/Aaron LL; PSA NM 7: 10 cards w/#'s 3 Aaron/Mays LL, 18 Buc Blasters, 25 Kaline, 72, 138 Mays/Musial, 173 Bombers' Best, 340 Berra, 345 Robinson, 501 and 505; **SGC 84 NM 7:** 1 card, #250 Musial; **PSA EX-MT 6:** 3 cards w/#'s 120 Maris, 200 Mantle and 537 Rose. **Ungraded Cards** - include #'s 2 Mantle LL (EX), 115 Yastrzesmki (EX), 210 Koufax (EX/MT), 228 Oliva (EX/MT), 242 Aaron/Banks (EX), 247 Yankees (EX/MT), 275 Mathews (EX), 300 Mays (EX), 320 Spahn (EX), 360 Drysdale (EX/MT), 390 Aaron (EX), 400 Robinson (EX/MT), 412 Dodgers' Big Three (EX), 446 Ford (EX/MT), 470 Tresh SP (EX), 472 Brock (EX/MT), 490 McCovey (EX/MT), 500 Killebrew SP (EX/MT), 540 Clemente (EX/MT), 544 Staub (EX), 550 Snider (EX/MT), 553 Stargell (EX). Grades 29% NM to NM/MT, 66% EX to EX/MT, 5% VG to VG/EX. **Minimum Bid: $500**

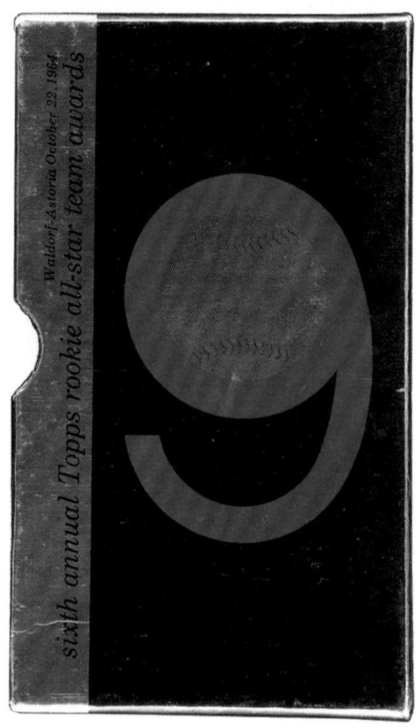

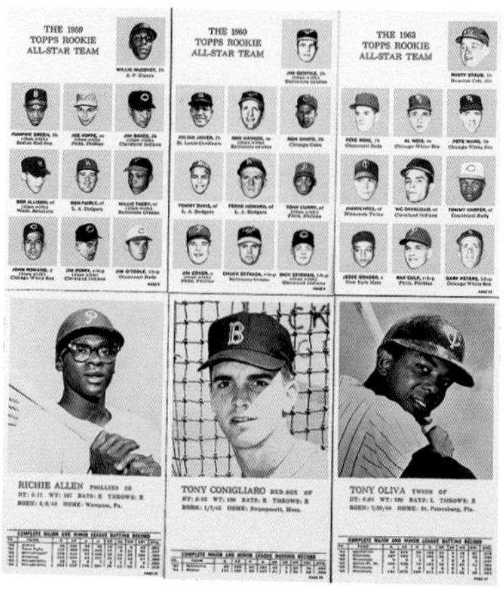

19227 **1964 Topps Rookie All-Star Banquet Boxed Set (36).** Since 1959 Topps has sponsored a formal post-season banquet to honor its annual Rookie All-Star team. In 1964, the gum company deviated from the traditional dinner program by issuing a 36-card boxed set. Each card in this unique dinner program measures 3" x 5-1/4" and is numbered as a "PAGE" in the lower right-hand corner. Highlights include #8 The 1959 Topps Rookie All-Star Team, 9 The 1960 Topps Rookie All-Star Team, 12 The 1963 Topps Rookie All-Star Team, 19 Richie Allen, 25 Tony Conigliaro, 27 Tony Oliva. The #1 Header Card and #35 Rookie All-Star Trophy cards are creased, but remaining cards grade NM or better. **Minimum Bid: $500**

19228 **1964 Topps Baseball Complete Set (587)** Although this set lacks the rookie fire power, it does contain all of the stars from this era, such as Mantle, Mays Aaron, Rose, Clemente, Koufax and much more. A total of 17 cards have been graded by SGC with an aggregate SMR value of $1,188. Highlights include: Graded Cards - **SGC 96 MINT 9:** 1 card, #257; **SGC 92 NM/MT+ 8.5:** 2 cards w/#'s 197 and 291; **SGC 88 NM/MT 8:** 2 cards w/#'s 146 John and 171; **SGC 86 NM+ 7.5:** 2 cards w/#'s 50 Mantle and 251; **SGC 84 NM 7:** 10 cards w/#'s 21 Berra, 35 Mathews, 125 Rose, 150 Mays, 200 Koufax, 210 Yastrzemski, 230 Robinson, 250 Kaline, 287 Conigliaro and 433 Yankees. **Ungraded Cards** - include: #'s 1 Koufax LL (EX), 5 Koufax/Drysdale LL (EX/MT), 9 Mays/Aaron LL (EX), 21 Berra (EX), 29 Brock (EX/MT), 55 Banks (EX), 120 Drysdale (NM), 155 Snider (EX), 167 Piniella (EX/MT), 177 Killebrew (EX/MT), 225 Maris (EX), 243 Allen (EX), 260 Robinson (EX/MT), 300 Aaron (EX), 206 Mays/Cepeda (EX/MT), 331 A.L. Bombers (miscut), 342 Stargell (EX), 350 McCovey (EX), 380 Ford (EX), 400 Spahn (NM), 423 Aaron/Mays (EX/MT), 440 Clemente (EX), 460 Gibson (EX), 468 Perry (EX/MT), 541 Niekro (EX). Grades 16% NM to NM/MT, 77% EX to EX/MT, 7% VG to VG/EX. **Minimum Bid: $700**

19229 **1964 Topps Stand-Up Baseball Complete Set (77) Plus Extras (8).** Stars are not lacking from this set which contain Mantle, Mays, Aaron, Banks, Clemente, Koufax, Yastrzemski and so much more. A total of 8 cards have been graded by PSA with an aggregate SMR value of $800. Highlights include - Aaron (PSA EX 5), Baldschun SP (VG/EX), Banks (VG/EX), Clemente (VG/EX), Clendenon SP (EX), Drysdale SP (EX/MT), Gonder SP (VG/EX), Gonzalez SP (EX/MT), Frank Howard SP (PSA NM 7), Kaline (EX), Killebrew (VG/EX), Koufax (PSA EX 5), Lock SP (EX/MT), Lumpe SP (EX/MT), Mantle (PSA NM-MT 8 MC), Marichal SP (EX), Mathews (VG/EX), Mays (PSA EX 5), McCovey SP (EX/MT), Pearson SP (EX/MT), Brooks Robinson (EX), Frank Robinson (PSA NM-MT 8), Roebuck SP (GD), Santo SP (EX/MT), Spahn SP (PSA EX-MT 6), Stuart SP (EX), White SP (EX/MT), Williams SP (PSA EX-MT 6), Woodeshick SP (EX/MT) and Yastrzemski SP (VG/EX). Grades 16% NM to NM/MT, 72% EX to EX/MT, 12% VG to VG/EX. Extras - 8 cards. Grades VG to EX. **Minimum Bid: $600**

19230 **1965 Topps Mickey Mantle #350 SGC 88 NM/MT 8.** This card appears to be exactly how it was the day it was produced at the Topps factory in 1965 and does not look to have ever been handled. Four sharp pack fresh corners highlight this high grade offering and the only thing holding it back from mint status would have to be the 65/35 left to right centering. **Minimum Bid: $250**

19231 **1965 Topps Baseball Complete Set (598).** There are plenty of stars and rookies in this set, including Jim Hunter, Tony Perez and Joe Morgan. A very evenly matched set, in terms of condition. A total of 17 cards have been graded by SGC with an aggregate SMR value of $$865. Highlights include: **Graded Cards - SGC 96 MINT 9:** 1 card, #551 Mets; **SGC 92 NM/MT+ 8.5:** 5 cards w/#'s 377 Stargell, 458, 517, 539 and 590; **SGC 88 NM/MT 8:** 7 cards w/#'s 130 Kaline, 193 Perry, 200 Torre, 236 McLain, 385 Yastrzemski, 400 Killebrew and 419; **SGC 86 NM+ 7.5:** 1 card, #134 Mantle WS; SGC 80 EX/NM 6: 2 cards w/#'s 477 Carlton and 526 Hunter; **SGC 70 EX+ 5.5:** 1 card, #350 Mantle. **Ungraded Cards** - include #'s 2 Clemente/Aaron LL (EX), 8 Koufax/Drysdale LL (miscut), 16 Morgan (miscut), 50 Marichal (EX), 120 Robinson (EX), 145 Tiant (EX/MT), 150 Robinson (EX), 155 Maris (EX), 160 Clemente (EX), 170 Aaron (EX), 176 McCovey (EX), 205 Spahn (EX), 207 Rose (EX), 220 Williams (miscut), 250 Mays (EX), 260 Drysdale (VG/EX), 282 Murakami (EX/MT), 300 Koufax (), 320 Gibson (EX/MT), 330 Ford (VG/EX), 460 Allen (GD/VG), 461 Niekro (GD/VG), 470 Berra (EX), 500 Mathews (miscut), 510 Banks (EX), 513 Yankees Team (VG/EX), 519 Uecker (EX), 533 McGraw SP (EX), 540 Brock SP (EX), 581 Perez SP (EX). Grades 10% NM to NM/MT, 80% EX to EX/MT, 10% VG to VG/EX (some lesser). **Minimum Bid: $600**

19232 **1965 Topps Baseball High Grade Complete Set (598).** A complete set of 598 cards in overall mid to high grade, with some high grade star cards. Some of the rookies that are featured in this set are Jim Hunter, Tony Perez, Luis Tiant and all of the stars of this era. A total of 37 cards have been graded by PSA with an aggregate SMR value of $4429. Highlights include: **Graded Cards - PSA MINT 9:** 8 cards w/#'s 8 Koufax/Drysdale LL, 31, 34, 305, 407, 423, 445 and 526 Hunter; **PSA NM-MT+ 8.5:** 4 cards w/#'s 72, 155 Maris, 350 Mantle and 380 Colavito; **PSA NM-MT 8:** 18 cards w/#'s 95 Mazeroski, 120 Robinson, 130 Kaline, 176 McCovey, 182, 194, 227, 233, 250 Mays, 313, 320 Gibson, 461 Niekro, 500 Mathews, 532, 533 McGraw, 540 Brock, 556 Schoendienst and 582; **PSA NM+ 7.5:** 1 card, #170 Aaron; **PSA NM 7:** 5 cards w/#'s 207 Rose, 300 Koufax, 347, 377 Stargell and 477 Carlton; **PSA EX-MT 6:** 1 card, #160 Clemente; **Ungraded Cards** - include #'s 2 Clemente/Aaron LL (EX/MT), 16 Morgan (EX), 50 Marichal (EX/MT), 74 Petrocelli (EX/MT), 134 Mantle WS (EX/MT), 145 Tiant (EX/MT), 150 Robinson (EX/MT), 205 Spahn (EX/MT), 220 Williams (EX/MT), 260 Drysdale (EX/MT), 282 Murakami (EX/MT), 330 Ford (small), 385 Yastrzemski (EX/MT), 400 Killebrew (NM), 460 Allen (EX/MT), 470 Berra (EX), 510 Banks (EX), 513 Yankees Team (EX), 519 Uecker (VG/EX), 581 Perez SP (EX). **Grades 38% NM to NM/MT,** 54% EX to EX/MT, 8% VG to VG/EX. **Minimum Bid: $750**

19233 **1966 Topps Sandy Koufax #100 SGC 96 Mint 9.** Koufax is notable as one of the outstanding Jewish athletes of his era in American professional sports. His decision not to pitch Game 1 of the 1965 World Series because game day fell on Yom Kippur, the Jewish Day of Atonement, garnered national attention as an example of conflict between social pressures and personal beliefs. Issued during Sandy Koufax's last season in 1966, his brilliant pitching career was cut short due to an arthritic elbow. Of the 158 submitted to SGC, this one ranks as the singular best. As the lone SGC 96 Mint 9 example (none graded higher), it should come as no surprise that the card displays all of the characteristics inherent in such a high grade. Beautiful colors, ultra-bright clean borders, four sharp corner and perfect registration are all readily apparent with this card. SGC registry collectors will not want to let this opportunity pass, it may be a long time coming before another of this quality is ever offered. **Minimum Bid: $300**

19234 **1966 Topps Baseball Complete Set (598).** Presented is a complete 1966 Topps Baseball set in overall mid to high grade. Rookie cards of Jim Palmer, Ferguson Jenkins and Don Sutton are represented along with a very tough high series. A total of 32 cards have been graded by SGC with an aggregate SMR value of $1,530. Highlights include: Graded Cards - **SGC 96 MINT 9:** 2 cards w/#'s 166 and 380 Conigliaro; **SGC 92 NM/MT+ 8.5:** 4 cards w/#'s 37, 251, 458 and 520; **SGC 88 NM/MT 8:** 13 cards w/#'s 120 Killebrew, 139, 243, 244, 311, 320 Gibson, 364, 386 Hodges, 390 Robinson, 460, 484, 523 and 582; **SGC 86 NM+ 7.5:** 2 cards w#'s 195 Morgan and 558 Scott; **SGC 84 NM 7:** 7 cards w/#'s 70 Yastrzemski, 100 Koufax, 200 Mathews, 410 Kaline, 415, 473 and 583 Tigers; **SGC 80 EX/NM 6:** 4 cards w/#'s 30 Rose, 50 Mantle, 126 Palmer and 254 Jenkins. **U**n**graded Cards** - include: #'s 1 Mays (EX), 28 Niekro (EX/MT), 36 Hunter (EX), 70 Yastrzemski (EX), 72 Perez (EX/MT), 91 Uecker (EX), 110 Banks (EX/MT), 125 Brock (EX), 160 Ford (EX), 195 Morgan (EX/MT), 215 Clemente/Aaron/Mays LL (EX/MT), 217 Mays/McCovey LL (EX/MT), 223 Koufax/Drysdale LL (VG/EX), 225 Koufax/Gibson LL (EX), 255 Stargell (EX), 288 Sutton (EX/MT), 300 Clemente (EX/MT), 310 Robinson (EX), 365 Maris (EX), 420 Marichal (EX/MT), 430 Drysdale (EX/MT), 469 Murcer (EX/MT), 526 Twins SP (EX/MT), 530 Roberts (EX/MT), 540 McLain SP (EX/MT), 547 Clark SP (EX/MT), 550 McCovey SP (EX), 580 Williams SP (EX/MT), 591 Jackson SP (EX/MT), 598 Perry SP (VG/EX). Grades 26% NM to NM/MT, 69% EX to EX/MT, 5% VG to VG/EX. **Minimum Bid: $500**

19235 **1966 Topps Baseball High Grade Complete Set (598).** A short-print of the final seventy-five cards in this large issue gives that late series a sizeable premium, and many of those appear here in EX/MT to NM condition. The Topps tradition of fine baseball photographic portraiture continues throughout. A total of 28 cards have been graded by PSA with an SMR value of $3,768. Highlights include: **Graded Cards - PSA MINT 9:** 5 cards w/#'s 132 Cepeda, 218 NL HR Leaders, 455 Lolich, 535 Davis and 541; **PSA NM-MT+ 8.5:** 1 card, #227; **PSA NM-MT 8:** 15 cards w/#'s 1 Mays, 125 Brock, 255 Stargell, 310 Robinson, 510 Wilhelm, 525, 526 Twins, 527, 533, 540 McLain, 547, 555, 558 Scott, 566 Cuellar and 577; **PSA NM+ 7.5:** 1 card, #195 Morgan; **PSA NM 7:** 6 cards w/#'s 50 Mantle, 72 Perez, 300 Clemente, 565 Piersall, 591 Jackson and 598 Perry. **Ungraded Cards** - include #'s 28 Niekro (EX), 30 Rose (VG), 36 Hunter (EX/MT), 70 Yastrzemski (NM), 91 Uecker (EX), 100 Koufax (VG/EX), 110 Banks (EX/MT), 120 Killebrew (EX), 126 Palmer (EX/MT), 160 Ford (EX/MT), 200 Mathews (VG/EX), 215 Clemente/Aaron/Mays LL (EX), 217 Mays/McCovey LL (NM), 223 Koufax/Drysdale LL (EX/MT), 225 Koufax/Gibson LL (NM), 254 Jenkins (EX/MT), 288 Sutton (EX/MT), 320 Gibson (NM), 365 Maris (EX/MT), 390 Robinson (NM), 410 Kaline (EX/MT), 420 Marichal (EX/MT), 430 Drysdale (NM), 469 Murcer (NM), 500 Aaron (EX), 530 Roberts (EX), 550 McCovey SP (EX/MT), 580 Williams SP (NM) and 583 Tigers SP (NM). **Grades 40% NM to NM/MT,** 55% EX to EX/MT, 5% Lesser. **Minimum Bid: $750**

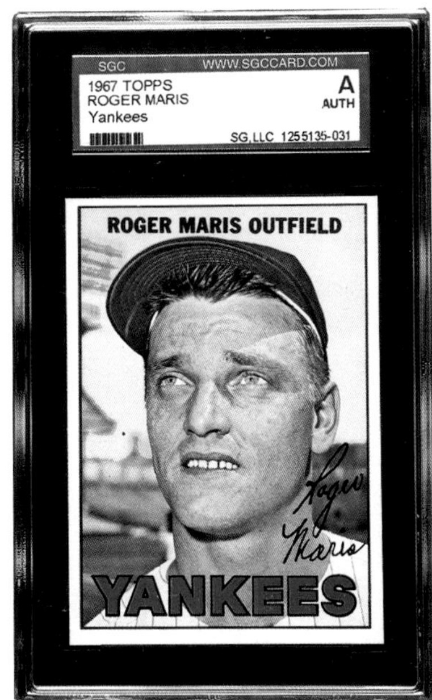

19236 **1967 Topps Roger Maris #45 "Yankees" Blank Back Proof Card SGC Authentic.** In 1967, Roger Maris was traded from the Yankees to St. Louis and as a result, the Topps card which designated him as a Yankee was only produced as a proof and was never issued. Only a short supply of these "Yankees" cards were ever printed and the vast majority of the cards were incinerated when the company's building and inventory were destroyed by fire in the late 1970's. Those that remain are blank backed and normally appear in extremely off-centered orientation. This is a superior example of the rarity, featuring uncommonly strong centering and NM/MT condition corners. An ideal specimen of this Topps rarity and absolutely one of the finest examples in the hobby. **Minimum Bid: $300**

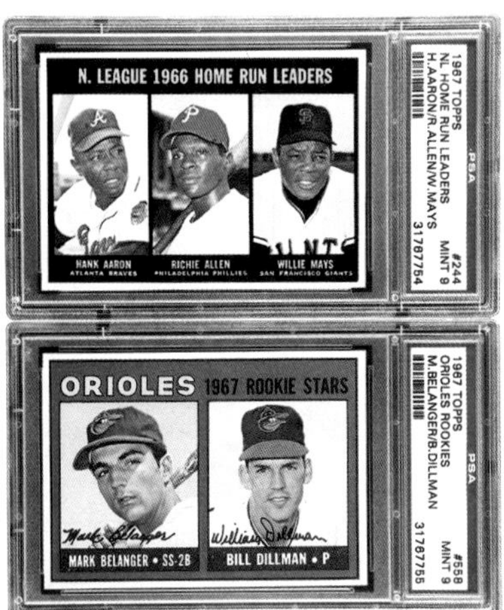

19237 **1967 Topps NL Home Run Leaders w/Aaron #244 and Mark Belanger #558 PSA MINT 9 Lot of 2.** Two superstar sluggers for the price of one and a short-print high number card share a Mint 9 designation, providing pack-fresh glossiness and a complete absence of wear rarely seen in the issue. Card #244 finds none overtaking its population chart supremacy, while card #558 has been surpassed a single time. **Minimum Bid: $150**

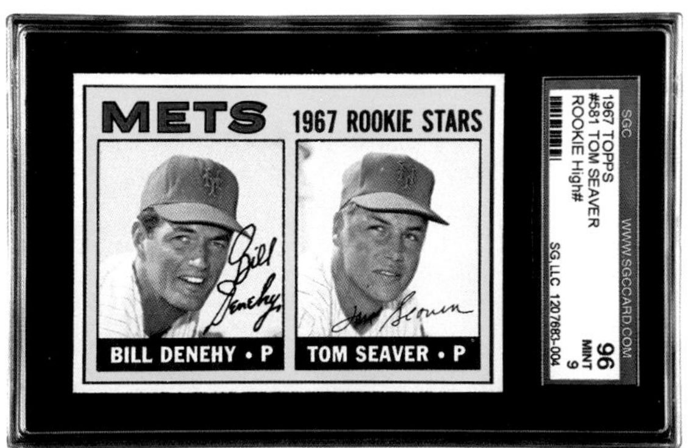

19238 **1967 Topps Tom Seaver Rookie #581 Mint SGC 96.** Of the 176 Topps Tom Seaver rookie cards submitted to SGC, only four (none higher) have captured the 96 Mint 9 designation. A terrific accomplishment, to be sure; much like the season a 24-year old Seaver posted during the Miracle Mets' magic run to World Series title in 1969. Seaver posted a record of 25-7 that regular season and, along with fellow pitching phenom Nolan Ryan, was instrumental in their postseason success as well. **Minimum Bid: $500**

19239 **1967 Topps Baseball High Grade Complete Set (609).** A pair of first-ballot Hall of Fame rookies, Tom Seaver and Rod Carew, are fan favorites in this set which likewise features high number rarities from Brooks Robinson, Rocky Colavito, Mark Belanger and Tommy John. A total of 78 cards have been graded by SGC with an aggregate SMR value of $3,285. Highlights include: **Graded Cards - SGC 96 MINT 9:** 6 cards w/#'s 17, 92, 293, 315 Williams, 390 and 485 McCarver; **SGC 92 NM/MT+ 8.5:** 20 cards w/#'s 118, 144, 153, 160, 193, 309, 320 Perry, 323, 420 McClain, 426, 488, 519, 537, 548, 556, 565, 574, 584 Piersall, 605 Shannon and 606; **SGC 88 NM/MT 8:** 31 cards w/#'s 16, 19, 45 Maris, 48 Freehan, 81, 124, 125, 131 Yankees Team, 154, 169, 183, 185, 198, 227, 231, 256, 308, 369 Hunter, 375, 387, 421, 445 Sutton, 498, 500 Marichal, 543, 571, 577, 578, 583, 589 and 593; **SGC 86 NM+ 7.5:** 13 cards w/#'s 55 Drysdale, 63 Brock/Flood, 87, 140 Stargell, 146 Carlton, 166 Mathews, 210 Gibson, 326 Uecker, 440, 450 Allen, 552, 555 and 600 Robinson; **SGC 84 NM 7:** 8 cards w/#'s 77, 100 Robinson, 150 Mantle, 200 Mays, 355 Yastrzemski, 430 Rose, 460 Killebrew and 569 Carew. **Ungraded cards** - include #'s 1 The Champs (EX, Robinson, auto), 5 Ford (NM), 30 Kaline (NM), 215 Banks (EX/MT), 216 Bengal Belters (EX), 236 Koufax/Gibson LL (NM), 242 Clemente/Aaron LL (EX), 244 Aaron/Mays LL (EX), 250 Aaron (EX/MT), 285 Brock (EX), 337 Morgan (EX), 400 Clemente (EX/MT), 423 Mays/ McCovey (EX), 456 Niekro (EX/MT), 475 Palmer (EX, auto), 476 Perez SP (miscut), 480 McCovey (EX/MT), 536 Niekro (EX), 540 Cash (EX/MT), 558 Belanger (EX), 560 Bunning (NM), 570 Wills (EX/MT), 580 Colavito (miscut), 581 Seaver (EX), 604 Red Sox Team (EX/MT), 607 Stanley (NM), 609 John (EX/MT). **Grades 49% NM to NM/MT,** 46% EX to EX/MT, 5% VG to VG/EX. **Minimum Bid: $750**

19240 **1968 Topps Baseball High Grade Complete Set (598).** This set contains the rookie cards of the flame throwing Nolan Ryan and one of the best catchers in Johnny Bench. A total of 66 cards have been professionally graded (63 PSA, 2 SGC and 1 BVG) with an aggregate SMR value in excess of $5,000. Highlights include: **Graded Cards - PSA GEM MINT 10:** 3 cards w/#'s 118 Belanger, 145 Drysdale and 388 Washburn; **PSA MINT 9:** 26 cards w/#'s 20 Robinson, 27 Hodges, 32, 81, 86 Stargell, 92, 116, 120 Stottlemyre, 140 Conigliaro, 154 Gibson WS, 158, 176, 184, 185, 244, 361 Killebrew AS, 373 Robinson AS, 389, 396, 418, 422, 439, 445, 452, 490 Killebrew/Mays/Mantle and 530 Bird Belters; **PSA NM-MT+ 8.5:** 2 cards w/#'s 147 and 465; **SGC 92 NM-MT+ 8.5:** 1 card, #408 Carlton; **PSA NM-MT 8:** 19 cards w/#'s 30 Torre, 125, 170, 183, 189, 226, 257 Niekro, 275, 280 Mantle, 285, 321, 330 Maris, 360, 364 Morgan AS, 365 Robinson AS, 381, 390 Mazeroski, 447 and 520 Brock; **SGC 86 NM+ 7.5:** 1 card, #374 Clemente AS; BVG 7.5 NM+: 1 card, #250 Yastrzemski; **PSA NM 7:** 12 cards w/#'s 50 Mays, 80 Carew, 110 Aaron, 150 Clemente, 162, 177 Ryan, 230 Rose, 273, 384, 480 Manager's Dream, 500 Robinson and 528 Tigers; **PSA EX-MT 6:** 1 card, #247 Bench. **Ungraded Cards** - include #'s 1 Clemente LL (EX/MT), 3 Clemente/ Aaron LL (NM), 45 Seaver (EX/MT), 58 Mathews (EX/MT), 100 Gibson (NM), 144 Morgan (NM), 205 Marichal (EX), 240 Kaline (NM), 290 McCovey (NM/MT), 355 Banks (EX), 363 Carew AS (NM), 369 Yastrzemski AS (NM), 370 Aaron AS (NM), 385 Hunter (NM), 575 Palmer (EX). **Grades 65% NM to NM/MT,** 30% EX to EX/MT, 5% VG to VG/EX. **Minimum Bid: $750**

19241 **1969 Topps Baseball High Grade Complete Set (664).** This set is headlined by cards of Hall of Famers such as Mantle, Mays, Aaron, Ryan, Seaver and Clemente, along with rookie cards of Reggie Jackson and Rollie Fingers. A total of 63 cards have been graded by PSA with an aggregate SMR value of $3063. Highlights include: **Graded Cards - PSA MINT 9:** 19 cards w/#'s 27, 28, 41,132, 161, 165 Brock WS, 221, 268, 287, 355 Niekro, 360, 379 Boyer, 385 Cepeda, 448, 504 Robinson CL, 557, 565 Wilhelm, 594 and 633; **PSA NM-MT+ 8.5:** 6 cards w/#'s 15 Powell, 169, 193, 230 Staub, 450 Williams and 619; **PSA NM-MT 8:** 30 cards w/#'s 40, 81, 95 Bench, 120 Rose, 147 Durocher, 162 Gibson WS, 200 Gibson, 209, 245, 305, 335, 354, 355 Niekro, 370 Marichal, 372, 400 Drysdale, 412 Mantle CL, 419 Carew AS, 420, 429, 456, 465 John, 471, 510 Carew, 532, 539 Ted Shows How, 545 Stargell, 643, 652 and 659; **PSA NM 7:** 8 cards w/#'s 2 Rose LL, 78, 85 Brock, 190 Mays, 255 Carlton, 260 Jackson, 533 Ryan and 550 Robinson. **Ungraded Cards** - include #'s 1 Yaz LL (EX), 20 Banks (NM), 35 Morgan (EX/MT), 50 Clemente (NM), 99 Nettles (EX/MT), 100 Aaron (EX/MT), 130 Yastrzemski (miscut), 250 Robinson (NM), 375 Killebrew (NM), 400 Drysdale (EX/MT), 410 Kaline (NM), 424 Rose AS (EX/MT), 425 Yastrzemski AS (EX/MT), 430 Bench AS (NM), 440 McCovey (NM), 480 Seaver (NM/MT), 500 Mantle (EX), 573 Palmer (NM), 597 Fingers (NM), 630 Bonds (EX), 650 Williams (EX). Grades 68% NM to NM/MT, 32% EX to EX/MT. **Minimum Bid: $500**

19242 **1970 Topps Pete Rose #580 PSA Gem Mint 10.** Due to the gray borders and the easily chipped paper that Topps used for the 1970 issue, this is undeniably one of the toughest contemporary Pete Rose cards to find in strong condition. Luckily this beautiful example has passed through the Topps factory and the following decades unscathed with four perfectly formed mint corners and flawless borders which helped it to garner the top grade of Gem Mint from PSA. One of only nine such examples to achieve Gem Mint status from PSA of the nearly 1,200 that have been graded. **Minimum Bid: $750**

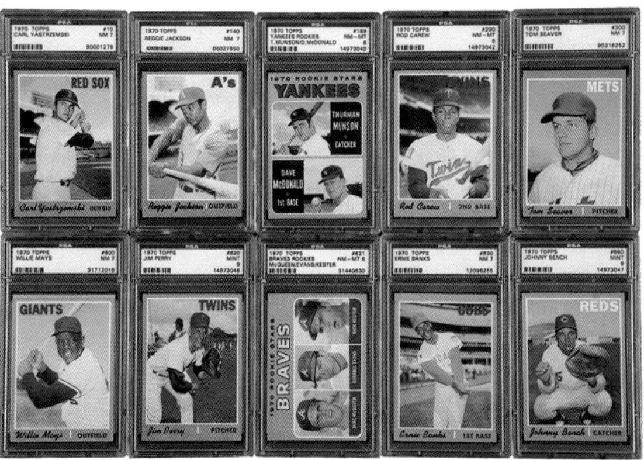

19243 **1970 Topps Baseball Complete Set (720).** This set features the Thurman Munson rookie card (graded PSA NM-MT 8). Also included are plenty of Hall of Famers such as Aaron, Clemente, Bench (awarded a PSA MINT 9), Jackson, Rose, Mays, Seaver, and several others. Twenty-two cards have been graded by PSA with an aggregate SMR value of $1,650. Highlights include: **Graded Cards - PSA MINT 9:** 4 cards w/#'s 277, 615, 620, 660 Bench; **PSA NM-MT 8:** 10 cards w/#'s 184, 189 Munson, 290 Carew, 332, 560 Perry, 588 CK, 621 Evans, 622 Sutton, 657, 696; **PSA NM 7:** 7 cards w/#'s 10 Yastrzemski, 140 Jackson, 230 B.Robinson, 300 Seaver, 450 McCovey AS, 600 Mays, 630 Banks; **PSA EX-MT 6:** 1 card, #350 Clemente. **Ungraded Cards** - include #'s 150 Killebrew (EX), 198 Ryan NL Playoff (NM), 211 Williams (EX/MT), 220 Carlton (EX/MT), 330 Brock (NM), 449 Palmer (EX/MT), 458 Rose AS (EX), 459 Jackson AS (EX), 462 Aaron AS (VG/EX), 464 Bench AS (EX/MT), 530 Gibson (EX), 580 Rose (EX), 640 Kaline (EX/MT), 700 Robinson (EX/MT), 712 Ryan (EX/MT), 713 Pilots Team (EX/MT). Grades 23% NM to NM/MT, 74% EX to EX/MT, 3% VG to VG/EX. **Minimum Bid: $300**

19244 1971 Topps Greatest Moments High Grade Complete Set (55). One of the most difficult sets of the 1970's to find in high grade, the 1971 Topps Greatest Moments issue is one of the toughest in the post-war era. The black borders, unusual size and centering difficulties make this a very desirable set when found in high grade. Over half of the set has been graded PSA NM 7 or higher. Thirty-eight cards, which represents 70% of the set, have been graded by PSA. Aggregate value for the graded cards is $2,650. Highlights include: **Graded Cards - PSA NM-MT 8:** 7 cards w/#'s 22, 24 Gibson, 28, 30, 35, 38, 54; **PSA NM 7:** 22 cards w/#'s 2 Wilhelm, 3, 7, 11, 12, 15 Rose, 18, 19 Kaline, 20, 21, 23, 26 Cepeda, 29, 31, 32, 34 Morgan, 36 Banks, 42, 43, 48, 50, 51 Aparicio; **PSA EX-MT 6:** 8 cards w/#'s 8 Killebrew, 9 Robinson, 13 Bench, 25, 27 Brock, 39, 44, 46; **PSA EX 5:** 1 card w/#41 Mays. **Ungraded Cards** - include #'s 1 Munson (EX), 40 Yaz (VG/EX), 47 Jackson (VG/EX), 52 McCovey (EX/MT). Overall grades **53% NM to NM/MT,** 27% EX to EX/MT, 20% VG to VG/EX. **Minimum Bid: $1,000**

19245 1971 Topps Baseball High Grade Complete Set (752). A very nicely preserved set with over 40% in NM to NM/MT condition. A total of 64 cards have been professionally graded (63 PSA and 1 GAI) with an aggregate SMR value of $1,800. Highlights include: Graded Cards - **PSA NM-MT+ 8.5:** 4 cards w/#'s 177, 286, 389 and 658; **PSA NM-MT 8:** 39 cards w/#'s 47, 64 Bench LL, 81, 105 Conigliaro, 140 Perry, 157, 188 Valentine, 238, 284, 343, 375, 387, 396, 401, 417, 437, 439 Luzinski, 486, 529, 541, 543 Yankees, 559, 570 Palmer, 602, 616, 619 CL, 620 Howard, 665, 666, 674, 676, 691, 692, 697, 698 Brewers, 707, 710, 739 and 747; **PSA NM+ 7.5:** 1 card, #163; **GAI NM+ 7.5:** 1 card, #525 Banks; **PSA NM 7:** 17 cards w/#'s 45 Hunter, 50 McCovey, 100 Rose, 105, 111, 160 Seaver, 196, 331, 341 Garvey, 400 Aaron, 446, 513 Ryan, 575, 594 Hrabosky, 615, 630 Clemente and 633; **PSA EX-MT 6:** 2 cards w/#'s 66 and 600 Mays. **Ungraded Cards** - include #'s 1 Orioles Team (EX/MT), 5 Munson (EX/MT), 14 Concepcion (EX/MT), 20 Jackson (EX), 55 Carlton (), 180 Kaline (EX), 210 Carew (NM), 230 Stargell (NM), 250 Bench (color added), 300 Robinson (EX), 325 Marichal (EX/MT), 380 Williams (NM), 450 Gibson (EX/MT), 530 Yastrzemski (EX), 550 Killebrew (EX), 580 Perez (EX), 625 Brock (EX), 640 Robinson (EX), 650 Allen SP (EX/MT), 709 Baylor/Baker SP (VG/EX). **Grades 43% NM to NM/MT,** 57% EX to EX/MT (some lesser). **Minimum Bid: $500**

19246 1972 Topps Baseball High Grade Complete Set (787). Presented is a very nice 1972 Topps complete baseball set. Although this set lacks the high ticket rookie cards, it does contain the Carlton Fisk rookie and a plethora of stars, including many with their In Action cards. This was the largest set that Topps produced to date. A total of 34 cards have been graded by PSA. A total of 34 cards have been graded by PSA with an aggregate SMR value of $1,311. Highlights include: **Graded Cards - PSA MINT 9:** 8 cards w/#'s 60, 141, 177, 267 Concepcion, 355, 441 Munson, 552 and 630; **PSA NM-MT 8:** 25 cards w/#'s 20, 49 Mays, 80 Perez, 98, 147, 204, 212, 227, 234, 315, 359, 366, 381, 403, 436, 444, 445 Seaver, 466, 504, 558, 594, 611, 624, 686 Garvey and 695 Carew; **PSA NM 7:** 1 card, #309. **Ungraded Cards** - include #'s 37 Yastrzemski (EX), 79 Fisk (EX/MT), 100 Robinson (EX), 130 Gibson (NM), 270 Palmer (EX/MT), 299 Aaron (NM), 300 Aaron IA (EX), 310 Clemente IA (NM), 420 Carlton (EX/MT), 433 Bench (EX), 435 Jackson (VG/EX), 550 Robinson (EX), 559 Rose (EX/MT), 560 Rose IA (VG/EX), 595 Ryan (EX), 600 Kaline (EX/MT), 696 Carew IA (NM), 751 Carlton Traded (NM), 752 Morgan Traded (EX/MT), 754 Robinson Traded (EX), 761 Cey (EX). **Grades 40% NM to NM/MT,** 55% EX to EX/MT, 5% VG to VG/EX. **Minimum Bid: $250**

19247 **1972 Topps Baseball High Grade Complete Set (787).** This set features the Carlton Fisk rookie card (graded PSA MINT 9) as well as several other All-Time Greats such as Aaron, Clemente, Rose, Ryan, Jackson and many others. 1972 is the first year Topps introduced "in-action" cards. Many of the top players have an "in-action" card in addition to the regular issue. Twenty-seven cards have been graded by PSA with an aggregate SMR value in excess of $2,000. Highlights include: **Graded Cards - PSA GEM MINT 10:** 1 card, #498 Brooks Robinson Boyhood Photo; **PSA MINT 9:** 13 cards w/#'s 79 Fisk, 188, 257, 273, 285 Perry, 380, 493, 500 Torre, 546, 547, 600 Kaline, 623, 772; **PSA NM-MT 8.5:** 1 card, #270 Palmer; **PSA NM-MT 8:** 8 cards w/#'s 299 Aaron, 447 Stargell, 474, 559 Rose, 626, 708, 752 Morgan Traded, 760 Mazeroski; **PSA NM 7:** 4 cards w/#'s 435 Jackson, 445 Seaver, 686 Garvey, 698. **Ungraded Cards** - include #'s 37 Yastrzemski (NM), 49 Mays (EX), 100 Robinson (NM), 130 Gibson (EX/MT), 300 Aaron IA (EX), 309 Clemente (EX/MT), 310 Clemente IA (EX/MT), 420 Carlton (EX/MT), 433 Bench (EX), 441 Munson (NM), 550 Robinson (EX/MT), 560 Rose IA (NM), 595 Ryan (EX/MT), 695 Carew (EX/MT), 696 Carew IA (EX/MT), 751 Carlton Traded (NM), 754 Robinson Traded (NM). **Grades 42% NM to NM/MT,** 58% EX to EX/MT (some lesser). **Minimum Bid: $300**

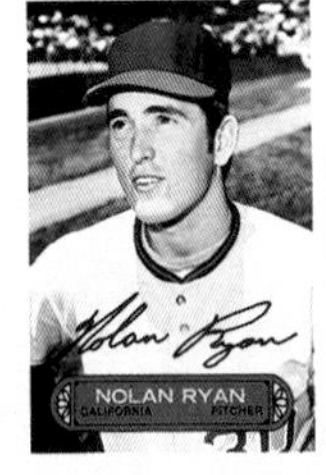

19248 **1973 Topps Pin-Ups Test Issue Complete Set (24).** A test issue from 1973, the 24 Topps Pin-Ups include the same basic format and the same checklist as the Comics test issue of the same year. The 3-7/16" x 4-5/8" Pin-Ups were actually intended to be used as the inside of a wrapper for a piece of bubblegum, and are therefore cut a little off-center. Highlights include - Aaron (NM), Bench (NM), Carlton (NM), Jackson (NM), Killebrew (NM), McCovey (NM), Robinson (EX/MT), Ryan (EX/MT), Seaver (NM), Stargell (EX/MT), Yastrzemski (EX/MT). The set grades overall EX/MT to NM. **Minimum Bid: $1,000**

19249 **1973 Topps Baseball Complete Set (660).** A total of 51 cards have been graded by PSA with an aggregate SMR value in excess of $2,400. Highlights include: Graded Cards - PSA GEM MINT 10: 3 cards w/#'s 83, 104 and 208; **PSA MINT 9:** 36 cards w/#'s 35, 39, 50 Clemente, 51, 69, 77, 78, 86, 97, 107, 109, 114, 119 Bowa, 133, 142 Munson, 144, 151, 162, 177, 205, 206, 210, 226, 235 Hunter, 255 Jackson, 316, 318, 320 Brock, 348, 394, 410 McCovey, 426, 429, 463, 474 Ruth ATL and 530; **PSA NM-MT+ 8.5:** 1 card, #350 Seaver; **PSA NM-MT 8:** 11 cards w/#'s 93, 100 Aaron, 130 Rose, 175 Robinson, 305 Mays, 376, 471 Cobb ATL, 499, 508, 591 and 615 Schmidt. Ungraded Cards - include #'s 1 Aaron/Mays/Ruth ATL (EX/MT), 90 Robinson (), 193 Fisk (NM), 220 Ryan (NM), 245 Yastrzemski (EX/MT), 280 Kaline (NM), 300 Carlton (NM), 380 Bench (), 613 Boone (NM), 614 Evans (EX/MT). Grades overall 71% NM to NM/MT, 29% EX to EX/MT (few lesser). **Minimum Bid: $200**

19250 **1973 and 1974 Topps Baseball High Grade Complete Sets (2).** This group features rookie cards of Mike Schmidt and Dave Winfield. Also features many Hall of Famers such as Aaron, Mays, Ryan, Rose, Clemente and many more. Twenty-four cards (23 PSA and 1 SGC) have been graded with an aggregate SMR value of $1,643. Highlights Include: 1973 Topps - complete set of 660 cards. **Graded Cards - PSA MINT 9:** 9 cards w/#'s 114, 160 Palmer, 165 Aparicio, 175 F.Robinson, 193 Fisk, 245 Yastrzemski, 330 Carew, 350 Seaver, 435; **SGC 92 NM-MT+ 8.5:** 1 card, #603; **PSA NM-MT 8:** 4 cards w/#'s 50 Clemente, 100 Aaron, 280 Kaline, 380 Bench; **PSA NM 7:** 3 cards w/#'s 220 Ryan, 614 Evans, 615 Schmidt. **Ungraded Cards** - include #'s 1 Aaron/Mays/Ruth ATL (EX), 90 Robinson (NM), 130 Rose (EX/MT), 142 Munson (EX/MT), 174 Gossage (EX/MT), 255 Jackson (NM),305 Mays (EX/MT). Grades 55% NM to NM/MT, 45% EX to EX/MT (some lesser). 1974 Topps - complete set of 660 cards w/#'s 1 Aaron (EX), 4 Aaron Special (PSA NM-MT 8), 10 Bench (NM), 20 Ryan (PSA NM 7), 55 F.Robinson (PSA MINT 9), 80 Seaver (EX), 130 Jackson (EX/MT), 131 Boone (PSA MINT 9), 207 Ryan/Seaver (EX), 280 Yastrzemski (NM), 283 Schmidt (PSA NM 7), 300 Rose (PSA NM 7), 456 Winfield (PSA NM-MT 8), 598 Griffey (EX/MT). Grades 42% NM to NM/MT, 57% EX to EX/MT, 5% Lesser. **Minimum Bid: $200**

19251 **1974 Topps Baseball Complete Set (660).** A total of eighty-eight cards have been graded by PSA with an aggregate SMR value of $. A total of 88 cards have been graded by PSA with an aggregate SMR value in excess of $2,000. Highlights include: **Graded Cards - PSA GEM MINT 10:** 9 cards w/#'s 189, 314 Brewers Team, 446, 497, 505 Buckner, 516, 544, 592 and 571; **PSA MINT 9:** 56 cards w/#'s 142, 154, 180, 181, 184, 186, 192, 208, 224, 225, 256, 260 Simmons, 276, 291, 292, 295, 298, 300 Rose, 301, 304, 312, 317, 335, 338 Jackson/Williams, 374, 382, 402, 403, 411, 412, 417, 419, 420, 434, 438, 445, 454, 461, 467, 482, 498, 514, 515, 520, 567, 572, 579, 587, 590, 591, 594, 595, 627, 628, 630 and 656; **PSA NM-MT 8:** 22 cards w/#'s 1 Aaron, 153, 191, 205, 224, 279, 285, 290, 308, 375, 425, 441, 462, 514, 527, 545, 556, 562, 565, 580, 585 and 655. **Ungraded Cards** - includes #'s 10 Bench (EX), 20 Ryan (EX/MT), 80 Seaver (EX/MT), 207 Ryan/Seaver (EX/MT), 280 Yastrzemski (EX/MT), 283 Schmidt (EX/MT), 456 Winfield (EX). Overall grades 63% NM to NM/MT and 37% EX to EX/MT (some lesser). **Minimum Bid: $200**

19252 **1975 Topps Baseball Complete Set (660).** Nineteen cards have been graded by PSA with an aggregate SMR value of $1,254. Highlights include: Graded Cards - **PSA MINT 9:** 10 cards w/#'s 20 Munson, 72, 110, 113, 142, 152, 160 Nettles, 180 Morgan, 186 and 228 Brett; **PSA NM-MT 8:** 8 cards w/#'s 7 Ryan HL, 185 Carlton, 230 Hunter, 241, 260 Bench, 500 Ryan, 600 Carew and 660 Aaron; **PSA NM 7:** 1 card, #223 Yount. Ungraded Cards - include #'s 1 Aaron HL (EX/MT), 61 Winfield (NM), 70 Schmidt (NM), 80 Fisk (NM/MT), 280 Yastrzemski (EX/MT), 300 Jackson (EX/MT), 320 Rose (EX/MT), 370 Seaver (NM), 616 Rice (EX/MT), 620 Carter (EX/MT). Grades 70% NM to NM/MT and 30% EX to EX/MT (some lesser). **Minimum Bid: $200**

19253 **1975 and 1976 Topps Baseball High Grade Complete Sets (2).** These sets feature rookie cards of George Brett, Robin Yount, Gary Carter, Dennis Eckersley and a plethora of stars such as Hank Aaron, Nolan Ryan, Pete Rose and much more. A total of 18 cards have been professionally graded (16 PSA and 2 SGC) with an aggregate SMR value of $582. Highlights include: 1975 Topps - complete set of 660 cards w/#'s 1 Aaron HL (EX/MT), 5 Ryan HL (PSA NM 7), 20 Munson (EX/MT), 50 B.Robinson (PSA NM-MT 8), 61 Winfield (EX/MT), 70 Schmidt (PSA NM 7), 223 Yount (PSA NM-MT 8), 228 Brett (PSA NM 7), 260 Bench (EX/MT), 280 Yastrzemski (EX/MT), 300 Jackson (NM), 320 Rose (EX/MT), 370 Seaver (PSA NM 7), 500 Ryan (PSA NM-MT 8), 540 Brock (PSA NM 7), 616 Rice (SGC 84 NM 7), 620 Carter (EX/MT), 660 Aaron (EX). Grades 44% NM to NM/MT, 56% EX to EX/MT. 1976 Topps - complete set of 660 cards w/#'s 1 Aaron RB (EX), 19 Brett (PSA NM 7), 98 Eckersley (PSA NM-MT 8), 230 Yastrzemski (PSA NM-MT 8), 240 Rose (SGC 84 NM 7), 330 Ryan (PSA NM-MT 8), 341 Gehrig ATG (PSA NM-MT 8), 345 Ruth ATG (EX/MT), 468 Alou (PSA MINT 9), 480 Schmidt (EX/MT), 500 Jackson (NM), 520 McCovey (PSA MINT 9), 550 Aaron (EX), 589 Rookie Pitchers (PSA NM 7), 600 Seaver (EX/MT). Grades 46% NM to NM/MT, 54% EX to EX/MT. **Minimum Bid: $200**

19254 **1982 Topps Traded Baseball Uncut Sheets Group Lot of 5.** This lot contains five uncut sheets from the 1982 Topps traded issue. Each sheet is 11 cards across and 12 cards down making them 132 cards total and each containing the full 132 card 1982 Topps Traded set. Each holds the super-desirable "Traded" rookie card depicting Cal Ripken, Jr snugly in the middle of the sheet, which has allowed them to stay in Mint condition for the past 25 years. This first solo Topps card of the first-ballot Hall of Famer was never available in packs, compelling collectors to buy entire 1982 Topps Traded sets in the quest to obtain a top-grade specimen of this single card. The percentages worked against those gamblers, because the overwhelming majority of the Ripken cards in this 1982 production have unsightly print blotches, random centering, or corners "dinged" by factory packing. These exceptionally rare factory sheets, picturing baseball's reigning "Iron Man," contain five stellar, unimprovable examples. **Minimum Bid: $600**

19255 **1935 National Chicle Knute Rockne #9 PSA NM-MT 8.** The second most valuable card in this earliest of football sets remembers the tragic Notre Dame coach who implored his team to "win one for the Gipper!" Marvelous color and registration, paired with sharp corners, sets this near the top of the 214 graded by PSA at the time of this writing. Only three unqualified examples have ever surpassed this magnificent specimen on the population charts. **Minimum Bid: $500**

19256 **1948 Leaf Football Near Set (85/96).** Offered is a 1948 Leaf Football Near Set of 85/96 cards (#'s 60-67, 72, 73, 75 are needed for completion) in overall solid middle grade. This near set contains many rookie cards, since it was one of the first football card productions in the post-war era. Some of the rookie contained in this near set are Baugh, Luckman, Waterfield, Lujack, Turner, Bednarik, Walker, Van Buren and so many more. The second series is much more scarce than the first series. A total of 15 cards have been graded by PSA with an aggregate SMR value of $1,520. Highlights include: **Graded Cards - PSA EX-MT 6:** 8 cards w/#'s 4 Walker, 40, 58, 68 La Force (Red Background), 78, 79, 81 (Yellow Pants) and 91 Hart; **PSA EX 5:** 4 cards w/#'s 13 Lujack, 19 McAfee, 52 Nomellini and 54 Bednarik; **PSA VG-EX 4:** 2 cards w/#'s 6 Layne and 53 Conerly; **PSA GOOD 2:** 1 card, #1 Luckman. **Ungraded Cards** - include #'s 3 Turner (VG/EX), 15 Justice (VG/EX), 16 Pihos (VG/EX), 17 Washington (GD), 22 Van Buren (VG/EX), 26 Waterfield (VG), 29 Trippi (EX), 34 Baugh (VG), 36 Dudley (EX), 37 Connor (VG/EX) and 98 DiMarco (EX). Grades 44% EX to EX/MT, 51% VG to VG/EX, 5% GD. **Minimum Bid: $500**

19257 **1950 Bowman Football High Grade Complete Set (144).** The first color football set. These cards were issued to the collecting public in six-card nickel packs with two pieces of gum, and are arranged so that trios of players from the same team are numbered together in sequence. Important rookies included in this set are Canadeo, Glenn Davis, Fears, Graham, Groza, Hirsch, Lavelli, Motley, Joe Perry and Tittle. A total of 42 cards have been graded by SGC with an aggregate SMR value of $5,115. Highlights include: **Graded Cards - SGC 96 MINT 9:** 1 card, #39; **SGC 92 NM/MT+ 8.5:** 4 cards w/#'s 14, 16 Davis, 107 Nomellini and 134 Pihos; **SGC 88 NM/MT 8:** 15 cards w/#'s 17 Waterfield, 26 Lujack, 27 Luckman, 37 Layne, 59, 61, 73, 77, 92, 100 Baugh, 102, 108, 123, 133 and 135; **SGC 86 NM+ 7.5:** 7 cards w/#'s 5 Tittle, 15 Younger, 20, 69, 72, 116 and 124; **SGC 84 NM 7:** 13 cards w/#'s 8 Speedie, 32, 45 Graham, 48, 54, 60, 71, 89, 96, 98, 101, 103 Conerly and 122; **SGC 80 EX/NM 6:** 1 card, #6 Groza; **SGC 50 VG/EX 4:** #38 Hart. **Ungraded Cards** - include #'s 1 Walker (EX/MT), 9 Canadeo (NM), 23 Van Buren (EX), 28 Turner (EX), 35 Perry (EX), 43 Motley (EX), 51 Fears (VG/EX), 52 Hirsch (EX), 78 Lavelli (VG/EX), 81 Rote (EX), 128 Finks (EX/MT), 132 Bednarik (EX). Grades 35% NM to NM/MT, 54% EX to EX/MT, 11% VG to VG/EX. **Minimum Bid: $750**

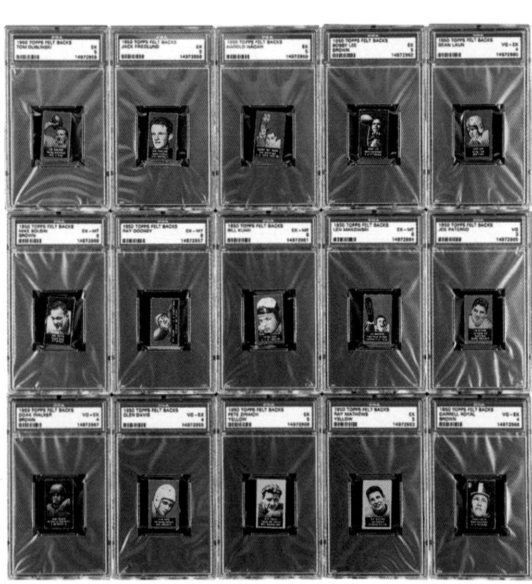

19258 **1950 Topps Felt Back Football Complete Set (100).** This is a set that is extremely difficult to find as a complete set in any condition, let alone a very pleasing example, such as this one. This set brought us the Rookie card of the legendary Joe Paterno, along with Doak Walker, Ernie Stautner and Darrell Royal. The cards were comprised of two materials one being the usually cardboard and the later with the felt backs that has a college pennant on the reverse. These cards measure a mere 1 7/16" by 7/8". A total of 15 cards have been graded by PSA with an aggregate SMR value of $1,595. Highlights include: Graded Cards - **PSA EX-MT 6:** 4 cards w/ Boldin/brown, Dooney, Kuhn and Makowski; **PSA EX 5:** 6 cards w/ Dublinski, Friedlund, Hagan, Lee/brown, Mathews/yellow and Zinaich/yellow; **PSA VG-EX 4:** 4 cards w/ Davis, Laun, Royal/brown and Walker/brown; **PSA VG 3:** 1 card, Paterno. **Ungraded Cards** - include: #'s 35 Hart (GD), 62 Nomellini (VG), 79 Stautner (VG). Grades 60% EX to EX/MT, 30% VG to VG/EX, 10 GD. **Minimum Bid: $500**

19259 **1951 Bowman Football High Grade Complete Set (144).** Issued both in six-card nickel packs and single-card penny packs, this issue experienced a growth spurt from previous years, with the cards now five-eighths of an inch taller, but with the same amount of cards. There are many notable rookie cards including Landry, Tunnell and Van Brocklin. A total of cards have been graded by SGC. A total of 54 cards have been graded by SGC with an aggregate SMR value of $4,470. Highlights include: **Graded Cards - SGC 92 NM/MT+ 8.5:** 2 cards w/#'s 5 and 70; **SGC 88 NM/MT 8:** 15 cards w/#'s 1 Humble, 6 Fears, 12 Bednarik, 16, 17, 29, 30, 34 Baugh, 51, 53, 58, 60, 67, 107 and 131; **SGC 86 NM+ 7.5:** 9 cards w/#'s 11, 14, 33, 80, 84, 89, 92, 94 and 130 Finks; **SGC 84 NM 7:** 22 cards w/#'s 3 Spedie, 4 Van Brocklin, 13 Turner, 15 Lujack, 19, 20 Landry, 24, 26 Hart, 27, 32 Tittle, 35, 38, 39, 49, 61, 69, 78, 83, 85, 102 Layne, 110 and 114; **SGC 80 EX/NM 6:** 6 cards w/#'s 50, 52, 66, 71, 77 and 97. **Ungraded Cards** - include #'s 2 Graham (EX), 4 Van Brocklin (EX/MT), 15 Lujack (EX/MT), 20 Landry (NM), 21 Weinmeister (EX/MT), 25 Walker (EX), 40 Waterfield (EX/MT), 42 Davis (EX/MT), 46 Pihos (EX/MT), 56 Conerly (EX), 75 Groza (EX), 76 Hirsch (EX), 91 Tunnell (EX), 96 Stautner (EX), 105 Perry (VG/EX), 109 Motley (VG/EX), 140 Nomellini (EX/MT), 144 Dudley (EX/MT). Grades **40% NM to NM/MT,** 55% EX to EX/MT, 5% VG to VG/EX. **Minimum Bid: $1,000**

19260 **1952 Bowman Small Norman Van Brocklin #1 SGC 88 NM/MT 8.** Offered is a high-grade number one card that is one of only two examples to achieve the grade of SGC 88 with none grading higher. Bowman decided to have Hall of Fame quarterback Norm Van Brocklin grace the first card for their 1952 set. This card is notoriously off-centered. When you are lucky enough to find one with equally sized borders then it is usually plagued with the general wear that nearly all #1 cards encountered. Then, if you are able to line up these two characteristics, it will inevitably have a print defect or a wax stain. Well, this card is proof that it can all be found in a single card. The bottom line is that this is a solid Near Mint to Mint card. Great centering, bold colors and exceptional eye appeal. **Minimum Bid: $300**

19261 **1954 Bowman Football High Grade Complete Set (128).** Within this set is the very tough mid series, which contains 32 cards and command a significant premium over the other cards. Many Hall of Famers are highlighted throughout the set including the likes of Blanda, Nomellini, Tittle, Groza, Layne, Gifford, Bednarik and so many more. A total of 66 cards have been graded by SGC with an aggregate SMR value of $2,503. Highlights include: Graded Cards - **SGC 96 MINT 9:** 1 card, #77; **SGC 92 NM/MT+ 8.5:** 10 cards w/#'s 5, 38, 48, 60, 80, 92, 99, 103, 115 and 125 White; **SGC 88 NM/MT 8:** 29 cards w/#'s 2, 3, 8 Van Brocklin, 9 Pihos, 12 Matson, 13, 14, 19, 22, 24, 31 Wietecha, 32 Hirsch, 35, 37, 39, 44, 45, 52 Groza, 62, 68, 69, 79, 100 Christiansen, 106, 107, 109, 124, 126 and 127; **SGC 86 NM+ 7.5:** 5 cards w/#'s 15, 34, 46, 49 and 59; **SGC 84 NM 7:** 16 cards w/#'s 11 Bratkowski, 17, 55 Gifford, 57 Bednarik, 63, 67, 70 Rote, 84, 96, 102 Tunnell, 84, 113 Conerly, 116, 119, 120 and 123; **SGC 80 EX/NM 6:** 4 cards w/#'s 27, 28, 40 Graham and 101; **SGC 70 EX+ 5.5:** 1 card, #23 Blanda. **Ungraded Cards** - include #'s 4 Atkins (NM), 6 Perry (GD/VG), 20 Fears (EX/MT), 41 Walker (EX), 42 Tittle (EX), 53 Layne (NM), 54 McElhenny (EX/MT), 76 Nomellini SP (EX), 118 Stautner (EX/MT), 128 Lattner (EX/MT). Grades 58% NM to NM/MT, 35% EX to EX/MT, 7% VG to VG/EX. **Minimum Bid: $750**

19262 **1957 Topps Bart Starr #119 SGC 88 NM/MT 8.** Offered here is a blazing specimen of Hall of Famer Bart Starr's rookie card from the 1957 Topps issue's scarcer "high number" series. This card delivers amazing surface gloss and an extremely fresh presentation of its production's memorable portrait and action dichotomy. Centering is a primary concern for this Topps issue, but that is not the case with this well centered example with 45/55 centering at both the top to bottom and left to right edges. **Minimum Bid: $300**

19263 **1957 Topps Johnny Unitas #138 SGC 86 NM+ 7.5.** Here we present the important rookie card of one the most famed NFL quarterbacks of all time, Johnny Unitas. Strong centering combined with bold color and the lack of the common snowy effect seen on the 1957 Topps football issue make this offering a true winner in NM+ condition. **Minimum Bid: $150**

19264 **1958 Topps Jim Brown #62 PSA NM 7.** The foundation upon which any serious football collection should be built; the Jim Brown rookie card features the greatest running back to ever carry the pigskin, posed in his Cleveland Browns uniform shortly after his dominant collegiate career at Syracuse University. Wonderfully centered; clean back; great colors. **Minimum Bid: $100**

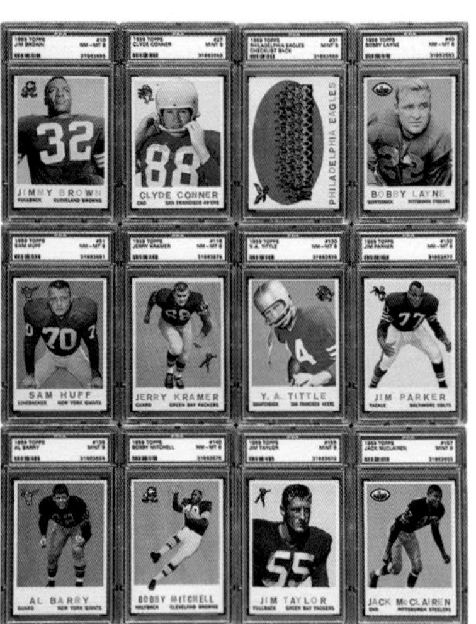

19265 **1959 Topps High Grade Football Complete Set (176).** Presented is a high grade 1959 Topps football set. This ever-popular set features all of the era's superstar players, as well as attractive "team pennant" cards and team cards with checklists on the back. A total of 41 cards have been graded by PSA with an aggregate SMR value of $2,401. Highlights include: **Graded Cards - PSA MINT 9:** 10 cards w/#'s 27, 31 Eagles Team, 108, 136, 138, 155 Taylor, 157, 158, 164 and 171; **PSA NM-MT 8:** 31 cards w/#'s 3 Lions Team, 10 Brown, 12, 29, 36, 37, 40 Layne, 41, 46 Packers, 48, 51 Huff, 62, 69, 73, 85, 94, 99, 104 Bears Team, 111 49ers, 116 Kramer, 129, 129, 130 Tittle, 131, 132 Parker, 133 Giants Team, 140 Mitchell, 144, 146 Steelers Team, 165 and 172. **Ungraded Cards** - include #'s 1 Unitas (EX), 4 McGee (NM), 20 Gifford (EX/MT), 23 Starr (EX/MT), 55 Berry (EX), 60 Groza (NM), 82 Hornung (NM) and 103 Karras (NM). Grades 56% NM to NM/MT, 44% EX to EX/MT (some lesser). **Minimum Bid: $300**

19266 **1961 Fleer High Grade Football Set (220).** The second Fleer football set is considered to be a giant step forward from the debut issue, with more stars, rookies and total cards. Highlights include rookie cards of Don Meredith, John Brodie, Don Maynard, Jim Otto and more. A total of 51 cards have been graded by SGC with an aggregate SMR value of $2,499. Highlights include: **Graded Cards - SGC 96 MINT 9:** 10 cards w/#'s 108, 143, 158, 159, 171 Cannon, 176, 188 Flores, 203 Haynes, 204 and 215 Maynard; **SGC 92 NM/MT+ 8.5:** 14 cards w/#'s 45, 48, 62, 96 Ringo, 99 Matson, 100, 141, 155 Kemp, 163, 164, 180, 183, 185 and 190; **SGC 88 NM/MT 8:** 12 cards w/#'s 20, 31 Ameche, 39 Donovan, 50, 64, 69, 121, 124, 132, 144, 160 Maguire and 181; **SGC 86 NM+ 7.5:** 11 cards w/#'s 6 Jones, 11 Brown, 30 Unitas, 71 Brown, 79, 91, 103, 115, 197 Otto, 200 and 214; **SGC 84 NM 7:** 4 cards w/#'s 1 Brown, 88 Starr, 125 Stautner and 199 Davidson. **Ungraded Cards** - include #'s 32 Moore (NM), 33 Berry (EX/MT), 41 Meredith (), 55 Bednarik (NM), 59 Brodie (NM), 74 Huff (EX), 89 Taylor (NM), 90 Hornung (NM), 117 Layne (NM), 166 Blanda (NM). **Grades 61% NM to NM/MT,** 39% EX to EX/MT. **Minimum Bid: $450**

19267 **1963 Topps Football Complete Set (170).** The 1963 Topps football set contains 170-standard sized cards of NFL players grouped together by teams. The key rookie cards in the set are defensive standouts Deacon Jones, Bob Lilly, Jim Marshall, Ray Nitschke, Larry Wilson, and Willie Wood. This is a very difficult set to find in high grade due to the color borders which were susceptible to easy chipping. A total of 10 cards have been graded by PSA with an aggregate SMR value of $592. Highlights include #'s 1 Unitas (PSA EX-MT 6), 14 Brown SP (PSA EX-MT 6), 19 Groza SP (EX/MT), 26 (PSA NM 7), 44 Jones (EX), 49 Tittle SP (EX), 52 (PSA NM-MT 8), 59 Huff SP (EX/MT), 62 Ditka (PSA NM 7), 74 Meredith SP (EX/MT), 82 Lilly SP (PSA NM 7), 86 Starr (EX), 87 Taylor (EX), 91 Ringo (PSA NM 7), 95 Wood (EX/MT), 96 Nitschke (PSA EX-MT 6), 98 Tarkenton (EX/MT), 103 McElhenny (PSA NM 7), 107 Marshall (EX), 110 Jurgenson SP (EX/MT), 129 Stautner SP (EX), 134 Brodie (VG/EX), 155 Wilson (PSA NM 7), 159 Mitchell (NM), 170 CL (EX/MT). Grades 16% NM to NM/MT, 79% EX to EX/MT, 5% VG/EX. **Minimum Bid: $200**

19268 **1964 Topps Canadian Football League Full Box GAI Mint 9.** Complete original unopened 36-count wax box of 1964 Topps Canadian football, printed in Canada by O-Pee-Chee, graded Mint 9 by GAI. The box contains thirty-six unopened wax packs. Great to keep as a full box or to have individual packs graded for resale. The 1964 Topps Canadian set includes stars of the day from the Canadian Football League including Joe Kapp. This extraordinary high-grade unopened wax box is in virtually perfect condition, looking exactly as it did when they left the factory in 1964. These boxes are rarely seen in unopened pristine condition. **Minimum Bid: $250**

19269 **1965 Topps Football Complete Set (176).** The 1965 Topps football set contains 176 oversized cards featuring only players from the American Football League The set is significant with football collectors for its inclusion of Joe Namath's rookie card; as well as those of Fred Biletnikoff, Willie Brown and Ben Davidson. A total of 76 cards have been graded by PSA with an aggregate SMR value of $3,796. Highlights include: **Graded Cards - PSA MINT 9 (OC):** 8 cards w/#'s 15, 18, 48, 49, 79, 129, 160 and 163; **PSA NM-MT 8:** 10 cards w/#'s 61, 63, 76, 87 Checklist, 97, 107, 124, 130, 131 (ST) and 172; **PSA NM-MT 8 (OC):** 6 cards w/#'s 12, 42, 101, 114, 115 and 140; **PSA NM 7:** 38 cards w/#'s 3 Buoniconti, 10, 16, 21, 24, 26, 30, 31, 35 Kemp, 36 Lamonica, 38, 47, 69 Blanda, 75, 77, 82, 85, 93, 98, 100, 103, 108, 110, 120, 121 Maynard, 123, 127 Snell, 128, 134 Cannon, 137 Davidson, 144, 145 Otto, 151, 156, 157, 162, 168 Mix and 176 Checklist; **PSA EX-MT 6:** 14 cards w/#'s 1 Addison, 13, 17, 29, 46 Brown, 55, 57, 68, 91 Bell, 99 Dawson, 122 Namath, 154, 155 Alworth and 159. **Ungraded Cards** - include 94 Buchanan SP (EX), 133 Biletnikoff SP (VG/EX), 161 Hadl SP (EX). Grades 35% NM to NM/MT, 52% EX to EX/MT, 13% VG to VG/EX. **Minimum Bid: $500**

19270 **1965 Topps Football High Grade Complete Set (176).** The "tall boy" format of this hugely popular football set made storage difficult, a fact which accordingly provides no shortage of condition problems for those cards that have survived to this day. The high powered rookie card of Joe Namath is presented in solid SGC 84 NM 7 condition here, and plenty of short printed cards appear in similarly fine condition. A total of 58 cards have been graded by SGC with an aggregate SMR value of $8,017. Highlights include - **Graded Cards: SGC 96 MINT 9:** 13 cards w/#'s 11 SP, 18 SP, 25 SP, 35 Kemp SP, 50 SP, 71 SP, 91 Bell SP, 92 Branch SP, 98, 126, 152 Williamson SP, 153 and 155 Alworth; **SGC 92 NM/MT+ 8.5:** 7 cards w/#'s 9, 16, 59, 130 SP, 140, 143 SP and 169 Mix SP; **SGC 88 NM/MT 8:** 21 cards w/#'s 7 SP, 21 SP, 22 SP, 24 SP, 26 SP, 32 SP, 36 Lamonica, 46 Brown SP, 53 Haynes SP, 75 SP, 81 SP, 100 SP, 104, 107 SP, 118 SP, 119 SP, 120, 123, 127 Snell SP, 131 SP and 166 Lowe SP; **SGC 86 NM+ 7.5:** 12 cards w/#'s 5 Cappelletti SP, 8, 15 SP, 38 SP, 68 SP, 69 Blanda SP, 80 SP, 82 SP, 106, 124 SP, 125 SP and 157 SP; **SGC 84 NM 7:** 5 cards w/#'s 37 Maguire SP, 122 Namath SP, 133 Biletnikoff SP, 138 SP and 172. **Ungraded Cards** - include #'s 87 CL (EX), 99 Dawson (VG/EX), 121 Maynard (NM), 137 Davidson (NM), 145 Otto (EX/MT), 161 Hadl (NM) and 176 CL (EX). **Grades 53% NM to NM/MT,** 42% EX to EX/MT, 5% VG/EX. **Minimum Bid: $1,000**

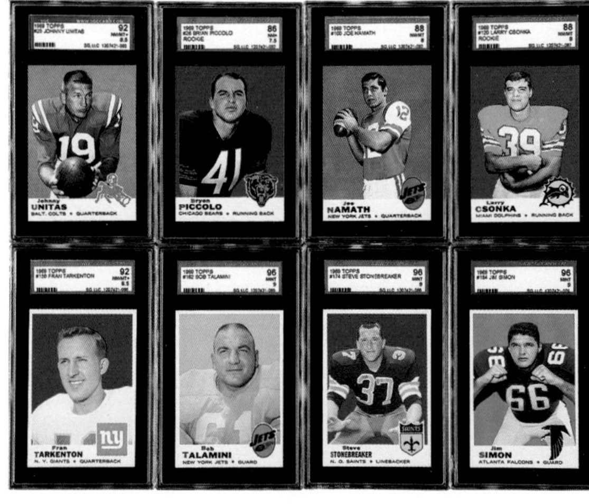

19271 **1969 Topps Football High Grade Complete Set (263).** The beautifully rendered 1969 Topps football set, released in two series, features brightly colored backgrounds and full-bleed printing in the first series (the second half has a white border). The issue includes rookie cards of Larry Csonka and Bryon Piccolo and star cards of Unitas, Starr, Griese, Sayers and Blanda. A total of 20 cards have been graded by SGC with an aggregate SMR value of $967. Highlights include: **Graded Cards - SGC 96 MINT 9:** 3 cards w/#'s 162, 174 and 184; **SGC 92 NM/MT+ 8.5:** 4 cards w/#'s 25 Unitas, 30, 150 Tarkenton and 238 Jones; **SGC 88 NM/MT 8:** 11 cards w/#'s 12, 16, 41, 53 Lilly, 62, 66, 100 Namath, 120 Csonka, 173, 179 and 194; **SGC 86 NM+ 7.5:** 1 card, #26 Piccolo; **SGC 84 NM 7:** 1 card, #75 Meredith. **Ungraded Cards** - include #'s 1 Kelly (VG), 20 Dawson (EX/MT), 51 Sayers (VG), 139 Butkus (EX/MT), 161 Griese (EX/MT), 215 Starr (EX/MT), 232 Blanda (EX/MT), 263 Lamonica (EX). Grades **43% NM to NM/MT,** 52% EX to EX/MT and 5% VG to VG/EX. **Minimum Bid: $200**

19272 **1970 Kellogg's Football Complete Sealed Sets (9), Unsealed (1).** The 1970 Kellogg's football set of 60 cards was Kellogg's first football issue. The cards could be obtained from boxes of cereal or as a set from a box top offer. Offered here are ten such sets, with nine still sealed in the original envelopes. We opened one set and it was amazing how nice they were, with many worthy of grading. Some of the stars contained in this set include O.J. Simpson, Bob Griese, Johnny Unitas, Larry Czonka, Dick Butkus, Gale Sayers and more. With the grades that came out of this one set, one can only imagine what lies within the other nine. A total of 16 cards were graded by PSA. Highlights include: **Graded Cards - PSA GEM MINT 10:** 3 cards w/#'s 2 Otto, 4 Nelsen and 20 Stenerud; **PSA MINT 9:** 13 cards w/#'s 1 Eller, 3 Matte, 6 Dawson, 10 Butkus, 17 Griese, 21 Warfield, 34 Mackey, 39 Hayes, 41 Czonka, 48 Simpson, 49 Hill, 51 Sayers and 55 Unitas. This set grades out at a MINT level. **Minimum Bid: $250**

19273 **1972 Topps Joe Namath #100 PSA GEM-MT 10.** Presented here is a flawless example of Broadway Joe's 1972 Topps issue. It exhibits perfect 50/50 centering on both the top to bottom and left to right borders as well as four razor sharp corners. The registration and gloss is defect free to boot. This is simply a stellar card and presents a great opportunity for a lucky collector to own the best of Broadway Joe. **Minimum Bid: $200**

19274 **1972 Topps Football SGC Partial First Series Graded Set Plus 400+ Singles.** Offered is a high grade presentation of 1972 Topps First series football, including 71 cards that have been graded by SGC. These cards were all pulled from a fresh unopened vending box and there are still plenty of cards that can still be graded. A total of 71 cards have been graded by SCG with an aggregate SMR value of $2,095. Highlights include: **Graded Cards - SGC 96 MINT 9:** 41 cards w/#'s 12, 14, 20 Eller, 22, 31, 33, 36, 39, 40 Gabriel, 41, 43 Buoniconti, 56, 57, 59, 62, 63, 64, 68, 69, 79 CL, 80 Griese, 83, 88, 95 Brown, 96, 98, 101 Greenwood, 107, 110 Sayers, 113, 114, 115 Yepremian, 117, 119, 120 Bradshaw IA, 121 Kiick IA, 122 Staubach IA, 123, 124 Brodie IA, 130 and 131; **SGC 92 NM/MT+ 8.5:** 11 cards w/#'s 11, 18 Kilmer, 85 Brockington, 90, 93 Hendricks, 97, 100 Namath, 111, 112 Gray, 126 Riggins IA and 129; **SGC 88 NM/MT 8:** 12 cards w/#'s 2, 6, 30, 42, 54, 75, 76, 81, 84, 127, 128 and 132 Griese IA; **SGC 86 NM+ 7.5:** 3 cards w/#'s 7, 49 and 73; **SGC 84 NM 7:** 4 cards w/#'s 3, 39, 47 and 65 Plunkett. **Ungraded Cards** - include #'s 13 Riggins (2: both NM), 55 Manning (3: NM/MT and 2 NM), 65 Plunkett (5: 2 NM/MT and 3 NM), 80 Griese (3: all NM/MT), 93 Hendricks (NM), 100 Namath (4: 2 NM/MT and 2 NM), 101 Greenwood (2 both NM), 106 Alzado (4: all NM), 110 Sayers (NM), 120 Bradshaw IA (3: all NM/MT) and 122 Staubach IA (2: NM/MT and NM). **Grades 90% NM to NM/MT,** 10% EX to EX/MT (mainly due to centering). **Minimum Bid: $250**

19275 **1972 Topps Football High Grade Complete Set (351).** The presented set is perfect for those high-grade set collectors. Over 85% of this set has been graded at the NM or higher level. This colorful issue includes a notoriously difficult high number series and key rookies of Staubach, Spurrier, Hendricks, Joiner, Little, Manning, Plunkett, Riggins and Upshaw. A total of 121 cards have been graded (119-PSA, 2-SGC)with an aggregate SMR value of $3,809. Highlights include: **Graded Cards - PSA MINT 9:** 33 cards w/#'s 43 Buoniconti, 52, 107, 158, 203, 264, 265 Yary AP, 266, 267 Little AP, 270, 271 Warfield AP, 272 Griese AP, 275, 276, 277 Eller AP, 278 Smith AP, 280 Lilly AP, 281 Hendricks AP, 284 Johnson AP, 285, 287, 288, 292, 293 Pardee, 300 Page, 302, 313, 314, 316 Wright, 321, 322 Boozer, 323 and 324; **SGC 92 NM/MT+ 8.5:** 1 card, #165 Unitas; **PSA NM-MT 8:** 77 cards w/#'s 2, 10, 11, 14, 15 Hadl, 24, 26, 28, 32, 34, 40 Gabriel, 47, 49, 56, 62, 63, 65 Plunkett, 68, 71, 73, 74, 75, 77, 88, 89, 92, 95 Brown, 96, 98, 99, 100 Namath, 105 Hayes, 110 Sayers, 112, 113, 115, 116, 117, 118, 121, 135, 141, 144, 153, 155, 160 Simpson, 163, 167 Warfield, 170 Butkus, 171, 181 Olsen, 182, 184, 188, 192, 193, 197, 205, 215, 216, 217, 219, 221, 226, 229, 232, 235 Blanda, 240 Little, 244 Joiner, 245 Dawson, 246, 249, 251 Unitas IA, 252, 256, 327 and 333; **PSA NM 7:** 9 cards w/#'s 1, 67, 84, 86 Otto, 104 Yary, 140 Czonka, 190 Smith, 209 and 248 Alworth; **SGC 84 NM 7:** 1 card, #200 Staubach. **Ungraded Cards** - include #'s 13 Riggins (NM/MT), 55 Manning (NM), 93 Hendricks (EX/MT), 106 Alzado (NM/MT), 120 Bradshaw IA (NM/MT), 122 Staubach IA (NM), 150 Bradshaw (NM), 186 Upshaw (NM), 230 Greene (NM), 279 Page AP (NM/MT), 291 Spurrier (EX/MT), 294 CL (NM), 338 Spurrier IA (EX/MT), 340 Dawson IA (EX/MT), 341 Butkus IA (NM), 343 Namath IA (EX/MT), 348 Blanda IA (EX/MT). Grades 86% NMto NM/MT, 14% EX to EX/MT (some lesser). **Minimum Bid: $1,000**

19276 **1948 Bowman Basketball SGC Graded Collection (55).** The 1948 Bowman basketball set was released in two series. This high grade selection includes cards from only the first series. Aggregate SMR value is in excess of $10,000. Highlights include: **Graded Cards - SGC 92 NM/MT+ 8.5:** 6 cards w/#'s 3, (2) 13, 19, 25, 29; **SGC 88 NM/MT 8:** 28 cards w/#'s 6, 7, 8, 9 Andy Phillip (R) (HOF), (2) 10 Bob Davies (R) (HOF), (2) 11, (2) 12, 13, (2) 14, (2) 15, (3) 16, 18, (2) 20, 22, 24, 25, 28, 29, 33, 35; **SGC 86 NM+ 7.5:** 4 cards w/#'s 11, 12, 19, 32; **SGC 84 NM 7:** 14 cards w/#'s 2, 4, 8, 9 Andy Phillip (R) (HOF), 10 Bob Davies (R) (HOF), 12, 14, 15, 26, 28, 30, 32 Red Holzman (R) (HOF), 33, 34 Joe Fulks (R) (HOF); **SGC 80 EX/NM 6:** 2 cards w/#'s 21, 29; **SGC 60 EX 5:** 1 card w/#'s 1 Ernie Calverley (R). **Minimum Bid: $1,000**

19277 **1948 Bowman Basketball Complete Set (72).** This set contains the high powered rookie card of George Mikan, along with Red Holzman, Joe Fulks and Carl Braun. This set is seldom seen complete and now is a great opportunity to own the first basketball set produced by the Bowman company. A total of 21 cards have been graded by PSA with an aggregate SMR value of $3,170. Highlights include: **Graded cards - PSA NM 7:** 3 cards w/#'s 14,60 and 62; **PSA EX-MT 6:** 13 cards w/#'s 13, 19, 20, 21, 32 Holzman, 40, 48 Sadowski, 50, 51, 56, 57, 61 and 68; **PSA EX 5:** 5 cards w/#'s 16, 63, 64, 66 Pollard and 69 Mikan. **Ungraded cards** - include #'s 1 Calverley (GD), 9 Phillip (EX), 10 Davies (EX), 34 Fulks (VG/EX), 38 Jeanette (VG/EX), 43 Halbert (EX), 46 McKinney (EX), 52 Simmons (EX), 54 Palmer (GD), 55 Zaslofsky (EX), 58 Risen (VG), 72 Braun (VG). Graded 4% NM, 68% EX to EX/MT, 28% VG to VG/EX (some lesser). **Minimum Bid: $500**

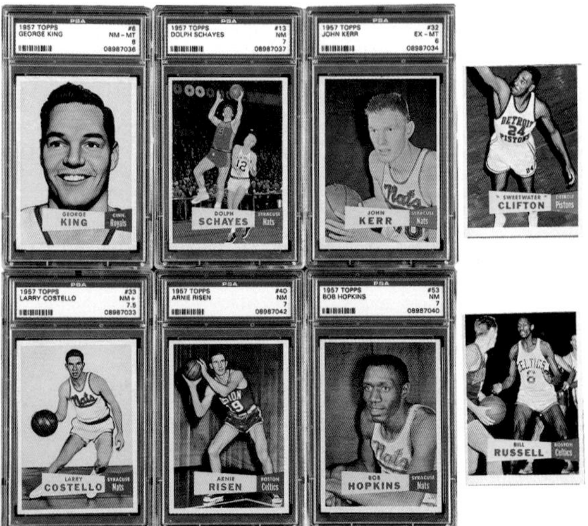

19278 **1957 Topps Basketball Complete Set (80).** This set contains an amazing amount of rookies being that it was the first Topps production. The set has sharp corners, tremendous color and clarity, but the centering remains a problem throughout. There are 25 cards that have centering that is worse than 100-0, which we would deem to be GD/VG. A total of 10 cards have been graded by PSA with an aggregate SMR value of $950. Highlights include #'s 1 Clifton (GD/VG), 2 Yardley (EX), 3 Johnston (VG/EX), 5 Sharman (GD//VG), 6 King (PSA NM-MT 8), 8 Ricketts (PSA EX-MT 6), 10 Arizin (EX), 12 Martin (GD/VG), 13 Schayes (PSA NM 7), 15 Ramsey (VG/EX), 16 McGuire (VG/EX), 17 Cousy (VG/EX), 19 Heinsohn SP (VG/EX), 24 Pettit (VG/EX), 28 Mikkelson SP (VG/EX), 32 Kerr SP (PSA EX-MT 6), 33 Costello (PSA NM+ 7.5), 37 Hagan SP (GD/VG), 39 Loscutoff SP (GD/VG), 40 Risen (PSA NM 7), 42 Stokes (GD/VG), 43 Hundley (GD/VG), 44 Gola (EX/MT), 47 Friend (PSA EX-MT 6), 51 Selvy (PSA EX-MT 6), 53 Hopkins (PSA NM 7), 56 Houbregs (PSA NM 7), 59 Bianchi SP (VG), 62 Gallatin (EX), 71 Twyman (GD/VG), 77 Russell SP (GD/VG), 78 Lovellette (VG/EX), 80 Schnittker SP (VG/EX). Grades 9% NM to NM/MT, 37% EX to EX/MT, 54% GD/VG to VG/EX. **Minimum Bid: $500**

19279 **1961-62 Fleer Jerry West #43 PSA Mint 9.** Jerry West starred at West Virginia, leading them to the 1959 NCAA championship, before serving as co-captain (with Oscar Robertson) of the 1960 U.S. Olympic gold medal team in Rome. West played in nine NBA Finals, but finished his career with only one championship, won in the 1971-72 season, the year the Lakers established a modern North American professional sports record of 33 straight wins. As any collector of the 1961 Fleer basketball set can tell you, finding a high-grade example is akin to finding the proverbial needle in a haystack. PSA has graded 605 examples of this Jerry West card and only three have ranked higher. Card displays flawless centering, four sharp corners; as well as brilliant color, contrast and gloss. **Minimum Bid: $500**

19280 **1969-70 Topps Basketball High-Grade Near Set (85/99).** One of the most collectible basketball sets in the hobby, this classic "tall boy" issue includes plenty of key Hall of Fame rookie cards including Alcindor, Thurmond, Hawkins, Cunningham, Lucas, Bing, Unseld, Reed, Hayes, Monroe and DeBusschere. Condition issues typically plague the set, so a high-grade offering like this is a rare occurrence. The Lew Alcindor rookie, issued before he even played a game with the Milwaukee Bucks, was the inspiration behind Topps reestablishing itself in the basketball card market with a 99-card issue. A total of 68 cards (46 SGC and 22 PSA) have been professionally graded with an aggregate SMR value of $2,819. A total of 68 cards have been graded by SGC with an aggregate SMR value of $2,819. Highlights include: **Graded Cards - PSA MINT 9 (OC):** 3 cards w/#'s 19, 76 and 77; **SGC 92 NM/MT+ 8.5:** 6 cards w/#'s 3 Russell, 16, 23 Adelman, 29 Erickson, 59 and 94 Loughery; **PSA NM-MT 8:** 13 cards w/#'s 11 (OC), 12, 15 Hawkins, 18, 24, 33, 37, 51 (ST), 62, 66 (OC), 68, 79 (OC) and 69 (OC); **SGC 88 NM/MT 8:** 12 cards w/#'s 13, 21, 28, 34, 49, 71, 73, 74, 82 Nelson, 85 Debusschere, 86 and 97; **SGC 86 NM+ 7.5:** 13 cards w/#'s 9, 10 Thurmond, 17, 32, 40 Cunningham, 44 Wilkens, 47, 50 Robertson, 54, 57, 61 Silas, 83 Hairston and 92; **PSA NM 7:** 6 cards w/#'s 2 Goodrich, 6, 31, 69, 78 Love and 81; **SGC 84 NM 7:** 14 cards w/#'s 1 Chamberlain, 4 Imhoff, 5, 8 Walker, 20 Havlicek, 25 Alcindor, 26 Marin, 36, 42, 70, 84 Greer, 90 West, 95 Bellamy and 96; SGC 80 EX/NM 6: 1 card, #56 Unseld. Ungraded Cards - include #'s 35 Baylor (EX/MT), 45 Lucas (EX/MT), 55 Bing (EX/MT), 60 Reed (NM) and 80 Monroe (EX/MT). Grades 80% NM to NM/MT, 20% EX to EX/MT. **Minimum Bid: $400**

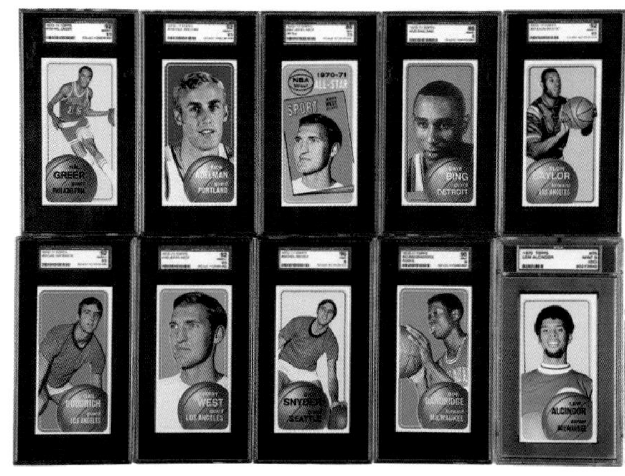

19281 **1970-71 Topps Basketball High Grade Complete Set (175).** Topps returned in 1970-71 with a 175-card "tall boy" set which included an equally intriguing rookie in Pete Maravich, who dominated the collegiate game while at Louisiana State University. Condition issues typically plague the set, so a high-grade offering like this is a rare occurrence. Highlights include: **Graded Cards - SGC 96 MINT 9:** 2 cards w/#'s 63 Dandridge and 64; **PSA MINT 9 (OC):** 1 card, #75 Alcindor; **SGC 92 NM/MT+ 8.5:** 10 cards w/#'s 42, 61, 65 Baylor, 83, 92, 93 Goodrich, 118 Adelman, 155 Greer, 159 and 160 West; **SGC 88 NM/MT 8:** 15 cards w/#'s 28, 48, 73, 76, 82, 98, 102, 116, 125 Bing, 132, 133, 141, 144, 153 and 157; **SGC 86 NM+ 7.5:** 17 cards w/#'s 5 Alcindor Rebound Ldrs. 18, 44, 51, 56, 96, 99, 107 West AS, 110 Reed AS, 121, 134, 147, 151, 154, 158 and 166; **SGC 84 NM 7:** 12 cards w/#'s 23, 30, 41, 43, 66, 71, 81, 105, 109 Hawkins AS, 127, 165 Haskins and 169; **PSA NM 7:** 2 cards w/#'s 10 Havlicek (OC) and 11; **SGC 80 EX/NM 6:** 3 cards w/#'s 20 Monroe, 114 Robertson AS and 136; **PSA EX-MT 6:** 2 cards w/#'s 6 and 50 Chamberlain. **Ungraded Cards** - include #'s 1 Alcindor/West LL (EX), 2 West/Alcindor LL SP (NM), 7 Bradley (EX/MT), 13 Riley (EX), 24 CL (VG/EX), 70 Hayes (EX/MT), 80 Wilkens SP (VG), 86 Nelson SP (EX/MT), 100 Robertson (EX/MT), 101 CL (EX), 112 Havlicek AS (EX/MT), 120 Frazier (EX), 123 Maravich (EX), 130 Hawkins (NM), 137 Murphy (EX). Grades 47% NM to NM/MT, 47% EX to EX/MT, 6% VG to VG/EX. **Minimum Bid: $300**

19282 **1986 Fleer Basketball Michael Jordan Collection (2).** Michael Jordan forever changed the face of basketball and popularized the sport at a higher level worldwide. His influence on the game is still being felt today and every up-and-coming star must face the inevitable comparisons. An opportunity to own both the card and sticker from Michael Jordan's first major set release, the 1986 Fleer basketball issue. 1986 Fleer #57 Michael Jordan rates PSA NM-MT 8 and 1986 Fleer Sticker #8 Michael Jordan rates PSA Mint 9. **Minimum Bid: $200**

19283 **1986 Fleer Michael Jordan #57 SGC 98 Gem Mint 10.** Presented is one of the most sought-after modern cards of any type, and arguably the most popular card from any era or sport: here's an opportunity for a basketball card collector to reach the pinnacle. The offered rookie is clearly a pack-fresh example, with impeccable centering and superb color. The bold, perfectly focused and brilliant image of Jordan absolutely radiates through its pristine layer of uninterrupted, original surface gloss. Four perfect and apparently never-touched edges culminate in pinpoint-sharp corners at each aspect. Of the over 900 examples that have been graded by SGC and this superior example is one of only 4 to achieve Gem Mint 98 status. **Minimum Bid: $1,500**

19284 **1910 C56 Imperial Tobacco Cards PSA & SGC-Graded Group Lot of 9.** The league that immediately preceded today's NHL was known as the National Hockey Association and dropped the puck on its first season in 1910. Here we present nine cards depicting players from the league's seven teams from what is the first known hockey set — the Imperial Tobacco C56 issue. Each of the nine cards from this 36-card set has been graded and encapsulated within a protective holder. Lot includes: **PSA GOOD 2** — #14 Tom Dunderdale, #19 Jim Jones, #21 Jack Laviolette, #31 Horace Gaul, #34 Bruce Ridpath. **PSA VG 3** — #9 Angus Campbell, #10 Harry Hyland, #13 Ed Decary. **SGC VG 40** — #25 Art Bernier. **Minimum Bid: $250**

19285 **1911 Jack Marshall Sweet Caporal Postcard.** The direct predecessor to North America's current professional hockey league — the NHL — was the National Hockey Association, which operated from 1909-1917. The 1911 Sweet Caporal postcard set featured 45 players from the WHA's five teams that played that season. Extremely rare in any condition, these photographic postcards featured the same images that were used for he hobby-favorite C55 tobacco issue. The subject of the currently-offered Sweet Caporal is Hall of Fame star Jack Marshall, who was the first man in the game's history to win six Stanley Cups. He was also the first and one of only three men who have won Stanley Cups for four different clubs. His prominent exemplar from the postcard issue remains in beautiful condition and serves as one of the true vintage gems of the hobby. This may be the first one of this issue to come up for auction and will command the requisite attention from hobby enthusiasts. **Minimum Bid: $300**

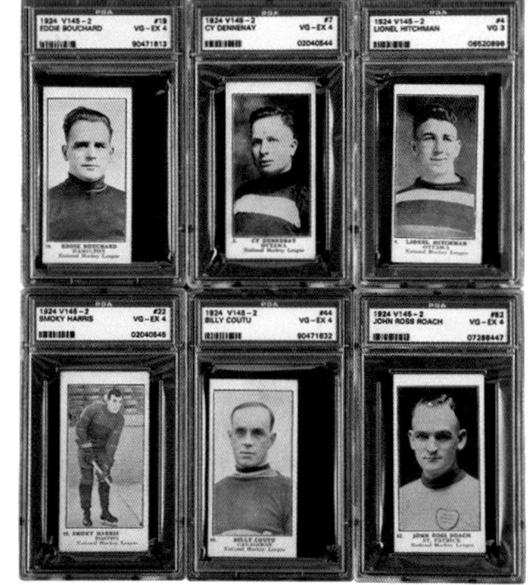

19286 **1924-25 V145-2 William Paterson Cards, PSA-Graded Group Lot of 6.** Redeemed in Paterson's chocolate bars, the V145-2 card issue featured NHL stars and were available from 1924-25. The 60-card set is highly coveted among collectors due to the impressive black and white photography that graces each entry. Here we present a glorious half-dozen PSA-graded cardboards from the V145-2 issue: **PSA VG-EX 4** — #7 Cy Dennenay, #19 Eddie Bouchard, #22 Smoky Harris, #44 Billy Coutu, #52 John Ross Roach. **PSA VG 3** — #4 Lionel Hitchman. **Minimum Bid: $150**

19287 **1963-64 Parkhurst High Grade Complete Hockey Set (99).** Offered is a high grade 1963/64 Parkhurst complete set. A total of 53 cards have been graded by PSA including several of the key HOF'ers. Over 50% of this set has been graded at a an astounding PSA NM-MT 8 or PSA MINT 9 level. A total of 53 cards have been graded by PSA with an aggregate SMR value of $3,700. Highlights include: **Graded Cards - PSA MINT 9:** 17 cards w/#'s 4, 5 Bower, 6, 10, 11, 16 Horton, 17 Mahavlich, 21, 33 Ferguson, 39 Worsley, 51, 54, 56, 58, 81, 87 and 89 Beliveau; **PSA NM-MT 8:** 34 cards w/#'s 8, 14, 18, 20, 23 Richard, 25, 28, 29 Geoffrion, 31 Tremblay, 34 Blake, 37, 45 Pronovost, 47, 48, 52 Ullman, 57, 62, 63 Kelly, 65 Bower, 67, 68, 70, 71, 72, 73 Armstrong, 74, 76 Horton, 77 Mahovlich, 79 Imlach, 82 Richard, 84, 90 Tremblay, 91 and 93 Blake; **PSA NM+ 7.5:** 1 card, #78; **PSA NM 7:** 1 card, #44. Ungraded Cards - include #'s 1 Stanley (EX), 30 Beliveau (EX), 42 Faulkner (), 53 Sawchuk (EX/MT), 55 Howe (), 69 Shack (VG), 75 Keon (), 88 Geoffrion (VG/EX), 92 Ferguson (EX), 98 Worsley (EX), 99 Maniago (GD, writing on reverse). **Minimum Bid: $500**

19288 **1953 – 1955 Topps World on Wheels Original Art (28).** Offered here is a good portion of the original artwork created by Topps artists for the 1953 issue known as World on Wheels. The set features vehicles from the past and present, as well as future concept cars. It was originally produced as a (160) card set in 1953, and then reissued in 1955 with an additional (20) cards to include newer models. Their phenomenal display character illustrates the care that was expended in the issue's planning and composing, and every one demonstrates concerted, painstaking artistry. Each hand-painted artwork measures about 5" x 3.5". Further, each has the expected, paste-up adhesive residue on the reverse. All of the artworks are extraordinarily vivid in color and detail, and all reflect minimally Near Mint preservation in their subject drawings. Designs and card numbers include: #37 Ford Model T, #41 Stanley Steamer, #57 VIM Stage, #64 Pierce Arrow, #70 Pumper Fire Engine, #76 Peerless Roadster, #105 Adams Farwell, #109 Leon Bolle, #112 De Deon Bouton, #113 Oldsmobile, #117 Ford La France, #120 Ohio Roadster, #121 Brewster, #129 Hoffman Vespa, #130 Volkswagen, #131 MG Sportscar, #133 Packard, #135 Reeves, #162, Thomas, #145 American Hosetruck, #147 Knox. The following (7) paintings have been hand-cut from the original 5"x 3.5" card: #31 Hose Truck, #36 Locomobile, #116 Knox runabout, #148 Apperson, #154 Pope, (2) Unidentified. **Minimum Bid: $2,000**

19289 **1944 R59 American Beauties Uncut Sheets Lot of 7.** Highly collectible war era pin-up set helped to remind the boys overseas what they were fighting for. Difficult to find in high-grade, this offering multiplies the rarity tenfold, providing seven uncut sheets in remarkably fine condition. Sheet 1: "Sitting Pretty" top left. Left six cards NM-MT, last column EX except for creased bottom right card. Sheet 2: "Out on a Limb" top left. NRMT to NM-MT throughout. Sheet 3: "Playing Safe" top left. Dings in three corners otherwise EX-MT to NRMT. Sheet 4: "Sport Model" top left. Ding at lower left corner, otherwise appears Mint. Sheet 5: "Sport Model" upper left. NRMT. Sheet 6: "Sitting Pretty" top left. VG. Sheet 7: "Ankles Aweigh" top left. EX to EX-MT. Slight crease on "No Stares" card. **Minimum Bid: $250**

19290 **Circa 1910 S67 Indian Chiefs Silks Large Premiums Lot of 6.** Super-rare large format (each approximately 4x6.5") silks utilize the same imagery as the N2 Allen & Ginter series issued in 1888, and while we've seen the smaller sized silks (2x3.25"), this is our first encounter with the expanded premiums. The silks are numbered "L-1" through "L-5," with the sixth trimmed below what we can only assume is "L-6," with signs of removed stitching running close to the borders as well. Other than the issues with this sixth specimen, the silks remain in splendid condition considering their age and delicacy, with only minor edge fraying and no staining, tearing or loss of brightness. A gorgeous, evocative sampling that speaks to the tremendous artistry of the early tobacco card hobby. **Minimum Bid: $250**

19291 **Circa 1910 S67 Indian Chiefs Silks Complete Set (50).** Utilizing the same artwork that appears on the N2 Allen & Ginter American Indian Chiefs series issued in 1888, these silks were issued by the American Tobacco Company - one per pack in Tokio cigarettes. Includes legendary American Indian figures Geronimo, Red Cloud, Sitting Bull, Chief Joseph and many others. An extremely attractive clean set with vivid coloring; it is beautifully framed at matted and ready for display. Nearly the entire set grades in the Excellent to Near Mint range. **Minimum Bid: $250**

BY LAND & BY SEA, PART ONE

19292 1955 Topps Rails & Sails Original Art (21). The Topps "Rails and Sails" set presents some of the most attractive gumcards ever made as the set's subjects are presented with historically accurate detail on 200 full-color cards, including 130 locomotives, railroad cars and other train-related items, as well as 70 military and civilian sailing ships. This lot offers one-of-a-kind painted artwork, measuring 5" x 3.5" and depicting (21) separate locomotives and railroad cars. All of the artworks are extraordinarily vivid in color and detail, and all reflect minimally Near Mint preservation in their subject drawings with standard working paste up residue on the verso. Designs and card numbers include: #1, #12, #18, #24, #39, #46, #58, #59, #71, #79, #80, #90, #92, #93, #95, #100, #109, #113, #114, #126, #129.. **Minimum Bid: $3,000**

BY LAND & BY SEA, PART TWO

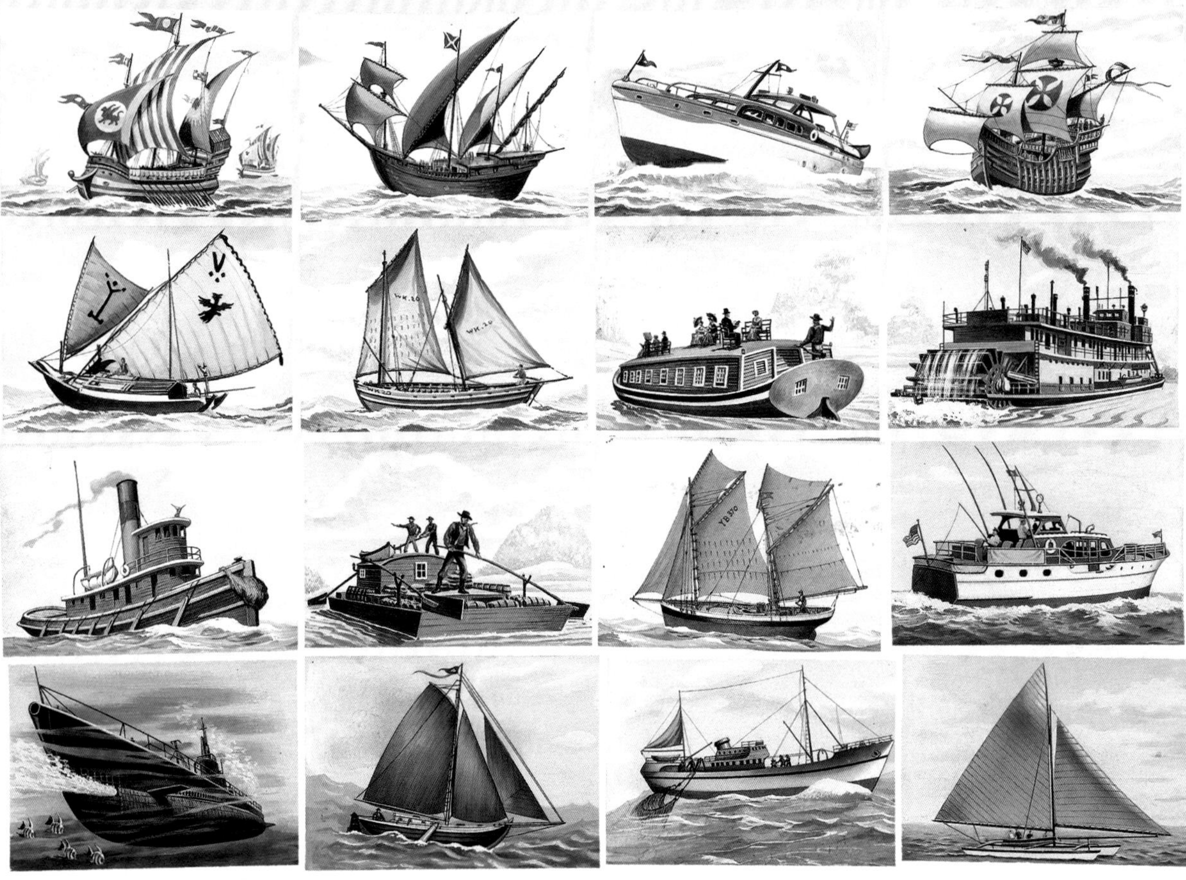

19293 **1955 Topps Rails & Sails Original Art (23).** The Topps "Rails and Sails" set presents some of the most attractive gumcards ever made as the set's subjects are presented with historically accurate detail on 200 full-color cards, including 130 locomotives, railroad cars and other train-related items, as well as 70 military and civilian sailing ships. This lot offers one-of-a-kind painted artwork, measuring 5" x 3.5" and depicting (23) separate military and civilian sailing ships. All of the artworks are extraordinarily vivid in color and detail, and all reflect minimally Near Mint preservation in their subject drawings with standard working paste up residue on the verso. Designs and card numbers include: #131, #134, #135, #137, #138, #139, #141, #142, #144, #145, #148, #153, #154, #158, #160, #164, #165, #167, #181, #182, #185, #192, #194. **Minimum Bid: $3,000**

19294 **1956 Topps Elvis Presley High Grade Complete Set (66).** Presented is a high grade complete set of the 1956 Topps Elvis Presley cards. These cards depicted "The King's" movies, personal preferences which helped his fans understand more about their idol. An impressive 55% of the cards are in the NM to NM/MT range. Additionally, 25 cards have been graded and encapsulated by PSA with an aggregate SMR value of $2,540. Highlights include: **Graded Cards - PSA NM-MT+ 8.5:** 1 card, #11; **PSA NM-MT 8:** 18 cards w/#'s 2 Elvis Checklist, 3, 4, 13, 14, 19, 20, 23, 27, 38, 41, 45, 46, 47, 48, 49, 62 and 63; **PSA NM 7:** 6 cards w/#'s 1 Go, Go, Go, Elvis, 26, 31, 37, 53 and 61. Grades **55% NM to NM/MT,** 45% EX to EX/MT. **Minimum Bid: $300**

19295 **1956 R749 Adventure Gum Products Inc. High-Grade Complete Set (100).** Offered is a high grade 1956 Gum Products Adventure Set. Scarce and desirable issue pictures the greatest pugilists of the day (and yester-year) against a patriotic backdrop of red, white and blue. Along with the pugilists, there are a whole other variety of cards that depicted other events. A total of 15 cards have been graded by PSA. Highlights include: **Graded Cards - PSA GEM MINT 10:** 1 card, #69 Shrine of Democracy; **PSA MINT 9:** 9 cards w/#'s 12, 38, 46, 52, 54, 55 Agganis, 59, 60 and 70; **PSA NM-MT 8:** 4 cards w/#'s 8, 23, 79 and 41 Louis; **PSA NM 7:** 1 card, #86 Schmeling. **Ungraded Cards** - include #'s 32 Johnson (NM), 34 Dempsey (NM), 44 Marciano (EX/MT), 76 Sullivan (NM). Grades 66% NM to NM/MT, 34% EX to EX/MT (some lesser). **Minimum Bid: $300**

19296 **1957 Target Moon Complete Set (88).** In late 1957 to early '58, Topps distributed a perplexing non-sport card issue. Hobbyists at the time acknowledged the release of an 88- card production called "Space Cards," but these were also presented with the title "Target: Moon." The two issues were exact twins in every respect, except for their identity. The sequence of their appearance is moot. For that matter, they were possibly retailed at the same time. To the production's credit, the imagery is colorful, and the futuristic narratives are creative. A total of 16 cards have been graded by PSA, including card #48 which is the only card that has attained the lofty PSA MINT 9 status. Highlights include: **Graded Cards - PSA MINT 9:** 1 card, #48; **PSA NM-MT+ 8.5:** 2 cards w/#'s 20 and 74; **PSA NM-MT 8:** 12 cards w/#'s 15, 26, 32, 35, 39, 46, 53, 54, 57, 75, 77 and 80; **PSA NM 7:** 1 card, #61. Grades 26% NM to NM/MT, 65% EX to EX/MT, 9% VG to VG/EX. **Minimum Bid: $200**

19297 **1959 Fleer Three Stooges High Grade Complete Set (96).** N'yuk, N'yuk! Woo, Woo, Woo! Unh, Unh, Unh! Soitenly the most successful comedy of all-time; Moe, Larry and either Curly, Shemp or Joe made a total of 195 Columbia Shorts between 1934 and 1958. The comedic giants made their cardboard debut a year later, when the Frank H. Fleer Corp. under license from Norman Maurer Productions, Inc. produced a 96-card full-color set. The cards were produced in soft pastel colors, which reminds us of the other 1959 Fleer issues, including the Ted Williams and Indian cards. A total of 38 cards have been graded by PSA with an aggregate SMR value of $5,675. Highlights include: **Graded Cards - PSA MINT 9:** 8 cards w/#'s 19, 28, 49, 52, 55, 57, 66 and 77; **PSA NM-MT 8:** 27 cards w/#'s 6, 8, 10, 16 Checklist, 20, 21, 24, 32, 33, 34, 35, 38, 50, 53, 54, 56, 71, 72, 74, 76, 78, 84, 85, 87, 89, 92 and 96 Trying The Squeeze Play; **PSA EX-MT 6:** 3 cards w/#'s 1 Curly, 2 Moe and 3 Larry. **Grades 59% NM to NM/MT,** 34% EX to EX/MT, 7% VG to VG/EX. **Minimum Bid: $500**

19298 **1962 Mars Attacks Burning Cattle #22 PSA Mint 9.** Not even the livestock is safe from the brutality of the Martian invaders, though Old McDonald appears ready to fight back with his shotgun at upper right. This twenty-second card in this comical and gory set is the finest known to exist, sharing that title with just one other card at the top of the PSA population charts. **Minimum Bid: $250**

19299 **1962 Mars Attacks Creeping Menace #37 PSA Mint 9.** A massive red-eyed insect lays waste to suburbia as a family scrambles for cover upon this simply flawless card from the beloved Kennedy-era "sci fi" set. Only one other example of this card has matched the perfection of the offered specimen, with none ever charting higher. **Minimum Bid: $250**

19300 **1962 Mars Attacks Terror in Times Square #8 PSA Mint 9.** The aliens do damage to the heart of Manhattan that not even Rudy Giuliani could clean up. But the Martian mess stands in stark contrast to the glossy perfection of the offered card, which stands alone without a single equal at the top of the PSA population chart. A true "one of one." **Minimum Bid: $250**

MARS STARS

19301 **1962 Topps High Grade Mars Attacks Complete Set (55).** Offered is a high grade 1962 Topps Mars Attacks Set. Simultaneously charming in its cartoonish design and horrifying in its depictions of extreme violence, this Kennedy-era set remains one of the collecting hobby's favorite non-sports issues. The fifty-five cards take us through the Martians' attempted conquest of earth, sparing not a drop of blood and gore, and culminates with Earth's eventual counter-attack that leaves our orbital neighbor wishing they'd never stepped into their spaceships. The quality of this high grade set is evident in the 25 cards slabbed by PSA, which have an aggregate SMR value of $3,900. The 3 cards that have been graded PSA NM-MT+ 8.5 are the highest graded by PSA, with no 9's. Highlights include: **Graded Cards - PSA NM-MT+ 8.5:** 3 cards w/#'s 2, 33 and 51; **PSA NM-MT 8:** 13 cards w/#'s 5, 12, 14, 23, 25, 28, 29, 35, 36, 41, 46, 48 and 52; **PSA NM 7:** 9 cards w/#'s 1 The Invasion Begins, 6, 10, 13, 15, 18, 34, 49 and 55 Checklist. Grades **46% NM to NM/MT,** 45% EX to EX/MT, 9% VG to VG/EX. **Minimum Bid: $1,000**

19302 **1964 Topps Beatles Collection (295).** When looking for a wise non-sports investment, The Beatles should be at the top of anyone's list - given their enduring popularity. The impact of the Beatles upon popular music cannot be overstated; they revolutionized the music industry and touched the lives of all who heard them in deep and fundamental ways. Includes Topps Beatles B&W, Series I - 60-card set with 33 extras; Series II - 50 of 55-card set with 35 extras; Series III - 50-card set with 67 extras. Lot totals 295 Beatles cards from the three series. Six 2nd Series cards have been graded by SGC and include - **SGC 96 Mint 9:** #83; **SGC 88 NM/MT 8:** #77, 104, 106, 110; **SGC 84 NM 7:** #86. Balance of the cards grade from EX to NM, 15% lesser (due to centering). **Minimum Bid: $200**

19303 **1965 Topps Battle High Grade Complete Set (66).** Difficult to find in any condition, the Topps Battle set from 1965 is similar in nature to its predecessor — the 1930s classic Horrors of War — with its often graphic depiction of the gore and violence associated with war. In a sense, the set was just mirroring parallel developments in the new popular medium of TV which was bringing the war into viewers' living rooms. A total of 23 cards have been graded by PSA. Card #'s 58 and 65 are the only PSA 9's. **Highlights include: Graded Cards - PSA MINT 9:** 6 cards w/#'s 14, 25, 51, 58, 63 Roosevelt (OC) and 65 Cloth Emblem Checklist; **PSA NM-MT+ 8.5:** 1 card, #54; **PSA NM-MT 8:** 15 cards w/#'s 1 Fight to the Death, 5, 6, 9, 20, 26, 27, 28, 34, 35, 42, 49, 53, 59 and 62; **PSA NM 7:** 1 card, #47. **Grades 61% NM to NM/MT,** 39% EX to EX/MT (some lesser). **Minimum Bid: $200**

19304 **1967 Topps Nutty Initial Stickers Original Art (30).** In 1967 Norman Saunders was hired to paint the "Love Letters" series for Topps and he proposed a new idea for a different alphabet series based on these twisted creatures, which are contorted into letter shapes that came to be known as Nutty Initial Stickers. Here we offer the original art for the set, which includes the entire alphabet as well as (4) symbols with the only missing art being the exclamation point. All of the images are designed and painted by Norman Saunders. Their phenomenal display character illustrates the care that was expended in the issue's planning and composing, and every one demonstrates concerted, painstaking artistry. Each hand-painted artwork measures about 4.5" x 3.5". Further, each has the expected, paste-up adhesive residue on the reverse. All of the artworks are extraordinarily vivid in color and detail, and all reflect minimally Near Mint preservation in their subject drawings. **Minimum Bid: $3,000**

THIS IS ONLY A TEST...

19305 **1973 Topps Comics Test Issue High Grade Complete Set (24).** Strictly a test issue, if ever publicly issued at all, the 24 players in the 1973 Topps Comics issue appear on 4-5/8" x 3-7/16" waxed paper wrappers. The design is similar to the popular Bazooka Joe comics and they were intended to be a wrapper for pieces of bubble gum. The inside of the wrapper combines a color photo and facsimile autograph with a comic-style presentation of the player's career highlights. Some of the lesser known players are listed for $200 a piece, while the Nolan Ryan lists for $3,500 in NM condition. With every comic graded by PSA, here is a golden opportunity to own the entire set in high grade. Highlights include: **Graded Cards - PSA MINT 9:** 11 cards w/Johnny Bench, Steve Carlton, Nate Colbert, Harmon Killebrew, Willie McCovey, Gaylord Perry, Lou Piniella, Tom Seaver, Willie Stargell, Joe Torre and Billy Williams; **PSA NM-MT+ 8.5:** 1 card, Reggie Jackson; **PSA NM-MT 8:** 10 cards w/ Hank Aaron, Dick Allen, Willie Davis, Mickey Lolich, Mike Marshall, Bobby Murcer, Brooks Robinson, Nolan Ryan, George Scott, Carl Yastrzemski; **PSA EX-MT 6:** 2 cards w/ Mike Epstein and Lee May. **Minimum Bid: $2,500**

19306 The Net 54 Vintage Baseball Card Forum Charity Auction Lot. This special lot consists of (64) items that were all donated by generous members of the Net 54 Vintage Baseball Card Forum and all of the proceeds from this lot, including the buyer's premium, will be donated to charity.

The lot is comprised of the following: **1)** 1888 N135 Talk of the Diamond "He Serves the Ball" (VG-EX) **2)** 1888 WG1 Pettit (Hand Cut) **3)** 1908 E102 Bescher PSA 2 Good 2 (MK) **4)** 1909 E97 Briggs Birmingham SGC 20 Fair 1.5 **5)** (7) 1909-1911 T206 Ball PSA 3, Clark SGC 50, Egan SGC 40, Lavender SGC 40, Liebhardt (VG), Mitchell (VG-EX), Titus (VG) **6)** (4) Circa 1910 T203 Mayos Baseball Comics (Paper loss on verso of each) **7)** 1910 T212 Obak Thorsen SGC 30 Good 2 **8)** 1910 T210 Old Mill Manion (Good - Pencil marks on verso) **9)** 1910-11 M116 Hoblitzel SGC 40 VG 3 **10)** 1911 T205 Blackburne SGC 40 VG 3 **11)** 1912 C46 Batch SGC 20 Fair 1.5 **12)** 1913 National Game Gregg PSA 8 NM-MT **13)** (10) 1914 B18 Blankets: Burns, Cutshaw, Fletcher, Hartzell, Hummel, Keating, Moeller, Pratt, Rucker, Wheat. **14)** 1914 Cracker Jack # 97 Benton (Poor, paper loss) **15)** 1916 M101-5 Bancroft SGC 10 Poor 1 **16)** 1919 T213 Coupon Dubuc (VG) **17)** 1920 W514 Jess Barnes (Hand Cut, Writing on verso) **18)** 1920 Zeenut Reilly (Hand Cut - VG-EX) **19)** 1921 E121 American Caramel George Kelly SGC 50 VG-EX 4. **20)** 1928 W565 Pugilists Complete Set of 5 (Hand Cut, EX-MT to NM) **21)** 1931 Giants Postcards Carl Hubbell (EX, pencil mark on verso) **22)** 1933 Goudey Luque # 209 SGC 20 Fair 1.5 **23)** 1933 Goudey Swanson # 195 SGC 20 Fair 1.5 **24)** 1933 Goudey Vaughan # 229 SGC 40 VG 3 **25)** 1933 Goudey Schulte # 190 SGC 40 VG 3 **26)** 1933 Tatoo Orbit Frank O'Doul SGC 40 VG 3 **27)** 1933 W574 Frank Grube (VG-EX) **28)** 1934-36 Diamond Matchbook Paul Waner (Good) **29)** (2) 1935 Diamond Star # 40 Ryan (good w/ pencil marks) #70 Trosky (VG) **30)** 1936 WWG Rowe 334 SGC 50 VG-EX 4 **31)** 1939 Play Ball # 113 Al Schacht (VG) **32)** (3) 1940 Play Ball #49 Weatherly (EX-MT)# 116 Schacht (Poor), #144 Vosmik (VG) **33)** 1946-50 D317 Oakland Oaks Team Set (14) (4 VG-EX or lesser, Hafey Trimmed, 10 Ex or better) **34)** 1948 Leaf Hermanski SGC 40 VG 3 **35)** 1948 Leaf Spahn (Good) **36)** 1951 Baseball Encyclopedia **37)** 1951 Topps Red Back Near Set (51/52) w/ wax wrapper, missing Snider (60% VG-EX or lesser, 40% EX) **38)** (3) 1955-60 Bill and Bob Postcards (EX): Burdette (Signed), Crandall (Signed), Haney **39)** (2) 1960's Exhibit Cards: Aaron (Ex-Mt), Banks (EX) **40)** 1963 Kahn's Frank Robinson (VG-EX) **41)** 1981 TCMA Wade Boggs PSA 9 Mint **42)** 1985 Topps Roger Clemens PSA 8 NM-MT **43)** Unidentified Hank Greenberg Postcard.

This project was conceived and coordinated by the members of the Net 54 Vintage Baseball Card Forum and we are proud that Heritage was chosen to contribute our services. We would like to acknowledge Kyle Bicking who came up with the concept and took the time to coordinate and accept all of the donated materials. In addition, we would like to acknowledge each of the twenty four following collectors who took time and made the effort to contribute valuable cards from their personal collections to make this a truly special auction offering: Bruce Babcock, Kyle Bicking, Mark Bowers, Dan Bretta, David Davis, Rob Dewolf, Ben Fisher, Rob Gutheil, Sean Besser Hank, Tom Hines, Leon Luckey, Bruce MacPherson, Darren Magness, Stephen R. Murray, Martin Neal, Trae Regan, Bob Shannon, Barry Sloate, David Stambaugh, Anthony Stephenson, Alan Ugal, Brian Weisner, Ricky Yoneda, and Scot York.

The charity that has been chosen by the Network 54 members is Surfers Healing, which seeks to enrich the lives of children with autism and the lives of their families by exposing them to the unique experience of surfing. Surfers Healing is a nonprofit organization with 501(c)(3) status. For additional information, please go to www.SurfersHealing.org. For this special charity lot we request that the winner make the check payable directly to "Surfers Healing". **Minimum Bid: $500**

End of Session One

VINTAGE SPORTS COLLECTIBLES

Live, Internet, and Mail Bid Signature Auction #709 • Session Two • Lots 19307-19884
Saturday, May 3, 2008 • 12:00 NOON CT • Dallas, Texas

A 19.5% Buyer's Premium ($9 Minimum) Will Be Added To All Lots.

Visit HA.com/Sports to view scalable images and bid online.

One of the most exciting "finds" of 2007 will present bidders in the Heritage Auction Galleries May 2008 Signature Sports Auction with the opportunity to own what are unquestionably the finest PM1 pins on the face of the earth. The nine pins were located by Heritage's consignors at an Arkansas flea market and purchased for a song, the seller unaware of the tremendous scarcity and importance of the treasures.

The discovery of these pins sheds a small beam of light upon an issue that still remains largely shrouded in mystery. Though it has been established that these Ornate-frame Pins date to 1915, the identity of the original issuer and the mode of distribution remain an enigma. This stunning assortment Mint pins adds a Hall of Famer to the known roster of PM1's, providing the hobby with its first look at a Chief Bender model. And the balance of the find, featuring Frank Baker, Frank Chance, Al Demaree, Ty Cobb, Johnny Evers (name only), Walter Johnson, Benny Kauff and Joe Tinker, each remain attached to its original 2x2" blank card, also never before encountered in the hobby.

Those few hobbyists who have met with this rare issue are well aware that condition problems are accepted as an inevitability when collecting PM1's, with oxidation and damage to the delicate metal frame and scratching of the central image present on essentially all existing specimens. The Mint condition of this Arkansas find is quite literally unprecedented, and should pique the interest of many elite collectors who demand nothing but the very best.

19307 **1915 PM1 Ornate Frame Pins Frank Baker.** After three World Series and four American League Championships, "Home Run" Baker would sit out the entire 1915 season that this pin was issued in a contract dispute with Connie Mack, effectively ending his Hall of Fame service to the Philadelphia Athletics. Here he demonstrates the form that earned him the long ball crown from 1911 through 1914. **Minimum Bid: $2,500**

19308 **1915 PM1 Ornate Frame Pins Chief Bender.** Arguably the most desirable of the stunning assortment of PM1's from "The Arkansas Find" is this specimen paying tribute to the Hall of Fame right-hander who spent the 1915 year of issue plying his trade for the Baltimore Terrapins of the Federal League. Until this pin's discovery late in 2007, the Bender model was unknown to the hobby. **Minimum Bid: $2,500**

19309 **1915 PM1 Ornate Frame Pins Frank Chance.** The 1913 season saw big changes for the New York Americans, who traded their "Highlanders" nickname and Hilltop Park home field for the "Yankees" and the Polo Grounds respectively. This is the man who took the reins at the start of that new era, striking a batting stance for a pin that would be issued the first year of his retirement. **Minimum Bid: $2,500**

19310 **1915 PM1 Ornate Frame Pins Ty Cobb.** The greatest name of the Dead Ball era demonstrates the wide stance and grip that gave birth to over 4,000 hits. The most extensively represented baseball figure from the tobacco days, Cobb is found in Mint condition in only a small handful of the thousands of surviving cards and pins of the era. Certainly this competes for the finest playing-days issue of all. **Minimum Bid: $2,500**

19311 **1915 PM1 Ornate Frame Pins Al Demaree.** He shared a pitching rotation with Mathewson, Marquard, Rixey and Alexander during his years in New York and Philly. Here he is captured at the close of the right-handed delivery that carried him through eight successful National League seasons. **Minimum Bid: $2,500**

19312 **1915 PM1 Ornate Frame Pins Johnny Evers.** The celebrated Chicago Cubs second baseman joins teammate Joe Tinker in this incredible find of PM1 pins, likewise sporting a uniform of 1907 design. The slightest degree of oxidation is apparent at the upper edge of the metal frame, but the pin is otherwise in magnificent shape. **Minimum Bid: $2,500**

19313 **1915 PM1 Ornate Frame Pins Walter Johnson.** The Big Train continued his fireballing dominance of the American League the season this pin was issued, taking the top position is such pitching categories as victories, strike outs, complete games and shut outs. **Minimum Bid: $2,500**

19314 **1915 PM1 Ornate Frame Pins Benny Kauff.** A member of the Federal League's Brooklyn Tip-Tops at the time of issue, Kauff led that rogue league in batting average and stolen bases in 1915. A touch of oxidation at the exterior metal frame is noted for accuracy's sake, but the pin remains in stellar condition otherwise. **Minimum Bid: $2,500**

19315 **1915 PM1 Ornate Frame Pins Joe Tinker.** One-third of the greatest double play combination in baseball history, Tinker lets one fly here in the uniform of the 1907 Chicago Cubs, a rather unusual photographic choice for a fellow representing the Federal League Chicago Whales at the time of issue. **Minimum Bid: $2,500**

19316 **Circa 1918 Babe Ruth Single Signed Baseball.** Magnificent and ancient rarity dates to the age when Babe Ruth was known as a superstar pitcher, and not the game's premier slugger as history remembers him today. Though wear subsequent to the baseball's signing has diminished the boldness of the autograph to a rating of 2/10 to 3/10, the autograph is unmistakable in its rookie-era styling, far smaller than the more commonly seen model dating from the mid-1920's and beyond. This signature carries particular intrigue for its placement upon an Official National League baseball, which would rather firmly suggest that the ball was autographed during the 1918 World Series, the only reasonable explanation for the Babe's proximity to a Senior Circuit sphere. The "Cork Center" stamping of the ball assures 1917-25 vintage, though, again, the signature style directs us to the earlier portion of that range. No serious collector need be told what a significant premium is attached to Ruth material from his Red Sox days, so we expect great bidding interest in this special artifact. *LOA from PSA/DNA. LOA from James Spence Authentication.* **Minimum Bid: $2,000**

19317 **Circa 1920 Grover Cleveland Alexander Signed Baseball.** The slanted "Cork Center" words that frame the Official National League stamping of the offered sphere allow us to pin the manufacturing date to the period between 1914 and 1925, ensuring that the Alexander signature it houses is of "playing days" variety. As tough as it is to find Old Pete on any baseball whatsoever, those that do arise are typically the result of his later barnstorming activities, making this piece all the more scarce and desirable. As a legitimate "single," the price tag for this ball would be off the charts, but the lovely 6/10 black fountain pen autograph was once joined by several others which have been expertly removed by a chemical process to leave not even a pale ghost of their former presence. Those trying to complete a run of singles from the Hall of Fame's inaugural class will find this troubled but brilliant right-hander to be the toughest by far, so expect some real competition when this ball reaches the auction block. *LOA from PSA/DNA. LOA from James Spence Authentication.* **Minimum Bid: $1,500**

19318 **Mid-1920's Sam Rice Signed Baseball.** The Ban Johnson stamping on this highly desirable red and blue stitched Official American League baseball allows us to date this offering definitively to the period prior to Ernest Barnard's 1928 assumption of the League presidency, suggesting a close proximity to the Washingon Senators' most glorious era. One of that club's most noteworthy stars, Hall of Fame outfielder Sam Rice, appears in 8/10 black fountain pen ink upon a side panel, providing the appearance of a $3,000+ single. We must confess that a chemical process has stripped the sphere of earlier neighbors to Rice, though this work has been done with such skill so as to be undetectable by the naked eye. Definitely a Senator worthy of your vote. *LOA from PSA/DNA. LOA from James Spence Authentication.* **Minimum Bid: $500**

19319 **1927 Babe Ruth & Lou Gehrig Signed "Stat" Baseball.** We've never seen anything quite like the offered sphere, and we don't expect to ever see another. While today it is commonplace for athletes to enhance their autographs with various facts, figures and notations, such was not the case back in 1927, when this special ball was signed. It appears that the ball was initially autographed in black ink by Ruth, Bob Meusel, Dazzy Vance and perhaps a few others, and while Ruth is still quite visible at 3/10, the same cannot be said of his black ink companions, which border on complete disappearance. At a later time, we believe, a blue ink pen was presented to Gehrig along with this ball, and, for some unknown reason, he was compelled to add his 1927 home run total of "47" below his autograph. We believe that, at this point, that pen was handed to Ruth, who added in blue ink beside his black autograph, "Oct. 27, 1927, 60 Home Runs." While a famous signed photo making reference to this historic record-setting accomplishment, sold in the famous Barry Halper auction in 1999, is known in the hobby, we are not aware of any baseball that does so. And we couldn't imagine any that might include Gehrig's stunning long ball total as well. Ruth and Gehrig's blue ink writing is a good bit stronger at 7/10, but a rarity such as this makes talk of condition seem almost crass. We're also a bit confused by the baseball, which clearly has "American League Ball" stamping, but further stamping just above that matches no known official ball, and black and red stitching besides (rather than blue and red, as is proper for period OAL balls). But all of these mysteries aside, we're left with one of the most exciting Ruth/Gehrig signed baseballs ever to reach the hobby's auction block. *LOA from PSA/DNA. LOA from James Spence Authentication.* **Minimum Bid: $4,000**

19320 **1927 Babe Ruth & Lou Gehrig Signed Baseball.** While the tremendous visual quality of this autographed baseball is certain to appeal to all fans of the sport's most fearsome slugging duo, the true Yankee historian is bound to fall desperately in love for yet another reason. From the minor variation present in the stamping of this ONL (Heydler) ball, we are able to peg it definitively to the 1927 season. And why would Lou and the Babe be in the presence of a National League ball? The only logical conclusion is that the venue of the signing was Pittsburgh's Forbes Field on either October sixth or seventh, the dates of the first two games of the 1927 World Series. This relic from the absolute pinnacle of New York Yankees glory features a brilliantly bold black fountain pen sweet spot signature from the sixty home run hero, projecting at a boldness of 8.5/10, touched only by a minor degree of surface wear. Below him we find an 8/10 Lou Gehrig, the American League's Most Valuable Player. This remarkable quality is due in some degree to a coating of shellac, which has mellowed to a caramel tone, adding to the vintage patina of this delectable piece. *LOA from PSA/DNA. LOA from James Spence Authentication.* **Minimum Bid: $3,000**

19321 **Circa 1928 Babe Ruth & Lou Gehrig Signed Baseball.** Equal in quality to Ruth and Gehrig signed spheres that have summited the $40,000 mark at auction, this outrageously high-grade specimen should realistically approach a similar level despite the addition of contemporary Boston Red Sox Bill Carrigan and Ira Flagstead, particularly given the fact that Carrigan managed Ruth in Boston upon his arrival in the Majors. Matching the ideal bold composition of the four black fountain pen autographs upon this "Brine's Official League Ball" are the signatures' ideal placement, each very effectively presenting as a single upon its own hemisphere of horsehide. The subtle variations in the formation of the Ruth and Gehrig autographs, paired with the fact that Carrigan and Flagstead shared a dugout just two and a half seasons, allow us to date the ball with great confidence to the period between 1927 and 1929, coinciding with the absolute height of Murderer's Row Yankeedom. We must note that our authenticators believe the ball was professionally cleaned to remove grime accumulated over the passing decades, though this will not be apparent upon display. A splendid addition to any high-end baseball autograph collection. *LOA from PSA/DNA. LOA from James Spence Authentication.* **Minimum Bid: $6,000**

19322 **1928 Babe Ruth & Lou Gehrig Signed Baseball.** In a time when Big League baseball ventured no further west than the Mississippi River, these Yankee Hall of Famers were the game's greatest ambassadors, touring the nation and later the world to showcase their talents. This Official International League ball dates from the pinstriped duo's American barnstorming days in the weeks following their four-game annihilation of the St. Louis Cardinals in the Series. Ruth and Gehrig are ideally positioned on a side panel for simultaneous display, with the black fountain pen ink still intensely bold, though affected to a degree by surface wear to rate a technical 7/10 and 5/10 respectively. Our catalog imagery should illustrate that the cracked brown horsehide, darkened on two panels by a coating of shellac, still presents very nicely. The panel to the north of the autographs is notated "Oct. 21, 1928" in an unknown hand. A fine artifact from the heart of the Murderer's Row era. *LOA from PSA/DNA. LOA from James Spence Authentication.* Minimum Bid: $2,500

19323 **Late 1920's Babe Ruth & Lou Gehrig Signed Baseball.** "They didn't get along," Tony Lazzeri once said of his fellow Hall of Fame Yankee teammates. "Lou thought Ruth was a big-mouth, and Ruth thought Gehrig was cheap. They were both right." Though despite the low-grade feud that followed the duo throughout much of their eleven seasons in pinstripes together, no two ballplayers remain linked quite so firmly in baseball's history book. This "Official Partridge League" sphere plays its small role in maintaining this troubled yet extraordinarily successful partnership, offering a sweet spot signature from the Babe and a side panel Gehrig specimen. Each is rendered in black fountain pen ink on the lightly and evenly toned horsehide surface, with Ruth rating an attractive 6/10, and Gehrig perhaps a shade lighter at 5/10. A clean and solid specimen from the most consistent investment performers in the sports collecting hobby. *LOA from PSA/DNA. LOA from James Spence.* Minimum Bid: $3,000

19324 **Circa 1930 Goose Goslin Signed Baseball.** A key component in the delivery of the Senators' only World Championship to the fans in our nation's capital in 1924, the Hall of Fame outfielder led the American League that season with an astounding 129 runs batted in. His tough 9+/10 blue ink signature is provided here for the cultured collector, one of the finest we've encountered from the 1968 Hall of Fame inductee on a baseball. Professional removal of all other signatures that once joined Goslin's upon this ball has also claimed the sphere's stamping, but the red and blue stitching strongly suggests this is a pre-1935 Official American League model. With genuine Goslin singles all but nonexistent in the hobby, this bold vintage offering should turn more than a few heads, and spirited bidding is expected. *LOA from PSA/DNA.* **Minimum Bid: $500**

19325 **Circa 1930 Lewis "Hack" Wilson Single Signed Baseball.** Although just five-foot six inches tall, Wilson tipped the scales at 195 pounds of muscle, with an eighteen inch neck but just size six shoes. One sports writer suggested he was built along the lines of a beer keg, and not wholly unfamiliar with its contents. Sadly, the Hall of Fame slugger's life was cut short by his alcoholism at age forty-eight soon after the close of the Second World War, and a full thirty-one years before Cooperstown came calling. One could point to these factors to explain the scarcity of his autograph in the hobby today, particularly in the single signed baseball format of the offered lot. Unquestionably the toughest member of the Fifty Home Run Club, Wilson provides a marvelous 9/10 black fountain pen signature on the side panel of this Pacific Coast League ball. Some surface wear flirts with the edges of the autograph but never intersects, as if understanding just how rare and special it is. A rare opportunity to elevate your collection to a level that few others match. *LOA from James Spence Authentication.* **Minimum Bid: $2,000**

19326 **1930's Bucky Harris Signed Baseball.** Pick your favorite Bucky Harris autograph and display it proudly as a single. There are two here from which to choose, while other signatures that once resided upon the "Dizzy Dean Major League" ball have been expertly removed by a chemical process that has left behind no hint of the former inhabitants. The Harris autographs rate 8/10 and 7/10 respectively, quality that would garner a price tag in the neighborhood of $5,000 as a legitimate single. Despite his long service to the game, Harris is very rarely found alone on a baseball, making this offering an appealing fall back plan for the collector looking to fill that gap in his holdings. *LOA from PSA/DNA. LOA from James Spence Authentication.* **Minimum Bid: $300**

19328 **Circa 1934 Babe Ruth Single Signed Baseball.** Now deep into his eighties, our consignor still clearly recalls the thrill of meeting his baseball idol as a young schoolboy at Washington D.C.'s Griffith Stadium. His charming notarized letter of provenance details the moment wonderfully, reading in part, *"I ran toward the Babe; at that moment a hostile looking usher appeared and ordered me off the field. Then I heard the Babe's friendly voice saying, 'That's OK. Come over here son.' He signed my ball. I thanked him profusely and he gave me that great big wonderful grin of his."* He also notes, though admits he cannot be completely certain, that this may have well happened on the final day of the 1934 season, which would ultimately prove to be the Babe's last in a Yankees uniform. Whether this was the last ball signed as a Yankee or not, the appeal is undeniable. The black fountain pen sweet spot signature still maintains a boldness of 7/10, and the ONL (Heydler) ball, brought from home by the young fan, is evenly toned with a few scattered spots of foxing well clear of the autograph. A rock-solid specimen of an essential ball, made all the more appealing by its sweet history. *LOA from PSA/DNA. LOA from James Spence Authentication.* **Minimum Bid: $2,000**

19327 **1932 Babe Ruth & Lou Gehrig Signed Baseball.** Note the faint remnants of the red John Heydler presidential stamping on the side panel of this Official National League ball? That's a single-year style, issued only during the year 1932. And we can think of only one occasion that would have brought this pair face to face with an NL ball, and that's the World Series at Wrigley, where the Babe taught the taunting Cubs a lesson with his famed Called Shot. Historical suppositions aside, however, there's still much to love about this fine specimen. The Babe's sweet spot signature, and Lou's offering to the west, each present at a strong 7/10, and the black and red stitched sphere provides a marvelous vintage patina of evenly toned horsehide. A special keepsake from the era of the Babe's most celebrated moment. *LOA from PSA/DNA. LOA from James Spence Authentication.* **Minimum Bid: $4,000**

19329 **1934 Dizzy & Daffy Dean Signed Baseball.** Ford Frick's ascendance to the National League presidency in 1935 assures that this ONL (Heydler) sphere could only have been autographed during these fraternal Gashouse Gangsters' glorious World Championship season of 1934, the rookie season for the younger Dean. One can't overstate the importance of Paul and Jerome Dean in the annals of St. Louis Cardinals history, as the pair combined for forty-nine regular season victories in 1934, and all four of the club's Series wins. Given this supreme historic relevance, the outstanding condition of this autographed sphere is practically overkill. Each signature presents with 9+/10 boldness, and the ball itself is wonderfully clean with a gorgeous creamy tone. We simply couldn't imagine a superior specimen. *LOA from James Spence Authentication.* **Minimum Bid: $1,000**

19330 **1934 Babe Ruth, Tris Speaker and More Signed Baseball.** Our consignor reports that this baseball was passed down to him with the story that it derived from a Toronto banquet recognizing Babe Ruth's 700th home run, and the twentieth anniversary of his first professional homer as a pitcher for the Providence Grays in an International League meeting with the Toronto Maple Leafs. The Babe (2/10) was forced to a side panel position by the stern Kenesaw Mountain Landis (9/10), who claimed Ruth's customary sweet spot position before the Babe got his hands on this Official National League ball. Other titans of the diamond who turned out to honor the Babe's long ball legacy include Speaker (7/10), Mack (8/10), Giles (6/10), Rickey (9/10) and Cleveland Indians manager Steve O'Neill. Seventeen autographs are here in total, with the balance mainly representatives of the International League, and tending toward the higher end of the boldness scale. A light coating of shellac has given the ball an amber tone but has served its intended purpose well. *LOA from PSA/DNA. LOA from James Spence Authentication.* Minimum Bid: $1,500

19331 **The Earliest Known Satchel Paige Single Signed Baseball, 1935.** Intriguing and important relic is perhaps the only known surviving piece of memorabilia from the inaugural "Little World Series" of the National Baseball Congress, the brainchild of Wichita sporting goods salesman Hap Dumont to bring top level semi-pro baseball to the Midwest during the Depression. In order to assure the first Series would be a success, Dumont offered the exorbitant sum of $1,000 to Satchel Paige's Bismarck (ND) touring team, an offer gladly accepted by the eventual Champs. Paige would strike out sixty batters and win four games, each mark still standing as a tournament record to this day. The ball is artfully emblazoned with the the words, "First Little World's Series, Aug. 1935, Wichita, Kansas," with Paige signing the southern panel in his early "Satchell" double-L format, adding "Bismarck Ball Club" below. Paige's autograph and inscription survive at an impressive strength of 7/10. The ball exhibits a degree of toning and surface abrasions, but neither issue is of any noteworthy concern. An exceedingly scarce Negro League playing-days single for the advanced autograph collector. *LOA from PSA/DNA. LOA from James Spence Authentication.* Minimum Bid: $1,000

19332 **Circa 1935 Hall of Famers Multi-Signed Baseball with Foxx, Lazzeri.** While we cannot date this "Official League Ball" with complete certainty, the cast of characters is likely explained by a mid-1930's meeting between the Philadelphia Athletics and the New York Yankees, as all resident autographs could be traced to those camps. Seven signatures are here in total: Foxx, Lazzeri, Combs, Dickey, Higgins, Warstler and Connie Mack, Jr. Both Foxx and Lazzeri display quite convincingly as singles, adding further appeal to a ball that has no shortage of such. Autograph strength varies from 6/10 to 8/10, clearly well inside the acceptable range for a septuagenarian sphere. *LOA from PSA/DNA. LOA from James Spence Authentication.* Minimum Bid: $600

19333 **Babe Ruth, Lou Gehrig & Joe DiMaggio Signed Baseball.** Numbers Three, Four and Five stack up in a row on this Official International League ball, answering the prayers that any serious Yankee collector would have never even dared to dream. The magical trio is the result of an autograph hunt spanning decades, as Ruth and Gehrig's black fountain pen signatures (rating 5/10 in strength) clearly predate DiMaggio's 9/10 blue ballpoint offering by half a century. Intriguingly, the anachronistic assortment doesn't end there. Another side panel features the 6/10 black fountain pen signature of Hall of Famer Bill McKechnie, which he dates "July 23/29." It's interesting to note that this marks the day that he was reinstated as manager of the St. Louis Cardinals, ending a failed experiment placing Billy Southworth at the reins. Another rotation of the ball finds legendary pugilist Jack Dempsey, who dates his 5/10 blue ink signature "5/16/60." Bob Feller and Lou Boudreau also appear to have been added in later years, and a final unidentifiable light black ink signature dates to the prewar era. Will the winning bidder put it in his trophy case, or keep the project going? Derek Jeter and Alex Rodriguez might be options to consider. Regardless, you can be sure you won't find a ball quite this intriguing any time soon. *LOA from PSA/DNA. LOA from James Spence Authentication.* Minimum Bid: $3,000

SPHERE OF INFLUENCE

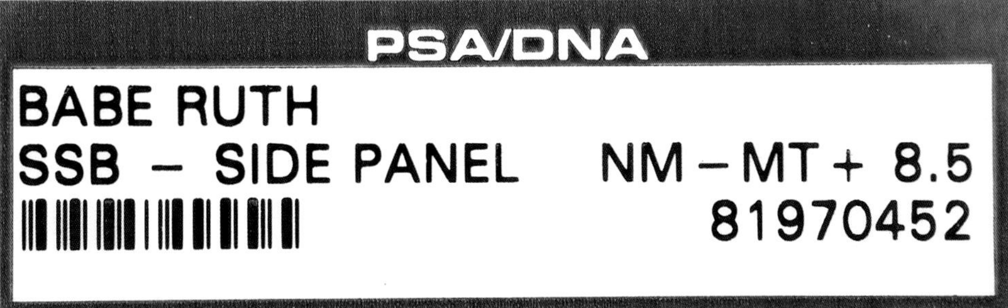

PSA/DNA
BABE RUTH
SSB – SIDE PANEL NM – MT + 8.5
81970452

19334 **Late 1930's Babe Ruth Single Signed Baseball, PSA NM-MT+ 8.5.** We'll never know the full identity of the "Malcolm" to whom the Bambino personalized this OAL (Harridge) ball, but we know he must have been a responsible fellow. Whereas so many of the Babe's baseballs were taken out to the sandlot, or left to rattle around dresser drawers for decades, the presented example was clearly tucked away in a dark,dry place and forgotten. The result is one of the highest grade Ruth singles you'll encounter, with the black fountain pen ink spelling, "To Malcolm From Babe Ruth" and the baseball itself each meriting grades of 8/10 from the tough graders at PSA/DNA. With an extra half-point added for "eye appeal," the result of NM-MT 8.5 is still probably a bit conservative. If condition is one of your major collecting concerns, this sphere should be prominent upon your auction radar. *LOA from PSA/DNA. LOA from James Spence Authentication.* **Minimum Bid:** $10,000

19335 Circa 1938 Chuck Klein & Honus Wagner Signed Baseball. Five autographs upon this ONL (Frick) ball were apparently garnered at a meeting between the two National League representatives of the state of Pennsylvania. From this small cast of Pirates and Phillies, two tough Hall of Famers catch the eye, namely superstar outfielder Chuck Klein and the Dead Ball era's greatest shortstop Honus Wagner. Phillies managers Hans Lobert and Jimmie Wilson are here as well, along with pitcher Claude Passeau. Signature quality ranges from 4/10 to 6/10, and the ball is lightly and evenly toned. *LOA from PSA/DNA. LOA from James Spence Authentication.* **Minimum Bid: $500**

19336 Late 1930's Rabbit Maranville Signed Baseball. Soon after having been named manager of the 1925 Cubs, he made his rounds through a Pullman car dumping water on sleeping players' heads and announcing, "No sleeping under Maranville management, especially at night!" Despite his irreverent nature, the tiny infielder is remembered as one of the era's top talents, earning a Hall of Fame plaque for his efforts. Sadly, that day came months after his passing in January of 1954, limiting the availability of his important autograph to the collecting hobby. This 6/10 side panel offering resides upon an Official International League sphere that has undergone a magical chemical process to remove all signatures but Maranville's. With quality singles reaching $5,000 at auction on the rare occasions that one surfaces, this should be an appealing alternative for the dedicated autograph hound. *LOA from PSA/DNA. LOA from James Spence Authentication.* **Minimum Bid: $1,000**

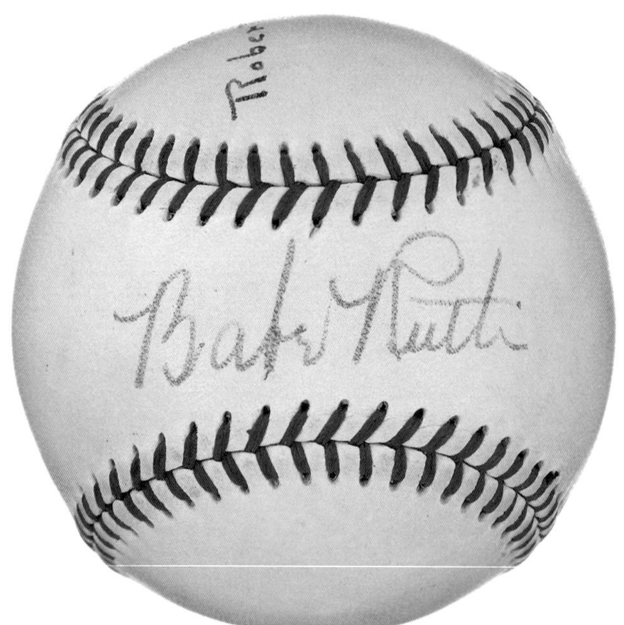

19337 Early 1940's Babe Ruth Single Signed Baseball. Absolutely exceptional specimen will serve as the cornerstone of the finest of Hall of Fame single signed baseball collections. Ideal in all regards, the offering pairs a clean and milky-white OAL (Harridge) ball and a bona fide 9/10 sweet spot signature rendered in flowing blue fountain pen ink. A black ink notation in the autograph seeker's hand gifts this treasure to a lucky young collector, who clearly took great interest in the baseball's care. Babe Ruth autographs, and particularly those of the utmost quality, have been the hobby's most consistent and unshakeable performers in the hobby market for years, a trend which will almost certainly continue as long as baseball is played. All indicators would suggest that this is one of the auction's safest investments. *LOA from PSA/DNA. LOA from James Spence Authentication.* **Minimum Bid: $7,000**

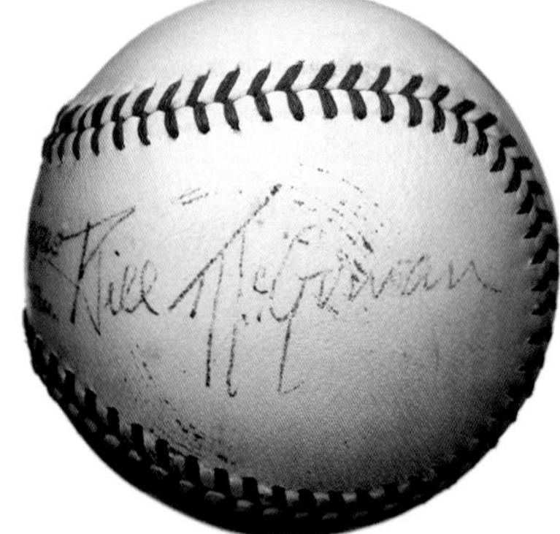

19338 1944 Bill McGowan Signed Baseball. Once signed by six members of the 1944 World Series umpiring staff, this ONL (Frick) ball has been magically transformed through chemical treatment to take on the appearance of a phenomenally scarce McGowan single, allowing one smart collector to fill a very tough gap in his autograph collection. McGowan's service to our National Pastime in an officiating capacity, paired with his early passing almost forty years prior to his Hall of Fame induction, has made his autograph a rare commodity, particularly on baseballs. This 8/10 black ink offering, applied upon an unobtrusive swirl of apparent game use, is as close as you're likely to come to a genuine single, which would certainly cost a small fortune if it did arise. *LOA from PSA/DNA. LOA from James Spence Authentication.* **Minimum Bid: $750**

19339 **1940's Cy Young Signed Baseball.** "All us Youngs could throw," the sole member of Major League Baseball's 500 Win Club once explained. "I used to kill squirrels with a stone when I was a kid, and my granddad once killed a turkey buzzard on the fly with a rock." While his popularity with woodland creatures may be lacking, collectors have never loved the Hall of Fame hurler more, making this 7/10 blue ink side panel offering a particularly appealing commodity. Young is quite tough on baseballs, and he presents here as a single though several other autographs have been removed through a chemical process, with two still faintly visible afterwards. The "Official League" ball is mildly and evenly toned throughout, supplying an attractive canvas for this important signature. *LOA from PSA/DNA.* **Minimum Bid: $600**

19340 **1947 Babe Ruth Single Signed Baseball, PSA EX 5.** This Official American League (Harridge) ball has found its way home again, signed by the Babe in 1947 at Dallas, Texas' Reverchon Park, literally across the street from the Heritage offices. It comes to us from the son of Harry Rubin, an early twentieth century European immigrant who embraced his adopted country's national pastime with a fervor, spending much of his young adult years at Yankee Stadium in awe of the Babe. In 1933, Rubin was forced to leave New York for Dallas, though his love of baseball, and the Yankees specifically, never faltered. So, when Rubin was trying to advance the sport in Dallas as the district athletic officer of the American Legion, he rather optimistically placed a call to his idol asking for assistance. Typical of Ruth's well-documented generosiity, he accepted the invitation, arriving at Dallas Love Field airport to huge crowds headed by Rubin and Dallas Mayor Jimmy Temple. Now, six decades later, the prized keepsake of that meeting arrives on our auction block. The black fountain pen sweet spot signature still projects wonderfully, garnering a rather stingy score of 6/10 from the PSA graders. The ball grades at 4/10 due to moderate toning and surface wear for the combined score as listed. A letter of provenance from the son of Harry Rubin is included in the lot. *Full grading LOA from PSA/DNA. LOA from James Spence Authentication.* **Minimum Bid: $3,000**

19341 **1948 Babe Ruth Single Signed Baseball.** Three days after he made his final appearance at Yankee Stadium to attend the ceremonies retiring his number "3" jersey, and less than two months before his death at age fifty-three, the greatest icon in baseball history autographed one of the last baseballs of his life for a fan. The "Official League" ball finds the dying Bambino in his customary sweet spot position, his hand still strong despite the cancer that ravaged his once powerful frame. The 8+/10 blue ink autograph is dated "6-19-48" in Ruth's hand, supplying the heartbreaking context. The ball exhibits a small degree of surface wear, but the writing remains all but entirely untouched by these minor concerns, as our catalog imagery will attest. A special piece from the final weeks of one of the most intriguing American lives of all. *LOA from PSA/DNA. LOA from James Spence Authentication.* **Minimum Bid: $4,000**

THE BAMBINO'S BEST

19342 **Circa 1947 Babe Ruth Single Signed Baseball, PSA NM-MT+ 8.5.** Absolutely stunning single from the Sultan of Swat dates to the final years of his life, as the unique stamping of the ONL (Frick) ball upon which his autograph resides was produced only between 1946 and 1951. As a cornerstone of a top-echelon baseball autograph collection, one couldn't choose a more worthy candidate, as the blue fountain pen autograph is flawlessly executed here, following decades of practice as the game's most sought after and generous signer. The baseball itself provides the creamiest tone of horsehide without a single distracting fault, and the manufacturer's stamping retains its original boldness. One merely states the obvious when proclaiming this as one of the very finest Ruth singles known to the hobby. Both the autograph and the baseball itself garner a frankly stingy grade of 8/10, with a half-point added for eye appeal to result in the score as posted. *LOA from PSA/DNA. LOA from James Spence Authentication.* Minimum Bid: $20,000

19343 **Circa 1950 Connie Mack Signed Baseball.** One of the most pristine signatures on a baseball you'll ever encounter from the grand old man of baseball, who dedicated sixty-six years of his life to the professional game. This OAL (Harridge) ball dates from close to the end of that epic run, as the unique stamping could be no earlier than 1946. The massive black fountain pen autograph commands almost a third of the sphere's equator, and resonates at a strength of 9+/10. It must be noted that other autographs once joining Mack's have been removed through a chemical process to leave not even the faintest sign of their former presence. The result is a ball that would challenge for the title of "finest known" if it were a true single, made affordable to the budget-minded hobbyist. *LOA from PSA/DNA. LOA from James Spence Authentication.* **Minimum Bid: $500**

19344 **Circa 1950 Connie Mack Single Signed Baseball, PSA NM 7.** The unique styling of this OAL (Harridge) sphere dates its birth to the final years of Mack's managerial reign or the earliest of his retirement. The sharp appearance of the ball matches the dapper wardrobe for which this long-serving legend was known, with a black fountain pen sweet spot signature rating an 8/10 on PSA/DNA's strict grading scale, and the ball netting a 6/10 for the composite score as listed. A top-tier specimen from the wise embodiment of baseball during the twentieth's century first half. *LOA from PSA/DNA. LOA from James Spence Authentication.* **Minimum Bid: $750**

19345 **Circa 1950 Cy Young Single Signed Baseball.** Perhaps the most famous Young single in the hobby, this exact sphere is pictured in the 1993 hardcover *Baseball Archaeology: Artifacts from the Great American Pastime.* One look and you can see how it was booked for the modeling gig, as the black ink sweet spot signature projects at a strength of 9/10. The ball exhibits a bit of staining, which helps to photo match this ball to the book, but nothing that adversely affects the autograph. The manufacturer's stamping has faded beyond visibility. Still a rock-solid example that will ably complete your collection of 500 Win Club singles. *LOA from PSA/DNA.* **Minimum Bid: $2,000**

19346 **1950's Nellie Fox Signed Baseball.** Booking at $3,000 in *Sports Market Report* for a legitimate single, the diminutive Chicago White Sox second baseman provides a more affordable option for the bargain hunting autograph hound. This gorgeous OAL (Harridge) ball has seen seventeen other autographs professionally removed with such skill and artistry as to fool all but the most suspicious of collectors. Fox' side panel blue ink offering rates a solid 8+/10, ready for a place of honor in any high-end Hall of Fame autograph collection. One of the toughest of post-war Cooperstown singles. *LOA from PSA/DNA. LOA from James Spence Authentication.* **Minimum Bid: $500**

19347 **1950's Rogers Hornsby Single Signed Baseball.** "Any ballplayer that don't sign autographs for little kids ain't an American," Hornsby once suggested. "He's a communist." The Hall of Fame second baseman did his part to stay in the good graces of Senator Joe McCarthy with this offering, a massive and flawlessly rendered blue ink sweet spot signature upon an "Official Sandlot League" sphere. The autograph rates an 8.5/10, with the red and blue stitching and gorgeously toned horsehide very effectively recalling the official balls of the prewar Big Leagues. Certainly one of the finest Hornsby singles to come down the pike in quite some time. *LOA from James Spence Authentication.* **Minimum Bid: $1,000**

19348 **1950's Tris Speaker Signed Baseball.** "If you put a baseball and other toys in front of a baby, he'll pick up a baseball in preference to the others," the Hall of Fame outfielder told *Baseball Magazine* in 1951. Certainly any baby worth his diapers would pick up this ball in particular, autographed in 7/10 blue ink on the side panel by Ty Cobb's greatest Dead Ball batting rival. It must be noted that other signatures once resided upon this Official American Association ball, but they have been chemically removed with such artistry and skill as to leave behind not even a hint of Spoke's former neighbors. No serious baseball autograph collection should be lacking this inaugural class Hall of Famer, and this is a rock-solid specimen to fill that void. *LOA from PSA/DNA.* **Minimum Bid: $1,000**

19349 **1950's Tris Speaker Single Signed Baseball.** It was a legendary career that almost never happened, as Speaker's left arm was so badly damaged in a college football injury that doctors initially suggested amputation. But Speaker recovered to become one of the greatest hitters the game has ever known, maintaining to this day the career record for doubles, and top ten positions in average, hits and triples. Much like the man who signed it, the offered baseball finds few rivals, and may just be the nicest Speaker single to reach the auction block in recent memory. The blue ink of the sweet spot signature maintains a boldness of 9/10, and the Official Southern League ball that serves as its home is only very lightly and evenly toned. A magnificent specimen that would adapt easily to a life within the finest of Hall of Fame collections. *LOA from James Spence Authentication.* **Minimum Bid: $3,000**

19350 **1950's Bill Veeck Single Signed Baseball.** Baseball's answer to P.T. Barnum, this pioneering Hall of Famer brought the American League fans everything from a midget batter to Disco Demolition Night during his wild executive career. For all the thrills and laughs, however, he delivered few single signed baseballs to the hobby, and we're pleased to present this example to fill the nagging hole in one collector's holdings. The blue ink side panel signature rates a strong 8/10, topped by a lightly toned layer of shellac, with the OAL (Harridge) ball moderately toned throughout. Display value is still terrific! *LOA from James Spence Authentication.* **Minimum Bid: $500**

19351 **1950's Lloyd Waner Signed Baseball.** The look of a $2,500+ single without the price tag to match. This ONL (Giles) ball is pretty enough to take home to mother, aided in part by an artfully rendered chemical processing that has removed all other signatures that once joined Little Poison's. The result is a solo 9+/10 blue ink autograph from the younger member of the Hall of Fame Pirate fraternal duo on an equally splendid expanse of pale white horsehide. A top-tier specimen for the discerning hobbyist. *LOA from PSA/DNA. LOA from James Spence Authentication.* **Minimum Bid: $300**

19352 **Early 1950's Bill McGowan Single Signed Baseball.** "Single signed?" you ask. "What about all those other autographs?" Well, we're sticking to our story, as each of the five autographs residing upon this OAL (Harridge) ball is rendered in the hand of the Hall of Fame umpire. It's clear that the three decade veteran of the American League was a far better umpire than he was a forger, but his Ted Williams, Mickey Mantle, Billy Martin and Vic Raschi impersonations are not without their charm. Of course it's his own signature that carries the greatest appeal though, placed alone on a side panel in the same 9/10 black fountain pen ink used throughout. McGowan's passing in 1954, a full thirty-eight years prior to his Hall of Fame induction, has resulted in just a tiny supply of surviving singles. One dedicated collector will fill a hole found in hundreds of collections with his winning bid. *LOA from PSA/DNA.* **Minimum Bid: $750**

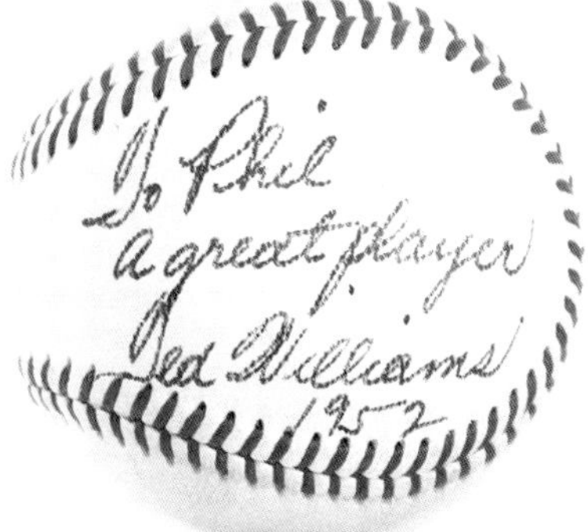

19353 **1952 Ted Williams Single Signed Baseball to Phil Rizzuto.** While "playing days" singles from Ted Williams are tough and highly desirable in any case, the offered example is particularly special, deriving from the personal collection of the Splinter's Hall of Fame compatriot Phil Rizzuto. Illustrating that the most famous rivalry in sports between the Red Sox and Yankees could still have its friendly moments, Williams inscribed the OAL (Harridge) ball with the words, "To Phil, A great player, Ted Williams 1952." Both the inscription and the ball itself remain in spectacular condition, clearly and justifiably having been a cherished possession of Scooter's. Accompanying the ball is a signed letter of provenance from Rizzuto's widow Cora. *LOA from PSA/DNA. LOA from James Spence Authentication.* **Minimum Bid: $500**

19354 **1950's Ty Cobb & 1976 Lou Brock Signed Baseball.** Linked in eternity as two of the greatest base thieves in our National Pastime's long history, this pair of fleet-footed Hall of Famers is likewise joined forever upon the offered OAL (Harridge) ball. Cobb's 9/10 blue ink side panel offering very ably presents as a single, as it indeed was until 1976, when a fellow named "Doug" asked Brock to add his autograph to the pale white sphere. Brock's dated inscription also retains 9/10 boldness, presenting as a single in its own right. The ball remains clean and white. One might seek out Rickey Henderson to further enhance the theme begun by Cobb and Brock. He'd surely be pleased for the opportunity to do so. *LOA from PSA/DNA. LOA from James Spence Authentication.* **Minimum Bid: $750**

19355 **Circa 1956 Mickey Mantle & Casey Stengel Signed Baseball.** We've seen no shortage of Ruth and Gehrig "duo balls" in our day, and more than a few Mantle and Maris, but this is the first time we can recall seeing this particularly pinstriped pairing. This OAL (Harridge) ball features 8+/10 vintage blue ink signatures from the Commerce Comet and the Ol' Perfesser, each applied to opposing sweet spots (Stengel resides over the heavily faded Harridge stamping). As such, each presents 100% convincingly as a single. Note that this short-lived Mantle signature variation conclusively dates the ball to the era of his Triple Crown season, and to his service to the inimitable Stengel. *LOA from PSA/DNA. LOA from James Spence Authentication.* Minimum Bid: $500

19356 **1957 Roy Campanella, Casey Stengel & Leo Durocher Signed Baseball.** Just two months before the tragic automobile accident that would end the Hall of Fame career of the Brooklyn Dodgers' superstar catcher, Campy joined Big League managers Casey Stengel, Leo Durocher and Fred Haney on the television variety show "Texaco Command Appearance." This ONL (Giles) baseball was presented to this impressive panel of diamond talent for signing, then skillfully notated with the details of this superstar summit. A fair degree of surface wear and toning has had some effect over the passing half century, with Campanella, Durocher and Haney rating a 7/10 as a result, and Stengel perhaps a point or two below. Still an impressive and historic piece, and likely one of the last baseballs signed by Campanella before that fateful January 1958 night. *LOA from PSA/DNA. LOA from James Spence Authentication.* Minimum Bid: $750

19357 **1960 Ty Cobb Single Signed Baseball.** Magnificent high-grade representation of one of the hobby's most essential singles ticks every box on the checklist for an ideal Cobb. The aging Peach fills an entire side panel of a clean white ONL (Giles) sphere with his 9+/10 inscription, reading "To William Lengfelder from Ty Cobb, 3/23/60." Almost half a century later, neither the writing nor the ball itself show anything more than the faintest hint of their advanced age, securing a place near the top of known examples. Smart collectors know that top quality examples of fundamental pieces such as this tend to be the most stable of investments, and we expect the steady incline of that market to continue for quite some time. *LOA from PSA/DNA. LOA from James Spence Authentication.* Minimum Bid: $3,000

19358 **1961 Cal Hubbard, Joe Cronin & Will Harridge Signed Baseball.** A vintage notation in an unknown hand upon this ONL (Giles) ball dates it to the 1961 World Series, which would go a long way toward explaining the rather unusual trio of autographs that adorn its side panel. Presumably the head of the umpiring corps, the current American League president and the former American League president attended this historic Series together, one of the only times all three of these Hall of Famers might meet outside of Cooperstown. The three signatures are ideally placed upon a single side panel, and project at a strength of 9+/10. The ball exhibits apparent game use, lending further appeal to this one of a kind artifact. *LOA from PSA/DNA. LOA from James Spence Authentication.* Minimum Bid: $400

19359 **1960's Satchel Paige Single Signed Baseball.** "Ain't no man can avoid being born average, but there ain't no man got to be common," the Negro League Hall of Famer once explained, and he himself was certainly anything but common. The same can be said for this "Energized League Ball," blessed with a 7/10 side panel blue ink signature from the greatest pitcher of his age (according to folks like Ted Williams, Joe DiMaggio and Bob Feller). The ball shows a slight dusting of foxing and minor surface wear, but nothing that is detrimental to the autograph, which presents wonderfully. A rock-solid example of a single that no serious baseball collection should be lacking. *LOA from PSA/DNA. LOA from James Spence Authentication.* Minimum Bid: $500

19360 **1960's Jimmie Foxx Single Signed Baseball, PSA EX+ 5.5.** Hall of Fame pitcher Lefty Gomez once joked, "When Neil Armstrong first set foot on the moon, he and all the space scientists were puzzled by an unidentifiable white object. I knew immediately what it was. That was a home run ball hit off me in 1933 by Jimmie Foxx." The first man to join the Babe in the 500 Home Run Clubhouse plastered his stylish blue ink signature across the side panel and sweet spot of this "Official League" baseball for a fan named "Vincent Maglio," to whom he personalized the offering on the northern panel. A moderate degree of surface wear to the ball accounts for the PSA score as listed, though our catalog photography should properly indicate that the autograph is not overly affected by these concerns. With Foxx and Ott far and away the toughest singles from the famed slugging Club, you can take one giant leap toward a complete set with this lot. *LOA from PSA/DNA. LOA from James Spence Authentication.* Minimum Bid: $2,000

19361 **1960's Nellie Fox Single Signed Baseball.** "Nellie was the toughest out for me," Hall of Fame pitcher Whitey Ford was once quoted as saying. "In twelve years, I struck him out once and I think the umpire blew the call." The diminutive second baseman's early passing at age forty-seven and posthumous Hall of Fame induction have resulted in a thin supply of available singles from the White Sox star, so we're pleased to present this "Official Little League" ball bearing a side panel inscription reading "Best Wishes to Walter Walker, Nelson Fox." The ink rates a consistent 7/10 in strength, with the lightly toned ball still residing in its original box. Many a Hall of Fame singles collection is missing the crafty Fox. *LOA from PSA/DNA.* Minimum Bid: $400

19362 **Late 1960's Roberto Clemente Single Signed Baseball.** He gave his Pittsburgh fans the privilege of witnessing his 3,000th career hit before giving his life in a tragic airplane accident during the subsequent off-season while on a humanitarian aid mission to Nicaragua. Joining the likes of Lou Gehrig and Jackie Robinson as the best and bravest in baseball history, Clemente should be considered an essential component of any quality autograph collection. Here we present an exceptional specimen, residing alone on the side panel of an ONL (Giles) baseball with 9+/10 boldness. Scattered scuffing and dirt on the baseball is almost certainly due to previous game use, as the autograph is affected by none of it. *LOA from James Spence Authentication.* **Minimum Bid: $3,000**

19363 **1969 Frank Frisch Single Signed Baseball.** The Fordham Flash illustrated his tremendous value by virtue of the fact that the flood of National League pennants followed him from New York to St. Louis following his trade from the Giants to the Cardinals, The beloved Hall of Famer applied this signature to the sweet spot of an ONL (Frick) ball apparently brought to the ballpark by a fan attending the All-Star Game in St. Louis in 1969, as a notation well clear of the autograph in an unknown hand attests. Frisch's autograph rates a fantastic 9+/10, and remains unharmed by a degree of water damage that has affected the opposing hemisphere of the ball. As our catalog photography will accurately attest, the visual strength of the ball is still first rate. A fine opportunity for the discerning collector. *LOA from PSA/DNA. LOA from James Spence Authentication.* **Minimum Bid: $1,000**

19364 **Circa 1970 Hall of Famers Multi-Signed Baseball .** We suspect that this ONL (Giles) ball derives from a Cooperstown induction ceremony, though the sizeable contingent of Cardinals also suggests the possibility of a St. Louis baseball event of some sort. Regardless, the cast of characters is impressive to say the least: Frisch, Medwick, Haines, Musial, Brock, Paul and Dizzy Dean, Ken Boyer, Feller, Boudreau, Gehringer, Stengel, Kaline and Mathews. That's a dozen Hall of Famers from a total of twenty autographs! Signature quality averages a bold 8/10, with Stengel and Mathews (each 6/10) the only listed names that drop more than a point below. A desirable ball for Cardinals fans and Hall of Fame collectors alike. *LOA from PSA/DNA. LOA from James Spence Authentication.* **Minimum Bid: $400**

19365 **Circa 1970 Mickey Mantle Single Signed Baseball.** While we freely admit that Mantle singles aren't exactly rare in the collecting hobby, this special offering is a cut above the typical example. The Mick's 10/10 black ink sweet spot signature clearly predates the autograph show era, perhaps even applied during Mantle's final seasons as a player. The ball itself is earlier still, an OAL (Harridge) sphere that could be no later than Joe Cronin's assumption of the American League presidential role in 1959. The ball appears to exhibit some game use but still presents very nicely, as our catalog photography should effectively indicate. *LOA from PSA/DNA. LOA from James Spence Authentication.* **Minimum Bid: $400**

19366 **1970's Lefty Grove Signed Baseball.** One of the game's greatest southpaws, Grove retired with a record of 300 wins against just 141 defeats, earning a trip to Cooperstown on his third ballot in 1947. Despite living almost thirty years beyond his induction, Grove makes for a tough single, and this ONL (Feeney) ball would be worth a mint if not for the chemically removed autographs that make this offering an affordable alternative. Grove's black ink sweet spot signature rates a strong 9/10, and we defy you to find a hint of his former neighbors with the naked eye. Better collecting through science. *LOA from PSA/DNA. LOA from James Spence Authentication.* **Minimum Bid: $750**

19367 **1970's Satchel Paige Single Signed Baseball, PSA NM-MT 8.** "I ain't ever had a job," the Hall of Fame pitcher once claimed, "I just always played baseball." And it certainly was a profession he practiced his entire life, getting his professional start in the 1920's, and striking out his last batter in a single scoreless inning of work for the 1965 Kansas City Athletics at his professed age of fifty-eight. Perhaps the greatest pitcher ever developed by the Negro Leagues, Paige applied his wonderfully bold black ink signature to the side panel of an "Official League" ball late in his life. While a NM-MT rating for such a desirable ball is surely cause for celebration, we frankly can't help but think the grade is a bit on the stingy side. You'll be hard pressed to locate a superior specimen. *LOA from PSA/DNA. LOA from James Spence Authentication.* **Minimum Bid: $600**

19368 **1980's 500 Home Run Club Signed Baseball.** It's rare to see a genuine example of this signed ball, arguably the most forged piece in the baseball autograph market. An authentic example such as this should turn more than a few heads, as such are becoming more and more scarce in the collecting hobby. This ONL (White) ball features the entire gang of eleven: Mantle, Williams, Aaron, Mays, Robinson, Mathews, Schmidt, McCovey, Killebrew, Banks and Jackson. The addition of Eddie Murray makes it an even dozen. Each blue ink signature rates 9/10 or better. The ball itself remains clean with just the faintest hint of scattered toning that is only visible upon the closest of inspection. One couldn't imagine a piece such as this doing anything other than rise in value with each passing year, so smart investors take note. *LOA from PSA/DNA. LOA from James Spence Authentication.* **Minimum Bid: $500**

19369 **500 Home Run Club Signed Baseball.** Nine of the "original eleven" are joined here by two new members of the elite club, with plenty of room left over for you to add guys like Griffey, A-Rod, Bonds, etc. The ONL (Feeney) ball features, in the boldest of blue fountain pen ink, Mantle, Williams, Aaron, Robinson, Mays, McCovey, Jackson, Mathews, Killebrew, Thomas and Thome. A fun project for the autograph seekers out there, as everyone you need but Ruth, Ott and Foxx are still available for signings. The ball itself remains clean and white, perfect for proud display. *LOA from PSA/DNA. LOA from James Spence Authentication.* **Minimum Bid: $400**

19370 **500 Home Run Club Signed Baseball Signed by Eleven.** With today's top sluggers laboring under a cloud of pharmaceutical suspicion, our affection for the Hall of Fame batsmen who populate this OAL (Brown) ball only continues to grow. All blue ink autographs are uniformly 9/10 or better, and include Williams, Mantle, Mays, Aaron, Schmidt, Killebrew, McCovey, Mathews, Banks, Robinson and Jackson. The ball remains as unblemished as the sluggers' stats, presenting exceedingly well. Plenty of room left to add more recent Club members should the mood strike. *LOA from PSA/DNA. LOA from James Spence Authentication.* Minimum Bid: $400

19371 **1980's Hall of Famers Multi-Signed Baseball with Williams, Mays.** Seventeen flawless ink signatures here, and not a single one lacking Cooperstown credentials. The snow-white OAL (Brown) ball begins with Ted Wiilliams and Lou Boudreau sharing the sweet spot, and goes on to feature Mize, Roberts, Herman, Snider, Mays, Aaron, Slaughter, Kiner, Appling, Kell, Irvin, Stargell, Spahn, Killebrew and Berra. There's still some room left for a few more autographs, so bring this beauty along to the next show and keep the project going. Any Hall of Famer would be proud to add his signature to this mix. *LOA from PSA/DNA. LOA from James Spence Authentication.* Minimum Bid: $400

19372 **1980's Joe DiMaggio, Mickey Mantle & Roger Maris Signed Baseball.** Numbers five, seven and nine will never ride upon Yankee pinstripes again in honor of these three iconic Bombers, who join forces here upon one of the only balls in existence to boast the trio's signatures. You'll certainly find none finer, as each signature is rendered in the boldest of black ink, literally unimprovable in its shade. DiMaggio claims the sweet spot of the OAL (MacPhail) orb, with Maris to the east, and Mantle below, adding "To Louis, Best Wishes" to his signature. A couple light fingerprints from handling the wet ink only add further appeal to this remarkable offering. Provenance is equally impressive, as the ball derives from the personal collection of Julie Isaacson, Maris' closest friend during the historic 1961 home run campaign, and a driving force behind Billy Crystal's biopic *61**. See also Isaacson's presentational plaque from Maris within this auction. *LOA from PSA/DNA. LOA from James Spence Authentication.* Minimum Bid: $1,000

19373 **1980's Joe DiMaggio & Mickey Mantle Signed Baseball.** Despite dozens of joint appearances at New York Yankees alumni events and the occasional autograph show together, this historic Yankee pair is rather rarely found pairing up on a baseball like their predecessors Ruth and Gehrig. Here we present an opportunity to add a bit of flair to your Yankee collection with this tough duo ball, providing a blue felt tip DiMaggio on the sweet spot of an OAL (Brown) sphere, and Mantle in blue ballpoint to the south. Each autograph rates 9/10 or better. DiMaggio's signature is bolstered by a thin coating of sealant which has yellow somewhat with time. Scattered toning affects the other panels as well. Three decades of Bronx center field greatness in the palm of your hand. *LOA from PSA/DNA*. Minimum Bid: $400

19374 **1980's Ted Williams "The Kid" Single Signed Baseball.** While the "golden years" spent by the likes of Williams, Mantle and DiMaggio on the autograph circuit have left the hobby with no shortage of standard singles, "variation" balls continue to rise in value as collectors realize just how relatively scarce these examples are. You surely won't see too many like this one, a gorgeous blue ink sweet spot signature on an OAL (Brown) ball tagged with the Red Sox legend's youthful nickname. All writing registers at a strength of 9+/10, and the ball itself exhibits no flaws of note. A Minimum Bid: $400

19375 **1995 Cal Ripken, Jr. Single Signed "2,131" Baseballs Lot of 12.** When the Iron Man overtook the Iron Horse in the most impressive display of fortitude and dedication the game has ever seen, special OAL (Budig) baseballs were printed to be used at the event. Here we present a dozen of these baseballs, each signed on the sweet spot in 9/10 or better blue ink by the man of the hour, who adds the historic "2131" notation as well. Each bears Ripken's personal holographic authenticating sticker. A terrific dealer's lot, or an investment for the future. *LOA from PSA/DNA. LOA from James Spence Authentication*. Minimum Bid: $500

19376 Circa 1906 Ty Cobb Signed Photograph to Grantland Rice. One early sporting legend sends his best regards to another. This exceptional century-old photograph of the Dead Ball Era's greatest superstar finds him at the infancy of his Major League career, with the white-collared navy jersey and pants he wears utilized only during Cobb's first two seasons (1905-06) in Detroit. The 7x9" image is inscribed to legendary sportswriter Grantland Rice, best remembered for naming the early 1920's Notre Dame backfield "The Four Horsemen of the Apocalypse," and other such grandiose journalistic phrasings. Rice should have checked his facts in this case however, as he captions the verso of this photograph, "The Georgia Peach playing semi-pro ball in Georgia at the age of 16." He repeats the mistake in his 1954 book *The Tumult and the Shouting, My Life in Sport,* which actually reproduces this very signed photo in the illustrated section at the center of the text. Perhaps it was from Cobb himself that he received the misinformation, but this is unquestionably an early Tigers photo, and perhaps the very earliest of Cobb in a batting posture.

The inscription to Rice is applied to the white area at the center of Cobb's wide batting stance. He writes, "To Grant, From His Friend, Ty." The ink maintains an average strength of 7/10, while any minor defects to the photo itself can only be spotted at certain angles to the light. By all accounts, this ancient print presents at a NRMT level. This "perfect storm" of condition, esteemed and rock-solid provenance, and status as perhaps the earliest signed Cobb image makes the offered lot one of the most significant autographed pieces from the Georgia Peach available in the hobby today. *LOA from PSA/DNA. LOA from James Spence Authentication.* **Minimum Bid: $2,000**

19377 1926 Babe Ruth Signed Photograph. The Babe works on his short game in this unique photograph snapped just weeks after he committed what historians contend to be the biggest gaffe of his baseball career, inexplicably and unsuccessfully attempting a steal of second base to record the final out of the Series' seventh game. We're tempted to forgive the Babe for this brief indiscretion, however, and instead focus upon the black fountain pen inscription which reads, To my friend Jim Boldt, From 'Babe' Ruth, Nov. 26, 1926." The strength of the ink ranges from 2/10 to 8/10 throughout the course of the writing, with "Babe" a little light but "Ruth" much bolder. The 7.5x9.5" photo is mounted to a cardboard backing, which has served its purpose admirably, warding off any tearing or creasing. A tough early signed photo from the game's greatest name. *LOA from PSA/DNA. LOA from James Spence Authentication.* **Minimum Bid: $1,500**

19378 1927 Babe Ruth & Lou Gehrig Signed Barnstorming Photograph. Those experienced in the baseball autograph collecting hobby have been trained to believe that Bustin' Babes and Larrupin' Lous dual-signed photos are actually modern reproductions, and for the most part that's true. Take a look on eBay and you'll find a dozen of them. Here we provide one of the rare breaks from that tradition, that instantly recognizable image of the barnstorming World Champs offering genuine, hand-signed autographs dating to the historic national tour. Pioneering sports agent Christy Walsh was the mind behind both this tour and this souvenir photograph that was sold at one of the ballparks the Home Run King and American League MVP visited in the weeks following the Yanks' four-game Series sweep. One wise fan took the opportunity to approach Ruth and Gehrig with this photo and a black ink fountain pen in hand, providing one collector eight decades later with a compelling reason to raise his bidding paddle high. Ruth's autograph rates a strong 8/10 in boldness, with Gehrig's, who adds an "Oct. 23, 1927" notation, a couple of shades lighter. The photo itself remains in remarkably fine condition with not a crease, stain or tear to be found. The 7x9" image is matted and framed to an elegant 15x17". *LOA from PSA/DNA. LOA from James Spence Authentication.* Minimum Bid: $7,500

19379 1930's Babe Ruth Signed Photograph. Remove one letter from the inscription and this signed photo goes from just fantastic to outrageously stupendous! But we've confirmed that the Babe didn't misspell the recipient's surname, and that this photo was not a gift to the Hall of Fame Washington Senators pitcher. But rather than dwell on what might have been, we'll instead celebrate the bona fide 10/10 strength of the bold fountain pen inscription that reads, "To My Pal Walter Johnston From Babe Ruth." It appears at upper left of this classic 8x10" image of the Bambino taking his cuts down at St. Petersburg's spring training camp. A vertical bend just right of center will only be apparent at certain angles to the light, and tape staining at top and bottom borders is likewise benign. A simple matting and framing job should result in a NRMT appearance for the photo, with the Babe's ink remaining a cut above even that lofty stature. *LOA from PSA/DNA. LOA from James Spence Authentication.* Minimum Bid: $2,000

19380 1930's Babe Ruth Signed Photograph. Classic image of the left-handed swing that launched 714 long balls is printed to dimensions of 8x10" and subsequently blessed by a brief inscription and signature from the subject. Ruth's black fountain pen ink reads, "To Jackie, From Babe Ruth," supplied at a strength of a conservative 8/10. The wide border at the lower left hand corner is chipped, but a simple matting job will hide that flaw entirely. The wonderful silver gelatin print is otherwise quite clean, with no creasing and only a slight instance of a surface abrasion which is effectively camouflaged by the white-shirted crowd in the background. Go ahead and tell your buddies that this photo came out of the Robinson estate. It's not the truth, but what's a harmless little fib between friends? *LOA from PSA/DNA. LOA from James Spence Authentication.* Minimum Bid: $2,000

THE "HERBIE & GERTIE COLLECTION" OF BABE RUTH AUTOGRAPHS

The five Babe Ruth autographed pieces that follow this brief introduction derive from the personal collection of Sanford Fitchman, whose Uncle Herbie and Aunt Gertie became close friends of the Babe in the late 1930's. The couple owned a tavern on Greenwood Lake in the Hudson River valley about fifty miles from New York City which was a frequent stop for Ruth upon his hunting trips, and the baseball legend sometimes even stayed in an apartment on the upstairs floor. This close friendship spawned some of the most unique and delightful Ruth autographed pieces we have yet to encounter. The collection comes to us directly from the Fitchman family, and is presented to the collecting community for the first time.

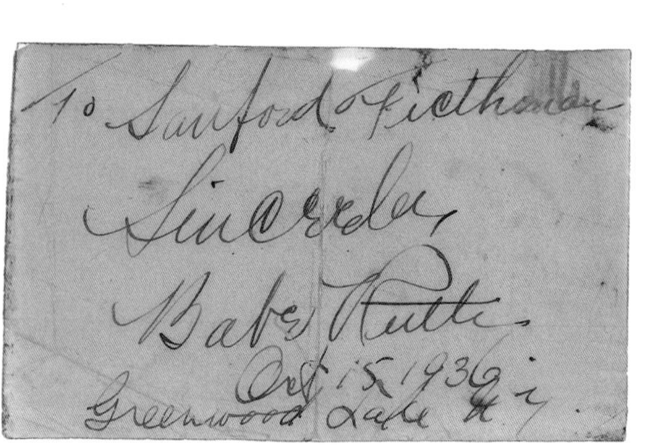
To Sanford Fitchman
Sincerely
Babe Ruth
Oct 15 1936
Greenwood Lake N.Y.

19381 **1936 Babe Ruth Signed Card.** After cherishing it for more than seven decades, our consignor passes on this childhood keepsake to a new generation of collector. The 3x5" piece of paper has been laminated to arrest its deterioration, but the ink remains as bold as the day it was penned, reading, "To Sanford Fitchman, Sincerely Babe Ruth, Oct. 15, 1936, Greenwood Lake, NY." Also included are two great photos of Ruth with young Sanford, a color 8x10" shot at the restaurant owned by Sanford's aunt and uncle (Sanford in green jacket), and a second snapshot (3x4") of Ruth and Sanford on a Manhattan street corner. Photos are VG. *LOA from PSA/DNA. LOA from James Spence Authentication.* **Minimum Bid: $1,500**

19382 **1940's Babe Ruth Signed Oversized Photograph.** Spectacular black and white portrait of the Babe at work should be familiar to most serious hobbyists, but the dimensions of the print (11x14") renders the offered lot anything but commonplace. Ruth makes fine use of the considerable girth of his pinstriped torso to place his 9+/10 black fountain pen inscription, which reads, "To My 'Pals,' Gertrude & Herbert, From Babe Ruth." Some minor tearing, wrinkling and foxes skirts the edges of the oversized cardstock print, but none of these faults have any significant effect upon the impressive appearance of this specimen. Accompanying the signed image is another (8x10") that finds the Babe framed by Herbert and his brother, owners of the restaurant the Babe frequented on trips to upstate New York. *LOA from PSA/DNA. LOA from James Spence Authentication.* Minimum Bid: $3,500

19383 **1940's Babe Ruth Signed Photograph at Age Twenty-Three.** A second youthful image from the "Herby & Gerty" collection, this shot pictures the Babe as he looked around the time of the historic Red Sox/Yankees trade that spawned the agonizing Curse of the Bambino. The black fountain pen inscription from Ruth notes, "To My Pals Herby & Gerty, Age 24, From Babe Ruth." A couple errant brushes of Ruth's hand before the 9+/10 ink dried are to be noted for accuracy, but these do nothing to override the unique and significant appeal. Some small flaws in the form of bends, border tears and tape stains are present at the edges, but could easily be matted out to approximate an EX-MT appearance at a minimum. Included is a photo of the Babe at the restaurant owned by Herby (standing third from left) and Gerty (between Herby & Ruth), measuring 8x10", Good. *LOA from PSA/DNA. LOA from James Spence Authentication.* Minimum Bid: $2,500

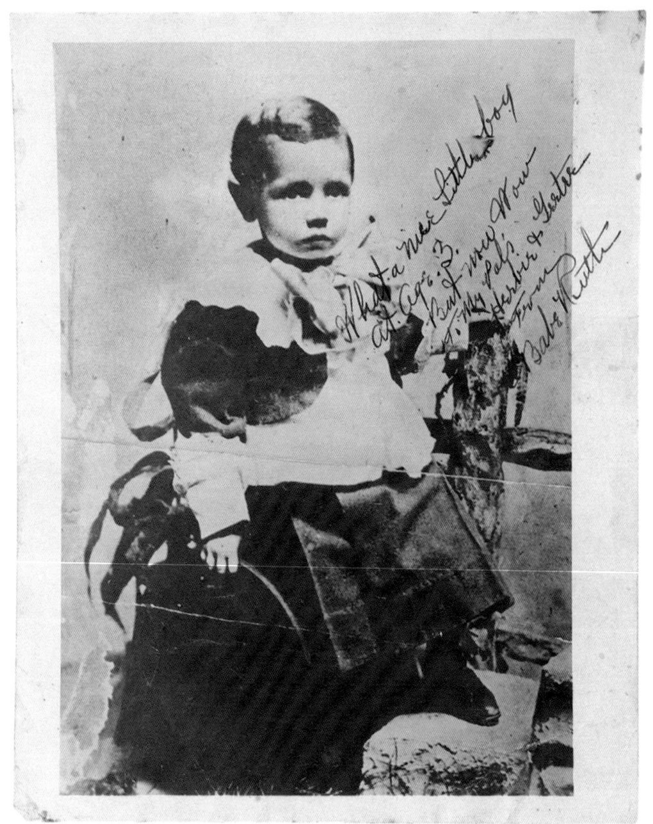

19384 **1940's Babe Ruth Signed Childhood Photograph.** Marvelous image of the Babe as a babe is instantly recognizable as the future Sultan of Swat. Ruth injects a bit of his famous humor into the inscription that appears in the upper right quadrant, writing, "What a nice little boy at age 3. But now, Wow. To my Pals Herbie & Gertie, From Babe Ruth." The blue fountain pen inscription is touched by a single droplet of water near the close of the first line, but is otherwise a bold and unimprovable 10/10. The 8x10" photograph exhibits a considerable degree of creasing, and some toning at the corners, but our catalog imagery should accurately reflect that these faults have little impact upon the visual strength of the piece. Certainly a one-of-a-kind piece for the Ruth collector who has everything. Consigned by the nephew of Herbie and Gertie. *LOA from PSA/DNA. LOA from James Spence Authentication.* Minimum Bid: $3,000

19385 **1940's Babe Ruth Signed Portrait Photograph.** From the "Herby & Gertie" collection of Babe Ruth signed photographs comes this all but unimprovable inscription from baseball's top star. The vast expanse of white background allows stunning contrast, with "To my Little girl friend Joan, From Babe Ruth" presenting at a legitimate 10/10. A small degree of chipping to the emulsion barely touches the first letter of the inscription, but leaves the rest unhampered. Some toning and bending at the edges could easily be disguised with a simple matting job. Photo measures 8x10" in size. *LOA from PSA/DNA. LOA from James Spence Authentication.* Minimum Bid: $3,000

19386 **1938 Minneapolis Millers Team Signed Photograph with Ted Williams.** On his final stop before the Show, a nineteen-year old Ted Williams made American Association history, becoming the first player to win the league's Triple Crown with a .366 average, forty-three homers and 142 runs batted in. Saddled with a youthful temper to match his tremendous skills, Williams became famous in Minneapolis for his outbursts, once shattering a glass water cooler with his fist after popping out, giving his teammates an early shower and almost ending his career when a shard of glass barely missed a nerve in his hand. It's been said that manager Donie Bush became so frustrated with the brash youngster that he told the team owner Mike Kelley, "Either that kid goes or I go." The reply: "We're going to miss you, Donie." Both the future legend and his manager are among the twenty Millers to sign this 8x10" photo issued for "Radio Appreciation Day" at Minneapolis' Nicollet Park, establishing this as among the earliest Williams signed baseball images in the hobby. While it must be noted that The Kid's autograph matches the others in its 2/10 to 3/10 boldness, it does remain fully legible and unmistakable. A few scattered creases are likewise noted, but, as with the light signatures, one must forgive imperfections in light of the great rarity and desirability of the piece. *LOA from PSA/DNA. LOA from James Spence Authentication.* Minimum Bid: $500

19387 **1940's Babe Ruth Signed Photograph.** This classic image from the lens of the era's most noteworthy baseball photographer George Burke is further improved by the addition of a bold inscription from the photo's subject. The Sultan of Swat writes, at lower left, "To My Pal Chas Koehler Jr From Babe Ruth, the ink still projecting at an impressive strength of 9/10. Purely for the sake of accuracy, we note that the pen's ink flow began to fail the Babe during the word "From," causing him to refuel his ink supply and restart the word. His autograph reaps the benefits of this pause with unimprovable boldness. The 7x9" photo is likewise in wonderful condition, though a thin sliver of the upper border may have been trimmed at some point, as we detect a slight waviness. Only the most eagle-eyed could spot this, however, and it has zero effect upon the visual power of the photo. Otherwise, there is not a crease, stain or tear to be found. A brilliant specimen. *LOA from PSA/DNA. LOA from James Spence Authentication.* Minimum Bid: $2,000

19388 **1940's Babe Ruth Signed Oversized Photograph PSA/DNA Graded 9.** While this stirring photographic portrait of the Babe should be familiar to most collectors, the enormous size of this high-quality print is certainly no common sight. There was surely some reason for this expensive print to be made, and one can only assume that the original recipient was a VIP of some manner. We can thank that person for giving the piece the care it deserves, as the 11x14" photo provides not a single flaw of note, and the black fountain pen "Sincerely, Babe Ruth" blasts from the pale background at a strength of 9/10. One of the most impressive autographed Ruth photos you'll encounter at auction in 2008. *LOA from PSA/DNA. LOA from James Spence Authentication.* Minimum Bid: $3,000

19389 **1940's Babe Ruth Signed Photograph in Boston Red Sox Uniform.** While the authenticators claimed that they could recall at least one other example of a Babe Ruth signed image in a Red Sox uniform, they were fairly confident that they had yet to encounter one of the Home Run King to be with a bat in his hands. The same certainly holds true for us here at Heritage, and we expect our most educated bidding clientele to understand what an exceptionally rare opportunity this offering presents. We readily note that both the print and the blue fountain pen inscription date to the later years of the Babe's life, though this later production date is largely to thank for the remarkable 9+/10 boldness of the "To Bob Lynn From Babe Ruth" inscription and the equally fine condition of the photo itself, printed upon an 8x10" sheet of photographic card stock. Clearly one of the most intriguing Ruth autographed pieces to come to market in 2008, this should set off a bidding war between Boston and New York residents almost as fierce as the Red Sox/Yankees rivalry itself. *LOA from James Spence Authentication.* **Minimum Bid: $5,000**

19390 **1948 New York Yankees Team Signed Photograph.** Valued at close to $1,000 in its unsigned state, this impressive oversized (12x20") team shot finds the Yanks on the brink of Major League Baseball's longest World Championship streak (1949-53). Note the black armbands on each player's left sleeve, worn to recognize the passing of the great Babe Ruth. Fourteen flawless blue sharpie signatures from this elite ballclub date from many years after the photo's issue date, but feature most of the biggest names, including DiMaggio, Rizzuto, Berra, Henrich, Crosetti, Reynolds, Lopat, Houk, Brown and more. The photo shows some creasing and minor tears in the wide white border, but the image area itself is free of any significant concerns, and the image could easily be matted and framed to approximate a NRMT appearance. *LOA from PSA/DNA. LOA from James Spence Authentication.* **Minimum Bid: $750**

19391 **1948 Babe Ruth Signed Photograph.** Just two months before succumbing to the cancer that had robbed the Babe of his once powerful slugging physique, Ruth demonstrated the generosity of spirit for which he was famous by signing this 8x10" shot of himself in happier times. The early 1930's spring training image is printed to dimensions of 8x10" and inscribed at upper left, "To Jimmy DiBetta, From Babe Ruth, 6-21-48." The bold fountain pen ink maintains a strength of 9/10, and a mild crease and tear at upper right remains well clear of both the autograph and the image's central focus. A top-tier example of a piece that should be on every collector's want list. Consigned by a family member of the original recipient. *LOA from PSA/DNA. LOA from James Spence Authentication.* **Minimum Bid: $2,000**

19392 **Early 1950's Mickey Mantle Signed Magazine Photograph.** The Golden Anniversary patch on the Mick's left sleeve dates this marvelous image to the 1952 season, corresponding perfectly with the 10/10 blue ink signature in the Hall of Fame slugger's rookie style. While Mantle signed photos are admittedly not rare, those dating to his first few seasons in the Majors most certainly are, and you'll be hard-pressed to find a superior example. The image measures just a fraction of an inch short of 8x10" in size, with tape stains at lower right and a small blemish above Mickey's shoulders causing not the slightest bit of concern. Definitely one of the most appealing Mantle signed piecces to surface in recent memory, recalling what is arguably the most glorious period of Yankees World Championship history. *LOA from PSA/DNA.* **Minimum Bid: $400**

19393 **1953 Roger Maras (Maris) Signed Photograph.** Early image finds the man who would be King in the first season of his professional baseball career, representing the Fargo-Moorhead Twins, the Northern League Cleveland Indians affiliate. While this tough vintage photo of the eighteen-year old slugger would be quite a find in its own right, its the "Roger Maras" autograph that should set collectors' hearts racing. Purportedly due to rude chants from fans in the grandstands, Roger changed the spelling of his surname to "Maris" in 1955, a full two years before his ascension to the Majors. Unsurprisingly, very few examples of his signature utilizing the early spelling are known today, particularly not on photographs. This 3x5" shot exhibits only minor corner wear that causes no concern, and the autograph itself is literally unimprovable. *LOA from PSA/DNA. LOA from James Spence Authentication.* **Minimum Bid: $1,000**

(NY51) NEW YORK, Sept. 26---MARIS MEETS WIDOW OF CHAMPION---Roger Maris kisses Mrs. Clare Ruth on meeting after game tonight at New York's Yankee Stadium. Between them they hold ball Maris hit during third inning of game against Baltimore for his 60th homerun of season. Mrs. Ruth, widow of Babe Ruth who holds record with 60 homeruns, congratulated the Yankee outfielder. Maris is second man in major league history to collect 60 homeruns in one season. By ruling of Ford Frick, based on extended season, Maris does not officially tie Ruth's record. (AP Wirephoto)(rwt32332stf)61 (See AP Sports Wire Story)

19394 **1961 Roger Maris Wire Photograph Celebrating Sixtieth Home Run, Signed.** The widow of Babe Ruth graciously accepts a kiss from Roger Maris as they pose with the baseball that he had just clubbed to match the Bambino's single season home run total of 1927. The printed caption at bottom gives the details, noting Ford Frick's ruling that would attach the asterisk to the Yankee slugger's accomplishment that was only removed after his passing. While it must be noted that Maris' 10/10 red sharpie autograph was applied to the photo years later, very few vintage images surrounding the historic 1961 home run chase are available to the hobby in autographed form. Only mild edge wear and lower corner bends are to be noted upon this Type 1 photo, nothing that could override its NRMT appearance of the image itself. *LOA from PSA/DNA. LOA from James Spence Authentication.* **Minimum Bid: $400**

19395 **1962 New York Yankees Team Signed Large Photograph.** Only the players and staff got one of these photos back in the day, with this specimen deriving from the personal collection of rookie shortstop Tom Tresh. His is one of thirty-two flawless 10/10 blue ink autographs from the back-to-back World Championship Yanks that dominate the wide white lower border of this special team shot. Also present is recently crowned Home Run King Roger Maris, his buddy Mickey Mantle, Berra, Ford, Crosetti, Skowron, Richardson, Kubek, Terry, Howard, Sain and Boyer. Tack holes and very minor bends are noted at the corners for the sake of accuracy, but the photo is otherwise beyond reproach in terms of condition, with the autographs untouched by even a hint of these small concerns. Certainly one of the most attractive and appealing team signed pieces from this important era of Yankees history to reach the auction block in recent memory. Size is 11x14". Pure Bronx gold. *LOA from PSA/DNA. LOA from James Spence Authentication.* **Minimum Bid: $3,000**

19396 **1980's Roger Maris & His Victims Signed Photograph.** Stylized black, white and gold image capturing the swing that made Maris the single season Home Run King is autographed in 10/10 blue sharpie by the pinstriped slugger and three of the pitchers who delivered his most significant blasts. Signing along with Roger are Paul Foytack, Jack Fisher and Tracy Stallard, who add brief inscriptions confessing to the responsibility for his first, sixtieth, and sixty-first homers of 1961 respectively. The 8x10" photo is triple matted and framed to a museum quality 15x18" in size. A unique piece that isn't likely to surface on the auction circuit any time soon. *LOA from PSA/DNA. LOA from James Spence Authentication.* **Minimum Bid: $600**

19397 **1980's Mickey Mantle Signed Large Photograph.** Brilliant studio portrait of a youthful Commerce Comet is expanded to dimensions of 16x20" and blessed with a stunning 10/10 blue sharpie inscription reading, "Best Wishes, Mickey Mantle, No. 7." The image is attractively matted and framed to final dimensions of 21.5x25". A rarely seen image, particularly at this size, made all the more appealing by the addition of more than just the standard simple autograph. *LOA from PSA/DNA. LOA from James Spence Authentication.* **Minimum Bid: $400**

19398 **1980's Mickey Mantle Signed Photographs Lot of 2.** Pair of 8x10" photos were signed by the New York Yankees legend to a golf buddy at the Desert Forest Golf Club in Carefree, Arizona. The first is an unassuming portrait of the pair, inscribed with the standard, "To Jim, My Best Wishes, Mickey Mantle." The second, however, gives a taste of the irreverent humor for which the Mick was known. He stands to the side of his buddy as he tees off, waving a finger in his direction. The inscription explains Mantle's maneuver, reading, "Jim, My zap didn't work, you lucky shit. Mickey Mantle." All writing is in 10/10 black sharpie, and the photos are likewise free of flaws. *LOA from PSA/DNA. LOA from James Spence Authentication.* Minimum Bid: $300

19399 **1990's Ted Williams Signed UDA Oversized Photograph.** Great rivals are made temporary teammates and co-celebrants at the 1941 All-Star Game, as Joe DiMaggio waits to congratulate Ted Williams at home plate after the latter clubbed a three-run walk-off homer to convert a five to four bottom of the ninth deficit into a seven to five American League victory. This joyful image has been printed to 16x20" in size using a special photographic process mixing silver and golden hues, then signed in 10/10 blue sharpie by the hero of the day. Bottom left holds the UDA authenticating holographic sticker (matching paperwork unavailable), and the limited edition numbering "35/300" is penned at bottom right. Photo is matted and framed to final dimensions of 24x27.5". *LOA from PSA/DNA. LOA from James Spence Authentication.* Minimum Bid: $300

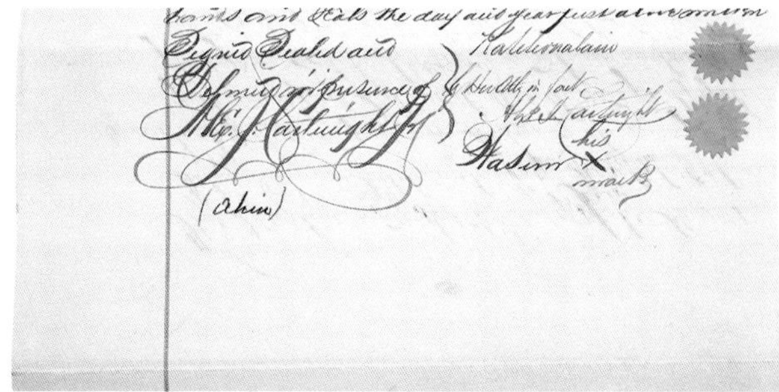

19400 **1881 Alexander Cartwright Signed Hawaiian Lease Agreement.** Essential autograph is likewise one of baseball's most attractive, the sport's equivalent of John Hancock. The man officially credited by the United States Congress in 1953 with the invention of the modern game of baseball signed his name to the offered lease agreement between Queen Emma of Hawaii and a local citizen for a parcel of land in Honolulu as the queen's attorney. As baseball historians are aware, Hawaii became Cartwright's home in the later years of his life when he fled the 1849 California gold rush cholera epidemic, subsequently becoming a close advisor to the Hawaiian royal family. The impressive handwritten document unfolds to a sizeable 24x8" in size, and remains in fine, undamaged condition with original fold lines. It must be stressed that this is not the far more common onion skin copy version of Cartwright's autograph that often surfaces in the hobby, but instead a legal document hand signed by the ultimate baseball pioneer. An elegant and important artifact for the most serious of collectors. *LOA from PSA/DNA. LOA from James Spence Authentication.* Minimum Bid: $1,000

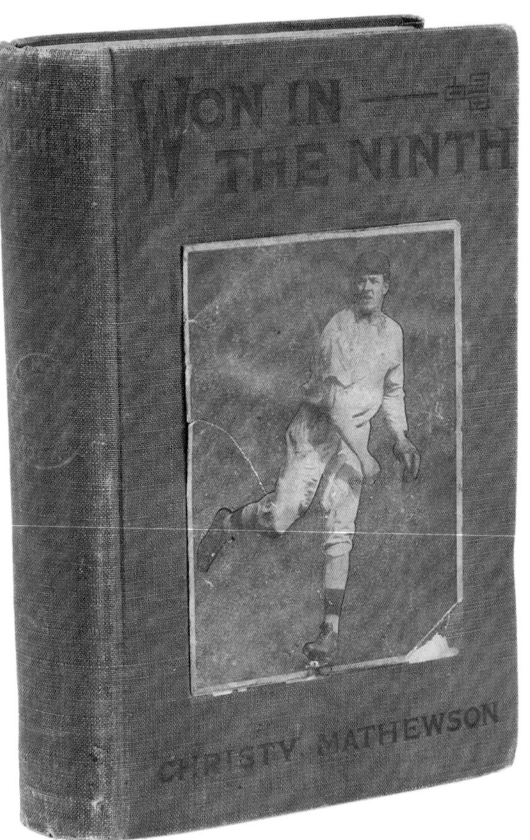

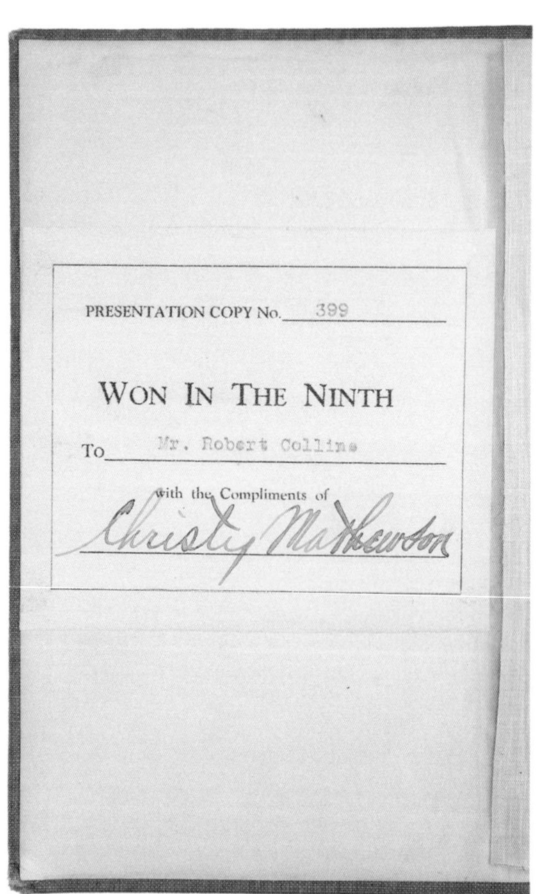
PRESENTATION COPY No. 399

WON IN THE NINTH

To Mr. Robert Collins

With the Compliments of
Christy Mathewson

19401 **1910 Christy Mathewson Signed Book.** "Mathewson was the greatest pitcher who ever lived," Connie Mack once explained. "He had knowledge, judgment, perfect control and form. It was wonderful to watch him pitch when he wasn't pitching against you." Matty's supreme relevance to the game of baseball and his early death in 1925 as a delayed reaction to a World War I gas attack have had dramatic effects on his autograph's demand and supply, with serious collectors skirmishing for the few quality examples that exist. We expect fierce bidding for the example we present here, a 9/10 beauty penned upon a book plate that remains affixed inside a presentational copy of Mathewson's 1910 book *Won in the Ninth*. Mathewson's elegant script is found at the bottom of the 3x4" card, which holds a typed attribution to its original owner and a "399" serial number from what one could reasonably expect is a limited run of either 500 or 1,000. The book shows the degree of wear one would expect for a century of life, but the volume remains tightly bound and any condition issues have no bearing upon the fine quality of the all-important signature. *LOA from PSA/DNA. LOA from James Spence Authentication.* **Minimum Bid: $5,000**

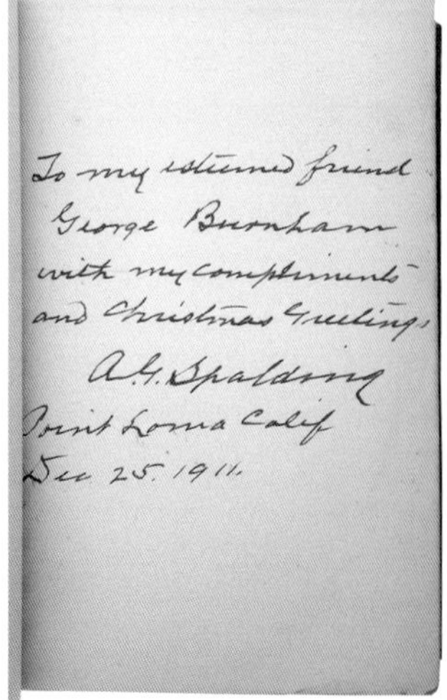
To my esteemed friend
George Burnham
with my compliments
and Christmas Greetings,
A.G. Spalding
Point Loma Calif
Dec 25. 1911.

19402 **1911 Albert Spalding Signed Book.** After a simple autograph clipped from a handwritten letter realized over $6,200 in our October 2007 Signature Auction, one smart consignor realized it might be time to part with this gorgeous autographed copy of the early baseball pioneers' *America's National Game*. Unquestionably a superior piece to the earlier offering, this fine hardcover bears a stunningly Mint black ink fountain pen inscription on a blank opening page, reading, "To my esteemed friend George Burnham with my compliments and Christmas Greetings, A.G. Spalding, Point Loma Calif, Dec 25, 1911." Our consignor was kind enough to point out that the volume is rebound, with a replaced spine, but the work was masterfully rendered and would only be apparent to the most eagle-eyed of collectors. No dust jacket. The front and rear covers are original, with the former sporting a fine early baseball image in gold against its deep blue background. All interior pages remain in fine undamaged condition with the exception of the panoramic fold-out, which does have tape reinforcement of the fold lines. Still one of the most solid examples we've encountered of this important early baseball book, a prize even in its unsigned state. *LOA from PSA/DNA. LOA from James Spence Authentication.*
Minimum Bid: $1,500

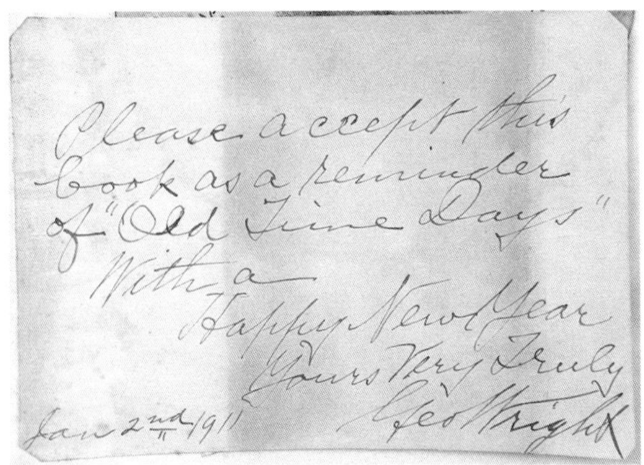

19403 **1911 George Wright Signed Book Dedication.** On April 22, 1876, George Wright became the first batter in National League history, serving as the Boston Red Caps' lead-off man and grounding out to the shortstop of the Philadelphia Athletics. Thirty-five years later, this Hall of Fame baseball pioneer made a gift of this hardcover edition of *The National Game* to an admirer, writing on a small (3x4.5") sheet affixed to an opening blank page, "Please accept this book as a reminder of 'Old Time Days' with a Happy New Year, Yours Very Truly, Geo. Wright, Jan 2nd, 1911." The black fountain pen ink remains wonderfully bold almost a century later, rating a legitimate 9/10 in strength. A column of toning affecting the dedication results from decades pressed against a yellowing newspaper column glued to the facing page recounting Wright's visit to Houston, Texas that gave birth to this treasure. The book itself shows some slight loosening of the binding and an expected degree of wear to the covers and spine, but nothing that troubles the all-important autograph. A tough and essential autograph for the avid baseball historian, provided with the finest provenance one could imagine for a signature of this vintage. *LOA from PSA/DNA. LOA from James Spence Authentication.* **Minimum Bid: $1,000**

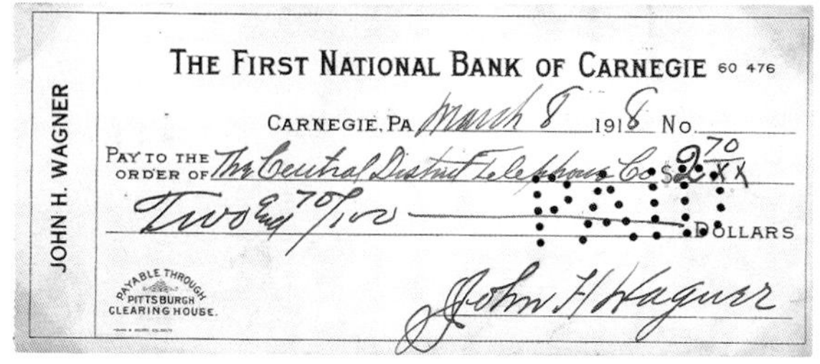

19404 **1918 Honus Wagner Signed Check.** Just six months removed from a Hall of Fame playing career that saw the Old Dutchman lead the National League in batting average eight times and register better than 3,400 hits, Wagner filled out this personal check drawn from a "Carnegie (PA) Trust Company" account. His unmistakable black fountain pen writing, paying "The Central District Telephone Co." the sum of $9.70, remains in splendid 9+/10 condition, closing with the desirable "John H. Wagner" authorizing signature. The check itself remains in the finest of condition, with no creases, stains or tears to report, and is attractively matted and framed with a second-generation photo of a Wagner/Cobb summit to final dimensions of 13.5x19". *LOA from PSA/DNA. LOA from James Spence Authentication.* **Minimum Bid: $400**

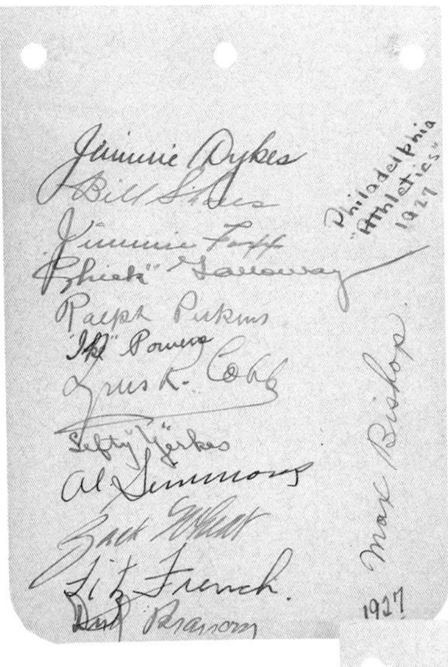

19405 **1927 Philadelphia Athletics Team Signed Album Pages.** Vintage autograph collecting at its essence. Provided for your hobby needs are two pages removed from a vintage autograph album, featuring sixteen signatures from Connie Mack's star-studded herd of White Elephants. Though the Championship seasons were still two years away at the time of the signing, the appearance here of aging veterans who retired before the brass ring was grasped makes this an arguably even more coveted prize for collectors. Cobb (penning his full "Tyrus R. Cobb" style), Wheat and Collins join up and coming Hall of Famers Foxx and Simmons, as well as Dykes, Bishop, French, Hale and Perkins. Autographs are applied in 9/10 and better black fountain pen ink, and the two album sheets (4.25x6" each) offer no condition troubles. *LOA from PSA/DNA. LOA from James Spence Authentication.* **Minimum Bid: $750**

BROTHERLY LOVE

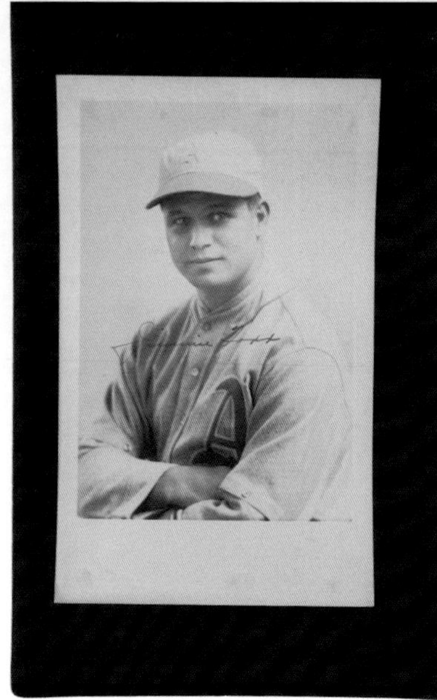

19406 **1929 Philadelphia Athletics Team Signed Photographic Portrait Album.** Magnificent photographic portraiture and a cast of World Championship legends collide here to produce one of the most exciting autographed pieces to be found within this auction. Presented only to team members and important figures in the Philadelphia baseball scene, volumes such as this one are the work of H. Madonna Wagner, whose photography bears more than a passing resemblance to legendary lensman George Burke. Embossed gold lettering upon the cover of the volume features Wagner's name and the text, "Snapshots, The World's Champions Baseball Club of 1929, To My Friends." Twenty-nine individual photos, each measuring 5x8" in size, are affixed to the black scrapbook pages within, with each photo signed by its subject in the boldest of fountain pen ink. All of this elite squad's legends are present and accounted for, with Foxx, Cochrane, Collins, Simmons, Grove and Connie Mack representing the Hall of Fame contingent. Other notables include the very tough Thomas Shibe, 1919 Black Sox manager Kid Gleason, Dykes, Earnshaw, Quinn, Walberg, Boley and more. All Hall of Famers rate 8/10 or better, with the balance ranging from 6/10 to 9/10. The photos uniformly remain in NRMT condition, though a few have come loose from the scrapbook pages. The most attractive keepsake we've yet to encounter from this number three rated club on "The Sporting News" list of baseball's greatest teams in history. *LOA from PSA/DNA. LOA from James Spence Authentication.*
Minimum Bid: $7,500

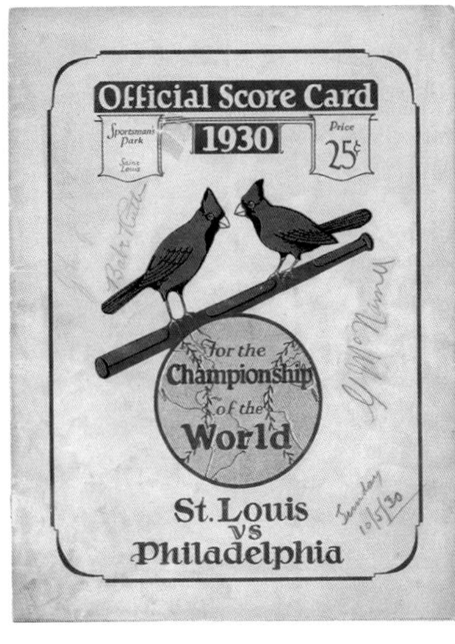

19407 1930 Babe Ruth & John McGraw Signed World Series Program. The playing field wasn't the only part of Sportsman's Park packed with Hall of Famers on the afternoon of October 5th, 1930—the grandstand was as well! One fan on hand to watch Lefty Grove and Jesse Haines battle it out in Game Four spotted two Big Apple legends among the spectators and secured pencil autographs on the cover of his program to commemorate the meeting. Babe Ruth's signature rates a bold 9/10, while the gruff John McGraw is several shades lighter at 3/10. A third unknown signature is here as well, along with the fan's penciled notation of the date. The program itself shows expected but acceptable wear, with vertical center fold that intersects no signatures, and remains tightly bound with no tearing or staining of note. Interior scorecard is filled out in pencil. No shortage of elite baseball history here. *LOA from PSA/DNA. LOA from James Spence Authentication.* **Minimum Bid: $1,000**

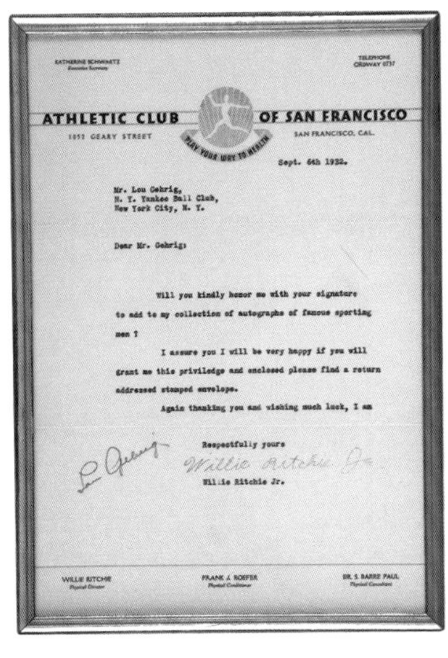

KATHERINE SCHWARTZ
Executive Secretary

TELEPHONE
ORDWAY 0737

ATHLETIC CLUB OF SAN FRANCISCO
1052 GEARY STREET — SAN FRANCISCO, CAL.
PLAY YOUR WAY TO HEALTH

Sept. 6th 1932.

Mr. Lou Gehrig,
N. Y. Yankee Ball Club,
New York City, N. Y.

Dear Mr. Gehrig:

Will you kindly honor me with your signature to add to my collection of autographs of famous sporting men ?

I assure you I will be very happy if you will grant me this priviledge and enclosed please find a return addressed stamped envelope.

Again thanking you and wishing much luck, I am

Respectfully yours

Willie Ritchie Jr.

WILLIE RITCHIE — FRANK J. ROEFER — DR. S. BARRE PAUL

19408 1932 Lou Gehrig Signed Autograph Request Letter. Mailed from San Francisco on September 6, 1932, this letter was likely waiting for the Yankee legend upon his return from a lengthy road trip that saw Gehrig club a grand slam and drive in four more runs in a fourteen-inning loss to the Detroit Tigers. The charming letter is typed upon the letterhead of the young collector's father, and reads, "Dear Mr. Gehrig: Will you kindly honor me with your signature to add to my collection of autographs from famous sporting men? I assure you that I will be very happy if you will grant me this priviledge (sic) and enclosed please find a return addressed stamped envelope. Again thanking you and wishing much luck, I am Respectfully yours, Willie Ritchie Jr." Besides young Willie's closing signature the Iron Horse provides his own, remaining in fine 9+/10 pencil three quarters of a century later. The letter is likewise in fine condition, with only original mailing folds to note, and is expensively matted and framed with a marvelous modern print of a batting portrait and an engraved plaque supplying a brief Gehrig biography. Total dimensions 26x28". *LOA from PSA/DNA. LOA from James Spence Authentication.* **Minimum Bid: $1,500**

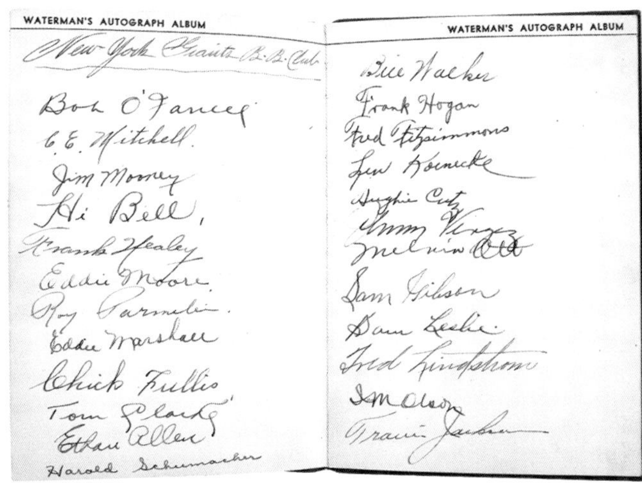

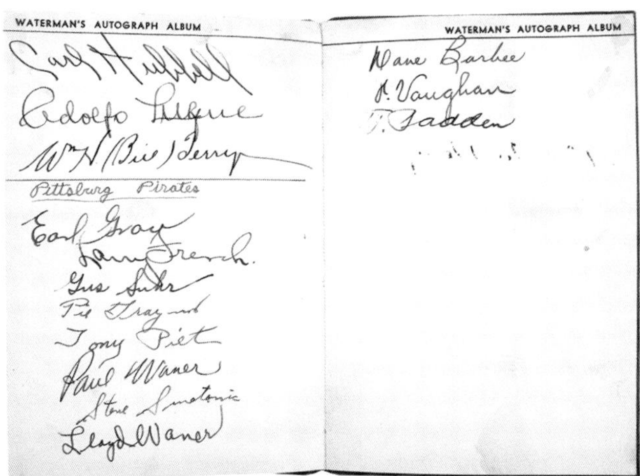

19409 Early 1930's Autograph Album Signed by Giants, Pirates, Cubs & Cardinals. One young New York City baseball fan made fine use of his "Waterman's Autograph Album," seeking out some of the National League's greatest names for inclusion in this charming little hardbound volume. Divided by teams, the album features the following: Giants, twenty-seven including Ott, Lindstrom, Jackson, Hubbell, Terry, Luque. Pirates, eleven including Traynor, both Waner brothers, Vaughan. Cubs, five including Hemsley, Malone, Smith. Cardinals, ten including Frisch, Bottomley, Dizzy Dean, Carleton. All autographs are 9/10 or better, and the pages occasionally show some mild age toning, but nothing that causes any concern. The book remains tightly bound. Some of the finest examples we've seen of these Depression-era legends. *LOA from PSA/DNA. LOA from James Spence Authentication.* **Minimum Bid: $750**

19410 **1930's Baseball Signed Autograph Lot of 123 with Ruth, Foxx, Cuyler.** Fantastic collection of prewar autographs from our National Pastime offers no shortage of the game's all-time greats, offering an intriguing look into one young man's hobby many decades ago. Most autographs are penned on colored album pages, often with an image of the player carefully trimmed from newspapers and magazines and pasted beside the signature. Quite a few autographs are placed directly on the image, and will be italicized if it is a signed image in the list to follow. Signature quality is a fantastic 9/10 and better throughout, with almost no exceptions. The brightest star, of course, is *Babe Ruth,* whose 1930's-era autograph appears upon an image of him in Red Sox uniform. The piece is encapsulated by PSA/DNA in a NM-MT 8 holder. Also featured: *Musial, Hartnett, Maranville, Schoendienst, Grimes,* Gomez, *Ruffing,* Gehringer, *Terry,* Rizzuto, Medwick, Stengel, Mack, *Manush,* Herman, Hubbell, Lyons, Lombardi, *Southworth,* Sisler, Greenberg, *Wheat,* Rick Ferrell, *Grove,* Lloyd Waner, *McCarthy,* Foxx, Bottomley, *Mize* (3), *Rixey,* Cuyler, Lopez. One of the finest treasure troves of vintage baseball autographs we've seen in some time, this collection affords one savvy hobbyist the opportunity to take his collection to the next level with a single bid. **Minimum Bid: $4,000**

19411 **1930's Lou Gehrig Signed Album Page.** Beautiful in its understated simplicity, this 10/10 pencil autograph paired with a delicately die-cut image of the Iron Horse at bat projects a cultured Depression era aspect. We've always been very fond of pieces such as this, clearly treasured by a young fan decades ago, and now destined to be treasured by a seasoned collector for decades to come. The 4.25x6" album page is masterfully framed between two panes of glass to allow viewing of the Mint pencil Joe Sewell autograph on verso, which is likewise paired with a cropped batting pose image. *LOA from PSA/DNA. LOA from James Spence Authentication.* **Minimum Bid: $1,500**

19412 **1930's Babe Ruth & Tris Speaker Signed Album Page.** "Ruth made a grave mistake when he gave up pitching," Tris Speaker once joked. "Working once a week he might have lasted a long time and become a great star." These two giants of early twentieth century baseball share space upon a blank 3.5x5.5" album page that has been glued to a larger scrapbook page along with an article naming these two (and Cobb) to the "All Time Outfield." The signatures are applied with the same 10/10 black fountain pen ink, providing elite examples for the discriminating collector. *LOA from PSA/DNA. LOA from James Spence Authentication.* **Minimum Bid: $1,500**

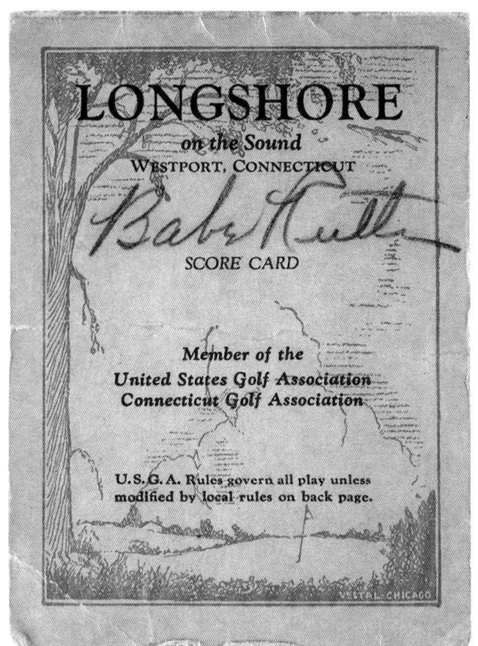

19413 **1930's Babe Ruth Signed Golf Scorecard.** The Sultan of Swat was indulging in his second great athletic love when spotted by a fan at Westport, Connecticut's Longshore on the Sound golf course about fifty miles from Ruth's Manhattan home. Armed with an unused scorecard and a pencil, the fan approached the Yankee legend and came away with this fine keepsake, bearing a 9/10 signature on the cover. The scorecard measures just over 3x4" in size (closed), and exhibits a degree of creasing and general wear, though nothing that diminishes the visual power of the autograph. A great piece to frame with your favorite photo of the Babe on the links. *LOA from PSA/DNA. LOA from James Spence Authentication.* **Minimum Bid: $1,000**

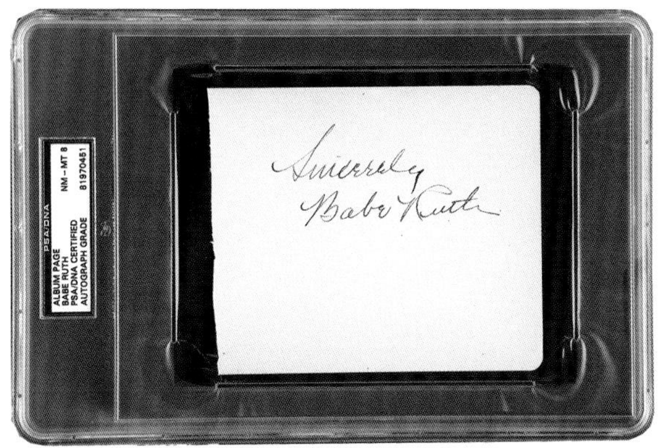

19414 **1930's Babe Ruth Signed Album Page, PSA NM-MT 8.** The essence of the sports collecting hobby is distilled here in the form of the quality Babe Ruth ink signature on paper. This one was acquired by a fan armed with a black fountain pen and an autograph album, with the page (4.5x5") since removed and waiting anxiously to be framed with your favorite Bambino photo. Delectable age toning skirts the edges of the creamy page, which otherwise exhibits none of the creasing, tearing or staining often found on paper of this vintage. A terrific example of the Babe's elegant, flowing penmanship. Encapsulated as NM-MT 8 by PSA/DNA for protection and unquestioned authenticity. **Minimum Bid: $1,000**

19415 **1930's Babe Ruth Signed Album Page, PSA NM-MT 8.** While legends of the Babe's home run promise to a hospital bedridden Johnny Sylvester and his 1932 World Series "Called Shot" are open to debate, the stories of his generosity with autographs most assuredly are not. Here we present a marvelous example of his essential signature, applied to a pink album page measuring 4.25x5" in size. Light age toning at the edges only adds vintage appeal, and the page is otherwise free of any flaws. Encapsulated as NM-MT 8 by PSA/DNA for protection and unquestioned authenticity. **Minimum Bid: $1,000**

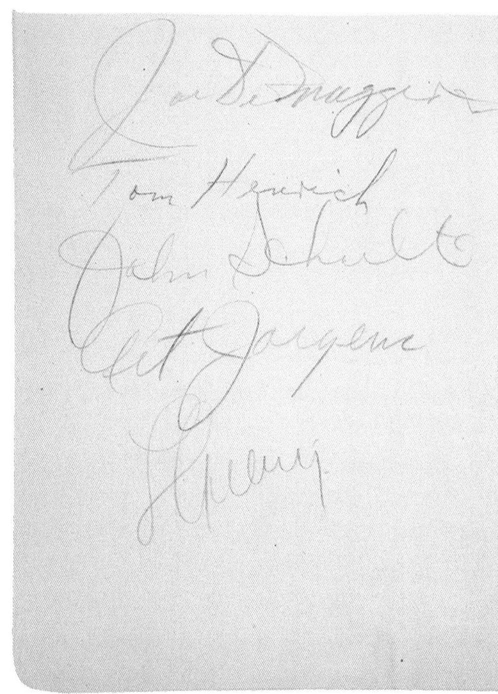

19416 **Circa 1938 Lou Gehrig & Joe DiMaggio Signed Album Page.** One lucky fan armed with an autograph album and a pencil earned this keepsake for future generations, providing this pale yellow 3.75x5" page to Joe DiMaggio, Tommy Henrich, John Schulte, Art Jorgens and Lou Gehrig for signing. The autographs remain as bold now as they had been on the day of their application, and represent three of the greatest Yankee figures of the day. The page itself is likewise mercifully free of any signs of age, absent the typical creasing or tearing of paper from this era. Only the faintest touch of toning at the page's edges suggest its advanced vintage. *LOA from PSA/DNA. LOA from James Spence Authentication.* **Minimum Bid: $1,000**

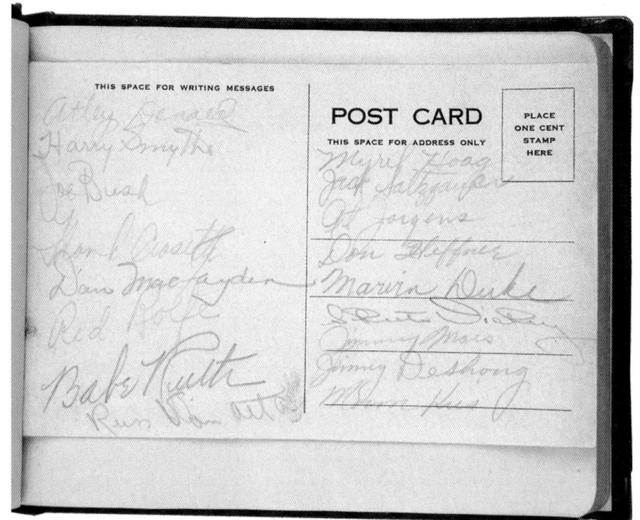

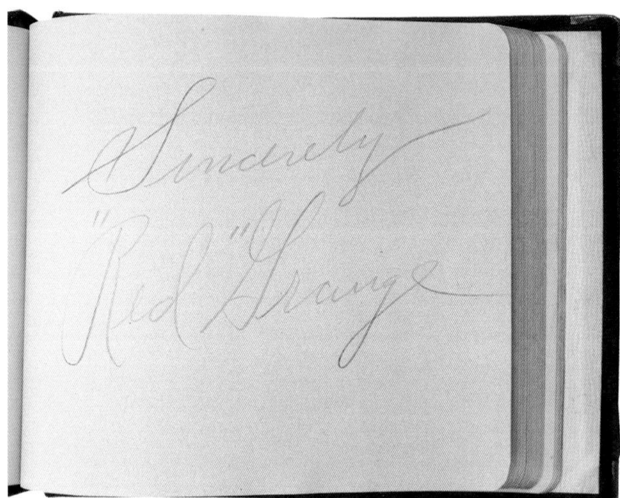

19417 Late 1930's Autograph Book Signed by Babe Ruth, Red Grange. Charming childhood volume is populated mainly by silly little poems from summer camp buddies and family members, though a few celebrities do find their way into its pages. Most notable is a postcard from a Clearwater, FL hotel autographed by an assortment of seventeen Big League ballplayers, almost certainly acquired during spring training festivities. The cast of characters is a mixture of several teams, though we expect that Babe Ruth, whose autograph remains in the boldest of pencil, was in service to the Brooklyn Dodgers as a coach at the time. Sharing space with him on the postcard, also in NRMT pencil, are the likes of Frank Crosetti, Danny MacFayden, Myril Hoag, Red Rolfe and Jimmy Deshong. Several pages later, signed directly on the pale pink album sheet, is a flawless Red Grange autograph, and deeper still into the volume we find big band leader Benny Goodman together with his top vocalist Martha Tilton (each 10/10 blue ink). The 5x6" leatherbound volume remains in wonderful condition, as does the entirety of its contents. *LOA from PSA/DNA. LOA from James Spence Authentication.* **Minimum Bid: $1,500**

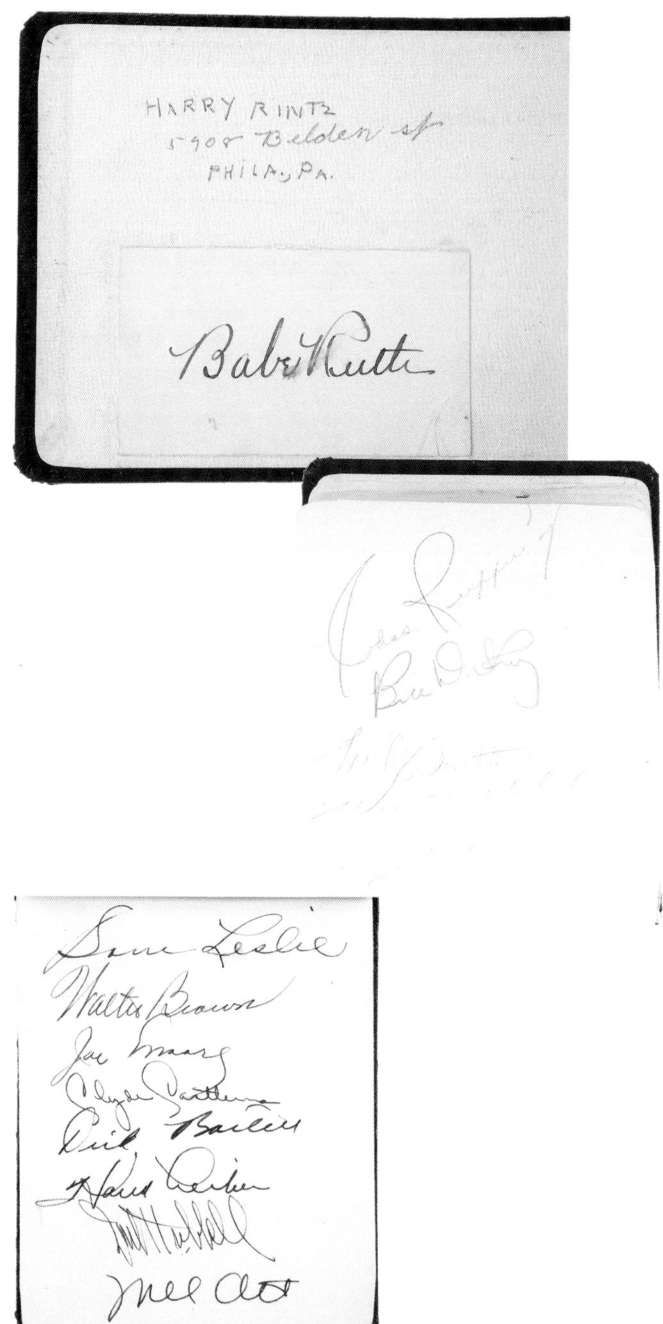

19418 Late 1930's Autograph Book Signed by Babe Ruth, Gehrig, Ott & More. Just short of two hundred signatures comprise this youthful project of an avid Philadelphia baseball fan, who sought out a sizeable contingent of legends and lesser-knowns to fill the pages of his autograph book. Beginning at the first page and continuing on, we encounter such names as Ruth (small smear, otherwise 9+/10), Chuck Klein (8/10), Cuyler (9/10 pencil), Averill, Feller, Wagner, Traynor, Hubbell, Ott, Combs (9+/10 pencil), Ruffing (9+/10 pencil), Dickey (9+/10 pencil), Gehrig (9/10 pencil), Gomez (9+/10 pencil), Mrs. Franklin D. Roosevelt (9+/10 pencil), Joe DiMaggio (9+/10 pencil), Greenberg (9+/10 pencil), Gehringer (9+/10 pencil), Mize (9+/10 pencil), Slaughter (9/10 pencil). Unless otherwise noted, all are in 9/10 or better ink. A wonderfully evocative archive of the prewar game. *LOA from PSA/DNA. LOA from James Spence Authentication.* **Minimum Bid: $2,000**

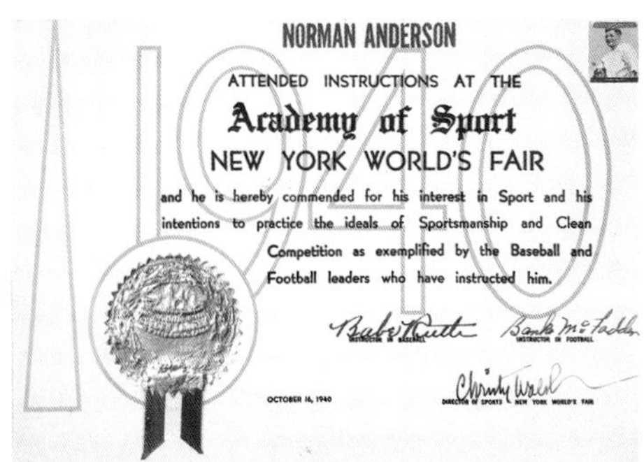

NORMAN ANDERSON

ATTENDED INSTRUCTIONS AT THE

Academy of Sport

NEW YORK WORLD'S FAIR

and he is hereby commended for his interest in Sport and his intentions to practice the ideals of Sportsmanship and Clean Competition as exemplified by the Baseball and Football leaders who have instructed him.

OCTOBER 16, 1940

19419 **1940 Babe Ruth Signed "Academy of Sport" Certificate.** The trylon and perisphere, celebrated symbols of the most famous World's Fair of them all, factor prominently into the design of this certificate bearing the autograph of another of the twentieth century's most recognizable symbols. A flawless 10/10 black fountain pen autograph from the great Babe Ruth appears along with Clemson football hero Banks McFadden and the Babe's sports agent Christy Walsh, certainly thrilling the young Norman Anderson, who was awarded this document by his instructors. In the interest of full disclosure, we must report that the top edge of the certificate appears to have been trimmed slightly, and the tiny image of a Babe Ruth Sport Kings card at upper right is likewise not original to issue. Neither of these concerns affects the visual strength in the least, however, and the certificate is otherwise entirely free of noteworthy flaws. **Minimum Bid: $1,500**

19420 **1941 Babe Ruth Signed World Series Program.** We wonder which side the Babe supported in this first of many great Subway Series between the Brooklyn Dodgers and the New York Yankees. After all, it was the Bums that gave the Babe his last Big League job, though one would hope that the Babe's heart was still wrapped in pinstripes. His 9/10 pencil autograph does appear on the Yankee side of the scale upon the cover of this program, and this is the Yankee version of the Fall Classic publication, if that gives any hint. The young collector's pencil autograph joins Ruth's on the cover, and a few marks are made to the interior scoresheet, but otherwise only typical edge, corner and spine wear is to be noted. A fine venue for this all-important autograph. *LOA from PSA/DNA. LOA from James Spence Authentication.* **Minimum Bid: $1,000**

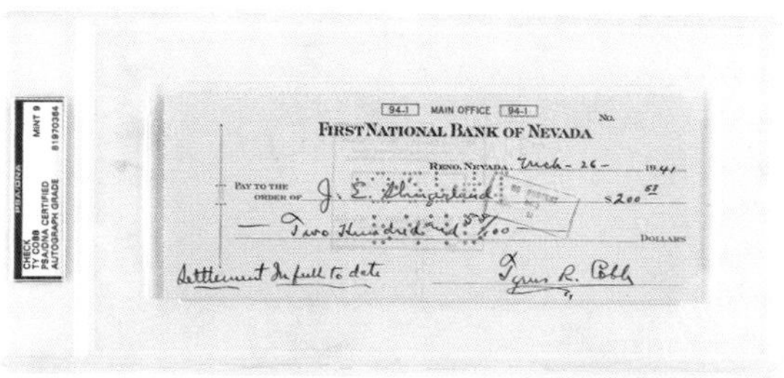

MAIN OFFICE

FIRST NATIONAL BANK OF NEVADA

RENO, NEVADA, March 26 — 1941

PAY TO THE ORDER OF J. E. Slingerland $200

Two Hundred — DOLLARS

Settlement in full to date — Tyrus R. Cobb

19421 **1941 Ty Cobb Signed Check.** Mint specimen should appeal to collectors who want nothing but the finest, as this personal check drawn against the Peach's "First National Bank of Nevada" account is slabbed in a PSA Mint 9 capsule. Cobb pays just over two hundred dollars to a "J.E. Slingerland," noting at the bottom margin, "Settlement in full to date." All black fountain pen ink is rendered in Cobb's hand, as is the authorizing "Tyrus R. Cobb" signature. The bank's stamping and punch coding remains clear of the autograph, with a single vertical fold line left of center the only condition issue of record. A flawless example of an essential autograph. **Minimum Bid: $500**

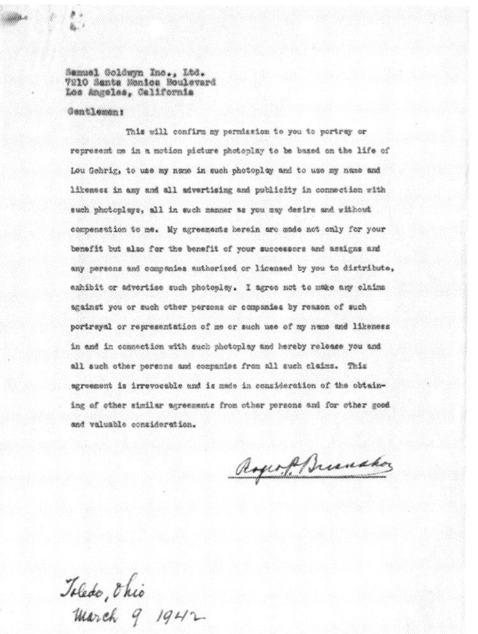

Samuel Goldwyn Inc., Ltd.
7210 Santa Monica Boulevard
Los Angeles, California

Gentlemen:

This will confirm my permission to you to portray or represent me in a motion picture photoplay to be based on the life of Lou Gehrig, to use my name in such photoplay and to use my name and likeness in any and all advertising and publicity in connection with such photoplays, all in such manner as you may desire and without compensation to me. My agreements herein are made not only for your benefit but also for the benefit of your successors and assigns and any persons and companies authorized or licensed by you to distribute, exhibit or advertise such photoplay. I agree not to make any claims against you or such other persons or companies by reason of such portrayal or representation of me or such use of my name and likeness in and in connection with such photoplay and hereby release you and all such other persons and companies from all such claims. This agreement is irrevocable and is made in consideration of the obtaining of other similar agreements from other persons and for other good and valuable consideration.

Roger P. Bresnahan

Toledo, Ohio
March 9 1942

19422 **1942 Roger Bresnahan Signed "The Pride of the Yankees" Contract Letter.** With the star catcher's professional career ending over nine decades ago, and his passing in 1944 predating his Cooperstown induction by a year, autograph collectors tend to find the Duke of Tralee a sizeable challenge. We're happy to present one of the more desirable examples you're likely to find in the form of this single-page typed letter granting permission "...to portray or represent me in a motion picture photoplay to be based on the life of Lou Gehrig..." Of course, this film would come to be known as "The Pride of the Yankees," perhaps the most beloved sports movies of all time. The autograph is rendered in 10/10 blue fountain pen ink, and a notation of "Toledo, Ohio, March 9, 1942" at the bottom of the page appears to be in another hand. The single 8.5x11" page exhibits two horizontal storage folds and a couple dots of foxing at upper left corner, none of which causes the slightest concern. A welcome sight for hundreds of Hall of Fame autograph collectors. *LOA from PSA/DNA. LOA from James Spence Authentication.* **Minimum Bid: $1,000**

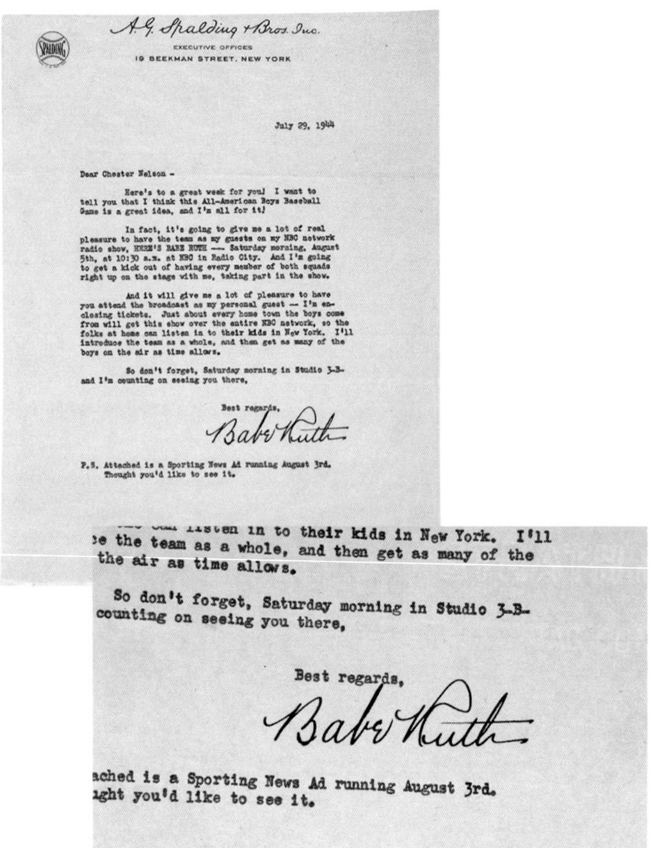

A. G. Spalding + Bros. Inc.
EXECUTIVE OFFICES
19 BEEKMAN STREET, NEW YORK

July 29, 1944

Dear Chester Nelson -

Here's to a great week for you! I want to tell you that I think this All-American Boys Baseball Game is a great idea, and I'm all for it!

In fact, it's going to give me a lot of real pleasure to have the team as my guests on my NBC network radio show, HERE'S BABE RUTH --- Saturday morning, August 5th, at 10:30 a.m. at NBC in Radio City. And I'm going to get a kick out of having every member of both squads right up on the stage with me, taking part in the show.

And it will give me a lot of pleasure to have you attend the broadcast as my personal guest -- I'm enclosing tickets. Just about every home town the boys come from will get this show over the entire NBC network, so the folks at home can listen in to their kids in New York. I'll introduce the team as a whole, and then get as many of the boys on the air as time allows.

So don't forget, Saturday morning in Studio 3-B- and I'm counting on seeing you there,

Best regards,

Babe Ruth

P.S. Attached is a Sporting News Ad running August 3rd. Thought you'd like to see it.

19423 **1944 Babe Ruth Signed Letter.** Simply the finest Babe Ruth autograph in existence, provided here upon a typed letter on "Spalding" letterhead inviting a young ballplayer to the Babe's NBC radio show. Nothing short of a 10/10 grade could possibly be rendered in this case, and the letter itself is equally fine, with original mailing folds and the slightest of inconsequential edge wear the only condition issues of note. Though the Babe signed hundreds of thousands of autographs in his life, autographed letters make up a surprisingly small percentage of that supply, and none could compete with the offered specimen. *LOA from PSA/DNA. LOA from James Spence Authentication.* Minimum Bid: $2,000

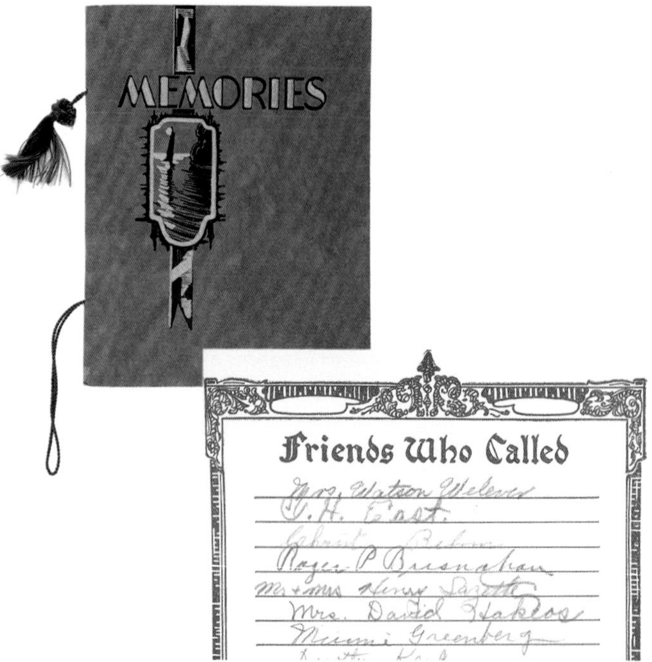

19424 **1944 Tully Frederick "Topsy" Hartsel Funeral Guest Book Signed by Roger Bresnahan.** The world bade farewell to this early Philadelphia Athletics great at the Garner Funeral Home in Toledo, Ohio on October 18, 1944, with scores of mourners turning out to pay their last respects. Offered is the guest book that was signed by those attending the services, each in pencil on seven lined pages. While almost all will be unrecognizable to those outside the Hartsel family, a flawless 10/10 pencil signature from Roger P. Bresnahan will attract the cultured baseball autograph collector. It is worth noting that this would be one of the last autographs that the Duke of Tralee would ever sign, suffering a fatal heart attack at his Toledo home just eight weeks later. The book also holds the text of the eulogy and what is purported to be the last photo ever taken of Hartsel. An envelope full of cards once attached to flowers sent to the funeral includes one from the Athletics. Condition of the softcover book and all of its contents remains perfect, with paper on back cover from scrapbook removal the only issue that may be worthy of note. This piece comes to us from the same Hartsel estate that has provided this auction with Topsy's game worn jersey and 1910 Championship trophy. *LOA from PSA/DNA. LOA from James Spence Authentication.* Minimum Bid: $400

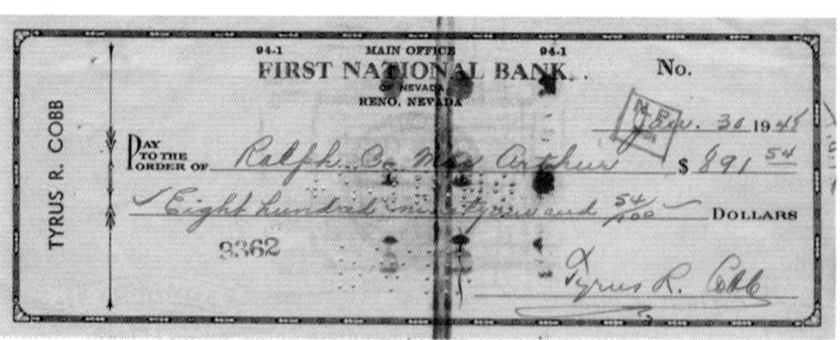

19425 **1945 Ty Cobb Signed Check.** The Hall of Fame's first inductee provides the boldest of his favored green ink upon this personal check from the First National Bank of Reno, Nevada. He makes $891.54 payable to "Ralph C. MacArthur," with all writing and his authorizing "Tyrus R. Cobb" signature rendered in his hand. The bank's red cancellation stamping remains mercifully free of the all-important signature, allowing for maximum visual appeal. Very slight paper loss on verso from scrapbook removal is not visible from the front. A top shelf example of this essential Cobb autograph format. *LOA from PSA/DNA. LOA from James Spence Authentication.* Minimum Bid: $400

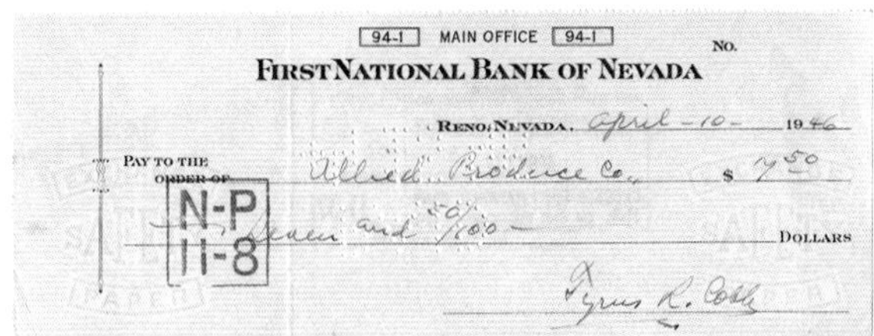

94-1 MAIN OFFICE 94-1 No.

FIRST NATIONAL BANK OF NEVADA

RENO, NEVADA, April -10- 1946

PAY TO THE ORDER OF Allied Produce Co. $ 7 50/

Seven and 50/100 DOLLARS

N-P 11-8

Tyrus R. Cobb

19426 **1946 Ty Cobb Signed Check.** For the autograph collector seeking the most solid assurance of authenticity, the cancelled personal check carries obvious appeal. Here we present a specimen from the man owning Cooperstown plaque number one, drawn from his personal account at the First National Bank of Nevada. All blank ink registers at a strength of 8/10 or better, and is applied entirely in Cobb's hand. The closing "Tyrus R. Cobb" signature, typical of his checks, is the most desirable of formats. A vertical fold line to the left of center is no cause for concern, and all bank stamping and punch coding remains well clear of the autograph. A very solid example. *LOA from PSA/DNA. LOA from James Spence Authentication.* **Minimum Bid: $400**

19427 **Early 1950's Cy Young Signed Index Card.** Unimprovable blue ink signature is ideally situated on the blank side of a 3x5" index card and ready for matting and framing with your favorite photo of this early legend. The card itself is likewise free of flaws, without a stain, crease or tear to be found. An essential component to any quality Hall of Fame autograph collection. *LOA from PSA/DNA. LOA from James Spence Authentication.* **Minimum Bid: $400**

19428 **1950's Bowman Mickey Mantle Cards Lot of 3, Signed.** Three early cards honoring the rising Yankee star, each signed years later in 10/10 blue sharpie by Number Seven himself. Included are 1952 Bowman #101 (Good), 1953 Bowman #59 (Poor) and 1955 Bowman #202 (Good). Each is encapsulated by PSA/DNA for protection and unquestioned authenticity. A great head start toward the project of collecting a complete Mantle signed run, or an opportunity for the smart investor/dealer. **Minimum Bid: $1,000**

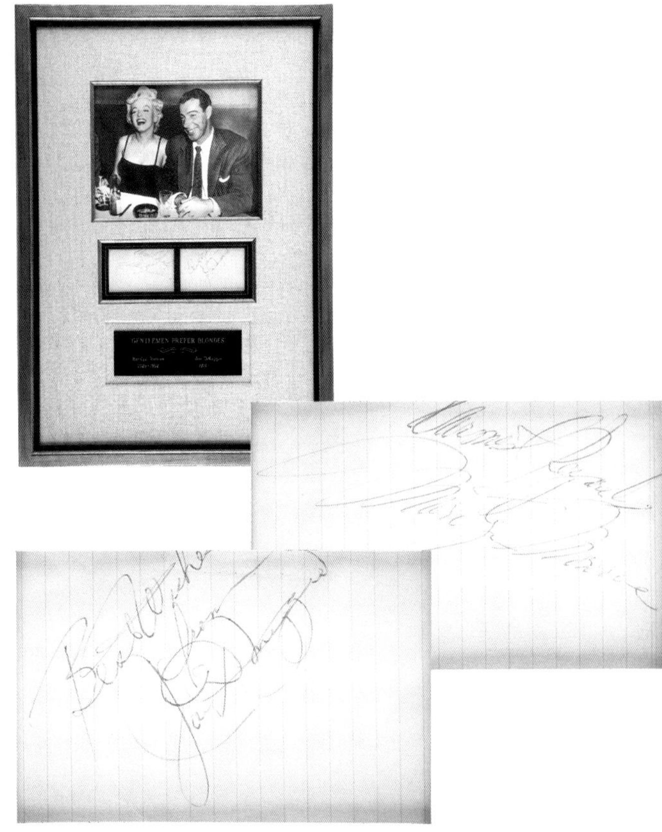

19429 **Circa 1954 Joe DiMaggio & Marilyn Monroe Signed Pages Display.** Almost certainly dating from this ultimate celebrity couple's 274-day marriage, this pair of identical signed pages (2.5x4" each) provides fantastic flowing signatures from Joe DiMaggio and Marilyn Monroe. The identical ink and identical lined paper leaves little doubt but that the autographs were acquired at the same time, and they have been expensively matted and framed beneath an 8x10" modern photographic print of the happy couple out for a night on the town. Marilyn adds "Warmest Regards" to her signature, while DiMaggio counters with "Best Wishes from." Each retains a fine 9/10 boldness, and the pages exhibit no creasing, tearing or staining. The full size of the framed display is 19x26". *LOA from PSA/DNA.* **Minimum Bid: $750**

NEW YORK April 3 1957 No. 438

CHEMICAL CORN EXCHANGE BANK 1-12/210

ROCKEFELLER CENTER OFFICE

PAY TO THE ORDER OF American Airlines $119 79/100

One Hundred nineteen and 79/100 DOLLARS

Jack R. Robinson

19430 **1957 Jackie Robinson Signed Check.** Just two weeks before the first Opening Day in a decade that would fail to feature the great Jackie Robinson, the future Hall of Famer made payment for tickets on "American Airlines" with this check drawn from his "Chemical Corn Exchange Bank" account. All ink is applied in Jackie's 9+/10 blue ink, as well as his flawless closing "Jack R. Robinson" signature. While bank stamping does obscure to some degree a portion of Robinson's writing, the autograph itself remains mercifully clear of these cancellations. No fold lines or other flaws to note. Included is a signed 1993 letter of provenance from Jackie's widow Rachel. *LOA from PSA/DNA. LOA from James Spence Authentication.* **Minimum Bid: $400**

A HERO'S FAREWELL

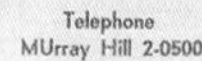

425 LEXINGTON AVENUE
New York 17, N. Y.

January 14, 1957

Mr. Horace Stoneham
New York Giants
100 West 42nd Street
New York City

Dear Mr. Stoneham:

After due consideration I have decided to request to be placed on the voluntary retired list as I am going to devote my full time to the business opportunities that have been presented.

My sincere thanks to you and to Mr. Feeney for your wonderful cooperation and understanding in this matter.

I assure you that my retirement has nothing to do with my trade to your organization. From all I have heard from people who have worked with you it would have been a pleasure to have been in your organization.

Again my thanks and continued success for you and the New York Giants.

Sincerely,

Jackie Robinson
Jackie Robinson

JR:cc

19431 **1957 Jackie Robinson Signed Retirement Letter.** The incredible saga of baseball's most culturally significant career came to a close when this letter was presented to New York Giants owner Horace Stoneham, who had acquired the pioneering Hall of Famer from the Brooklyn Dodgers for the sum of Dick Littlefield and $30,000 cash. In the ten years since his heroic transversal of baseball's color line, the superstar infielder had won over most of the sporting world with his talent and dignity, inspiring an outcry from baseball fans at his departure from the Major Leagues quite different but almost as vocal as was heard upon his arrival. Dodgers general manager Buzzie Bavasi would explain that that the dismissal of Robinson from his beloved Bums had been team owner Walter O'Malley's idea alone, and Jackie would characterize the 2008 Hall of Fame inductee in his 1972 autobiography *I Never Had It Made* as "viciously antagonistic." Bavasi was personally opposed to the trade, noting, "The only reason he was traded was because Walter O'Malley and Jackie never got along. It was a personal feud between Walter and Jackie, and I was asked to trade him. Walter wanted a trade a year earlier, but I told Walter we could win the pennant in '56 with Jackie and wouldn't without him. So he put it off a year."

Though the popular story in baseball culture is that Robinson considered the Polo Grounds the enemy camp and chose retirement over the treasonous act of suiting up in a Giants uniform, the truth is that his denial of such rumors in the text of his January 14, 1957 letter to Stoneham is likely genuine. He writes:

Dear Mr. Stoneham:

After due consideration I have decided to request to be placed on the voluntary retired list as I am going to devote my full time to the business opportunities that have been presented.

My sincere thanks to you and to Mr. Feeney for your wonderful cooperation and understanding in this matter.

I assure you that my retirement has nothing to do with my trade to your organization. From all I have heard from people who have worked with you it would have been a pleasure to have been in your organization.

Again my thanks and continued success for you and the New York Giants.

Sincerely,

(signed) Jackie Robinson

It has been well established that Robinson had signed a two-year contract to become a vice president and director of personnel for Chock Full o' Nuts, a chain of New York-based lunch counters, in December of 1956, and his letter of retirement appears on company letterhead. A story leaked by *Look Magazine,* written weeks before the trade, was to break the news of Robinson's retirement, though Bavasi would irk Jackie by publicly surmising a few weeks after the December 13th trade announcement that it was a ruse intended to loosen Giants purse strings. And so, days later, this letter arrived at Stoneham's Times Square office, ending all such speculation. Stoneham was gracious in his acceptance of the disappointing news, telling Jackie, "I can't help but thinking it would have been fun to have had you on our side for a year or two."

Rarely does a document of such historical importance find its way into the public domain, and Heritage is honored by the opportunity to present it to the collecting world. There is no question but that the career of Jackie Robinson has had an enormous effect upon American culture that extends far beyond the grandstands of Major League Baseball. When Robinson bade farewell to the game with this letter, it was far different than it had been upon its arrival, and far more worthy of its characterization as our National Pastime.

The 8.5x11" page exhibits minor toning at the edges and insignificant wrinkling at the lower edges, presenting flawlessly. Robinson's signature is 10/10. *LOA from PSA/DNA. LOA from James Spence Authentication.* **Minimum Bid: $4,000**

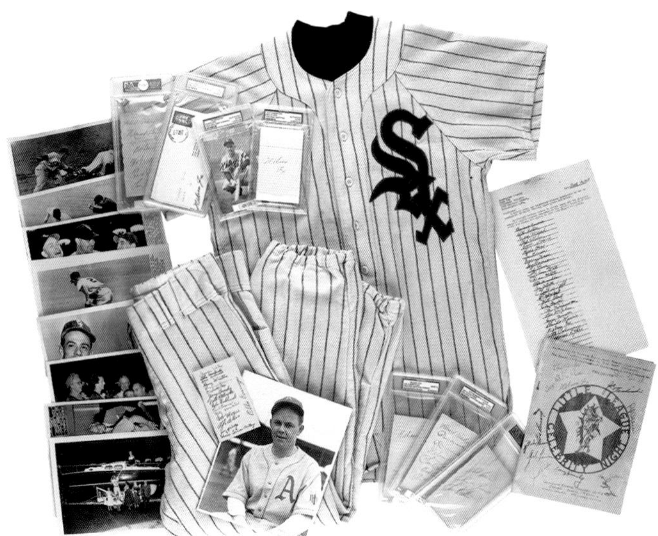

19432 **Nellie Fox Memorabilia Archive with Multiple Autographs, Photographs & Uniform Pieces.** The first ever American League MVP to wear a White Sox uniform, this spunky little Hall of Fame second baseman is best remembered for his dependable glove work and the ever-present wad of tobacco between his cheek and gum. One fan's lifelong collection of Fox artifacts are compiled into this single lot for the collector and dealer alike. Presented are: 1) Circa 1959 salesman's sample Nellie Fox uniform jersey and pants. Tagged "Wilson 36" and "Wilson 32" respectively. White pinstriped flannel exhibits minor age toning but no other flaws of note. 2) Game worn sleeveless undershirt. Number "2" in marker on "Wilson [size] medium" tag, "Fox" written on equipment tape applied above rear hem. Good wear. 3) Seven autographs from Fox encapsulated in PSA/DNA holders. Four in ink, three in pencil. All NRMT or better. 4) 1953 "Little League Celebrity Night" program signed on cover by Fox, Chief Bender and others. Autographs are 9/10 or better, program VG. 5) 1949 Philadelphia Athletics team signed sheet signifying permission for use of images by Sportstamp Company. Autographs include Fox, Al Simmons, Jimmie Dykes. Autographs 9/10 or better, sheet is EX. 6) 1944 Jamestown Falcons team signed index card with Fox (minor league, age seventeen), NRMT. 7) Eight wire photos picturing Fox, dating from 1951 to 1959. Average size 7x9", EX+. *LOA from PSA/DNA (autographs). LOA from James Spence Authentication (autographs).* Minimum Bid: $1,000

19433 **1962 "Safe at Home" Lobby Card, Signed by Mantle & Maris.** While this charmingly clumsy tale didn't exactly challenge "Lawrence of Arabia" for Best Picture honors in 1962 Academy Award voting, the casting of the M&M Boys has secured this film a place in the hearts of millions of movie buffs. Presented here is a classic image of Roger and Mickey with the film's young protagonist, posted upon one of the film's lobby cards issued at the time of the original release. Years later came the 10/10 blue sharpie signatures from the Yankee legends, elevating the piece to the heights of collectibility. The lobby card measures a standard 11x14" in size, with a four-inch vertical tear at bottom center barely noticeable, and well clear of the autographs. From any distance, the piece exudes a NRMT appearance. Skillfully matted and framed, with an engraved informational plaque, to final dimensions of 20x22". *LOA from PSA/DNA. LOA from James Spence Authentication.* Minimum Bid: $1,000

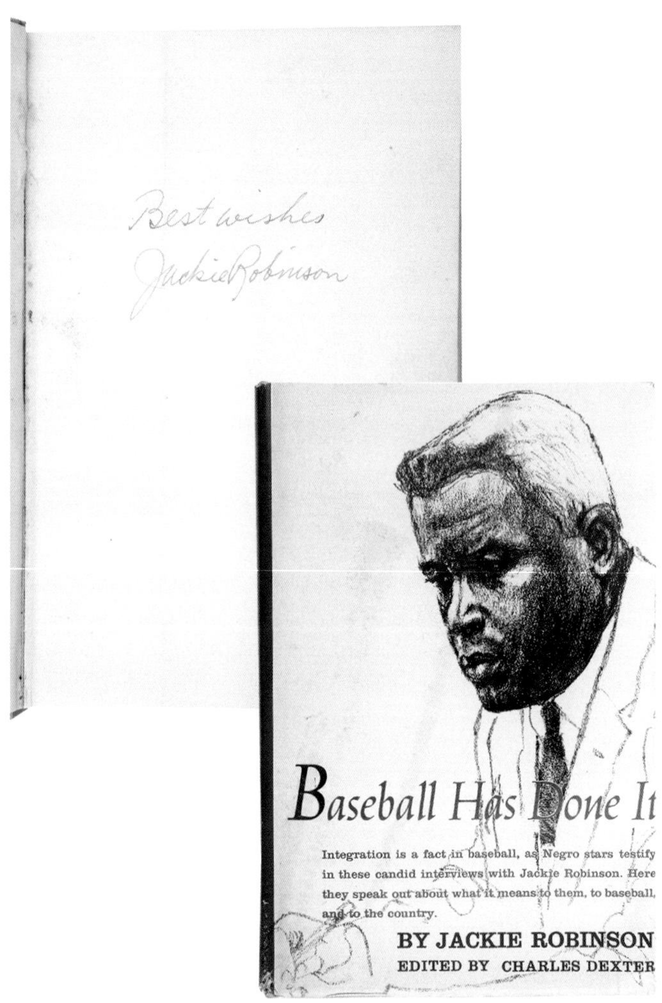

19434 **1964 Jackie Robinson Signed Book.** "The right of every American to first-class citizenship is the most important issue today," begins the brave racial pioneer's *Baseball Has Done It,* recounting his historic crossing of our National Pastime's color barrier and the challenges that still lay ahead. Given Robinson's supreme relevance to the integration of baseball, this book is widely considered to be one of the most attractive media for his autograph. We find on the opening blank page of this first edition hardcover, with "Best Wishes, Jackie Robinson" provided in 10/10 blue ink. A small degree of toning is evident on this page but to no visual detriment, and the book is otherwise in fine condition with the original dustjacket showing some toning and edge wear but remaining complete and solid. An important keepsake from one of the most important and inspiring figures of the twentieth century. *LOA from PSA/DNA.* **Minimum Bid: $600**

19435 **1969 New York Mets Signed "Portfolio of Stars."** This collection of individual portraits by Ron Stark that was distributed by New York City's *Daily News* has long been popular with autograph hounds, who worked to seek out all members of this miraculous World Championship squad to secure their signatures. One collector has done just that, successfully tracking down sixteen of the twenty Mets pictured and acquiring 10/10 black sharpie signatures on each 9x12" print. Highlights include Ryan, Seaver, Agee, Koosman, Swoboda, Shamsky, Kranepool, Jones, Harrelson, Grote, Gentry and Clendenon. Only Hodges, Taylor, McGraw and Cardwell are present in unsigned state. The portfolio folder is also signed by Ryan is 10/10 blue ink. A few of the prints exhibit minor bends at the corners that should be invisible upon framing. A great way to fill a wall of your trophy room with Amazin' memories. *LOA from PSA/DNA. LOA from James Spence Authentication.* **Minimum Bid: $400**

19436 **1970's Hilton Smith Signed Index Card.** With a known record of 161 victories against just twenty-two losses, and a reputation for the most effective curveball in Negro League history, Smith ranks high on that League's list of greatest pitchers ever. Sadly, the Hall of Fame induction he so richly deserved came eighteen years after his passing, with the volume of available autographs being one of the casualties of this lengthy oversight. Here we present one of the most attractive examples we've encountered from the skimpy supply, a lengthy inscription penned in 10/10 blue ink on a blank 3x5" card. It reads, "Hilton Smith pitcher, played in 6 All Star games, 2 Negro World Series, Won 2 games in each." Index card itself is likewise NRMT-MT. *LOA from PSA/DNA. LOA from James Spence Authentication.* **Minimum Bid: $300**

19437 **1970's Hilton Smith Signed Index Card.** Cooperstown's long overdue correction that brought a flood of Negro League talent into the Hall has complicated the lives of many autograph collectors who were forced to seek out the rare autographs from these underappreciated superstars. This lined 3x5" index card will make one such collector's day, as the 10/10 black ink signature is made further appealing by a notation that reads, "Pitcher, Kansas City Monarch, 1945 won 28 lost 4, 1941 won 25 lost 1." The index card is likewise free of flaws. *LOA from PSA/DNA. LOA from James Spence Authentication.* Minimum Bid: $600

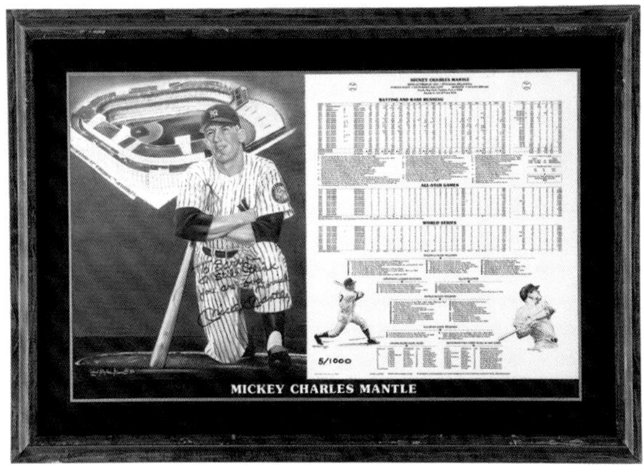

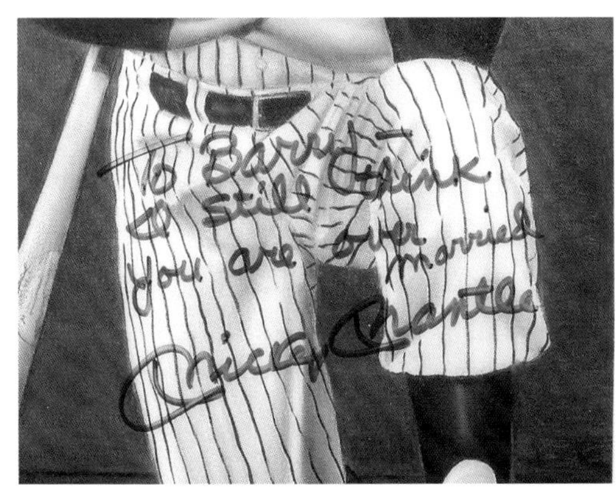

19438 **1980's Mickey Mantle Signed Print to Barry Halper.** The Mick pays tribute to the wife of esteemed late collector Barry Halper upon this unique print pairing a Robert Simon portrait and a lengthy stat sheet recounting the Hall of Famer's storied career. In 10/10 blue sharpie, Mantle writes, "To Barry, I still think you are over-married, Mickey Mantle." A "5/1000" limited edition notation to the right appears to relate to the print itself, which measures 12x20" in size. Complete framed dimensions: 18x25". A unique piece that once held a place of honor in arguably the finest private baseball collection ever assembled. *LOA from PSA/DNA. LOA from James Spence Authentication.* Minimum Bid: $400

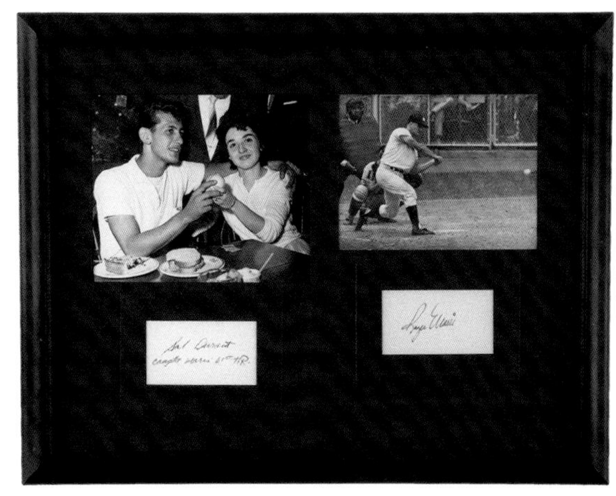

19439 **1980's Roger Maris & Sal Durante Signed Index Cards.** Unique display piece features the hero of the 1961 home run chase and that season's most famous fan. Unimprovable blue ink signatures from the pair each reside upon their own blank 3x5" index cards, with Durante adding a notation to his autograph reading, "Caught Maris 61st HR." Matted above each autographed index card is a photo taken at this remarkable time in baseball history. Durante poses with his fiancee and the historic home run ball, their ticket lucky stubs on the table between them, while Maris prepares to send one skyward. Quality matting and framing extends the total dimensions of the piece to 18x24". *LOA from PSA/DNA.* Minimum Bid: $300

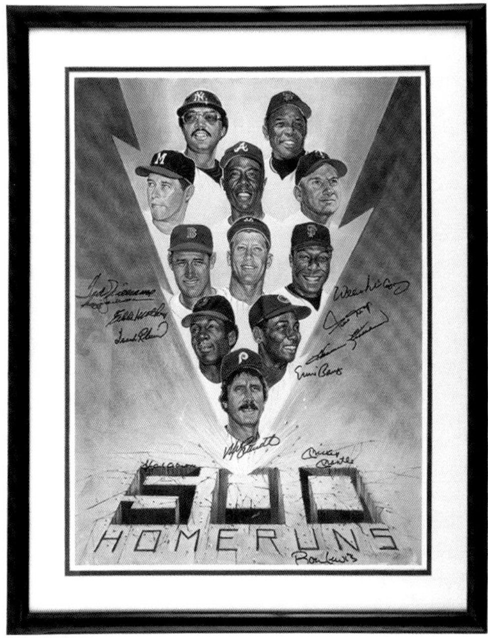

19440 **500 Home Run Club Poster Signed by Eleven.** The classic 1986 Ron Lewis "lighting bolt" artwork picturing the Elite Eleven offers the finest sharpie autographs you'll ever find from Williams, Robinson, Killebrew, Jackson, Mantle, Mays, Aaron, Schmidt, Banks, Mathews and McCovey. An equally fine autograph from the artist brings the total to an even dozen. The poster presents not a single fault to mention, and is tastefully matted and framed to final dimensions of 23.5x29". *LOA from PSA/DNA. LOA from James Spence Authentication.* Minimum Bid: $500

19441 **Holtzman Sports Classics Signed Sports Books Lot of 10.** Attractive matched set compiles ten of the best sports titles issued in the last half century, bound in attractive red and blue leather with golden embossing. Each book is signed in unimprovable blue ink by the author. Featured are: *Instant Replay* by Jerry Kramer, *Eight Men Out* by Eliot Asimov, *Babe* by Rober Creamer, *Paper Lion* by George Plimpton, *The Long Season* by Jim Brosnan, *Veeck—as in Wreck* by Bill Veeck, *Farewell to Sport* by Paul Gallico, *The Sweet Science* by A.J. Liebling, *The Boys of Summer* by Roger Kahn, *The Glory of Their Times* by Lawrence Ritter. An elegant addition to your study/trophy room, or a great gift for the literate sports fan in your life. *LOA from PSA/DNA. LOA from James Spence Authentication.* **Minimum Bid: $400**

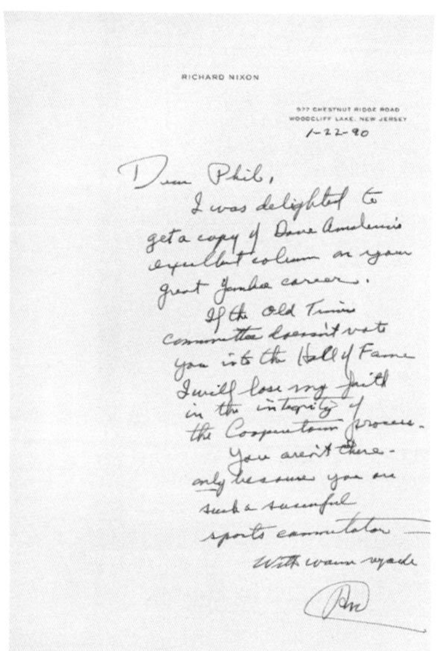

RICHARD NIXON

577 CHESTNUT RIDGE ROAD
WOODCLIFF LAKE, NEW JERSEY

1-22-90

Dear Phil,
I was delighted to get a copy of Dave Anderson's excellent column on your great Yankee career.
If the Old Timers committee doesn't vote you into the Hall of Fame I will lose my faith in the integrity of the Cooperstown process.
You aren't there - only because you are such a successful sports commentator —
With warm regards
RN

19442 **1990 Richard Nixon Handwritten Letter to Phil Rizzuto.** "I don't know a lot about politics," President Nixon was once quoted as saying, "but I do know a lot about baseball." Battling only our current Commander in Chief for recognition as the greatest baseball supporter ever to occupy the White House, Nixon sent this handwritten letter of support to Phil Rizzuto, letting Scooter know that he thought he had earned his bronze plaque. "If the Old Timers committee doesn't vote you into the Hall of Fame I will lose my faith in the integrity of the Cooperstown process," he writes, in part. The single handwritten page on Nixon's personal letterhead is signed simply "R.N." Both the blue ink and the page itself remain in flawless condition, with original mailing folds. From the personal collection of Phil Rizzuto, with a letter of provenance from his widow Cora. *LOA from PSA/DNA. LOA from James Spence Authentication.* **Minimum Bid: $400**

19443 **Early 1990's Mickey Mantle Signed Jacket.** Fine replica by the "Mitchell & Ness Cooperstown Collection" is a dead ringer for the warm-up jacket that greeted the young Commerce Comet when he came up to the Yankees in 1951. But this high-quality navy wool letterman style jacket goes one step better, providing upon the chest a 9+/10 blue sharpie autograph from the esteemed Hall of Fame slugger. While signed jerseys are fairly commonly seen from this iconic Yank, this is the first signed example we can recall of this highly collectible garment. Size Large. An opportunity not to be missed! *LOA from James Spence Authentication.* **Minimum Bid: $750**

19444 **1990's Joe DiMaggio Signed Jersey.** Exacting replica of Joltin' Joe's 1939 home New York Yankees jersey could only be the work of Mitchell & Ness, well established in the hobby as the top craftsmen of vintage replica shirts. This one is made all the more appealing by the 9+/10 blue sharpie signature that joins the gorgeous Centennial patch on the sleeve and number "5" on verso. The autograph is positioned below the logo "NY" for ideal display, and leaves the jersey ready for framing or placement upon a mannequin in your trophy room. *LOA from PSA/DNA. LOA from James Spence Authentication.* **Minimum Bid: $750**

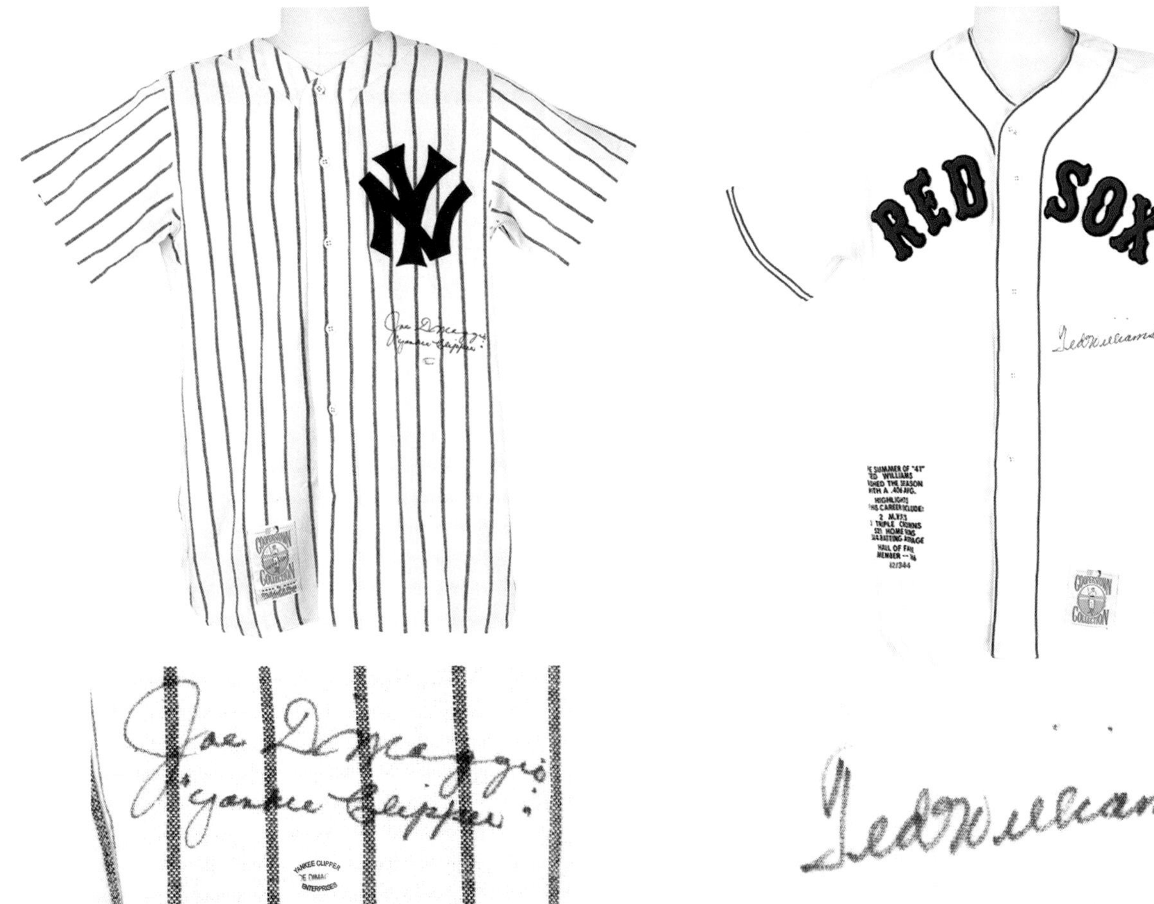

19445 **1990's Joe DiMaggio "Yankee Clipper" Signed Jersey.** Red Schoendienst once noted of Joe DiMaggio, "He was a solid ball player in every way. I never saw him make a mistake, but there was a smooth way he had of going about everything. That's why they put that name on him, the Yankee Clipper." Presumably this also explains the smooth, flawless application of the blue sharpie signature on the chest of this Mitchell & Ness Cooperstown Collection flannel jersey, underscored with the famous nickname rarely seen on DiMaggio's autographed collectibles. Authenticating sticker and paperwork attribute the creation to "Yankee Clipper Enterprises," DiMaggio's personal marketing company. A fine memento of Marilyn Monroe's ex. *LOA from PSA/DNA. LOA from James Spence Authentication.* **Minimum Bid: $750**

19446 **1990's Ted Williams Signed Jersey.** Top quality limited edition replica of The Kid's rookie Red Sox gamer is blessed with a 10/10 blue sharpie signature from the greatest hitter that ever lived. A full paragraph of statistics and career highlights is embroidered at lower right tail, noting that the piece is "62/344" of a limited edition. With the classic and colorful Baseball Centennial patch on the left sleeve, the display value of this highly collectible piece is off the charts. Produced by Williams' "Green Diamond Sports, Inc." marketing company, with a photograph of Williams at this signing. *LOA from PSA/DNA. LOA from James Spence Authentication.* **Minimum Bid: $750**

19447 **1996 New York Yankees Team Signed World Series Full Ticket, PSA Mint 9.** Eighteen years of frustration in the Bronx came to an end this October as the Yanks took a page from General Sherman's playbook, bringing sorrow to the hearts of the residents of Atlanta. With this Game Seven ticket made obsolete by the Series-clinching victory in Game Six, one fan decided to put it to good use by seeking out the autographs of this World Championship squad that launched the latest Bronx dynasty. Twenty-four black and silver sharpie autographs decorate the front and back of this oversized ducat, with all major figures accounted for: Jeter, Torre, Rivera, Mendoza, Gooden, Fielder, Martinez, O'Neill, Wetteland, Cone, Williams, Girardi, Boggs, Rains, Leyritz, Strawberry, Posada and more. Encapsulated by PSA/DNA in a Mint 9 holder for protection and unquestioned authenticity. **Minimum Bid: $400**

19448 **1998 Joe DiMaggio & Leroy Neiman Signed Lithograph.** The unmistakable impressionistic style of sports' most celebrated artist captures the prettiest swing in baseball history, framed against a flaming yellow background of Cleveland's League Park grandstands. Entitled, "The DiMaggio Cut," the masterful work is numbered "62/200" of a limited edition, and signed first by the subject in 10/10 blue sharpie, then by the artist in 8/10 black felt tip which has taken on an amber hue. The 19x24" print has been expertly matted and framed to final dimensions of 29x34", ready to take on a place of honor in your study or trophy room. Distributed by Yankee Clipper Enterprises, DiMaggio's personal marketing company, with a letter of provenance from DiMaggio's lawyer Morris Engelberg. *LOA from PSA/DNA. LOA from James Spence Authentication.* **Minimum Bid: $750**

THE HOWARD LYON AUTOGRAPHED GOVERNMENT POSTCARD COLLECTION

Now well into his eighties, Howard Lyon was just a young boy in Connecticut when he undertook the hobby of collecting autographs from the greatest stars of the baseball diamond through the mail. As was the common method utilized at the time, young Howard would deliver to his heroes self addressed penny postcards, better known to the hobby as government postcards, in the hope that they would one day return with an autograph. And many did. On the pages that follow, we present the fruits of this labor, certainly one of the finest and freshest collections of GPC's to reach the auction block in quite some time.

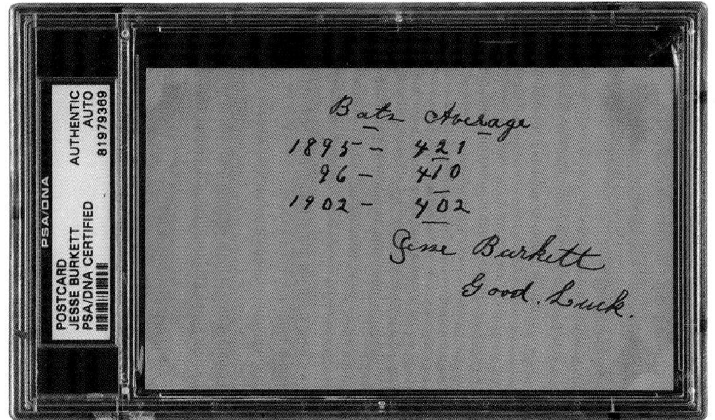

19449 **Circa 1936 Jesse Burkett Signed Government Postcard.** Though this 1946 Hall of Fame inductee began his professional baseball career as a particularly promising pitcher, compiling a thirty-nine and six record for a Worcester, Massachusetts minor league franchise, Burkett is best remembered today for his three seasons posting batting averages north of the magical .400 mark. Though later research would lower his 1899 average to .396, Burkett provides an historically inaccurate recollection to a young autograph collector that misses the year entirely. Joining Burkett's 10/10 black fountain pen autograph and "Good Luck" wishes, he writes "Bats Average: 1895 - 421, 96 - 410, 1902 - 402," the final stat being a full ninety-six points more generous than his recorded mark for that season. We'll forgive the mistake, however, and instead concentrate on the quality and intense scarcity of this amazing GPC. One of many government postcards from the collection of young Howard Lyon presented within this auction. Encapsulated by PSA/DNA for protection and unquestioned authenticity. **Minimum Bid: $1,000**

19450 **1936 Lou Gehrig Signed Government Postcard.** The Iron Horse's blistering home run pace this season, averaging better than one long ball for every twelve at bats, earned him the well deserved second MVP award of his career, and helped to power the Yanks to the World Championship in October. His 9+/10 pencil inscription offers greetings to the boy who sent this self-addressed postcard, reading "Best Wishes Howard, Lou Gehrig." Postmark is from Gehrig's New Rochelle, New York hometown. A small degree of paper loss on verso is the result of scrapbook removal. One of many government postcards from the collection of young Howard Lyon presented within this auction. Encapsulated by PSA/DNA for protection and unquestioned authenticity. **Minimum Bid: $1,500**

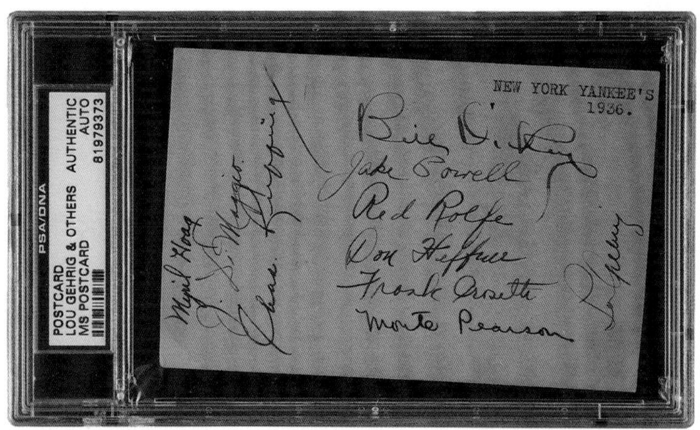

19451 **1936 New York Yankees Signed Government Postcard with Gehrig, DiMaggio.** One of two postcards blessed by the hands of the World Champion 1936 Yankees, this example is somewhat more comprehensive, providing four Hall of Fame autographs in the form of Gehrig, the rookie DiMaggio, Ruffing and Dickey. Six more are here as well: Hoag, Powell, Rolfe, Heffner, Crosetti and Pearson, all in 9/10 or better black fountain pen ink. One of many government postcards from the collection of young Howard Lyon presented within this auction. Encapsulated by PSA/DNA for protection and unquestioned authenticity. **Minimum Bid: $1,500**

19452 **1936 New York Yankees Signed Government Postcard with Lou Gehrig.** Six members of the World Championship Yankees conspired to make the day of one lucky fan who sent this self-addressed GPC to the fabled Bronx ballpark they called home. Gehrig's 9+/10 black fountain pen signature is joined by equally strong specimens from Heffner, Hadley, Selkirk, Crosetti and Rolfe. Each player's position is identified by the collector's neat typing. One of many government postcards from the collection of young Howard Lyon presented within this auction. Encapsulated by PSA/DNA for protection and unquestioned authenticity. **Minimum Bid: $1,000**

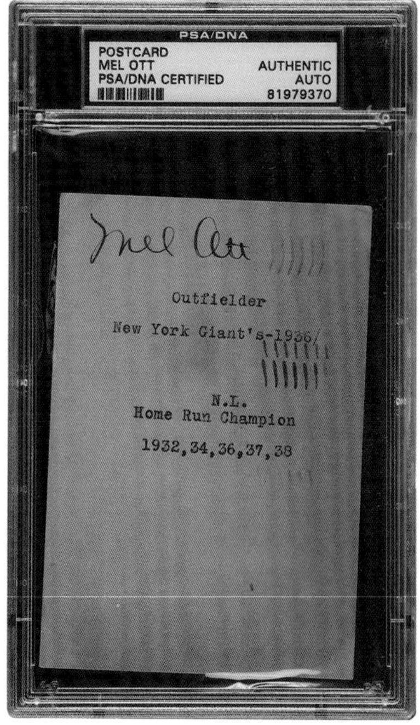

19453 **1936 Mel Ott Signed Government Postcard.** The third man to enter the elite brotherhood of 500 home run hitters provides a 10/10 black fountain pen signature midway through a season that would see his New York Giants claim the National League pennant and face the Yanks in an historic Subway Series. The collector's typed notations are joined by postmark stamping on the autographed side, but none affects the signature in any regard. One of many government postcards from the collection of young Howard Lyon presented within this auction. Encapsulated by PSA/DNA for protection and unquestioned authenticity. **Minimum Bid: $600**

19454 **1937 Jim Bottomley Signed Government Postcard.** The star first baseman for the great St. Louis Cardinals teams of the 1920's, Bottomley provides a significant challenge to modern autograph collectors due to his 1959 passing, a full fifteen years prior to his Hall of Fame induction. His black fountain pen ink signature, mailed from St. Louis in May of his final season in the game, is a 10/10 marvel. One of many government postcards from the collection of young Howard Lyon presented within this auction. Encapsulated by PSA/DNA for protection and unquestioned authenticity. **Minimum Bid: $400**

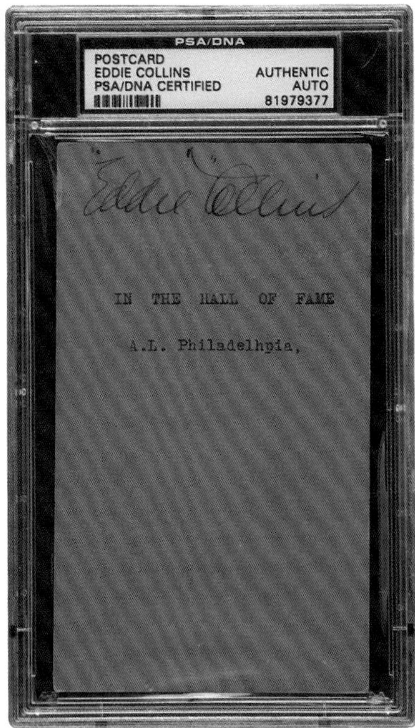

19455 **1939 Eddie Collins Signed Government Postcard.** Considered one of the greatest bunters and lead-off men in baseball history, "Cocky" Collins finished his career with 3,315 hits, 744 steals and a lifetime average of .333. The 1914 American League MVP provided a 9+/10 black fountain pen signature for a collector the year of his Hall of Fame induction, mailed from the city of Boston where he would pass away in 1951. Very minor paper loss on verso from scrapbook removal. One of many government postcards from the collection of young Howard Lyon presented within this auction. Encapsulated by PSA/DNA for protection and unquestioned authenticity. **Minimum Bid: $300**

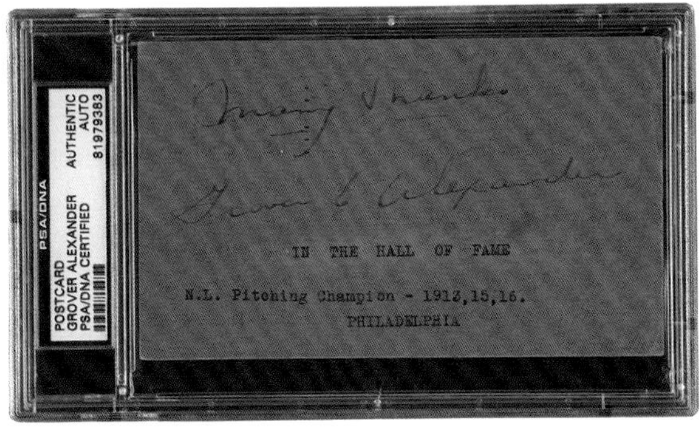

19456 **1941 Grover Cleveland Alexander Signed Government Postcard.** Had he not lost a season and a half to military service during the first World War, Old Pete almost certainly would have joined Cy Young and Walter Johnson as the only men in Major League history to tally four hundred victories. Still the bronze medalist in that event, the troubled hurler is remembered with this 7/10 "Grover C. Alexander" autograph to a fan penned beneath a "Many Thanks" sentiment. One of many government postcards from the collection of young Howard Lyon presented within this auction. Encapsulated by PSA/DNA for protection and unquestioned authenticity. **Minimum Bid: $600**

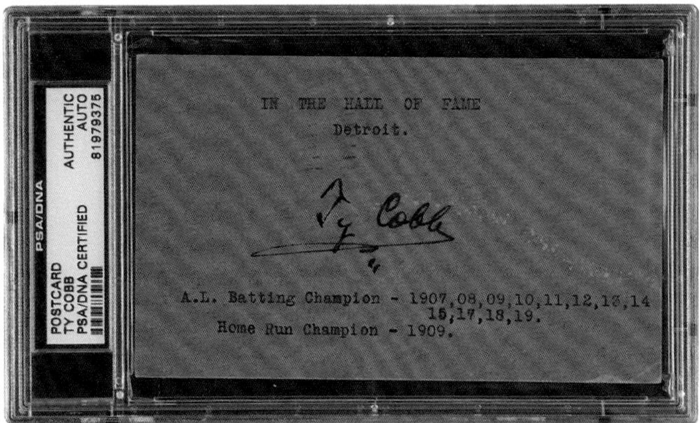

19457 **1941 Ty Cobb Signed Government Postcard.** A booming black fountain pen signature from the greatest talent of our National Pastime's Dead Ball Era was mailed from the Peach's home in Menlo Park, California on the thirtieth anniversary of Cobb's first ever grand slam. A small degree of paper loss on verso is likely attributed to removal from a scrapbook, otherwise the postcard shows no noteworthy condition faults. One of many government postcards from the collection of young Howard Lyon presented within this auction. Encapsulated by PSA/DNA for protection and unquestioned authenticity. **Minimum Bid: $500**

19458 **1941 Hugh Duffy Signed Government Postcard.** Inducted to the Hall of Fame four years after mailing this postcard to a fan, Duffy posted one of the greatest seasons in baseball history in 1894, winning the Triple Crown with eighteen home runs, 145 runs batted in and an outrageous .440 average. His 10/10 black fountain pen signature is notated "Red Sox Coach" in Duffy's hand, and bears a postmark from his Boston hometown. One of many government postcards from the collection of young Howard Lyon presented within this auction. Encapsulated by PSA/DNA for protection and unquestioned authenticity. **Minimum Bid: $300**

19459 **1937 Rogers Hornsby Signed Government Postcard.** Just three months to the day before this Hall of Fame second baseman would take his final swings in a Major League uniform, Rajah mailed this massive 9+/10 black fountain pen signature to a fan. Postmark is from the city of St. Louis, where Hornsby made his case for immortality. One of many government postcards from the collection of young Howard Lyon presented within this auction. Encapsulated by PSA/DNA for protection and unquestioned authenticity. **Minimum Bid: $300**

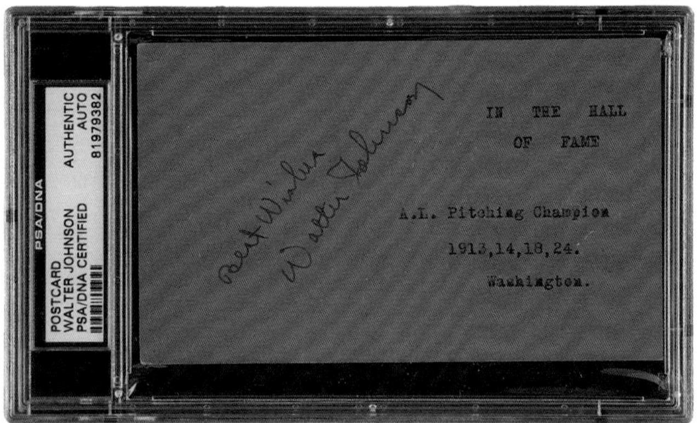

19460 **1941 Walter Johnson Signed Government Postcard.** "The first time I faced him," Ty Cobb once said of Johnson, "I watched him take that easy windup. And then something went past me that made me flinch. The thing just hissed with danger. We couldn't touch him... every one of us knew we'd met the most powerful arm ever turned loose in a ball park." The Big Train's 8+/10 black fountain pen signature resides below a "Best Wishes" greeting upon this rare GPC mailed from Johnson's Germantown, Maryland hometown. One of many government postcards from the collection of young Howard Lyon presented within this auction. Encapsulated by PSA/DNA for protection and unquestioned authenticity. **Minimum Bid: $600**

19461 **1941 Napoleon "Larry" Lajoie Signed Government Postcard.** Number twenty-nine on *The Sporting News'* 1999 list of the one hundred greatest baseball players of all time, Lajoie was considered the leading contender for Cobb's title of the American League's greatest hitter, following him into the Hall of Fame in 1937. He provides his less formal "Larry Lajoie" autograph here in 9+/10 black ink, adding the date of "April - 29/41" below. One of many government postcards from the collection of young Howard Lyon presented within this auction. Encapsulated by PSA/DNA for protection and unquestioned authenticity. **Minimum Bid: $300**

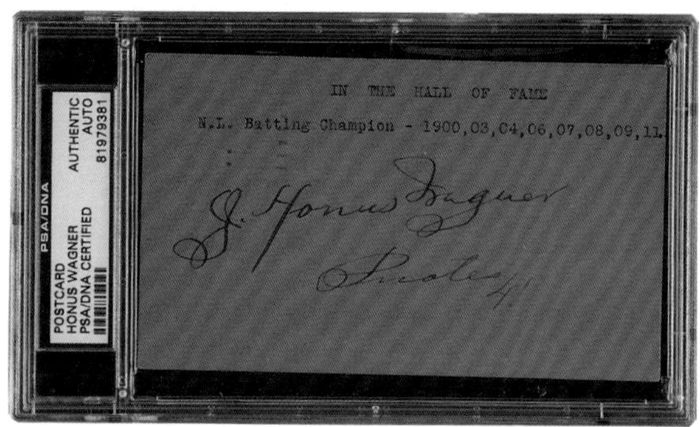

19462 **1941 Honus Wagner Signed Government Postcard.** The brilliant Hall of Fame shortstop remains to this day one of the Steel City's most beloved sporting icons, and his gorgeous 9+/10 black fountain pen signature proudly notes his allegiance with a "Pirates 41" notation below. Postcard is mailed from Philadelphia, which coincides with a Bucs doubleheader at Shibe Park. One of many government postcards from the collection of young Howard Lyon presented within this auction. Encapsulated by PSA/DNA for protection and unquestioned authenticity. **Minimum Bid: $600**

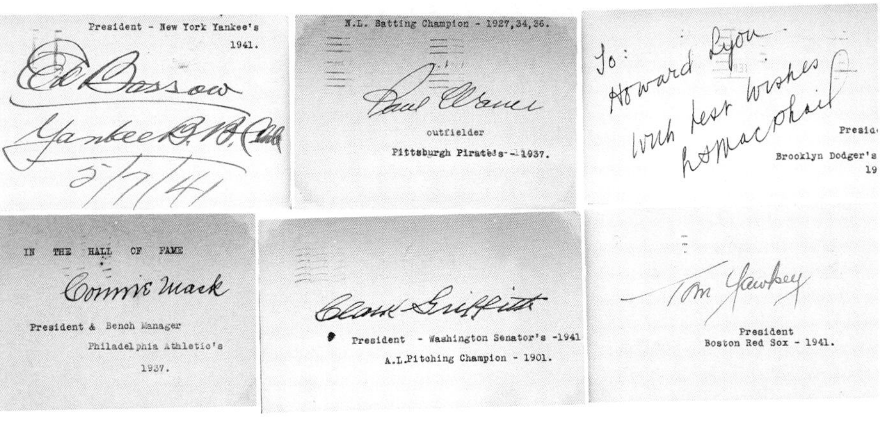

19463 1930's-40's Major League Baseball Players Signed Government Postcards Lot of 249 with Ruth, Wagner, Walter Johnson. Perhaps the finest vintage collection of autographed government postcards we've ever encountered, this thrilling grouping is offered for the first time to the collecting hobby, having been consigned to us by the elderly gentleman who personally collected them seven decades ago. While the very finest specimens from this collection are being offered as individual lots within this auction, there is still absolutely no shortage of magnificent specimens within this massive lot. There is far too much to list or image within the pages of this catalog, so we strongly recommend that interested parties visit our offices to peruse the collection personally if at all possible. Unless otherwise noted, all autographs appear in 9/10 or better blue ink, with the mailed postcards toned with age but otherwise free of any concerning defects.

Highlights: Ruth (2/10), Wagner, Walter Johnson, Lazzeri (postcard slightly trimmed), Ted Williams, Speaker (3/10), Mack (2/10), Vaughan, Vance, Musial, Manush, Barrow, Ruffing, Gomez, Joe DiMaggio, Hoyt, Rizzuto, Ernie Bonham (tough, d. 1949), McCarthy, Mack, Simmons, Harry Davis (d. 1947), Lyons, Griffith, Harris, Rick Ferrell, Appling, Walsh, Greenberg, Gehringer, Goslin (7/10 pencil), Eric McNair (d. 1949), Cochrane, Feller (signed in 1937), 1939 Indians with 14 including Feller, 1941 Indians with 16 including Boudreau, Boudreau (8/10), Jim Bagby Jr. (tough, d. 1954), Landis, Harridge, Frick, MacPhail Sr., Reese (2 different), Herman, Wheat, Medwick, Grimes, Klein, Stengel, Averill, Paul Waner, Dizzy Dean, Dahlgren, Root, Mize, Southworth, Slaughter (2 different), Haines, Martin, McKechnie, Lombardi, Lloyd Waner, Vander Meer, Luque, Roush, Kelly, Hubbell, Terry, Hartnett (9/10 pencil), Frisch, Lopez, 1942 White Sox with13 including Appling, Ruffing, Red Barber, Hafey and many, many more.

Turn of the century names are here, as are various All-Stars and borderline Hall of Famers. All postcards have typed identifiers on them, showing just how serious young Howard Lyon was with his hobby. Included is the large leatherbound scrapbook in which the vast majority of the postcards still reside, held with corners rather than glue so that removal will be simple and danger-free. Exceptional break down value here, though the collection is so appealing in its entirety that the true baseball historian may wish to preserve it as a whole. A prewar autograph collector's dream lot. *LOA from PSA/DNA. LOA from James Spence Authentication.*
Minimum Bid: $5,000

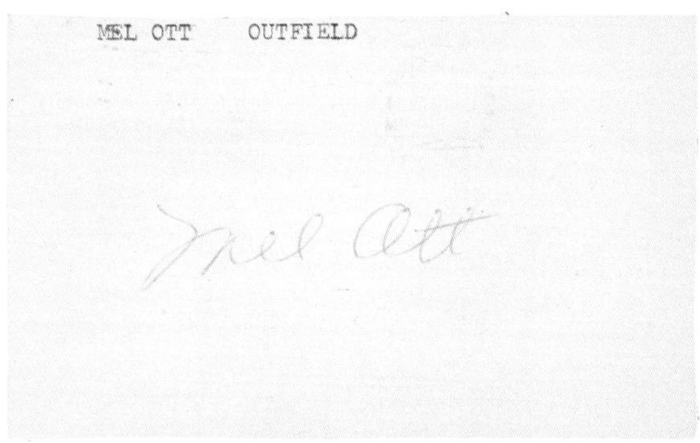

19464 **1951 Mel Ott Signed Government Postcard.** The July 7, 1951 postmark from Oakland, California suggests this penny postcard was mailed by the 500 Home Run Club member just before he made the trip east to be honored at the Baseball Hall of Fame induction ceremonies. Ott's simple black ink signature rates a solid 8/10, and a couple of mild vertical creases have no significant effect upon the display. A nice specimen from a significant time in this superstar slugger's short life. *LOA from PSA/DNA. LOA from James Spence Authentication.* **Minimum Bid: $500**

19465 **Circa 1939 Walter Johnson Signed Black & White Hall of Fame Plaque Image.** Let us begin this description by stressing that the offered piece is not technically an Artvue plaque as are the others presented in adjacent lots within this auction, but rather a clipping from the 1939 Hall of Fame Grand Opening magazine which has been subsequently backed with thin cardboard to approximate the appearance of an Artvue. Remember that Artvues were first issued in 1947, a year after Johnson's passing, and are impossible to acquire in autographed form as such. This is an entirely convincing alternative, however, and the black ink signature that fills the bottom white border of the "card" is as fine as can be. Absent any creasing, tearing or staining, the 4x6" piece itself also leaves no room for improvement. *LOA from PSA/DNA. LOA from James Spence Authentication.* **Minimum Bid: $750**

19466 **1940's Ty Cobb Signed Black & White Hall of Fame Plaque.** The first man through the gates of Cooperstown, Cobb could rightfully be considered the most important of all signed Hall of Fame plaques. We've located a beauty for you here, with the Peach's blue ink signature at the lower white margin presenting at a 9+/10 level. Notations in ink and pencil on verso in an unknown hand, otherwise only the lightest edge and corner wear to note. *LOA from PSA/DNA. LOA from James Spence Authentication.* **Minimum Bid: $1,000**

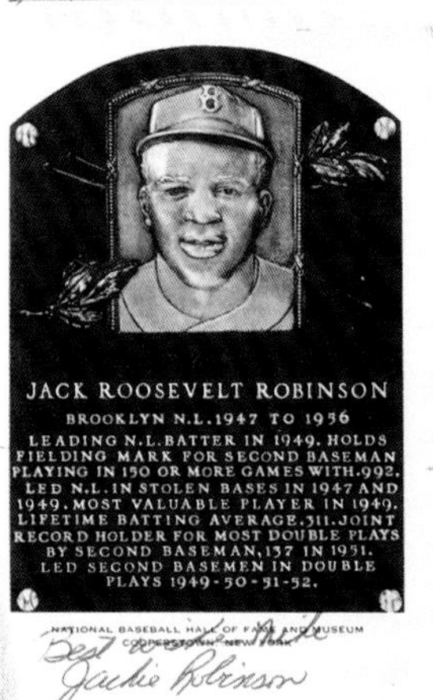

19467 1940's-60's Hall of Fame Black & White Signed Plaques Lot of 33. Issued between 1947 and 1963, the black and white Artvue Hall of Fame plaque postcards quickly caught on as a favored medium for autograph seekers, and continue to rise in popularity with every passing year. The appeal is obvious, as the images of the plaques on display at Cooperstown speak to the very nature of each legend's greatness. This exciting collection should carry great appeal to both collectors and dealers alike. Unless otherwise noted, all autographs are in 9/10 or better ink, and the postcards present no noteworthy flaws. Included: Jackie Robinson (personalized, postcard creased and stained at lower left edge), Ott, Hornsby, Lajoie, Baker, Paul Waner, Traynor, Cochrane, Walsh (personalized "To Mother"), Griffith, Clarke, Sisler, Frisch (8/10), Hubbell, Grove, Gehringer, Terry, Dickey, DiMaggio, Lyons, Hartnett, Schalk, Greenberg (7/10), Cronin, McCarthy (personalized), Crawford, Wheat, Carey, McKechnie, Feller, Roush, Rice, Flick. All are signed on front for ideal display. *LOA from PSA/DNA. LOA from James Spence Authentication.* **Minimum Bid: $6,000**

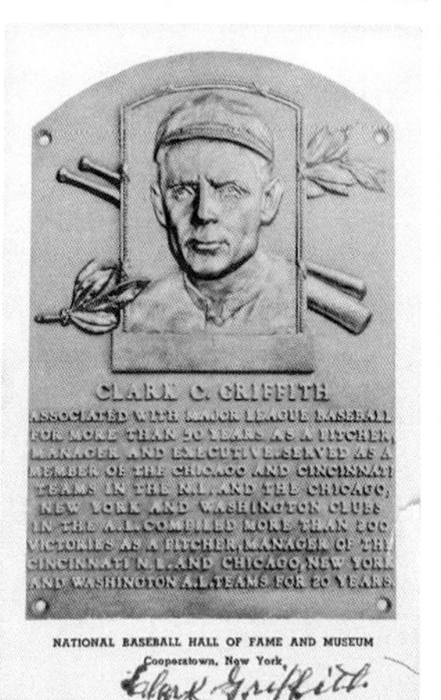

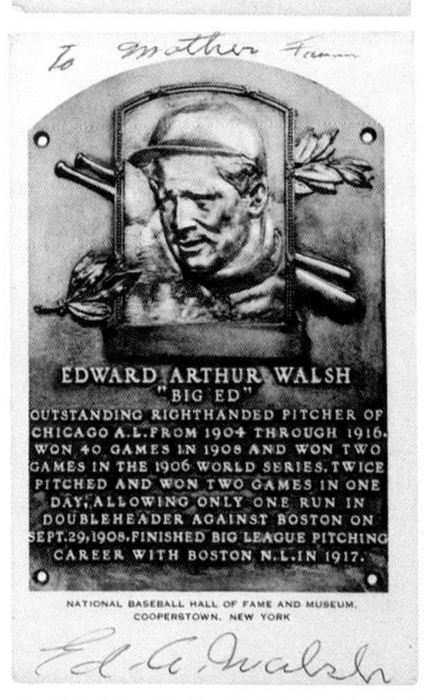

19468 **Circa 1950 Jesse Burkett Signed Black & White Hall of Fame Plaque.** Spectacularly rare offering is almost certainly the only example in the collecting world, acquired from this titan of the Dead Ball era during the brief period between his 1946 Cooperstown and his passing in 1953 at the age of eighty-four. Just about any baseball autograph collector worth his salt knows that Burkett, whose career spanned the period between 1890 and 1905, is an exceedingly tough signature in any format. But the modestly proportioned yet flawlessly rendered 10/10 black fountain pen ink signature presented here is truly one of a kind. A light lower right corner bend and mild edge toning do nothing to diminish the exceptional eye appeal of this singularly unique artifact which will serve to establish its eventual owner as a peerless collector. *LOA from PSA/DNA.* **Minimum Bid: $1,500**

19470 **Circa 1950 Tris Speaker Signed Black & White Hall of Fame Plaque.** Another fine offering from the Baseball Hall of Fame's inaugural class. The legendary outfielder's blue ink signature appears just below his image, and while the contrast is somewhat compromised by the darker background, the ink maintains a technical rating of 9+/10 and still presents exceedingly well. The postcard itself exhibits mild corner wear but nothing that diminishes in any significant manner the fantastic visual appeal. *LOA from PSA/DNA. LOA from James Spence Authentication.* **Minimum Bid: $500**

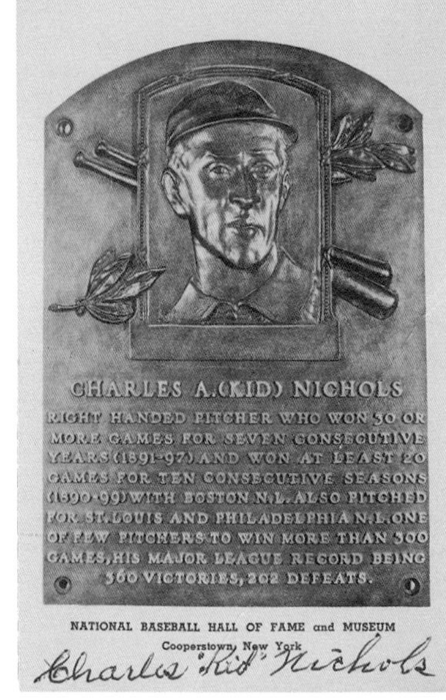

19469 **Circa 1950 Charles "Kid" Nichols Signed Black & White Hall of Fame Plaque.** Despite notching 361 career victories on the mound for the Braves, Cardinals and Phillies, Nichols waited forty-three years following his 1906 retirement from the Majors before he entered the Hall. Four years later, at age eighty-three, he was gone. This tough plaque was autographed during that narrow stretch of time that Nichols could enjoy the honor, and the blue ink signature at the lower margin appears that it will remain as immortal as the man himself. The 10/10 autograph is not diminished by a diagonal crease that runs from bottom center to right center, the only flaw of note. *LOA from PSA/DNA. LOA from James Spence Authentication.* **Minimum Bid: $1,000**

19471 **Circa 1950 Cy Young Signed Black & White Hall of Fame Plaque.** A splendid specimen from the man whose name is synonymous with pitching greatness. The sole member of pitching's 500 Win Club provides the boldest of black ink signatures, with an all but imperceptible brush of the ink at the letter "n" the only fault one could possibly note. The postcard itself is entirely beyond reproach. *LOA from PSA/DNA. LOA from James Spence Authentication.* **Minimum Bid: $500**

19472 **Circa 1955 Al Simmons Signed Black & White Hall of Fame Plaque.** With six home runs in just seventy-three World Series at bats, this Hall of Fame slugger for the Athletics and Reds outpaced even the great Mickey Mantle in October long ball effectiveness. "Bucketfoot Al" passed away just three years after Cooperstown's call, resulting in a tragically short supply of signed plaques such as this. The black fountain pen signature at the lower white border presents at an impressive 9/10, and the plaque itself exhibits just light, inconsequential edge and corner wear. *LOA from PSA/DNA. LOA from James Spence Authentication.* Minimum Bid: $750

19473 **Early 1950's Jimmie Foxx Signed Black & White Hall of Fame Plaque.** The second man to gain entry into Babe Ruth's 500 Home Run Club provides a 9/10 black ink signature at the white bottom border of this Artvue plaque. Very minor edge and corner wear is noted for the sake of accuracy, but these small faults are only noticeable upon close inspection. A solid example of a tough and valuable commodity. *LOA from PSA/DNA. LOA from James Spence Authentication.* Minimum Bid: $500

19474 **1950's Mel Ott Twice Signed Hall of Fame Plaque.** Beginning a sad trend in 1958 of New York Giants Hall of Famers perishing in automobile accidents, teammates Frank Frisch (1973) and Carl Hubbell (1988) would likewise suffer mortal injuries behind the wheel. But while the latter two were well into their golden years at the time of their passing, Ott was just forty-nine, and only seven years removed from his Cooperstown induction. As a result, his autograph is by far the toughest of the three, particularly in this format. His blue ink signature is a magnificent 10/10 on both front and verso, and the postcard, though evidently mailed to a collector from Ott's New Orleans hometown, exhibits no creasing or other noteworthy faults. One of just a small handful of Ott signed plaques, and perhaps the only dual-signed model. *LOA from PSA/DNA. LOA from James Spence Authentication.* Minimum Bid: $1,000

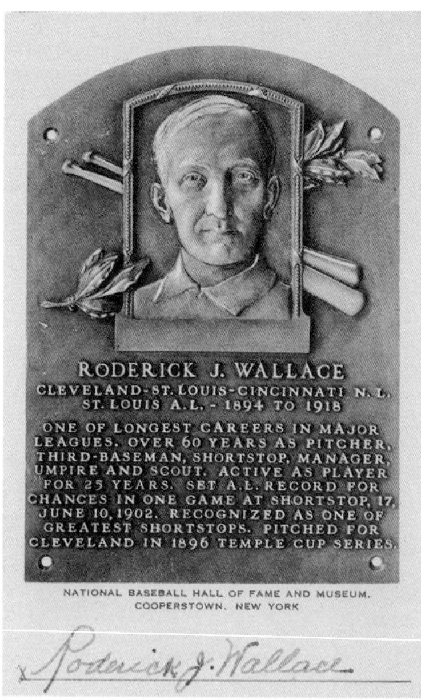

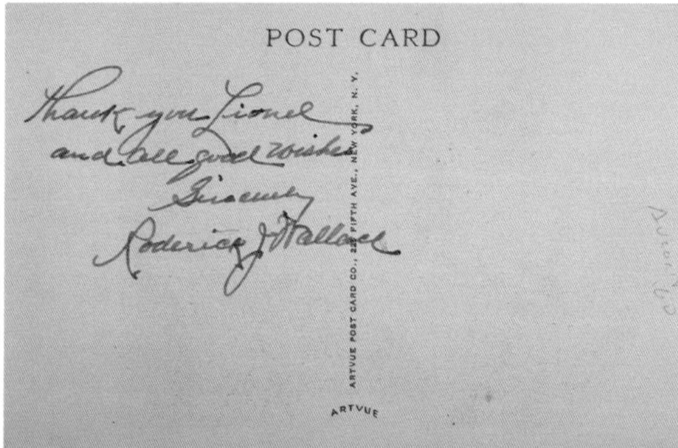

19475 1950's Roderick "Bobby" Wallace Twice Signed Black & White Hall of Fame Plaque. To the best of our knowledge, we present here the only known authenticated example of a Bobby Wallace signed plaque, allowing one dedicated hobbyist to raise his collection to a level that no other could match. The scarcity is no surprise. Wallace was eighty years old at the time of his induction and living in Torrance, California, making Cooperstown appearances all but impossible. This one appears to have been acquired to the mail, which would explain the line drawn for signature placement on the front, and the inscription on back that reads, "Thank you Lionel, and all good wishes, Sincerely Roderick J. Wallace." The signature on front rates a solid 9/10, with the inscription on verso perhaps a half-point stronger still. Certainly one of the finest Artvues in the hobby, period. *LOA from PSA/DNA. LOA from James Spence Authentication.* Minimum Bid: $1,000

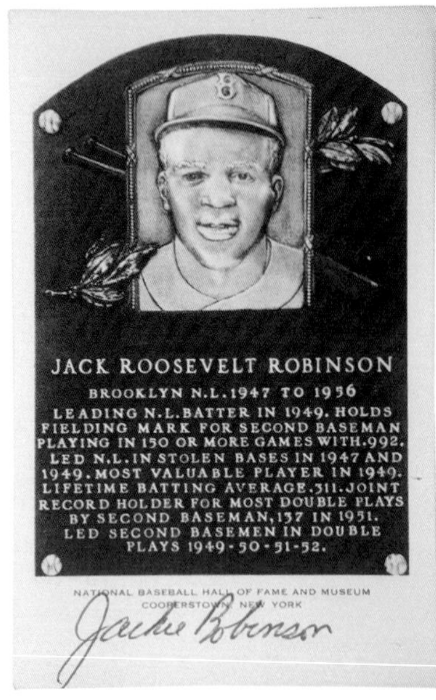

19476 1960's Jackie Robinson Signed Black & White Plaque. The Major League's first black ballplayer was likewise the first to cross Cooperstown's color line, and here we present his highly collectible Artvue black and white postcard picturing the bronze prize for his brilliance. Robinson's bona fide 10/10 blue ink signature appears in the white margin below, creating the standard by which all other Jackie plaques should be judged. The postcard itself exhibits only the faintest hint of wear and age toning at the extreme edges, with some yellowing at upper region of verso that doesn't affect the display whatsoever. A real gem here. *LOA from PSA/DNA. LOA from James Spence Authentication.* Minimum Bid: $750

19477 Circa 1970 Jackie Robinson Signed Gold Hall of Fame Plaque. The first black player in Cooperstown bronze, the great Jackie Robinson appears here in pure gold. He adds a "Best wishes" to his 9/10 blue ink signature at the lower border of this NRMT postcard. A rock-solid example of a collecting essential. *LOA from PSA/DNA. LOA from James Spence Authentication.* Minimum Bid: $400

19478 **Circa 1972 Dave Bancroft Signed Gold Hall of Fame Plaque.** "Beauty" Bancroft's death just a year after his 1971 Hall of Fame induction makes his signed plaque one of the toughest in the hobby, but the rare few that do exist are all but universally signed on the verso. This specimen makes hen's teeth seem as common as dirt, and boasts a spectacular 9+/10 blue ink signature to boot. Postcard itself is equally fine. Our auction results database finds not a single front-signed example selling within a major auction this millenium, and it wouldn't be a great surprise if this were the last as well. An exciting find for the plaque collecting willing to go the extra mile toward completion. *LOA from PSA/DNA. LOA from James Spence Authentication.* Minimum Bid: $1,000

NATIONAL BASEBALL HALL OF FAME AND MUSEUM
COOPERSTOWN, NEW YORK
plaque of
ROBERT CAL HUBBARD
Elected to National Baseball Hall of Fame
1976
Baseball Hall of Fame Committee on Veterans

POST CARD

PLACE STAMP HERE

19479 **Circa 1976 Cal Hubbard Twice Signed Gold Hall of Fame Plaque.** The only man enshrined in both the Football and Baseball Halls of Fame, this masked authoritarian made it to Cooperstown as an umpire just a year before his passing in 1977. Given this fact, it should surprise few that signed Hall of Fame plaques from Hubbard are a tough commodity, and we're pleased to present one of the few examples here. The black sharpie signature on the front is ever so slightly hazy, but still a legitimate 8+/10. The offering on verso finds no such troubles, rating a perfect 10/10. The postcard itself is likewise free of difficulties. *LOA from PSA/DNA. LOA from James Spence Authentication.* Minimum Bid: $500

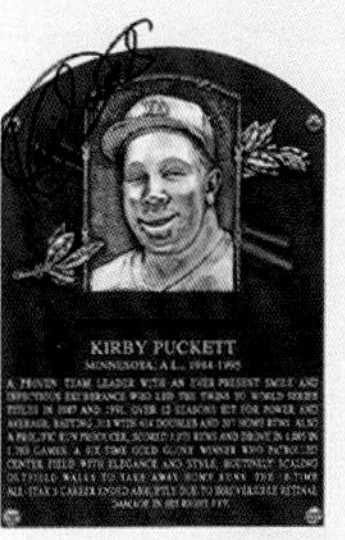

19480 **1983-2006 Inductees Signed Gold Hall of Fame Plaques Lot of 60.** Willie Mays is the only legend missing from this remarkably comprehensive collection of plaques bearing signatures from every enshrinee alive to sign. Matching the theme of excellence in baseball abilities is the quality of the postcards themselves, which appear in NRMT condition with 9/10 or better ink or sharpie autographs unless otherwise noted. The roster: Alston, Kell, Brooks Robinson, Marichal, Aparicio, Drysdale, Killebrew, Ferrell, Reese, Slaughter, Wilhelm, Brock, McCovey, Doerr, Billy Williams, Hunter, Dandridge (8/10), Stargell (8/10), Bench, Barlick, Yastrzemski, Schoendienst, Palmer, Morgan, Jenkins, Carew, Perry, Newhouser, Fingers, Seaver, Reggie Jackson, Rizzuto, Carlton, Schmidt, Ashburn, Weaver, Bunning, Niekro, Lasorda, MacPhail (7/10), Doby, Sutton, Cepeda, Brett, Ryan, Yount, Fisk, Anderson (8/10), Perez, Puckett, Mazeroski, Winfield, Ozzie Smith, Murray, Carter, Molitor, Eckersley (7/10), Sandberg, Boggs, Sutter. *LOA from PSA/DNA. LOA from James Spence Authentication.* Minimum Bid: $600

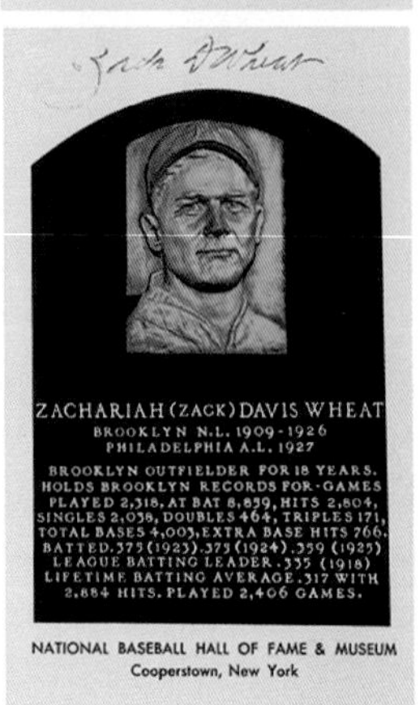

19481 **1939-82 Inductees Signed Gold Hall of Fame Plaques Lot of 70.** The Gold series of Hall of Fame plaques debuted in 1964, though signed examples can be had for those who gained enshrinement in the preceding decades as well, as this collection illustrates. In some rare cases the Gold version is even tougher than the Black & White to acquire, though any collector working toward building a complete set will find this lot to be a tremendous help. Only thirteen possibles are missing from those inducted during this forty-three year stretch. Unless otherwise noted, all autographs are in 8/10 or better ink or sharpie, and the postcards present no noteworthy flaws. Included: Sisler, Grove, Frisch (7/10), Hubbell, Traynor (7/10), Gehringer, Dean, Dickey, Terry, Hartnett (6/10), Schalk (personalized), Lyons, Greenberg, Cronin, McCarthy, Crawford, Wheat, Carey, Feller, Roush, Rice, Flick (tape at left edge), Faber, Manush, Grimes, Appling, Stengel, Lloyd Waner, Ruffing, Medwick, Coveleski, Musial, Hoyt, Combs, Boudreau, Haines, Frick, Marquard, Hooper, Hafey, Paige, Gomez, Leonard, Koufax, Wynn, Kelly, Irvin, Spahn, Mantle, Ford, Conlan, Bell, Judy Johnson (6/10), Herman, Averill, Kiner (7/10), Roberts, Lindstrom, Lemon, Lopez, Sewell, Mathews, Mays, Snider, Kaline, Mize, Bob Gibson, Chandler, Frank Robinson, Travis Jackson. All are signed on front for ideal display. *LOA from PSA/DNA. LOA from James Spence Authentication.* **Minimum Bid: $1,500**

19482 **1980's-90's Hall of Famers Signed Perez-Steele Postcards Lot of 124** Massive collection of signed Perez-Steeles is one man's labor of love, as all autographs were acquired in person over years of time. Aaron, Anderson, Aparicio, Appling, Banks, Barlick (2), Bell, Bench (2), Berra, Boudreau, Brett, Brock, Bunning, Carew (3), Carlton (2), Cepeda, Chandler, Conlan, Dandridge (2), Dickey, DiMaggio, Doby, Doerr (2), Drysdale, Feller, Ferrell (2), Fingers (2), Fisk, Ford (2), Gehringer, Gibson (2), Gomez, Herman, Hubbell, Hunter (2), Irvin, Reggie Jackson (2), Travis Jackson (3), Jenkins (2), Judy Johnson, Kaline, Kell, Killebrew, Kiner, Koufax (2), Lasorda, Lemon, Leonard, Lopez, McPhail, Mantle, Marichal (2), Mathews, Mays, Mazeroski, McCovey (2), Mize, Morgan (2), Musial, Newhouser (2), Niekro, Palmer, Perez, Perry (2), Puckett, Reese (2), Rizzuto (2), Roberts, Brooks Robinson, Frank Robinson, Roush, Ryan (2), Schmidt, Schoendienst (2), Seaver (2), Sewell, Slaughter (2), Snider, Spahn, Stack, Stargell (2), Steele/Steele/Perez, Sutton, Terry (2), Weaver, Wilhelm, Billy Williams (2), Ted Williams, Winfield, Wynn, Yastrzemski (3), Yount. Condition is uniformly NRMT or better throughout. One of the most comprehensive Perez-Steele collections to reach the auction block in some time. *LOA from PSA/DNA. LOA from James Spence Authentication.* **Minimum Bid: $600**

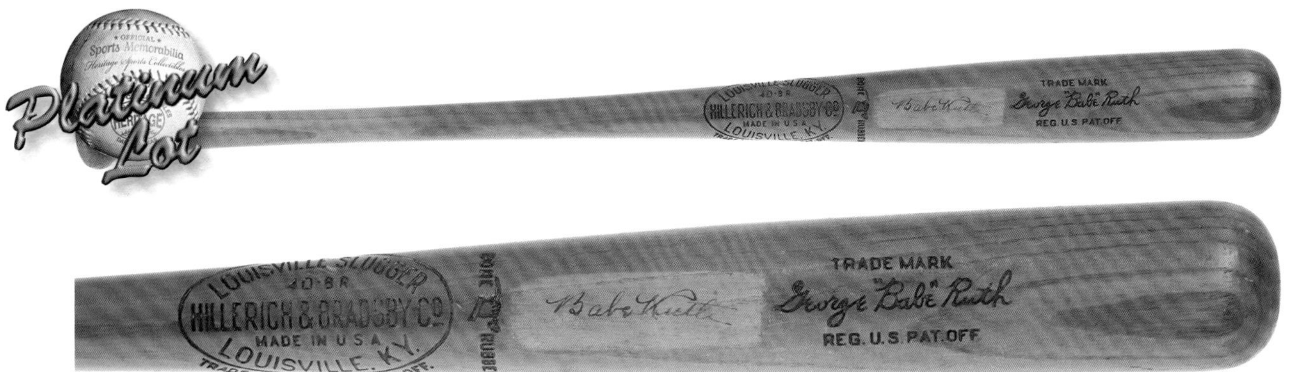

19483 **Late 1920's Babe Ruth Signed Bat.** While our national pastime's most noteworthy figure laid pen to the horsehide of tens if not hundreds of thousands of baseballs during his lifetime, it is a particularly rare and exciting occurrence when one encounters a bat bearing the mark of the Babe. Autographing bats just wasn't something that was typically done back in the days before permanent markers were in vogue, so those collecting pre-war signed wood are a brave and ambitious lot. They'll have cause to celebrate now, however, as we present a remarkably strong signature from Ruth on a signature model Hillerich & Bradsby 40 B.R. retail issue. On the rare occasions when bats were autographed during the pre-war era the glossy finish of the area to be signed was often filed away to present a more welcoming home for fountain pen ink, and such is the case here. The Babe centers his autograph within a 1.5x4" filed patch, with his signature surviving in remarkably strong 8/10 condition to this day. The bat itself likewise presents beautifully, and measures thirty-five inches in length. As it was with a Hillerich & Bradsby in his hands that Babe carved himself a heaping slab of athletic immortality, we couldn't think of a better home for his autograph than some Louisville lumber. *LOA from PSA/DNA.* Minimum Bid: $4,000

19484 **1966 Ted Williams All-Star Game Issued Coach's Bat, Signed.** Worth an absolute fortune if dating from the Splinter's Hall of Fame playing days, this bat issued to Williams in his capacity as a coach for the American League still offers plenty to love. The signature model Hillerich & Bradsby W215 is crafted to the exact specifications of those that the Red Sox legend used to establish himself as the game's greatest hitter, with "All Star Game, 1966 - St. Louis" framing his facsimile signature in bold block lettering. While an absence of use is to be expected from the man who would enter the Hall of Fame this year, a later and literally flawless blue sharpie signature on the barrel provides the ultimate final touch to this special artifact. Certainly one of the most desirable Ted Williams signed bats available in the hobby market. *LOA from PSA/DNA. LOA from James Spence Authentication.* Minimum Bid: $1,000

19485 **1977 & 1978 New York Yankees Team Signed Bats Lot of 2.** As the Son of Sam terrorized the streets of New York City, the Bronx Bombers did the same to the competition, dominating the Disco Age after the longest World Championship drought since Babe Ruth arrived on the scene. Each bat is specially engraved with identifying text, then signed by twenty Series winners in the boldest of blue sharpie. Among the notable names: Jackson, Guidry, Gossage, Lyle, Berra, Chambliss, Rivers, Nettles, White and more. Each full-sized bat presents flawlessly, ready for proud display. *LOA from PSA/DNA. LOA from James Spence Authentication.* Minimum Bid: $500

19486 **Joe DiMaggio Signed "1941" Bat.** The most desirable of Joltin' Joe autographed lumber is represented here as number 1773 of a limited edition of 1941, a figure which should bring to mind the historic fifty-six game hitting streak to all but the most casual baseball historian. Exacting in every detail to the signature model Hillerich & Bradsby wielded by the Yankee great during that campaign, this one differs only in the edition stamping and the 9+/10 blue sharpie signature that resides just above. *LOA from PSA/DNA. LOA from James Spence Authentication.* Minimum Bid: $500

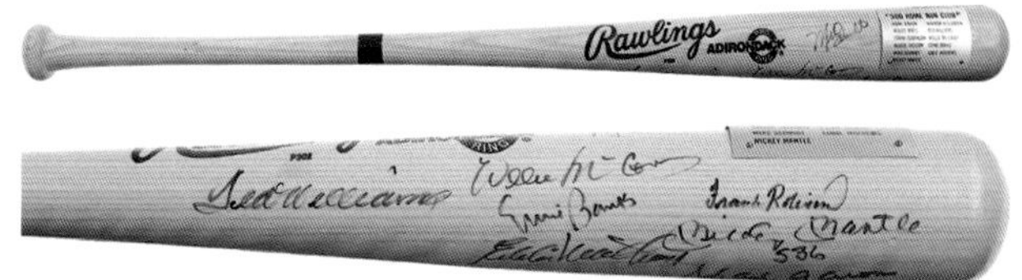

19487 1980's 500 Home Run Club Signed Bat. When you consider the tremendous desirability and value of bats signed by either Mickey Mantle or Ted Williams, the remarkable appeal of this lumber signed by both (and nine more long ball leviathans) comes into focus. This Rawlings Big Stick offers the greatest of the pre-pharmaceutical era sluggers, with 9/10 and better blue sharpie signatures from Mantle (who adds a "536" notation), Williams, Aaron, Mays, Robinson, Jackson, Schmidt, Killebrew, McCovey, Banks and Mathews. An engraved brass plaque affixed to the barrel identifies the legends (as if they needed any introduction). The 500 Home Run Club might be much larger now, but none of the new crowd can hold a candle to this bunch. *LOA from PSA/DNA. LOA from James Spence Authentication.* **Minimum Bid: $750**

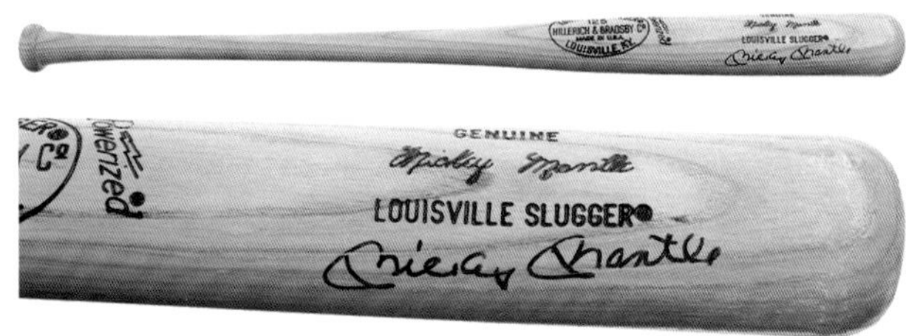

19488 1980's Mickey Mantle Signed Bat. While the Mick could work magic with a Louisville Slugger, he hated to sign them, and tried to discourage autograph hounds by demanding what was then considered an exorbitant sum to apply sharpie to wood. This example rates as one of the finest examples you'll find, with the perfect replica of Mantle's Hillerich & Bradsby M110 sporting a 9+/10 blue sharpie signature from the Yankee great. As more and more of these bats find a home in permanent collections, it will be tougher and tougher to locate prime specimens like this one, so bid now. *LOA from PSA/DNA. LOA from James Spence Authentication.* **Minimum Bid: $1,000**

19489 1980's Mickey Mantle Signed Vintage Store Model Bat. Worth a pretty penny in its unsigned state, this Mint condition 1965-68 Mantle store model Hillerich & Bradsby ups the ante with the addition of a 9/10 blue sharpie signature from its celebrity endorser. As most baseball autograph collectors are aware, the Mick had a particular aversion toward signing bats, charging an astronomical fee in order to dissuade signature seekers from requesting them. The resultant thin supply has left collectors scrambling for the top examples, a characterization that certainly applies here. Definitely one of the finest Mantle signed bats on the market. *LOA from PSA/DNA. LOA from James Spence Authentication.* **Minimum Bid: $1,000**

19490 Baseball Hall of Famers Multi-Signed Bat from Phil Rizzuto Collection. A torch carried for years by the pinstriped legend can now be passed on to you, to add to the collection of forty-plus blue sharpie autographs acquired by Scooter himself. The full-size Rawlings Big Stick is emblazoned with a logo of the Hall of Fame, which is surrounded by 9/10 and better signatures from the likes of Mays, Bench, Brock, Fingers, Seaver, Killebrew, Ford, Palmer, Puckett and Rizzuto himself. There's still plenty of room left for more though, and any Hall of Famer would be honored to add his John Hancock to this treasured keepsake from the Yankee shortstop. Letter of provenance from Rizzuto's widow Cora is included. *LOA from PSA/DNA. LOA from James Spence Authentication.* **Minimum Bid: $500**

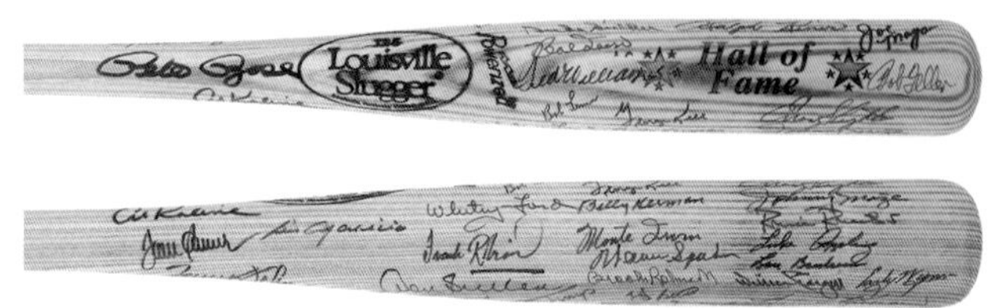

19491 1980's-90's Hall of Famers Multi-Signed Bat with Ted Williams. Hundreds of miles of driving and dozens of hours of waiting in lines at autograph shows can be saved for the cost of one winning bid upon this special Louisville Slugger signed by thirty-seven members of Cooperstown's illustrious brotherhood. Names like Ted Williams, Mathews, Spahn, Drysdale, Stargell and Mize make this one impossible to replicate. Also here are Mays, Seaver, Kaline, Ford, McCovey, Musial, Gibson, Banks, Carlton, Palmer, Killebrew, Snider, Brooks and Frank Robinson and Berra, to name a few. Only Boudreau, Rose and Tommy John (not included in count of thirty-seven) lack a plaque. There's still plenty of room left to add more, and any Hall of Famer would be honored to join these blue sharpie ranks. Signature quality is uniformly 9/10 or better, continuing the theme of greatness. *LOA from PSA/DNA. LOA from James Spence Authentication.* **Minimum Bid: $750**

19492 **Early 1990's Mickey Mantle "No. 7" Signed UDA Bat.** From a market standpoint, few so-called "production pieces" in the sports collecting world have performed as strongly and consistently as the Mickey Mantle signed bat. This is particularly true of the rare few examples that boast some form of notation along with the signature, and for those created under the auspices of memorabilia purveyor Upper Deck. And so this fabulous lumber hits on all cylinders, providing not only a "No. 7" notation to join the 9/10 blue sharpie autograph on the barrel of the signature model Hillerich & Bradsby, but also the full contingent of UDA stickering, paperwork and packaging. We expect plenty of bidding action upon this one. *COA from Upper Deck. LOA from PSA/DNA. LOA from James Spence Authentication.* **Minimum Bid: $1,000**

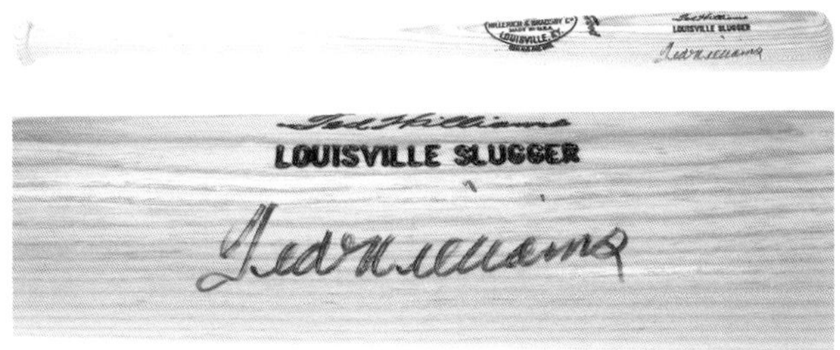

19493 **1990's Ted Williams Signed UDA Bat.** Picture-perfect reproduction of The Kid's trusted Hillerich & Bradsby W215 game bat is further improved by the addition of a 9/10 blue sharpie signature from the game's greatest hitter. Collectors know that the Upper Deck credentials of this offering add even more appeal, with holographic authenticating stickering, certificate and original cloth storage bag all present and accounted for. A fitting tribute to the iconic Red Sock. *COA from UDA. LOA from PSA/DNA. LOA from James Spence Authentication.* **Minimum Bid: $300**

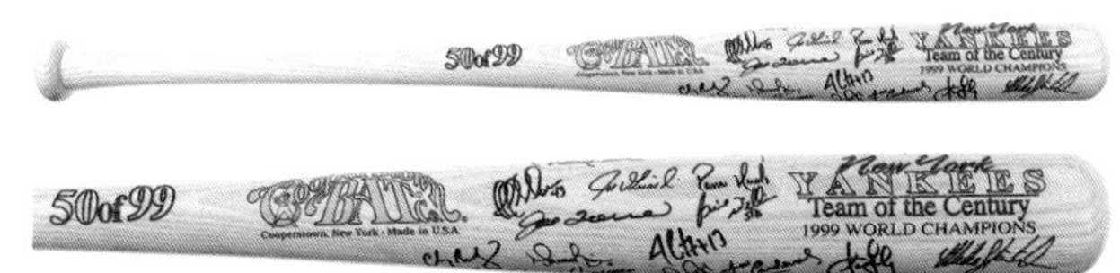

19494 **1999 New York Yankees Team Signed Bat.** The most dominant playoff edition of all from the modern Bronx dynasty, the 1999 Yanks played just a single game beyond the minimum in October in their unstoppable march to the World Championship. Twenty-four members of this pinstriped juggernaut appear in 10/10 blue sharpie upon the offered Cooperstown Bat Co. lumber, numbered "50" of a limited run of ninety-nine. Highlights include Jeter, Torre, Williams, Cone, El Duke, Knoblauch, Rivera, Strawberry, Mendoza, Leyritz and more. There's still room to chase down a few stragglers, and any of them would be thrilled to be reminded of these glory days. *LOA from PSA/DNA. LOA from James Spence Authentication.* **Minimum Bid: $400**

19495 **1927 Washington Senators Team Signed Baseball.** The legendary Walter Johnson added the final five victories to his career total of 417 this season, closing out twenty-one seasons of brilliance on the Major League mound. His black fountain pen ink signature projects at an impressive 8/10 on the side panel of this OAL (Johnson) ball inhabited by twenty-six members of this Golden Age juggernaut. Plenty of 1924 World Champs remain on this later model, including Hall of Famers Rice, Goslin and Harris, star catcher Muddy Ruel, Judge, Bluege and Marberry. Rounding out the Hall of Fame outfield, in his single season of service to the Senators, is Tris Speaker on the sweet spot. Signature quality averages a solid 7/10, with only Marberry of the noted names dipping more than a point below that figure. A coating of shellac has provided the ball with an antique tobacco shade, but has served its intended purpose admirably. A tough ball with no shortage of prewar icons. *LOA from PSA/DNA. LOA from James Spence Authentication.* **Minimum Bid: $600**

19496 1927 Philadelphia Athletics Team Signed Baseball. After competition from the rogue Federal League forced Connie Mack to dismantle what may have been the finest compilation of baseball talent ever to inhabit a single dugout in the mid-Teens, the Tall Tactician was steadily building toward his second great masterpiece that would eclipse even the Yankees of Ruth and Gehrig in the coming seasons. This OAL (Johnson) sphere may be even more desirable to collectors than the World Championship models to come, as it features a selection of iconic veterans who helped pave the way but retired before the glory days arrived. Marvelous offerings from Ty Cobb, Eddie Collins and Zack Wheat are counted among the twenty-one 7/10 and better black ink offerings, joined by the likes of Cochrane, Mack, Grove, Gleason, Dykes, Hale, Perkins, Boley and Rommel. *LOA from PSA/DNA. LOA from James Spence Authentication.* Minimum Bid: $1,000

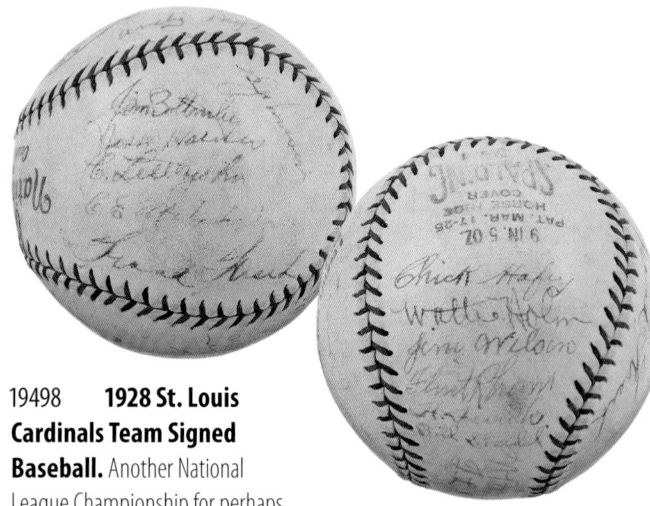

19498 1928 St. Louis Cardinals Team Signed Baseball. Another National League Championship for perhaps the greatest dynasty in St. Louis baseball history. This ONL (Heydler) ball goes a long way toward explaining the club's winning ways, as the Sportsman's Park dugout was packed to the rafters with Hall of Fame talent. Among the twenty-one signatures found here are such legends as Frisch, Hafey, Bottomley, Haines and McKechnie. Signature quality ranges from 2/10 to 7/10, with all but a few within two points of the top end of the scale. Along with the Yankees and the Indians, the class of 1920's Major League Baseball. *LOA from PSA/DNA. LOA from James Spence Authentication.* Minimum Bid: $750

19497 1928 Chicago Cubs & Pittsburgh Pirates Signed Baseball with Hack Wilson, Ki Ki Cuyler. Some very tough prewar legends make this ONL (Heydler) ball pure gold for the Hall of Fame autograph collector. Dating to a 1928 edition of the historic Cubs/Pirates rivalry, the moderately toned sphere boasts the likes of Wilson, Cuyler, Hartnett, Traynor, Grimes, both Waner brothers, Root and Gonzales among its inhabitants. Twenty autographs are here in total, averaging 5/10 with none listed ranging more than a point in either direction. Joe McCarthy is the sole clubhouse signature. Light shellac has served its intended purpose well. A special Golden Age keepsake from the Senior Circuit's best. *LOA from PSA/DNA. LOA from James Spence Authentication.* Minimum Bid: $750

19499 1928 New York Yankees Team Signed Baseball. The Murderer's Row Yankees were at their homicidal height at the time this sphere was passed around the Bronx clubhouse, in the midst of back-to-back World Series sweeps and record-shattering offensive production. This OAL (Johnson) baseball provides the signatures of twenty-four members of that illustrious squad, with Ruth (4/10) taking his customary sweet spot position, and fellow Hall of Famers Gehrig (4/10), Combs (4/10), Pennock (3/10), Lazzeri (5/10), Dickey (1/10), Durocher (1/10) and the very tough Miller Huggins (2/10) nearby. Waite Hoyt is also present, but has been enhanced at some point, as has teammate Tom Zachary. All other autographs remain untouched by later hands, and range from barely visible to 8/10. Not a pristine example, but an affordable opportunity for the collector wishing for his own brush with Golden Age greatness. *LOA from PSA/DNA. LOA from James Spence Authentication.* Minimum Bid: $1,000

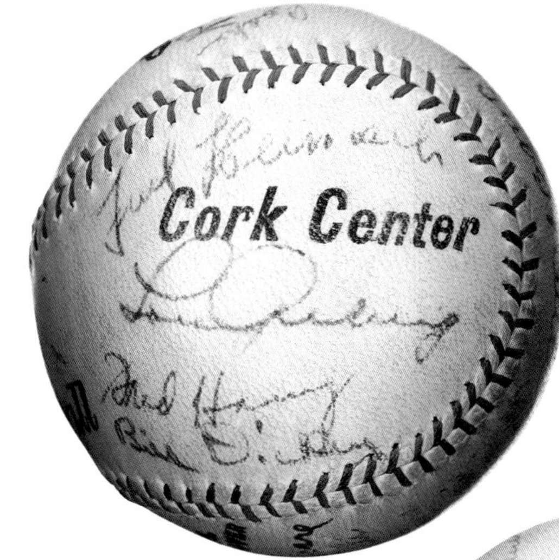

19500 **Circa 1929 Babe Ruth, Lou Gehrig & G.C. Alexander Signed Baseball.** We can't quite solve the riddle of this baseball, as our initial theory that the presence of the three Hall of Famers listed in the auction lot title would suggest 1926 or 1928 World Series vintage was derailed by others who arrived on the Major League scene afterwards. But while the origins remain in question, the tremendous appeal does not. The Ruth signature upon the sweet spot of the "Official League Ball" would make for a $15,000 single in its 8/10 condition, and his sidekick Gehrig is equally strong on the southern panel. The very tough Grover Cleveland Alexander resides to the north of the Babe, projecting at an even more impressive 9/10. Other notables include Combs (3/10), Dickey (9/10), Lazzeri (6/10) and Wilcy Moore (8/10). Eighteen autographs are here in total, with the average a solid 6/10. A fine chance to bring some qualiity pre-war Hall of Fame autographs into your collection. *LOA from PSA/DNA. LOA from James Spence Authentication.* Minimum Bid: $3,000

19501 **1929 New York Yankees Team Signed Baseball.** Though one could argue that, technically, the 1950's was the greatest decade in Yankees history, the fiercest collecting love centers around the 1920's Murderer's Row days. Here we provide a witness to those glorious Golden years, an OAL (Barnard) sphere autographed by twenty-one early pinstripers. Most notable, of course, are Ruth (7/10) and Gehrig (4/10), who occupy the sweet spot and southern side panel respectively. Following this pair into Cooperstown are Hoyt, Pennock, Combs, Dickey, Durocher and Lazzeri. Durst, Grabowski, Bengough and Pipgras are also worthy of note. Signature quality ranges from 3/10 to 8/10, with all easily identifiable. With the Stadium falling at the close of the 2008 season, we expect early Yankee artifacts such as this to surge on a wave of nostalgia, so there's never been a better time to invest. *LOA from PSA/DNA. LOA from James Spence Authentication.*
Minimum Bid: $1,500

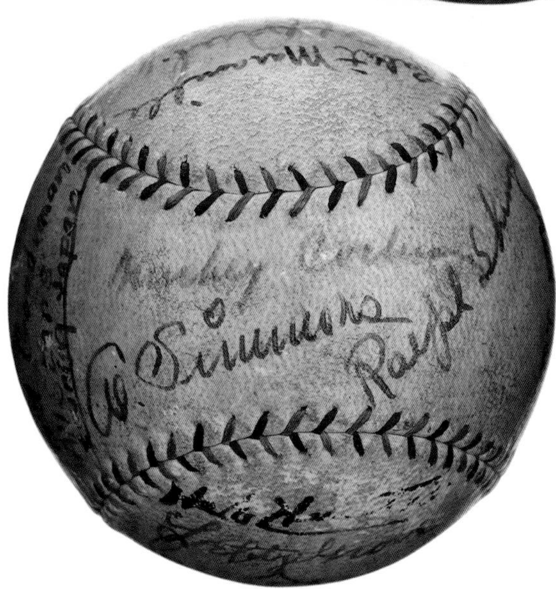

19502 **1931 Tour of Japan Team Signed Baseball with Gehrig.** Far scarcer than team balls from the more widely recognized 1934 Tour are those from the trip across the Pacific three years earlier, featuring a smaller (but still star-studded) cast of diamond icons. Presented is one of the finest specimens we've encountered from that limited supply, boasting seventeen bold black fountain pen signatures on an "Official Six University League of Tokyo" baseball. Most noteworthy is an 8/10 offering from the great Lou Gehrig, who would make the trip again in '34. He's joined by fellow Hall of Famers Cochrane (5/10), Simmons (8/10), Grove (8/10), Frisch (9/10), Kelly (3/10) and Maranville (8/10). 1924 World Series hero Muddy Ruel (7/10) is here as well. The balance of signatures average a solid 7/10, with only a single deviation from that impressive theme. A large inscription in an unknown hand fills a side panel, and reads, "To our good Friend Fred Goodman, All Stars touring Japan '1931.'" A light coating of shellac has provided an amber tone, but has served its duty of autograph preservation admirably. As a memento documenting a key step in the globalization of the sport of baseball, this sphere carries tremendous historical importance, and should garner significant bidding accordingly. *LOA from PSA/DNA. LOA from James Spence Authentication.* **Minimum Bid: $4,000**

THE BABE'S LAST CHAMPIONSHIP

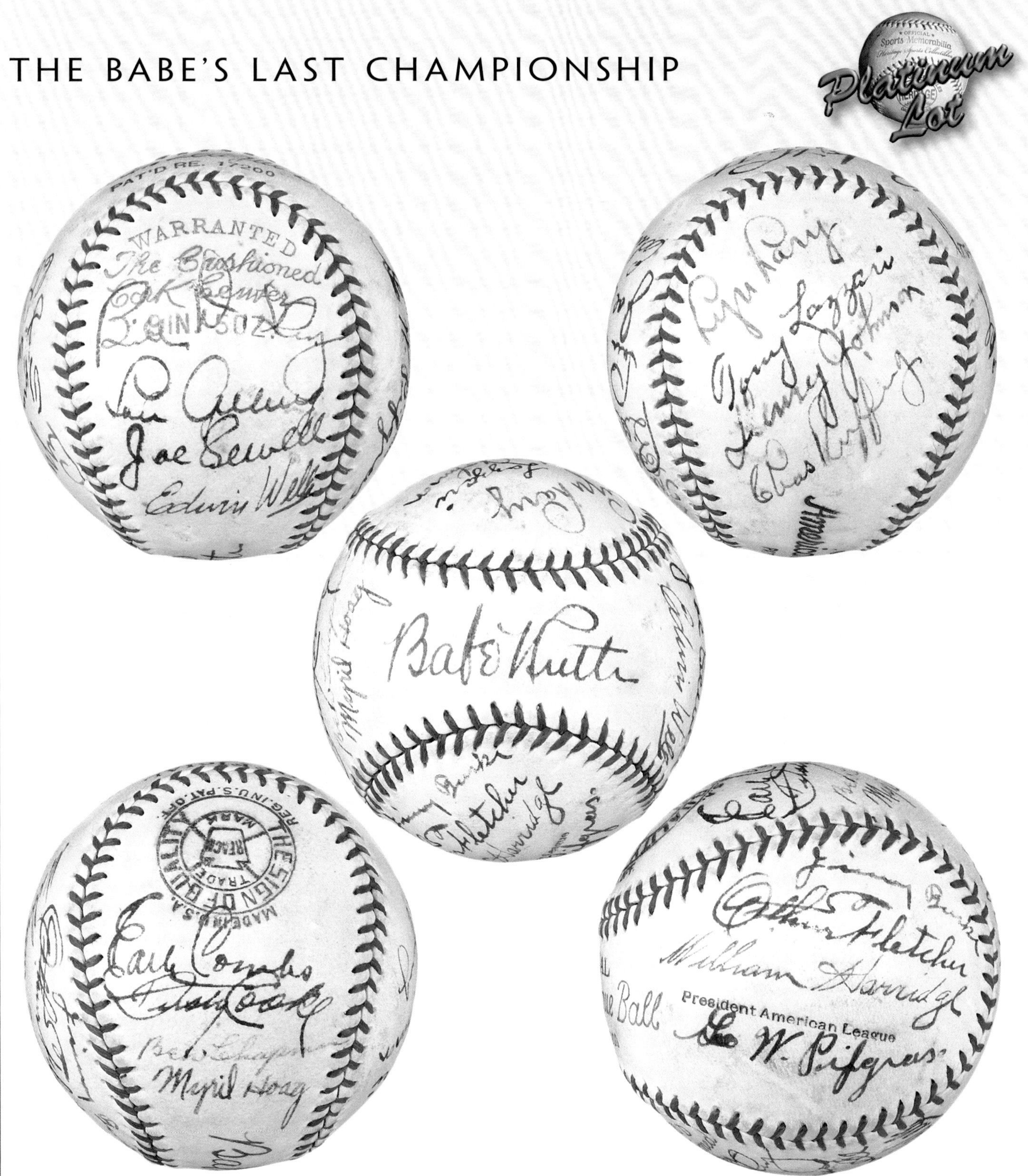

19503 **1932 New York Yankees Team Signed Baseball.** Exceptional high-grade sphere may well be the finest honoring the Babe's final World Championship team ever to reach the auction block. Ruth occupies his customary position on the sweet spot of this gorgeous OAL (Harridge) ball, joining fifteen other teammates that only once (Ben Chapman at 6/10) veer more than a point from the 9/10 strength that characterizes the Bambino's offering. All the pinstriped icons are present and accounted for: Gehrig, Lazzeri, Combs, Dickey, Sewell and Ruffing, proving this ball is far more than just a pretty face. The ball itself has mellowed only slightly to a light tobacco shade, and the manufacturer's stamping remains vivid and pronounced. As glorious and unexpected as Ruth's World Series Called Shot, this ball is destined for a place of honor in the finest of private baseball autograph collections. *LOA from PSA/DNA. LOA from James Spence Authentication.*
Minimum Bid: $7,500

19505 **1932 New York Giants Team Signed Baseball with Ott, McGraw.** Essentially the same ballclub that would defeat the Washington Senators the following season to claim the World Series title, one notable departure from that club two months into the 1932 season makes this offering arguably even more desirable than a Championship sphere. After thirty-one years at the helm of the New York Giants, the great John McGraw would turn over control to Bill Terry, ending one of the longest and most successful managerial tenures in the game's history. Clearly this "Pacific Coast League" sphere predates McGraw's June 3, 1932 resignation, as he appears as one of the thirty-three ultra-high grade autographs that coat the ball's surface. Also appearing in 9+/10 blue ink are Ott (signing with his full "Melvin" name), Hubbell, Lindstrom, Terry, Bancroft, Travis Jackson, Fitzsimmons, Luque, Moore, Marshall, Critz and Hogan. A patch of foxing upon one panel does nothing to undermine the strength of the autographs with which it shares space, and a few fingerprints dabbed the wet ink on occasion, likewise to no significant effect. A coating of shellac has remained perfectly clear and has served its intended purpose marvelously. Almost assuredly the highest quality sphere in the hobby to boast the full contingent of Depression-era Hall of Fame Giants, this is one for the collector who demands nothing but the best. *LOA from PSA/DNA. LOA from James Spence Authentication.* **Minimum Bid: $2,000**

19505 **1932 Chicago Cubs Stars Signed Baseball with Tris Speaker.** With just eight signatures taking up residence upon this "Official League" ball, the terminology "team signed" doesn't quite apply, but the savvy Depression-era autograph hound definitely picked the top names from this National League Championship squad. Hall of Famers Ki Ki Cuyler, Rogers Hornsby and Gabby Hartnett represent Wrigley's best and brightest, and Tris Speaker sneaks in as well, each surviving in the same 9+/10 blue fountain pen ink that characterizes the totality of the autographs. Others present are Smith, Jurges, English and Taylor (8/10). Ball is evenly toned to an attractive tan shade. *LOA from PSA/DNA. LOA from James Spence Authentication.* **Minimum Bid: $600**

19506 **1933 American League All-Star Team Signed Baseball.** Thrilling relic recounts the outrageous assortment of American League legends that convened at Chicago's Comiskey Park to participate in the inaugural All-Star Game, arguably the most talent-packed team ever assembled on a single diamond. Highlighted with a sweet spot signature from Babe Ruth (small chip affects final letter), who gave fans their money's worth with the delivery of the Midsummer Classic's first long ball, this OAL (Harridge) ball features nineteen bold black fountain pen autographs averaging 8/10 in strength. Other notables include Gehrig, Lazzeri, Foxx, Simmons, Collins, Cronin, Dickey, Grove, Rick Ferrell, Averill, Gehringer, McCarthy (light) and even National League manager John McGraw. That's fourteen Hall of Famers! A coating of shellac has provided the ball with a deep tobacco tone but has served its purpose of autograph maintenance admirably. A top-tier artifact from one of the most significant single events in twentieth century baseball. *LOA from PSA/DNA. LOA from James Spence Authentication.* **Minimum Bid:** $4,000

19507 **1933 New York Giants Team Signed Baseball.** After a decade playing second fiddle to their Yankee neighbors to the east, the Giants finally reasserted themselves as the toast of the Big Apple, claiming the World Championship with a four games to one victory over the Washington Senators in the Fall Classic. Twenty-five black ink signatures from the world-beating Giants appear upon this ONL (Heydler) ball, including all of your favorites like Ott (4/10), Hubbell (4/10), O'Doul (3/10), Ryan (4/10), Luque (3/10) and Fitzsimmons (4/10). The balance of autographs average 3/10, and range between 1/10 and 6/10 in strength. The last Championship at the Polo Grounds until Willie Mays brought back the glory days twenty-one seasons later. Included is a VG-EX *Baseball Magazine* premium (9.5x12") picturing this immortal ballclub. *LOA from PSA/DNA. LOA from James Spence Authentication.* **Minimum Bid: $400**

19508 **1933 New York Yankees Team Signed Baseball.** The second to last year for the historic Hall of Fame pairing of Ruth and Gehrig, who appear together upon this toned OAL (Harridge) orb with a selection of their Yankee teammates. While a significant degree of surface wear to the southern panel makes an exact signature count impossible, the rest of the ball has survived the passing decades with greater aplomb, and a dozen autographs are discernible at the least. Besides Ruth and Gehrig, who present at 7/10 and 2/10 respectively, we also can report the appearance of Ruffing (2/10), Gomez (1.5/10), Combs (3/10), Lary (5/10) and Farrell (5/10). While no beauty prizewinner, the presence of Golden Age Yankee greats makes this one a winner regardless. **Minimum Bid: $750**

19509 **1930's Tour of Japan/Hawaii Signed Baseball with Ruth, Gehrig, Foxx.** The handwritten date of October 11, 1932, penned by parties unknown, throws us for a bit of a loop here, as the collection of autographs that coat the surface of this OAL (Harridge) ball appear to be those of 1931 and 1934 Tourists, as well as some who were a part of neither. We'll accept this bit of mystery, though, and turn our concentration toward the princely assortment of names that decorate its surface. As is the case with any great "Tour ball," this one begins with Ruth (1/10) and Gehrig (2/10), moving on to the likes of Foxx (3/10), Mack (7/10), Gehringer (3/10), Cochrane (2/10), Appling (1/10), Lyons (3/10), Kelly (6/10), McNair (3/10) and more. Signature quality dips low enough at times that an exact count is impossible, but all listed above are readily legible. Some staining and surface wear are noted. Certainly not a pristine sphere, but an opportunity for the budget-minded collector to bring many of the game's greatest names into his private collection. *LOA from PSA/DNA. LOA from James Spence Authentication.* **Minimum Bid: $600**

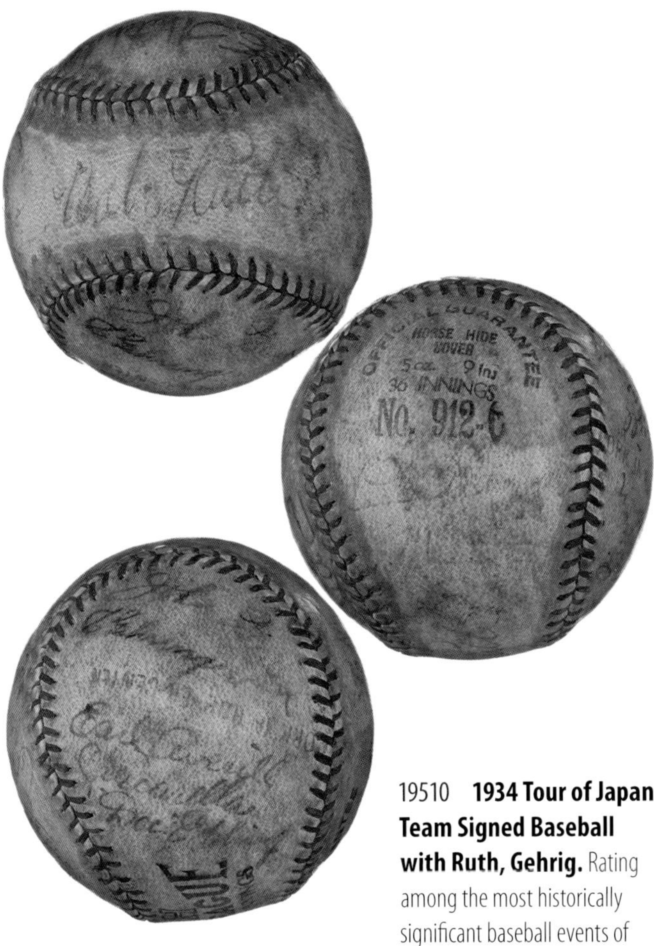

19510 **1934 Tour of Japan Team Signed Baseball with Ruth, Gehrig.** Rating among the most historically significant baseball events of the pre-war era was the 1934 Tour of Japan, which served as the catalyst for the sport's burgeoning popularity in that country today. Collectors also love relics of that Tour for the iconic stature of its participants, who are documented in vintage fountain pen ink upon this shellacked "Worth Official League" ball. Inhabiting his traditional sweet spot position is Babe Ruth, with Lou Gehrig likewise in his usual position to the east. Also to be found among the fourteen legible autographs are Gehringer, Mack, Averill, Gomez, Miller, McNair, Cascarella and Ebling. Signature quality of these fourteen signatures averages 5/10, and range from 2/10 to 7/10 in boldness. The ball itself provides the rich vintage patina of milky coffee, only furthering the aesthetic appeal. An essential keepsake for the true baseball historian. *LOA from PSA/DNA. LOA from James Spence Authentication.* Minimum Bid: $2,000

19511 **1935 Chicago Cubs Team Signed Baseball.** Since before the First World War, only a single Cubs team has posted triple-digits in the win column for a season, and here we present an ONL (Heydler) ball celebrating that historic National League Championship club. Though Heydler's National League presidency ended in 1934, we're certain this ball dates from the subsequent season due to the presence of Larry French and Fred Lindstrom, who were traded to Chicago from the Pirates in November of 1934. Thirteen other autographs join these new Wrigley arrivals, notably Klein, Herman, Grimm, Root, Warneke, Hack and Demaree. Autograph quality finds an impressive average of 8+/10, providing quality of ink to match that of the team. A warm vintage patina further serves the visual cause. *LOA from PSA/DNA. LOA from James Spence Authentication.* Minimum Bid: $600

19512 **1935 New York Giants Team Signed Baseball.** Essentially the same team that would capture the flag each of the next two seasons to come, this Polo Grounds powerhouse certainly was Giant in terms of Hall of Fame talent. Four prewar legends are among the nineteen autographs decorating this ONL (Frick) ball: Ott, Hubbell, Terry and Jackson, with lesser stars like Luque, Mancuso, Critz, Bartell and Cuccinello nearby. All Hall of Famers present at a strength of 9/10 or better with the exception of Travis Jackson (6/10). The balance ranges from 6/10 to 9/10, with most at the upper end of that range. *LOA from PSA/DNA. LOA from James Spence Authentication.* Minimum Bid: $600

19513 **1936 New York Yankees Team Signed Baseball.** The arrival of a rookie from San Francisco named Joe DiMaggio signalled the dawning of a new age in the Bronx, with a new superstar to fill the void left by Babe Ruth's departure. Joltin' Joe is one of twenty-five autographs on this OAL (Harridge) ball documenting the World Championship Yanks, joining captain Lou Gehrig, Ruffing, Combs, McCarthy, Gomez, Henrich, Dahlgren and more. Signature quality is admittedly light, averaging 3/10, though all listed are identifiable, and Gehrig on the sweet spot is the strongest at 5/10. Still a very desirable sphere, with an enormous helping of top names to be had. *LOA from PSA/DNA. LOA from James Spence Authentication.* **Minimum Bid: $500**

19515 **1930's Multi-Signed Baseball with Lazzeri, Joe DiMaggio.** We haven't quite been able to crack the code that would explain the unusual concoction of baseball talent that decorates this ONL (Frick) sphere, but perhaps the enterprising baseball historian will enjoy the project. The mystery certainly does nothing to diminish the obvious appeal, particularly in regard to the two Yankees Hall of Famers who anchor the roster. Lazzeri and DiMaggio appear in 7/10 and 6/10 black fountain pen ink respectively, well in line with the balance of the twenty-nine that join them. More notables: Ernie Lombardi, Dick Bartell, Gus Suhr and Cookie Lavagetto. The ball is very lightly and evenly toned, with no flaws of note. *LOA from PSA/DNA. LOA from James Spence Authentication.* **Minimum Bid: $500**

19514 **1936 Cincinnati Reds & Pittsburgh Pirates Signed Baseball with Wagner, Cuyler.** A small notation in an unknown hand dates this ONL (Frick) ball to April 15, 1936, the second game of the season, an eight to six loss for the Crosley Field home team. A sampling of twenty-eight combatants fill all panels in blank fountain pen ink that diverges from a strength of 3/10 to 7/10 only on rare occasion. Falling solidly within that range are such legends as Wagner, Cuyler, Lombardi, Traynor, Kelly, Vaughan and both Waner brothers. Chick Hafey also appears at 2/10. That's nine prewar Hall of Famers! The ball itself remains clear and undamaged, presenting very well for its advanced age and serving as a fitting home for such a regal cast of characters. *LOA from PSA/DNA. LOA from James Spence Authentication.* **Minimum Bid: $600**

19516 **1937 American League All-Star Reunion Team Signed Baseball.** Twenty-five years after the American League squad topped its older brother at Griffith Stadium, the Midsummer Classic made its way back to our nation's capital and invited the victorious '37 squad along for the festivities. Though the Americans couldn't repeat their winning ways on this Silver Anniversary day, fans of the Junior Circuit nonetheless have reason to cheer in the form of this OAL (Cronin) ball blessed by twenty-three All-Star Old Timers. Sharing the sweet spot are Hall of Fame legends Grove and Foxx, with Averill, Joe DiMaggio, Feller, Dickey, Gehringer, Greenberg and Gomez nearby. The inspirational Monty Stratton, the original owner of this important baseball, is here as well. Signature quality ranges from 3/10 to 9/10, with all offerings easily legible. The ball has suffered a few abrasions in its travels, but still presents nicely and remains impressively white. No shortage of prewar legends here, making this a fine choice for powering up your autograph collection in a hurry. *LOA from PSA/DNA. LOA from James Spence Authentication.* **Minimum Bid: $600**

19517 **1937 New York Giants Team Signed Baseball.** The National League Champs once again found their World Championship dreams stymied by their neighbors across the Harlem River, as Joe, Lou and the rest of the Yankees took the Series in five games. A quick look at the Giants roster should give some indication of what a fearsome battle that Fall Classic must have been, as we find Ott, Terry, Hubbell, McCarthy, Ripple, Ryan and Bartell among the signers upon this International League sphere. Nineteen autographs are present in total, with all listed rating 8/10 or better, a score shared by all but three of the signatures, which dip two points below the mark. An even coating of shellac is largely to thank for the fine quality of the black fountain pen ink. A fine Subway Series keepsake. *LOA from PSA/DNA. LOA from James Spence Authentication.* **Minimum Bid: $500**

19519 **1938 Brooklyn Dodgers Team Signed Baseball with Ruth.** After realizing that the Boston Braves would never hand the managerial reins to him, the Babe was burnt a second time by the Brooklyn Dodgers, who dangled the same hope before him and then hired Leo Durocher to replace manager Burleigh Grimes instead. While Ruth did serve as first base coach, in the end he would come to realize he was hired as little more than a side show attraction, meant to bring the curious to Ebbets for a chance to watch him knock out a few homers during pre-game batting practice. It would be the last time the Babe would wear a Major League uniform. Almost seven decades later his 9/10 autograph is still the sight to see on this ONL (Frick) ball he shares with twenty fellow Bums. Following the theme of hiring legends past their prime, we find a final season KiKi Cuyler among the signers, as well as Grimes, Phelps, Frankhouse, Hassett, Rosen and more. Signature quality averages 5/10, with only four (none listed) dipping below this level. Light shellac. *LOA from PSA/DNA. LOA from James Spence Authentication.* **Minimum Bid: $3,000**

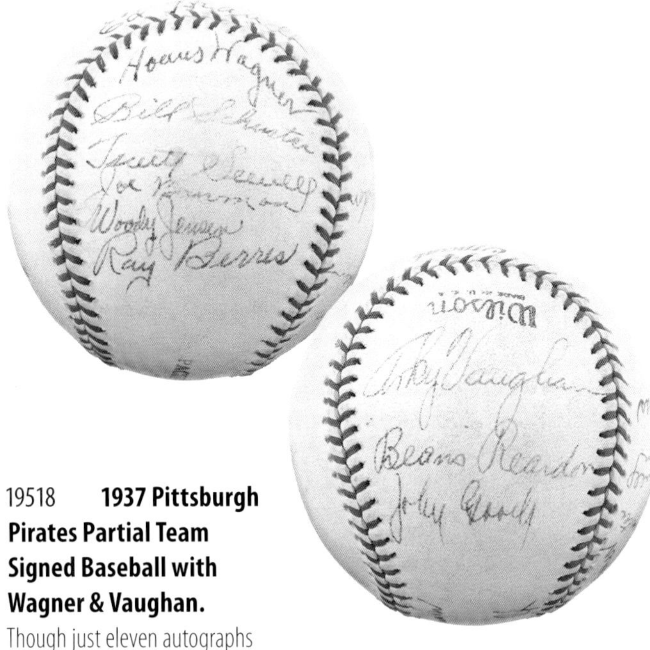

19518 **1937 Pittsburgh Pirates Partial Team Signed Baseball with Wagner & Vaughan.** Though just eleven autographs inhabit the pearly white surface of this Official Pacific Coast League orb, two of them stand more than a cut above the rest in terms of value and collectibility. Each at the top of his respective panel are the ageless legend Honus Wagner, and fellow Hall of Fame Pirates shortstop Arky Vaughan, whose accidental early death over three decades before his induction makes his signature even tougher than that of his esteemed predecessor. Other names include Schuster, Berres and Bowman. All autographs rate at an impressive strength of 7/10 or better. A clean and exotic beauty. *LOA from PSA/DNA. LOA from James Spence Authentication.* **Minimum Bid: $400**

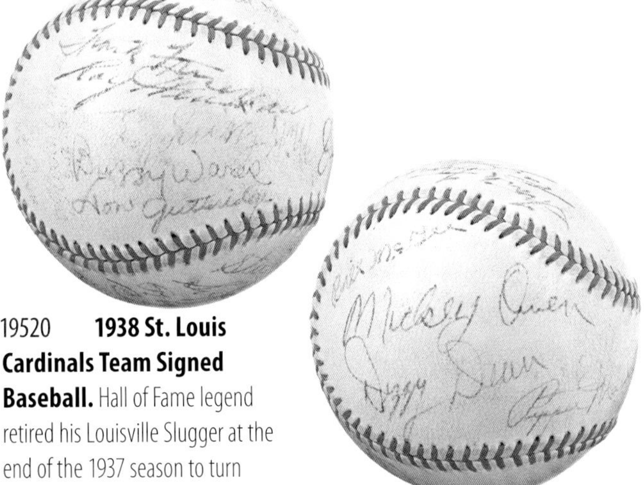

19520 **1938 St. Louis Cardinals Team Signed Baseball.** Hall of Fame legend retired his Louisville Slugger at the end of the 1937 season to turn his attentions completely to his managerial duties, and while this 1938 squad didn't quite conquer the National League, he did keep fantastic company during his struggles. Joining The Flash upon this "Official League" ball are the autographs of seventeen others, including Dizzy Dean, Slaughter, Mize, Medwick, Pepper Martin, Bush, Wares, Gonzalez and Owen. Signature quality remains strong throughout, ranging from 6/10 to 9/10, and the ball has retained its innocent white shade admirably. *LOA from PSA/DNA. LOA from James Spence Authentication.* **Minimum Bid: $600**

19521 **1938 New York Giants Team Signed Baseball.** Top Polo Grounds draws Mel Ott and Carl Hubbell share a side panel of this ONL (Frick) ball, providing ideal display for the smart collector. Their signatures, rating 8/10 and 7/10 respectively, join twenty-one others who, for the most part, share that same theme of autograph strength. Also presenting impressively are fellow Hall of Famer Bill Terry, Mancuso, Bartell, Moore, Coffman, Melton, Kampouris and Jumbo Brown. Perhaps five signatures dip to levels of 2/10 to 5/10, but none are listed above. A solid specimen that appears to have seen Big League action before taking on its second life as an autographed artifact. *LOA from PSA/DNA. LOA from James Spence Authentication.* **Minimum Bid: $600**

19522 **1938 New York Yankees Team Signed Baseball.** After running away with the American League flag, the Bombers made short work of the National League flag bearing Cubs, needing just four games to three-peat as World Champs. The star-studded cast that made ultimate glory all but a foregone conclusion from the opening bell gathers upon this "Official Joe DiMaggio League Ball," most notably captain Lou Gehrig who finds his appropriate position upon the sweet spot. Among the twenty-three that join the celebrated first baseman are Ruffing, Dickey, Henrich, Crosetti, Selkirk, Rolfe, Gordon and Babe Dahlgren, who would become the first Yankee other than Gehrig to start at the three position since 1925. Gomez and DiMaggio appear in secretarial format. Signature quality averages a conservative 6/10, with all present easily legible, thanks in part to a carefully applied coating of shellac. A solid example of an important team ball. *LOA from PSA/DNA. LOA from James Spence Authentication.* **Minimum Bid: $750**

19523 **1938 New York Yankees Team Signed Baseball.** The final taste of World Championship glory for the great Iron Horse, whose muscular frame was already beginning the imperceptible downward slide that would end his Hall of Fame career the following season. Gehrig fittingly claims the sweet spot of this "Official Joe DiMaggio League Ball" for himself, surrounded by twenty-two teammates including DiMaggio, Gomez, Ruffing, Dickey, Dahlgren, Crosetti, Henrich, Hoag, Chandler and Selkirk. Autograph quality ranges from 3/10 to 8/10, with most closer to the upper end of that spectrum and all easily identifiable. Dickey and Gomez are secretarial. The ball itself is gently toned with a few scattered spots of foxing that do little to detract. A solid specimen recalling the great Yankee captain's last hurrah. *LOA from PSA/DNA. LOA from James Spence Authentication.* **Minimum Bid: $1,000**

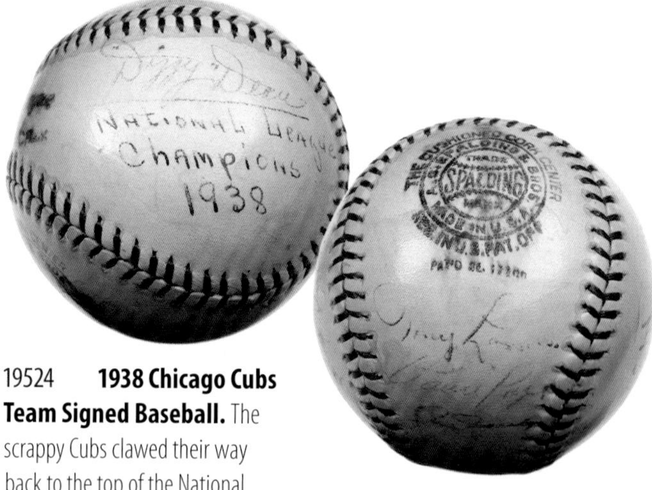

19524 **1938 Chicago Cubs Team Signed Baseball.** The scrappy Cubs clawed their way back to the top of the National League for the sixth time since their last Series victory thirty years early, but the World Championship hibernation would continue thanks to a four-game Yankee sweep. Cardinals Gashouse Gang pitchers Tex Carleton and Dizzy Dean reunite here, with Gabby Hartnett and Tony Lazzeri adding further star power. Other notables: Galan, Collins, French and Russell. Fourteen autographs are here in total, averaging 7/10 on a lightly shellacked ONL (Frick) sphere, which remains housed in its original and complete Spalding box. *LOA from PSA/DNA. LOA from James Spence Authentication.* **Minimum Bid: $400**

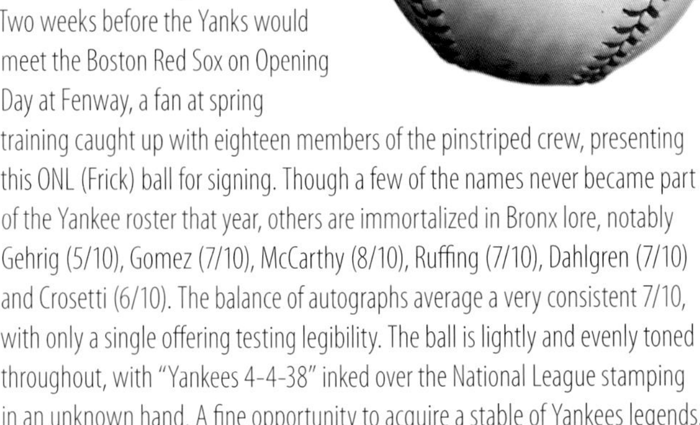

19525 1938 New York Yankees Team Signed Baseball. Two weeks before the Yanks would meet the Boston Red Sox on Opening Day at Fenway, a fan at spring training caught up with eighteen members of the pinstriped crew, presenting this ONL (Frick) ball for signing. Though a few of the names never became part of the Yankee roster that year, others are immortalized in Bronx lore, notably Gehrig (5/10), Gomez (7/10), McCarthy (8/10), Ruffing (7/10), Dahlgren (7/10) and Crosetti (6/10). The balance of autographs average a very consistent 7/10, with only a single offering testing legibility. The ball is lightly and evenly toned throughout, with "Yankees 4-4-38" inked over the National League stamping in an unknown hand. A fine opportunity to acquire a stable of Yankees legends. Complete original "Spalding" baseball box (VG) is included. *LOA from PSA/DNA. LOA from James Spence Authentication.* **Minimum Bid:** $750

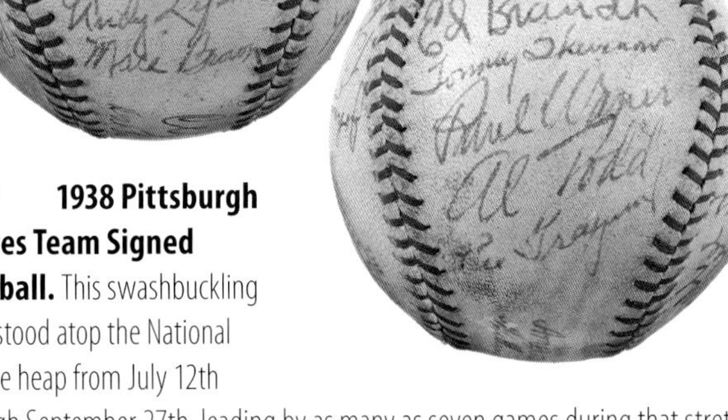

19527 1938 Pittsburgh Pirates Team Signed Baseball. This swashbuckling crew stood atop the National League heap from July 12th through September 27th, leading by as many as seven games during that stretch, before being nipped at the wire by the surging Chicago Cubs. Twenty-three signatures from these runners-up find a home on an OAL (Harridge) ball, almost as if to suggest that they should have visited the Bronx in October to use such a ball in the Series. All autographs project at a stunning 9/10 or better, and include many of the day's greatest figures: Wagner, both Waner brothers, Traynor, Manush and more. The ball shows apparent game use that clearly predates the autograph session. You'll rarely see prewar signed balls boasting autograph boldness such as this. *LOA from PSA/DNA. LOA from James Spence Authentication.* **Minimum Bid:** $750

19526 1938 St. Louis Cardinals Team Signed Baseball. An extraordinary compilation of Cooperstown talent paired with phenomenal condition makes this ball a hot commodity on the sports collectibles market. While a small number of autographs derive from other clubs, suggesting possible spring training vintage, all the big Cardinals stars are here, notably Mize, Medwick, Slaughter, Frisch, Paul Dean, Pepper Martin, Owen, Johnson and Bordagaray. Despite his 1938 move to the Cubs, Dizzy Dean is here as well, bringing the Hall of Fame total to five. Twenty-four autographs are here in total, averaging 8/10 in boldness, with no listed name dipping more than two points below that mark. The ONL (Frick) ball is likewise impressive in its condition, clean and unblemished in its original box (missing lid). A rock-solid example of a tough pre-war team ball. *LOA from PSA/DNA. LOA from James Spence Authentication.* **Minimum Bid:** $400

19528 1940 National League All-Star Team Signed Baseball. A first inning home run by Max West proved to be all the Nationals would need at this Sportsman's Park Midsummer Classic, as five NL pitchers joined forces to blank an American League line-up stacked with the likes of DiMaggio, Foxx, and Ted Williams. The hero of the day appears just below Mel Ott on the side panel of this ONL (Frick) ball, joined by twenty-three other members of the victorious Senior Circuit. Other notables: Mize, Medwick, McKechnie, Stengel, Hubbell, Walters, Herman and Durocher. That's nine Hall of Famers! Autograph quality ranges from 4/10 to 9/10, with all Hall of Famers at the upper end of that expanse. A light coating of shellac and the original complete Spalding box are to thank for the fine quality. *LOA from PSA/DNA. LOA from James Spence Authentication.* **Minimum Bid:** $600

19529 **1940 Boston Red Sox Team Signed Baseball.** In 1939, with the arrival of Ted Williams at the gates of Fenway, Major League Baseball would find two future 500 Home Run Club members sharing a dugout for the first time. This boldly autographed orb features splendid signatures from the second and fourth players to reach the mark, with Foxx a bona fide 10/10 and Williams just a point behind. Twenty-nine signatures appear on the OAL (Harridge) ball in total, with all but a few comparable in quality to the iconic Hall of Famers. These include Cronin, Grove, Doerr (light), coach Hugh Duffy, Dom DiMaggio, Cramer and more. A coating of shellac and some scattered surface wear are to be noted, but neither issue causes any significant visual concern. A great way to bring some top quality Red Sox Hall of Fame autographs into your collection with a single bid. *LOA from PSA/DNA. LOA from James Spence Authentication.* **Minimum Bid: $600**

19531 **1942 "The Pride of the Yankees" Cast Signed Baseball with Babe Ruth, Gary Cooper.** Widely considered the most important sports film of all time, the Lou Gehrig biopic featured a tantalizing convergence of stars from the diamond and silver screen joined to honor the fallen Iron Horse. This OAL (Harridge) sphere is one of the few known to have been birthed upon the set of that film, featuring a magnificent sweet spot signature (conservative 8/10) from the Babe on the sweet spot and leading man Gary Cooper in 7/10 condition on the panel just above. Former Yanks and noteworthy Hollywood figures comprise the balance of the eleven autographs, and include Bill Dickey, Mark Koenig, Bob Meusel, Babe Herman, Lefty O'Doul, Walter Brennan and Dan Duryea. Average signature quality is 7/10. A light coating of shellac has performed admirably in its intended purpose of autograph maintenence, and provides a handsome tone to the horsehide. We'll let the baseball fans and movie buffs fight it out for this one. *LOA from PSA/DNA. LOA from James Spence Authentication.* **Minimum Bid: $3,000**

19530 **1941 St. Louis Cardinals Team Signed Baseball.** Stan the Man (or perhaps "the Boy" in this case) made his Major League debut on September 17th of this year, assuring that this will be one of the only '41 Cardinals balls to bear the rookie Hall of Famer's autograph. His youthful 10/10 black fountain pen offering joins twenty-five teammates from the National League runners-up, including Southworth, Brecheen, Marion, Cooper, Lanier. Wares and more. Signature quality averages a consistent 9/10, and the "Amateur League" ball remains clean with no noteworthy flaws. *LOA from PSA/DNA. LOA from James Spence Authentication.* **Minimum Bid: $400**

19532 **1942 New York Yankees Team Signed Baseball.** Posting 101 victories in this final year before the Second World War would claim much of the game's greatest talents, the Bronx Bombers cruised to its sixth American League Championship in seven seasons in 1942. An examination of the superstar roster that appears upon this OAL (Harridge) sphere explains this dominance convincingly. Twenty-seven black ink autographs include DiMaggio, Gomez, Rizzuto, Ruffing, McCarthy (clubhouse), Bonham, Borowy, Chandler, Crosetti, Selkirk and more. Signature quality averages 7/10 in strength, and the few that dip more than a couple points below that mark are secondary figures not listed above. A fine specimen from the last great prewar Yankee team. *LOA from PSA/DNA. LOA from James Spence Authentication.* **Minimum Bid: $600**

COMPLIMENTS OF THE BABE

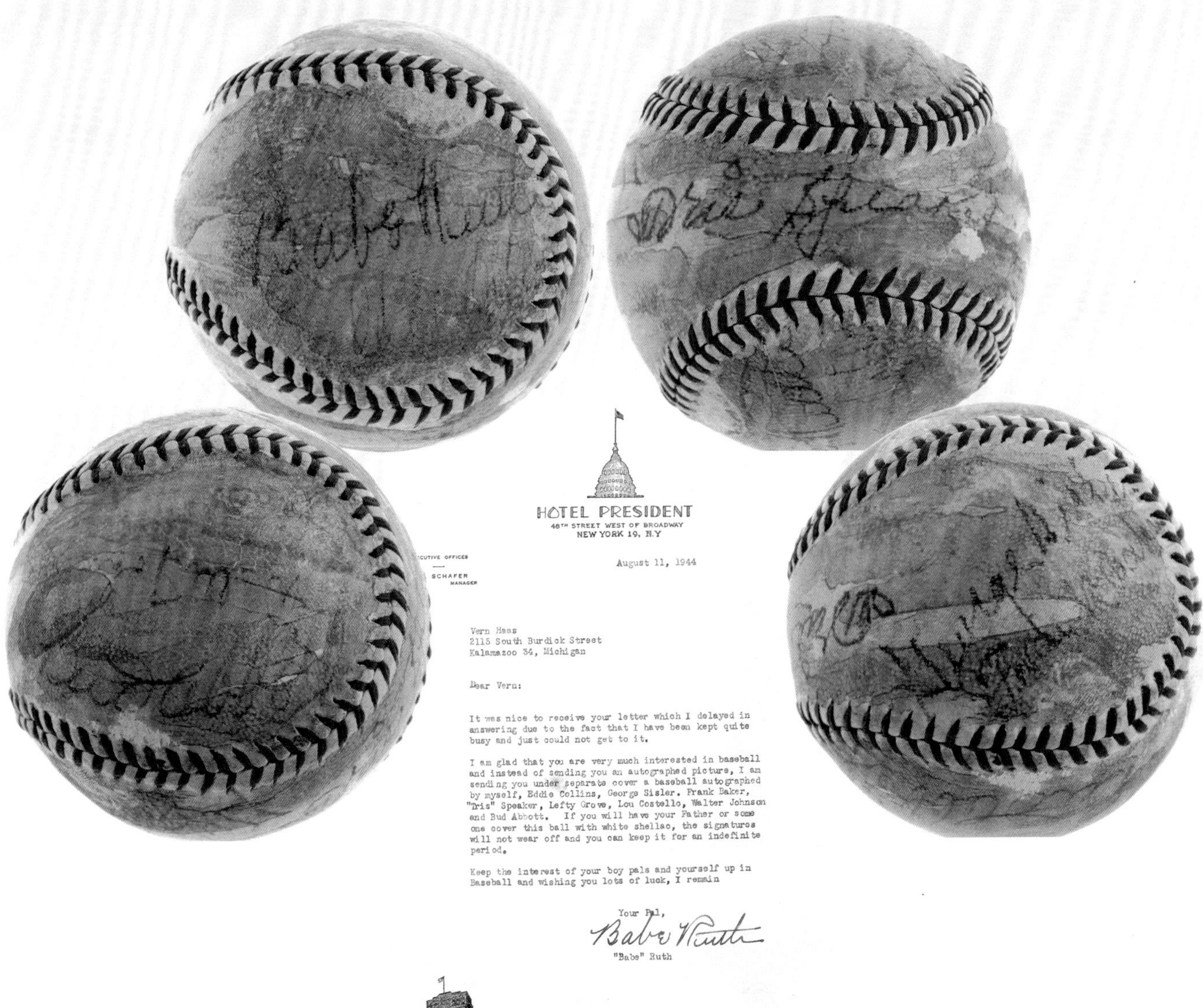

HOTEL PRESIDENT
48TH STREET WEST OF BROADWAY
NEW YORK 19, N.Y

CUTIVE OFFICES
SCHAFER
MANAGER

August 11, 1944

Vern Haas
2115 South Burdick Street
Kalamazoo 34, Michigan

Dear Vern:

It was nice to receive your letter which I delayed in answering due to the fact that I have been kept quite busy and just could not get to it.

I am glad that you are very much interested in baseball and instead of sending you an autographed picture, I am sending you under separate cover a baseball autographed by myself, Eddie Collins, George Sisler. Frank Baker, "Tris" Speaker, Lefty Grove, Lou Costello, Walter Johnson and Bud Abbott. If you will have your Father or some one cover this ball with white shellac, the signatures will not wear off and you can keep it for an indefinite period.

Keep the interest of your boy pals and yourself up in Baseball and wishing you lots of luck, I remain

Your Pal,
Babe Ruth
"Babe" Ruth

MAKE NEW YORK YOUR VACATION CITY AND MAKE THE PRESIDENT HOTEL YOUR HOME

19533 **1944 Hall of Famers Signed Baseball with Babe Ruth Signed Letter of Provenance.** Spectacular lot is best described in the words of the great Bambino himself, whose typed letter to a fan reads, in part, "...I am glad that you are very much interested in baseball and instead of sending you an autographed picture, I am sending you under separate cover a baseball autographed by myself, Eddie Collins, George Sisler, Frank Baker, 'Tris' Speaker, Lefty Grove, Lou Costello, Walter Johnson and Bud Abbott. If you will have your Father or some one cover this ball with white shellac, the signatures will not wear off and you can keep it for an indefinite period..." The letter, on New York City's Hotel President letterhead, is signed at the close in flawless 10/10 fountain pen ink. The baseball of which Ruth writes is an OAL (Harridge) model, featuring each of the inaugural class Hall of Famers and the "Who's on First" comedians that he promises. His advice to shellac the ball was heeded by the young fan, causing somewhat pronounced and uneven toning, but maintaining a boldness of 7/10 or better for Ruth, Speaker, Sisler, Baker and Abbott. Costello, Grove, Collins and Johnson are all still entirely legible, but range from 3/10 to 5/10 instead. Now, over six decades later, one winning bidder will be able to experience the same rush of finding these autographed treasures in the mail as did young Vern Haas from Kalamazoo in August 1944. *LOA from PSA/DNA. LOA from James Spence Authentication.* Minimum Bid: $7,500

19534 **1946 St. Louis Cardinals Team Signed Baseball.** Seems like Harry "The Hat" Walker should have given Enos Slaughter sole possession of this ONL (Frick) ball if you ask us—after all, it was Country's "Mad Dash" that served as the nail in the Red Sox' coffin and secured baseball's greatest prize for the birds. Twenty-three members of the World Championship squad appear in total, including young Hall of Famers Musial and Schoendienst, Garagiola, Marion, Brecheen, Kurowski, Moore and Dusak. To a man, the autographs present at a strength of either 7/10 or 8/10, and the ball itself is likewise consistently fine in condition. A fine memento of one of the most noteworthy Cardinals teams ever. *LOA from PSA/DNA. LOA from James Spence Authentication.* **Minimum Bid: $400**

19535 **1947 New York Yankees Team Signed Baseball with Medwick.** For the Yankee team ball collector who has everything, we present a piece that only the most educated of baseball historians even knew was possible. Positioned on the sweet spot of this OAL (Harridge) ball is the bold black fountain pen autograph of Joe "Ducky" Medwick, the only Hall of Fame player in Yankee history that never saw Yankee action. The legendary Gashouse Gang outfielder was picked up as a free agent in December of 1946 and released just a few weeks into the 1947 season, having never seen an inning's work for the club. He's joined by a jam-packed roster of thirty-four others, including more familiar Bronx faces like DiMaggio, Rizzuto, Berra, Henrich, Crosetti, Chandler, Silvera, Bevens and Dressen. Signature quality is quite strong throughout, averaging 8/10 and only rarely dipping as low as 6/10. You can bet you won't have too much luck finding another such Yankee ball, in any condition whatsoever, and definitely not one as nice as this. *LOA from PSA/DNA. LOA from James Spence Authentication.* **Minimum Bid: $600**

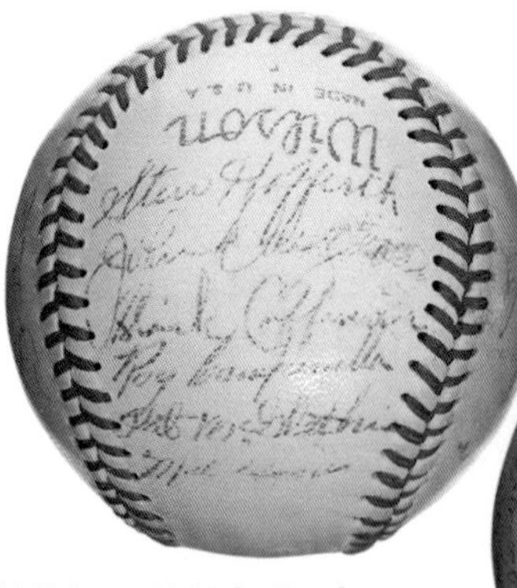

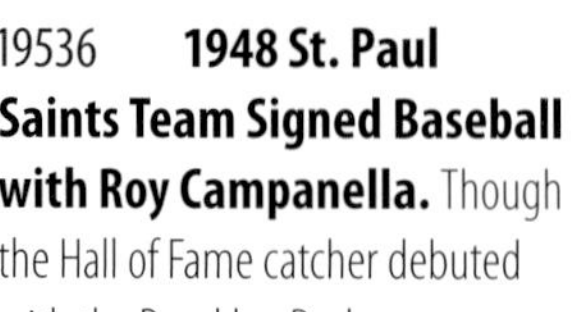

19536 **1948 St. Paul Saints Team Signed Baseball with Roy Campanella.** Though the Hall of Fame catcher debuted with the Brooklyn Dodgers on Opening Day of 1948, Hall of Fame executive Branch Rickey soon decided to give Campy the "Jackie Robinson treatment," tapping him to break the American Association color barrier with a trip to St. Paul in May. After a brief stay in Minnesota he was back at Ebbets, but not before he would apply his signature to this tremendously scarce Official American Association ball recounting the '48 Saints club. Fellow Dodgers Hall of Famer Walt Alston is among the nineteen autographs joining the star catcher, rating at the same 6/10 to 7/10 strength that is consistent throughout. The ball itself is clean and wonderfully white. With only a single other Campy/Saints piece selling in a major auction in the past several years, it's a safe bet that you won't have too many more chances at such a unique offering as this. *LOA from PSA/DNA. LOA from James Spence Authentication.* **Minimum Bid: $1,000**

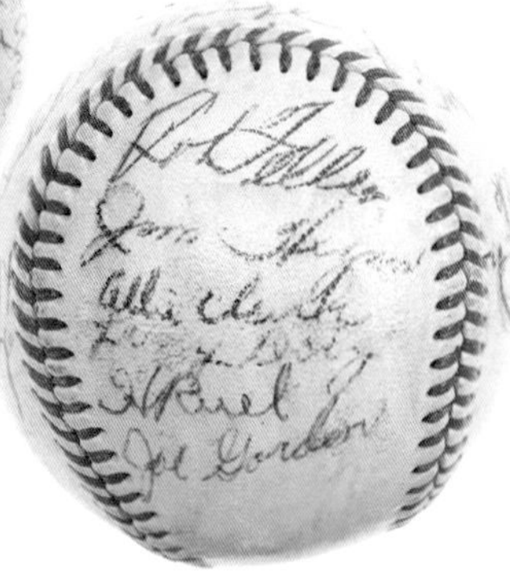

19537 **1948 Cleveland Indians Team Signed Baseball.** In a city starved for World Championship sports glory, this last ballclub to celebrate a World Series victory remains close to the hearts of millions of Ohioans. Boasting perhaps the most stacked pitching rotation in Major League history, the 1948 Indians brought three Hall of Famers to the mound as starters. Ancient rookie Satchel Paige joins manager Lou Boudreau on the sweet spot of this OAL (Harridge) ball, with Lemon and Feller stationed nearby. Other notables include Paige's fellow Negro League standout Doby, Keltner, Hegan, Gordon, Robinson and coach Muddy Ruel. Gordon, Kuel, Black and Peck are secretarial. Signature quality averages 7/10 under a yellowing layer of shellac. A solid example of a ball no true Indians fan should be without. *LOA from PSA/DNA. LOA from James Spence Authentication.* **Minimum Bid: $750**

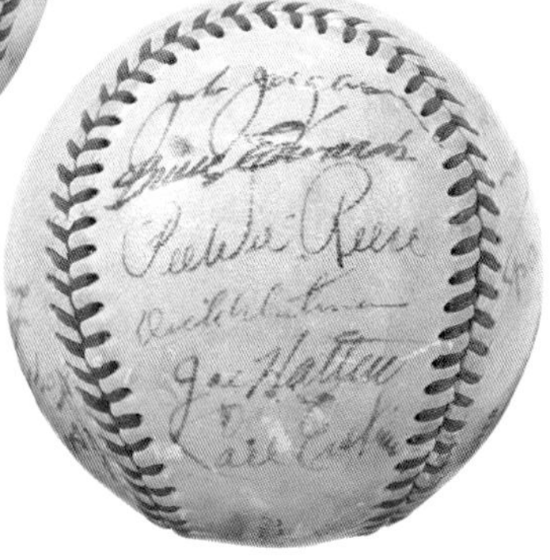

19538 **1949 Brooklyn Dodgers Team Signed Baseball.** Almost as if they could read the minds of twenty-first century collectors, the noble duo of Jackie Robinson and Roy Campanella chose to stack their 8+/10 blue ink signatures upon this ONL (Frick) ball to provide the ideal format for display. These pioneering Hall of Famers join thirteen other National League Champs upon the toned and partially shellacked relic, including Snider, Reese, Hodges, Branca, Erskine and Jorgenson. Signature quality ranges from 5/10 to 9/10, with most close to the upper end of that scale. *LOA from PSA/DNA. LOA from James Spence Authentication.* **Minimum Bid: $600**

19540 **1952 New York Yankees Team Signed Baseball.** With Joe DiMaggio settling into his first year of retirement, the torch was officially passed this season to a twenty-year old Mickey Mantle, who topped the American League with sixty-seven extra base hits to take the bronze medal in MVP voting. His highly desirable early signature joins twenty-nine other members of this World Championship squad on an OAL (Harridge) ball, including Mize, Berra, Dickey, Rizzuto, Martin, Crosetti, Reynolds, Raschi, McDougald, Lopat, Houk and Sain. Autograph quality ranges between 4/10 and 8/10, with most closer to the higher end of that scale. A solid specimen from the most dominant World Championship era in Yankee history. *LOA from PSA/DNA. LOA from James Spence Authentication.* **Minimum Bid: $600**

19539 **1949 New York Yankees Team Signed Baseball.** Though Casey Stengel's appointment to the Yankee managerial position was met with almost universal scorn by Bronx boosters in early 1949, those folks were singing a different tune as the Ol' Perfesser led the Bombers back to the promised land for the first of five consecutive Octobers. Many Yankee collectors are aware that Stengel is typically found in clubhouse format on team balls, but such is not the case here, and he joins twenty World Champs here in authentic format. Joe DiMaggio claims the sweet spot, with Mize (twice), Berra, Dickey, Rizzuto, Reynolds, Raschi, Crosetti and Collins nearby. Autograph quality ranges from 5/10 to 8/10 with just two exceptions, neither of which is among the names listed above. OAL (Harridge). The beginning of what is arguably the greatest dynasty in baseball history. *LOA from PSA/DNA. LOA from James Spence Authentication.* **Minimum Bid: $600**

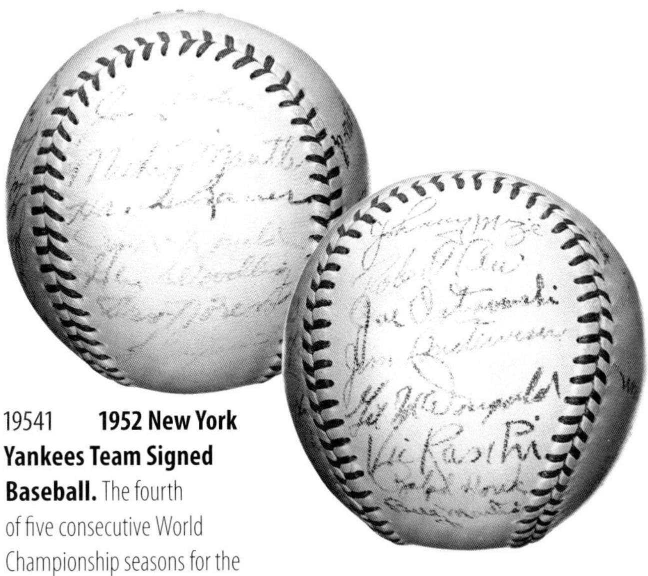

19541 **1952 New York Yankees Team Signed Baseball.** The fourth of five consecutive World Championship seasons for the mighty Bronx Bombers, who kept the streak going despite the departure of Joe DiMaggio at the close of the previous season. Of course young Mickey Mantle was starting to make his case for immortality, and his highly desirable early signature is one of the twenty-five autographs that decorate this OAL (Harridge) ball. Other notables include Rizzuto, Berra, Mize, Martin, Reynolds, Raschi, McDougald, Houk and Bauer. Signature quality ranges from 2/10 to 8/10, with all Hall of Famers rating at least 4/10. An entirely respectable specimen from arguably the most dominant era in Bombers history. *LOA from PSA/DNA. LOA from James Spence Authentication.* **Minimum Bid: $600**

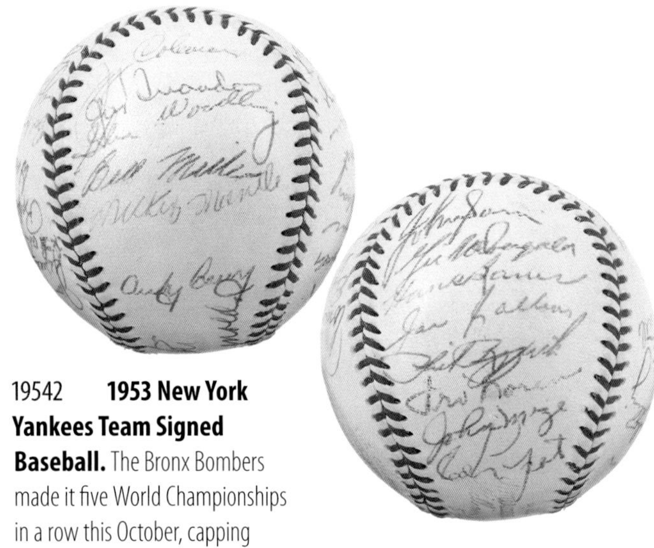

19542 **1953 New York Yankees Team Signed Baseball.** The Bronx Bombers made it five World Championships in a row this October, capping the most dominant run in Major League history that featured the transition from one Hall of Fame center fielder to another. The young Mickey Mantle, who ably accepted the reins from a retiring Joe DiMaggio, is present on this OAL (Harridge) ball as one of twenty-eight strong (8/10 average) ink signatures. Other notables include Mize, Ford, Rizzuto, Berra, Houk, McDougald, Sain, Woodling and Coleman. Autograph quality is strong and consistent throughout, all falling within the range of 7/10 to 9/10. *LOA from PSA/DNA. LOA from James Spence Authentication.* **Minimum Bid: $750**

19544 **1954 Cleveland Indians Team Signed Baseball, PSA NM-MT+ 8.5.** Time has literally stood still for this outrageous OAL (Harridge) ball since the Indians laid claim to the American League flag with an outrageous 111-43 record, preserving perfectly the winningest team of the twentieth century. A full roster of thirty-one achieves an autograph grade of 9/10 from the stingy graders at PSA/DNA, and includes Lopez, Feller, Lemon, Doby, Newhouser, Wynn, Avila, Rosen, Wertz, Hegan and Glynn. The ball itself rates an 8/10 on the full PSA letter of authenticity, accounting for the composite score of NM-MT+ 8.5. Perhaps the best team sphere in existence from what is arguably the greatest roster ever fielded in Cleveland. *LOA from PSA/DNA. LOA from James Spence Authentication.* **Minimum Bid: $600**

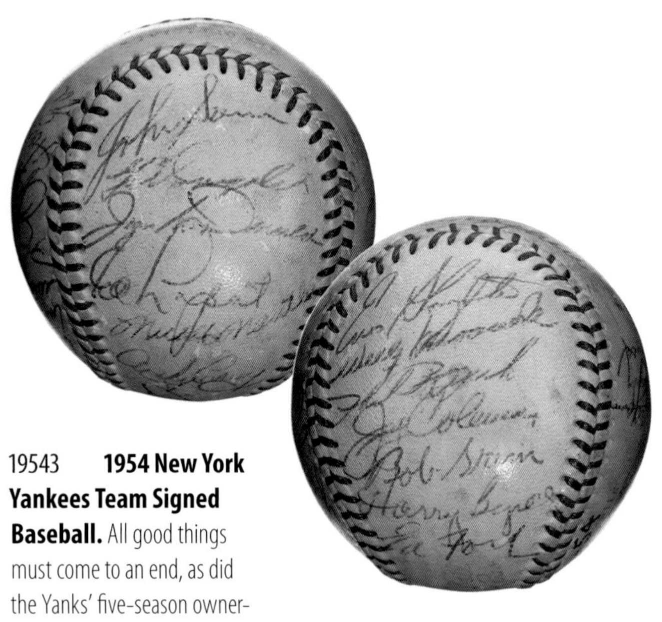

19543 **1954 New York Yankees Team Signed Baseball.** All good things must come to an end, as did the Yanks' five-season ownership of the American League flag and the World Championship the season this OAL (Harridge) ball made the rounds of the Bronx dugout. But their loss could be one smart collector's gain, as the brilliant cast of characters remains largely unchanged from its more expensive Championship vintage brethren. Most important is the early format of Mickey Mantle's signature, applied in 5/10 black ink upon a side panel. The balance of autographs are in blue, averaging 8/10 and including Slaughter, Rizzuto, Ford, Berra, Sain, Lopat, Skowron and more. Stengel is present in clubhouse form. Twenty-seven autographs are here in total, nicely preserved under a thin coating of shellac. A small amount of surface wear causes no major concern, leaving the ball to present remarkably well for its advanced age. *LOA from PSA/DNA. LOA from James Spence Authentication.* **Minimum Bid: $400**

19545 **1955 Brooklyn Dodgers Team Signed Baseball.** The sixth time was a charm for the long-suffering Bums, who finally got the best of the hated Yanks this October after five stinging defeats at the hands of Joe, Mickey and the gang. The club that finally brought joy to Flatbush is memorialized for eternity here on this ONL (Giles) ball featuring twenty-four signatures from the likes of Jackie, Campy, Koufax (tough rookie signature!), Alston, Hodges, Podres, Labine, Erskine, Furillo, Gilliam, Newcombe and the important Frank Kellert, whose single season of Brooklyn service assures 1955 vintage. Snider, Reese, Furillo, Bessent and Loes have been deemed clubhouse variety. Autograph quality is superb for a ball cruising past the half-century mark, with a remarkable average of 9/10. No more "wait 'til next year." The time to bid is now. *LOA from PSA/DNA. LOA from James Spence Authentication.* **Minimum Bid: $1,500**

19546 **1955 New York Yankees Team Signed Baseball.** The long-suffering Brooklyn Dodgers finally got the best of the boys from the Bronx this season, but the fact still remains that this sphere represents perhaps the most dominant dynasty in American sport. What a "blazer" it is too, with none of the twenty-four signatures dipping below 8/10 in boldness, thanks in part to an expertly applied coating of shellac that has given an amber tone to the OAL (Harridge) ball. Best is the early signature variation of the great Mickey Mantle, though we can't forget the likes of Berra, Ford, Howard, McDougald, Lopat, Bauer, Turley and Skowron, who check in here as well. *LOA from PSA/DNA. LOA from James Spence Authentication.* **Minimum Bid: $750**

19548 **1956 New York Yankees Team Signed Baseball.** Mickey Mantle wrote a book calling the 1956 season *My Favorite Summer,* and, given his Triple Crown coronation and World Championship ring to boot, the sentiment is not surprising. The switch-hitting superstar shares the sweet spot with fellow Hall of Famer Yogi Berra, with twenty-four teammates gathering around the pair upon this OAL (Harridge) sphere. Other notables: Ford, Slaughter, Martin, Larsen, Howard, Skowron, Carey and Bauer. Mickey and Yogi reside near the top of the quality range of 2/10 to 8/10, with most just above the center point of that span. A solid reminder of perhaps the greatest era to be a baseball fan in the Big Apple. *LOA from PSA/DNA. LOA from James Spence Authentication.* **Minimum Bid: $600**

19547 **1956 Brooklyn Dodgers Team Signed Baseball.** The club that delivered the last National League flag to the borough of Brooklyn convene here upon an ONL (Giles) ball autographed by twenty-three. Departing veteran Jackie Robinson joins a rookie Don Drysdale and five more Hall of Fame legends: Campanella, Koufax, Reese, Snider and Alston. Also present are Hodges, Furillo, Erskine, Gilliam, Labine, Maglie and more. Signature quality is fantastic throughout, with the 9/10 average due in large part to a successful application of shellac which has supplied the ball with a healthy amber glaze. Our experts assert that the following are secretarial: Reese, Snider, Koufax, Gilliam, Amoros, Cimoli. Though a year removed from World Championship glory, the '56 edition represents the Bums at their Hall of Fame height and is arguably the finest of any Dodger club to call Ebbets home. *LOA from PSA/DNA. LOA from James Spence Authentication.* **Minimum Bid: $500**

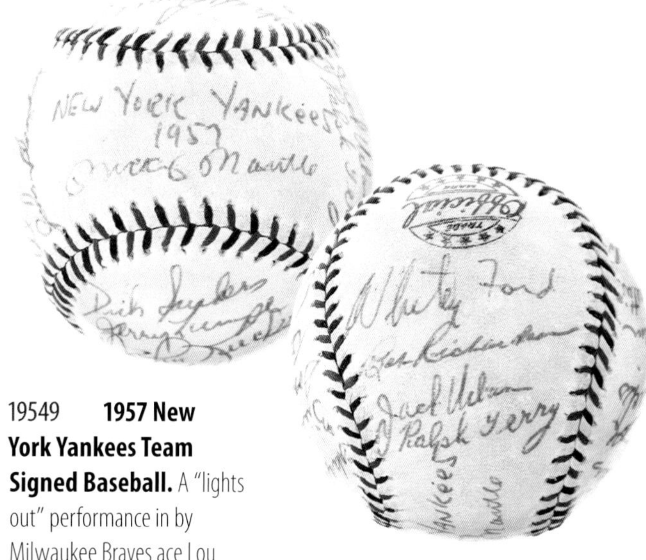

19549 **1957 New York Yankees Team Signed Baseball.** A "lights out" performance in by Milwaukee Braves ace Lou Burdette in Game Seven of the 1957 World Series denied this American League Championship club yet another World Series ring, but the Yanks would get their revenge in the 1958 October rematch. Here we find the cast of one of the great Bomber dynasties, anchored, of course, by the legendary Mickey Mantle who claims his rightful sweet spot position upon this "Official Special League" baseball in his coveted early signature style. Joining him are twenty-one teammates in equally brilliant 9/10 and better blue ink, including Rizzuto, Ford, Martin, Terry, Crosetti, Bauer, Kubek, Richardson and more. The ball is clean and white, and particularly attractive with it's "old school" black and red stitching. *LOA from PSA/DNA. LOA from James Spence Authentication.* **Minimum Bid: $1,000**

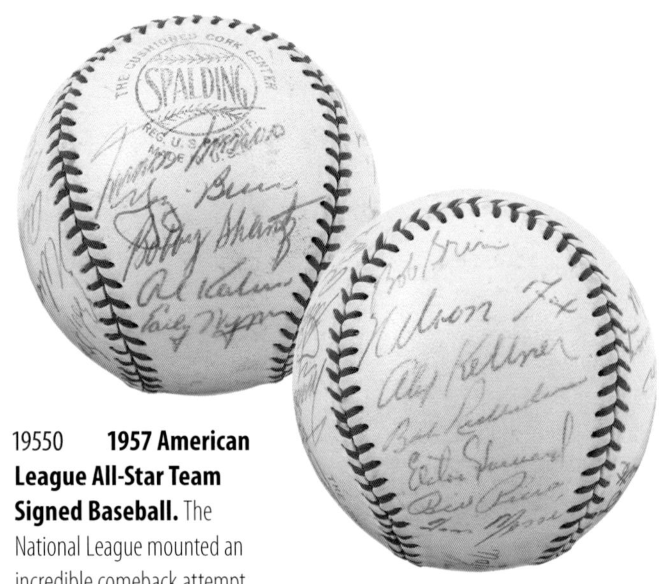

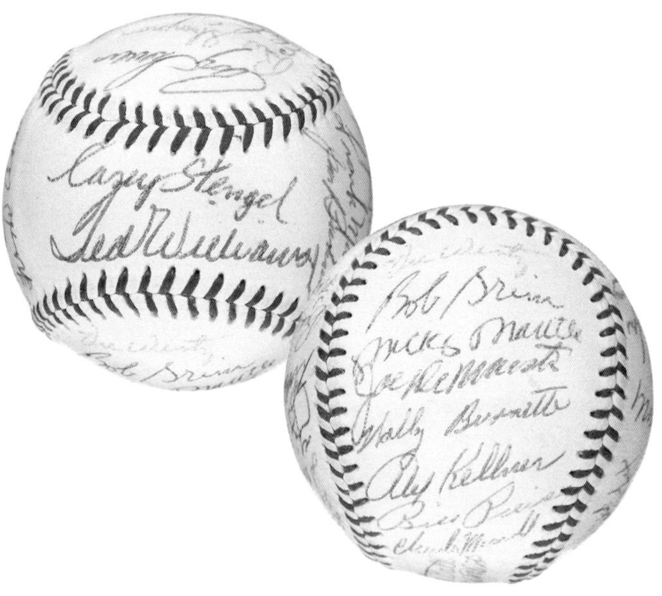

19550 **1957 American League All-Star Team Signed Baseball.** The National League mounted an incredible comeback attempt in the bottom of this St. Louis contest's ninth inning, but a spectacular catch in left center by Minnie Minoso preserved the victory for the Junior Circuit. The Cuban-born savior of the A.L. win is joined by twenty-two fellow stars upon this ONL (Giles) ball, with other notables including Berra, Kaline, Wynn, Kell, Bunning, Fox, Howard, Richardson, Skowron and Kuenn. Not a single autograph dips below a strength of 8/10, and the ball is likewise in fine condition. *LOA from PSA/DNA. LOA from James Spence Authentication.* Minimum Bid: $400

PSA/DNA
CASEY STENGEL
MS BASEBALL NM – MT + 8.5
81971134

19551 **1957 American League All-Star Team Signed Baseball, PSA NM-MT+ 8.5.** One of the more controversial Midsummer Classics, this Cincinnati affair was complicated by the locals' stuffing of the ballot box, electing nearly the entire Reds team to the National League's starting roster. League president Ford Frick was forced to step in to minimize the effects, stating, "I can take it if we lose, but I strongly object to our league making a burlesque out of the All-Star Game." But while the Senior Circuit may have fielded a watered-down team, the same could not be said for the eventual winners. This OAL (Harridge) ball features the full roster of thirty-one American Leaguers, highlighted by the likes of Ted Williams and Casey Stengel on the sweet spot, and Mantle, Kaline, Fox, Bunning, Kell, Berra, Wynn, Howard and Wertz nearby. The remarkable condition is no optical illusion, with PSA/DNA assessing 8/10 grades for both the autographs and the ball itself, resulting (somewhat cryptically) in a composite score of NM-MT+ 8.5. *LOA from PSA/DNA. LOA from James Spence Authentication.* Minimum Bid: $750

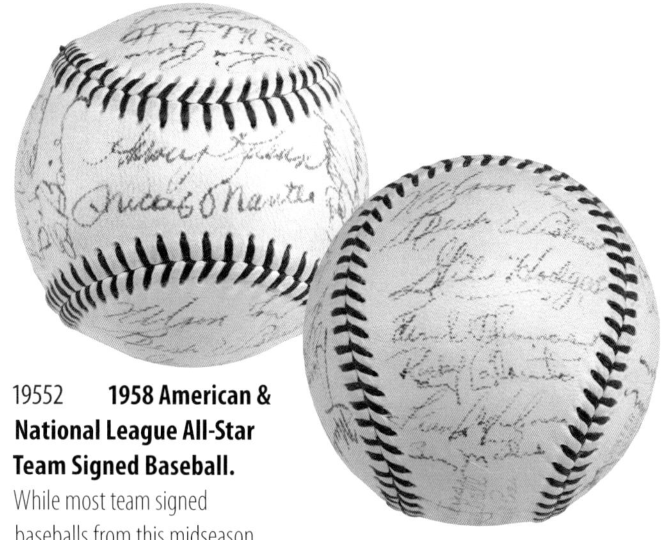

19552 **1958 American & National League All-Star Team Signed Baseball.** While most team signed baseballs from this midseason event are segregated by League, one unbiased fan delivered this OAL (Harridge) baseball to both dugouts, coming away with a brilliant assortment of the best ballplayers of the Eisenhower era. Thirty-one blue ink signatures are highlighted by a sweet spot Mantle, Ford, Mazeroski, Fox, Banks, Hodges (who adds "Best Wishes"), Colavito, Martin, Podres, Vernon, Newcombe, Gilliam, Kuenn and more. Signature quality varies little from an average of 8/10 in boldness, and the ball itself remains pale and attractive with only a couple unobtrusive dots of toning. A special keepsake direct from the diamond at Baltimore's Memorial Stadium. *LOA from PSA/DNA. LOA from James Spence Authentication.* **Minimum Bid: $1,000**

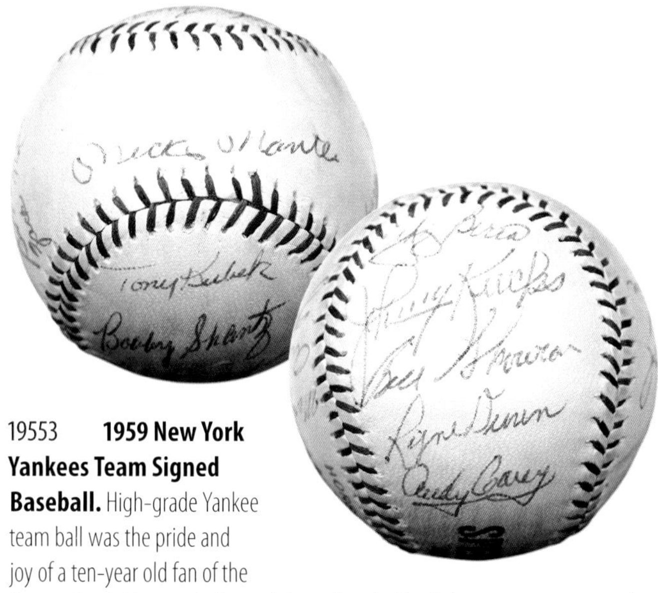

19553 **1959 New York Yankees Team Signed Baseball.** High-grade Yankee team ball was the pride and joy of a ten-year old fan of the Kansas City Athletics who learned that a friend of his father was a waitress at the hotel where the visiting clubs stayed when visiting Municipal Stadium. Wisely, the youngster supplied the waitress with this "Official Special League" ball and asked that she pass it around the breakfast tables as she served them. Seventeen members honored her request, with their signatures remaining in incredible 9/10 condition almost half a century later. Notables include Mantle, Berra, Ford, Duren, Skowron, Howard, Turley, Carey, Richardson, Houk and more. A top-quality sphere for collectors who prize condition. *LOA from PSA/DNA. LOA from James Spence Authentication.* **Minimum Bid: $600**

19554 **1963 New York Yankees Team Signed Baseball.** A fourth consecutive American League flag for the boys from the Bronx, who powered their way to the top of the Junior Circuit with the thunderous bats of the M&M boys. Mantle and Maris appear in authentic form here, bucking the trend of secretarial format that one so often encounters in Yankee balls of this era. Only Bridges, Kunkel and Gibbs are ghost signed on this OAL (Cronin) sphere, with the balance of the twenty-seven total signatures on the ball the genuine article. Signature quality rates an impressive average of 8/10, and a number "15" marked on the Reach stamping attributes this ball to Tom Tresh, from whose personal collection it (and several other contemporary Yankees signed pieces within this auction) derives. Other notables upon this ball include Berra, Howard, Pepitone, Bouton, Boyer, Richardson, Terry, Blanchard, Kubek and Tresh himself. *LOA from PSA/DNA. LOA from James Spence Authentication.* **Minimum Bid: $750**

19555 **1965 New York Yankees Team Signed Baseball.** One of several Yankee balls presented within this auction from the personal collection of outfielder Tom Tresh comes this high-grade OAL (Cronin) sphere recounting the '65 Bronx Bombers. While the club's fortunes took a significant southern turn this season after five straight American League pennants, the greats of the era are still present and accounted for, most notable the superstar pairing of Mickey Mantle and Roger Maris, who appear on the sweet spot and side panel respectively. Also here are Ford, Howard, Boyer, Bouton, Stafford, Richardson, Stottlemyre, Pepitone, Kubek, Tresh and new manager Johnny Keane. It's interesting to note that the number on the Reach stamping, which typically indicates the uniform number of the player for whom it is intended, is "9" in this case, suggesting that Tresh may have grabbed Roger Maris' team ball by mistake. Regardless, the condition is absolutely stunning, with all autographs rating 9/10 or better and the horsehide remaining as clean and white as newly fallen snow. Definitely one for the "condition freaks" in our collecting audience. *LOA from PSA/DNA. LOA from James Spence Authentication.* **Minimum Bid: $750**

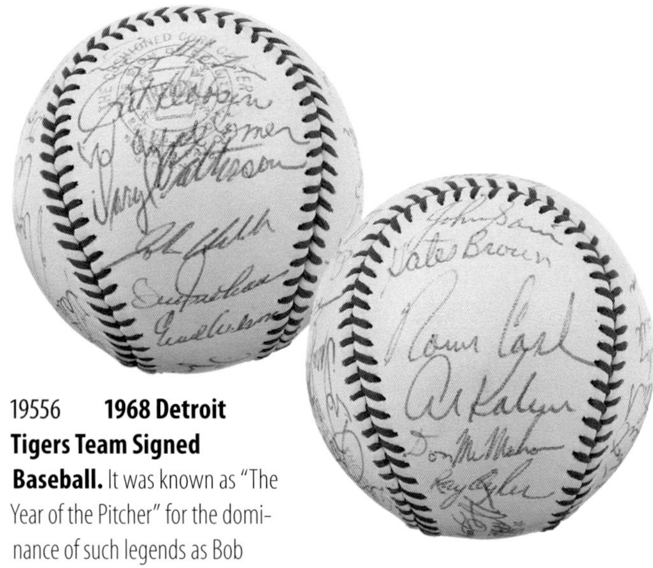

19556 **1968 Detroit Tigers Team Signed Baseball.** It was known as "The Year of the Pitcher" for the dominance of such legends as Bob Gibson of the St. Louis Cardinals and Denny McLain, who won an outrageous thirty-one games for the ballclub that is celebrated here. The 1968 American League Cy Young winner appears as one of twenty-nine blazing blue signatures upon this stunning OAL (Cronin) ball, almost assuredly the finest dedicated to this World Championship squad available in the hobby today. Other notables include Lolich, Kaline, Cash, Horton, Stanley, Wilson and Brown. Manager Mayo Smith signs over the Cronin stamping. This is no trick photography—the ball really is that perfect! *LOA from PSA/DNA. LOA from James Spence Authentication.* Minimum Bid: $400

19557 **1969 New York Mets Team Signed Baseball.** Amazin' ONL (Giles) sphere is one of the finest we've ever encountered from the team that ensured that fans in the borough of Queens would remember 1969 as "The Summer of Love." Not a single signature dips below a booming 9/10 in strength, nor is anybody forgotten with a full roster of thirty-two checking in. Even Casey Stengel, who famously asked his hapless 1962 squad "Can't anybody here play this game?!" joins the festivities, sharing space with Ryan, Seaver, Berra, Weiss, McGraw, Koosman, Shamsky, Swoboda, Kranepool, Harrelson, Agee, Yost and anybody who was anybody during this miraculous season. A side panel dedication reads, "To Mr. Baseball, Our Own Robbie, With Thanks, St. Pete, Mets 1969." Stunning in its quality and comprehensiveness, this is an absolutely essential purchase for the orange and blue-blooded Mets fan. *LOA from PSA/DNA. LOA from James Spence Authentication.* Minimum Bid: $750

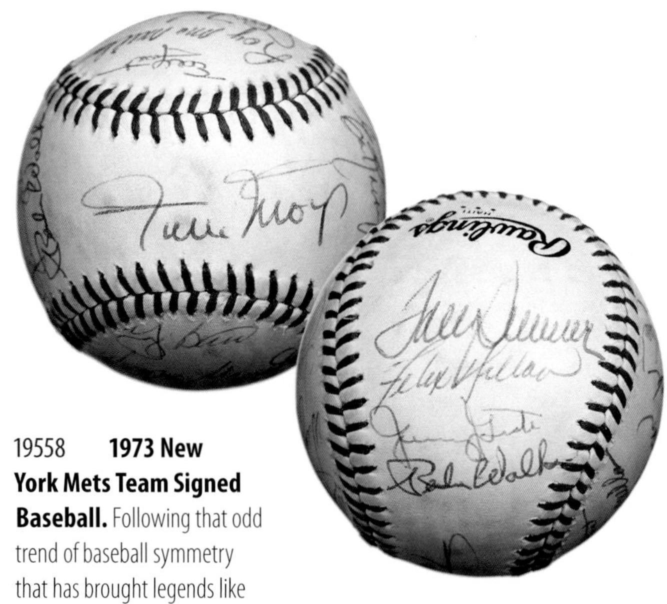

19558 **1973 New York Mets Team Signed Baseball.** Following that odd trend of baseball symmetry that has brought legends like Babe Ruth, Hank Aaron and Dizzy Dean back to the towns where their careers had begun to finish out their playing days, the great Willie Mays said goodbye to baseball in grand Big Apple style, helping to secure the National League pennant for his final team. Mays fittingly claims the sweet spot of this ONL (Feeney) ball for himself, joined by twenty teammates including Seaver, Berra, McGraw, Jones, Koosman, Matlock, Grote and Staub in the boldest of blue ballpoint ink. A few scattered patches of light toning are noted for the sake of accuracy, but do little to detract from the tremendous visual appeal. A top-quality specimen bursting with historical significance in several regards. *LOA from PSA/DNA. LOA from James Spence Authentication.* Minimum Bid: $500

19559 **1979 Negro Leaguers Multi-Signed Baseball with Turkey Stearnes.** Fantastic multi-signed sphere is highlighted by the appearance of the rare and important 2000 Hall of Fame inductee Norman "Turkey" Stearnes, who appears alone on the side panel of this "Official League" ball. We must stress that Stearnes is almost never found on baseballs, nor is he typically seen signing with his celebrated nickname. And, when one considers how convincingly this offering displays as a single (of which we've never seen a genuine example), the tremendous appeal is evident. Stearnes keeps impressive company here, joined by twelve Negro League luminaries including Banks, Leonard, Day, Dandridge, Irvin, Judy Johnson, Ted Page and even former barnstormer Bob Feller. An unknown hand dates the ball to "7/3/79." All autographs rate 9/10 or better. Definitely one of the toughest balls in the hobby dating to the last thirty years. *LOA from PSA/DNA. LOA from James Spence Authentication.* **Minimum Bid: $1,500**

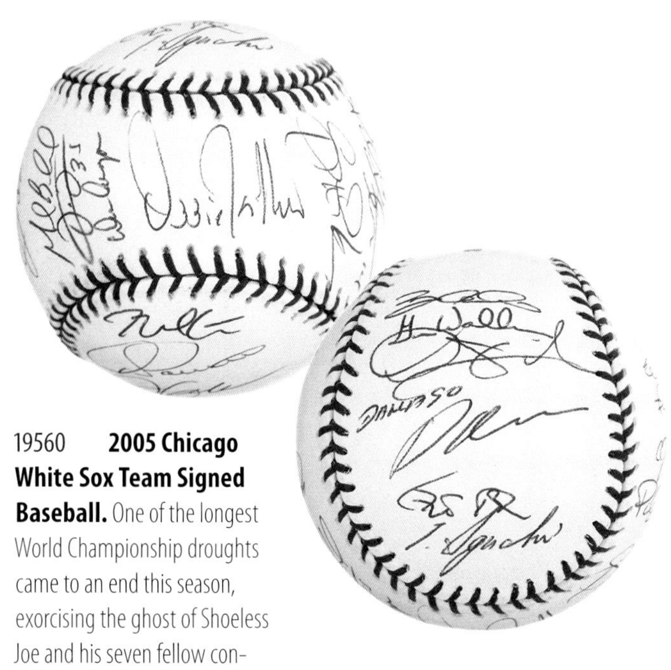

19560 **2005 Chicago White Sox Team Signed Baseball.** One of the longest World Championship droughts came to an end this season, exorcising the ghost of Shoeless Joe and his seven fellow conspirators who haunted almost nine decades of dashed dreams for White Sox faithful. Twenty-six 10/10 blue ink signatures appear upon this Dead Mint OML sphere, highlighted by manager Ozzie Guillen, Pierzynski, Konerko, Dye, Podsednik, Iguchi, Crede, Jenks and more. Holographic authenticating sticker from Schwartz Sports, who orchestrated the signing of the World Champs, is affixed. *LOA from PSA/DNA. LOA from James Spence Authentication.* **Minimum Bid: $300**

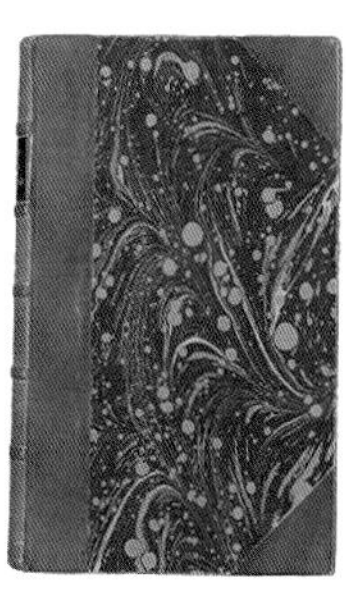

19561 **1841-1889 Boxing Books Lot of 4.** The avid bare knuckle boxing historian will have hours of reading ahead of him should he place the winning bid upon this lot detailing the early days of the sweet science. In order of publication date, we find: 1) *Fistiana, or The Oracle of the Ring* by Vincent George Dowling, 1841. Very rare first edition in Good condition, sturdy and intact, owner signed. 2) *A Lecture on the Art of Self-Defence* by Pierce Egan, 1845. First edition in fair condition. 3) *Fights for the Championship of England, or Accounts of the Prize Battles for the Championship, from the Days of Figg and Broughton to the Present Time* by Frank Lewis Dowling, 1855. Very rare first edition in Good condition. 4) *Prize Ring Champions from England* by Richard K. Fox, 1889. Signed by the author. Fair condition with tape reinforcement of spine. **Minimum Bid: $750**

19562 **1881 John L. Sullivan Cabinet Card.** Glorious photograph of the greatest figure in 19th century pugilism is notated in vintage ink on verso, "Mar. 17, 1881, 188 lbs., 188," dating the piece to the earliest stage of the Heavyweight legend's fame. It was this month that Sullivan took up residence at Harry Hill's Dance Hall and Boxing Emporium in Manhattan, offering fifty dollars to any man who could last four rounds with him under the Queensberry rules. The sepia image finds the Boston Strong Boy in formal garb, looking far more dapper than one might expect of the world's most dangerous fist fighter. Studio stamping at bottom recognizes the Boston suburb where the image was snapped. Condition is absolutely remarkable, a legitimate NRMT without even the typical edge rounding one finds on virtually all cabinet cards of the day. Size is 4x7". Unquestionably one of the finest Sullivan images to surface in recent years. **Minimum Bid: $400**

FIGHT OF THE CENTURY

19563 **1910 Jack Johnson vs. Jim Jeffries "Dana" Postcards Lot of 118.** Simply the most complete and incredible collection of Dana postcards from this most historic of Heavyweight Championship bouts ever to reach the auction block. Text and a selection of images couldn't possibly convey the magnitude and splendor of this collection that will serve as the best visual record of the Reno, Nevada event until somebody invents a time machine. The collection begins with fine portraits of the two battlers, then continues on to images of each sparring, President Teddy Roosevelt enjoying pre-fight festivities, and the legions of spectators packing themselves into the wooden arena. Several images of the announcements before the fight begins feature John L. Sullivan and Tex Rickard. Then we come to images of Johnson and Jeffries entering the ring. Various shots finds a smiling Johnson in his corner before the opening bell, and a determined Jeffries on his stool. Then the bell rings and we come to forty-five action shots detailing the bout round by round, beginning with the opening parries and ending with Jeffries on the canvas and Johnson standing above him. Images of Johnson being declared Champ and Johnson's white wife cheering for him, the only joyous spectator, close out the remarkable collection.

While these are sometimes seen in small quantities, rarely more than a dozen, we believe that the presentation at auction of such a comprehensive set is unprecedented. All show the edge and corner wear typical of postcards of this era, and they appear to have all been tacked to a wall at some point in their past. It must be noted, however, that only a small percentage actually bear tack holes—the rest have small rust stains where they were held to the wall by the flat part of the tack, rather than having been punctured by it. Not a single postcard shows wear that proves significantly detrimental to its visual power. Perhaps five duplicates are present, and two portraits of Johnson may not be Dana, but the rest most assuredly are. All have been arranged chronologically by the consignor, allowing us to experience this incredible event in sporting history in a way that few since the 1910 bout have been able to do. Without question, one of the most intriguing boxing lots to be offered in recent history.
Minimum Bid: $4,000

19564 1910 John L. Sullivan Handwritten Letters Lot of 5. Thrilling archive derives from the nephew of the last bareknuckle Heavyweight Champ, who mailed these letters back to Boston while on a journey to the British Isles. Those well schooled in the boxing collecting hobby are aware of how tough and desirable Sullivan letters are considered, and an opportunity to acquire a grouping such as this is all but unprecedented in the auction world. The "tale of the tape," so to speak, is as follows: 1) Four pages. Discusses conditions in Ireland, his pay for stage appearances. Signed "John." 2) Two pages. Explains the financial and business ramifications of the term "limited," similar to term "incorporated." Mentions "William Morris Vaudeville Office." Signed "Uncle John." 3) Two pages. Recounts highlights of his touring, seeing Blarney Castle, churches, etc. Signed "Uncle John." 4) Two pages. References return to New York City to work for *The New York Times* to cover the Jeffries vs. Johnston (sic) fight, "if the fight ever takes place." He signs "Uncle John," then adds a postscript, signing "John" again. 5) Two pages. Returning to United States. Wants his nephew to see about getting him a hotel in Boston for a week. Desires "quietness." Signed "Uncle John." All black fountain pen ink remains as bold as the day it was applied, and the letters have no noteworthy flaws outside of original mailing folds. Each letter retains its original mailing envelope, addressed in Sullivan's hand but unsigned. Also included is a marvelous 5x7" period photograph that finds Sullivan and his nephew posing along with Jake Kilrain and others. Each gentleman is identified on back in period ink in an unknown hand. *LOA from PSA/DNA. LOA from James Spence Authentication.* Minimum Bid: $2,000

19565 1911 Barney Oldfield & Jim Jeffries Signed Large Photograph. The first man to drive a car a mile a minute poses with the boxer best remembered as Jack Johnson's victim when becoming the first black Heavyweight Champ in 1910. This photo was signed just seven months after that historic Reno match, as a "Feb. 14 - 1911" notation at upper left notes. Oldfield has penned above his image, "To my friend Lardner, You know me, Barney Oldfield." Jeffries adds, "To my southern friend, Yours, Jas. J. Jeffries." The "Lardner" in question is the famed sportswriter Ring Lardner, who maintained friendships with such literary elite as F. Scott Fitzgerald and Ernest Hemingway. This photo that once resided in his collection measures 10x12" in size, with the mounting board extending the final dimensions to 12x15". Minimal wear is evident at the corners, and would be hidden when the piece is framed. The ink of the inscriptions and signatures remains wonderfully bold, registering at a strength of 8/10 or better. A fine piece that joins three of the biggest names in pre-World War I American sports. *LOA from PSA/DNA.* Minimum Bid: $500

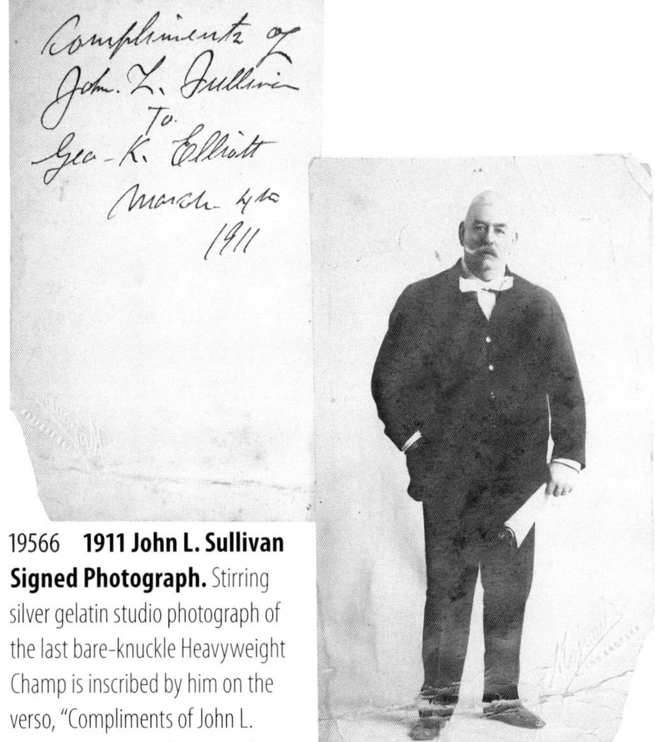

19566 1911 John L. Sullivan Signed Photograph. Stirring silver gelatin studio photograph of the last bare-knuckle Heavyweight Champ is inscribed by him on the verso, "Compliments of John L. Sullivan To Geo. K. Elliott, March 4th, 1911" in the boldest of black fountain pen ink. While the 3.5x6" image exhibits a certain number of condition challenges, most notably creasing and paper loss in the lower third, these issues remain entirely clear of the inscription. As such, it remains an ideal example of this essential boxing autograph. *LOA from PSA/DNA. LOA from James Spence Authentication.* Minimum Bid: $500

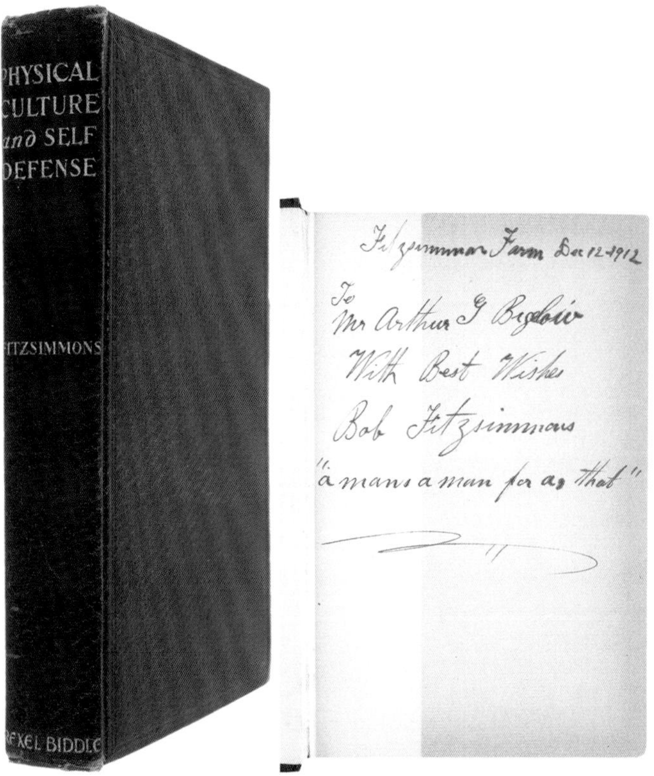

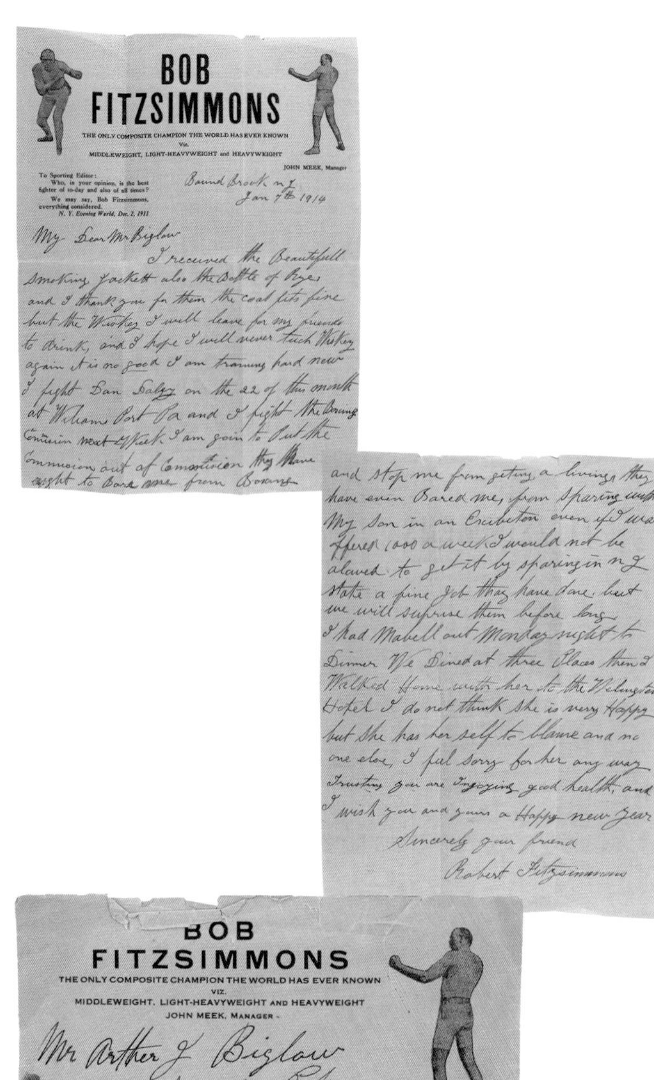

BOB
FITZSIMMONS
THE ONLY COMPOSITE CHAMPION THE WORLD HAS EVER KNOWN
VIZ.
MIDDLEWEIGHT, LIGHT-HEAVYWEIGHT and HEAVYWEIGHT
JOHN MEEK, Manager

To Sporting Editor:
Who, in your opinion, is the best fighter of to-day and also of all times?
We may say, Bob Fitzsimmons, everything considered.
N. Y. Evening World, Dec. 2, 1911

Bound Brook n.J.
Jan 7th 1914

My Dear Mr Biglow
I received the Beautifull Smoking Jackett also the Bottle of Rye and I thank you for them the coat fits fine but the Wiskey I will leave for my friends to Drink, and I hope I will never tuch Wiskey again it is no good I am training hard now I fight Dan Daley on the 22 of this month at William Port Pa and I fight the Boxing Comission next week I am goin to Put the Commission out of Comission they Have ought to Bare me from Boxing and stop me from geting a living they have even Bared me from Sparing with My Son in an Exibition even if I was offered 1000 a week I would not be alowed to get it by sparing in N.J. State a fine Job they have done but we will suprise them before long I had Mabell out Monday night to Dinner We Dined at three Places then I Walked Home with her to the Welington Hotel I do not think She is very Happy but She has her self to blame and no one else, I feel Sorry for her any way Trusting you are Enjoying good health, and I wish you and yours a Happy new Year

Sincerely your friend
Robert Fitzsimmons

BOB
FITZSIMMONS
THE ONLY COMPOSITE CHAMPION THE WORLD HAS EVER KNOWN
VIZ.
MIDDLEWEIGHT, LIGHT-HEAVYWEIGHT AND HEAVYWEIGHT
JOHN MEEK, MANAGER

Mr Arthur J Biglow
53 Temple Place
Boston
Mass

19567 **1912 Robert Fitzsimmons Signed Book.** Listed at number eight on the *Ring Magazine* list of the one hundred greatest punchers of all time, Fitzsimmons finds himself sandwiched between Jack Dempsey and George Foreman, whose devastating power is the stuff of legend. In fact, nine years before making a gift of this first edition copy of his *Physical Culture and Self Defense* book to a friend, his first-round knockout of Con Coughlin, known as "The Irish Giant," proved fatal, as Coughlin would succumb to his injuries the following day. Fitzsimmons' tremendous relevance as one of the sport's all-time greats is essentially inversely proportional to the availability of his autograph, and we must stress that the appearance of two signed pieces in this auction is due solely to the fact that both derive from the same source. Predating the handwritten letter also in this auction is this important hardcover volume, inscribed upon the opening page, "Fitzsimmons Farm, Dec. 12 - 1912, To Mr. Arthur J. Bigelow, With Best Wishes, Bob Fitzsimmons, 'a man's a man for a' that.'" The literary quotation at the end is a line from celebrated Scottish poet Robert Burns' work "Is There For Honest Poverty," which was adopted as a form of Scottish national anthem, though its use by a British-born New Zealander in this instance is a bit of a mystery. Regardless, the inscription remains marvelously bold in black fountain pen ink, and the "Fitzsimmons Farm" reference at the start could quite reasonably be considered a second example of this tough and important autograph. The rightmost two-thirds of the page is toned, most likely from a dust jacket that has since been lost, but the effect causes little visual concern. The leather covered volume is otherwise in fine shape, tightly bound with only typical edge and spine wear. *LOA from PSA/DNA. LOA from James Spence Authentication.* **Minimum Bid: $750**

19568 **1914 Robert Fitzsimmons Handwritten Letter.** With a powerful torso forged at the fires of his blacksmith shop, Fitzsimmons rode his tremendous punching power to World Championship titles in the Middleweight, Light-Heavyweight and Heavyweight divisions. While Fitzsimmons' death in 1917 has assured the thinnest of supplies for boxing autograph collectors today, the offered piece multiplies that scarcity by ten-fold. The first Fitzsimmons handwritten letter to reach the auction block in recent memory, this remarkable missive would be a treasure even without the fantastic content it provides. "Ruby Robert," who had been denied a boxing license at the advanced age of fifty-one, rails against the authorities behind the decision, writing in part, "...I am training hard now to fight Dan Daley on the 22 of this month at Williams Port Pa and I fight the Boxing Commission next week. I am going to put the Commission out of commission..." The letter is penned in 9+/10 black ink on front and back of Fitzsimmons' wonderful personal letterhead, which remains in terrific condition with only a half-inch separation at one of the original mailing folds. Closing "Robert Fitzsimmons" autograph is superb. Original mailing envelope is likewise penned in the Boxing Hall of Famer's hand. An absolutely superb piece of boxiana for the elite collector. Please see also the Robert Fitzsimmons book signed to the letter's addressee presented within this auction. *LOA from PSA/DNA. LOA from James Spence Authentication.* **Minimum Bid: $1,000**

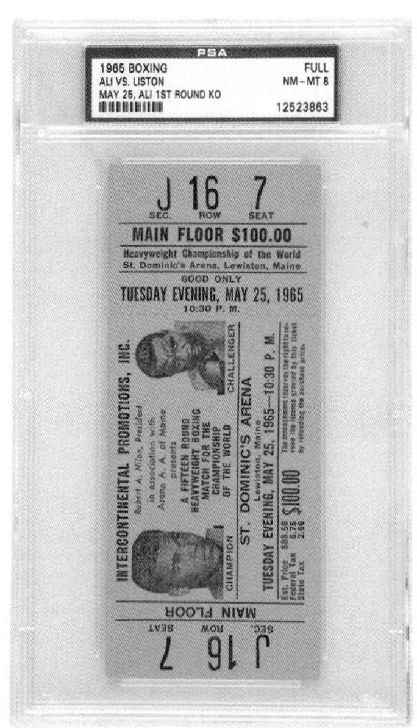

19569 **1965 Ali vs. Liston Full Ticket PSA NM-MT 8.** Phantom punch or legitimate knock out, this decisive victory for Ali in his Lewiston, Maine rematch with Sonny Liston remains one of the most famous events in post-war pugilism. This high-grade ticket would have granted one spectator entry to St. Dominic's Arena for the brief but important spectacle. You'll be hard-pressed to locate a superior example. Encapsulated in a NM-MT 8 holder by PSA for protection and unquestioned authenticity. **Minimum Bid: $750**

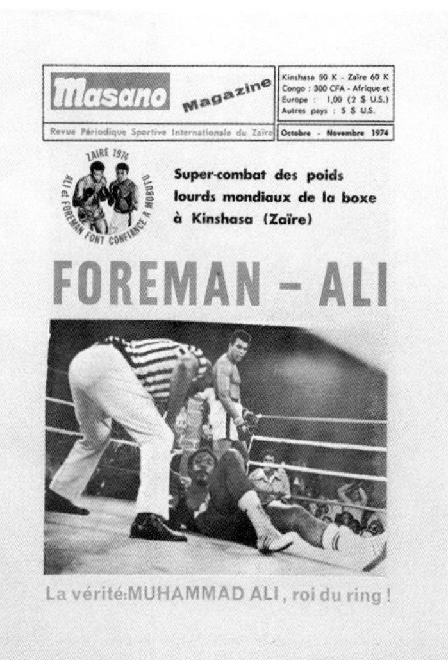

19571 **1974 "Rumble in the Jungle" Post-Fight Publication from Zaire.** This is the first example we've ever encountered of this intriguing publication, issued in the wake of the famous Ali vs. Foreman bout in Kinshasa, Zaire. This "Masano Magazine," subtitled (translation) "The International Sports Periodical Review of Zaire" presents a round by round coverage in both photographs and French language text of this legendary fight, printed in the same town that served as its venue. Only a tiny handful of these magazines could have made it back to the States, with this one coming courtesy of Boxing Hall of Famer Archie Moore, who inscribes the magazine to a friend on page twenty-nine. Even more scarce within the hobby than the official on-site programs, this African publication remains in stellar condition, with fifty-two pages dedicated to Ali's greatest victory. It's a safe bet that you will never see one of these again. **Minimum Bid: $200**

19570 **1974 Muhammad Ali Trunks Worn in Training for Foreman Bout.** White satin trunks in Ali's unmistakable black trim on white style date from the weeks leading up to his greatest triumph, his upset victory over George Foreman in the Kinshasa, Zaire battle known forever after as "The Rumble in the Jungle." The center front waistband holds a white "Everlast" manufacturer's label with the slogan "Made Expressly for Muhammad Ali" in block lettering at the lower edge. On the right leg is found a vintage black marker inscription which reads, "Muhammad Ali, Peace, 6/25/74, Deer Lake, Pa," the location denoting that of Ali's rural training camp. When one considers the fact that Ali was working to reacquire the Heavyweight Championship belt which had been unfairly stripped from him seven years earlier for his refusal to participate in the Vietnam draft, the significance of the offered lot becomes quite clear. A letter from noted boxing expert Craig Hamilton expresses that the trunks had been given as a gift to a female friend of Ali at the time, and were originally acquired from her directly. The trunks exhibit fine wear and very minor staining, but still present marvelously, with the inscription maintaining the same boldness it enjoyed upon its application. A special piece from one of the most important periods in post-war pugilistic history. *LOA from Craig Hamilton. LOA from James Spence Authentication (autograph).* **Minimum Bid: $2,000**

19572 **Mid-1970's Muhammad Ali Training Worn Robe.** From the same source that provided the "Rumble in the Jungle" training trunks featured within this auction comes this terrycloth training robe utilized the "The Greatest" at approximately the same period of his illustrious career. The luxurious garment is tagged at the collar from "The Four Seasons Hotel," with the hotel's logo tree embroidered over the heart. One can reasonably conclude that Ali acquired the robe during a stay at the five-star hotel, and converted it for training use. The black tackle twill "Muhammad Ali" sewn to the back of the robe exactly matches other training robes of the era, and the size is proper, with sleeves wide enough to accomodate boxing gloves. The robe is heavily stained and soiled, though this could be attributed in at least some degree to its sweaty use by the greatest figure in postwar boxing. An important artifact from one of the most exciting times in Heavyweight history. *LOA from Craig Hamilton.* **Minimum Bid: $1,000**

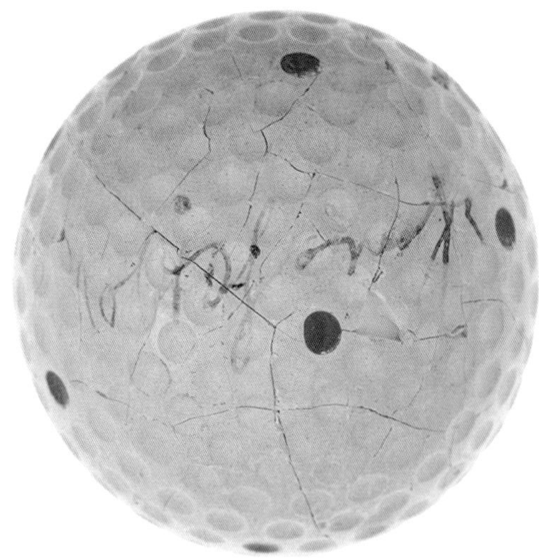

19573 **1931 Bobby Jones Signed Golf Ball.** It is stories like this one that make us love the collecting hobby. The year was 1931, and a small North Carolina town was abuzz with the news that the legendary golfer Robert Tyre Jones, Jr., fresh from his sweep of the Grand Slam of golf, was to visit. Golf, we must remember, was one of the great spectator sports of the era, on a par with baseball and boxing, and Jones was even more beloved and admired than Tiger Woods is today. A twelve-year old boy, anxious to meet this Golden Age god, crouched in the brush and brambles that lined the fairway of the local golf course on the day that Jones was to play, and waited. Finally, in the distance, the dashing young golfer appeared on the tee, and launched his ball to a point in the fairway not far from where the boy was waiting. As Jones strode toward his ball in preparation of the second shot, the boy emerged from the woods. Trembling a bit with the nerves of coming face to face with his idol, the boy produced a golf ball from his hip pocket and extended it toward Jones. "Will you please sign this ball for me, sir?" he asked. Jones, ever the gentleman, kindly obliged, though he did question the medium. "The ink will never last on a golf ball, son," he told him. The youngster was undeterred, however. "I'll be really careful with it," he assured the golfing legend.

And so he was. The boy packed it in a cotton-filled matchbox, autograph side up, and there it remained for seventy years, before finally finding its way into the collecting hobby. The result is one of the most exciting golf artifacts to reach the auction block, a single signed "Robt Jones, Jr." golf ball, remaining in remarkable 5/10 to 6/10 condition due to the young collector's promised diligence. There is some crazing to the "Spalding Kro-flite" blue-dotted ball's surface, and while it does cross the path of Jones'ink, it does little to detract. Infinitely more rare than the Babe Ruth single signed baseball, this piece offers the serious golf collector the opportunity to play the next part in this fascinating and charming story that all began with a boy crouching in the North Carolina underbrush, waiting for a legend to arrive. *LOA from PSA/DNA. LOA from James Spence Authentication.* Minimum Bid: $1,500

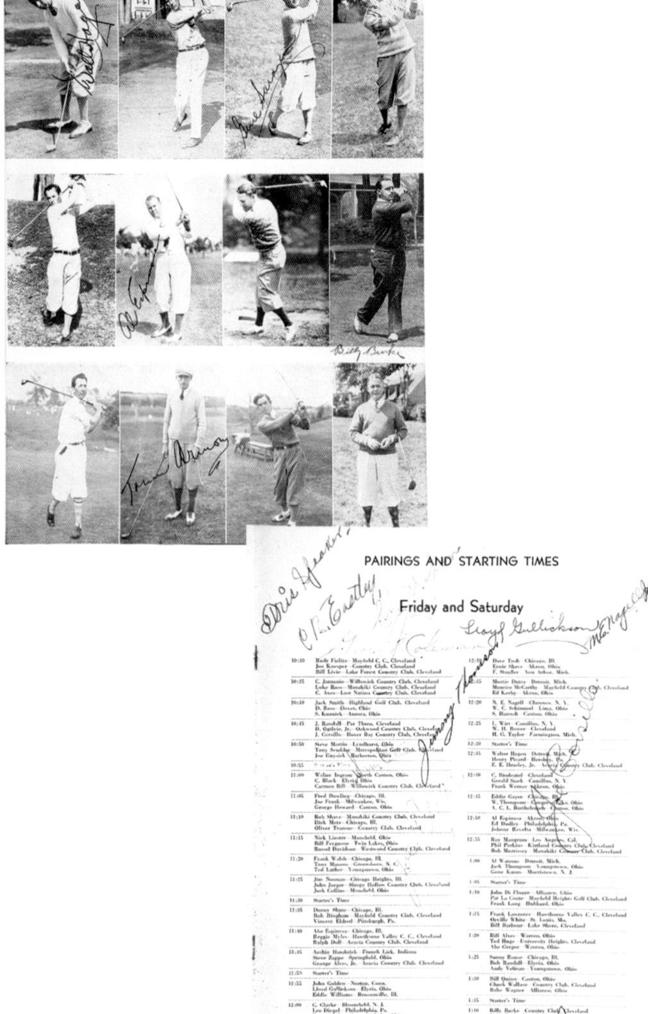

19574 **1935 PGA Open Tournament Programs (2) Signed by Hagen, Armour & More.** Worth a nice little sum in unsigned condition, this pair of programs for the August 1935 PGA Open at Cleveland, Ohio's Acacia Country Club finds further appeal with the addition of thirty-eight autographs (spread over both programs) from those present for the event. Most appealing is a page of small photographs entitled "Famous Stars of Golf," which provides flawless black fountain pen autographs from Walter Hagen, Gene Sarazen, Al Espinosa, Billy Burke and Tommy Armour. Most notable among the balance of autographs, which include golfers, PGA staffers and tournament attendees, are John Revolta, who signs the cover of the second program "To a Lovely Waitress," and Baseball Hall of Famer Tris Speaker. All autographs noted, and practically all present, remain in splendid 9+/10 condition. The programs themselves exhibit minor paper loss on the back covers from scrapbook removal but are otherwise free of any troubling flaws. *LOA from PSA/DNA. LOA from James Spence Authentication.* Minimum Bid: $400

THE TRADITION BEGINS

19575 **1938 Henry Picard First Masters Championship Gold Medal.** While for decades the prize for victory at Augusta has been the glorious Green Jacket, this longstanding tradition does not date to the inception of the sport's most noteworthy event. For his victory in the tournament's fifth edition, legendary golfer Henry Picard was awarded this ten karat gold medal, certainly one of the most significant golf artifacts ever to be offered for public sale. And it bears noting that though the tournament began in 1934, it had been called the Augusta Invitational through 1937. As such, this represents, by strict definition, the very first Master's medal.

In one of the tournament's most thrilling finishes, Picard began the final round of the 1938 Masters with a one-stroke lead over Gene Sarazen, Ed Dudley, Ralph Guldahl and Harry Cooper. While the iconic Sarazen was unable to keep pace, Guldahl and Cooper each posted rounds of seventy-one for totals of 287. Picard never faltered, however, shooting a final-round seventy for a two shot victory.

And so awaiting Picard at the Augusta clubhouse was this very medal, picturing the location of the prize's presentation on the face, with the words "Augusta National Golf Club" ringing the perimeter in raised text. On the verso the raised text continues, spelling the words "Masters Tournament" above the logo of the Masters and the engraved words "Henry Picard 1938." The medal tips the scales at two ounces, with a diameter of two and a quarter inches, though its appeal and significance are immeasurable. Included is its simple original presentational case.

The medal comes to us through the son of Mr. Picard's nephew by marriage, whose father was a very close confidant and golfing partner of the legendary linksman. A notarized letter of provenance from this Picard family member will accompany the medal.

Now thishistoric artifact, once the most prized possession of Henry Picard, is ready to find a home in an advanced golf memorabilia collection. Heritage is pleased to offer one of just a scant few of Grand Slam Championship prizes ever to be made available to the collecting hobby. **Minimum Bid: $5,000**

19576 **1942 Sam Snead PGA Championship Tournament Used Golf Bag.** Rated the third greatest golfer (behind Nicklaus and Hogan) by *Golf Digest* in 2000, Snead is best remembered today for his "Perfect Swing," which generated thousands of imitators over his many decades of service to the game. Though his record eighty-two PGA Tour victories span the period between 1936 and 1965, his first and therefore arguably his most important Major victory came in 1942 at the PGA Championship at Seaview Country Club in Atlantic City, New Jersey. Snead mentions this event in the handwritten letter of provenance that accompanies the offered bag:

9-22-90

Hello! Cricket:

The bag your Dad will give you I used during my early Spring of 1942 and during my stay in the Navy and a while after. I finally got a new Bag after they/Wilson resumed making golf equipment. I won the 1942 P.G.A. using the bag and several other P.G.A. Tournaments before I changed.

I hope you are well. My best to the John Deer's.

Cheers, Sam.

The original mailing envelope and a second letter of provenance from Cricket Gentry are included as well. The leather and canvas bag shows heavy use with some fraying of the shoulder strap but nothing else that could rightfully be considered damage. Our catalog imagery should accurately illustrate that the strength of display is still considerable. Snead's name is screened in black script on the rear of the bag, along with the "Wilson Sporting Goods Co." manufacturer's markings. A plastic identification tag clipped to the back of the bag reads, "Claude Harmon, Member of P.G.A., Winged Foot Golf Club, Mamaroneck, N.Y., SAM SNEAD, Rack No. 449." With supreme historic relevance and ironclad provenance to match, this bag rates among the most important and desirable to reach the auction block in recent memory. *Letter of provenance from Sam Snead.* **Minimum Bid: $5,000**

IKE HITS THE LINKS

19577 **1950's President Dwight D. Eisenhower Game Used Golf Clubs.** Some months after the end of his term as President of the United States, a journalist asked Eisenhower if leaving the White House had affected his golf game. "Yes," he replied, "a lot more people beat me now." The thirty-fourth President is properly recognized as the greatest golf enthusiast to occupy our nation's highest office, and can be credited in large degree with the increase in popularity that transformed the sport from the sole property of the upper class to a nationwide phenomenon. In this regard, this full set of five woods, eight irons and a putter takes on a significance that is equally political and athletic. The high-quality "Spalding" clubs bear the stamped facsimile signature of the President, with the irons holding that of Ike's friend and ultimate golf icon Bobby Jones as well. Only the putter is free of either name. All clubs show fine use but no damage, with even the rubber grips remaining free of condition problems. Included are letters of provenance from both Eisenhower's son and daughter-in-law, each of whom attest that the clubs were used by the President, then given as a gift to their neighbors after they had inherited them following Ike's death. The fantastic provenance is further assured by the gorgeous custom leather golf bag in which the clubs currently reside, stamped with the name "John Eisenhower," Ike's son. While we can't expect this lot to reach the same astounding level as the $770,000 realized in 1996 for clubs used by President John F. Kennedy, this well-loved and perfectly provenanced set from his Oval Office predecessor could properly be considered within the same elite league. **Minimum Bid: $5,000**

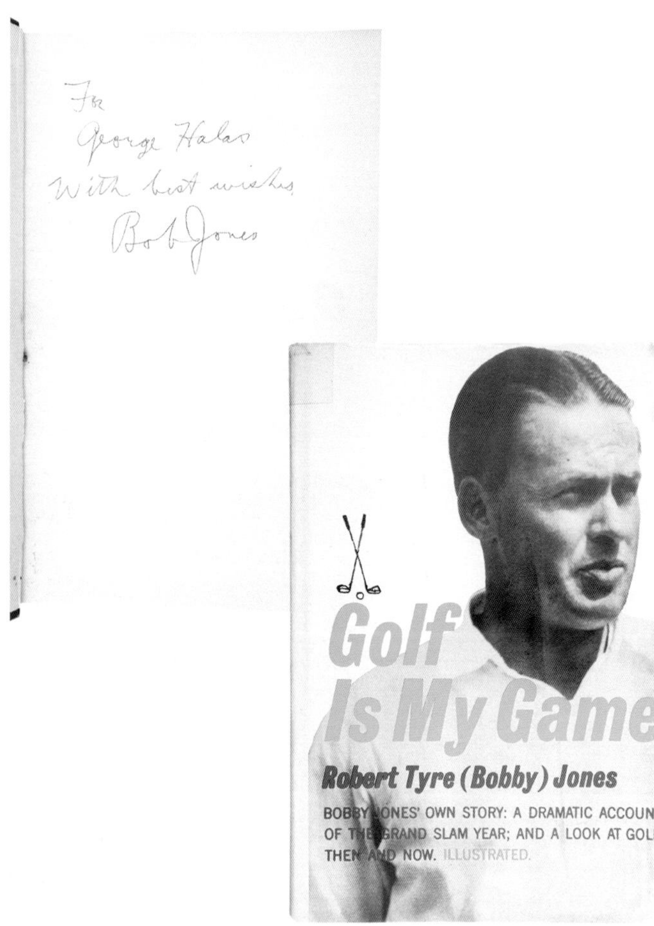

19578 **1960 Bobby Jones Signed Book to George Halas.** One of the great sportsmen of the twentieth century, Jones once dismissed plaudits rendered to him for taking a penalty stroke for an infraction during the US Open which nobody else had witnessed with the statement, "You may as well praise a man for not robbing a bank." Here we find a bold and spacious autograph from the author of *Golf is My Game* on the book's opening page, rating an unimprovable 10/10 in black ink. He signs, "For George Halas, with best wishes, Bob Jones," gifting this volume to a fellow early sports icon, a name synonymous with Chicago Bears football. The volume remains in marvelous condition, with its rare dust jacket in place though bearing an occasional crease and bolstered by a small tape repair. The inscription is unaffected by any condition concerns. An essential autograph from one of the Golden Age of Sport's key figures to another. *LOA from James Spence Authentication.* **Minimum Bid: $750**

19579 **1970's Jack Nicklaus Tournament Used Golf Bag.** Golf's equivalent of Mickey Mantle, the flaxen-haired Golden Bear was the American dream of a sports superstar, with movie star looks and boy next door charm to match his unparalleled athletic abilities. The offered green and white leather MacGregor bag accompanied the legendary linksman at the crest of his storied career, a period that saw him capture six of his record eighteen Major Championship victories. It comes to us from the Professional Caddies Association, which is consigning the historic piece to raise funds for its charitable interests, and informs us that this bag was used by Nicklaus from January 1971 through December 1975. Interior "MacGregor" factory coding lists this bag as serial number "002," attributing the bag definitively to this iconic golfer far more than even the "Jack Nicklaus" applied in vintage black tackle twill to the center striping could allow. Wear is fantastic throughout, recalling a long life in the presence of a legend, but could still ably render service to its new owner if required. Originally sourced through Nicklaus' long time personal caddie "Angie" Argea. **Minimum Bid: $2,500**

19580 **Augusta National Golf Club Member/Masters Tournament Green Jacket.** In the golfing world, the most coveted prize one can earn is the fabled Green Jacket, presented annually to the victor in The Masters Tournament at the Augusta National Golf Club. Dating back to 1937, members at Augusta wore green jackets so fans would know whom they could approach with questions during the annual tournament. But, beginning in 1949, the celebrated garment took on greater significance as the winner of The Masters Tournament was presented with one at the award ceremonies. Only club members and Masters winners are issued these jackets, and they are not to be allowed off site. This jacket belonged to a former club member.

Highlighting the front is the unmistakable logo of the Augusta National in the form of a circular patch displayed over the heart. It is tailored to "42 Long," indicated with a black marker on the inside lining. The interior lining holds dual tagging, representing Cincinnati based tailor "Hamilton" and the logo of the Augusta National, which once held the name of the original owner (since deled with black marker). The jacket's buttons—three on the front and two smaller ones on each sleeve cuff—are all original, and again, cast in the image of the Masters logo. The back of each button reveals creation by "The Waterbury Button Company" of Cheshire, Connecticut. Overall, the condition of this exclusive jacket presents without a single objection.

Only golf's most accomplished figures have been able to capture the Green Jacket, but this offering allows one lucky bidder to own one for himself, regardless of the size of his handicap. Minimum Bid: $1,000

19581 **Circa 1998 Tiger Woods Single Signed Baseball.** Any knowledgeable sports autograph collector is well aware that Tiger remains one of the most elusive autographs of all living sports figures, as well as one of the most commonly forged. Here we present a particularly scarce and 100% authentic example for the collector looking for something different. Woods' 10/10 black ink signature appears upon the sweet spot of an ONL (Coleman) ball which is itself in the same unimprovable condition. A submission for grading may be in order here. *LOA from PSA/DNA.* Minimum Bid: $500

19582 **2005 The Presidents Cup Team Signed Flag with Woods, Nicklaus.** The United States yet again asserted its links dominance over the rest of the world, taking the victory in this tournament at the Robert Trent Jones Golf Club in Gainesville, Virginia. Our expert golf consignor assures us that such team signed flags are tremendously scarce, and few could match the offered specimen for condition or stature of those who signed. Fourteen flawless black sharpie signatures are here in total, and feature Woods, Mickelson, Nicklaus, Leonard, Couples, Perry, Toms, Sluman, Verplank, Funk, Furyk, DeMarco, Love and Cink. The souvenir flag measures 13x19" in size, and presents flawlessly. *LOA from PSA/DNA. LOA from James Spence Authentication.* Minimum Bid: $500

19583 **1932 Los Angeles Summer Olympics Flag.** Fantastically preserved banner once welcomed spectators to the famed 1932 Olympic Games in Los Angeles, the second installment of this international competition to be held within the borders of the United States. With massive dimensions (204x42") to match its historic importance and collecting appeal, this banner most likely spanned a large archway to announce, "Welcome, Citius, Fortius, Altius, Olympic Games, Los Angeles, Visitors." The banner is fashioned from eleven pieces of fabric in the colors of the Olympic rings, with golden fringe running the lower edges. Typical age toning is to be noted, but the stunning piece is absent the staining and tearing so often found in textiles of this vintage. A couple of the seams have been professionally reinforced, but this is only evident when viewed from verso.A stunning piece of Depression-age artistry, and a real treasure for lovers of The Games. **Minimum Bid: $500**

19584 **1960's-2000's Formula One Drivers Signed Index Cards Lot of 16.** Nerves of steel and feet of lead are the common themes of this autograph collection celebrating the best and brightest of the Formula One circuit. Unless otherwise noted, the autographs rate 9/10 or better, and are applied to blank 3x5" index cards either near or over "Wheels of Freedom" 1960 US postage stamps. Featured are: Bignotti, Brabham (one index card, one picture postcard), DeFerren, Fangio, Fittipaldi, Hill (2), Johncock, Luyendyk, Mansell, Martin, Montoya, Moss (one index card personalized to "Michael," one typed letter), Shelby. All pieces are free of creases, tears or other condition concerns. *LOA from PSA/DNA. LOA from James Spence Authentication.* **Minimum Bid: $400**

THE INTIMIDATOR

19585 **1996 Dale Earnhardt, Sr. Daytona 500 Race Worn Uniform.** Certainly one of the most significant and desirable artifacts from the realm of American motorsports is presented here for your consideration, the uniform worn by The Intimidator on the very track where he would lose his life in a last-lap crash five years later. While the elder Earnhardt had long been considered a leading figure upon the NASCAR circuit prior to his tragic and untimely death, his sudden loss has served to elevate him to true iconic status among the millions of racing fans who followed his twenty-seven year career, and to make him a household name even among those who never watched a single lap in their lives.

Dale Senior had to settle for second place at the 1996 Daytona 500, unable to pass the legendary Dale Jarrett to take the checkered flag. After the race, a relieved Jarrett announced to reporters, "The last lap was close to 500 miles itself. I'd rather look in the mirror and see anybody but that number 3 car back there." It would be the fourth second-place finish for Earnhardt at the storied Florida racetrack, the best he would realize until finally crossing the line first at the 1998 event. "It's Daytona," Earnhardt explained as Jarrett celebrated. "We just didn't have enough. Our car was super all day, but those Fords were super, too."

The unmistakable jumpsuit Earnhardt was wearing that February 1996 day on Florida's east coast is dominated with logos of "GM Goodwrench," Earnhardt's lead sponsor, with a constellation of smaller patches including Snap-On, Food City, Goodyear and McDonalds scattered nearby. Fabric wear is apparent at the surfaces where the G-forces directed the most friction, particularly in the seat of the uniform and the backs of the legs. A mysterious markered code inside the zipper path of the chest reads an apparent "JAPPA 96." A flawlessblack sharpie signature on the right chest adds the final bit of appeal to this picture perfect specimen.

Impeccable provenance is delivered as well, in the form of four letters that trace the history of the uniform. These include two 1996 letters from Earnhardt's general counsel detailing their donation of this uniform to a charitable organization, a letter from that charity to the winning bidder of the charity auction, and a letter from that winning bidder himself. The result is a piece that should serve as a centerpiece for the finest of private racing collections. *LOA from PSA/DNA (autograph).* Minimum Bid: $10,000

19586 **Circa 1860 "Lemon Peel" Model Baseball.** Before the "Figure Eight" stitching style that has dominated the game's signature centerpiece, this model populated our National Pastime's earliest days. The reasoning behind the "lemon peel" moniker should be immediately apparent, as the stitching style follows the natural contours of a citrus skin. One will also note the slightly smaller dimensions of the ball, typical of the day. This example remains in remarkably strong condition, with tight stitching and no noteworthy defects to the brown leather hide. An essential purchase for the serious baseball historian. **Minimum Bid: $750**

In destroying some very old papers of my fathers, I found the enclosures. If you're not interested, you may know some one who will be; some one who is interested in the early history of baseball—amateur and prof.—in this area.

Yours truly
B.O.M. DeBeck

(my name is the same as my father's, who countersigned these tickets)
D

(Box 93, RR2 Loveland, Ohio)

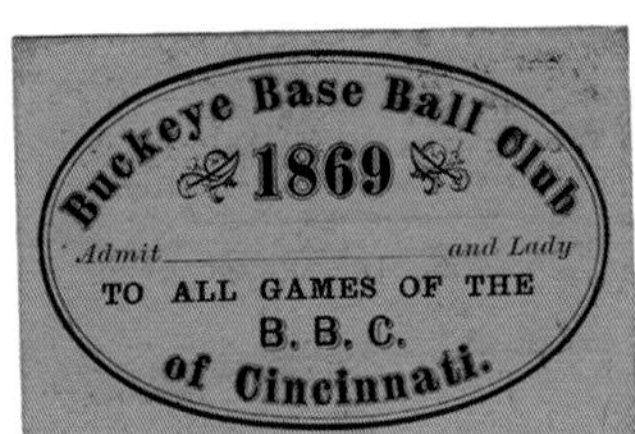

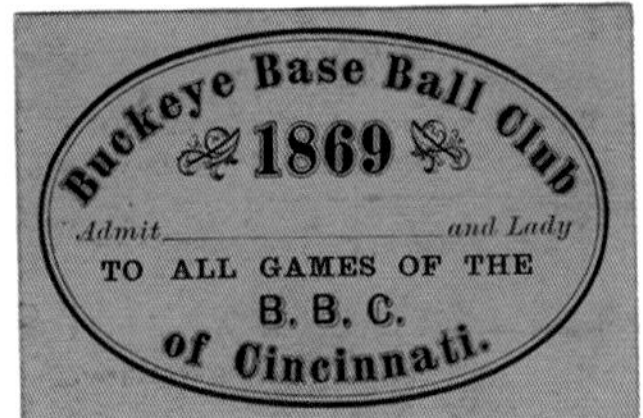

19587 **1869 Buckeye Base Ball Club of Cincinnati Passes Lot of 2.** This monumentally historic pair of passes is about all that remains of this early competitor to the first professional baseball team, the Cincinnati Red Stockings. The Buckeyes, founded in 1860, actually predate the Reds, arriving on the scene a full six years before the latter team was established. Yet sadly, it was the Red Stockings that would prove to be the Buckeyes' undoing. When the Reds decided in 1869 to field an all-salaried team many of the Buckeyes players jumped ship for the money, and the mighty Buckeyes were left with no option but to fold. But records do show that the teams met twice on the field of battle in 1869 before the Buckeyes called it quits, with the Reds winning both contests by the comical scores of seventy-one to fifteen, and one-hundred three to eight.

Presented here are two passes for entry to games from the Buckeyes' final season (perhaps the meetings with the Red Stockings!). Each reads, "Buckeye Base Ball Club, 1869, Admit ____ and Lady to All Games of the B.B.C. of Cincinnati" on the face, and are signed by the team Treasurer B.O.M. DeBeck on verso. According to Harry Ellard's "Base Ball in Cincinnati," B.O.M. DeBeck played third base for the 1866 Buckeyes, and must have later become an executive with the club. The passes remain in marvelous, undamaged condition, and are accompanied by a 1957 handwritten letter from the son of the Buckeye Treasurer to a writer for the Cincinnati Post. He notes that he found the passes in some old papers of his father's, and wonders if he may know "some one who is interested in the early history of baseball—amateur and prof.—in this area."

Well, we think that we might know a few of those folks, so we are thrilled to be able to present what may well be the earliest baseball tickets ever offered for public sale. With the origins of professional baseball historically established as 1869 Cincinnati, to find this date and this town in print on any baseball-related artifact is a discovery on a par with King Tut's tomb, and a pair of NRMT tickets for one of the earliest baseball teams, bar none, is beyond most collectors' wildest dreams. **Minimum Bid: $2,000**

19588 **Circa 1870 Lemon Peel Baseball.** The infancy of our National Pastime is represented by this ancient homemade sphere used in the years immediately following our American Civil War. You'll first note the unique stitching pattern, quite different from the figure-eight model that has dominated the game for well over a century, and then the enormous heft of the ball despite the fact that the circumference is actually smaller than modern examples. Those collectors with an affinity for the earliest history of baseball must consider this offering strongly, as the archeology of the sport begins here. Condition remains remarkably strong for the ball's advanced vintage, with the stitching still intact and the shape remaining perfectly round. **Minimum Bid: $300**

19589 **Circa 1880 "Figure Eight" Model Baseball.** Spectacular ancient baseball artifact represents the first evolutionary step away from the "lemon peel" style that dominated the game of baseball until this point. The ball is skillfully constructed, perfectly spherical and well-balanced, and wonderfully preserved with every last stitch solidly in place. The importance of this piece is difficult to overstate—after all, such innovations as the curve ball and split-fingered fastball would never have become part of the game's lexicon. An important relic of baseball's archaeology. **Minimum Bid: $300**

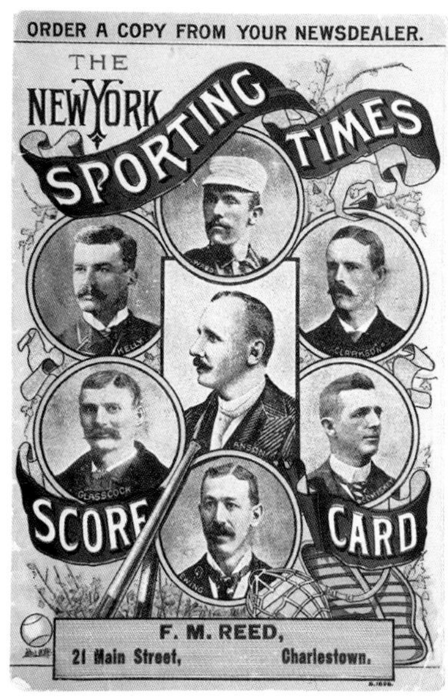

19590 **1887 New York Giants vs. Boston Beaneaters Scorecard.** One of just a small handful of surviving scorecards from nineteenth century National League action, this incredible rarity recounts a nine to three victory for the visiting Boston club at upper Manhattan's Polo Grounds. Penciled into this gorgeous lithographed scorecard are the names of such early legends as Billy Hamilton, Hugh Duffy, Chick Stahl and Kid Gleason, best remembered as the manager of the notorious 1919 Chicago White Sox. Fantastic cover imagery pictures future Hall of Famers Kelly, Ward, Clarkson, Anson, Comiskey and Ewing, and advertises leading Big Apple newspaper *The New York Sporting Times*. A degree of wear is to be expected, and the spine of the 7x9.5" (when opened) scorecard flirts with separation but does remain attached. All pencil writing remains entirely legible, however, and the wonderful cover graphics are none the worse for wear. Certainly a miracle in any condition, and a great treasure for the early baseball enthusiast. **Minimum Bid: $500**

19591 Circa 1889 Irv Ray (Boston NL) Cabinet Photograph. The five-foot six inch Boston Beaneaters shortstop was known as "Stubby" for his fire hydrant build, and his abridged strike zone helped to rank him as one of the toughest in the game to strike out. The cabinet from "T. Waldon Smith" studios of Boston shows typical edge wear and minor corner chipping, and a small constellation of spots dot Ray's chest and the area around his head, though all remain clear of his serene face. Ray's name is written in an unknown hand in bold black ink at the lower border, and "Copyrighted" is penned on verso. Size is 4.25x6.25". An evocative glimpse into professional baseball's earliest days. **Minimum Bid: $1,000**

19592 1889 Tom Brown (Boston NL) Cabinet Photograph. Scarce early cabinet pictures Boston Beaneaters outfielder Thomas Brown, who shared a dugout with such nineteenth century Hall of Famers as Dan Brouthers and Mike "King" Kelly during his two seasons of service to the club. Though not quite on the same elite level as these teammates, Brown was no fly-by-night figure either, representing a combination of American Association, National League and Players League squads for a career of seventeen seasons. He appears straight out of central casting for a Victorian age ballplayer, complete with laced-front jersey and mustache, captured in gorgeous sepia tones. The cabinet from "T. Waldon Smith" studios of Boston shows typical edge wear and minor corner chipping, and a two-inch tear arches toward Brown's face, but the central focus of the image is unimpaired by these concerns. Brown's name is written in an unknown hand in bold black ink at the lower border, and "Copyrighted 1889" is penned on verso. Size is 4.25x6.25". A highly collectible image from the infancy of Major League Baseball. **Minimum Bid: $1,000**

19593 Circa 1890 Frank Dwyer (Chicago PL) Cabinet Photograph. Acquired by our consignor as part of an ensemble of outrageously scarce Players League cabinets from the Chicago Pirates roster, this fine image of right-handed pitcher Frank Dwyer almost assuredly dates to the single season of that defunct League's operation, though we must note that Dwyer had also served the Chicago White Stockings of the National League during the previous two seasons. In any regard, this wonderful sepia image is a nineteenth century treasure, providing razor sharp contrast and a local Chicago studio's stamping at lower border. Dwyer's name and position are penned in an unknown hand at top, with his name repeated by hand on verso, which offers gorgeous period studio graphics. Small chips at each corner and a freckling of toning are to be noted in terms of condition, but our catalog imagery should properly illustrate that the visual strength of the piece survives with grace. Size is 4.25x6.25". **Minimum Bid: $1,000**

19594 1890's Reach Button-Back Glove. Fine early specimen was state of the art during the era of King Kelly and Cap Anson despite the fact that it bears a closer similarity to a pot holder than baseball gloves of today. These ancient button-back gloves are typically fraught with condition problems, with many losing the delicate wrist strap or the webbing between the thumb and index finger. Such is not the case here, as the deep brown leather has weathered the passing decades with few problems. Only the seam that holds the palm padding in place is at issue here, and this has no real effect upon the display. The proper period "Reach" label remains firmly affixed at the base of the wrist strap, and the original button holds that strap in place. A tremendously attractive piece for the avid baseball historian. **Minimum Bid: $600**

19595 **1895 Rockford Open Face Baseball Pocket Watch.** For the sophisticated gentleman with an appreciation for the early game, we present this elegant timepiece once owned by a 19th century baseball enthusiast. The fifteen jewel, eighteen size Rockford features nickel full plate movement, a lever set and fancy dial. Verso is the true charm, however, featuring a period uniformed batsman rendered with exquisite artistry upon the fourteen-karat gold-filled case. The watch movement is in excellent mechanical condition, and will do its part in getting you to the game on time, and in high style to boot. Fine, undamaged condition but for a hairline crack to the crystal. With an estimated value of $500 purely as a fine vintage watch, this engraved model should set the bar significantly above for its greatly heightened scarcity and collecting desirability. **Minimum Bid: $500**

19596 **1902 Chicago Orphans vs. Pittsburg Pirates Program.** Tremendously scarce "Official Score Card" documents a visit by Honus Wagner's National League Championship Pirates to Chicago's West Side Park the year before the club would take on its new "Cubs" moniker. The twenty-page booklet remains in remarkably strong condition, with the pencil marked center score pages listing legends from Tinker to Chance to Fred Clarke. This center spread has loosened from, but still remains affixed to, the center staples, though the booklet remains otherwise tightly bound. All other pages show a remarkable absence of wear. The color lithography on front and rear covers is simply out of this world. Definitely one of the finest from the very short supply of turn-of-the-century scorecards surviving in the hobby today. And, with a record of 103 victories and thirty-six losses, this season marks the highest winning percentage (.741) in Pirates history. **Minimum Bid: $400**

19597 **1904 Fan Craze Baseball Board Game.** Just a year before Ty Cobb emerged upon the Major League scene, this charming little board game hit the retail shelves, bringing baseball to kids stuck inside on a rainy day. All fifty-two playing cards, complete with 19th and early 20th century baseball trivia on each, are present and accounted for, as is the wooden playing field, the envelope with nails for marking the strike count, runs and players, and an unused (though toned) scorecard. The exterior box shows some water staining and edge wear, but still presents quite nicely and remains solid and intact. Pencil writing on underside of box will have no effect upon display. A nice example of a very tough game. **Minimum Bid: $400**

19598 **Circa 1905 Tully Frederick "Topsy" Hartsel Studio Cabinet Photograph by Horner.** From the estate of the early Philadelphia Athletics star that provided the 1910 World Series trophy and game worn jersey also offered within this auction comes this artful photographic portrait snapped by the era's most celebrated baseball photographer. Carl J. Horner, whose name and Boston studio address are stamped on the lower mount, is responsible for many of the Dead Ball Era's most recognizable portraits, with scores of his images (including the famous Honus Wagner T206) reproduced on trading cards of the day. This was Topsy's personal copy of his own Horner portrait, measuring 5x7" in size including the cardboard mount. Some paper remnants from scrapbook removal are evident on the verso, but the front presents at an incredible NRMT level. **Minimum Bid: $1,500**

19599 **Circa 1905 Al Bridwell Studio Portrait Photograph by Joseph Hall.** The most collectible baseball photographer of the nineteenth century, Hall was responsible for many of the images utilizted in the famous Old Judge trading card issues. This fine photographic portrait, dating to the early years of the twentieth century, likewise found a home in packs of tobacco, reproduced for the T206 Al Bridwell No Cap card. The offered specimen finds the young infielder captured in razor-sharp sepia tones, with the image affixed to a "Hall's Studio" mount that measures 4.5x6.5" in size. Condition is spectacular, with minor wear at the corners the only issue of note. Identifying pencil writing is found on verso, as well as stamping for "The Ring, Inc.," tracing this piece back to the archives of the famous boxing magazine. **Minimum Bid: $1,500**

19600 **Circa 1906 Tully Frederick "Topsy" Hartsel Studio Photograph.** Another fine offering from the personal estate of this key figure in Connie Mack's first great Philadelphia Athletics dynasty. As are the 1910 team cabinet photograph and Topsy's funeral guest book, this photo was removed from a Hartsel family scrapbook, and pictures the young ballplayer in formal attire. We suspect this is the work of celebrated baseball photographer Carl Horner, and the fact that the image was reproduced for the 1906 Lincoln Philadelphia A's Postcards set would seem to lend credence to this theory, as Horner's work was often used for trading card issues of the day. The oval image measures approximately 3.5x5" at its largest dimensions, and has been trimmed from its cardboard mount to a half inch border. Otherwise the photo remains in flawless shape, with scrapbook paper remnants remaining affixed to verso. **Minimum Bid: $300**

19601 **1910 Philadelphia Athletics Team Cabinet Photograph in Cuba.** Previously unknown image was removed from the personal scrapbook of Frederick "Topsy" Hartsel, whose jersey, 1910 Championship trophy and several other artifacts are featured within this auction. We must thank the Philadelphia Athletics Historical Society for their generous assistance in shedding some light upon the history of this photograph, which had initially confused us due to the Spanish language studio stamping that appears on the reverse. The society informed us that in December 1910, just several weeks after their World Series victory, most of the Athletics travelled to Cuba where Cincinnati business manager Frank Bancroft had lined up exhibition games against the Detroit Tigers and the top Cuban professional teams. Certainly this is the photograph's derivation. A listing of players in uniform was also generously provided. Standing: Derrick, Bender, Lap. Seated: Plank, McInnis, Hartsel, Davis, unidentified (probably Morgan), Thomas, Barry, Murphy. The fine sepia image measures 5x7" and presents razor-sharp contrast with not a single flaw of note. Hartsel is identified in an unknown hand as "Topsy" in blue ink. The cardboard mount shows typical edge and corner wear with some paper loss at lower right corner and scrapbook remnants on verso, 7x9". A unique view into one of baseball's great dynasties, as well as one of its earliest foreign excursions. **Minimum Bid: $750**

PHILADELPHIA PRIDE

19602 **1910 Philadelphia Athletics World Championship Trophy Presented to Tully Frederick "Topsy" Hartsel.** One of the earliest and most impressive Major League Baseball Championship trophies ever to reach the auction block, this stunning specimen was the prize awarded to Connie Mack's feisty little left fielder Frederick "Topsy" Hartsel following the White Elephants' five-game Series victory over Tinker, Evers, Chance and the rest of the Chicago Cubs ballclub. The tri-handled loving cup is boldly engraved upon its face, "Presented by The Citizens of Philadelphia to T. Frederick Hartzel (sic), World's Champions, The American Baseball Club of Philadelphia, Season 1910." The raised seal of the City of Philadelphia rests at center. The two remaining sides of the cub feature a crossed bats and ball motif and a team logo pennant respectively, the latter exhibiting some loss to the enameling but none to the enormous visual appeal. The body of the cup is crafted from silver-plated base metal and measures eight inches in height, with the mouth of the cup at a diameter of six inches. A dent at the edge of the base, below the right arm in the catalog photograph, must be noted, but is barely noticeable upon display. A weighty and impressive piece even without its tremendous baseball significance, and the ultimate memento of Connie Mack's first great dynasty. Please also see Hartsel's game worn jersey, personal photographs and funeral guestbook also featured within this auction. **Minimum Bid: $4,000**

19603 **Circa 1910 Eddie Collins Full Size Decal Bat.** They called him "Cocky," and with a lifetime batting average of .333 and 3,315 career hits, he could be forgiven for a bit of arrogance. The offered artifact dates from early in the Hall of Famers' quarter-century playing career, when he was representing Connie Mack's first great Athletics dynasty. The full size (35") J.F. Hillerich & Son. Co. lumber features a well-preserved decal image of Collins at the barrel, retaining 85% of its original state. The bat itself is likewise in fine condition, with a small chip at the knob but no other issues of note. **Minimum Bid: $600**

19604 **Circa 1910 Napoleon Lajoie Decal Bat.** Tough full-size model was found by our consignor tucked away for decades in an old cabinet of a home in Cleveland, where this Hall of Fame second baseman was so popular in his day that the ballclub was called the "Naps" during his tenure with the American League representative. The image utilized on his valuable T206 tobacco card is likewise used here, upon the barrel of this "J.F. Hillerich & Son Co. 40L" model, which shows clear Dead Ball era use but none of the cracking or dead wood typical of century-old lumber. The decal remains seventy-five to eighty percent intact, still well within the acceptable and desirable range for these delicate rarities. While a couple full-body pose Lajoie decal bats have hit the auction block in recent years, we can find no examples of this style having been offered, so there's every reason to believe that the wait for another after this one will be quite long. **Minimum Bid: $500**

19605 **1912-19 Baseball Magazine Photographs Lot of 10.** Marvelous assortment of Dead Ball photography derives from the archives of *Baseball Magazine*, and provides the viewer with a unique view of the early game. Four are the work of Charles Conlon, denoted by stamping or his own personal handwritten notations on verso. Early baseball photography afficionados are certainly familiar with Conlon, who is widely recognized as the premier lensman of early twentieth century baseball. The Conlon photos: Jesse Barnes, Lum Davenport, George Gibson, Hugo Bezdek. The balance: Doc Johnston, John Henry, Jack Martin, Art Nehf, Red Smith, Earl Yingling, Bob Berman. Condition ranges from VG to EX-MT, with the faults present typically confined to corner wear or chipping, leaving the central focus of the image unhampered. Size ranges from 5x7" to 8x10". All are top-quality images providing brilliant clarity and razor-sharp contrast. **Minimum Bid: $500**

19606 **1912 Boston Red Sox World Series Pinback & Sock.** "As I look back upon the 1912 series, when we lost to the Boston Red Sox, I see it was the same. Pitchers, outfielders, the whole team collapsed under the strain," Christy Mathewson was once quoted on saying, who himself uncharacteristically lost both starts in the Giants' four game to three defeat by the Red Sox. But while it was all doom and gloom for the Big Apple boys, the opposite was true for the original owner of this special souvenir, which paired an exquisitely rare pinback button with a charming little red sock. The celluloid pin measures 1.25" in diameter and presents very well despite a degree of foxing on the face that only adds to the vintage patina. The original paper backing is found on verso, advertising local Boston retailer "A.R. Lopez & Bro." The child-size sock presents a few small moth holes but also displays quite nicely despite the few flaws, and provides a fine home for the pin. Together, the pin and sock very effectively evoke the spirit of the Dead Ball game. **Minimum Bid: $400**

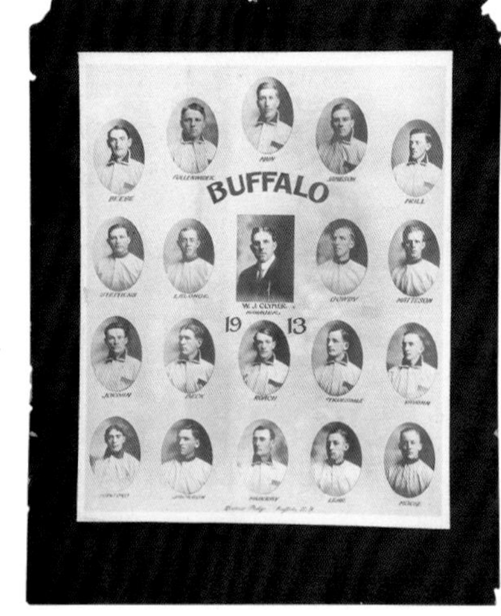

19607 **1913 Buffalo Bisons Imperial Cabinet Photograph.** Thrilling International League artifact pictures the members of the club that would take the League crown in two years time, presented in the composite format often seen in similar pieces of the era. Each player appears in his own oval portrait, with manager W.J. Clymer positioned at center. The photographic print, bearing the Buffalo photographer "Weasner Photg" markings at bottom center, measures a bold 12x15" in size, strongly suggesting that this was intended for team personnel or VIP's only due to the significant cost of producing such a large image. The cardboard mount extends the complete dimensions to 16x20", and shows some chipping at the upper corners and general wear typical of oversized cabinets from the time. Definitely one of the most impressive Dead Ball Era display pieces we've encountered from the game's most important minor league. **Minimum Bid: $750**

RUTH ON THE RISE

19608 **1914 Providence Grays Imperial Cabinet Photograph with Babe Ruth.** Perhaps the most convincing evidence in existence to prove the popular maxim, "If at first you don't succeed, try, try again," this exceptional photograph finds a nineteen-year old George Herman Ruth upon a trip back down to the minors after failing to convince the Boston Red Sox, in twenty-three innings of pitching work, that he was ready for the Big Leagues just yet. Less than a year removed from his days at St. Mary's Industrial School for Boys, the baby-faced Babe towers over his teammates at back row center in one of the earliest known images of baseball's greatest star as a professional. It was with the Providence Grays of the International League that the Babe would swat his first professional homer, during a September 5, 1914 meeting with Toronto. Despite this early hint at his destiny as the greatest slugger of his age, Ruth would continue in his pitching role for the Grays, helping to lead them to the International League Championship with a personal eight and three record.

One of just a handful of such images known to survive to this day, this spectacular specimen is almost assuredly the finest of that tiny supply. It comes to Heritage from the descendants of former Detroit Tiger Matty McIntyre, who had shared an outfield with Ty Cobb before a trade to the Chicago White Sox, eventually closing out his career in Providence before his early death in 1920 from tuberculosis. McIntyre stands second to right in the image, beside the boy in dark pants. With an image size of 10.5x13.5 (complete dimensions including mount 14.5x18.5"), this image would have been very costly to produce in 1914, and would have been issued only to players and VIP's, explaining the highly endangered status today. But again we must stress that this example has done far more than simply survive—it remains inoutrageous NRMT condition, exhibiting only the most inconsequential wear at the edges of the mount to suggest its approaching centennial. The image itself is free of even a hint of a blemish. "General Photo Co., 131 Washington St., Providence R.I." stamping appears at lower right mount.

A letter of provenance from the family of Matty McIntyre is included in this lot. **Minimum Bid: $4,000**

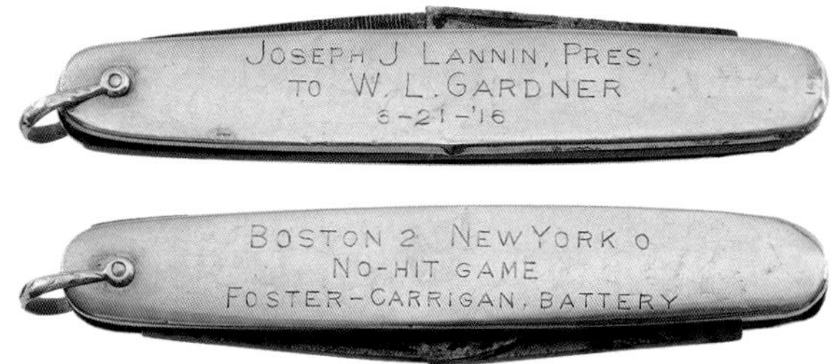

19609 **1916 Rube Foster No-Hitter Pocket Knife Presented to Boston Red Sox Player.** The first example we've ever encountered of this exciting relic, which is actually referenced in the essential Internet baseball research site, www.BaseballLibrary.com. The chronology section notes, for Wednesday, June 21st, 1916, *"Rube Foster of the Red Sox no-hits the Yankees 2-0 for the first no-hitter in Fenway Park, beating Bob Shawkey 2-0. Harry Hooper leads the offense with three hits. Red Sox president Lannin hands Rube a $100 bonus and each of his Sox teammates receive a gold handled pocket knife engraved with the date."* The offered example was presented to the club's third baseman, as the engraving on one side attests: "Joseph J. Lannin, Pres. to W.L. Gardner, 6-21-16." The opposing side is engraved, "Boston 2 - New York 0, No-Hit Game, Foster - Carrigan, Battery." While we must note that one of the two folding blades is broken, the fourteen-karat gold case is unaffected by this concern, as is the tremendous visual appeal. Minor surface wear to the gold case causes no concern. One of the more intriguing artifacts from this World Championship season to surface in the hobby in recent memory, and one of the earliest to document the greatest rivalry in professional sports. **Minimum Bid: $1,000**

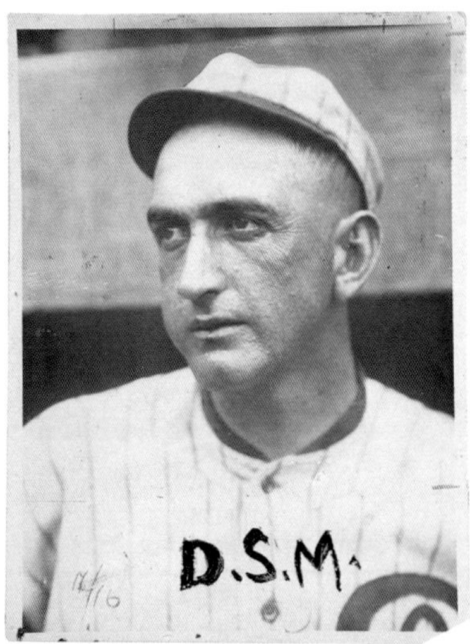

19610 **Circa 1919 Joe Jackson Photograph by Conlon.** Is there a terrible secret burning behind those dark eyes? This masterful portrait of the immensely talented Shoeless Joe dates from the era of his tragic fall, as he and seven teammates conspired to throw the World Series for underworld gamblers. A tough baseball life is evident in the lines of Jackson's face, which are captured with crystal clarity by the famous Sporting News photographer Conlon. Various editors markings are evident on the chest of Joe's White Sox jersey and at the upper borders. Verso has twin "Charles M. Conlon" stamps. Clipped bottom right corner is the only condition issue of note, otherwise wear is confined to touches at the edges and corners. Type 2 print appears to date circa 1940. Photo measures 6.5x8.5". **Minimum Bid: $200**

19611 **1919 Cincinnati Reds Publications Lot of 4.** So much has been made of the "Eight Men Out" of the Chicago Black Sox that one can almost be forgiven for overlooking the tremendous talent of the team that served as the beneficiary of the World Series fix. Though this Fall Classic victory may not be the proudest for the fans of Cincinnati, it will always stand as the first, and the first is always the sweetest. Presented here is an intriguing assortment of publications issued during that season that almost tore our National Game apart. 1) 1919 World Series program, Cincinnati model. The cover suffers from previous mold damage which has caused a speckling effect, and a ballpoint doodle appears at lower right corner. Wear to the spine and some paper loss to rear cover. Center four-page spread is loose from staples, otherwise the program remains tightly bound. 2) *Official Players Souvenir, The Reds of 1919.* Small green booklet provides colorized images and biographies of all team members. Fine EX-MT+ condition. 3) *Wells Theatre* handbill for the Week of Sept. 29, 1919, announcing that it will be providing "World's Series Returns By Innings." Measures 3.5x5.5". EX. 4) *Base Ball in Cincinnati, A History* by Harry Ellard. Hardcover first edition, published 1907, Very scarce in first edition format. Minor soiling to the spine, owner name written on endpaper. No dust jacket. Near fine. **Minimum Bid: $1,000**

19612 **1920's Christy Mathewson Personally Owned Portrait of Himself with Wife.** Finely rendered portrait of Big Six and his bride finds the former in his World War I military uniform, returned from the front after suffering the training accident that would ultimately bring a premature end to his life. The damage caused to his lungs by the inhalation of chlorine gas while serving as a Captain in the newly established Chemical Service would bring Matty to develop tuberculosis, and lead his doctor to prescribe clean, fresh air as a method of rehabilitation. It is this move that allows us to definitively authenticate the painting, as it comes to us along with its original shipping crate, addressed to "Mrs. Christy Mathewson, Old Military Road, Saranac Lake, New York," where Mathewson would pass away in 1925 at the age of forty-five. Further proof comes in the form of a second affixed shipping label, directing the crate to an address in Lewisburg, PA, where Christy's widow passed away in 1967 at eighty-seven years of age. The oil on canvas work has been carefully preserved over the decades, and exhibits no flaws of note. The original frame shows some weathering, but this only adds to the vintage charm. The wooden shipping case shows expected handling wear, but serves perfectly in its role of provenance establishment. One of the few Christy Mathewson owned articles ever to make it to public auction, and among the best for display. **Minimum Bid: $1,500**

19613 **1921-32 Baseball Magazine Photographs Lot of 21.** The Golden Age of our National Pastime is documented with this stirring compilation of images from the famed *Baseball Magazine* archives. Six are the work of Charles Conlon, denoted by stamping or his own personal handwritten notations on verso. Early baseball photography afficionados are certainly familiar with Conlon, who is widely recognized as the premier lensman of early twentieth century baseball. The Conlon photos: George Case, George Caster, Ripper Collins, Tony Cuccinello, Bucky Walters, Lon Warneke (missing upper left corner). The balance: Lee Meadows, Rabbit Maranville, Bill McKechnie, Tom Hughes, Carmen Hill, Charlie Grimm, Larry Gardner, Jim Bivin/Erv Brame, Bill Brenzel, Hy Myers, Steve O'Neill, Gus Suhr, John Stone, Steve Swetonic, Doc Cramer. Condition ranges from VG to EX-MT, with the faults present typically confined to corner wear or chipping, leaving the central focus of the image unhampered. Size ranges from 5x7" to 8x10". All are top-quality images providing brilliant clarity and razor-sharp contrast. **Minimum Bid: $1,000**

19614 **1922 Cupar Baseball Team Cabinet Photograph with Eddie Shore.** Terrifically scarce cabinet photograph finds a nineteen-year old future ice legend posing as a member of the Cupar baseball club in his Saskatchewan hometown. The remarkable image derives from the personal collection of Shore himself, and is presented with a letter of provenance from Shore's son. The Hockey Hall of Fame confirms that they have never encountered this image before, and there is every reason to believe that none others exist. The image area measures approximately 6x10", with the mount extending the total dimensions to 10x14". Each player is identified at the lower border, with "E. Shore" seated cross-legged at far left. Second from left is his brother, dressed in a dark suit and bowler hat. The image stands as one of the earliest known to picture this iconic hockey star, and is all the more desirable given the fact that it was Shore's own. A small stain at lower right mount is of no concern, and the piece otherwise presents no noteworthy condition flaws. **Minimum Bid: $400**

19615 **The Ultimate Yankee Stadium Seat.** Close your eyes and picture in your mind the finest Yankee Stadium seat in the hobby, and it will likely be a carbon copy of the offered specimen. Purchased during the mid-1970's stadium renovation sale, this seat remains exactly as it was during its days of service with the sole exception of the brass plaque affixed, reading "Yankee Stadium, 'The House That Ruth Built,' 50th Anniversary, 1923-1973, Bronx, N.Y." The Yankee blue overcoat of the paint gives way in a beautiful mottled pattern to reveal an earlier turquoise coat underneath, and Mickey Mantle's heroic number "7" is stenciled to the uppermost slat. The wrought iron sides are similarly and charmingly worn, with just the proper sprinkling of oxidation. One of the slats of the seat is cracked, but not to the degree that it threatens structural integrity, and it certainly does not affect the unbeatable display value. So much more desirable than the repainted, reworked seats much more commonly seen in the hobby. **Minimum Bid: $1,000**

19616 **1923 Yankee Stadium Terra Cotta Figural Piece.** For five decades, from the birth of The House that Ruth Built until the 1973 renovations, this treasure of baseball archaeology kept watch over the millions of fans passing through the home plate gates of Yankee Stadium. The 16x19x5" slab of baseball history should be instantly recognizable to those fans fortunate enough to have visited the Stadium during its first half century of life, and now that the game's most important venue is mere months from its destruction, the importance and appeal becomes all the more vivid. Those thinking that more will become available when the wrecking ball comes should be advised that none still remain on the Stadium's walls, though these pieces are clearly visible in vintage photography, and Yankee Stadium blueprints (copies of which are always available on eBay) present this design above the text "Terra Cotta Panels on Balconies." The decorative design consists of two baseballs in the center of a scrolled pattern backed by a golden oval that was meant to convey a sense of glowing light. It's a stunning display piece that conveys better than any stadium chair or featureless brick the majesty of this Golden Age monument to our National Pastime. Fifty years of weathering is apparent upon its surface, but the weighty piece (perhaps seventy-five pounds) remains solid and undamaged, ready for a place of distinct honor in even the finest of private collections. **Minimum Bid: $4,000**

19617 **1929 Philadelphia Athletics Panoramic Team Photograph.** Only one American League team could stand toe to toe with the mighty Murderer's Row Yankees of the late 1920's, and you will find them here, standing in a long line with their wise leader Connie Mack in his customary dark suit at center. Fellow Hall of Famers Collins, Foxx, Cochrane, Grove and Simmons are likewise captured in the crispest sepia tones, framed against the background of the Shibe Park grandstands. A two-inch square area of staining at upper left remains mercifully clear of the white-uniformed players and is frankly of minor concern. Otherwise the 7x29" image presents in fantastic NRMT condition, mounted for protection to a cardboard backing. **Minimum Bid: $750**

19618 **1929 Chicago Cubs Panoramic Print.** If you've ever wondered what it was like to sit in the center field bleachers of Wrigley Field back in 1929, now you know. This magnificent image takes in the entirety of one of the sport's most hallowed grounds, with white-shirted fans filling every seat, and even camped out on the grass, deep in the outfield in fair play. Orbiting the perimeter of this marvelous vista are vignette photographs of the gentleman who brought the National League pennant to the Windy City that season, with legends like Hack Wilson, Rogers Hornsby, Ki Ki Cuyler, Gabby Hartnett and manager Joe McCarthy among them. The print, issued on paper by "Kaufmann & Fabry Co." of Chicago, remains in its original wooden frame, which has preserved the piece in fine EX-MT order. The frame itself shows a definite degree of wear, but this only adds to the period charm. **Minimum Bid: $400**

19619 **1920's Major League Baseball Player Photographs by Conlon Lot of 9.** Neal McCabe, the author of *Baseball's Golden Age: The Photographs of Charles M. Conlon,* asserts Conlon's status as the greatest baseball photographer of all time, describing his images as "worthy of comparison to the classic works of Southworth and Hawes, Matthew Brady, Julia Margaret Cameron, August Sander and Lewis Hine." The vintage Conlon photos presented in this lot are true original prints, actually developed and printed by Conlon himself. They may be the only known original examples. Conlon's signature and/or stamp can be found on the reverse side of each photo, along with a player identification. All derive from the archives of *Baseball Magazine*. Presented are Sparky Adams, Vic Aldridge, Clyde Barnhart, Dick Bartell, Lyle Bigbee, Max Bishop, Donie Bush, Ike Boone and George Earnshaw. Some have vintage editing marks upon the image, and all have *Baseball Magazine* authenticating stickers from the 1996 auction of the archives on verso. Image size ranges from 5x6.5" to 8x10". Condition issues are confined mainly to edge/corner wear and insignificant occasional wrinkles. All would present at EX-MT or better with simple matting and framing. **Minimum Bid: $1,000**

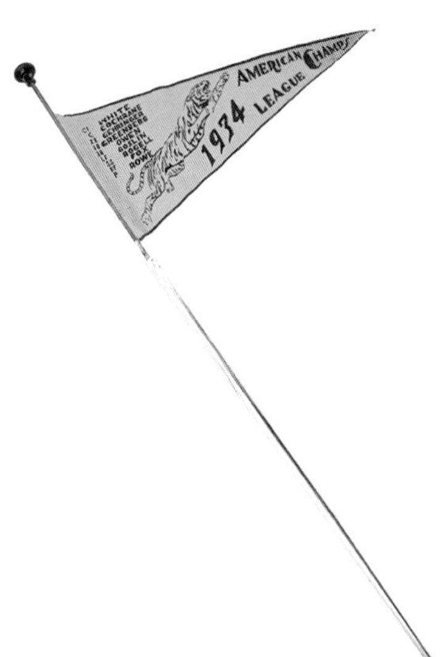

19620 **1934 Detroit Tigers A.L. Championship Pennant in Cane.** Fabulous walking stick was almost certainly sold at Navin Field as Cochrane, Gehringer, Greenberg and Goslin were visited by Dizzy Dean's Gashouse Gang in the 1934 World Series. Measuring 37" when closed, the cane expands to 52" when fully extended, and unfurls to reveal a 23" long orange silk flag listing the team roster, an image of the mascot, and the words "1934 American League Champs." The pennant remains free of any tearing or significant staining after seventy-plus years coccooned inside the cane. A wonderfully evocative piece of Depression-era baseball. **Minimum Bid: $400**

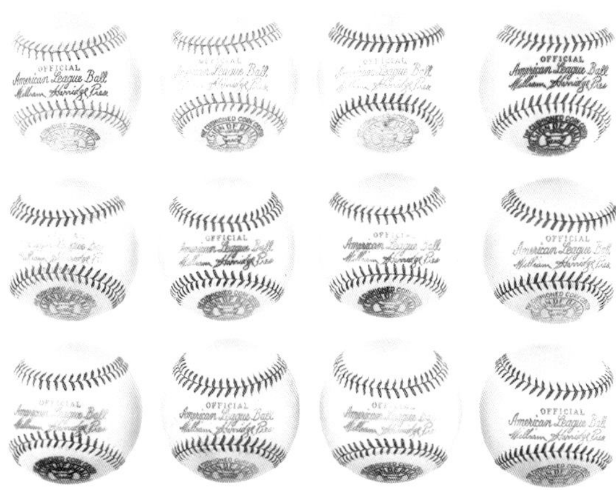

19621 **1934-39 Official American League (Harridge) Baseballs in Boxes (12).** A dozen baseballs ready for action on the diamond with Gehrig, DiMaggio and Foxx. Though all of the boxes have been opened, we can assure you that the baseballs inside are as virginal as can be, perhaps a bit toned by seven decades in seclusion but bearing fierce navy stamping and not a speck of use or wear. All but a couple of the boxes are in comparably superb condition. They definitely don't make them like this anymore, and the available supply of untouched Harridges dwindles with every passing year. Blink and they'll be gone forever. **Minimum Bid: $1,000**

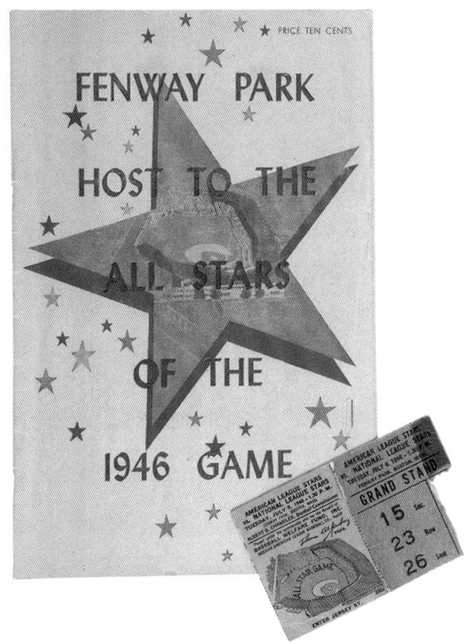

19622 **1946 All-Star Game Program & Ticket Stub.** The great Ted Williams thrilled his hometown crowd by clubbing two long balls for the Fenway Midsummer Classic, leading the American League to a lopsided twelve to nothing shutout of the hapless Nationals. Presented is the very scarce program for that first postwar All-Star Game, and a matching stub. The program is considered the toughest of all issued for the All-Star Game following the Second World War, certainly due in large part to the fragile newsprint stock utilized. Our example is curled from having been rolled up for decades (though it could surely be flattened over time, and shows some chipping and smalll tears along the right edge of the cover. Program is unscored. The ticket stub has some paper loss at lower right and tape repairs, as well as creasing. In light of the tremendous scarcity, however, condition concerns for both pieces must be largely overlooked. **Minimum Bid: $300**

19623 1947 Ben Chapman All-Star Game Presentational Wristwatch. Gold-plated Lord Elgin wristwatch was awarded to National League coach Chapman for his efforts in a two runs to one loss to the American League at Wrigley Field. The attractive timepiece features a black face and engraving on back of case that reads, "Ben Chapman, N.L. All-Stars, 1947." Light wear does not diminish the fine eye appeal, and the watch still keeps time nicely. Matching band is likewise fully functional. Included is a letter of 2003 provenance from Chapman's sons, and a 9/10 black ink cut signature from the diamond veteran. *LOA from James Spence Authentication (autograph).* **Minimum Bid: $400**

19624 1940's-50's Putnam Team Biographies Complete Hardbound Set. The literate baseball historian will have many hours of reading ahead of him should he find himself casting the winning bid upon this tough complete run of Putnam baseball biographies. This sixteen-volume hardcover set is complete down to the original dust jackets, and includes the following: *The Baltimore Orioles* (1955); *The Boston Braves* (1948); *The Boston Red Sox* (1947); *The Brooklyn Dodgers* (1945); *The Chicago Cubs* (two, 1946); *The Chicago White Sox* (Signed by author Warren Brown, 1952); *The Cincinnati Reds* (1948); *The Cleveland Indians* (2 diff. from 1949); *The Detroit Tigers* (1946); *The New York Giants* (1952); *The New York Yankees* (1943); *The Philadelphia Phillies* (1953); *The Pittsburgh Pirates* (1948); *The St. Louis Cardinals* (1944); *The Washington Senators* (two,1954). Also thrown in is *Connie Mack, Grand Old Man of Baseball* (1945). Nineteen books in total, averaging VG-EX to EX-MT. **Minimum Bid: $500**

19625 Circa 1950 Phil Rizzuto Original Cartoon Artwork by Mullin. Exceptional pen and ink work is unmistakably that of *The Sporting News'* esteemed cartoonist Willard Mullin, best remembered today as the creator of the famous Brooklyn Dodgers "Bum." Here we find his charming study of the Hall of Fame Yankees shortstop, drawn for publication in advance of Phil Rizzuto Day at the Stadium. The work measures 14x15" on artist's paper, and is signed by Mullin in the lower right quadrant. A simple framing job extends the complete dimensions to 19x20". Given as a gift to Rizzuto by Mullin following the cartoon's publication, it is offered today with a signed letter of provenance from Rizzuto's widow Cora. **Minimum Bid: $400**

19626 1953 New York Yankees World Championship Presentational Platter from Rizzuto Estate. Direct from the Scooter Estate, with a letter of provenance from Phil's widow Cora, comes this silver plated copper platter issued only to players and staff members of the 1953 Yanks. The platter measures just short of thirteen inches in diameter, and features the facsimile engraved signatures of all members of the team, making proud note of their four previous consecutive World Championships as well. Only the slightest edge wear is to be noted in terms of condition. An incredible memento recounting the greatest dynasty in Yankee history, from one of that era's brightest stars. **Minimum Bid: $300**

19627 George Sosnak Folk Art Baseball, Signed by Mickey Cochrane. Perhaps only Leroy Neiman's name is more recognizable to collectors when it comes to the field of sports art. And while the styles of these two celebrated artists couldn't be more different, their love and appreciation for the subjects of their work is evident. George Sosnak began his career in baseball as an umpire of military games in Germany after the Second World War, later attending umpiring school in Florida, where he called balls and strikes at Detroit Tigers Spring Training games. It was around this time that Sosnak began to develop his distinctive folk art style, characterized by charmingly crude figures and painstakingly rendered text and statistics applied with almost mathematical precision. Wonderful work by this talented folk artist is made all the more appealing by the presence of a 6/10 side panel signature from the subject it celebrates. Aside from this coveted autograph, the theme is standard Sosnak, with a Hall of Fame plaque, another great portrait (actually an action scene!) and endless miniature text and statistics. The early work is signed "Geo. H. Sosnak, '62." A thin coating of shellac has served very well to maintain the condition of the artwork. *LOA from PSA/DNA. LOA from James Spence Authentication.* **Minimum Bid: $500**

19628 1961 Roger Maris Sixty-First Home Run Program. "Fastball hit deep to right. This could be it! Way back there! Holy cow! He did it! Sixty-one for Maris! Look at 'em fight for that ball out there!" Though the famous call of radio announcer and fellow Yankee great Phil Rizzuto is remembered by millions today, only 23,154 fans were actually on hand to witness the historic event first hand in the Bronx. With the Yankees clinching the pennant almost two weeks earlier, attendance for this 162nd and final game of the 1961 season was particularly light, resulting in a correspondingly thin supply of artifacts from that game today. Here we present one of the few available programs purchased and scored by a lucky spectator on October 1st, 1961, with Maris' fourth inning home run circled and notated as the record-breaker. The program shows a mild degree of external wear but no damage, and remains solidly bound. This is one of the toughest post-war programs in the hobby, so any opportunity to own one should be taken very seriously. **Minimum Bid: $500**

19629 **1961 Roger Maris Sixty-First Home Run Ticket Stub.** When ranking the most memorable moments in post-war baseball history in terms of fan attendance, the game that saw Roger Maris supplant the Babe at the top of single season home run ladder rates right at the bottom. The 1961 Yanks had wrapped up the American League pennant eleven days earlier, shaving the crowd for the final regular season game to just 23,154. So it's little wonder that stubs such as this rarely surface within the hobby, nor is it a surprise that bidding for the few available specimens is uniformly spirited. Short of typical edge and corner wear, this modest little stub presents marvelously, with no creases, tears or stains to note. Included in the lot are two oversized (approximately 11x14") vintage photos taken of Maris that season, one crossing home plate after one of his many long balls, and the other posing with the widow of Babe Ruth and the sixtieth home run baseball. Photos are EX or better. **Minimum Bid: $400**

19630 **1961 Roger Maris Sixty-First Home Run Ticket Stub.** This 1.5x3" slab of paper represents one of the most inspiring moments in our National Pastime, as a quiet and humble midwestern boy secured his place in history during the game it recalls. The final match of a Yankee season that saw Maris excoriated by the press and booed by his own fans was attended by just over 23,000 fans, leaving the Bronx ballpark more than half empty for that heroic moment. As such, only a handful of tickets from the game exist today, and just a scant few could possibly match the NRMT condition of the offered specimen. Included in the lot is a fantastic 11x14" print capturing the moment of impact, with Maris' number "9" clearly visible in the batter's box and the sparsely populated outfield bleachers in the distance. Mat and frame them together for an impressive display. **Minimum Bid: $400**

19631 **1962 Mickey Mantle Nodder.** The tiniest chip at the front of this highly agreeable Mick in miniature is the only fault one encounters when inspecting this highly collectible souvenir from the era of the fabled home run record chase and back-to-back World Championships. Otherwise this baby looks like its right out of the box, with not even a flaw to the paint job, and the uniform as white as Opening Day. One dab of navy paint and it's a NRMT-MT marvel. **Minimum Bid: $300**

19632 **1962 Roberto Clemente Nodder.** Uncommonly clean example finds only the slightest touches of wear at the left edge of this heroic Pittsburgh Pirates' cap and sleeve to suggest it was born during the Kennedy administration. Otherwise you'll be hard pressed to locate any signs of age. Even the uniform, which so often takes on a tan shade with the passing years, remains snow white here. A top specimen for the discriminating collector. **Minimum Bid: $600**

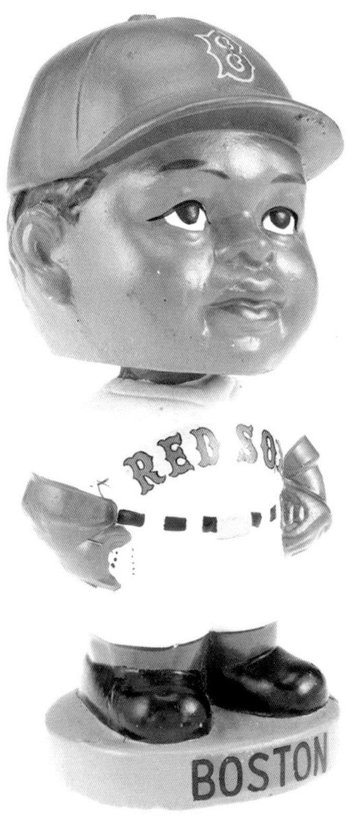

19633 **1963-65 Boston Red Sox Black Face Nodder.** The long and noble history of the Boston Red Sox franchise is marred by one unhappy distinction. Of the sixteen original Major League clubs, the Sox were the very last to integrate, signing Pumpsie Green a full twelve years after Jackie Robinson broke the color barrier. So while the black face nodders were anything but popular during the Jim Crow days in which they were issued, arguably none found a smaller audience than the Boston version we present here. The bobbing head doll presents marvelously, with only light surface wear and some minor toning of the white uniform apparent to the eye. The head needs to be reglued to the spring, but this could be easily accomplished without any sign of the restoration visible. A particularly scarce keepsake that serves as an artifact of both our National Pastime and a racially charged period in American history. **Minimum Bid: $600**

19634 **1970 Johnny Bench "Player of the Year" Presentational Wristwatch.** The Hall of Fame Cincinnati Reds catcher posted one of the finest offensive seasons ever realized by a masked man in 1970, hammering National League-topping figures of forty-five home runs and 148 RBI's while helping to raise the National League flag over the Crosley Field grandstands. Along with his first of two National League MVP Awards, Bench earned for his troubles this Longines watch, engraved upon the verso, "Johnny Bench, 1970 Baseball's Player of the Year." The seventeen-jewel timepiece features a ten karat gold filled case and fourteen karat gold plated band, though clearly its value extends well beyond its jewelry content. Watch shows typical wear, but no damage, and functions perfectly. As a symbol of the ultimate personal single season honor for an iconic Hall of Fame figure, this is a piece that should raise more than a few bidding paddles of Big Red Machine enthusiasts. **Minimum Bid: $1,000**

19635 **1975, 1978 & 1985 All-Star Game Rings.** Trio of rings comes to Heritage from the collection of Dick Butler, who earned them in his capacity as the American League's third Executive Director of Umpires. Each is crafted from base metal with colored semi-precious stones upon the face ringed by text that reads either "All-Star Game" or "Baseball All-Star." The shanks note the year of issue, with two of the three likewise engraved with Butler's surname. Two rings are size eight, the third size nine. An exciting opportunity for the collector concentrating on this annual convergence of the game's greatest stars. Please see also Butler's World Series umpire's ring presented within this auction. **Minimum Bid: $600**

19636 **1982 World Series Umpire Presentational Ring.** It may seem like umpire's get nothing but abuse, but here's proof to the contrary. In his capacity as Supervisor of Umpires, noted "man in black" Dick Butler was presented this ten karat gold ring for service to the 1982 Series. A real diamond is set at the center of a miniature baseball diamond upon the ring's face, ringed by the words "World Series Umpire." The shanks announce the two competing teams in that Fall Classic—the St. Louis Cardinals and the Milwaukee Brewers—with charming baseball imagery of bats, gloves and ballplayers interspersed. Butler's name and "Balfour" markings are found within the band, which measures to a size nine. Please see also Butler's collection of All-Star Game rings likewise presented within this auction. **Minimum Bid: $1,000**

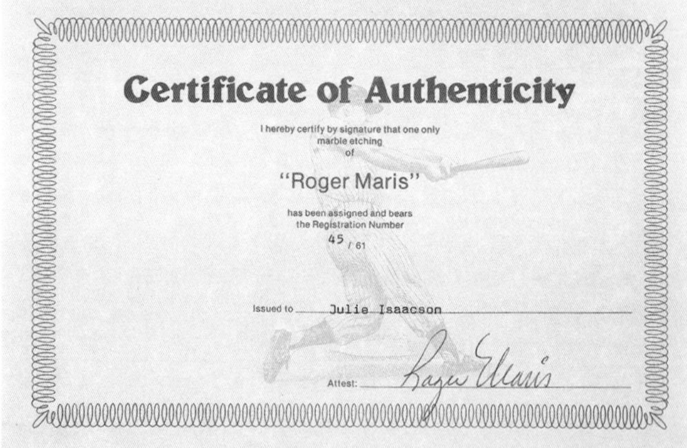
Certificate of Authenticity

I hereby certify by signature that one only marble etching of

"Roger Maris"

has been assigned and bears the Registration Number 45/61

Issued to Julie Isaacson

Attest: Roger Maris

19637 **1984 Roger Maris Marble Plaque Presented to His Best Friend.** Breathtaking limited edition display is consigned to Heritage directly by Julie Isaacson, known to any serious Yankee fan as Maris' best buddy from his arrival on the New York scene in 1960 until his passing in 1985. "When Roger was going for the home run record he would eat only bologna and eggs for breakfast," Isaacson recalled. "Every morning we would have breakfast together at the Stage Deli. We had the same waitress, and I'd leave her the same five dollar tip every time. After, I would drive Roger up to the Stadium." Years later, in gratitude for his long and important friendship, Maris presented Isaacson with this remembrance of that incredible season, a wonderful likeness of the record-breaking swing etched in white marble. Isaacson explained that he chose number "45" of the limited edition of sixty-one, as the numbers added up to his buddy's uniform number "9." To the best of our knowledge, this is the only example ever to surface in the hobby, and Isaacson strongly suspects that far fewer than the supposed run of sixty-one was ever completed. The heavy marble plaque measures 12x16" in size, and is attractively framed to complete dimensions of 20x25". Included is a Certificate of Authenticity noting Isaacson as the recipient, signed in 10/10 blue ink by Maris himself. A truly special piece for the advanced Yankees collector who wishes to set himself apart from the rest. *LOA from PSA/DNA (autograph). LOA from James Spence Authentication (autograph).* **Minimum Bid: $1,500**

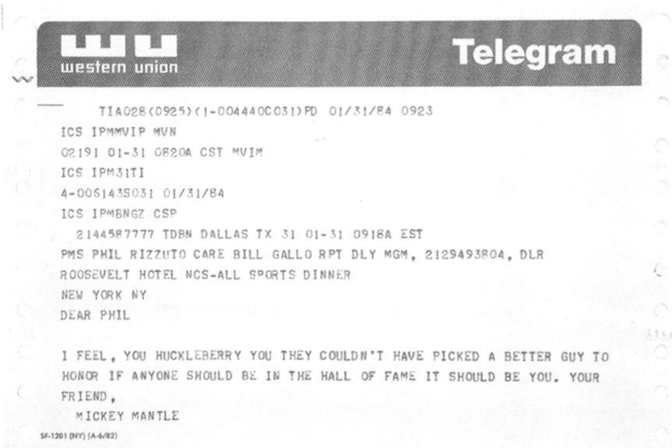

western union Telegram

TIA028(0925)(1-004440C031)PD 01/31/84 0923
ICS IPMMVIP MVN
02191 01-31 0820A CST MVIM
ICS IPM31TI
4-006143S031 01/31/84
ICS IPMBNGZ CSP
2144587777 TDBN DALLAS TX 31 01-31 0918A EST
PMS PHIL RIZZUTO CARE BILL GALLO RPT DLY MGM, 2129493804, DLR
ROOSEVELT HOTEL NCS-ALL SPORTS DINNER
NEW YORK NY
DEAR PHIL

I FEEL, YOU HUCKLEBERRY YOU THEY COULDN'T HAVE PICKED A BETTER GUY TO HONOR IF ANYONE SHOULD BE IN THE HALL OF FAME IT SHOULD BE YOU. YOUR FRIEND,
MICKEY MANTLE

SF-1201 (NY) (A-6/82)

19638 **1984 Mickey Mantle Congratulatory Telegram to Phil Rizzuto.** Scooter and the Mick once again find themselves on the same team, as the scrappy little shortstop was granted entry to the hallowed halls of Cooperstown. Direct from Rizzuto's collection, with his personal signed letter of provenance, comes this telegram he received from Mantle, who writes, "Dear Phil, I feel, you huckleberry you, they couldn't have picked a better guy to honor. If anyone should be in the Hall of Fame it should be you. Your friend, Mickey Mantle." The Western Union telegram presents a few minor fold lines, but nothing that diminishes either the visual strength or the touching sentiment. **Minimum Bid: $400**

19639 **1985 Babe Ruth Perez-Steele Original Artwork by Dick Perez.** Probably the most significant work by this gifted sports artist ever to reach the auction block, this gorgeous watercolor of a young Babe Ruth was reproduced as card number one in the 1985 Perez-Steele Great Moments set. Recognizing the conventional wisdom that a picture is worth a thousand words, we'll allow Perez' watercolor mastery to speak for itself. The work on watercolor paper measures 13.5x17.5" in size, with a suitably dignified framing extended the final dimensions to 21x25". Included in the lot is an example of the Great Moments card the painting spawned. A genuine masterpiece that would represent well in the finest of sports and fine art collections alike. **Minimum Bid: $1,000**

19640 **1987 Sandy Koufax Dodger Stadium Silver Anniversary Ring.** The rocket-armed lefty is considered by many to be the most dominant pitcher of his age, posting microscopic ERA's that were the National League-best each season between 1962 and 1966, when he hung up his spikes at the top of his game. This era of dominance coincided exactly with the debut of Dodger Stadium, which celebrated its twenty-fifth birthday with presentational rings for a cast of Old Timers on hand for the festivities. A letter from our consignor, who was in the employ of the company tapped to create the rings, states, "When Sandy Koufax stopped by my station and was signing the baseballs, I asked him to let me measure his finger for the ring. At that time he said 'you keep the ring, I have more than enough rings.' That is how I came to own the ring." The simple design features a blue enamel face applied to white metal, with "Los Angeles Dodgers" ringing the perimeter of the face and "Koufax Dodgers 32" engraved at left shank. Right shank features a miniature Dodger Stadium. Size 10.5. No Koufax Championship rings have ever surfaced in the hobby, and there is no reason to expect that any ever will. As such, this may be the only Koufax ring presented by the Dodgers ever to find its way to the auction block. **Minimum Bid: $1,500**

19641 **1999 New York Yankees World Series Championship Trophy.** "A pop in to left...the New York Yankees...World Champions. Team of the decade. Most successful franchise of the century." That was Bob Costas' call as the Yanks closed out a four-game annihilation of the National League Champion Atlanta Braves, becoming the first team to win the Fall Classic with consecutive sweeps since the 1938-39 Bronx editions. This shimmering trophy was the spoils of war for one team staffer, who was fortunate enough to be on the payroll for the twenty-fifth World Championship season. The design should be familiar to any collector, but it still never fails to send up a chill. Pennants rising up to a foot tall and representing all Major League teams surround crown and baseball figurals at center of a circular base, upon which the press pins for both the Yankees and the Braves are applied. A golden band cinches the base, engraved with the celebratory phrase, "World Series Champions, New York Yankees, 1999." Unless you know how to hit, pitch or otherwise cater to the strict demands of The Boss, this auction may be the only way one of these will ever sit upon your mantle. **Minimum Bid: $3,000**

19642 **Circa 2000 Shoeless Joe Jackson Original Artwork by Arthur Miller.** Stirring masterwork derives from the studio of Arthur K. Miller, an eminently skilled New England painter whose work has been exhibited as a one-man show at the Baseball Hall of Fame in Cooperstown since the year 2000 and is likewise featured in many upscale galleries and private collections worldwide. This portrait of the brilliant but troubled Shoeless Joe is arguably the cream of the crop, and has been used to create one of his top-selling lithographs at his website www.ArtoftheGame.com. Though Miller's style could be characterized accurately at photorealism, his works suggest far more than hypersensitivity to detail, with his brilliant command of light and shadow providing a soulfulness that no photograph could muster. This 24x32" acrylic on board seems to capture the strain and sadness of the 1919 scandal in Jackson's gaze with the subtlety and humanity of Mona Lisa's smile. Unquestionably one of the most arresting works of sports art we have encountered. Framed to 27x36". **Minimum Bid: $3,000**

19643 "Ebbets Field" Original Artwork by Glaubach. Celebrated Big Apple folk artist Harry Glaubach's unmistakable style is put to wonderful effect with this piece recalling the beloved Flatbush ballpark and the legendary players who once called it home. Commissioned works from this witness to decades of New York baseball history reside in the personal collections of such notable figures as James Cagney, Darryl Strawberry and Lou Piniella. A line-up of white uniformed Dodgers join Abbott and Costello and the Brooklyn Bum in the foreground, with a packed grandstand and charming early advertising signs dominating the rear. Constructed from die-cut wood and painstakingly applied paint, this large and impressive three-dimensional work measures 26x48x5". One of two original works by Glaubach presented within this auction, each signed by the artist on verso. **Minimum Bid: $1,000**

19644 "The Polo Grounds" Original Artwork by Glaubach. Celebrated Big Apple folk artist Harry Glaubach's unmistakable style is put to wonderful effect with this piece recalling the beloved Coogan's Bluff ballpark and the legendary players who once called it home. Commissioned works from this witness to decades of New York baseball history reside in the personal collections of such notable figures as James Cagney, Darryl Strawberry and Lou Piniella. A chorus line of Giants appear in the foreground, with a packed grandstand and charming early advertising signs dominating the rear. Constructed from die-cut wood and painstakingly applied paint, this large and impressive three-dimensional work measures 25x48x5". One of two original works by Glaubach presented within this auction, each signed by the artist on verso. **Minimum Bid: $1,000**

19645 1861 Pioneer Base Ball Club Token. It is reported that just 150 pieces of this white metal token were ever minted, done in commemoration of the third anniversary of the formation of the Pioneer Base Ball Club in Springfield, Massachusetts, the town which ironically would give birth to the game of basketball three decades later. Surely it goes without saying that baseball artifacts dating to the Civil War era are tremendously scarce and desirable, and this piece has the marvelous visuals to match its ideal collecting vintage. The face of the token features an image of a period batter, complete with pillbox cap and wagon tongue bat, with "Pioneer Base Ball Club" text navigating the perimeter. Further text on verso reveals, "Organized April 30, 1858, Play Ground on Hampden Park, Springfield, Mass." Minor surface wear causes no concerns, with the piece still displaying quite convincingly at an EX-MT level. **Minimum Bid: $500**

19646 1922 New York Giants Silver Season Pass. A bold stylistic departure from earlier (and later) examples, the 1922 season pass issued to Manhattan VIP's incorporated colorful enamel work upon the obverse, fashioning a wind-whipped pennant spelling the words "N.Y. Giants 1921 World Champions." A small chip to the blue border enamel is noted, though the visual power is not undermined by this fault. The reverse announces, "The Giants Bid You Welcome, 1922, 50, Robt. Stein & One, Chas.H. Stoneham, Pres."Maker's mark, "Lambert Bros, Sterling," is at bottom verso. **Minimum Bid: $300**

19647 **1923 New York Giants Silver Season Pass.** The Polo Grounds celebrated a National League pennant this season, to the surprise of few. One lucky fan was afforded free entry to see a roster packed with Hall of Famers (Kelly, Frisch, Bancroft, Youngs, Jackson, Stengel, Wilson and Terry!) merely by flashing this badge to the turnstile tender at the uptown Manhattan baseball palace. The obverse announces, "Giants, Worlds Champions, 1921-1922, Chas.H. Stoneham, Pres," with verso engraved with serial number "190," presentee's name "Wm. Collier & One" and the year of "1923." Maker's mark, "Lambert Bros, Sterling," is at bottom verso. Light surface wear affords a very conservative rating of EX-MT. **Minimum Bid: $300**

19648 **1924 New York Giants Silver Season Pass.** One flash of this charming silver trinket and the gates would swing open for its bearer, providing Polo Grounds access during yet another National League Championship season. The obverse announces, "Giants, 1924, Open Gate, Chas.H. Stoneham, Pres," with verso engraved with serial number "209," presentee's name "Miss Helen Brown & One." Maker's mark, "Lambert Bros, Sterling," is at bottom verso. Marvelous NRMT condition. **Minimum Bid: $300**

19649 **1925 New York Giants Silver Season Pass.** Magnificent craftsmanship from "Lambert Bros, NY," whose mark appears on verso, provides a remarkably detailed miniaturized view of the Polo Grounds grandstands on its face, joined by the text, "Pennant Winners, 1925 NY Giants, Chas. A. Stoneham, Pres." Verso is engraved with the identity of the lucky original owner, "H.A. Ferguson & Party," and the pass' unique serial number "606." Minor tarnishing is the only condition issue worthy of mention. **Minimum Bid: $300**

19650 **1925 World Series Press Pin (Pittsburgh Pirates).** Presenting a NRMT appearance to the naked eye, this scarce and gorgeous relic recalling the World Championship glory days of Traynor, Cuyler and Carey requires magnification in order to reveal a few scattered instances of surface scratching. The enamel remains complete and uncracked, however, and the golden plating is only lightly worn at the edges. Most importantly, as this tends to be a problem with most specimens from the small surviving supply, the original "Whitehead & Hoag" stamped nut remains on verso. Certainly among the finest surviving examples of this tough pin. **Minimum Bid: $750**

19651 **1926 New York Giants Silver Season Pass.** A welcoming hand extended the offer of a season's worth of games at the famed Polo Grounds to "George Odom," whose name is engraved on verso along with the pass' "433" serial number. This charming little charm reads, "Welcome 1926, Giants, Chas. A. Stoneham, Pres." on obverse, and remains in splendid, undamaged condition with a touch of tarnishing the only issue of any note. An important relic that recalls the debut of a seventeen-year old kid named Melvin Ott. **Minimum Bid: $300**

19653 **1928 World Series Press Pin (St. Louis Cardinals).** Pins with spacious fields of white enamel are commonly found pink-toned, porous and discolored. Additionally, the convex surface which accommodates the vast white enamel field and the red enamel-filled cardinal lends itself to sensitivity issues when even minimal external force or contact is applied. The result is a pin which is often found with cracking that ranges from hairline to missing pieces in severity. The offered pin possesses only a minimum of discoloration in the white field, as it otherwise remains in an exceptional state of preservation. It rates among the finest of its issue both technically and aesthetically. Further adding to the aesthetics of the offered pin the presence of the fragile gold plating which still remains on most of the obverse, a testament to the care this pin received over the past eighty years. Includes original "St. Louis Button Co. " nut on back. **Minimum Bid: $600**

19652
1927 New York Giants Silver Season Pass. Though the big story that season was just across the Harlem River where Babe Ruth was making history as leader of Murderer's Row, one lucky fan surely made good use of this pass in support of his National League club. An attractive "fan" design offers an oddly singular "Giant" on obverse, with "1927" and "Chas. A. Stoneham, Pres." Verso features engraved owner's name and serial number, "Mr. & Mrs. H. McAleenan Jr. 166" Maker's mark, "Lambert Bros, NY, Sterling," is at bottom verso. Fine NRMT condition. **Minimum Bid: $300**

19654 **1928 World Series (New York Yankees) Press Pin.** The Yanks make it eight October wins in a row as they sweep their National League opposition for the second consecutive season. The wearer of this pin got to watch Lou Gehrig take Grover Cleveland Alexander deep in the first inning of Game Two! We must resort to the magnifying glass to hunt down any faults, which come only in the form of a few oxidation pinpricks to the metal face that may well be removable. The enamel remains essentially pristine, with just a sliver of toning underneath the number "8." Threaded post on verso with Dieges & Clust stamped nut. A stunning NRMT example. **Minimum Bid: $1,500**

19655 **1929 World Series Press Pin (Chicago Cubs).** The bat-wielding bear displays exceptional detail and is free of any wear that is commonly found along the high points of this popular high relief design. The red and white enamel about the periphery remains true throughtout, thus allowing the lettering within to remain unusually legible for the issue. A tiny spot of white enamel overflow remains on the edge below the "o" in Chicago. Ranks among the finest '29 Cubs extant, a fine memento of a hard-fought meeting with Connie Mack's unstoppable white elephants. "Hipp & Coburn" maker's mark and original threaded post and nut on verso. **Minimum Bid: $400**

19656 **1930 World Series Press Pin (Philadelphia Athletics).** Generally considered the rarest post-1920 press pin. The vast areas of uninterrupted enamel upon a convex surface made this pin extremely prone to cracking and chipping in both the blue and white enameled areas, though this example remains mercifully free of any such concerns. The gold plating remains entirely intact throughout. It would be difficult to imagine a finer 1930 Athletics press pin exists. Original threaded post and nut on verso. October action with Foxx, Cochrane and the rest! **Minimum Bid: $500**

19657 **1939 World Series (New York Yankees) Press Pin.** The Centennial season was one of baseball's most notable, and despite the loss of the services of team captain Lou Gehrig, the Yanks still managed to bring the year's Championship home to the Bronx. Spectacular Dieges & Clust pin offers flawless enamel and metal free from oxidation, resulting in a NRMT appearance. Threaded post and nut on verso. **Minimum Bid: $300**

19658 **1943 World Series Press Pin (St. Louis Cardinals).** Like its older brother from the 1942 Series, this tremendously scarce relic is a dying breed, with most examples lost due to the flimsy construction that war-time restrictions on metal usage necessitated. An indication of the perils faced by the pin is evident in the wrinkling of the paper beneath the clear celluloid, but it still presents very nicely despite this. The simple brooch pin on verso is present and accounted for. Chances to own one of these do not come around often. **Minimum Bid: $1,000**

19659 **Circa 1910 Industrial League Game Worn Uniform with Photo Match.** While our research into the exact identity of the Toronto, Ohio baseball team represented here has come up short, our consignor informs us that the offered uniform belonged to a young ballplayer named Alex Stewart, who kneels second from the left in the pair of accompanying cabinet photographs. It may not be professional issue, but complete uniforms from this period are quite tough to come by, and particularly so with photographic documentation dating back a full century. The top-quality heavyweight white flannel jersey spells "Toronto" in black felt lettering down the collar's button path, with some form of craftsman's tool logo over the heart. A period "Spalding" tag appears inside the collar, above a label that identifies the owner as "Mr. A.T. Stewart, Toronto, O." Matching pants are identically tagged. Both jersey and pants exhibit a mild degree of age and infield dirt toning, but, remarkably, none of the damage almost assured when dealing with clothing of this vintage. The cabinet photograph images measures 5x7", with the chipped mounts extending the final dimensions to 8.5x10.5". Finally, we have a studio portrait of Stewart acquired as part of the same estate box lot, which enabled us to pick Stewart out of the line-up of eleven ballplayers in the cabinet photo. **Minimum Bid: $400**

TOPSY TURVY

19660 **Circa 1911 Tully Frederick "Topsy" Hartsel Game Worn Jersey.** One of just a tiny handful of jerseys dating to Connie Mack's first great Philadelphia Athletics dynasty known to survive today, this incredible home white flannel shared the diamond with the likes of Frank "Home Run" Baker, Eddie Plank and Charles "Chief" Bender when the City of Brotherly Love was the center of the baseball world. It comes to us from the descendants of Hartsel, who served the cause of the White Elephants for ten seasons, though it would stand to reason that this was his last jersey that he kept, dating it to the World Championship season of 1911.

The simple style, however, with the black felt letter "A" over the heart and pullover/buttoned tailoring, is correct for Hartsel's entire term of Athletics service. The ancient "Spalding" manufacturer's tag appears at rear interior collar, with a pale "Hartsel" chain stitched just below. Button holes at the sleeve cuffs recall a day when removable long sleeves were in baseball vogue. Sadly, the decision was made at some point to trim the jersey of its collar. But, outside of this alteration and a single missing button, the jersey remains exactly as it was worn during the fabled Dead Ball days.

Wear is strong throughout, but the jersey is free of the heavy staining and moth damage so often seen on ancient flannel uniforms. A few light spots, likely tobacco-related, are noted for accuracy but cause no visual concern. Provenance is spectacular, as this jersey shares space with several other lots from the Hartsel estate, including his 1910 World Series trophy, also found within this auction. Included with the jersey is an 8x10" mounted photograph (Good) picturing Hartsel wearing what may very well be the offered jersey. *LOA from Lou Lampson.* **Minimum Bid: $5,000**

FREDDIE'S FLANNEL

19661 **1936 Freddie Lindstrom Game Worn Jersey.** The Hall of Fame third baseman spent the bulk of his career in the service of the New York Giants, and was remembered by his teammates as one of the very few players with the nerve to square off against the legendary gruffness of manager John McGraw. He would attribute his premature grey streak in his blonde hair to McGraw, and was quoted as saying that his greatest thrill in baseball "...came the day Mr. McGraw named his twenty all-time players. I'm ninth on that list and that is thrill enough to last me a lifetime."

Though we have never encountered a game worn jersey of Lindstrom's from the Giants or any other team prior to this example, simple mathematics would suggest that the offered lot is the rarest possible. Lindstrom appeared in just twenty-six games, the last of his career, as a member of the Brooklyn Dodgers, making his final appearance on a Major League diamond on May 15, 1936. The Dodgers were at home at Ebbets Field on that day, facing the Pirates club Lindstrom had represented two years earlier, so there is a very genuine possibility that this home white pinstriped flannel is the very last jersey worn by this early legend in competition. Visually, the jersey is an absolute masterpiece of Depression-age baseball couture, with navy and red felt lettering spelling "Brooklyn" across the chest in the most elegant of fonts, and the number "31" on verso likewise the height of art deco style. Double navy piping rings the collars, cuffs and button path, furthering the aesthetic cause. "F. Lindstrom" is artfully chainstitched into the body of the collar beside the small and simple "Spalding" manufacturer's label, matching the year "36" designation sewn directly into the lower front left tail. Short of a small degree of uneven trimming of the rear tail, which does not draw the eye to any significant degree,the jersey remains 100% original and unaltered from its issued state. Very possibly the only chance the elite hobbyist might ever have to bring this tough Hall of Famer into his flannel collection. *LOA from Lou Lampson.* **Minimum Bid: $10,000**

RED ALERT

19662 **1945 Albert "Red" Schoendienst Game Worn Rookie Uniform.** The red-headed Hall of Famer wore the uniform of the St. Louis Cardinals in six different decades, but this was the first of them all, issued to the 1989 Hall of Fame inductee upon his arrival at Sportsman's Park in 1945. Though signed as a free agent in 1942 at the age of nineteen, military service delayed Schoendienst's Big League debut, and a serious eye and shoulder injury almost ended his brilliant career before it started. His rookie season provided a sign of his greatness to come, as he would lead the National League with twenty-six stolen bases and help his club finish just three games short of the pennant.

The simply stunning home white flannel uniform offered here would be a treasure even without its regal heritage, as the classic chenille birds and bat chest logo joins the patriotic World War II stars and bars patch on the left sleeve to create an aesthetic marvel. Number "6" is applied in red and navy to the jersey verso, with "Schoendienst 45" elegantly scripted in red embroidery at the left front tail. Proper "Rawlings St. Louis" label inside collar rests beside a "42 Regular" size tag. The matching pants bear an identical manufacturer's label at interior waistband, framed by "Dry Clean Only" and "38 Regular" tags. Two other names are inked inside the waistband, and while we are convinced that the pants first belonged to Schoendienst, we must admit that no physical evidence of this does exist. At the very least, it is the proper style, and provides the required visuals for display.

Wear is solid and consistent throughout the uniform, though it must be stressed that there are no stains or holes to report short of an apparent blood stain at the pants' right knee where the wound to the flannel has been patched, and the condition could not possibly be any more ideal. Few players in baseball history have given more to a single team than has Red Schoendienst, and we suspect that this first offering of his rookie uniform to the collecting public will cause the appropriate and well-merited stir in the City of St. Louis. *LOA from Lou Lampson.* Minimum Bid: $10,000

19663 **1940's-50's Boston Red Sox Game Worn Warm-up Jacket.** The days of Ted Williams, Dom DiMaggio and Johnny Pesky are vividly recalled with the sight of this navy wool letterman style jacket owned and worn by one of these legends' teammates on cold days at Fenway. While we cannot identify the specific player, it must be stressed that this jacket was team-issue only, and never available to the general public. A fantastic "red socks" chenille patch is sewn over the heart, and red, white and blue elasticized cuffing appears at collar, waist and sleeve ends. Fully operational snap-button front. "Tim McAuliffe [size] 48" tagging appears inside collar. Light wear is evident, but the jacket remains in splendid undamaged condition, without so much as fraying of the cuffs typically seen on jackets from this era. This is a piece that will function equally well in your trophy room or your personal wardrobe. *LOA from Lou Lampson.* **Minimum Bid: $300**

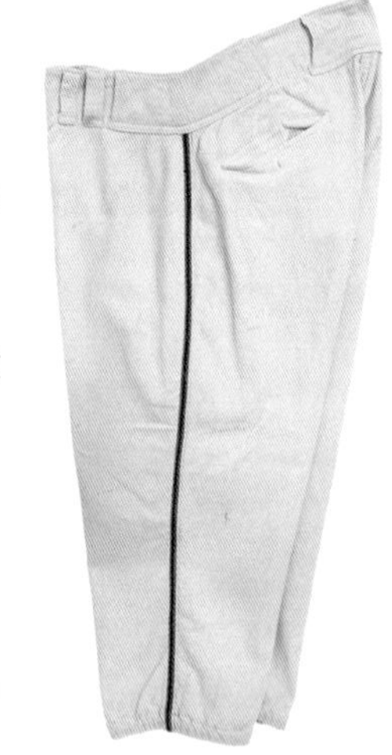

19664 **1950 Jack Maguire Game Worn Uniform.** We could legitimately point out that the offered home white flannel is Maguire's rookie model, though the appeal here is clearly the gorgeous New York Giants style, given Maguire's brief service to the Major Leagues. Despite the fact that the jersey's former owner is no household name, we are nonetheless transported back to the Polo Grounds by the sight of his shirt, which proclaims "Giants" with black and orange felt in the classic Old English font. Number "29" appears upon verso, though we must note that the second digit has been changed from its original "4." The "2" remains original and unmoved, and the number change clearly was rendered soon after, or perhaps even during, the 1950 season. "Maguire 24" is embroidered upon a felt swatch inside the collar, below the "MacGregor Goldsmith size 42" maker's label. A "Set 1 1950" flap tag is affixed to the interior button path. The jersey shows fine wear but surrenders none of its beauty to age, remaining free of staining or cloth damage. The matching pants have no player attribution or year tagging, but provide "A.G. Spalding & Bros." manufacturer's tagging framed by "Dry Clean Only" and size "36" labels. Vintage team repairs are noted, but the pants otherwise present wonderfully and make a perfect visual complement to the jersey. *LOA from Lou Lampson.* **Minimum Bid: $1,000**

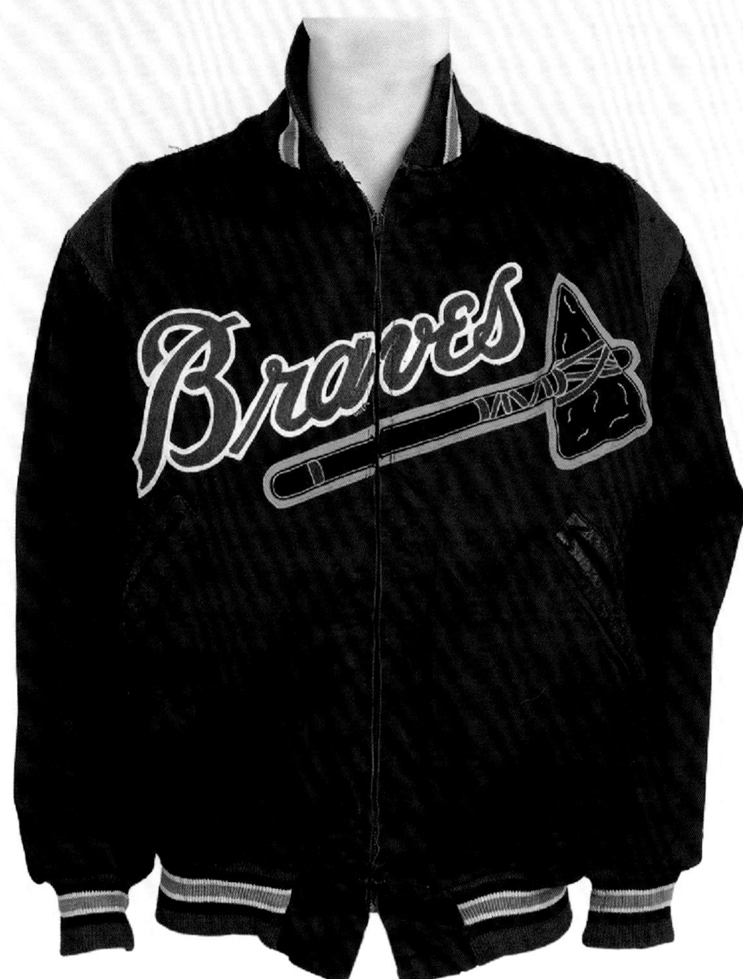

19665 **Early 1950's Milwaukee Braves Game Worn Jacket Attributed to Rookie Hank Aaron.** In an age when the average Major League salary tops $2 million annually, it's hard to believe that once upon a time even the greatest stars of the game were issued "hand me down" uniform pieces, but this was a well-documented practice. When a player left a club behind, the man taking his place would often assume his uniform if the size was right, and jersey numbers were often assigned based purely upon who fit the jersey upon which it was placed. But there was an added component to the decision of who received what uniform pieces back in this era. Many white ballplayers refused uniforms that had been worn by an African-American, and, as such, we often see the path of jackets such as this one following racial bloodlines.

This high-quality letterman style Braves jacket was never intended to be a single season uniform piece—photo documentation shows this same jacket being used for a number of years. This one almost surely dates to the 1953 season. It couldn't be any earlier, as the Braves were in Boston in 1952, at which point they used the Indian head logo. It was only upon their move to Milwaukee in '53 that the tomahawk came into vogue. We can then attribute this jersey to Sam Jethroe, who did not play in 1953, but was still the property of the Braves. His number "5" is found embroidered on a black felt swatch on the inner left tail. It is almost certain that Aaron was issued number "5" in 1954 because he was Jethroe's size, and he would not be bothered by the fact that the former owner of his uniform had dark skin. Uniform authenticator Lou Lampson notes this in his highly detailed letter of authenticity, which traces the probably progression of the jacket from Jethroe to Aaron. The jersey number "5" was not worn by any other Brave until 1956, too late for this jacket to have been originally issued. As such, we can assert with a good amount of confidence that this jacket belonged to Aaron during his rookie season.

As to the specifics of the jersey itself, we need not state just how beautiful it is—our catalog imagery will tell this tale. The black heavyweight satin body offers a wonderful felt script team nickname and tomahawk, which displays only the slightest scattering of pinpoint holes. The neck and sleeve elasticized trim is complete and undamaged, and the zipper operates perfectly. "Wilson [size] 44" tagging appears in the collar, and the number "28" markered below further proves the long life of this piece as it was sent down to the minors after Major League action. The tan chamois leather lining shows fine wear but remains undamaged to this day. In short, this is about as good as it gets for the serious Aaron collector, combining rookie history with tremendous visual appeal. One look and you'll see why the Braves wanted to use these jackets forever. *LOA from Lou Lampson.* **Minimum Bid: $4,000**

19666 **1956 Jim Hearn Game Worn Uniform.** Less than a week after Bobby Thomson hit his "Shot Heard 'round the World," Hearn earned a Game Three victory over the mighty Yanks in the 1951 World Series, arguably the highlight of his thirteen-season career on the Big League mound. The offered jersey dates from five seasons later, and his last of seven as a representative of New York National League club. The gorgeous creamy white flannel provides the original Old English "Giants" in a shallow black and orange arc across the chest, with number "27" appearing on verso. It must be noted that Hearn wore number "21" while with the Giants, and the second digit has been swapped out, though the number "2" is original and unmoved. All other details are likewise original and unaltered, from the "Hearn" embroidered swatch inside the collar to the "Tim McAuliffe Inc." label in the tail that rises above the chainstitched sizing and year information, "46 5 in 56." Matching pants are attributed inside the waistband by way of black embroidery to Johnny Antonelli, whose twenty and thirteen record in '56 earned him his second of five All-Star nods. The year and sizing information of "56" and "36 28 ins" respectively frame the "Tim McAuliffe Inc." manufacturer's label. Strong wear is evident, particularly in the pilling of the fabric at the crotch, resultant of Antonelli's pitching motion. Together, the jersey and pants offer the modern viewer a trip back in time to Coogan's Bluff and the departed yet immortal Polo Grounds. *LOA from Lou Lampson.* Minimum Bid: $1,000

19667 **1957 Roy Campanella Game Worn Pants.** From the same source that provided the incredible 1958 Duke Snider game worn jersey presented within this auction comes this important garment worn by the tragic Brooklyn Dodgers Hall of Fame catcher in what would prove to be his final season in baseball. Considering the fact that players of this era were issued just two home and two road uniforms, and that the Dodgers played their final game as representatives of Brooklyn at Philadelphia's Shibe Park, one can conclude that there is a 50-50 chance that these pants were the last ever worn by Campy in competition. The grey flannel pants exhibit fantastic wear, with heavy pilling in the crotch one will see on any starting catcher's pants during the flannel era. Some of the blue piping at the outseams has come loose, but to no major visual detriment. The interior waistband is tagged with the proper "Spalding" label and Dry Cleaning tag. with the felt swatch below embroidered "Campanella" in blue thread showing tremendous wear but still hanging on by a thread. The double heartbreak for Brooklynites of losing both their beloved Bums and their superstar catcher following the 1957 season remains among the most poignant in sports history, while Campy's reaction to his misfortune remains one of the most inspiring. As such, these pants should occupy a place of honor in even the finest of private collections. *LOA from Lou Lampson.* Minimum Bid: $2,000

THE DUKE OF LOS ANGELES

19668 **1958 Duke Snider Game Worn Jersey.** "We wept," the Hall of Fame Dodgers outfielder said of his teammates' reaction to their departure from Ebbets. "Brooklyn was a lovely place to hit. If you got a ball in the air, you had a chance to get it out. When they tore down Ebbets Field, they tore down a little piece of me." Even today, a full half century since the hated Walter O'Malley pulled up stakes and headed west, you'll find the borough of Brooklyn full of senior citizens who have yet to get over the betrayal. But, in many ways, those tears shed back in 1957 were the nourishment needed for the game to grow, and for the fulfillment of baseball's Manifest Destiny. Today we couldn't imagine the Major Leagues confined to one side of the Mississippi River.

Dating to what may well be, in retrospect, the most important season in our National Pastime's history, this road grey Los Angeles Dodgers jersey might even have seen action during the first Major League game on the West Coast. The Dodgers would celebrate Opening Day, 1958 as the visitors to the newly christened San Francisco Giants at Seals Stadium. Though the club wouldn't see anything close to the same level of success in 1958 that the following World Championship season would bring, this first-year style is clearly the most desirable of all Los Angeles models. The supple grey flannel body provides the classic "Dodgers" on the chest, the only year the road model would not announce "Los Angeles" instead. Snider's retired number "4" appears on verso. While most jerseys from this era were sent down to the minors following the season and reworked with the new team's design, this example remains 100% original and unaltered. The tail holds the proper "Wilson [size] 44" label beneath a blue chainstitched "#4 D Snider, 1958 Set 2." Wear is solid and consistent throughout, following in the theme of supreme desirability. The jersey was sourced through a gentleman close to the Dodgers organization, who also provides the Roy Campanella game worn pants offered within this auction. *LOA from Lou Lampson.* **Minimum Bid: $5,000**

WEST COAST WILLIE

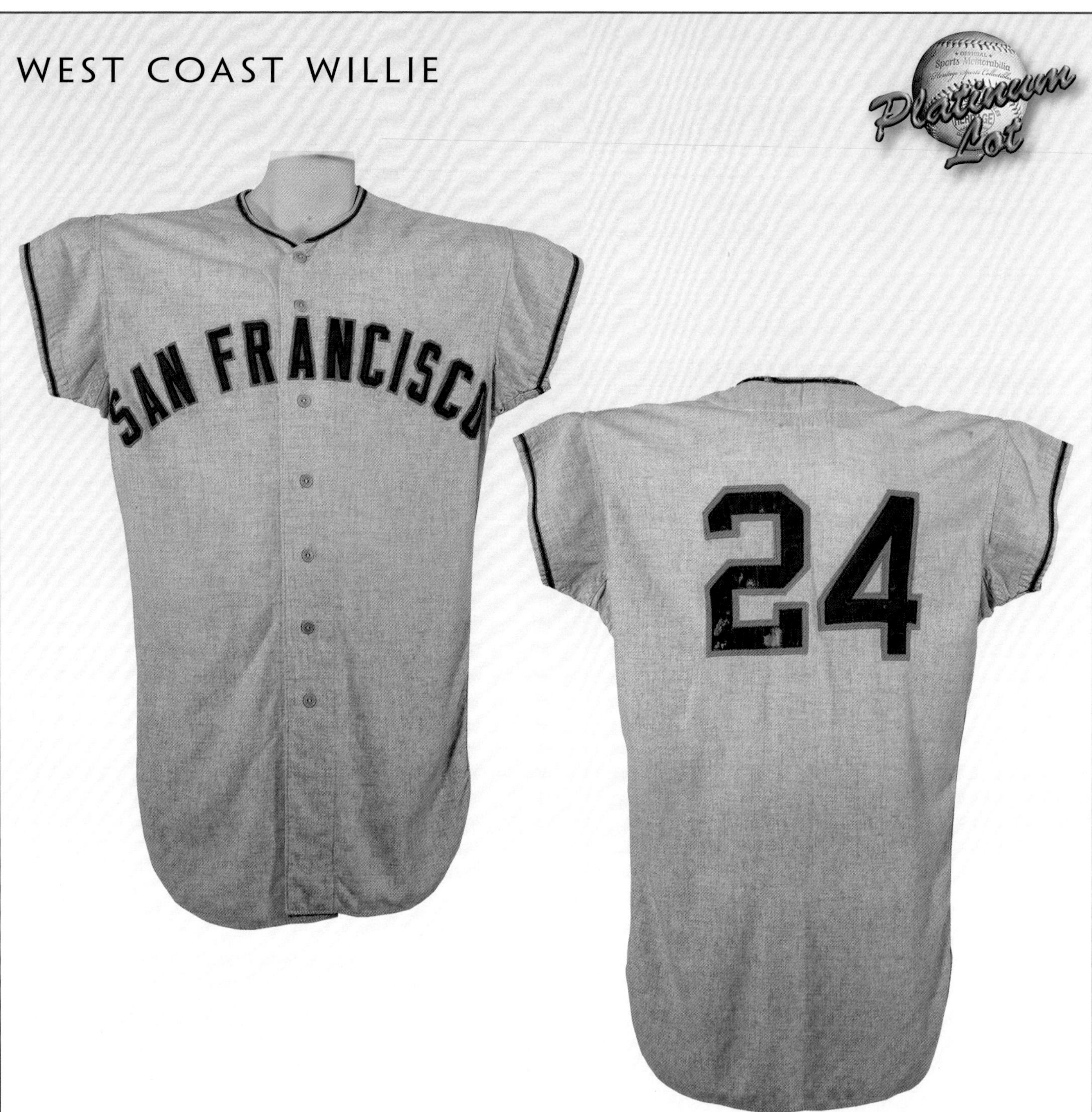

19669 **1958 Willie Mays Game Worn Jersey.** One of the most significant artifacts within this auction, both for the great stature of the player who once owned it and for the historic westward shift of the game that it heralded. This incredible grey flannel was the first roadster issued to the Giants' superstar center fielder after abandoning the Polo Grounds, announcing upon its chest a California town that had forever prior remained two thousand miles removed from the nearest Major League action. While it was a heartbreaking development for millions of Big Apple baseball fans who had suddenly seen their baseball options diminished by two-thirds, Mays thrived in the Pacific air, posting a career-best .347 batting average and leading the National League in stolen bases and runs scored.

Fine wear is evident from this key season in a career with no shortage thereof, with a team repair at the right shoulder and consistent softening of the tackle twill identifiers announcing "San Francisco" on the chest and "24" on verso. We must note here that the identifier on chest has been restored. A "MacGregor size 42" label appears within interior collar, with an artfully chainstitched "Mays" properly applied to a white felt swatch an inch and a half below. Left front interior tail houses the small but important flap tag proclaiming "Set 2 1958." A small amount of loss to the black and orange piping at the back of the collar and some bleaching of the rear numerals are mentioned for accuracy's sake and do not materially diminish the stunning visual or historic appeal. Post-war baseball collectibles don't get much more significant than this jersey, and we expect that the eventual winning bidder will give it the place of honor that it deserves within his trophy room. *LOA from Lou Lampson.*
Minimum Bid: $10,000

19670 **1963 St. Louis Cardinals Game Jersey.** The birds and bat logo that establishes St. Louis Cardinals jerseys as arguably the most beautiful of all Major League models first appeared in 1922 and continues on to this day, undergoing only the slightest of modifications over the past eight and a half decades. The gorgeous chenille design is in full effect here, applied to the silky soft grey flannel of this unused road jersey. The red and navy number "7" on both front and verso is a digit that didn't see action during this final season of Stan Musial's Major League career, hence no embroidered player attribution is to be found. A "Rawlings [size] 44" label appears in lower front tail, with a washing instructions label and "Set 1 1963" flap tag affixed to the interior tail. A rare Mint condition relic for the jersey style collector. *LOA from Lou Lampson.* Minimum Bid: $300

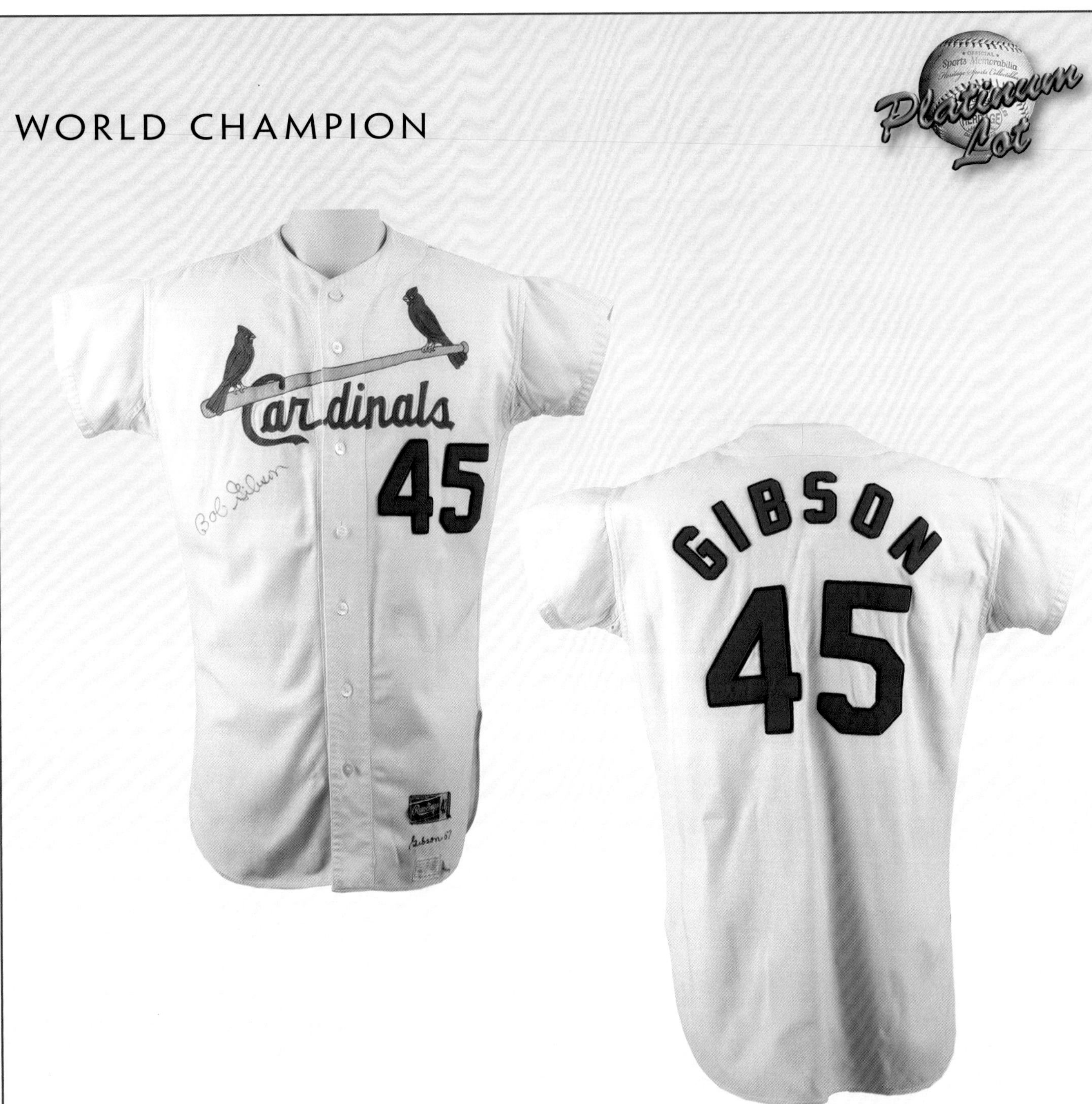

19671 **1967 Bob Gibson Game Worn Jersey.** One of the fiercest competitors in the game's long history, Gibson one explained "I've played a couple of hundred games of tic-tac-toe with my little daughter and she hasn't beaten me yet. I've always had to win. I've got to win." And win he did. While his career total of 251 is certainly impressive enough, perhaps even more so is his record of seven and two in World Series games, including three he notched the year he wore this incredible jersey, giving up just three runs in twenty-seven innings of work. Quite possibly this is the very jersey he wore for his Game Four shut-out performance against Carl Yastrzemski and his American League Championship Red Sox. A season's worth of wear is clearly evident in the creamy white flannel that composes the body of the shirt, which remains 100% original and unaltered right down to the buttons on the chest. The Cardinals' chenille bird and bat logo has retained its colorful look as have the two-color felt identifiers. The name on back is particularly critical as the majority of Cardinals' flannels had the names removed prior to the following spring training. This one has survived gloriously, and the steeply arched "Gibson" above the "45" on the verso is unaltered, original, and majestic. A "Rawlings [size] 42" label in the lower left front tail is accompanied by a washing instructions label with a "Set 1 1967" flap tag attached to its right vertical quadrant edge. In between is a chain link stitch in Cardinals red reading "Gibson 67." It is perfect in all respects, matching all 1967 and 1968 exemplars. The cherry on top comes in the form of a 10/10 black sharpie signature from Gibson on the chest. A simply unimprovable Hall of Fame home white flannel from a World Series MVP season. Can it get any better? *LOA from Lou Lampson.* Minimum Bid: $20,000

19672 **1968-69 Curt Flood Game Worn Uniform.** The superstar Cardinal's 1,861 hits, .293 lifetime average, three All-Star appearances, and seven Gold Gloves tell the story of an excellent major league player, but fails to address his even greater relevance in baseball history as an instrumental figure in overturning the Major Leagues' reserve clause. Though the Supreme Court voted against his case and it disrupted his career and changed his life, it was an important battle which provided the union strength and platform for its mid '70's victories which opened up the salary floodgates. Every current player should salute Curt Flood and also salute his '68/'69 uniform which is not only earth-shaking in its beauty, but pristine in its condition.

Unlike most cotton/wool blend flannels of the era, this one has just a slight cream hue to the white flannel. All seven buttons are original and the red bird and bat chenille stitched front logo retains its colorful brilliance. The same holds true for the original front and back 2-color felt numerals and the all important arched name on back.

Notorious for quick removal of NOB's at season's end, this Cardinals' gem retains its original "Flood" with spectacular arch and spacing. The front tail sports some of the most beautiful decorative highlights of any 1960's flannel. A "Rawlings [size] 38" label was apropos for the diminutive but powerful 5' 9", 165 pound centerfielder. The washing instructions label with "Set 1 1968" flap tag are straight stitched beneath, leaving ample space for a "Flood 68" chain link identifier which rates a "10" on the calligraphy scale. A bonus feature is the presence of an original MLB 100th anniversary patch on the left sleeve, indicating use or backup use during the 1969 campaign.

Taking the superlatives a step further is a matching pair of Flood's flannel pants with 1/4" red braid side piping. Again, the inner waistband provides the best in 1960's flannel tailoring and decoration. A "Rawlings [size] 30" label, washing instructions and "Set 1 1968" flap tag are affixed in tandem. Accompanying this tagging schema is a 6" felt swatch (fully intact) with red chain link identifiers "Flood 68 30 22 ins" signifying player's name, year, size, and inseam. Flood has autographed the jersey front in bold black sharpie.

The only blemish, if one can call it such, is a well faded, quarter-inch tall markered name "Somerfeld." Whether that was a "cup of coffee minor leaguer" or a recipient of the jersey is unknown. But for sure, the jersey never saw more than a day in the minors, the condition is superb and as an all original representation, ranks as a 10+. And lest we forget in all the flannel hoopla, it represents an extremely talented and important figure in baseball history, and is eminently displayable. *LOA from Lou Lampson.* Minimum Bid: $7,500

19673 **1969 Gil Hodges Game Worn Jacket.** Originally acquired directly from the family of the beloved Brooklyn Dodgers player and New York Mets manager, this blue wool jacket was on hand during that Amazin' Autumn when the Mets became Champions of the World. It is possible that this jacket had a few owners before Hodges, as these durable uniform pieces were typically handed down year after year, though authenticator Lou Lampson notes that the tagging style dates to the 1962-67 era, leaving open the strong chance that Hodges was issued the jacket as a player that first hopeless season at the Polo Grounds. The design is pure vintage Mets, with the orange chenille interlocking "NY" over the heart and the team logo patch on the left sleeve. "MacGregor [size] 48" label inside has vintage number "14" penned to its surface. Wear is very strong, again leading to the conclusion that the jacket saw multiple seasons of use. Lowermost snap is missing, but jacket is otherwise solid, complete and undamaged. Letter of provenance from noted uniform expert attests to Hodges family derivation. *LOA from Keith Vari. LOA from Lou Lampson.* Minimum Bid: $4,000

19674 **1976 Mike Schmidt Game Worn Jersey.** While this Hall of Fame slugger is understandably best remembered for his membership within the exclusive 500 Home Run Club, it does bear mention that the Philadelphia Phillies star would earn the first of ten Gold Gloves for his work at third base the season he suited up in this home white pinstriped gamer. Lovers of the long ball will likewise note that Schmidt's thirty-eight home runs and seventy-three extra base hits were likewise tops in the National League. The classic zipper-front style offers red tackle twill number "20" and logo "P" on the chest, with "Schmidt 20" properly placed on verso. The fantastic sleeve patches recall the nation's Bicentennial and National League Centennial at left and right respectively. Interior collar sports an embroidered "Schmidt" swatch, which matches the "76 2" placed in the tail below the "Wilson [size] 46" labeling. Marvelous wear throughout suggests a full season's use. Finally, a 10/10 blue sharpie autograph, tagged "500 HR" appears at upper right chest to round out the package. *LOA from Russek & Imperato. LOA from Lou Lampson. LOA from PSA/DNA (autograph). LOA from James Spence Authentication (autograph).* Minimum Bid: $1,000

19675 **1979 Steve Carlton Game Worn Jersey.** He's number eleven on the all-time victories list with 329, and number two for southpaws with only the great Warren Spahn above him. This home white pinstriped gamer dates from a season that saw Lefty add eighteen W's to his historic total, exhibiting fine pitcher's wear from that impressive campaign. His number "32" and Phillies logo "P" appear in red tackle twill upon the zippered chest, with "Carlton 32" balancing the design from the rear. A cloth swatch applied to the interior collar holds a black embroidered "Carlton," matching the "79 1" that appears in the lower left front tail below a "Wilson [size] 44" label. Applied just above is an unimprovable example of Carlton's blue sharpie signature, to which he has added a "HOF 94" notation to celebrate his Cooperstown enshrinement. *LOA from Russek & Imperato. LOA from Lou Lampson. LOA from PSA/DNA (autograph). LOA from James Spence Authentication (autograph).* **Minimum Bid: $1,000**

19676 **1983 Robin Yount Game Worn Jersey.** Home white pinstriped Milwaukee Brewers gamer dates from a season that saw the 1999 Hall of Fame inductee take the starting shortstop position at the All-Star Game, adding an RBI to the American League's winning score of thirteen to three. The pullover knit features a blue and yellow tackle twill "Brewers 19" on the chest, with number "19" repeated on verso. "Medalist Sand-Knit" exclusivity and size "40" tagging are affixed at front left tail, displaying a softness perfectly matching the fine wear on the jersey overall. A strip sewn to interior rear tail reads, "83 * Yount 40S." A picture-perfect Hall of Fame gamer from a man who joins the likes of Bart Starr and Brett Favre as one of Wisconsin's most favorite sporting sons. *LOA from Lou Lampson.* **Minimum Bid: $1,000**

19677 **1984 Pete Rose Game Worn Batting Practice Jersey.** Charlie Hustle's excursion north of the border lasted just ninety-five games, making any relics from that brief Montreal Royals tenure a tough commodity in the collecting world. Here we present his red knit pullover BP jersey, joined by a handwritten letter of provenance from the Hit King himself. The "Expos" name and logo appear over the heart, with number "14" applied in white and blue tackle twill to left sleeve and verso. "Wilson [size] 44" label resides inside collar. A 10/10 black sharpie signature from Rose decorates the front, which has a few small stains from his use. Use is appropriately light given the term and nature of service. *LOA from Pete Rose. LOA from Lou Lampson.* **Minimum Bid: $300**

19678 **Mid-1980's Ozzie Smith Game Worn Jersey.** Widely considered one of the greatest defensive infielders of all time, with thirteen consecutive Gold Gloves to prove it, the "Wizard of Oz" was a fixture of the St. Louis Cardinals line-up for a decade and a half. This road grey gamer dates from early in that lengthy tenure, sporting the number "1" on front and back that will never again grace a Cardinals uniform. The classic chenille birds and bat logo on chest is balanced on verso by a gently arching "O. Smith" across the shoulders at rear. For reasons unknown, the name was repositioned by the team at some point, leaving the outline of its former placement visible, though the fine, consistent wear and the "Game Worn" inscription added to Smith's 10/10 blue sharpie signature on the chest assure action upon his Hall of Fame frame. "Rawlings" label inside front left tail holds Smith's proper size "38" designation, but is missing the year tag, suggesting, along with the repositioning of the name, that the shirt was reconditioned for use as a back-up in a later season. Fine wear and regal parentage makes this a Cooperstown-quality collectible. *LOA from Lou Lampson. LOA from PSA/DNA (autograph). LOA from James Spence Authentication (autograph).* **Minimum Bid: $750**

19679 **1991 Barry Bonds Game Worn Jersey.** There are great Barry Bonds Giants gamers in the marketplace, and there are so-so versions. Bonds has even marketed them himself. For certain, there are many from his late-career era, perhaps too many. But there are precious few from his early career in Pittsburgh, and even fewer with solid wear and a unique differentiator. Offered here is one of the finest early career representations of baseball's new home run king, a 1991 home Pirates button down knit worn when Aaron's fabled record was still over six hundred homers in the distance. The six-button front sports the highly styled "Pirates" in black on yellow tackle twill. Bonds' number "24" appears in proper rounded block font on the jersey front and verso, with "Bonds" name on back affixed to an arched plate. The inner front tail sports a "Rawlings [size] 42" label with a "Set 2 1991" flap tag affixed to its right vertical quadrant edge. The Pirates' gold based team patch resides on the left sleeve, and the right sleeve sports the very rare "H" memorial patch in recognition of the late season passing of John Hallihan, the long-serving Pirates equipment manager affectionately known as "Hoolie." The overall wear is solid, and the presence of the "H" patch makes this early Pirates knit one of the most important Bonds extant. *LOA from Lou Lampson.* Minimum Bid: $5,000

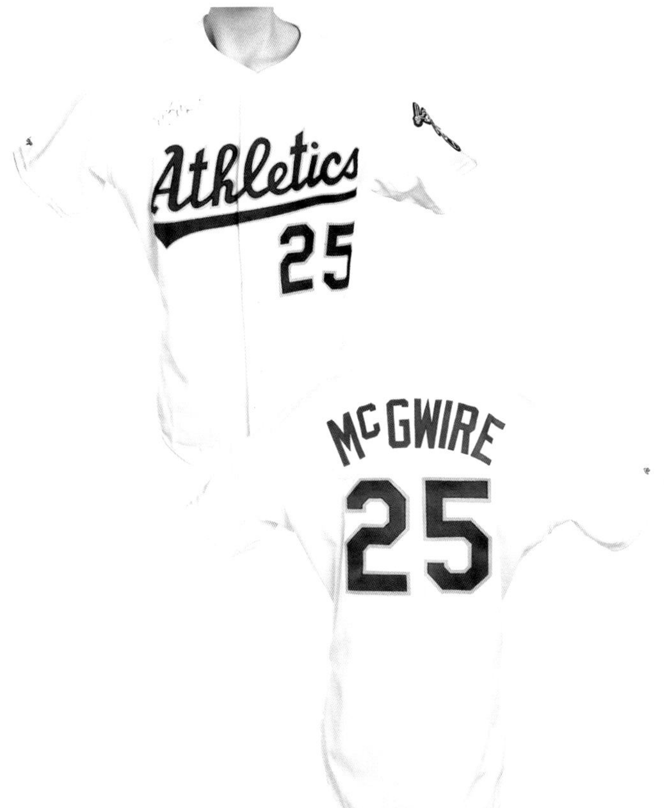

19680 **1991 Mark McGwire Game Worn Jersey.** A fifth consecutive All-Star season for the burly Bash Brother who would briefly reign as the single-season Home Run King during the final years of his career. This home white Oakland Athletics knit exhibits strong wear apparent in the yellowing sweat stains that are concentrated in the collar and armpit areas. "Athletics 25" is applied in green and yellow tackle twill to the chest, with "McGwire 25" on verso. Green logo elephant patch appears at left sleeve. Proper "Rawlings [size] 50" label is applied at inner front left tail, with "Set 1 1991" flap tag at lower right edge. A 9+/10 blue sharpie signature at upper right shoulder dates to the period, closing the book on a picture-perfect representation from this probable future Hall of Famer. *LOA from Lou Lampson. LOA from PSA/DNA (autograph). LOA from James Spence Authentication (autograph).* Minimum Bid: $600

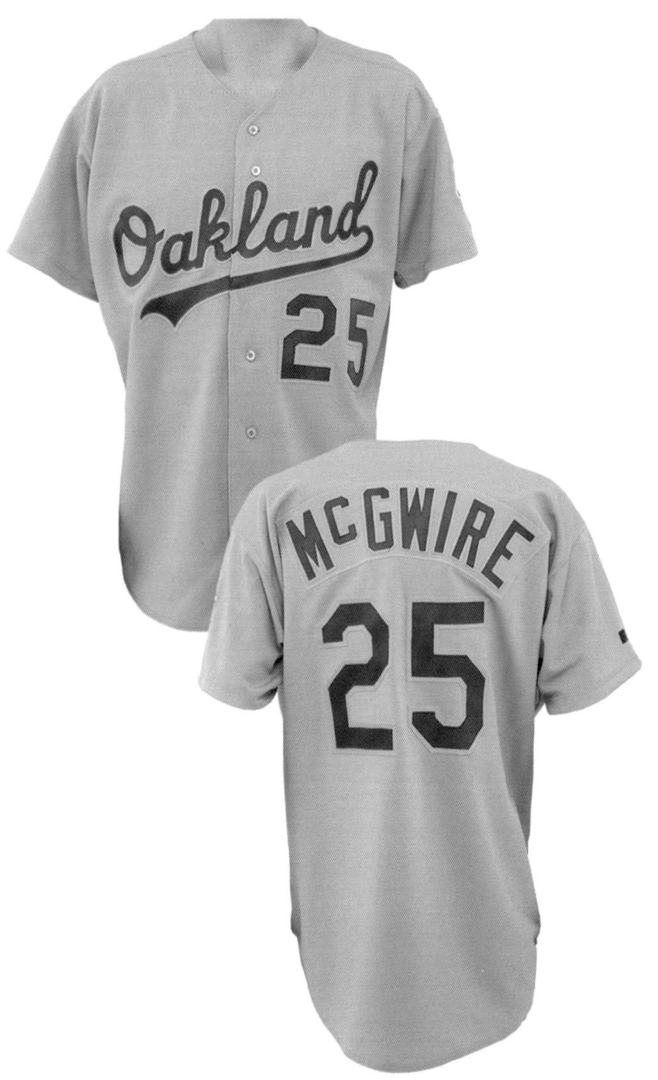

19681 **1994 Mark McGwire Game Worn Jersey.** Tough patch style makes this road grey Oakland A's jersey a hot commodity even without its superstar heritage. The elephant patch on the left sleeve saw just two seasons of action before its redesign, though the "Oakland 25" in green and yellow tackle twill should be instantly recognizable. "McGwire 25" appears on verso. Wear is clearly evident but understandably light for a strike season that saw Big Mac appear in just forty-seven games. "Russell Athletic Diamond Collection [size] 48" label in tail sprouts "100% Polyester" and "2" Extra Length" flap tags below. While the market for McGwire is admittedly not at its height at present, baseball history has shown that controversial superstars tend to emerge as the most collectible (and valuable) as the years pass, so the investment outlook on this jersey is strong. *LOA from Lou Lampson.* **Minimum Bid: $600**

19682 **1996 Mike Piazza Game Worn Jersey.** Widely considered the greatest offensive catcher in the game's long history, this sure-fire future Hall of Famer posted outrageous numbers the season he made use of this road grey knit, blasting thirty-six homers and 105 runs batted in, all while maintaining a .336 batting average, third best in the National League. Classic Bums styling is present throughout, with "Dodgers 31" appearing in patriotic tackle twill upon the chest, and "Piazza 31" filling the rear. A colorful patch applied to the left sleeve celebrates the thirty-fifth season at Dodger Stadium. The rear interior tail tagging centers around the "Russell Athletic Diamond Collection [size] 50" label, with "1996" year swatch above and flap tags denoting "2" Extra Length" and "1" Extra Sleeve Length" below. Light, consistent wear is evident throughout. With the understanding that all Piazza game material will surge when his induction is announced, smart investors are buying today. *LOA from Lou Lampson.* **Minimum Bid: $600**

19683 **Circa 1998 Ken Griffey, Jr. Game Worn Batting Practice Jersey.** Junior will almost certainly enter the elite 600 Home Run Club during the 2008 season, his twentieth in the Majors, bringing the membership to an even half dozen. His future Hall of Fame status assured, Griffey makes for an appealing investment for the collector with an eye on the market. This navy mesh pre-gamer shows nice wear, with a sparkling "Mariners" applied to the chest and "Griffey 24" appearing on verso, complete with a 9+/10 blue sharpie signature. Team logo patch is affixed to the left sleeve, and proper "Majestic Authentic Diamond Collection" labeling finds a home in the tail, with a size "48" flap tag below. Rounding out the package is a letter of authenticity signed by Griffey himself. *LOA from Ken Griffey, Jr. LOA from Lou Lampson. LOA from PSA/DNA (autograph). LOA from James Spence Authentication (autograph).* Minimum Bid: $600

19684 **Circa 1998 Alex Rodriguez Game Worn Batting Practice Jersey.** Navy mesh Seattle Mariners jersey shows fine pregame wear from this supremely talented three-time American League MVP, dating to the era that saw A-Rod enter the ultra-exclusive 40/40 club. Shimmering silver "Mariners" decorates the chest, with "Rodriguez 3" applied to verso. A 9/10 blue sharpie signature from the superstar infielder appears on verso as well. Team logo patch decorates the left sleeve. "Majestic Authentic Diamond Collection" label in tail holds a proper size "48" flap tag. A nice worn and signed jersey from what will almost assuredly be a first-ballot Hall of Fame career. *LOA from Lou Lampson. LOA from PSA/DNA (autograph). LOA from James Spence Authentication (autograph).* Minimum Bid: $600

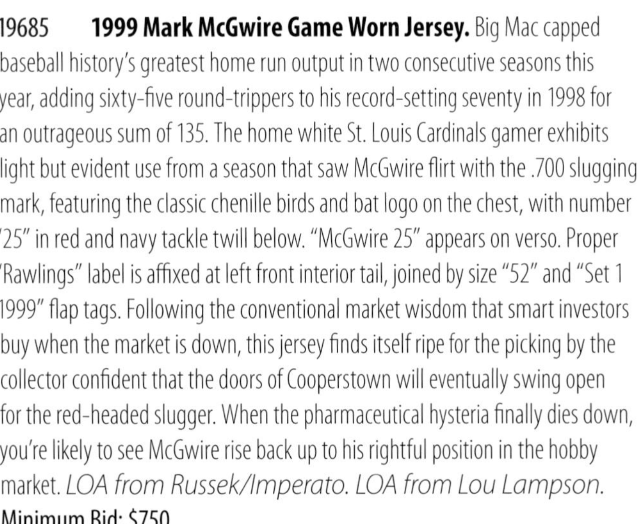

19685 **1999 Mark McGwire Game Worn Jersey.** Big Mac capped baseball history's greatest home run output in two consecutive seasons this year, adding sixty-five round-trippers to his record-setting seventy in 1998 for an outrageous sum of 135. The home white St. Louis Cardinals gamer exhibits light but evident use from a season that saw McGwire flirt with the .700 slugging mark, featuring the classic chenille birds and bat logo on the chest, with number "25" in red and navy tackle twill below. "McGwire 25" appears on verso. Proper "Rawlings" label is affixed at left front interior tail, joined by size "52" and "Set 1 1999" flap tags. Following the conventional market wisdom that smart investors buy when the market is down, this jersey finds itself ripe for the picking by the collector confident that the doors of Cooperstown will eventually swing open for the red-headed slugger. When the pharmaceutical hysteria finally dies down, you're likely to see McGwire rise back up to his rightful position in the hobby market. *LOA from Russek/Imperato. LOA from Lou Lampson.*
Minimum Bid: $750

19686 **2001 Barry Bonds Career Home Run #553 Game Worn Jersey.** Home white San Francisco Giants jersey is the very one worn by the controversial slugger as he deposited the first pitch of his seventh inning at bat against Arizona's Miguel Batista into McCovey Cove 420 feet from home plate. It would bring Bonds' season total to fifty-nine home runs, well en route to his record-setting seventy-three. As Bonds notes along with his black sharpie signature and home run total on the jersey's rear, the date was "9/4/01," just one week before the attacks that would change the course of American history forever. While Bonds' current status in our National Pastime is the source of heated debate, as are the legitimacy of his home run records, one could be reasonably assured that Bonds' 2001 home run jerseys will one day be viewed much like artifacts from the 1919 White Sox due to the tremendous relevance, positive or negative, within the game's history. And, of course, the jersey's proximity in action to September 11, 2001 will likewise assure its future value.

The massive off-white knit gamer sports the Old English "Giants" in tri-color tackle twill across the chest, and Bonds' number "25" on verso. Team logo patch is affixed at left sleeve. "Russell Athletic Authentic Collection" label is straight-stitch affixed at lower left front tail, with Bonds' personal marketing company patch sewn just below. Wear is definite, but understandably light for a season that saw Bonds changing uniforms often for marketing purposes. Included is Bonds' authentication certificate, autographed in his hand. *LOA from Lou Lampson. LOA from PSA/DNA (autograph). LOA from James Spence Authentication (autograph). COA from Barry Bonds.*
Minimum Bid: $2,000

19687 **2001 Albert Pujols Game Worn Rookie Home "Flag" Jersey.** Don't tell Ted Williams, but there has been talk that this devastating Dominican slugger might just be the greatest hitter that ever lived. Now, it may be a bit too early to make such a pronouncement, but if he is one day remembered as such you'll wish you had purchased this rookie gamer when you had a chance. Pujols absolutely ran away with the Rookie of the Year voting the year he made use of this home white jersey, claiming all thirty-two first place votes for the landslide victory. The front of the jersey presents the classic chenille birds and bat logo and the tackle twill number "5" below. Verso reads, "Pujols 5." Interior tail tagging features a "Rawlings Authentic Collection" label with size "48" and "Set 1 2001" flap tags affixed. The American flag patch at rear collar honors the lives lost in the terror attacks of September 11, further establishing the tremendous significance of this rookie gamer. Wear is light but evident, with no alterations of any kind. Grade A5. *LOA from Dave Bushing. LOA from Lou Lampson.* Minimum Bid: $1,500

JOE'S LAST JOLT

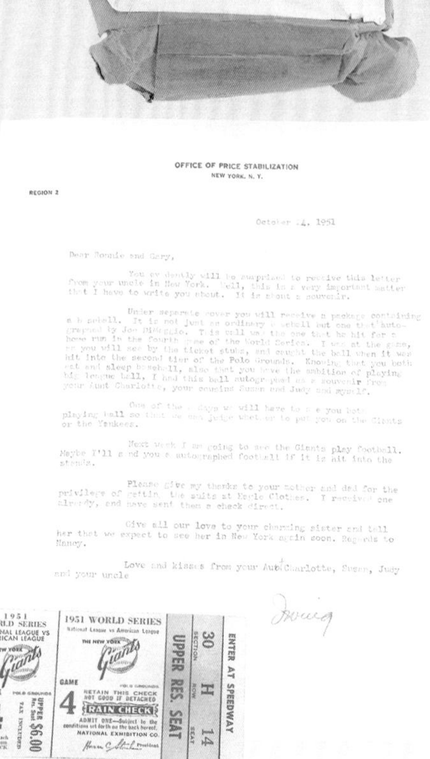

OFFICE OF PRICE STABILIZATION
NEW YORK, N. Y.

REGION 2

October [illegible], 1951

Dear Ronnie and Gary,

You evidently will be surprised to receive this letter from your uncle in New York. Well, this is a very important matter that I have to write you about. It is about a souvenir.

Under separate cover you will receive a package containing a baseball. It is not just an ordinary baseball but one that autographed by Joe DiMaggio. This ball was the one that he hit for a home run in the fourth game of the World Series. I was at the game, as you will see by the ticket stubs, and caught the ball when it was hit into the second tier of the Polo Grounds. Knowing that you both eat and sleep baseball, also that you have the ambition of playing big league ball, I had this ball autographed as a souvenir from your Aunt Charlotte, your cousins Susan and Judy and myself.

One of these days we will have to see you both playing ball so that we can judge whether to put you on the Giants or the Yankees.

Next week I am going to see the Giants play football. Maybe I'll send you an autographed football if it is hit into the stands.

Please give my thanks to your mother and dad for the privilege of getting the suits at Eagle Clothes. I received one already, and have sent them a check direct.

Give all our love to your charming sister and tell her that we expect to see her in New York again soon. Regards to Nancy.

Love and kisses from your Aunt Charlotte, Susan, Judy and your uncle

Irving

19688 **Joe DiMaggio's Final Home Run Baseball, Hit in Game Four of 1951 World Series.** The sweetest swing in baseball history was responsible for 369 home runs in Big League competition, with 361 coming during the regular season and the balance of eight dating to the Fall Classic. Here we present what is arguably the most significant of them all, the ball that recorded the 369th and final round-tripper for the man they called the Yankee Clipper. Just across the Harlem River from the stadium that he consecrated with thirteen seasons of Hall of Fame service, DiMaggio launched this ONL (Frick) delivered by pitcher Sal Maglie into deep left field to open up a four to one lead and move one step closer to ending the 1951 Giants' fairy tale story punctuated by Bobby Thomson's "Shot" on the same Polo Grounds field five days earlier.

Historic home run artifacts continue to capture the imagination of the collecting world unlike any other baseball collectibles, with Mark McGwire's 1998 record-setting ball and Babe Ruth's first Yankee Stadium home run bat the only two non-card lots to top one million dollars at auction. Surely it goes without saying that the final home run baseball from one of the most iconic figures in American sports carries tremendous historical import. The connection to this unforgettable Subway Series, which brought Big Apple legends DiMaggio, Mickey Mantle and Willie Mays together in combat for the only time, is just the icing on the cake.

Ironclad provenance is delivered in several forms. First, we have a typed, signed letter dated October 24, 1951 from the gentleman who caught the baseball to his nephews, making note of the gift. He writes, in part, "Under separate cover you will receive a package containing a baseball. It is not just an ordinary baseball but one that is autographed by Joe DiMaggio. This ball was the one that he hit for a home run in the fourth game of the World Series. I was at the game, as you will see by the ticket stubs, and caught the ball when it was hit into the second tier of the Polo Grounds..." And, sure enough, still keeping company with the letter and the baseball is a pair of adjacent ticket stubs in the "Upper Res. Seat" section of the fabled Manhattan ballpark. Amazingly, even the original packaging that delivered the baseball from lucky fan Irving Stein to his nephews in North Dakota has survived within this collection.

We must note that the autograph to which Mr. Stein refers is unfortunately not that of DiMaggio himself, but rather of a clubhouse worker ghost signing for the future Hall of Famer. This was quite common at the time, and seasoned autograph collectors are well aware that many Yankee team balls of the era bear a secretarial DiMaggio. Top autograph authenticator James Spence does confirm, however, that the "October 1951, To Ronnie & Gary, Joe DiMaggio" inscription is applied in vintage ink, and is no modern contrivance. While a genuine DiMaggio signature would be ideal, the clubhouse version does not in any way detract from the stature of this horse-hide sphere in the book of baseball history. A fundamentally important artifact of our national game, worthy of placement within the finest of private collections. *LOA from James Spence Authentication.* **Minimum Bid: $5,000**

19689 **1966 Mickey Mantle Career Home Run #485 Baseball.** The included letter of provenance tells the story better than we could, so we transcribe it here:

"During the years from 1964 to 1966, I was the batboy for the old Washington Senators Baseball Club. Fortunately, I saved a few souvenirs during that time. On July 1, 1966, the New York Yankees were in town (D.C. Stadium, later became R.F.K. Stadium) playing a series with the Senators. Phil Ortega pitched for Washington on that day. During the game, Mickey Mantle hit a home run (Home run #485) off Ortega that hit the mezzanine and bounced back onto the playing field. The left fielder threw the ball to the Yankee dugout. The Yankee batboy threw the ball to me in our dugout (home teams supplied the game balls). I put the ball in my back pocket.

After the ball game, I asked Phil Ortega if he wanted the baseball. Ortega had no interest in keeping the ball, so I asked him if he would get Mantle to sign the ball for me (growing frustrated of signing autographs later in his career, it was increasingly difficult to get Mantle to sign, except for fellow ballplayers). Ortega asked me what I wanted Mantle to sign on the ball. I asked for him to sign, "To Al, Best Wishes, Mickey Mantle." Phil Ortega sent the baseball to the Yankee clubhouse for the autograph. Either Mantle or the messenger became confused. The ball was sent back to me signed, *"To Phil, Best Wishes, and thanks for throwing this one easy, Mickey Mantle."* I decided to keep the baseball anyway, because it had Mickey Mantle's signature on it.

Now over forty years later, the OAL (Cronin) baseball that the great Mickey Mantle sent on its wild ride still presents exactly as described, its toned hide carrying the clever inscription at a boldness of 7/10. As one of just a handful of Mantle home run balls ever to reach the auction block,this offering presents the advanced collector with a rare opportunity to bring a Cooperstown-quality artifact into his personal portfolio. *LOA from PSA/DNA (autograph). LOA from James Spence Authentication (autograph).* **Minimum Bid: $4,000**

19690 **1973 Willie Mays Career Home Run #656 Baseball.** Back in the Big Apple after a decade and a half on the West Coast, the greatest slugging talent of his age was able to supply his former hometown with the last of his home run heroics. Presented is the ONL (Feeney) ball that Mays launched for hsi 656th round tripper, supporting a ten to two victory at Shea over the San Diego Padres. The well-worn sphere, clearly showing the bruise of its historic bludgeoning on a side panel, was retrieved and supplied to Mays for an autograph, which appears on the sweet spot in black felt tip that has mellowed to an 8+/10 shade of brown. The same pen was used to neatly notate the ball's wild ride into the record books, reading, "Willie Mays' 656th Home Run, 6-16-73" on the northern panel, and "At: New York, Pitcher: Randy Jones" to the south. Game used baseball collectors are well aware that post-500 home run balls are very scarce, and post-600 examples are all but non-existent in the hobby. And Mets fans will fondly recall the 1973 season for its National League Championship victory as well, adding the last little bit of appeal to a ball with no shortage thereof. *LOA from PSA/DNA (autograph). LOA from James Spence Authentication (autograph).* **Minimum Bid: $2,000**

19691 **1977 Willie McCovey Career #470 Home Run Baseball.** The man whose proficiency with directing home runs over the right field wall at Candlestick earned him naming rights of AT&T Park's "McCovey Cove" recorded his 470th round-tripper when his Louisville Slugger met with this ONL (Feeney) ball. It derives from the collection of San Francisco Giants catcher Mike Sadek (1973-81), who was able to grab the sphere when it bounded into the bullpen where Sadek was at work. Sadek's bold markered "#470" appears opposite the panel he notated "5-1-77, Willie McCovey's 470th Homerun vs. Larry Christiansen & Phillies." A third panel holds the slugger's inscription, "To my Friend Mike, Best Wishes, Willie McCovey." The inscription projects at a strength of 7/10, and the ball shows fine use from its historic flight. Included is a signed letter of provenance from Sadek. Home run balls from members of the 500 Club are highly desirable, and the fine provenance of this example makes it particularly appealing. *LOA from PSA/DNA (autograph). LOA from James Spence Authentication (autograph).* **Minimum Bid: $1,000**

19692 **1987 Mike Schmidt Career Home Run #523 Baseball.** Magnificent provenance and historical importance make this offering a very attractive commodity to lovers of the long ball. The ONL (Giamatti) ball comes to us from a long-serving bat boy for the Philadelphia Phillies club, to whom Schmidt inscribed the sphere, "Bruce, Fond Memories at Dodger Stadium, #523, 8/31/87." His 10/10 autograph fills the adjacent side panel. The ball exhibits nice use from its flight into baseball's record books, with number "523" inked on another side panel to mark the ball immediately after it settled beyond the outfield wall at Chavez Ravine. Included in the lot is a photo of Schmidt and our consignor in their Phillies uniforms back in '87, and another of our consignor holding the ball shortly before delivering it to Heritage for auction. Post-500 home run baseballs are always highly sought after by the collecting world, particularly from those who labored prior to the pharmaceutical era. We expect great bidding interest for this special piece. *LOA from PSA/DNA (autograph). LOA from James Spence Authentication (autograph).* **Minimum Bid: $1,000**

19693 **1998 Alex Rodriguez Season Home Run #20 Baseball.** Historic long ball was number twenty of a forty-two total for the 1998 season, a year during which the speedy slugger would also record forty-six steals to become just the third player to enter the exclusive 40/40 Club. The OAL (Budig) ball, which likewise stands as A-Rod's eighty-sixth career homer, is signed in 10/10 blue ink upon the sweet spot and notated in his hand, "HR #20, 1998." Fine use is clearly evident. Even Barry Bonds himself believes that this supremely talented star will one day be crowned Career Home Run King, at which point any of his home run balls will surge in value dramatically. Investors take note. *LOA from PSA/DNA (autograph). LOA from James Spence Authentication (autograph).* **Minimum Bid: $750**

19694 **2007 World Series Game One Dustin Pedroia Home Run Baseball.** The defining moment of Pedroia's 2007 American League Rookie of the Year season came just two pitches into that year's Fall Classic, as he took Colorado Rockies ace Jeff Francis deep over Fenway Park's fabled Green Monster, only the second time in history that the first batter in a World Series has homered. Presented here is that very baseball that set the dominant tone for the 2007 Series, which the Sox led for all but four of the thirty-six innings it took to secure its second World Championship in four seasons. The Official World Series baseball is nicely rubbed up for its brief, dramatic service to Red Sox history, with the golden stamping seeming particularly appropriate in this context. Pedroia's 10/10 black felt tip signature adorns the sweet spot, and his notation "Laser show," a reference to an earlier boast about his slugging abilities that made the newspaper rounds, stretching across the eastern side panel. The airtight provenance comes in the form of an Official Major League Baseball holographic authenticating sticker with the serial number "BB 680452." This number can be referenced at the www.MLB.com website by choosing "MLB Authentication" from the drop-down menu entitled "Auction" at the top banner of the homepage. As fitting a symbol as any for the Sox' transformation from heartbreak kids to heavyweight champs, this baseball will surely cause quite a stir among the Fenway faithful. We'll see who's the biggest Red Sox fan of all when the hammer falls on this lot. *MLB Authentication sticker. LOA from PSA/DNA (autograph). LOA from James Spence Authentication (autograph).* **Minimum Bid: $1,500**

19695 **1922-25 Babe Ruth Game Used Bat.** There's nothing quite like the thrill of holding a Babe Ruth bat in one's hands, and this is a scarce early example dating to the era of the New York Yankees' first World Championship season. The signature model Hillerich & Bradsby exhibits excellent use with a professionally repaired handle crack, suggesting that the Babe may have launched a few into the cheap seats with this historic lumber. Several ball marks are visible on the right and left barrel, with the latter showing evidence of spike marks as well. Though Ruth typically utilized bats measuring thirty-five or thirty-six inches in length, he is quoted in an article on batting that he did sometimes use shorter bats as well. At a length of thirty-four inches and weight of thirty-seven ounces, this specimen certainly falls within the acceptable range. With examples matching Ruth's most commonly used attributes routinely approaching and surpassing the $100,000 mark at auction, this specimen boasting slightly more modest dimensions becomes all the more attractive. A key artifact from the beginning of the New York Yankees reign as baseball's most noteworthy franchise. Graded GU5. *LOA from Taube & Malta.* Minimum Bid: $7,500

19696 **1928-30 Honus Wagner Game Used Coach's Bat.** Hillerich & Bradsby labeling dates this important lumber to the Old Dutchman's mid-fifties, a decade after he hung up his Hall of Fame spikes. Of course it's well documented that Wagner lent his skills to the coaching profession following the close of his playing career, and this signature model gamer exhibits heavy use from that period. The authenticating paperwork makes note of "heavy use with a handle crack and four and a half inch piece missing and severe checking (grain separation) on the back barrel." It also notes four vintage nails used to repair the barrel, and missing wood on the knob and barrel end. Despite these imperfections, the fact remains that this bat did see action in the hands of one of the game's most noteworthy figures, and as such it offers a rare chance to possess a genuine Wagner bat at a price significantly below that which one of the few playing-days models would command. Graded GU2. *LOA from Taube & Malta.* Minimum Bid: $1,000

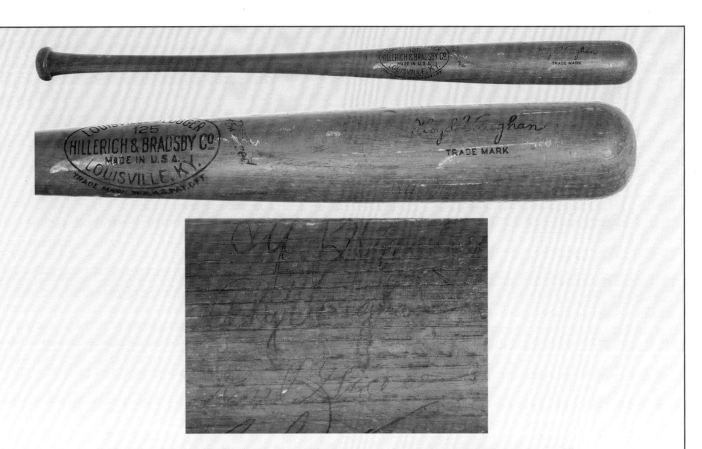

19697 **1935 Arky Vaughan Game Used Bat Signed by Pittsburgh Pirates Team.** Exceedingly scarce signature model Hillerich & Bradsby dates to the most productive offensive season in the career of this Hall of Fame shortstop, one in which he posted National League-leading numbers in batting average (.385), slugging percentage (.607), and runs created (147). While the details of the Hillerich & Bradsby center trademark date the model to the 1934 or 1937 labeling period, the thrilling addition of eight bold black ink signatures (average 8+/10) allow us to peg the bat's use to the 1935 season. Joining the autograph of Arky himself are both Paul and Lloyd Waner, Jensen, Blanton, Grace, Herman and Suhr. As Babe Herman's service to the Pirates franchise was limited to just twenty-six games of the 1935 season, the evidence linking this bat to the 1935 campaign is airtight. The bat shows evidence of outstanding use, with an area of punished wood presenting ball marks and grain separation just below Vaughan's facsimile signature in accordance with his left-handed swing. A cracked handle ended the bat's long service to the Buccaneer cause. A small amount of paint upon the bat's surface must be noted in the interest of full disclosure, though this is of no real concern. Length and weight are thirty-five inches and thirty-four and a half ounces respectively. The bat comes to us directly from Vaughan's cousin, who was just two years old when Arky tragically lost his life at age forty in a fishing boat accident. She still lives in the state that gave Floyd his distinctive nickname, and supplies a letter of provenance to accompany this marvelous offering. It has been reported that fewer than ten Vaughan game used bats are known to the hobby, and surely this must be the only autographed example. An elite piece as worthy of a place in Cooperstown as Arky himself. Graded GU8. *LOA from Taube & Malta. LOA from PSA/DNA (autographs). LOA from James Spence Authentication (autographs).* Minimum Bid: $4,000

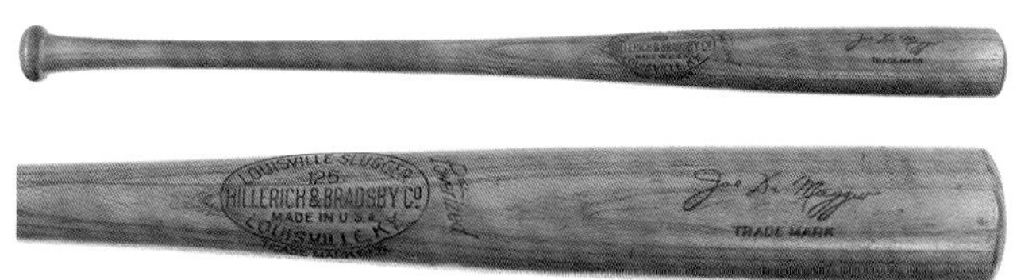

19698 **1939-43 Joe DiMaggio Game Issued Bat.** Identical in style to the bat used during DiMaggio's famed 1941 streak that sold in 2004 for just over $300,000, the offered example will not cause the winning bidder to open his pocketbook quite so wide. The signature model Hillerich & Bradsby was unquestionably created for use by the Yankee Clipper, but never made it into his capable hands, remaining unblemished by the impact of horsehide. We must also note that, for reasons unknown, the top seven-eighths of an inch have been trimmed from the barrel end, shedding about an ounce of weight from the proper thirty-five in the process. There is still much to love, however, particularly the chance for mere collecting mortals to own true DiMaggio lumber. Graded GU4. *LOA from Taube & Malta.* Minimum Bid: $750

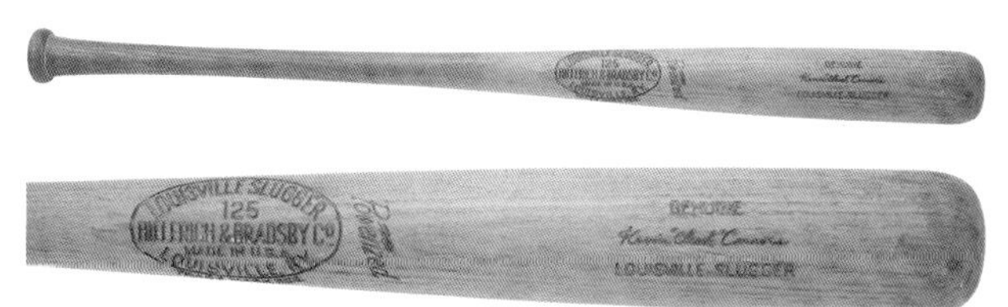

19699 **1949 Kevin "Chuck" Connors Game Used Bat.** Though better remembered to history as television's "The Rifleman," Connors was also an athletic Renaissance man of sorts, providing brief service to the Boston Celtics of the Basketball Association of America, and to the Brooklyn Dodgers and Chicago Cubs of Major League Baseball. Here we offer what may well be the only bat dating to Connors' days as a Bum, as the Hillerich & Bradsby labelling period for this signature model O16 was only utilized in 1948 and 1949. Could this be the bat wielded during Connors' single game as a Dodger, during his only at-bat? We can't state that with certainty, though the excellent use and slight grain separation on the back of the barrel suggests Connors at least took a good bit of batting practice with this exciting artifact. Leading bat authentication John Taube notes strong ball marks and a scored handle as well. No cracks. Length and weight are thirty-five inches and thirty-two ounces respectively. The bat derives from the collection of a gentleman close to the Dodgers organization which also provided this auction with the fine Gilliam rookie lumber. Possibly the scarcest bat that will reach the auction block in 2008. Graded GU7. *LOA from Taube & Malta.* Minimum Bid: $1,000

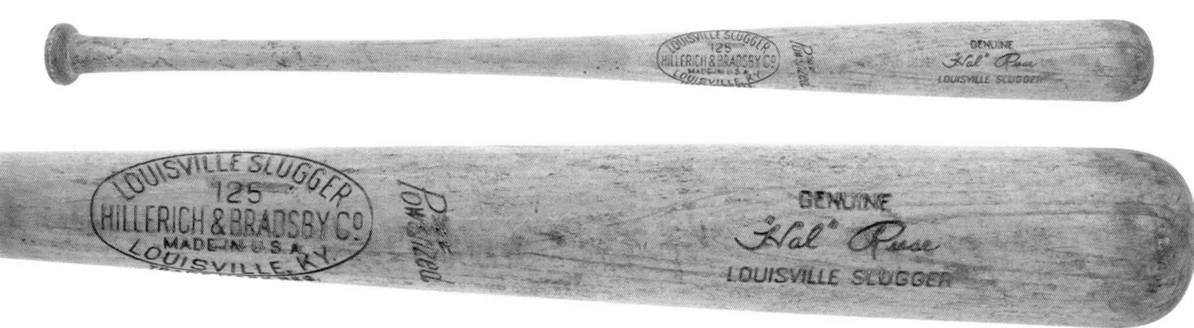

19700 **1949 Pee Wee Reese Game Used Bat from Phil Rizzuto Collection.** Six times these diminutive Hall of Fame shortstops faced off in baseball's greatest contest, developing a mutual respect and friendship through the course of these Big Apple civil wars. Here we present a gift made to the iconic Yankee by the beloved Bum, a piece that provides the finest provenance imaginable through its dual parentage of greats. The signature model Hillerich & Bradsby center brand markings denote a production period of 1943 to 1949, but factory records show that Reese first ordered this M117 model in 1949, allowing us to narrow its usage to that single season. With career-best totals posted by Reese in both hits (172) and homers (16), and National League Championship pedigree besides, 1949 would rank among the most desirable vintages for a Pee Wee gamer. Dave Bushing characterizes the use as "Significant," noting heavy ball marks and deeply imbedded stitch marks. Some dead wood on the barrel further attests to the fine use at Ebbets and beyond. Length and weight of thirty-four inches and thirty ounces are both proper for Reese's ordering records. The physical attributes and spectacular provenance of this lumber rates it easily among the most desirable Reese gamers in the hobby, suitable only for the finest of private collections. Graded A9.5. Letter of provenance from Rizzuto's widow Cora is included. *LOA from Dave Bushing.* Minimum Bid: $2,500

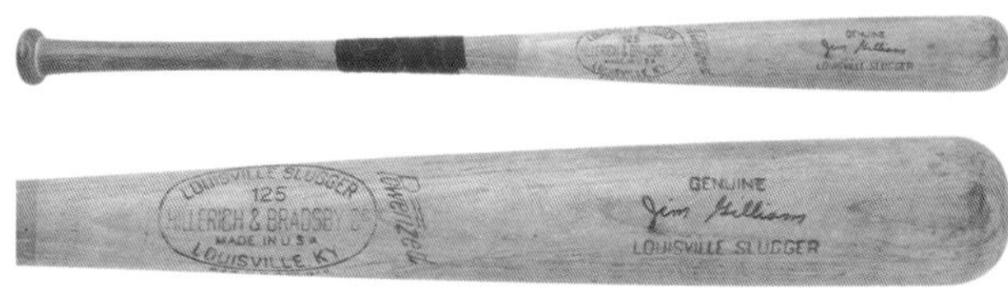

19701 **1953 Jim "Junior" Gilliam Game Used Rookie Bat.** With the Hillerich & Bradsby labelling period of 1950 to 1953 in evidence, we are able to definitively date this historic lumber to the Brooklyn Dodgers youngster's fantastic 1953 Rookie of the Year campaign, easily establishing this offering as the most desirable Gilliam bat to surface in recent memory. Appropriately honored by the Dodgers in 1978 with the retirement of his number "19" jersey, Junior was the Bums' lead-off hitter for most of the 1950's, and one of the club's leading run scorers, reaching home over one hundred times during each of his first four seasons. This signature model H&B 117 exhibits "outstanding" use according to bat expert John Taube, who notes ball marks on left, right and back barrel as is appropriate for Gilliam's switch-hitting style. Red and green bat rack streaks appear on the barrel, and the handle and left and right barrel have been scored. The upper handle has been taped to repair the crack that ended the bat's long service to this National League Championship season. Length: thirty-four and a half inches. Weight: Thirty-two and a half ounces. Graded GU7. This bat is presented for the first time to the collecting community, deriving from the same personal collection of a Dodgers insider that provides the Chuck Connors bat also found within this auction. *LOA from Taube & Malta.* **Minimum Bid: $750**

19702 **1956 Mickey Mantle Game Bat Signed by the Kansas City Athletics.** The Mick called it his "Favorite Summer," and clearly 1956 represented the legend at the height of his greatness, as the season's end saw not only another World Championship for the Yanks, but the Triple Crown placed upon his blonde head. Here we present a bat ordered by the Yanks for Mickey's use, though adorned by the autographs of approximately twenty-five Kansas City A's before it could participate in Mantle's outrageous 1956 campaign. A letter of provenance from the daughter of A's manager Harry Craft reads in part, "The 1956 team was especially dear to my dad. Although the A's decal is embedded into the bat along with the genuine autographs of team members, the actual bat belonged to Mickey Mantle. The bat was a gift to Daddy. Daddy was Mick's first-ever manager in 1949. The two were close friends right up until the day Daddy died." The unused Mickey Mantle signature model Hillerich & Bradsby K55 could not present more perfectly, with average signature quality a stunning 10/10. Notables include Craft, Boudreau, Boyer, Lopez, Melillo, Shantz and Ditmar. A rather charming Athletics decal is affixed to the upper handle, where the year "1956" is artfully penned. Bat is thirty-four inches and thirty-five ounces respectively. LOA from Dave Bushing A5. *LOA from Taube & Malta.* **Minimum Bid: $3,000**

19703 **1956 Roger Maris Game Used Pre-Rookie Bat.** Presented for your consideration is almost certainly the earliest Roger Maris game used bat ever to reach the auction block. Louisville Slugger factory records show that Maris' orders for this block lettered style of Hillerich & Bradsby O16 in the Spring of 1956, before moving on to signature models for his Major League career beginning in the Spring of 1957. The thirty-five inches of length and thirty-five ounces of weight perfectly match the records for this era, as does the round knob style and standard finish. Expert John Taube notes the omission of the "Powerized" markings to the right of the trademark, but states in his letter that he believes this to be "a factory error, which does not affect the authenticity of the bat." Fellow bat expert Dave Bushing choose the adjective "Significant" to describe use, pointing to heavy ball marks and deeply embedded stitch marks, as well as a fourteen-inch crack in the handle that ended the bat's service to the future single season Home Run King. For those collectors who wish to stand apart from the rest, this historic lumber is calling your name. Graded PSA GU6. *LOA from Dave Bushing A7. LOA from Taube & Malta.* **Minimum Bid: $1,000**

19704 **1958 Ted Williams Game Used Bat.** "I hope somebody hits .400 soon," the famously irritable Williams once said. "Then people can start pestering that guy with questions about the last guy to hit .400." Well, the Kid didn't live to see that day, nor should any of us expect to see it either. The tool of Williams' artistry is presented here for the collector concentrating on the hobby's most fundamental pieces, a signature model Hillerich & Bradsby O1 ordered by the Boston Red Sox in the late years of its star slugger's career. Williams favored the O1 model between 1940 and 1947, and the length and weight of thirty-five inches and thirty-three and a half ounces match his preferred specifications, though we cannot state definitively, due to lack of provenance and identifiable player use characteristics, that the bat was indeed used by Williams himself. Outstanding use is evident, however, with many ball marks and stitch impressions on right, left and back barrel, along with spike marks at the front barrel. Graded GU5. *LOA from Taube & Malta.* **Minimum Bid: $500**

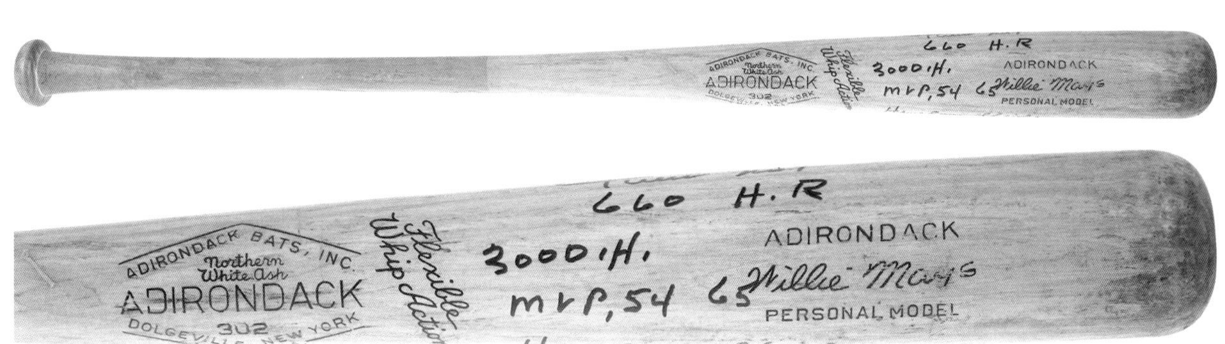

19705 **1958-60 Willie Mays Game Used Bat.** One of just four players in Major League history with keys to both the 3,000 Hit and 500 Home Run clubhouses, Willie Mays also brought one of the game's best gloves to the outfield, putting him high on the short list of greatest ballplayers ever. Here we present a tool from the offensive half of that equation, exhibiting moderate use from a period that saw him posting Top Ten figures in every significant batting category. The Adirondack 63A matches Mays' factory ordering records in its model number and specifications of thirty-five inches and thirty-three ounces, favored during this tremendously productive time in his Hall of Fame career. Several ball marks and stitch impressions are visible on the right and back barrel, as well as a streaking of red and green bat rack marks. The handle is lightly scored to improve grip. A handle crack (repaired) ended a long, productive life in the hands of a legend, beginning a second incarnation as a top-shelf collectible. A lengthy inscription upon the barrel furthers the tremendous appeal, with 10/10 blue sharpie spelling, "Best Wishes, Willie Mays. 660 H.R., 3000 H, MVP 54 65, Home Run Champ #24." Mays' number "24" appears in marker on the knob, though our authenticators believe this was applied after Mays' retirement. Graded GU6.5. *LOA from Taube & Malta. LOA from PSA/DNA (autograph).* **Minimum Bid: $3,000**

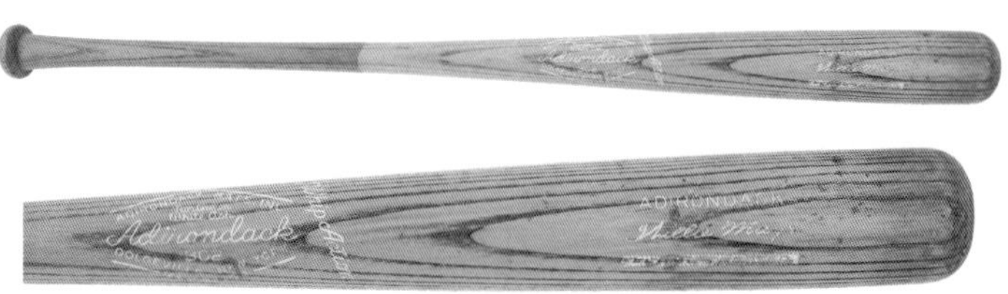

19706 **1961-63 Eddie Mathews Game Used Bat.** One of the most beloved Braves in team history, Mathews represented the club in three different cities, providing the team with 493 of his career's 512 home runs. The tremendous use evident in the abused grain of this signature model Hillerich & Bradsby S2 suggests that several of those long balls were delivered from its surface before a crack in the handle ended its long tenure in Eddie's Hall of Fame hands. Many ball and stitch impressions are visible upon the right, left and back barrel, and the ghost of spiral grip tape, since removed, can been seen on the handle. A small degree of chipping at the end of the barrel causes no concern. Number "41" appears in vintage marker on knob. Length and weight are thirty-five inches and thirty-two ounces respectively. A 9+/10 blue sharpie signature on the barrel is bolstered by a "512 HRs" notation in Mathews' hand. A solid example of a tough Hall of Fame bat, graded GU6.5. *LOA from Taube & Malta (bat). LOA from PSA/DNA (autograph). LOA from James Spence Authentication (autograph).* **Minimum Bid: $750**

19707 **1961-63 Willie Mays Game Used Bat.** A glorious job perk for one young St. Louis Cardinals bat boy, who compiled an impressive collection of gamers from visitors to Sportsman's Park during his early 1960's years of service. Here we present the jewel of that collection, an Adirondack M63 that exhibits phenomenal use from one of the greatest sluggers in Major League history. Heavy ball and stitch marks coat a barrel swollen from many games of punishment. A small amount of dead wood on the back barrel is likewise the result of this hard-hitting use, and does not affect the display in the slightest. The historic hardwood clocks in at thirty-four ounces and thirty-five inches, each proper for Mays' preferred specifications. His number "24" appears in vintage marker on the knob. A photocopied letter of provenance from the bat boy adds a point to the perfect base grades for model specs and use, with a half-point deduction for dead wood resulting in a grand total grade of A8.5. A top-tier artifact from an era that saw Mays average forty-two homers and 122 runs batted in annually. *LOA from Dave Bushing.* **Minimum Bid: $2,500**

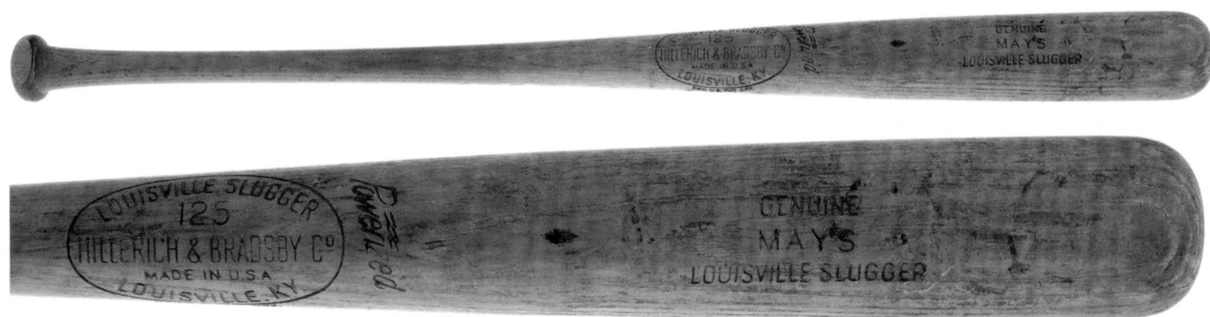

19708 **1961-63 Willie Mays Game Used Bat.** "If he could cook," Hall of Fame manager Leo Durocher said of his rookie star back in 1951, "I'd marry him." Almost certainly the finest five-tool player in the game's long history, Willie Mays was at the height of his considerable powers when he stood at the plate with this Hillerich & Bradsby S2 at the ready, the labeling period of the bat coinciding with a three-season stretch that saw Mays average over forty-two homers annually. Experts John Taube and Vince Malta characterize the use as "outstanding," suggesting very strongly that at least a couple of those four-baggers were launched from the bat's battered surface. Ball marks and stitch impressions coat the barrel, which is swollen from the punishment. We must note that our experts surmise that some degree of this use postdates Mays' ownership of the bat, suggesting action in another individual's hands as well. Red and green bat rack marks are apparent, and the knob is slightly chipped though the handle remains uncracked. The length of thirty-five inches and weight of thirty-five and a half ounces are prime Mays specifications, and match factory records perfectly. The back of the barrel features a 10/10 blue sharpie inscription from this greatest of all living players, reading, "Best Wishes, Willie Mays, 660 HR, 65 MVP." It appears that the number "24" on the knob dates to the same time as the inscription, well after Mays' playing days concluded. A solid specimen that could rightfully be considered one of the key artifacts of the 1960's game. Graded GU6. *LOA from Taube & Malta. LOA from PSA/DNA (autograph). LOA from James Spence Authentication (autograph).* **Minimum Bid: $3,000**

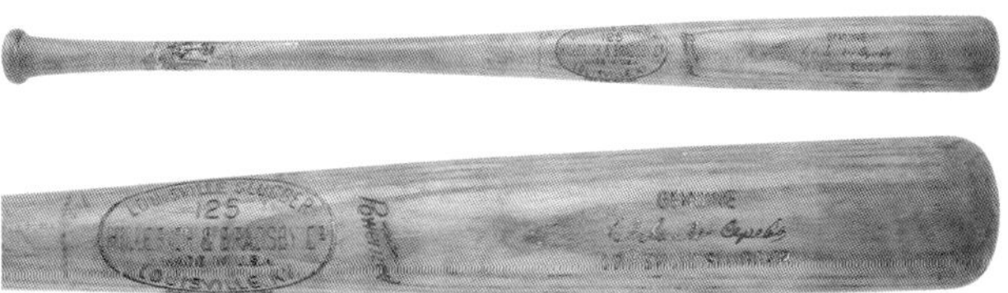

19709 **1964 Orlando Cepeda Game Used Bat.** Factory ordering records for this Hillerich & Bradsby signature model O16 allow us to pinpoint the mailing date to March 18, 1964, the beginning of a sixth consecutive All-Star season for the Hall of Fame first baseman. Excellent use is evident throughout, with grain separation and ball and stitch marks coating the left and back barrel. It must be noted that the ghost of tape removal at the barrel suggests that the bat was used for at least part of its life in a batting practice capacity, until a handle crack (one-inch piece missing) brought an end to its usefulness. Length is thirty-five and a half inches, at a Ruthian weight of forty-one inches. Quality Cepeda gamers rarely surface, with just one or two offered at major auctions annually. A fine addition to any high-end game used bat collection. *LOA from Taube & Malta.* Minimum Bid: $600

19710 **1965-69 Roberto Clemente Game Used Bat.** A top ten MVP candidate four of the five seasons this bat may have seen action (and winner of the Award in 1966), Clemente almost certainly worked some true magic with this signature model Hillerich & Bradsby G105. Fine use, evident in ball, stitch and spike marks dotting the barrel, suggests that this is true, as does the expertly repaired crack on the handle. The length of thirty-six inches and weight of thirty-five ounces are each proper for Clemente gamers of this model and era, perfectly matching factory records. In short, a solid representation of a highly desirable Hall of Fame gamer from a man whose greatness on the field was only challenged by his greatness off of it. Sticker on upper handle establishes provenance to the famous Louisville Slugger auction. *LOA from Taube & Malta.* Minimum Bid: $4,000

19711 **1965-68 Willie Mays Game Used Bat.** One of just four players in Major League history with keys to both the 3,000 Hit and 500 Home Run clubhouses, Willie Mays also brought one of the game's best gloves to the outfield, putting him high on the short list of greatest ballplayers ever. Here we present a tool from the offensive half of that equation, exhibiting use characterized as "heavy" by authenticator Dave Bushing. The block-lettered Hillerich & Bradsby S2 matches Mays' factory ordering records in its model number and specifications of thirty-four and three-quarter inches and thirty-four and a half ounces, favored during a tremendously productive time in his Hall of Fame career. Deeply imbedded ball and stitch marks coat the barrel, with some swelling of the grain from Mays' abuse of National League baseballs. A handle crack ended a long, productive life in the hands of a legend, beginning a second incarnation as a top-shelf collectible. Graded A7.5. *LOA from Dave Bushing.* Minimum Bid: $3,000

PURE PERFECTION

19712 **1966 Mickey Mantle Game Used Bat Graded Perfect 10 by PSA/DNA & MEARS.** One of the finest examples of Mantle lumber ever to reach the auction block, this signature model Hillerich & Bradsby W215 finds all leading bat authenticators united in their assessment that the offered specimen is the standard by which all other late-career gamers should be judged. Provenance, documentation in factory records and tremendous game use converge to establish the joint perfect ratings, with each firmly linking the bat to this most beloved Yankee of all. Experts Vince Malta and John Taube note that half a dozen W215's were ordered by Mantle on May 6, and another six on May 10th, with the length of thirty-five inches and weight of thirty-four ounces that match identically the example presented here. Heavy use is evident in deeply embedded stitch marks coat which coat both sides of the barrel in accordance with Mantle's switch-hitting style, and the patch of pine tar on the handle and fading number "7" in marker on the knob are likewise ideal Mantle traits. Green bat rack marks are noted as well. The handle remains uncracked despite the significant trauma suffered in the hands of the pinstriped slugger. Dave Bushing's letter of opinion notes that this was one of two Mantle bats sold to an Atlanta collector at the National Sports Collectors Convention by a former Cleveland Indians bat boy, who acquired the bat from Mantle directly. This bat was sold at auction in June 2006 for the sum of $60,000, which still stands as a record price for a regular season Mantle gamer. An offering that should appeal to the most sophisticated and discerning of game used bat collectors. *LOA from PSA/DNA. LOA from MEARS.* **Minimum Bid: $20,000**

19713 **1967 Mickey Mantle Game Used Bat.** Important signature model Hillerich & Bradsby K55 dates from the season that the Mick earned his key to the 500 Home Run Clubhouse. Though Mantle's offensive production was beginning to hit the downward slide that would lead to his retirement at the close of the 1968 season, it is noteworthy that the use on this lumber is characterized by top expert John Taube as "outstanding," suggesting the likelihood that at least a few of the legendary slugger's twenty-two home runs that season were launched from its barrel. A handle crack, since expertly repaired, brought the end to this bat's lengthy service, joining plentiful ball and stitch marks on both sides of the barrel that indicate Mantle's switch-hitting style. Also to be found are red and blue bat rack streaks and a moderate coat of pine tar on the handle, the latter of which appears to have been applied during the repair process. Mantle's number "7" appears in marker on the knob. Weight of thirty-one and a half ounces is correct for Mantle's records. A 9+/10 blue sharpie signature on the barrel, notated "No. 7," is the tasty cherry on top of this delicious package, though we must note that the signature has been enhanced at some point. Graded GU7.5. *LOA from Taube & Malta (bat).* **Minimum Bid: $7,500**

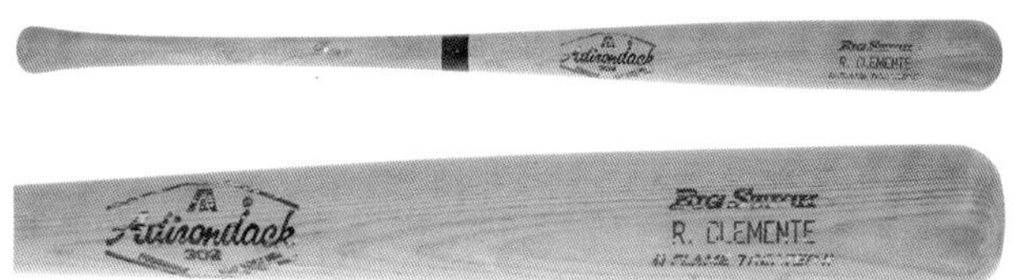

19714 **1968-70 Roberto Clemente Game Used Bat.** One of American sports most tragic figures, Roberto Clemente's brilliance upon the field of play was matched only by his great humanity, with his martyrdom in the cause of delivering relief to Nicaraguan earthquake victims securing his status as one of the game's true heroes. The offered Adirondack 234X formed a brief partnership with the Pittsburgh Pirates Hall of Famer during the late 1960's, earning a few ball marks and green bat rack streaks before a handle crack ended its term of service. Number "21" appears in vintage black marker at the knob and barrel end. Length of thirty-six and a half inches and weight of thirty-five ounces are correct for Clemente's preferred specifications, and match the manufacturer's ordering records. A solid late-career gamer, earning a grade of GU6 from the experts at PSA/DNA. *LOA from Taube & Malta.* **Minimum Bid: $2,000**

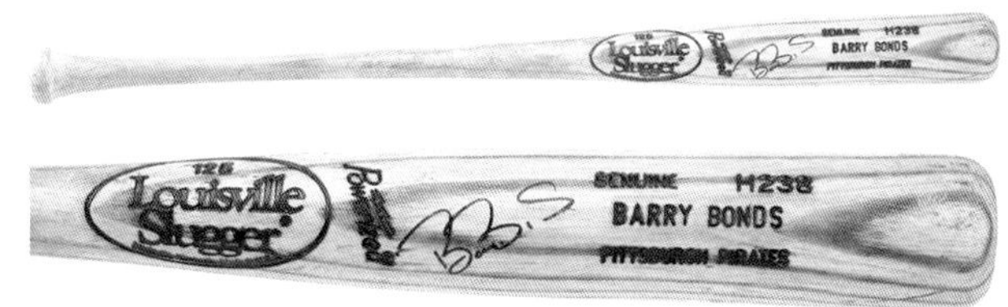

19715 **1991-92 Barry Bonds Game Used Bat.** The possible two-year span during which this block lettered Louisville Slugger H238 saw action in the hands of the game's most prolific and controversial slugger found him taking second and first place in MVP voting respectively, so you can bet some good work was done with it. The evidence bears this out as well, as hearty ball marks, complete with black ball stamping transfers, dot the left, right and back barrel. Stitch impressions likewise coat the surface of the grain, and a crack snakes through the pine-tarred handle. Number "24" appears in marker on knob and barrel end. The length and weight of thirty-four inches and thirty and a half ounces are correct for Bonds' early career preferences, helping to establish a strong rating of GU7 from the experts. A blue sharpie signature on the barrel is ever so slightly touched by an errant hand, otherwise flawlessly bold. A top-caliber example from the early days of Bonds' ascension to the pinnacle of slugging's ranks. *LOA from Taube & Malta. LOA from PSA/DNA (autograph). LOA from James Spence Authentication (autograph).* **Minimum Bid: $500**

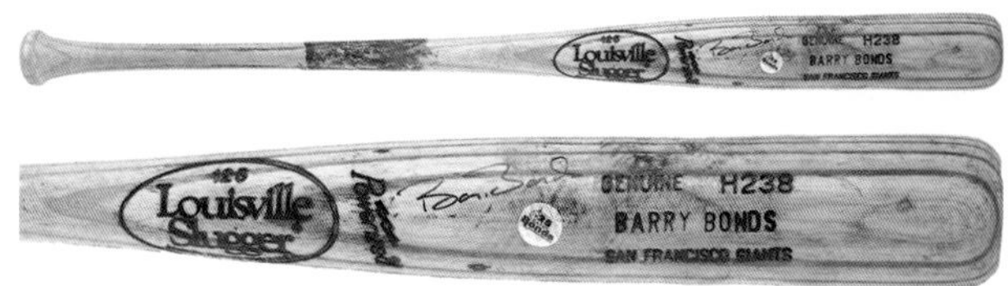

19716 **1993-97 Barry Bonds Game Used Bat.** Brutal, pounded use evident upon the barrel of this Louisville Slugger H238 speaks to the tremendous power the young Bonds could generate even before his physique underwent its controversial transformation. Ball and stitch marks dot the swollen barrel, and there's even a small chunk of white baseball leather and red stitching trapped in the separated grain. Red and green bat rack streaks reside nearby, and a moderate coating of pine tar appears mid-handle. Length is thirty-three and three-quarter inches. Weight is thirty-two and a half ounces. A rock-solid example of an early Bonds gamer, made all the more appealing by a 9/10 black sharpie signature, complete with Bonds' personal holographic authenticating sticker. Graded GU7. *LOA from Taube & Malta. LOA from PSA/DNA (autograph). LOA from James Spence Authentication (autograph).* **Minimum Bid: $750**

19717 **1999 Ken Griffey, Jr. Season Home Run #31 Game Used Bat.** Experts were still figuring Junior to be the eventual career Home Run King back in 1999, and with good reason. Before injuries began to slow his progress beginning in 2001, there was nobody launching more long balls than this supremely gifted slugger, who topped the American League with forty-eight the season this Louisville Slugger signature model C271 saw action. Griffey himself notates this bat as being responsible for "HR 31, 99" along with the 9/10 silver sharpie signature on the barrel, with features a scattering of ball and stitch marks. Excellent use is likewise evident in a handle crack (small piece missing), along with cleat and teal bat rack marks. Griffey's unmistakable criss-cross tape job is still apparent at the handle. Length and weight of thirty-three and three-quarter inches and thirty and a half ounces respectively. Graded GU8. *LOA from Taube & Malta. LOA from PSA/DNA (autograph). LOA from Jame Spence Authentication (autograph).* **Minimum Bid: $600**

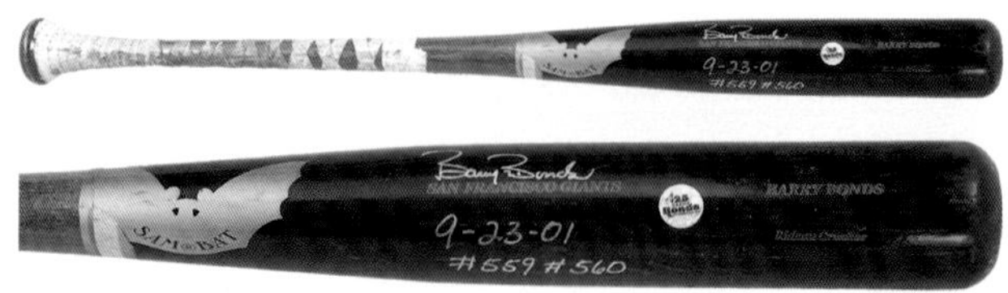

19718 **2001 Barry Bonds Career Home Runs #559 & #560 Game Used Bat.** Rookie San Diego pitcher Jason Middlebrook was victimized twice by the game's most prolific long ball artist on September 23, 2001 with the bat we present here, wielded by Bonds as he moved within four homers of Mark McGwire's short-lived single season record. Though Bonds has since found himself at the center of one of the game's greatest scandals, we prefer to see that glass as half full, understanding that a Barry Bonds home run bat from 2001 will one day be seen in the same light as Joe Jackson's from the 1919 Series. The fact that the homers came less than two weeks after one of the most significant events in American history further establishes the offering as one for the ages. The bat is uncracked and shows excellent use, with several ball and stitch marks evident on left, right and back barrel. Bonds' preferred manner of taping the handle is also in effect here. Sam Bat's unique style of notating all specs by hand on the barrel's end are in place, reading "34, 31.7 oz, 06 09 01, B2K1, B.B.," to indicate length, weight, manufacturing date, model number and Bonds' initials respectively. The barrel is signed by Bonds in flawless silver sharpie, and notated in his hand, "9-23-01, #559 #560." Bonds' personal holographic authenticating sticker is affixed nearby. The fine use, historical relevance and ironclad provenance result in a perfect GU10 grade. Love him or hate him, Barry Bonds will always be the face of baseball at the start of the new millenium. Smart investors will take this under advisement. *LOA from Taube & Malta. LOA from PSA/DNA (autograph). LOA from James Spence Authentication (autograph).* **Minimum Bid: $2,000**

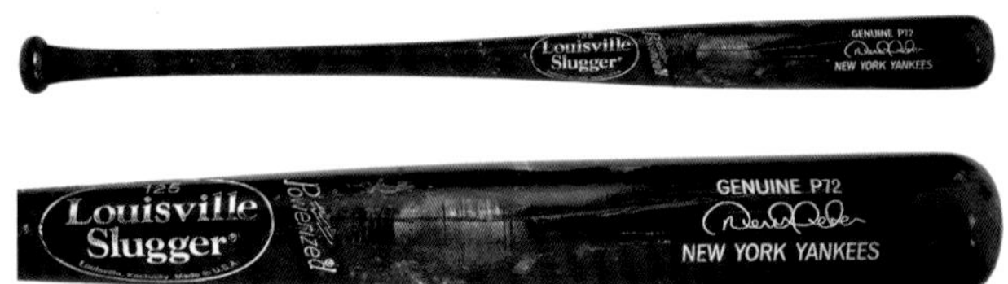

19719 **2004-05 Derek Jeter Game Used Bat.** Perhaps the most idolized Yankee since the days of Mickey Mantle, this All-Star shortstop is certainly Cooperstown bound and is likely the only reasonable candidate for the assumption of Pete Rose's career hit crown. Any bat from the beloved D.J. carries tremendous collecting appeal, and this specimen, showing "evidence of outstanding use" according to experts John Taube and Vince Malta, is particularly special. Ball and stitch marks coat the barrel of this signature model Louisville Slugger P72, with bat rack streaks also clearly evident. A moderate coating of pine tar is found on the handle. Tale of the tape: thirty-four inches and thirty-one ounces. Now go get his autograph on it and you'll have the ideal Jeter gamer! *LOA from Taube & Malta.* **Minimum Bid: $1,000**

19720 **1920-21 New Edinburg Hockey Club Team Photograph.** Brilliant vintage studio photo featuring the 1920-21 New Edinburg Hockey Club, who were a junior side in Ottawa. The 13x16" sepia print features the team's players and executives and was created by Pittaway Photo. Pictured players Rene Joliat (brother of Hall of Famer Aurel), Duncan Munro and Gerald Munro each enjoyed short stints in the NHL during the mid-1920s. The original mount has begun to deteriorate around the edges, bringing final dimensions to 19x22". **Minimum Bid: $200**

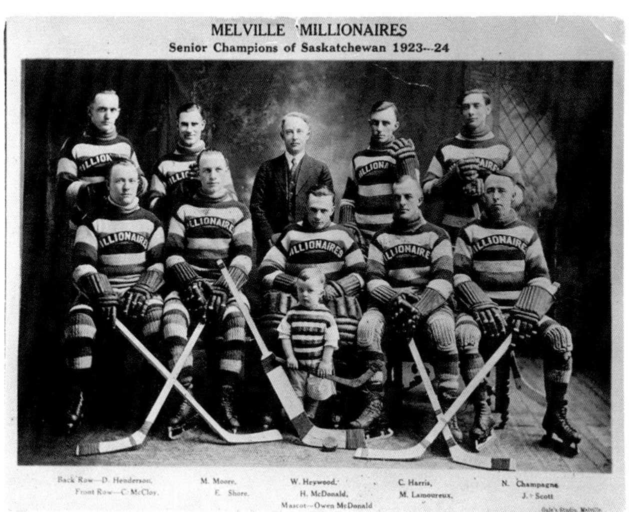

19721 **1923-24 Melville Millionaires Photo Postcard from the Eddie Shore Estate.** Before he became one of the most-lauded players in the history of hockey, Eddie Shore cut his teeth with the well-known amateur team the Melville Millionaires for the 1923-24 season. The original postcard seen here depicts the Hall of Famer with his team, who were the Saskatchewan Champions of that year. This offering originates from the personal collection of Eddie Shore and comes to us by way of his son Eddie Shore, Jr., who has provided a signed letter to that effect. A stunning rarity with fine historical significance. **Minimum Bid: $250**

19722 **1924-25 Regina Pats Composite Studio Photograph.** An apt representation of the time from which it derives, this fabulous 1925 photograph features the incumbent Canadian Junior Champs — the 24-25 Regina Pats. The Pats hold the distinction of being the oldest major junior hockey franchise in the world that have continuously operated from their original location and use the same name after being founded in 1917. Beautiful composite places in-uniform portraits of each player against a makeshift hockey stadium background. Portraits team's executives and mascot line the bottom edge of the photo. Created by Royal Photo, the 11x14" print has been affixed to a decorative mount, which has suffered some damage to the corners with the lower right one being completely missing. Scattered spots of moisture have also met the photo. Despite these issues, this piece remains one of the more visually impressive and historically meaningful vintage hockey photos we've seen in some time. **Minimum Bid: $250**

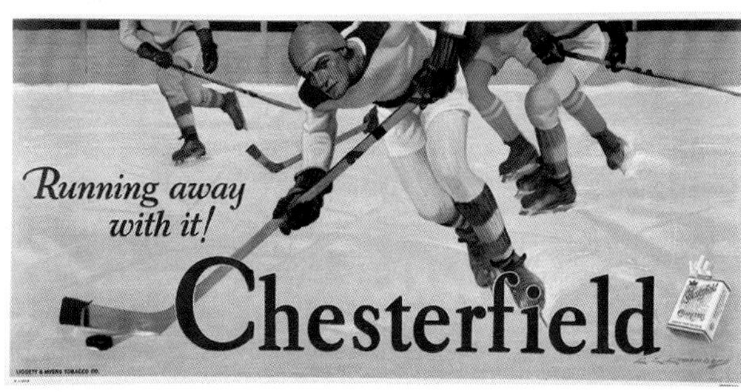

19723 **Circa 1925 Chesterfield Cigarettes Tobacco Advertisement.** Extremely rare Chesterfield Cigarettes advertisement dates from 1920 and has a hockey theme. Measuring 10x20", the full-color piece features the tag line "Running away with it, Chesterfield." Condition remains of the utmost quality as the poster has been professionally attached to a canvas backing for preservation. These posters were originally used on 1920s trolley cars. The original poster is a prime candidate for display given its extraordinary condition. **Minimum Bid: $600**

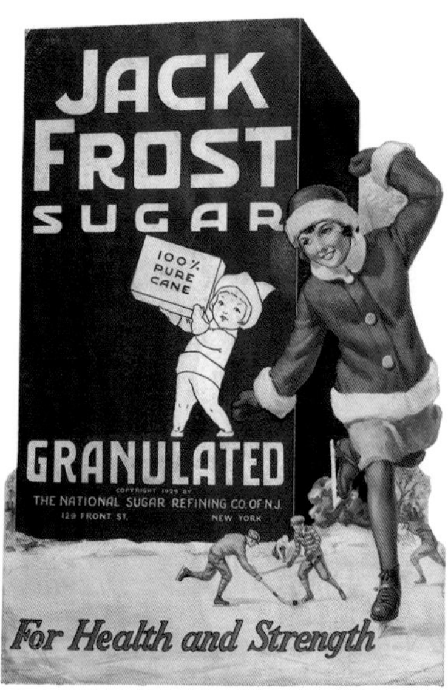

19724 **Circa 1929 Jack Frost Sugar Advertising Piece.** Glorious in its appearance, this 21x30" advertising sign for Jack Frost Sugar features young hockey players skating on a frozen over pond — a familiar activity for many of the game's young aspirants. Ad has been produced on a heavy stock material and has outstanding retention of color, making this a prime candidate for framed display. Endorsements of this quality from the 1920s and 1930s simply do not appear in this condition often enough to pass up your shot at this piece. **Minimum Bid: $300**

19725 **Circa 1930s Jimmy Ward Signed Photograph by Rice.** Montreal hockey legend Jimmy Ward is the focus of this fine vintage photograph which emanates from the studio of another prominent Montreal staple — the Rice Photography Studio. The 7x9" photo features Ward in his Montreal Maroons uniform and comes in original presentational sleeve from Rice Studio. While the sleeve has become somewhat tattered due to the ravages of time, the great sepia photo remains in glorious condition, which multiplies the appeal when considering the 10/10 fountain ink signature and inscription that reads "To a friend indeed". *LOA from PSA/DNA. LOA from James Spence Authentication.* **Minimum Bid: $300**

19726 **1930s CCM Advertising Sign.** Eye-catching die-cut 1930s advertising sign from an in-store display is highlighted by its excellent color retention and classic black-and-white photography. Measures roughly 21x33" and appears to be only a portion of the entire display, but the appeal is undeniable. At the bottom of the ad is text reading "Ice-Hockey, Skating and Ski Equipment". **Minimum Bid: $400**

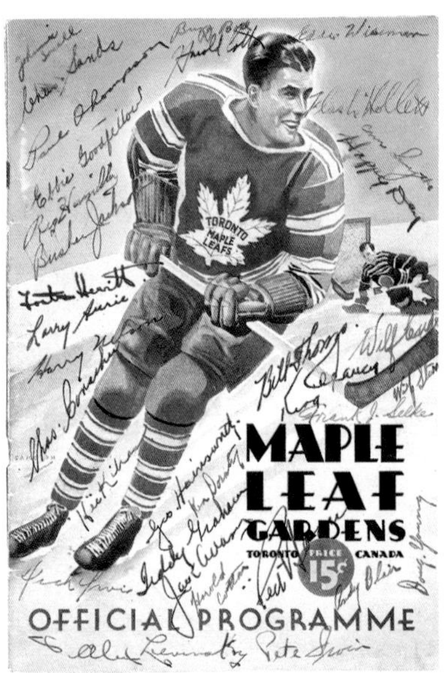

19727 **1934 Toronto Maple Leafs/Detroit Red Wings Team Signed Program.** Just after the close of the 1933-34 NHL season the Toronto Maple Leafs toured Western Canada playing against a Detroit Red Wing squad that was reinforced by three stars of the region as well as the entire top line of the IHL's Detroit Olympics — all playing due to some Red Wing regulars being unable to participate in the exhibition. Here we present a glorious example of one of the programs that were used for that tour, a Maple Leaf Gardens publication with the updated team lineup cards insert inside. What amazes is the stellar collection of black fountain ink signatures that populate the front cover, which includes such highlights as Busher Jackson, Charlie Conacher, George Hainsworth, King Clancy, Jack Adams, Conn Smythe, Happy Day, Paul Thompson (Chicago star playing with Detroit) and more. A slight vertical crease is the only condition issue, however the appeal of the cover makes it nearly insignificant. *LOA from PSA/DNA. LOA from James Spence Authentication.* **Minimum Bid: $600**

19728 **1934-43 Bee Hive Group 1 Trophy Photos Lot of 6.** From the original Bee Hive photograph promotion that ran from 1934-43 we present this collection of images of the utmost attractiveness and rarity. While condition may cause a small amount of concern, that doubt should be alleviated considering that each of these in its own right serves as a desirable hobby gem that would cause any serious collector of hockey vintage to clamor. Each photograph has been mounted to final measurements of 5 3/8" x 7 3/8". Included are photos of the Byng Trophy (x2), Calder Trophy, Vezina Trophy, Hart Trophy and the Memorial Cup. Simply breathtaking collection of tough photos rarely, if ever, seen at auction. **Minimum Bid: $400**

19729 **1934-43 Bee Hives Group 1 New York Americans Photos Lot of 14.** Issued from 1934-43, Group 1 Bee Hive promotional photographs remain some of the most desirable collectibles in this branch of the hobby and the current offering of 14 photos from that set is sure to impress. The New York Americans photos seen here have risen in appeal due to their toughness — the last year of the team's existence was in 1941 and thus entries featuring this team are understandably more scarce. Each of the offered candidates presents as a stellar visual example, with none of the expected condition issues from cards of this age. **Minimum Bid: $350**

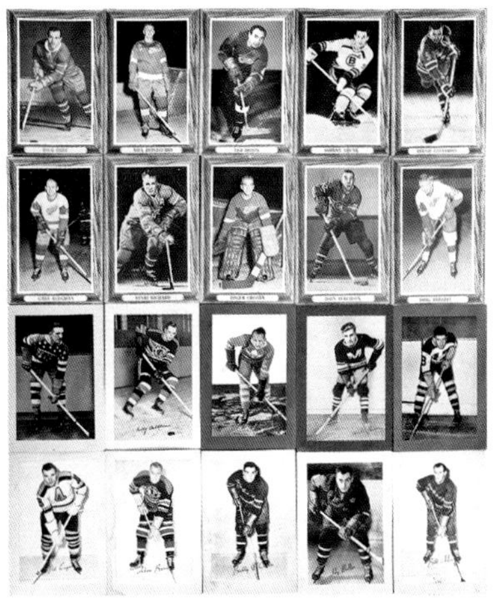

19730 **1934-67 Bee Hive Photos Massive Group Lot of 101.** Due to their size, use of attractive photography, and comprehensiveness of including all NHL teams and trophies, the Bee Hives photograph promotion serves as a staple for enthusiasts of vintage professional ice hockey. Any collection would be fueled by this prominent infusion of 101 of the photos, with exemplar originating from each of the three subsets of the Bee Hives. Lot breaks down as follows: **Group 1 (1934-43)** — 37 photos, **Group 2 (1944-64)** — 41 photos, and **Group 3 Wood Grains (1964-67)** — 23 photos. Includes many stars and Hall of Famers, with such noteworthy highlights present as Dick Duff, Alex Delvecchio, Leo Boivin, Boom-Boom Geoffrion, Red Horner, Neil Colville, Ehrhardt Heller, Harvey Jackson, Herb Cain, Jimmy Ward, Dave Schriner, Eddie Wiseman, Henri Richard, Woody Dumart, Red Kelly, Tim Horton, Allan Stanley and Tod Sloan. Average condition is EX or better, with condition limited some minor staining here and there and a few cards with pinholes at the corners. In any event, this group would make for an excellent display opportunity. **Minimum Bid: $500**

19731 **1937 Howie Morenz Memorial All-Star Game Original Turofsky Photograph.** Brilliant piece of hockey history is seen here with this original photograph taken by the acclaimed sports photographer Turofsky. Dating from 1937, this 8x10" photo depicts the team of NHL All-Stars that took on a squad of Montreal Canadiens and Maroons in the Howie Morenz Memorial Game. One of the most-beloved players in the game at the time, Morenz passed away earlier in the year due to complications suffered after he broke his leg during a game in Montreal. Pictured in their team uniforms, the All-Stars include a bevy of Hall of Fame talent with such inclusions as Eddie Shore, Happy Day, Charlie Conacher, Gordon Drillon, Busher Jackson, Dit Clapper, Ebbie Goodfellow, Frank Boucher, Jack Adams and more. The pinholes at the corners are the only detractors from visual appeal, however they do little to lessen the overall appeal of this attractive vintage photo. **Minimum Bid: $400**

NEW YORK RANGERS -- 1939-40
TOP ROW (LEFT TO RIGHT)
Frank Boucher (assistant manager and coach), Lynn Patrick, Neil Colville, Ott Heller,
Art Coulter, (captain), Babe Pratt, Murray Patrick, Alf Pike, Lester Patrick (manager and coach)
BOTTOM ROW (LEFT TO RIGHT)
Alex Shibicky, Phil Watson, Kilby MacDonald, Bryan Hextall, Dave Kerr, Mac Colville,
Clint Smith, Dutch Hiller, Harry Westerby (trainer)

19732 **1939-40 New York Rangers Team Photograph Signed by Lester Patrick.** From the turn of the 20th century Lester Patrick played a large role in the history of organized professional hockey, first as a player and later as a coach and executive. Taking over coaching duties of the New York Rangers in 1926 in place of the exiled Conn Smythe, Patrick saw immediate and abundant success. winning the Stanley Cup in only the organization's second year of existence. Patrick continued to pilot the team until 1939 when he stepped down to concentrate on his duties as general manager. Rare 8x10" photograph depicts the Stanley Cup winners from the 1939-40 season and still identifies Patrick, who has signed a glorious 10/10 black fountain ink signature, as one of the team's coaches. Furthering the historical significance, this is the team that many attribute are the originators of the dreaded Curse of 1940. Having paid off their mortgage for Madison Square Garden, the Ranger management burned the deed in the cup of the Stanley Cup trophy, consequently angering the Hockey Gods and preventing the team from lifting the Cup again for another 54 years. Attractive piece with outstanding appeal. *LOA from PSA/DNA. LOA from James Spence Authentication.* **Minimum Bid: $200**

19733 **1945-54 Quaker Oats Max Bentley #7B Home Dressing Room Photograph.** Part of a promotion that Quaker Oats ran from 1945-54, the Max Bentley 8x10" glossy print that we present here ranks as one of the more desirable of the entire issue and is rarely seen in any condition, let alone the sparkling presentational shape that the given offering exhibits. The 1946 Hart Memorial Trophy winner Max Bentley has a total of three variations in this set, which was available for order from Quaker between 1945-54. Presented here is the rarest of all of those variants, a shot of the Hall of Famer taping up in the dressing room. A small 1/2" tear at the photo's right edge remains the only visual detractor. The finest exemplar of this tough premium that we have ever seen. **Minimum Bid: $600**

19734 **Circa 1949 Jack Gordon Bee Hives (Group 2) Photograph.** The popular Bee Hives photos were presented as a hockey premium for thirty years, and the Group 2 entries account for more that half of them. What we present here is one of the most unique gems in the hobby in the form of a Bee Hive featuring the New York Rangers' Jack Gordon. Card is mounted, bringing final measurements to 5.5x8". The unconfirmed card was initially not even known to be part of the issue and is one of only five Gordon exemplars believed to exist in the hobby to date. Three are presently in private hands, so the chance to get your mitts on this incredible unicorn of a card will likely not happen again. One of the top 10 most desirable Bee Hive cards in the hobby. **Minimum Bid: $1,500**

19735 **1950-51 Cal Gardner Game Worn Jersey.** It was with the Toronto Maple Leafs that Cal Gardner enjoyed his moment in the sun, skating with enough skill to earn a pair of All-Star appearances and helping his team collect two Stanley Cups. Here we present Gardner's white home sweater from the Leafs' 1950-51 championship campaign. While it is well worn, it remains one of the most desirable and tough Toronto designs. Inner left seam of the garment carries remnants of the Doug Laurie manufacturer's tag. The classic Maple Leafs logo has been embroidered to the chest in a fabulous two-color felt and remains in fine presentational condition. Several moth-eaten holes and stains have ravaged the garment's lower half, a testament not only to the Gardner's on-ice grit but also the terrors of time. Blue-on-white felt "17" has been affixed to the verso of the sweater and remain as aglow as the front identifiers. Two small team repairs can be found in the rear tail. Significant for the Bill Barilko Game 5 Stanley Cup goal that clinched for the Maple Leafs over the Montreal Canadiens, Toronto's '51 championship has an added sentimental twist as Barilko passed away four months later, a victim of a plane crash. Here then, is a beautiful rare sweater worn by one of Barilko's last on-ice comrades. *LOA from Rich Ellis.* **Minimum Bid: $1,500**

19736 **1951-52 Marcel Paille Quebec Junior All-Star Game Worn Jersey.** Long-time professional hockey goaltender Marcel Paille got his start in junior hockey with the Quebec Citadels of the QJHL in 1948, sharing the ice with future Hall of Fame center Jean Beliveau. He starred for Quebec during the 1951-52 campaign, earning himself a spot in the league's All-Star Game. From that All-Star game we present an exceptional vintage sweater, a white shirt with red sleeve stripes and details at collar and waist hem. "JAHA" crest occupies the chest logo with three blue-on-red felt stars spanning the area just above that. Likewise-styled felt "1" on the verso. Wear is apparent in the form of several slash and puck marks which have resulted in many small unrepaired holes. Also includes the nice detail of a lace-up collar, making this one of the more attractive vintage sweaters you'll see for some time. **Minimum Bid: $500**

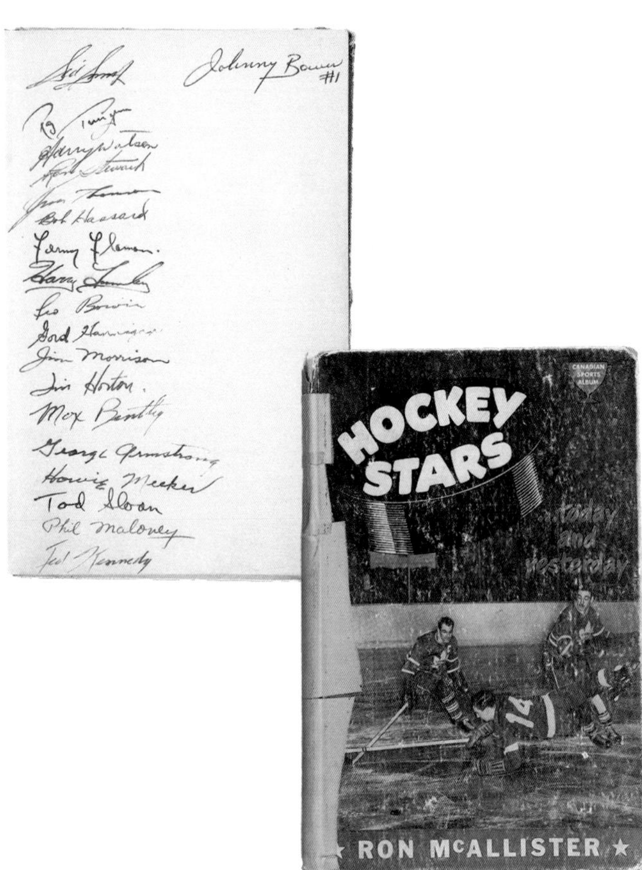

19737 **1952-53 Toronto Maple Leafs Team Signed Book.** While the 1950 first edition of the book *Hockey Stars ... Today and Yesterday* leaves something to be desired in the way of outward physical appearance, the real appeal is in the 19 compelling autographs found in the inner front cover — each applied by a member of the 1952-53 Toronto Maple Leafs squad. This particular team was significant for a number of reasons — with the Maple Leaf organization freshly mired in the adverse effects of the Barilko Curse, the team was in a period of transition with new faces such as long-time Leaf Tim Horton coming on board and veterans such as Max Bentley moving on. Both Bentley and the rookie Horton have checked in here, with other such noteworthy inclusions as fellow Hall of Famers Ted Kennedy, George Armstrong, Harry Watson, Leo Boivin, Fern Flaman, and Harry Lumley. The badly damaged spine of the book is of little consequence when considering the overall value of these vintage Toronto signatures. *LOA from PSA/DNA. LOA from James Spence Authentication.* **Minimum Bid: $450**

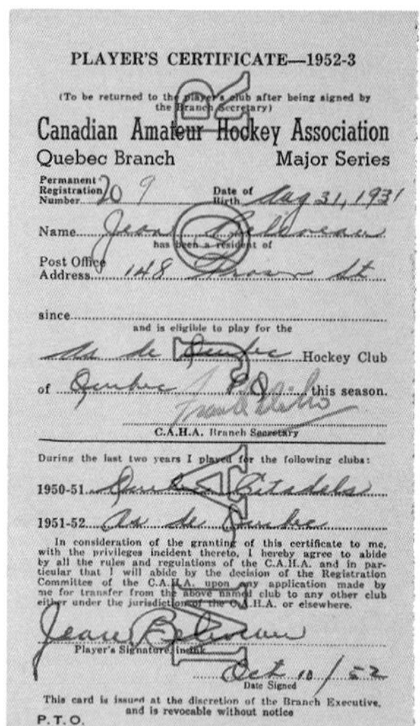
PLAYER'S CERTIFICATE—1952-3

(To be returned to the player's club after being signed by the Branch Secretary)

Canadian Amateur Hockey Association

Quebec Branch Major Series

Permanent Registration Number 209 Date of Birth Aug 31, 1931

Name ....

has been a resident of

Post Office Address 148 ....

since ....

and is eligible to play for the

.... Hockey Club

of .... this season.

C.A.H.A. Branch Secretary

During the last two years I played for the following clubs:

1950-51 ....

1951-52 ....

In consideration of the granting of this certificate to me, with the privileges incident thereto, I hereby agree to abide by all the rules and regulations of the C.A.H.A. and in particular that I will abide by the decision of the Registration Committee of the C.A.H.A. upon any application made by me for transfer from the above named club to any other club either under the jurisdiction of the C.A.H.A. or elsewhere.

Player's Signature (in ink)

Oct 10/52
Date Signed

This card is issued at the discretion of the Branch Executive, and is revocable without notice

P.T.O.

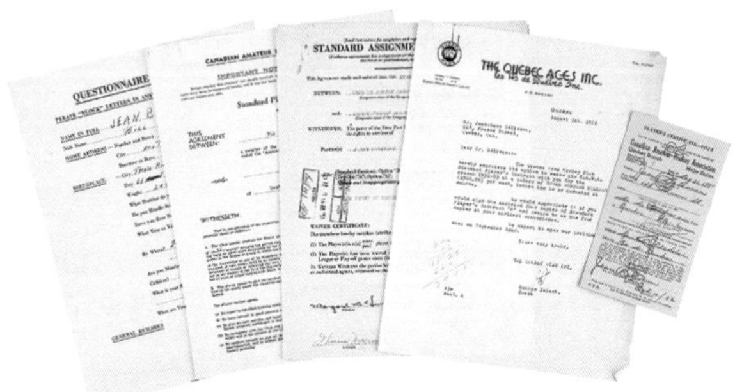

19738 **1952-53 Jean Beliveau Signed CAHA Player's Certificate with Official Contacts/Letters Lot of 5.** In what was one of the more circuitous routes taken into professional hockey, Jean Beliveau finally joined Montreal Canadiens in 1953 for good, never to play amateur hickey again. Beliveau's story began as a 15-year-old when he initially drew the attention of the Montreal Canadiens' general manager Frank Selke. Although he was a star for the Quebec Aces of the Quebec Senior Hockey League, led the team in scoring in 1953 and was called up for a couple brief stints to play with the Habs, Beliveau had little interest in pursuing a professional career, which drew the ire of a Selke who was intent on having the phenom play for him. To ensure that Selke would secure the services of the future Hall of Famer, the GM hatched a plan — the Canadiens would buy the entire QSHL and convert it into a professional league. This meant that under the terms of the B-form that he had previously signed, Beliveau would have to honor the Habs' ownership of his professional rights beginning with the 1953-54 season. Here we present perhaps the rarest group of material to emerge in the hobby in the form of several official documents from Beliveau's early forays into professional hockey. Included is his signed player's certificate from 1952-53, a 1951 agreement that sent Beliveau from his brief stint with the Canadiens back to the Aces with letters from each GM (signed by Selke), a signed letter from Aces coach George Imlach that offers a renewal of contract to Beliveau for the 1952-53 season with the mentioned contract, and a questionnaire for players filled out in fountain ink by the Hall of Famer himself, with such quirky answers as "golf & women" to the "What are your Hobbies?" line. Supremely scarce offering from on of the most-celebrated figures in the history of the game. *LOA from PSA/DNA. LOA from James Spence Authentication.* **Minimum Bid: $1,000**

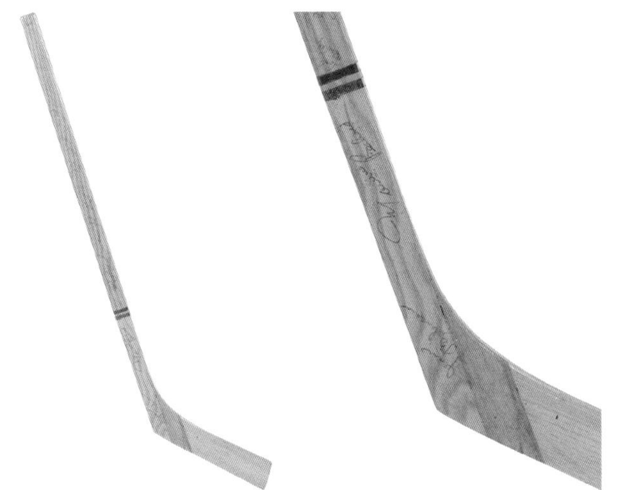

19739 **1953-54 Montreal Canadiens Team Signed Souvenir Stick.** Star-studded gathering of signatures from the historically significant Stanley Cup Finals 1953-54 Montreal Canadiens team comes to us here on the surface of a vintage souvenir hockey stick. Despite basically shunning the Canadiens and professional hockey as a whole, Jean Beliveau was happy to continue to play for his Quebec Senior Hockey League amateur squad the Quebec Aces, drawing the ire of Montreal head man Frank Selke, who had been trying for some time to secure the full-time services of the future Hall of Famer for years. In an unprecedented move, Selke purchased the entire QSHL, turned it into a professional league, and used his ownership of Beliveau's pro rights to make the star a Hab for the remainder of his career beginning with this '53-54 season. A total of 15 members of the team have checked in, including Beliveau, Rocket Richard, Boom-Boom Geoffrion, Doug Harvey, Bert Olmstead, Elmer Lach, Paul Meger, Floyd Curry and more. Each signature is distinct, with average for the group rating a solid 8/10. *LOA from PSA/DNA. LOA from James Spence Authentication.* **Minimum Bid: $400**

19740 **1955-59 Blueline Hockey Magazine Lot of 19.** *Blueline* magazine was long known as the standard monthly publication for the serious fan of NHL hockey. What we present here amounts to quite a treasure of back issues from *Blueline's* catalog detailing some of the most memorable years during the Original Six era. Dating from 1955-59, here we present a fine collection of 19 *Blueline* issues, all in great condition considering their age. Group includes such acclaimed stars on their covers as Jean Beliveau, Boom-Boom Geoffrion, Jacques Plante, Ted Lindsay, Gordie Howe, Andy Bathgate, Frank Mahovlich, Maurice Richard, Henri Richard, Fleming Mackell, Bill Gadsby, and Dickie Duff. Tremendous offering ripe for any advanced collector of Original Six era memorabilia. **Minimum Bid: $300**

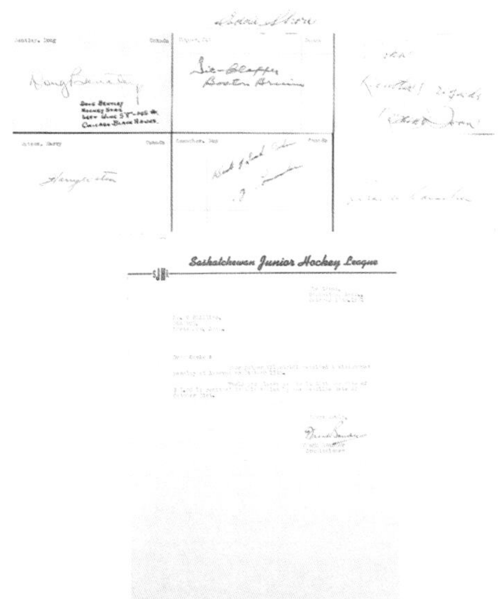

19741 **Deceased Hall of Famers Autograph Lot of 8.** Afford yourself a flirtation with the ghosts of hockey's storied past with this classic offering of eight signatures courtesy of eight deceased Hall of Famers. Each singular entry in its own right appears with an appealing combination of toughness and clarity — together this collection is nothing short of blue-ribbon. Honored contributors to this collection included a signed typed letter from Frank Boucher, a cut signature from Eddie Shore, and signed index cards from Roy Conacher, Charlie Conacher, Harry Watson, Tommy Ivan, Dit Clapper, and Doug Bentley. An appetizing pick-up for the serious hockey collector. *LOA from PSA/DNA. LOA from James Spence Authentication.* **Minimum Bid: $750**

19742 **1956-57 Detroit Red Wings Team Signed Advertisement.** Top-notch collection of 15 signatures from the 1956-57 Detroit Red Wings, who finished the regular season with the league's best record and top scorer in Gordie Howe with his 88 points. The autographs include seven Hall of Famers and come applied to a vintage advertisement for Export Cigarettes. Checking in here are Ted Lindsay, Marcel Pronovost, Alex Delvecchio, Gordie Howe, Murray Costello, Red Kelly, Glenn Hall, Earl Reibel and more. Ad measures about 10x15" and has been mounted to a thick piece of illustration board. Lineup sheet here comes from a 1956 exhibition between the Red Wings and the Winnipeg Warriors. A small hole exists near the upper left and right corners of the piece. Exceptional chance to obtain several classic Hall of Fame autographs in one fell swoop. *LOA from PSA/DNA. LOA from James Spence Authentication.* **Minimum Bid: $250**

19743 **1958-59 Johnny Bower Toronto Maple Leafs Cardigan Sweater.** It took over a decade of toil at the levels below the NHL, but Johnny Bower proved his skill as a top-tier goaltender and got his chance to prove it when the New York Rangers called him up in 1953. It was with the Toronto Maple Leafs that he would enjoy his most productive years in the net, collecting four Stanley Cups with the team. From his first season with the Leafs in 1958-59 we offer this brilliant team-issued cardigan sweater. The white sweater is highlighted by the impressive team logo applied over the heart and includes two blue stripes on each sleeve and blue cuffs. Wear is evident and tiny spots of staining affect the garment in areas, however it must be said that little has been done to knock down the display potential. Fantastic Hall of Fame apparel courtesy of one of the finest netminders to date. Includes handwritten and signed LOA from Bower himself. **Minimum Bid: $2,000**

19744 **1960 Hockey Stars Album Signed by 15 Hall of Famers.** Near Mint publication called *Hockey Stars 1960* features cartoons and statistics from several of the era's most celebrated stars of the "Original Six" era. With a total of 19 signatures appearing on the front cover and interior pages, this offering jumps in desirability by many degrees. All but two of the signatures come from renowned Hall of Famers, with a total of 15 inductees members having penned high-quality examples of their signatures. Included are superior autograph specimens from the likes of Jean Beliveau (signed twice), Andy Bathgate, Bobby Hull (signed twice), Maurice Richard, Gordie Howe, Fernie Flaman, Bob Pulford, Frank Mahovlich, Red Kelly, Gump Worsley (deceased), Doug Mohn (non-HOFer), Alex Delvecchio, Boom-Boom Geoffrion, (deceased), Ted Lindsay, Bill Gadsby, Dickie Moore and Ed Litzenberger (non-HOFer). One of the more impressive collections of Hall of Fame autographs that you're likely to see for some time. *LOA from PSA/DNA. LOA from James Spence Authentication.* **Minimum Bid: $400**

19745 **1960-61 Chicago Black Hawks Team Signed Program.** In 1961 the Chicago Black Hawks muscled their way to the franchise's first title in 23 years, with Chicago legends Bobby Hull and Stan Mikita each making their first Stanley Cup Finals that year. From a late-season visit that the Black Hawks made to Toronto's Maple Leaf Gardens during that championship season we present this official game program, signed on the front cover by over fifteen members of the Chicago side. Highlight signatures, which all appear in blue ink, include Hull, Mikita, Pierre Pilote, Bill Hay, Murray Balfour, Ron Murphy, Ken Wharram, Tommy, Ivan Moose Vasko and more. Interior score card has been filled. Tremendous championship autograph collection. *LOA from PSA/DNA. LOA from James Spence Authentication.* Minimum Bid: $350

19746 **1961 York Peanut Butter Montreal Canadiens Premium Photos Lot of 19.** Just before the 1961 Stanley Cup Playoffs, the York Peanut Butter Company released the first of their desirable premiums — a double-barreled promotion that included 5x7" photos from the league's top two teams as well as a series of glass tumblers that also featured those same Toronto Maple Leafs and Montreal Canadiens. The entire collection of 19 photos featuring Montreal Canadiens is offered here, all remaining in exceptional presentational condition despite the years that have passed since their original issue. In exchange for peanut butter and salted nut chevron labels, Canadian fans could request these attractive photos, each of which includes the pictured player's facsimile autograph. Highlights here include Hall of Famers Bernie Geoffrion, Jean Beliveau, Henri Richard, Tom Johnson, Jacques Plante, and Doug Harvey. A tremendous find of this tough edition, complete in its inclusion of the Habs' players. An appealing grab for those looking to complete the set with the remaining 18 Maple Leaf photos. Minimum Bid: $400

19747 **1961 Phil Goyette York Peanut Butter Glass.** Part of a popular two-tiered premium promotional that the York Peanut Butter launched just before the 1961 Stanley Cup Playoffs, here we offer one of the gem pieces of the collection. The glass peanut butter tumblers included a total of 21 different players from the Toronto Maple Leafs and Montreal Canadiens, and the Phil Goyette exemplar seen here rates among the toughest of them all. Rarely seen and in exceptional condition, hobby enthusiasts will surely clamor to own this fine prized possession. This precious memento will make for a top-notch highlight in any collection. Minimum Bid: $550

19748 **1961 Jacques Plante and Frank Mahovlich York Peanut Butter Glasses Series #1 Lot of 2.** In an effort to boost their sales, the York peanut butter company launched a promotion that saw them package their product in attractive glass tumblers featuring members of the Toronto Maple Leafs and the Montreal Canadiens. Since their initial release just before the 1961 Stanley Cup Playoffs, these mementos have become quite the lightning rod for collectors, always causing excitement among the more serious hockey hobbyists. Here we present a pairing of these fine tumblers, each exhibiting outstanding visual appeal and devoid of any flaws to speak of. Entries from Hall of Famers Jacques Plante and Frank Mahovlich are presented here, representing two of the more desirable pieces from the collection. Each comes from series #1 as indicated by the "F" imprinted on the bottom of each tumbler. Minimum Bid: $400

19749 **1962 Saskatoon Sr. Quakers Blazer Worn by Wally Patrick.** In what was one of the earliest instances of a touring hockey team, the 1962-63 Saskatoon Quakers of the Saskatchewan Senior Hockey League were selected as Canada's representatives for a tour that visited Czechoslovakia, Switzerland and Sweden. Created by Elwood Flynn, Ltd. of Saskatoon, the blazer that we offer was worn overseas by the team — an impressive show of the team's solidarity both on and off the ice. The black jacket has been fitted with a team logo over the left breast pocket and is a modified golf garment as seen by the interlocking flag and club logo on each button. Condition remains strong despite the age of the piece with no noteworthy flaws to mention. This particular offering was worn by Wally Patrick, a member of the touring squad. Sure to add a bold international flavor to a discriminating collector's stash. **Minimum Bid: $250**

19750 **Circa 1960s Pierre Pilote Game Used & Signed Stick.** Along with fellow Chicago Black Hawk Elmer "Moose" Vasko, Pierre Pilote helped to form one of the most formidable defensive pairing in the history of the game. Pilote's individual play was rewarded as well as he finished either winning the Norris Trophy, given to the league's best defenseman, or was the runner-up each year from 1962-67. From that stellar run we present one of Pilote's sticks that he wielded when he established himself as one of the most avoided defenders of Original Six hockey. The left-handed Northland Custom Pro stick exhibits clear indications of game use and remains with original taping at blade and upper handle. Lower shaft has been signed to read "To Hal, Best Regards and Good Luck, Pierre Pilote". Quite a rare stick from one of the game's more respected Hall of Famers. Also accompanied by a signed 8x10" photograph from the Hall of Famer. *LOA from PSA/DNA. LOA from James Spence Authentication.* **Minimum Bid: $450**

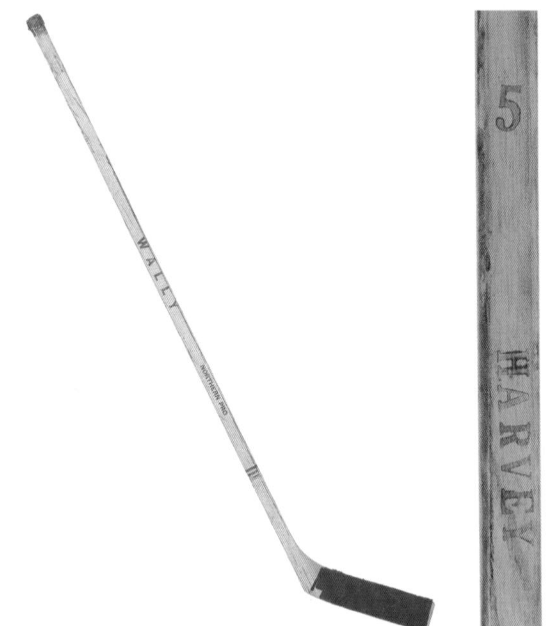

19751 **1960s Doug Harvey Game Used Hockey Stick.** Used by the legendary Doug Harvey while he was playing in the Quebec Aces of the American Hockey League, the stick has his stamped name and "5" jersey number and exhibits nice use and original taping at the blade and handle. Along with Bobby Orr and Eddie Shore, Harvey probably had the greatest impact of any player at that position. His dramatic rushes and superior defensive work allowed him to dominate the game. In a franchise deep in heroes, Harvey gained an immortal place in the history of the Montreal Canadiens. Harvey's reasons for leaving the NHL came about due to his being blacklisted after an attempted formation of a players' association. It is from this era that the Hall of Famer's stick that we present here originates, as he played with Quebec from 1963-65. A must-have for fans of the Habs. **Minimum Bid: $600**

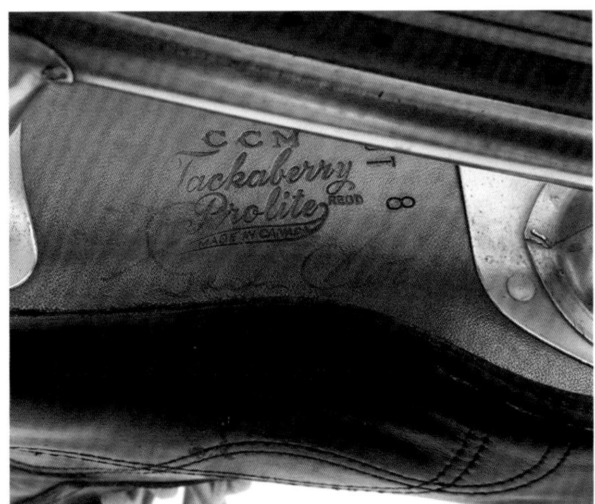

19752 **Gordie Howe Signed Skates.** A dominating force from his first NHL season, Gordie Howe used his tremendous size and hockey intelligence to score top 5 in league scoring for a whopping 20 straight seasons. This feat has never been matched by another athlete in any sport. Mr. Hockey quickly became a Detroit favorite and one of the game's most popular characters overall. Some lucky fan was the recipient of the Hall of Famer's signature, which he applied here to the outer sole of the right skate from a pair of vintage CCM Tacks skates from the 1960s. Signature has been applied in an attractive blue fountain ink and remains in fine presentational condition. *LOA from PSA/DNA. LOA from James Spence Authentication.* **Minimum Bid: $300**

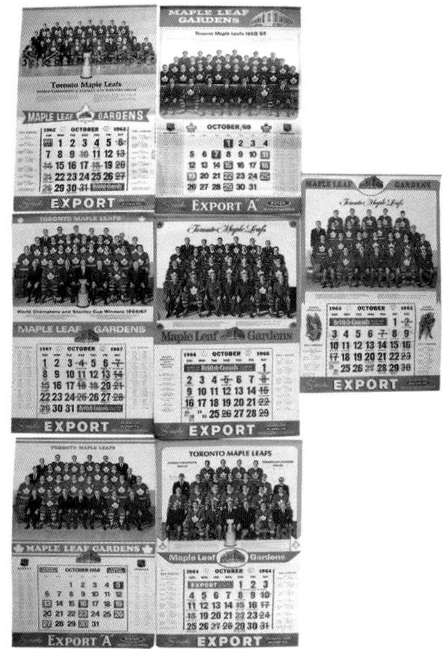

19753 **1962-70 Maple Leaf Gardens Export Calendars Lot of 7.** Toronto's 1960s Maple Leaf teams represented the strongest era in the franchise's storied past, winning four Stanley Cup titles in the last six years of the Original Six period. The Cup passed hands exclusively between the Leafs and the Montreal Canadiens during this period. What we present here is a run of the Maple Leaf Gardens Export Calendars spanning 1962-70, missing only the 1963-64 calendar. Some minor condition issues around the edges of the calendars do little to detract from the overall aesthetic appeal and desirability of the calendars, which mark an important era in NHL hockey in more ways than one. A noteworthy condition flaw is the stray writing that invades the front of the 1964-65 calendar. Many of the Maple Leaf Stanley Cup winners of the 1960s are pictured. **Minimum Bid: $300**

19754 **1964-67 Bee Hive Group 3 "Wood Grains" Trophy Photos Lot of 15.** Stunning assembly of the hobby-favorite Bee Hive Group 3 "Wood Grains" includes seven different trophy photographs for some of the most prestigious awards presented by the National Hockey League. Each example measures 5.5x8" and entries includes the Norris Trophy, the Byng Trophy, the Vezina Trophy, the Ross Trophy, the Hart Trophy, the Calder Trophy, the Prince of Wales Trophy and the beloved Stanley Cup. Duplicates exist for all except the Stanley Cup photo. Despite over a half century since their original production, condition issues for this top-notch collection are a non-factor. **Minimum Bid: $400**

19755 **1964-67 Bee Hive Group 3 "Wood Grains" Photos Lot of 94.** From the "wood grains" photo premiums released between 1964 and 1967 we present this fine collection of 94 featuring players from the New York Rangers, Toronto Maple Leafs and Montreal Canadiens. Several stars and Hall of Famers are represented including Jacques Plante, Phil Goyette, Ed Giacomin, Bernie Geoffrion, Terry Sawchuk, Frank Mahovlich, Ted Kennedy, Red Kelly, Tim Horton, Brian Conacher, George Armstrong, Gump Worsley, Maurice Richard, Henri Richard, Jean-Claude Tremblay, Jacques Laperriere, Bernie Geoffrion, and Jean Beliveau. Condition remains strong among the photos in this lot, with average of EX-MT across the group. **Minimum Bid: $300**

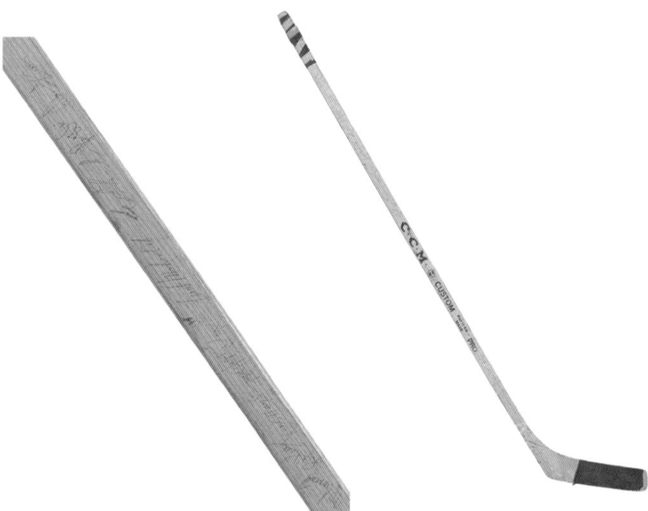

19756 **1966-67 Toronto Maple Leafs Team Signed Hockey Stick.** Despite employing a veteran group of players — Johnny Bower and Allan Stanley has already eclipsed the 40-year mark — the 1966-67 Toronto Maple Leafs secured the franchise's thirteenth Stanley Cup with a team average age of 31. This remains as the oldest championship team. Furthering the significance of the team piece, the 1966-67 season marked the last year of the Original Six era, with another six teams added to the NHL in '67 by way of expansion. What we present here amounts to a remarkable vintage memento to mark the Leafs' last Stanley Cup triumph with one of Stanley's game used sticks complete with 15 signatures from the team. Stick retains original taping and has Stanley's name stamped on the shaft. Autographs average 9/10 in strength and include several stars including Stanley, Terry Sawchuk, captain George Armstrong, Frank Mahovlich, Red Kelly, Tim Horton, and more. *LOA from PSA/DNA*. **Minimum Bid: $600**

19757 **1967-68 Jacques Laperriere Game Worn Jersey.** Few can argue that the timeless design of the Montreal Canadiens hockey sweaters can rival any uniform in any sport in its overall attractiveness. As the 100th anniversary of the franchise's existence approaches we shall celebrate by offering a rare number "2" sweater from the Habs' 1967-68 campaign. A 25-year-old Jacques Laperriere wore Doug Harvey's old jersey number, now retired, and enjoyed a magnificent season en route to collecting his third Stanley Cup. The beautiful red wool sweater exhibits the Canadiens' trademark stripe design and has the immediately recognizable red-on-white-on-blue three color tackle twill interlocking "C" and "H" logo on the chest. White-on-blue "2" numerals are found on verso as well as on either shoulder. This style Canadiens jersey is a lace-up collar version, but the original string has since become missing. Tease Knitting Company tag sewn in inside left hem. Great wear is apparent in the collar area, as well as by the numerous holes and advanced identifier puckering. Two team repairs are also found on the right sleeve. Fans of hockey will delight in this chance to acquire such a historically and aesthetically attractive exemplar. *LOA from Mei-Gray*. **Minimum Bid: $3,250**

19758 **Early 1960s Terry Sawchuk Signed J.D. McCarthy Postcard.** The over 600 stitches to the face are a testament to the vigor that Terry Sawchuk employed when he minded the net for professional hockey teams in Detroit, Boston and Toronto. Nicknamed "Uke" because of his Ukranian heritage, Sawchuk tattooed his impression on the game everywhere that he went, nowhere more evident than in the trio of Rookie of the Year awards that he won in each of three leagues — the first person to accomplish that feat. From the J.D. McCarthy postcard issue released in the early-1960s we present this quality Sawchuk exemplar, signed in 9/10 blue ink by the Hall of Famer. Card measures 3.5 x 5.5". Fine memento courtesy of a hard-nosed goaltender who retired with more wins than anyone else. *LOA from PSA/DNA. LOA from James Spence Authentication.* Minimum Bid: $250

19759 **Circa Late-1960s Gilles Marotte/Bill White Game Worn Jersey.** One of the most iconic pieces of hockey memorabilia remains the beautiful design of the Chicago Black Hawks. Here we present an often-sought style, worn both by Gilles Marotte and Bill White. The two were part of a trade between Chicago and the Los Angeles Kings that saw them swap teams. The rare one-year style jersey comes from the 1969-70 Chicago Black Hawks season, as evidenced by the "Gunzo's Berwyn, Ill." tag in the collar. Gunzo's used this tag for only one season as a 1970 fire forced them to move to River Forest, which is reflected on the tags of the later versions. The white home gamer is highlighted no doubt by the classic twill logo with hand-sewn detailings. Small light spots of blood are found throughout the chest and back area, and pronounced puckering to the logo and shoulder "2" twill identifiers is evident. Stick marks to the chest and the rear twill "2" also lend to the game use. General Athletic tag found in rear tail. Beautifully chain-stitched tomahawk logos found at either shoulder. While Marotte had the majority of the use of this garment with over 51 games logged, seven-year Black Hawk player and stint head coach Bill White played his first 21 games with the team in this shirt. A fine rarity with tremendous appeal. *LOA from Rich Ellis.* Minimum Bid: $1,500

19760 **1970 Don Awrey Stanley Cup Finals Game Worn Jersey.** A brutal defender who delivered crushing checks and stifled many opponent shots for the Boston Bruins, Don Awrey was rewarded for his efforts by having his name engraved on the Stanley Cup twice while with the team — once in 1970 and again in '72. From his first championship foray we advance this top-notch gamer which a 26-year-old Awrey donned during the '70 Stanley Cup Finals, a thrilling example with solid wear. This garment is one of two in this auction that was worn on the same ice as Bobby Orr during the legendary playoff run that was highlighted by Orr's famous goal, Awrey was on the line that observed "The Goal" in close proximity. The Wilson gamer carries the Bruins' trademark three-color tackle twill spoked "B" logo with pronounced deterioration, while similar wear is also evident on the rear gold-on-white rear numerals. Advanced sleeve pilling and team repairs in the right sleeve, left shoulder, front tail and back further the evidence of game use. Inner yoke remains intact with thorough oxidation staining from the inner clips. Not only is this a first-class example of one of the most distinguished uniform designs in sports, serious hobbyists will also enjoy its historical significance of the utmost degree from its proximity and contribution to Orr's legend. *LOA from Rich Ellis.* **Minimum Bid: $1,750**

19761 **1970 Wayne Cashman Stanley Cup Finals Game Worn Jersey.** A teammate who played alongside Bobby Orr in their junior hockey days with the Oshawa Generals, Wayne Cashman rejoined his Hall of Fame mate when he skated with him as a member of the Boston Bruins. Cashman was part of the legendary 1969-70 Bruin squad that ended a 29-year Stanley Cup drought and was one of the first men to mob Orr when he scored his championship-winning overtime goal in the most heroic of fashions. Here we present the jersey that Cashman donned that day, a glorious well-worn Bruins Wilson gamer with numerous team repairs and advanced puckering to the numerals and front logo. The right wing's numeral "12" has been applied in gold-on-white tackle twill on each shoulder as well as the verso, while the chest area is dominated by the Bruins' signature eight-spoke logo in three-color tackle twill. The black garment sports the vintage lace-up collar. A fight strap inside has been removed. A fine opportunity to own a classic exemplar of one of hockey's most attractive uniform designs, complete with the added distinction of its proximity to such a momentous athletic event. Comes from the personal collection of Cashman himself. *LOA from Rich Ellis.* **Minimum Bid: $2,500**

19762 **1970-71 Phil Esposito Game Used Stick Signed by Boston Bruins Team.** During his glory years with the Bruins, Boston hockey fans proudly displayed bumper stickers on their cars which announced, "Jesus saves, Espo scores on the rebound." The first player to reach one hundred points in a season, Esposito would top the century mark six times during his Hall of Fame career, with his greatest total of 152 coming the year he made use of the Northland Custom Pro stick we are privileged to present here. The stick exhibits fine use, suggesting that a fair quantity of that season's seventy-six goals and equal number of assists were registered by its taped blade. "Esposito" is emblazoned in block lettering at mid-shaft, with more original tape found at handle end. A faded red number "77" is found at upper shaft. Adding another layer of desirability to what could already be considered one of the most desirable Esposito sticks in the hobby is the addition of twenty signatures from the Bruins team, most notably Espo himself, Orr, McKenzie, Smith, Cashman, Cheevers, Stanfield, Hodge and Awrey. This is widely considered to be the greatest hockey team of all time, featuring four one-hundred point players just two years after Esposito became the first to ever reach that mark, and setting an NHL record for victories in a season. With tremendous appeal to both game used and autograph collectors alike, this is a stick that should garner serious bidding attention when its time on the auction block arrives. *LOA from PSA/DNA (autographs). LOA from James Spence Authentication (autographs).* Minimum Bid: $750

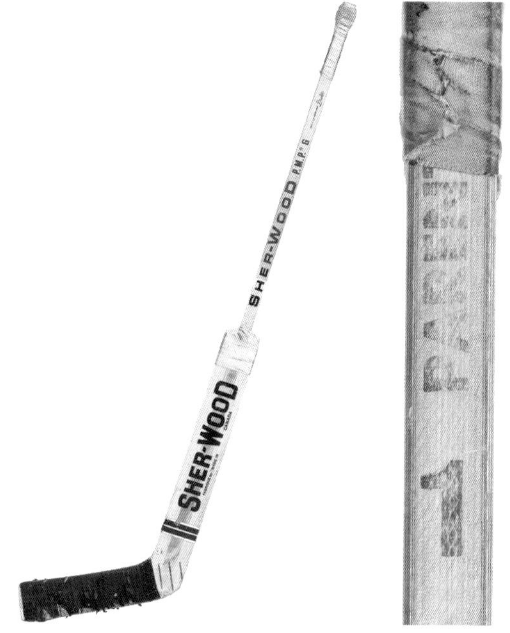

19763 **1972-73 Bernie Parent Game Used Stick.** The NHL's first defector to the fledgling World Hockey Association, Bernie Parent played the league's first season as a goaltender for the Philadelphia Blazers. Parent served as one of the WHA's only stars and was forced to compete with the Philly hockey limelight with his former team, the Flyers. A lesser level of defensive ability in front of him caused Parent a ton of work in the goal that season, culminating in his return to NHL ice the following campaign.

From Parent's only WHA season, 1972-73, we present this game-used Sher-Wood goalie stick with fine evidence of game use. Original taping at blade and handle remains in place, and the shaft has become cracked where it meets the blade. Heavy checking and divots pepper the back edge of the blade. An overall impressive piece from the Hall of Fame netminder. Minimum Bid: $400

19764 **1970s World Hockey Association Pennants Lot of 27.** Near complete collection of 30" felt pennants chronicles the short life of the World Hockey Association, which operated as a direct competitor to the NHL from 1972-79. The league suffered many financial woes, though — endorsing multi-million contracts on one hand while the franchises that supported them floundered with financial instability. Numbering 27 in total, just about every team that played in the league is represented, with some variants present. Entries include pennants from the Hew England Whalers (two variations), Birmingham Bulls, Minnesota Fighting Saints (two variations), Calgary Cowboys, Houston Aeros, Indianapolis Racers, Chicago Cougars, Ottawa Nationals, Winnipeg Jets (two variations), Cleveland Crusaders, Michigan Stags, New York Raiders, Cincinnati Stingers, New York Golden Blades, Alberta Oilers (two designs), Phoenix Roadrunners, Los Angeles Sharks, Denver Spurs, Quebec Nordiques (two designs), Toronto Toros, San Diego Mariners and Vancouver Blazers. Condition issues are limited to pin holes on some examples and some staining to the LA Sharks pennant, however several remain in mint presentational condition. Unique collection from this long-gone, but not forgotten, hockey league. **Minimum Bid: $450**

19765 **1970s Chicago Cougars Team-Issued Ring.** One of the original franchises of the World Hockey Association, the Chicago Cougars began operation in 1972. Though they only remained a franchise for three seasons, they did achieve a taste of success when they made it to the 1974 Avco World Trophy Finals against Gordie Howe and his Houston Aeros. Here we present a ring issued by the team during those early 1970s years, a gold ring with a green stone bearing the team's logo. A figure of a hockey player has been engraved on either wide, with "F. Potvin," presumably a front-office man, engraved on the left side banner. Impressive presentational piece remains in top condition **Minimum Bid: $300**

19766 **1970s Valeri Kharlamov Worn Soviet National Team Jacket.** A star among stars, Valeri Kharlamov used his incredible speed and hockey IQ to establish himself as the premier left winger for his CSKA Moscow side during an era that Soviet hockey was at its strongest. Forced to find other ways to excel due to his lack of brawn, Kharlamov elevated his on-ice play to the cerebral level, outwitting his opponents with trickery and guile. A terror in international play, few liked to see Kharlamov as he dominated his appearances against American professionals — collecting 19 goals and 29 assists for 48 points in 40 games played against them. This led to a nasty rash of on-ice brutality that saw Kharlamov suffer many injuries due to his rivals' cheap shots. The team-issued CCCP national jacket that we present here comes from an early 1970s tour of Canada and the United States embarked upon by the Soviets and is Kharlamov's personal garment. The red nylon jacket was manufactured by Winnipeg's New West Sportswear and includes embroidered "C.C.C.P." and criss-crossed hockey stick and puck over the heart. Embroidered verso reads "KHARLAMOV 17 C.C.C.P.", with additional embroidered "17"s on each sleeve. Wear is light but apparent in the form of wear to the embroidery and some light staining. The area of the "17" on verso appears to have undergone some sort of number change. Tremendous rarity courtesy of one of the most-feared and gifted players to emerge from the powerful Soviet hockey machine. **Minimum Bid: $750**

19767 **1975 Bernie Parent Game Worn All-Star Jersey.** Following his return to the NHL from the burgeoning World Hockey Association in 1973, Bernie Parent enjoyed one of the best stretches of his career. His prowess in the net earned him the Vezina and Conn Smythe Trophies in both 1974 and 1975 in addition to his All-Star berths. The All-Star jersey that we present here was worn by Parent in the 1975 All-Star Game — a fine orange Gerry Cosby shirt with expected moderate All-Star wear. A large embroidered NHL logo dominates the chest and is flanked by smaller logos set atop white tackle twill stars. Twill stars also encircle the waist and are found at each elbow. Black-on-white numeral "1" can be found on verso and on each shoulder, while "PARENT" in black twill outlined in white stitching is sewn directly to the jersey back. All twill identifiers exhibit pronounced puckering and the rear numeral has some nice abrasion marks. Puck marks can be found at the front chest. Fine Hall of Fame All-Star jersey from Parent in his prime. *LOA from Rich Ellis. LOA from Bernie Parent.*
Minimum Bid: $2,000

19768 **1976-77 Montreal Canadiens Miniature Stanley Cup Championship Trophy.** Glorious exemplar of one of the most sought-after mementos that exists in the hobby — this 13" was presented to a member of the 1976-77 Montreal Canadiens. Emanating from a particularly powerful streak in the franchise's history, the Habs took home the '77 Stanley Cup by way of their second consecutive four-games-to-none manhandling. Under the guidance of head coach Scotty Bowman, Montreal would stretch its stretch of consecutive championships to four. While it cannot be determined with absolute certainty who this award was originally awarded to, but the desirability still lies in the year issued as well as the sparkling condition that this piece exhibits given the thirty years since its presentation. Absent is the tarnish that would be expected in a piece of this age. The fantastic memento calls to mind such Montreal greats as Guy LaFleur, Jacques Lemaire, Steve Shutt. Larry Robinson and more. Will make for an attractive highlight for the serious hockey enthusiast. **Minimum Bid: $1,750**

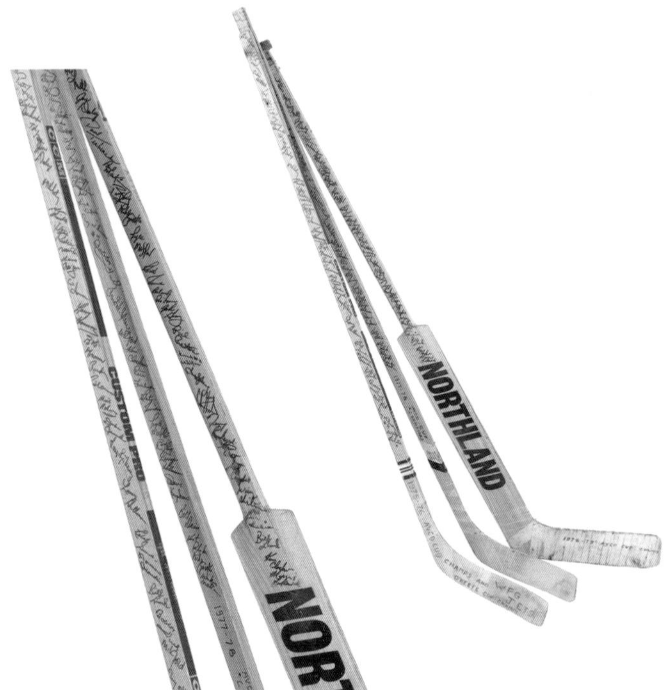

19769 **1976-79 Winnipeg Jets Team Signed and Avco Cup Finals Game Used Sticks Lot of 3.** Here we present a fabulous collection that honors the waning years of the NHL's most successful rival league, the World Hockey Association. Here we present a team signed stick from each of the three years that the Winnipeg Jets took home the Avco World Trophy — each having been used on the ice for the championship series. Lot includes: 1) Lyle Moffat's CCM Custom Pro signed by the 1975-76 Jets including Bobby Hull, Ulf Nilsson, Anders Hedberg, Veli-Pekka Ketola, Peter Sullivan, Joe Daley, and Mike Ford. 2) Lynn Powis' Northland stick signed by the 1977-78 Jets including Hull, Nilsson, Hedberg, Wally Lindstrom, Sullivan, Gary Bromley, and Kim Clackson. 3) Joe Daley's Northland goalie stick signed by the 1978-79 Jets in the final WHA season including Nilsson, Hull, Morris Lukowich, Daley, Lindstrom, Terry Ruskowski, and Rich Preston. Beautiful collection of WHA Champions team signed items, ripe for display in their present condition. *Autograph LOA from PSA/DNA.* **Minimum Bid: $500**

19770 **1977-78 Gordie Howe New England Whaler Warm Up Suit.** Given that his 26-year NHL career included numerous awards and accomplishments, it seemed that the book had closed on a stellar hockey career. Not one fan would have felt shorted, as Howe's prowess was enough that he essentially already racked up the statistics for two Hall of Fame careers. The superior athlete gave up retirement to return to competitive hockey with the WHA's Houston Aeros, an impressive for a man in his mid-40s. From the personal collection of long-time Whalers equipment man Skip Cunningham we present this quirky hockey memento — Howe's personal New England warm-up suit from the 1977-78 season. That particular campaign marks not only the season that Howe turned 50, but also saw him score his 1,000th career goal. The green Sand-Knit jacket and pants worn by Mr. Hockey show wear in the form of areas of pilling throughout as well as some small holes on the jacket back. The jacket's left chest has the signature white-on-gold twill whale logo as well as Gordie's full name and number in iron-on felt lettering below. The upper right portion of the "G" in "GORDIE" has been torn away. With Howe's game used material commanding a premium due to his dignified status in the sport, the offering here makes for a great Hall of Famer-worn memento for those perhaps not able to afford a top-notch piece worn by Howe. *LOA from Rich Ellis. LOA from Game Worn Auctions.* **Minimum Bid: $1,000**

MR. HOCKEY

19771 **1977-78 Gordie Howe Game Worn Jersey.** The size of Gordie Howe's body of work is so expansive that the only appropriate nickname — Mr. Hockey — encompasses the whole of the sport that made him famous. A bit of the opposite can also be said, as Howe had few rivals for popularity during his extensive career. A crushing presence on the ice during his heyday, Howe confounded with his amazing combination of toughness and goalscoring. More than impressive even in his 40s, Howe showed that the ravages of time could do little to affect his god-like talent as he widened the breadth his legend even further. From his WHA days with the New England Whalers we present this road green durene gamer manufactured by Wilson. Game use on this example consists of fine pilling and stick marks throughout, as well as some board burns. Stylized "W" logo on chest and whales on shoulders make for exceptional instances of graphic design. Verso has white-on-gold tackle twill identifiers with numeral "9" and full name "GORDIE HOWE" sewn directly to the jersey above, indicating that his sons also played on the team. Jersey is size 48 and has the fight strap removed — a detail indicative to Howe gamers. Not only did Howe turn 50 years old during the campaign which this jersey was worn, but he also recorded his 1,000th career goal that season — which he did while wearing a green Whalers sweater. The chance to own a top-notch Hall of Fame gamer worn in a milestone game such as this one will quite possibly never come again. It is believed that this jersey originates from the collector Steve Reyson, who was a personal acquaintance of Howe's and a well-known hobbyist in the Detroit area and a friend of Gordie Howe's. *LOA from Rich Ellis. LOA from Game Worn Auctions.*
Minimum Bid: $10,000

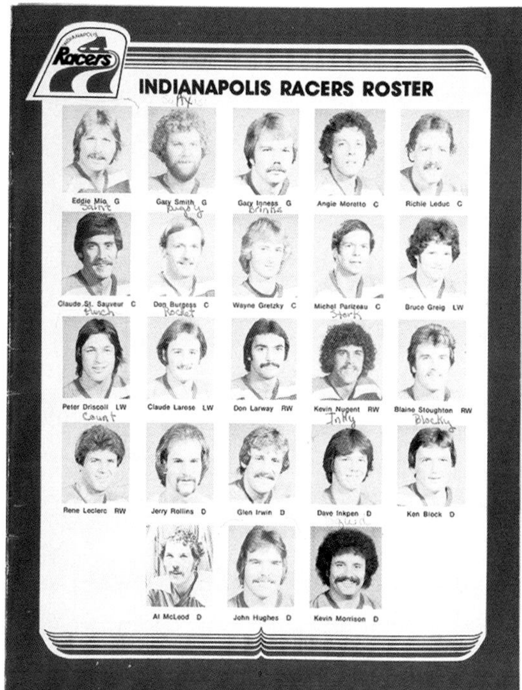

19772 **1978 Indianapolis Racers Official Game Programs with Wayne Gretzky.** With stirring skills that many equated to a "magic touch," Wayne Gretzky was one of the most-celebrated hockey phenoms in memory by the time that he was 16, which ensued in his recruitment by a number of WHA teams. League rules prohibited the NHL from signing sub-18 year old players, resulting in the Great One signing with the WHA's Indianapolis Racers at age 17. But at the time the league, and the team, were floundering and Racers owner Nelson Skalbania was forced to sell Gretzky's rights to the Edmonton Oilers to make up for his financial troubles. As a result, the indomitable number 99 only logged eight games for the Racers, switching teams very early in the 1978-79 season. Here we present a collection of five official game programs from late 1978. One of the programs comes from one of the Great One's few games in Racers uniform and thus commands a premium as these are prized in the hobby. The other highlight of the lot comes with the December 10 program, which also features Gretzky in his return to Indy as a member of the Oilers. Some of the earliest professional acknowledgements from the man regarded as perhaps the best ever. Minimum Bid: $350

19773 **1979-80 Wayne Stephenson Game Worn Jersey.** A star for the St. Louis Blues and Philadelphia Flyers for much of the 1970s, Wayne Stephenson enjoyed NHL success after tending the goal with the Canadian National Team early in his career. "Goodman & Sons" and "Bill Vanderburg" tags found in collar of the orange mesh sweater. Philadelphia's stylized flying "P" design has been applied to the gamer's front. Wear is evident by material pilling and stick marks on the arms and advanced puckering to the rear white-on-black twill "35". Board burns and several tears of the verso numbers further lend to the game use of this piece. An incorrect name plate was added to verso, but it has since been removed and jersey is now all original. Stephenson has placed a blue felt pen signature to the right shoulder. *LOA from Rich Ellis. LOA from PSA/DNA (autograph). LOA from James Spence Authentication (autograph).* Minimum Bid: $650

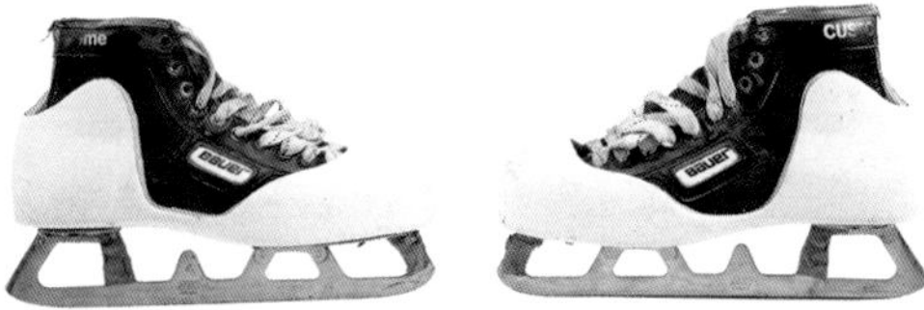

19774 **1980s Billy Smith Game Worn Goalie Skates.** While Billy Smith was considered one of the premier NHL goaltenders during the 1970s and early 1980s, he managed to build on his legend with some of the finest post-season performances that a netminder has ever known. The anchor for the New York Islanders dynasty of the 1980s, Smith ensured that the team would keep the Stanley Cup each year from 1980-83. Here we present a pair of Bauer goalie skates worn by Smith in the early to mid-1980s — perhaps they were part of the epic Stanley Cup run. Presented to 1970s Black Hawks great and Chicago sports bar owner Phil Russell, these skates come with a letter to that effect, signed by Russell. A dazzling piece of NHL history with loads of evidence of game use from an acclaimed Hall of Fame goalie. *LOA from Phil Russell.* **Minimum Bid: $400**

19775 **1981-82 Danny Gare Game Worn Jersey.** Though many will remember the 17-year career of Danny Gare for his dynamite goalscoring days with the Buffalo Sabres, he also enjoyed some great seasons with the Detroit Red Wings, beginning in the middle of the 1981-82 season during which he was traded. From the year of Gare's trade we present this top-quality red mesh Red Wings gamer, a thoroughly impressive example with ample evidence of game use. The classic "winged wheel" logo, with thread tattering and some puckering of the red tackle twill, is mounted on the jersey's front along with a patch honoring 50 years of ownership under the Norris family. White twill identifiers are attached to the verso to read "GARE" on a nameplate above the jersey numerals "18", which also appear in smaller form at each shoulder. All identifiers exhibit ample fraying and puckering and have been appropriately stained given the heavy use. Board burns and slash marks pepper each of the garment's sleeves, with a small team repair in the left arm. Tagging collar has been removed and the fight strap remains in the rear tail, exhibiting some minor oxidation staining. **Minimum Bid: $600**

19776 **Mid-1980s Wayne Gretzky Game Used Stick.** Wayne Gretzky's impact on the NHL was nothing short of miraculous, gaining a great amount of respect by proving the critics wrong that predicted that his success at the lower levels would flop in the face of bigger and stronger NHL competition. To show them that his game was superior at any level, Gretzky won the Hart Memorial Trophy as the league's MVP during his 1979-80 rookie year. Then he won it again each season for the next season. The Great One was born. From the early 1980s we present this Titan TPM2020 stick, wielded by the one and only Wayne Gretzky during his time with the Edmonton Oilers. Signs of use are evident by the abrasions to the shaft and blade, ad well as the wear to the original taping at the blade and handle. With the frequency with which Gretzky scored points during his NHL career, the mind fairly boggles when contemplating how many of his record-setting points were produced by the provided wooden gem. **Minimum Bid: $750**

19777 **1980s Denis Potvin Game Worn and Signed Gloves.** In what was one of the most impressive stretches enjoyed by any NHL team in recent history, the New York Islanders won four consecutive Stanley Cups from 1980-83, establishing themselves immediately as the team to beat for the early 1980s. Due in large part to the prowess of their captain Denis Potvin, the Isles established a dynasty that saw them win a whopping 19 consecutive playoff series, which stands as a record in pro sports. Without the grit of their star defender and on-ice leader Potvin, it's doubtful that any of this would have been possible. Here we offer a pair of Potvin's game worn gloves, signed and personalized and exhibiting extraordinary wear. Nearly every surface of the gloves is covered with abrasions and the right palm has been completely torn through and repaired — a testament to the defender's hard-nosed style of play. The inscription and signature span both gloves and reads: "To Rusty's, My Best Always, Good Luck 'Phil', Denis Potvin". A small handwritten "5" also in found inside each glove at the wrist. Originally presented to ex-Black Hawks defenseman Phil Russell for his Chicago sports bar, these gloves were worn at some point during those stellar Stanley Cup seasons. Includes a photo matched 8x10" print showing Potvin sporting the same gloves. A fine addition to any top-rate collection. *LOA from Phil Russell. LOA from PSA/DNA (autograph). LOA from James Spence Authentication (autograph).* **Minimum Bid: $500**

19778 **1980s Denis Potvin Game Used Skates.** When defenseman Denis Potvin came to New York as a member of the Islanders, the expectations were piled high upon him as he was there to save a struggling franchise. Add to that the pressure of being the next Bobby Orr and you'd come close to knowing what it was like to be Potvin in the 1970s. The player did not wilt in the face of his fan's huge hopes, instead he carved out one of the most accomplished careers from any backline player and even scored over 100 points for the 1978-79 season. He eventually broke Orr's record for all-time points by a defenseman, presumably in these skates. The captain excelled in virtually every aspect of the game and was one of the more heady men to play in his era. From the circa the mid-1980s we offer this fantastic pair of Tacks skates, worn on-ice by the Hall of Famer. Each skate s well-worn with advanced scuffing and abrasions found throughout. A black sharpie "5" has been written on the frame of each skate to indicate Potvin's now-retired jersey number. Includes photo match of Potvin wearing the same skates with the Islanders. Comes with letter from former Black Hawk and Chicago restauranteur Phil Russell, who was presented the skates by Potvin during the 1986 World Championships in Moscow. *LOA from Phil Russell.* Minimum Bid: $900

19779
Circa 1983 Raymond Bourque Game Used Stick. One of the greatest scoring defensemen in the history of professional hockey, Raymond Bourque completely endeared himself to Boston Bruins fans by simply being the best defender around. The league agreed with this sentiment and awarded him the Norris Trophy five times during his career, more than any player not named Orr or Harvey. From circa 1983 we present a fabulous early career stick used by the Hall of Famer. The Sher-Wood PMP 5073 stick dates both from before his captaincy of the Boston Bruins as well as before he changed his jersey number to "77," giving up his original "7" to honor the Boston great Phil Esposito. "BOURQUE 7" appears stamped on the shaft, with a black sharpie handwritten "7" located just above that. The player's original taping remains at the blade and the handle, with the expected signs of use found throughout. Fantastic chance for devout fans of the Bruins to own an early career Bourque piece. Minimum Bid: $350

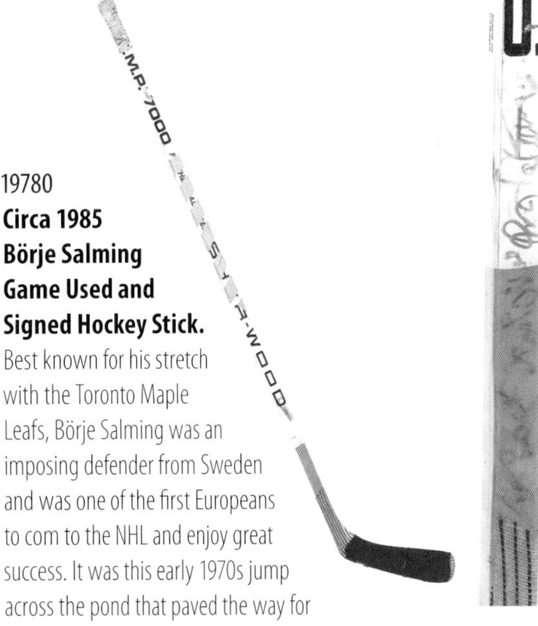

19780
Circa 1985 Börje Salming Game Used and Signed Hockey Stick. Best known for his stretch with the Toronto Maple Leafs, Börje Salming was an imposing defender from Sweden and was one of the first Europeans to com to the NHL and enjoy great success. It was this early 1970s jump across the pond that paved the way for the numerous foreign players that populate the league today. Here we present one of Salming's preferred on-ice companions — a game used Sher-Wood stick dating from circa the 1985-86 season. Nice use can be observed at various points up and down the shaft and on the blade and the player's original taping is found at the handle, shaft and blade. The Hall of Famer has added to the shaft his signature as well as inscription that reads "To Rocky, Best Wishes." Fine Hall of Fame game used material. *LOA from PSA/DNA (autograph). LOA from James Spence Authentication (autograph).* Minimum Bid: $350

19781 **1987-88 Mike Vernon Game Worn Jersey.** By the time that the 1987-88 NHL season had rolled around, Mike Vernon had already gathered much NHL experience and clout, backstopping his Flames to the NHL Finals against fellow rookie goaltender Patrick Roy and the Montreal Canadiens in 1986. By his third season he was a bona fide premier goalie, earning Calgary an impressive 39 wins for the 1987-88 season. From that particular campaign we present this white mesh gamer with desirable goaltender use. The red-on-yellow-on-white tackle twill Calgary Flames team logo takes its spot on the garment's chest, while verso identifiers are made up of a red-on-yellow twill "30" underneath a likewise-styled "VERNON" on a name plate. Numeral "30" is also found on each shoulder, the left of which is also home to a patch commemorating Calgary's hosting of the 1988 Winter Olympiad. Exceptional use is apparent in the form of advanced identifier puckering and staining to the right front shoulder area. CCM logo has been embroidered to rear tail and the inner fight strap remains attached. In 2007, the Calgary Flames organization retired Vernon's number 30, pushing this gamer to an even higher level of desirability **Minimum Bid: $500**

19782 **1988-89 Dave Manson Game Worn Hockey Jersey.** Exceptional white CCM Ultrafil knit jersey size 54 comes to us from the first full season that defenseman Dave Manson played with the Chicago Black Hawks. The iconic team logo is affixed to the jersey's front while black twill "MANSON" resides on a verso name plate above black-on-white tackle twill "3". Some light staining and material pilling is evident on the garment's front and underarms. Fight strap remains intact in rear tail and has light salt deposits. The Black Hawks' chain-stitched tomahawk logo is found at each shoulder, next to two-color twill "3" on each side. Maska Ultrafil tag in collar has a handwritten "54" presumably penned there by an equipment man. CCM logo is stitched in the rear right tail. The classic Black Hawks gamer is a staple for serious hobby enthusiasts. This offering is no different, providing some lucky collector the chance to bolster their stock with such an attractive shirt. *LOA from Rich Ellis.* **Minimum Bid: $400**

19783 **Early 1990 Raymond Bourque Signed Game Used Gloves.** The game's top scoring defenseman of all-time used the gloves presented here to rack up some of his record-setting numbers during his lengthy stretch with the Boston Bruins. Each of this pair of Sher-Wood SG-5040 Sher-Grip glove has also been signed in pen by the Hall of Famer. Dating from the early 1990s, the pair shows incredible wear throughout and each has been personalized by the defenseman's surname and jersey number. With Bourque becoming only the third defenseman to eclipse the 1,000-point mark in 1992, it seems likely that these gloves could have been used to collect some of the vital scores that contributed to that milestone. Great chance to own this piece from one the game's best ever. *LOA from PSA/DNA (autograph). LOA from James Spence Authentication (autograph).* **Minimum Bid: $400**

19784 **1990-91 Tomas Sandstrom Game Used Stick Signed by Los Angeles Kings Team.** The superstar Swede put fine use into this Sherwood P.M.P. 7000 gamer before providing it to his Smythe Conference-winning teammates for the application of twenty-four 9/10 and better black sharpie autographs. Among them we encounter Sandstrom himself, Gretzky, Duchesne, Hrudey, Robinson, Taylor, Elik, McSorley, Prajster and Laidlaw. A terrific display piece that will find game used collectors battling with autograph hounds for high bid domination. *LOA from PSA/DNA (autographs). LOA from James Spence Authentication (autographs).* **Minimum Bid: $300**

19785 **Mid-1990s Wayne Gretzky Game Used & Signed Stick.** Many who saw Gretzky play for the first time would swear that he had intimate contact with those who invented the sport — no vocabulary could amply describe his prowess more than simply applying the moniker of "The Great One". The amazing scoring talent utilized the provided Easton HXP 5100 while with the Los Angeles Kings circa the early to mid-1990s. Classic Gretzky Jack the Ripper handle and black tape covering the blade with evidence of powder having been applied there. Black sharpie signature has been applied to the blade, which also has "GRETZKY" stamped near the connection with the aluminum shaft. Obvious, yet light, signs of game use are evident throughout. Handle end has black handwritten "C31". Phenomenal exemplar from perhaps the game's foremost scoring threat of all-time. *LOA from PSA/DNA (autograph). LOA from James Spence Authentication (autograph).* **Minimum Bid: $600**

19786 **1990s Steve Yzerman Signed Game Used Gloves.** Through the eyes of the Detroit faithful, their long-time captain Steve Yzerman approached a God-like status. From the hands of that deity we present this fine pair of Louisville TPS gloves, alluring visually in their signature Red Wing crimson. Moderate wear is apparent in the form of several nicks and scrapes, as well as the appropriate palm wear caused by Yzerman's prodigious stickhandling. The "LOUISVILLE" branding that encircles each wrist has begun to crack and fade, however this region of each glove has been enhanced by the future Hall of Famer's black sharpie signature and jersey number "19" inscription. Rarified chance to own a piece worn by perhaps the Motor City's most-celebrated athletic hero. *LOA from PSA/DNA (autograph). LOA from James Spence Authentication (autograph).* Minimum Bid: $350

19787 **1990s Rob Blake Signed Team Canada World Championships Game Worn Jersey.** A premier defenseman whose talent needs no introduction, Rob Blake was given the job of captain of the Los Angeles Kings following the departure of Gretzky. This honor alone should insinuate the leadership that Blake does possess, however we will indulge with details of his patriotic servings with Team Canada in numerous World Hockey Championships throughout the 1990s. Manufactured by Tackla, the white mesh jersey presented here is a gamer courtesy of one of Blake's appearances in that tournament with sublimated maple leaf Canada logo on the chest. "BLAKE" resides on a name plate on the gamer's verso, next to which the star has applied a blue sharpie signature and jersey number "4", which is found below. "Allianz" sponsor patches have been sewn to each shoulder. Wear is light, but evident and shows itself especially by the slash marks on the right sleeve. Comes with letter of provenance from Hockey Canada official Marvin Goldblatt. *LOA from Rich Ellis. LOA from PSA/DNA (autograph). LOA from James Spence Authentication (autograph).* Minimum Bid: $400

19788 **Circa 1991 Raymond Bourque Game Used Stick.** Bourque consistently provided leadership from his spot on the Boston blue line. Through twenty seasons with the Bruins, twelve as team captain, Bourque dominated, earning 17 selections the NHL All-Star Game. He was also a five-time recipient of the Norris Trophy as the NHL's best defenseman, an honor only Bobby Orr and Doug Harvey have bested. In a memorable move, Bourque surrendered his original jersey number 7 during a December 1987 ceremony that honored Phil Esposito. At center ice in front of Esposito and the Boston faithful, Bourque removed his jersey to reveal a second Bruins sweater — this one numbered "77." Esposito's number could then be retired as Bourque went on to establish the double seven as his own. From circa 1991 we present one of Bourque's game used sticks, a black Sher-Wood model with "Bourque 77" applied to the shaft. Light signs of use are apparent and the original taping remains at the blade and handle. Shaft has a small crack about 18" up from the blade. A supreme exemplar from the Hall of Famer. **Minimum Bid: $250**

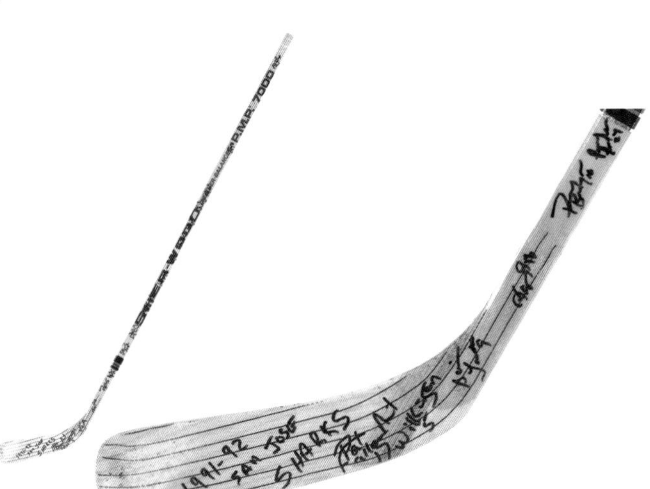

19789 **1991-92 San Jose Sharks Team Signed Stick.** Sports executives George and Gordon Gund had ownership of the Minnesota North Stars throughout the late 1970s and 1980s and sought to move the team to the Bay Area. While the powers that be in the league office did not allow this move, the Gunds were awarded an expansion team that would begin play for the 1991-92 season in exchange for selling the North Stars to Howard Baldwin. The expansion team in question was the San Jose Sharks, the league's first expansion team since '79. Here we present a Sher-Wood stick that has been signed by members of the team in perfect black sharpie. Includes entries from such first-year Sharks as Pat Falloon, Brian Lawton, Pat MacLeod, Neil Wilkinson, David Williams, Paul Fenton, Mike Sullivan, and Claudio Scremin. Stick was used on-ice by Scremin, who logged a total of 13 games with the Sharks that season. Would have prominent spot in any Bay Area hockey enthusiast's collection. *LOA from PSA/DNA (autograph). LOA from James Spence Authentication (autograph).* **Minimum Bid: $250**

19790 **1992-93 Jimmy Carson Stanley Cup Finals Game Worn Jersey.** Having had to deal with the pressure of being part of the trade that took Wayne Gretzky away from the Edmonton Oilers, Jimmy Carson was later able to team up with the Great One when he rejoined the Kings for the 1992-93 season. His first campaign back was a successful one as first-year head coach Barry Melrose led his team to a Stanley Cup clash against the strong Montreal Canadiens. The white Kings gamer that we present here was worn during those Stanley Cup Finals by Jimmy Carson with outstanding signs of wear in the form of numerous stick and puck marks and some great team repairs on the left arm. Jersey front includes the Kings silver and black crest on chest as well as the 100th Anniversary Stanley Cup patch worn by participants of the Finals. Rear numerals are composed of three-color black-on-white-on-silver tackle twill, with "CARSON" spelled in simple black twill above that. Swatch in tail carries an official embroidered Kings logo as well as text that reads "92-93 SET P" and a "PM" initials from the team's equipment manager. Great oxidation on the fight strap buttons. Overall, a perfect Stanley Cup exemplar from a mate of the Great One who once achieved All-Star status. Also offered with the lot is a DVD containing a video match of Carson wearing the sweater during the '93 Stanley Cup Finals. *LOA from Rich Ellis. LOA from Game Worn Auctions.* **Minimum Bid: $750**

BEANTOWN BOURQUE

19791 **1993-94 Raymond Bourque Game Worn Jersey.** Fans of the Bruins' gold and black can revel in the fact that their defense was anchored by one of the true geniuses of the game whose nose for the goal few back line men in NHL history could trump. His aggressiveness on the defensive end rounded him into one of the most total players in the game's history. Twenty-one remarkable chapters in Boston cemented his legacy, and his black CCM gamer from the 1993-94 campaign stands out here as a tremendous Hall of Fame offering. Any top-tier Bourque sweater will have many of the remarkable attributes that can be observed here, including interior and exterior pilling wear, team repairs in each sleeve and the back, slash marks, and board burns throughout — a testament to the player's hearty on-ice demeanor. Bruins' team logo "B" and gold-on-white tackle twill captain's "C" are the jersey front's design elements, while the same style tackle twill has been used on the verso for the "77" and "BOURQUE" which resides on the name plate above. The velcro button fight strap remains in place and demonstrates light rust. These extreme indications of game use make this amazing gamer one of the finest known in the hobby — the pinnacle Bourque shirt for the distinguished collector. NHL and CCM logos are embroidered to the right rear tail, while the left interior rear tail has a Custom Crafted logo and official team stamping. Amazing exemplar considering the numerous fakes that are known to exist from the '93-94 season. Dutiful hobbyists will do well to put forth their wager for this gamer, certified to be worn by one of the sport's most-honored during his final Norris Trophy season. *LOA from Rich Ellis. LOA from Milt Byron.* **Minimum Bid: $1,500**

19792 **1994 Wayne Gretzky European Exhibition Tour Game Worn and Signed Jersey.** In an attempt to jar the powers that be at the league offices, Wayne Gretzky organized a six-game tour of Finland, Sweden, and Norway during the 1994 NHL lockout. Officially earmarked as a tour of goodwill and charity, "Wayne Gretzky & Friends" included several high-profile stars such as Mark Messier, Brett Hull, Sergei Federov, and Steve Yzerman. A classy design of the eccentricity, the red and white striped sweater presented here is the on-ice garment for the Great One for that '94 tour. Script wording spelling Gretzky's famous jersey number is embroidered across the chest, which also is home to an NHLPA logo at right breast and a 4" white-red-white three-color tackle twill captain's "C" at left breast. Red twill stars complete the design of the jersey front as two flank the neck and four more form a horizontal line near the waistline. The player's surname "GRETZKY" is affixed to a red name plate on the jersey's verso along with white-red-white "99". A pair of CCM logos have been stitched into the rear tail, which also carries the customization of a velcro swatch on the inside right. The fight strap has been appropriately removed. As can be expected from an exhibition jersey, only light signs of wear can be discerned, however the white portions have picked up a bit of staining, especially near the waist on the reverse. A photograph is included depicting Gretzky himself presenting the jersey and the stained area can be accurately photo matched. A 10/10 Gretzky signature and "Tour 94" inscription has been added to the eastern "9" on the verso. We can't imagine a more attractive and unique exemplar from the Great One than this slick gamer. *LOA from Rich Ellis. LOA from PSA/DNA (autograph). LOA from James Spence Authentication (autograph).* Minimum Bid: $2,500

19793 **1997 NHL All-Stars Multi-Signed Street Banner.** Massive in dimensions and in the hockey talent it boasts, this heavy nylon flag was produced to welcome fans to this San Jose meeting of the NHL's best. The brightly colored display piece measures 29x94" in size, and features forty-two 10/10 black sharpie signatures from the men who combined for eighteen goals in a thrilling eleven to seven victory for the East at San Jose Arena. Among the more notable hockey icons: Gretzky, Lemieux Yzerman, Hull and Chelios. Included is a letter on NHL letterhead donating this piece to help raise funds for the American Cancer Society in memory of celebrated sportswriter Dick Dobbins. *LOA from PSA/DNA. LOA from James Spence Authentication.* Minimum Bid: $400

19794 **1997-98 Ray Bourque Game Worn Jersey Signed by Boston Bruins Team.** A staple of the Boston Bruins defense for over two decades, Bourque rates near the top of most experts' lists compiling the greatest NHL players of all time. This fantastic specimen dates from Bourque's nineteenth of twenty-one seasons in gold and black, and exhibits wonderful use that illustrates the hard-hitting style with which he paved a path to the Hall of Fame. All of the key factors in an ideal Bourque jersey are present here, with custom shortened sleeves, team repairs, stick marks, board burns and interior pilling wear all in evidence. The team logo "B" on the chest is joined by his captain's "C," with "Bourque 77" likewise applied in gold and black tackle twill on verso. Number "77" is repeated on each sleeve, below team logo bear patches. A velcro button style fight strap is in place in rear tail. Proper "Starter" tagging is found in interior collar, with "56-R" size designation. The jersey provides superb provenance to match its regal heritage, sourced from the personal collection of team trainer Kenny "Doc" Flager. Twenty-two black NRMT and better black sharpie signatures decorate the chest of the jersey, many personalized to Doc. Among the signers are Bourque himself, Samsonov, Donato, DiMaio, Axelsson and Thornton. The end result is a Bourque jersey that would only be at home in the finest of private collections. *LOA from Rich Ellis. LOA from PSA/DNA (autograph). LOA from James Spence Authentication (autograph).* **Minimum Bid: $3,000**

19795 **1999-2000 Luc Robitaille Game Worn Jersey.** His future Hall of Fame induction assured, Robitaille should rank high on the "want list" for collectors looking for solid investment material. This striking purple, black and silver gamer derives from Lucky Luc's second of three tours of duty with the Los Angeles Kings franchise, for which he holds the all-time club record for goals scored. He is properly honored here with an assistant captain's letter "A" upon upper left chest, balanced by the futuristic "2000 NHL" patch at upper right above the shimmering team crest at front and center. "Los Angeles" is spelled in distinctive font across lower front exterior hem. "Robitaille 20" is boldly affixed to the verso. Logo crown and number "20" appear upon each sleeve, which exhibit a nice scattering of board burns and stick marks. Further stick marks on the chest and light interior pilling bear further witness to icy battle. Velcro button fight strap remains affixed to rear interior tail. A 10/10 black sharpie signature on rear numerals provides that extra bit of appeal. A picture-perfect specimen from the most prolific goal scoring left winger in NHL history. *LOA from Rich Ellis. LOA from PSA/DNA (autograph). LOA from James Spence Authentication (autograph).* Minimum Bid: $500

19796 **2002-03 Milan Hejduk Game Worn Jersey.** Important gamer dates to the Czech superstar's finest season, one in which he earned the Maurice "Rocket" Richard Trophy as the NHL's top goalscorer. Fine wear upon his home white Colorado Avalanche jersey is evident within a sizeable collection of stick and board marks decorating the chest and sleeves, suggesting that at least a few of his fifty goals must have been netted in this shirt. Team logo patches are applied to chest and shoulders, with number "23" appearing on each sleeve and verso. Distinctive font spells "Hejduk" across rear nameplate. Manufacturer's "CCM" patch appears on rear collar, with size "56" Canadian flag tag inside collar. Fight strap is in place in rear tail. Unbeatable provenance is provided by "MeiGray Group" authentication, the marketing company with exclusive ties to the Colorado Avalanche franchise. Their authenticating patch is applied to inner tail hem, with matching serialized paperwork included. A top specimen from this young superstar. *LOA from MeiGray Group.* Minimum Bid: $400

19797 **2004 Yanic Perreault Game Worn Throwback Jersey.** For the 2003-04 season the Montreal Canadiens were one of the teams that took part in the NHL's Vintage jersey program, specially branded with the "V" patch. This Canadiens red jersey was designed to imitate the circa 1960 Habs' sweater, complete with tie-up collar. The current offering comes from center Yanic Perreault and carries with it light signs of wear. Excellent throwback exemplar. Minimum Bid: $200

19798 **2005-06 Ziggy Palffy Game Worn Jersey.** Road white gamer dates to Ziggy Palffy's final NHL season, one in which he decided to announce his retirement after playing 42 games with the Penguins. Team logo patches on chest and each shoulder, while evidence of patch removal exists over the right chest. Tremendous wear is evidenced in the form of numerous puck and stick marks that sprinkle the jersey front and sleeves. Verso name plate reads "PALFFY" in two-color tackle twill, with the player's "33" affixed below. Fight strap remains in the rear tail, with Cutting Edge Sports swatch in rear tail. Swatch indicates that this gamer is the "Set #1" exemplar from the '05-06 season and includes equipment manager Steve Latin's name. A solid contributor on the offensive end for over a decade at the NHL level, the given gamer provides a fine opportunity to own perhaps the final professional jersey worn by Palffy. *Includes team letter from the Pittsburgh Penguins.* Minimum Bid: $300

19799 **2006-07 Ryan Malone Game Worn Jersey.** The Pittsburgh fans' beloved "Bugsy" Malone is part of a rich Penguin heritage as he is the second member of his family after his father to play with the organization. The left winger is part of a deadly on-ice combination that pairs himself and the dominant star Sidney Crosby. This well-worn white road gamer from the 2006-07 season was sported by Ryan Malone. Team logos are found at the chest and at each shoulder, while the reverse identifiers are made up of black tackle twill with gold trim to read "MALONE" "12". Player's surname is attached to a nameplate. Wear to the garment is advanced and includes numerous slash marks and board burns peppering virtually every part of it. Several unrepaired holes dot the jersey front and sleeves, while obvious material pilling and identifier fraying secure its game-worn origin. Tail tagging from Steve Latin at Cutting Edge Sports indicates "Set #3 2005-06", and provenance is further cemented by the signature of Penguins equipment manager Dana Heinze found on the fight strap. Superb example of one of the most representative hockey designs with appropriate NHL star wear. *Includes team letter from the Pittsburgh Penguins.* Minimum Bid: $400

19800 **2006-07 Mark Recchi Game Worn Jersey.** Drafted in 1988 by the Pittsburgh Penguins, Mark Recchi has spent many of his better season as a member of that team, figuring largely in the team's 1990-91 Stanley Cup-winning side. The long-time winger has been playing NHL hockey ever since and has the robust career stats to back that up, which include over 1,300 points and 500 goals. From the 2006-07 NHL campaign we present this Reebok home black jersey. Front includes the team logo at chest as well as three-color white, black and gold tackle twill assistant captain's "A". Similarly-styled twill "RECCHI" has been applied to a name plate on the gamer's reverse, which spans the area above the verso "8". Each sleeve bears advanced evidence of slash marks and board burns, with many unrepaired holes showing the results of this in-game damage. Nice material pilling in the waist area. Tagging in tail from Cutting Edge Sports with Dana Heinze's name, whose signature has been applied to the fight strap. Own this marvelous gamer from one of the league's most-respected veterans. *Includes team letter from the Pittsburgh Penguins.* Minimum Bid: $400

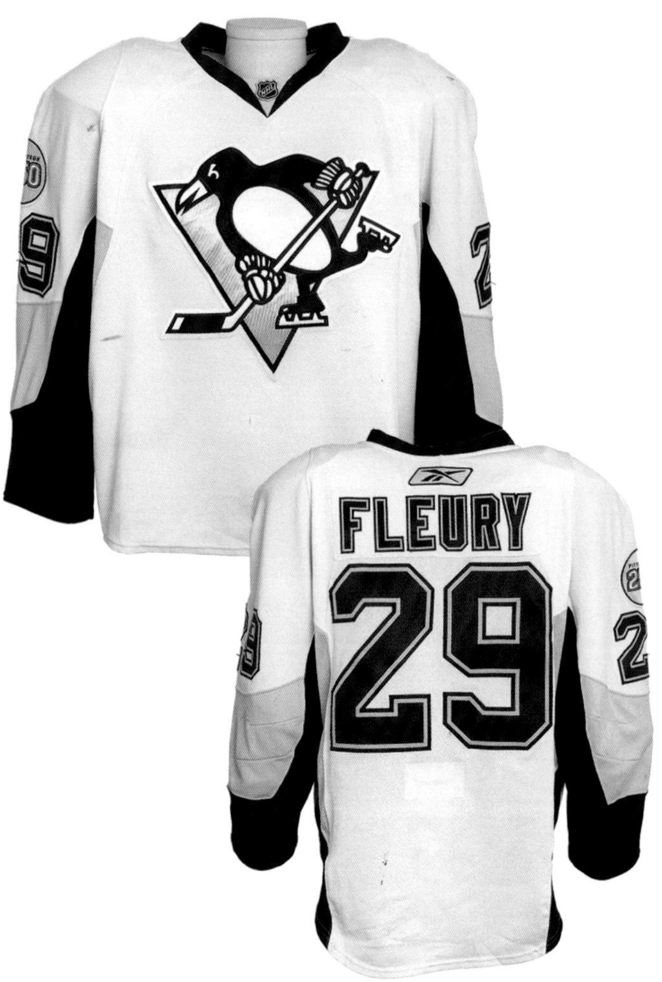

19801 **2007 Gary Roberts Game Worn Jersey.** A mid-season trade between the Florida Panthers and the Penguins saw league veteran Gary Roberts finish the 2006-07 season as a member of the Pittsburgh squad. Roberts has come to represent longevity in a league where careers average five years — Roberts is still in the NHL despite initially retiring following the 1995-96 season. Furthermore, Roberts has overcome his latest injury — a broken leg — to try to help his Penguins close the season strong and perform well in the playoffs. From his 2007 season that he finished with the Penguins we present this black home gamer, with nice wear in the form of stick marks and board burns resulting in several small unrepaired holes, mostly in the sleeve and shoulder regions. Further helping the evidence of game use is the pronounced material pilling near the waist hem. Team logo identifiers found on chest and both shoulders. Verso has tackle twill identifiers that read "ROBERTS" and "10" attached in three-color white, gold, and black. A "2006-07 Set #2" Cutting Edge Sports swatch with equipment manager Dana Heinze's name is found in the rear tail, which is also home to a Heinze-signed fight strap. Well-worn gamer courtesy of one of the game's long-time solid contributors. *Includes team letter from the Pittsburgh Penguins.* **Minimum Bid: $500**

19802 **2007-08 Marc-André Fleury Game Worn Jersey.** Another member of the young and talented stable of players employed by the Pittsburgh Penguins, Marc-André Fleury instilled enough confidence from the team's higher-ups that they used their number 1 pick in the 2003 Entry Draft to select him. Fleury has ensured that the pick was well worth it, playing his way to the team's top netminder and helping his team near the top of the Eastern Conference — a fantastic ascent in the table from the cellar-dwelling Penguin teams that Fleury cut his teeth with. From early in the current season we present this fine white gamer — a prime exemplar of the new Reebok NHL design with fantastic goalie wear. The jersey includes Penguins team logo at chest, with "29" and "FLEURY" affixed to a name plate on verso appear in a black twill with gold trim. Likewise-styled twill "29" also affixed to each shoulder, with a "Pittsburgh 250" patch attached to the right sleeve. Numerous stick and puck marks pepper the jersey front and sleeves, with material pilling at the collar and red goal paint residue on the upper back and sleeves adding to the game use. Fight strap remains attached in rear tail. A fine gamer from one the sport's premier young talents. *Includes team letter from the Pittsburgh Penguins.* **Minimum Bid: $300**

19803 **2007-08 Evgeni Malkin Game Worn Jersey.** Part of a powerful young Russian contingent that includes Alexander Ovechkin, Evgeni Malkin is already one of the most exciting and prolific scorers in the league today. The number 2 overall draft in the 2004 NHL Entry Draft, disputes with the Russian Hockey Federation delayed his NHL debut until 2006. His arrival to the league came with a bang, and he won the Calder Trophy for Rookie of the Year in his first season with the Pittsburgh Penguins. From the current season, which at the time of this writing sees him atop the scoring race with only Ovechkin ahead of him, we present this home black jersey in the new Reebok style debuted last year. The Pittsburgh team logo occupies the chest, while "EVGENI" and "71" are applied to the verso in three-color white, black and gold tackle twill. Wear is light, but evident. Right shoulder includes patch honoring the 250th anniversary of the founding of Pittsburgh. Tail includes "2007-08 set #2" tagging from Cutting Edge Sports and includes the name of equipment manager "Dana Heinze". Heinze has also signed the affixed fight strap. A stellar find from one the game's most-promising stars. *Includes team letter from the Pittsburgh Penguins.* Minimum Bid: $2,000

19804 **2008 Erik Christensen Winter Classic Game Worn Jersey.** On the first day of 2008 hockey history was made when the Buffalo Sabres and Pittsburgh met for a clash at Orchard Park, New York's Ralph Wilson Stadium for the first regular-season outdoor professional ice hockey game to be played in the United States. The participating teams played on a temporary rink built on the stadium's football field, drawing an NHL-record 71,217 attendance. Penguins and Sabres players all wore vintage uniforms, with the currently offered powder blue gamer representing the first time Pittsburgh has been outfitted in that hue since 1973. The 1-1 game was played for the most part in falling snow and culminated in a Penguins shootout win. Prodigious stickhandler Christensen was the first Pittsburgh shooter, but his miss mattered little when his team emerged on top 2-1. The young and skillful Erik Christensen, part of a Pens rookie class that included Sidney Crosby, Colby Armstrong, and Ryan Whitney, sported this anomaly of an offering for the game. Vintage team logo occupies the jersey front, joined by the special logo created for the event. Lace-up collar adds to the uniqueness of the piece. Verso has white twill "16" and "CHRISTENSEN" attached to a name plate, all outlined in a navy blue trim. As can be expected from this one-game style, wear is barely discernible, however the provenance in undisputable. Tag in inner tail comes from Cutting Edge Sports and includes a Winter Classic Logo as well as name of equipment manager Dana Heinze. Heinze has also placed a blue sharpie signature to the garment's fight strap. Mei-Gray tag also resides in the rear left tail. Be one of the first in the hobby to own one of these significant gamers, which will be sure to capture a hefty premium as we distance ourselves from the event. *Includes team Letter from the Pittsburgh Penguins.* Minimum Bid: $750

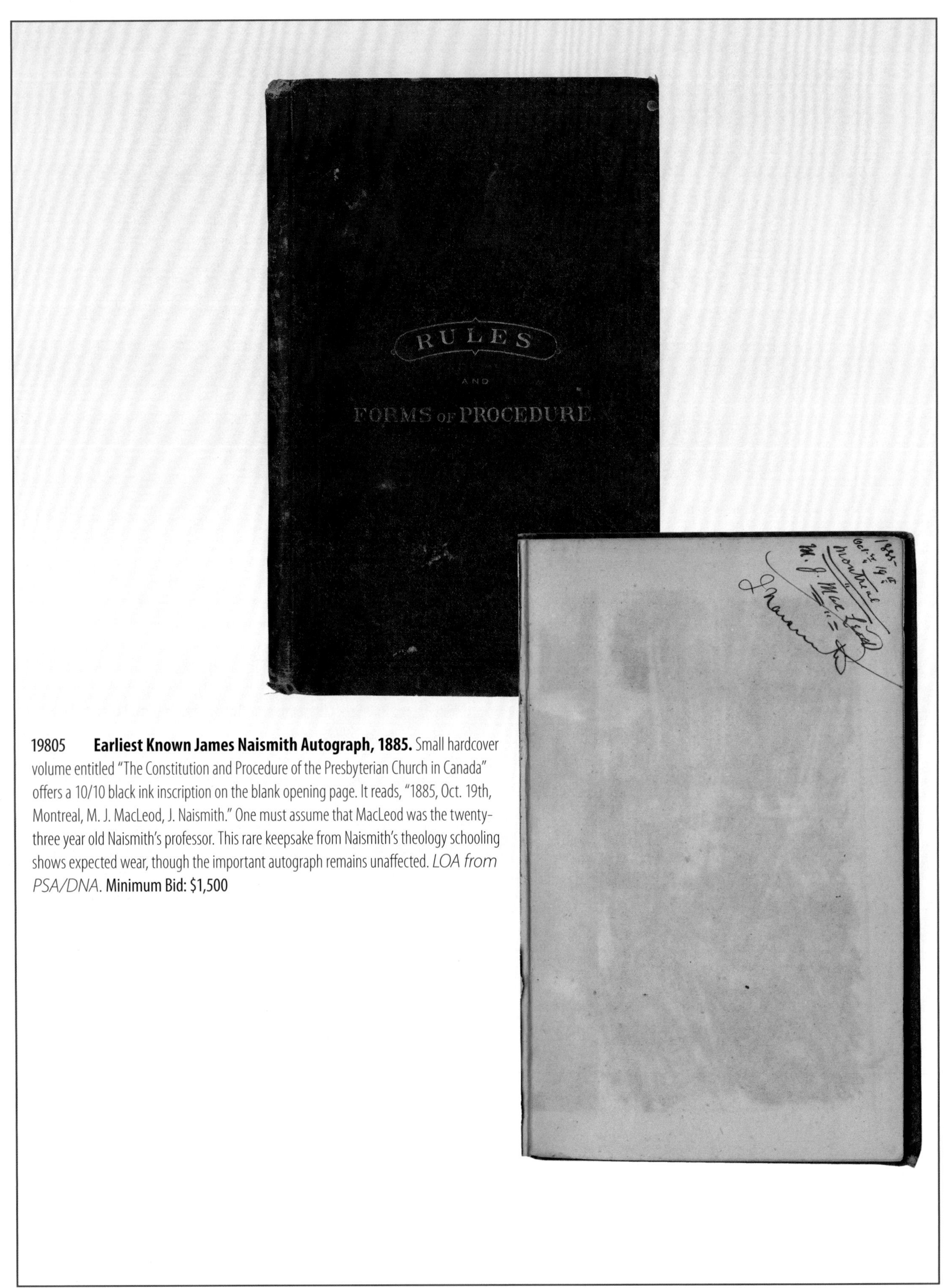

19805 **Earliest Known James Naismith Autograph, 1885.** Small hardcover volume entitled "The Constitution and Procedure of the Presbyterian Church in Canada" offers a 10/10 black ink inscription on the blank opening page. It reads, "1885, Oct. 19th, Montreal, M. J. MacLeod, J. Naismith." One must assume that MacLeod was the twenty-three year old Naismith's professor. This rare keepsake from Naismith's theology schooling shows expected wear, though the important autograph remains unaffected. *LOA from PSA/DNA.* **Minimum Bid: $1,500**

James Naismith
Center
Harvey Smith
Quarter
1891.

19806 1891 James Naismith Signed Football Cabinet Photograph. Naismith's second most important contribution to the world of sport is apparent here as he strikes a scrimmage pose while wearing the earliest prototype of a football helmet. It was actually Naismith's wife who requested such an innovation, lamenting the "cauliflower ears" her husband was developing as a result of his gridiron exploits. Playing the role of quarterback is his friend Harvey Smith, who is also identified in 10/10 black fountain pen writing in Naismith's hand on verso. Writing reads, in full, "James Naismith Center, Harvey Smith Quarter, 1891." This is arguably the finest Naismith autograph offered within this auction, if not the most pristine example in the hobby, bar none. The fantastic sepia cabinet photo bears the mark of a Springfield, Mass. studio at the left border, and remains in remarkable NRMT condition. Dimensions are 5x7". *LOA from PSA/DNA. LOA from James Spence Authentication.* Minimum Bid: $5,000

19807 **1951 Marques Haynes MVP Trophy - "Second Place Award" from the Marques Haynes Collection.** In 1951, after the success of the inaugural year before, the Harlem Globetrotters resumed their series of exhibition games versus the College All-Americans. Marques continued to excel and was the critical factor in leading the Globetrotters to victory. However, unlike the 1950 series, when he was named "Most Valuable Globetrotter," in 1951 the award went to his outstanding teammate, Reece "Goose" Tatum. Clearly, Goose had played extremely well and, as usual, entertained the audiences while doing so. However, a number of players on the team felt that Marques should have repeated. Abe Saperstein had wanted to reward and motivate one of his star attractions by giving the MVP award to Goose Tatum (Saperstein held the only vote, incidentally). However, he didn't want to create any dissension within an amazingly successful team. To address the issue, he decided to create the "2nd Place Award - Most Valuable Player" and presented it to Marques Haynes. This was the only time this was ever done. The trophy itself is in outstanding condition, with only a few minor marks on the walnut base and on the shining gold ball. The base where the player is attached to the ball has moderate chipping, with the darker metal showing through. It stands approximately thirty inches high, with a width at the base of approximately sixteen inches. Overall, it remains a beautiful display piece. **Minimum Bid: $750**

19808 **Late 1960's Geese Ausbie Game Worn Harlem Globetrotters Jersey.** Ranking as this country's top goodwill ambassadors in the field of athletics are the beloved Harlem Globetrotters, who have paired top-quality basketball with side-splitting comedy over six continents and eight decades. Here we present a jersey worn by one of the biggest names of the late 1960's and early 1970's, a team that featured the likes of Curly Neal and Meadowlark Lemon. This one was Hubert "Geese" Ausbie's, known as the "Clown Prince of Basketball" for his fine skills and irrepressible sense of humor on the court. The classic styling is unmistakable, with a patriotic color scheme and a spangling of stars. "Original Harlem Globetrotters" is spelled on the front in bold tackle twill, with Ausbie's number "35" on verso below a tackle twill and chenille globe. "Wilson" label in tail has typed size designator reading "42, +3." Wear is outstanding, typical for a team that toured two hundred fifty days a year and did not have a vast wardrobe of jerseys. Included in the lot is a pair of trunks with a later "Wilson" tagging style in the waistband (size 36), but perfect for display with the jersey. There are no identifiers, so we cannot attribute them definitively to Ausbie, though they do derive from the same source. *LOA from Lou Lampson.* **Minimum Bid: $1,500**

YOUNG GUN

19809 **1970-71 Pete Maravich Game Worn Rookie Jersey.**

If I have a choice whether to do the show or throw a straight pass, and we're going to get the basket either way, I'm going to do the show.

With all the struggles, success and tragedy of any great Hollywood movie, the short, brilliant life of Pete Maravich remains one of the most compelling in the history of American sport. Born in 1947 in a small Pennsylvania steel town, young Pete was molded by his loving yet domineering basketball coach father into an LSU standout and first round NBA draft pick, a journey that started when he was just three years old and so small he could only shoot the ball with a great heave from his hip, like a six-shooter. So they called him "Pistol."

Presented for the elite hobbyist is the one and only known example of Pistol Pete's rookie jersey, which, by default, must also be labeled the most important and appealing Maravich artifact ever to be offered at public auction. Simply ideal in every conceivable regard, the heavyweight blue knit treasure is as worthy of display at Springfield as any piece currently residing within the Basketball Hall of Fame.

The glorious aesthetics of the jersey is the first jewel in the crown, indicative of the Atlanta Hawks desire for a new and striking image for this inaugural season of the 1970's. The tri-color striping in an asymmetrical design seems an appropriate complement to the addition this season of the flamboyant young superstar, as the look bears comparison to the uniforms of the flashier ABA, an imitation by the Hawks that was likely not entirely unintentional. The small and stylish font spelling "Atlanta" upon the chest is applied in white tackle twill, as is the number "44" that appears on both front and verso. It should be noted that the 1970-71 season was the last in which the NBA failed to require player names on its teams' jerseys, allowing definitive dating of the offered example to Maravich's rookie year.

The spectacular wear raises the bar yet further, suggesting many games of use during Pete's freshman term in the NBA. The tackle twill identifiers exhibit the surface reactions that can only come from lengthy, sweaty wear, a perfect match to that of the interior tail "Rawlings [size] 40" and Dry Cleaning labels.

Provenance is the final point to celebrate, as the jersey derives from the personal collection of Pete's dentist, who was given the jersey by Maravich himself upon his return to Baton Rouge at the close of the 1970-71 NBA season. For a time, the jersey was on public display at an upscale New Orleans restaurant owned by the dentist's father, noted boxing mogul "Diamond Jim" Moran.

Pistol Pete Maravich's sudden and shocking passing at age forty robbed the sporting world of one of the greats of the game long before we were ready to say goodbye. One lucky bidder will be able to connect to this iconic figure in a very personal way every time he enters his trophy room, and will instantly establish himself as one of the elite collectors in the field with ownership. *LOA from Lou Lampson.* **Minimum Bid: $12,500**

WILL

I, PETER MARAVICH, also known as PETE MARAVICH, also known as "PISTOL PETE" MARAVICH, of Atlanta, Georgia, do make this my Will, hereby revoking any and all Wills at any time heretofore made by me.

FIRST: I direct that the expenses of my last illness and funeral be paid out of my estate as soon as may be convenient after my death.

SECOND: I give the sum of Five Thousand ($5,000.00) Dollars to Jackie Elliser in remembrance of the love and companionship we have shared with one another.

THIRD: I give, devise and bequeath all the rest, residue and remainder of my estate to my father, Press Maravich, if he survives me. If he does not survive me, I give, devise and bequeath my residuary estate aforesaid in equal shares to my mother, Helen Maravich; my brother, Ronnie Maravich; and my sister, Diana Maravich, or to the survivors or survivor of them who may be living at the time of my death.

FOURTH: I appoint my father, Press Maravich, Executor of this my Will. No bond shall be required of my Executor in any jurisdiction.

IN WITNESS WHEREOF, I have hereunto set my hand and seal this 29th day of July, 1972.

(SEAL)
Peter Maravich

also known as
(SEAL)
Pete Maravich

also known as
(SEAL)
"Pistol Pete" Maravich

Signed, sealed, published and declared by the above named Testator to be his Will in the presence of us, who, at his request, in his presence, and in the presence of each other, have hereunto set our hands as subscribing witnesses.

Residing at Aliquippa, Pa.
Residing at Aliquippa, PA.
Residing at Aliquippa, Pa. 15001

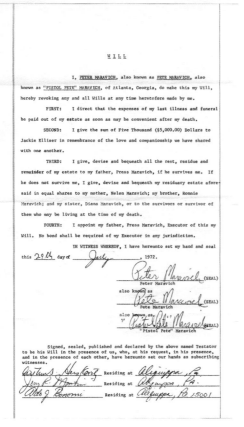

19810 **1972 Peter Maravich Triple-Signed Last Will & Testament.** Just twenty-five when he signed this brief legal document bequeathing his possessions to friends and family, the young superstar couldn't possibly have imagined that the end would come so soon. Though a later will would replace this one, the poignance of this offering is impossible to miss, as Pistol Pete would be struck down at the youthful age of forty while playing the game he loved. Beyond that extraordinary appeal, autograph collectors will thrill at the sight of three variations of Maravich's signature, stacked near the bottom of the single page document in 9/10 and better blue ink. Signatures of three witnesses appear below. The page itself measures 8.5x13.5, and remains in flawless condition, with original storage folds, and is stapled to a sleeve from the law offices of Roth & Herskovitz in Aliquippa, PA. One of the most interesting and important Maravich documents to surface in the hobby market in quite some time. *LOA from PSA/DNA. LOA from James Spence Authentication.* **Minimum Bid:** $750

19811 **1972-73 Mike Maloy Game Worn Dallas Chaparrals Jersey.** One can't help but love the American Basketball Association, with its red, white and blue basketball and wide-open, flashy style of offensive play, and the rare artifacts from the rogue league remain highly sought after by thousands of collectors. Offered here is the jersey worn by the six-foot seven inch forward out of Davidson named Mike Maloy, who represented the Virginia Squires for two seasons before finishing out his professional career in Dallas in 1972-73. True to the shoestring budget of the league, the jersey was reconditioned for use after Maloy, and a faint outline of "San Antonio" is visible under the replaced "Dallas" on the chest, illustrating that the shirt followed the team to its new home in 1974. The number "54" on chest and verso, and the "Maloy" sewn across the shoulders, are original and unrestored. Wear is very solid, as could be expected from multiple seasons of wear, with the "Rawlings [szie] 46" and washing labels loose at the interior tail but still affixed. With ABA gamers reaching the auction block with greater infrequency each passing year, collectors would be well advised to pay close attention to this offering. *LOA from Lou Lampson.* **Minimum Bid:** $400

19812 **1970's Basketball Superstars Multi-Signed Basketball with Maravich.** One young hardcourt fan really knew how to pick them, seeking out only the best and brightest of the professional hardcourt for inclusion upon this "Revelation" roundball. Black sharpie signatures appear from the esteemed dozen that follows: Maravich, Gervin, Barry, Erving, Drew, Malone, Hayes, David Thompson, Westphal, Gilmore, Cowens, Dawkins. Signature quality averages 7/10, and all are easily legible. A fantastic memento from the days just following the ABA/NBA merger. *LOA from PSA/DNA. LOA from James Spence Authentication.* **Minimum Bid: $600**

19813 **1975-76 ABA Game Used Basketball.** Who could forget the sight of Dr. J driving to the hoop with an afro as big as a prize-winning pumpkin and a red, white and blue basketball in his hand? This iconic symbol of the 1970's game is becoming more and more scarce upon the auction circuit, and this example dating to the presidency of Hall of Famer Dave Debusschere, whose facsimile signature adorns the patriotic orb, presents perfectly three decades after the NBA merger that halted production. It still holds air beautifully too, which may inspire you to take it to the court yourself, but we'd advise against. Rarities such as this deserve protection, and perhaps the autographs of the superstars who made this defunct league such an exciting chapter in the book of basketball history. **Minimum Bid: $600**

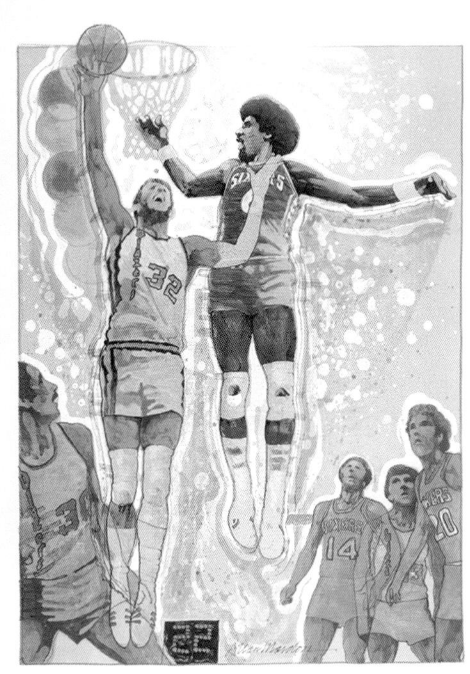

19814 **1977 NBA Finals Lithograph by Mardon.** Two of the greatest roundball stars of the era, Bill Walton and Julius "Dr. J" Erving, face off in this psychedelic masterwork by noted sports artist Allan Mardon. Walton, a fan of the Grateful Dead, had few peers when healthy and evoked comparisons to Wilt, Kareem, and Bill Russell. During the magical 1977 season under the guidance of their coach, Dr. Jack Ramsay, Walton and his Blazer teammates found a chemistry that combined with an exciting rebounding and running package led them to a championship. Walton finished off the series with an epic performance — 20 points, 23 rebounds, 8 blocks and 7 assists, garnering the respect of Julius Erving after a particularly heated and sometimes ugly series that included several ejections and near ejections. Released in only limited numbers in the months immediately following the Portland Trailblazers historic victory over the Philadelphia 76ers, the 22" x 28" lithograph has steadily increased in value and rarity in the quarter-century since, and is currently listed at $1500. This strong specimen offers just a touch of wear in the wide white borders, and could easily be matted and framed to appear Mint. A marvelous work, so evocative of the era when "Blazermania" swept across the Northwest following Portland's decisive victory over one of the most talented pro teams ever assembled. A great piece to have signed—it would be worth a small fortune if it were. **Minimum Bid: $300**

19815 **1978 George "Iceman" Gervin Game Worn Sneakers from Sixty-Three Point Game.** It was the last game of the NBA season, and the playoff match-ups had already been set, leaving personal pride and season records as the only variables of note. For weeks, George Gervin of the San Antonio Spurs and David Thompson of the Denver Nuggets had battled for the scoring title, with the latter leading by fifty-seven points after recording seventy-three in his final game earlier in the day. Though Gervin scoffed at the notion of scoring fifty-eight in a single game, a figure he had never met on any level of competition, his fellow teammates were intent upon feeding the Ice Man the ball at every opportunity in the same manner that Thompson's had done for him hours earlier.

Any basketball historian knows how the story ended. Gervin provided the most dominating performance of his Hall of Fame career, putting up an outrageous sixty-three points, including an NBA-record thirty-three in the second quarter alone!) to take the season's scoring crown by a razor-thin margin. Presented here are the Nike high-top sneakers that carried the supremely talented guard through his most famous game. Like the other offerings of NBA game worn sneakers presented in adjacent lots within this auction, these derive from the personal collection of the Spurs' ball boy from 1972 to 1982, who travelled with the team to New Orleans for this last game of the 1978 season, and bore witness to history in the making. The white leather gamers show a season's worth of wear, with Gervin's chilling nickname emblazoned across the rear ankle of each. No size markings are evident inside, but we'd estimate them at about a size twelve. Both are signed "George Iceman Gervin #44" in vintage ink, though we must note that the ink has faded considerably and currently rates about a 4/10 and 2/10 on the left and right respectively.

Joining the shoes are the official pre-game press briefings for the April 9, 1978 battle, as well as the post-game journalists' score sheets (laminated) recounting the history-making events. A letter of provenance from the ball boy who personally acquired the shoes is included as well. *LOA from Lou Lampson. LOA from PSA/DNA (autographs). LOA from James Spence Authentication (autographs).* Minimum Bid: $1,000

19816 **Late 1970's Philadelphia 76'ers Game Worn Sneakers Collection with Erving, Dawkins.** Another fine offering from the San Antonio Spurs ball boy who provided this auction with the historic sixty-three point game sneakers from George Gervin. The best of the City of Brotherly Love are presented for your consideration. Featured in this lot: 1) Julius Erving "Converse" single shoe, inscribed "To Andrew Smart, Julius 'Dr. J.' Erving. Custom "Dr. J." stamping just below. Good wear. Inscription 9+/10. 2) Darryl Dawkins "Pro-Keds" pair of shoes, right is inscribed "To Andrew, Darryl Dawkins #53." Strong wear. Inscription 9+/10. 3) Doug Collins "Adidas" pair of shoes, right is inscribed "To Andrew, My little buddy, Doug Collins, 76ers." Heavy wear. Inscription 9+/10. 4) Darryl Dawkins single shoe, unsigned with no player attribution, but identical (other than color) to pair presented in this lot. Strong wear. Letter of provenance from the Spurs ball boy is included. *LOA from Lou Lampson.* Minimum Bid: $500

19817 **Late 1970's NBA Superstars Game Worn Sneakers Collection with David Thompson, Lanier.** From the same long-serving (1972-82) San Antonio Spurs ball boy that provided this auction with George Gervin's historic sixty-three point game worn sneakers comes this intriguing assortment of footwear from the days of afros and short shorts on the NBA hardcourt. Featured in this lot: 1) David Thompson "Super Pros" single shoe, inscribed "To Andrew, See you next time, Your Buddy, David Thompson." Great "DT" customization on outer ankle. Strong wear. Inscription 9+/10. 2) Bob Lanier "Adidas" single shoe, inscribed "Peace, Bob Lanier." Massive shoe shows surface degradation at ankle, otherwise fine. Inscription 9+/10. 3) George McGinnis "Converse" single shoe, signed. Strong wear evident, no damage. Autograph 9+/10. 4) Artis Gilmore "Nike" single shoe, inscribed "To Andrew, Artis Gilmore [illegible]." Customization at rear ankle reads "Artis." Strong wear evident, no damage. Inscription 7/10. 5) Jo Jo White "Pro-Keds" pair of shoes, no autograph or other player attribution evident. Strong wear, no damage. Letter of provenance from the Spurs ball boy is included. *LOA from Lou Lampson.* **Minimum Bid: $500**

19818 **1981 Larry Bird NBA Championship Salesman's Sample Ring.** "I don't know if I practiced more than anybody," Bird once said, "but I sure practiced enough. I still wonder if somebody, somewhere, was practicing more than me." All of that practice finally made perfect in 1981, when the lanky kid from French Lick led his Boston Celtics to the first NBA Championship of his Hall of Fame career. This is the ring that Balfour designed for the occasion, identical in appearance to the one that was presented to the superstar forward. The ten-karat gold prize sports a faux diamond at center of the face, set in a green stone and surrounded by the raised text, "NBA World Champions." The left shank offers the NBA logo and year "1981," while the right provides an engraved "Bird" and a logo shamrock reading "XIV Celtics," noting the fourteenth team Championship. The word "Pride" is engraved below. "Balfour 10K" is stamped inside the band, which measures to a size ten. Mint condition, in original box. **Minimum Bid: $500**

19819 **1983-84 University of North Carolina Tarheels Team Signed Basketball with Jordan.** Michael Jordan earned All-America honors the year seventeen members of this powerhouse NCAA hardcourt program put sharpie to the white and Tarheel blue of this Official Spalding sphere. Matt Doherty, Kenny Smith and legendary coach Dean Smith are also present, in the same 9/10 black sharpie that characterizes all the other autographs as well. While there is no shortage of material from Jordan's glory days in Chicago, pieces relating to his collegiate career are quite rare and carry tremendous appeal among serious collectors of his artifacts. *LOA from PSA/DNA. LOA from James Spence Authentication.* **Minimum Bid: $600**

19820 **1984 Michael Jordan Olympics Game Worn Jersey.** A piece drenched in basketball relevance and collecting appeal, this wonderfully scarce USA team basketball jersey should arguably achieve a similar level to the $46,000 result realized by a 1984-85 Chicago Bulls rookie jersey in a 2004 auction. The future king of the hardcourt was still a Tarheels standout when he defended our home turf at the Los Angeles Games, leading the American side with an average of 17.1 points per game en route to the Gold Medal. This final relic from Jordan's amateur career was sourced from a veteran USA basketball executive and was first sold in 2001 after seventeen years in his collection. It bears mentioning that the United States wore blue for the Gold Medal game against Spain, and there is a very real possibility that this is the jersey Jordan wore that day. Use is appropriately light but evident, with the midnight navy micro knit body offering red and white tackle twill "USA 9" on chest and "9" again on verso. The "Descente" manufacturer's logo appears at right shoulder, and size "44" tagging at lower front left tail. A black sharpie signature on the chest rates a perfect 10/10, and bears a holographic authenticating sticker from UDA with matching certificate. Clearly one of the most desirable Jordan artifacts to reach the auction block in recent years. *LOA from Lou Lampson. COA from UDA (autograph). LOA from PSA/DNA (autograph). LOA from James Spence Authentication (autograph).* **Minimum Bid: $10,000**

19821 **1987-88 Michael Jordan Game Worn Jersey.** The 1987-1988 season was a defining one for Michael Jordan. His first three years in the league saw him ascend to the cusp of N.B.A. royalty, but there were some who still regarded him strictly as an electrifying player who put more stock in the number of points he scored rather than the number of games his team won. Michael changed quite a few minds in 87-88, leading the Bulls to a 50-32 record, and getting them out of Round One of the playoffs for the first time since his arrival in Chicago. His performance in the first round of the playoffs against Cleveland, where he averaged forty-five points per game, is the stuff of which legends are made.

Like a great film at the Oscars, when it came to award time, Jordan swept all categories. First team All-N.B.A. for a second consecutive year, League Most Valuable Player, and Defensive Player of the Year. The All-Star Game was held in front of his hometown Chicago fans that year, and he did not disappoint, walking away with M.V.P. honors and, of course, retaining his title as Slam Dunk Champion, with the famous leap from the free throw line which is the source of one of the most famous basketball images ever.

This Chicago Bulls home white gamer exhibits moderate use, which still sets it apart from and above the majority of Jordan jerseys that show minimal wear. The supremely memorable number "23" is screened in bold red and black on chest and verso, where the words "Bulls" and "Jordan" are announced respectively. The jersey and shorts are properly tagged with "Sand-Knit 44 Bulls Exclusivity" labels, with the "87" year and "3" L.B." alteration noted on embroidered swatches to the left. Early Jordan gamers are becoming increasingly scarce upon the auction circuit, and this is one of the finest we've encountered. Jersey expert Dave Bushing agrees, assigning a grade of A8, with points lost only to the "moderate" use he notes. In every other regard, this is a perfect ten, and a piece worthy of display at Springfield or the finest of private collections. *LOA from Dave Bushing. LOA from Lou Lampson.* Minimum Bid: $5,000

19822 **1988 Michael Jordan Signed UDA Jersey.** Limited edition (2/88) throwback jersey by Mitchell & Ness recalls the first All-Star jersey worn by basketball's greatest name. A 10/10 silver sharpie signature from Jordan appears just above the UDA holographic authenticating sticker. At bottom center, a skillfully embroidered paragraph of text notes the highlights of the event on the Bulls' home court, which in many ways served to introduce the outrageous talents of the six-time NBA Champion to the basketball world. A top-notch display piece with Upper Deck's ironclad guarantee of authenticity. UDA paperwork and packaging not included. *Authenticating sticker from UDA. LOA from PSA/DNA. LOA from James Spence Authentication.* Minimum Bid: $400

19823 **1990's Michael Jordan Single Signed UDA Basketball.** Arguably the most significant figure to stride upon the American athletic stage since Babe Ruth, the legendary Michael Jordan offers up here the definitive collectible by which to remember him. The large 10/10 black sharpie signature upon this "Wilson" ball was witnessed by an Upper Deck staff member, providing the ironclad provenance one must demand for an autograph so commonly forged in the hobby. All authenticating stickering and paperwork is here as well, along with the original UDA velvet pouch and storage box. *COA from UDA. LOA from PSA/DNA. LOA from James Spence Authentication.* Minimum Bid: $400

19824 **1991-92 Larry Bird Game Worn Jersey.** A thirteen-season Hall of Fame career came to an end the season the great Larry Bird hit the hardwood in this home white mesh jersey, worn as the leader of the venerable Boston Celtics team. The twelve-time All-Star who had delivered three World Championships to the city of Boston put light but definite wear into this special shirt, offering classic "Celtics 33" in green tackle twill on the chest, and "Bird 33" on verso. The "NBA" logo patch finds its proper home at the left shoulder, and tail tagging reveals dual "Champion" labels reading "Year 1991, ID#, Body Length +3" and size "46" respectively, all proper for Bird gamers of this era. Affixed to the lower left inside gusset side seam is a flap tag noting "100% Nylon," showing curling consistent with sweaty wear. Surely sharing the court as the legend sunk some of the final buckets of his career, the jersey is an inspiring piece to any basketball fan, and practically a religious artifact to the die-hard Celtic booster. A large black sharpie signature on the front rates a perfect 10/10. *LOA from Lou Lampson. LOA from PSA/DNA (autograph). LOA from James Spence Authentication (autograph).* **Minimum Bid: $1,000**

19825 **Michael Jordan Signed Peter Max Lithograph with Remarque.** The acclaimed pop artist Max, whose bright, vibrant style has garnered him international fame and appearances in permanent collections of many of the world's most prominent museums, takes on the subject of the world's most prominent basketball player. In his inimitable style, Max captures MJ making the jump shot that earned his Chicago Bulls their sixth and final NBA Championship with Jordan at the helm. This very limited edition (103/123) litho on heavy paper stock, entitled "Farewell Shot," is signed in perfect black sharpie by both Jordan and the artist himself, who adds a hand-drawn sketch (remarque) of Jordan in black marker, a little bit of Peter Max original art! Measures 26x33" in dimension. Mint. *LOA from PSA/DNA. LOA from James Spence Authentication.* **Minimum Bid: $1,000**

19826 **Michael Jordan Signed Peter Max Lithograph.** Limited edition (111/423) lithograph proves that Leroy Neiman isn't the only skilled impressionist to take a crack at the sporting world. Acclaimed artist Peter Max captures Air Jordan's defining moment as he delivers the jump shot that elevated his Chicago Bulls to World Championship status for the sixth time. Adding to the tremendous visual appeal are flawless black sharpie signatures from artist and subject alike, with the latter's authenticity further assured by a holographic authenticating sticker from Jordan's preferred marketing firm, Upper Deck. Dimensions are 26x33", and condition is Mint. *LOA from PSA/DNA. LOA from James Spence Authentication.* **Minimum Bid: $750**

19827 **1996 Dominique Wilkins "Sportsman of the Year" Trophy & 2000 Atlanta Hawks Presentational Artwork.** One of the game's most prolific scorers and most esteemed slam dunk artists, the man they called "The Human Highlight Film" released these two personally owned artifacts to the hobby in recent years. First, we have a trophy presented by Mayor of Atlanta Andrew Young to the young Hawks superstar, engraved at the base with the words, "1986 Sportsman of the Year, Presented to Dominique 'Unique' Wilkins." A life-size golden basketball sits atop a wooden base for this striking display piece. A small dent at the north pole of the ball causes little visual distraction. Joining the trophy is a large and colorful artwork presented to Wilkins in the year following his retirement from the game he dominated. Matted and framed to an impressive 32x38", the piece is dedicated with an engraved brass plaque at the bottom border, which reads, "Dominique Wilkins, Congratulations on a Stellar Career from the Atlanta Hawks Organization, January 23, 2000." Minor wear to the frame, otherwise NRMT. **Minimum Bid: $400**

19828 **1997-98 Michael Jordan NBA Finals Game Worn Jersey.** It all ended with a fade-away jumper in Game Six of the NBA Finals, perhaps Air Jordan's most defining moment, earning the Chicago Bulls their sixth and final NBA Championship under his leadership. The following year found this legendary team scattered to the wind, and Jordan claiming retirement, but this monumentally important road red mesh gamer lives on to help us remember the magic. The offered jersey derives from a season that saw Jordan do far more than bring home yet another World Championship, as he tallied his third straight scoring title and tenth overall, his second triple crown with his fifth MVP award, third all-star game MVP, and sixth Finals MVP award. If there was ever a jersey worthy of a home in Springfield, it's this one.

"Bulls 23" is sewn to the chest in red and black tackle twill, giving way to "Jordan 23" on verso. The player name letters are correct at 3.25" in height. It should be noted that the positioning drop of the name on back is critical in differentiating game worn jerseys from the "Pro Cut" versions, which often are mistaken for gamers. The "NBA Finals" patch appears in its proper location at right shoulder. While the wear of the jersey is light, this is not abnormal for a Michael Jordan representation, and appropriate for a jersey likely used only in a single Finals game. Though Jordan wore size "46" when "Champion" manufactured Bulls jerseys, the size "48" found on the "Nike" label in the tail is correct for the new maker, as is the customization noted by the "Length +4" flap tag.

While we can offer nothing concrete to substantiate that this is indeed *the* jersey, it does bear mentioning that Jordan drained "The Shot" that sealed the Championship for the Bulls in front of a hostile Utah crowd, where he wore a road red uniform. So we're left to wonder, is this the very shirt His Airness was wearing at the absolute pinnacle of his greatness and fame? *LOA from Lou Lampson.* **Minimum Bid: $3,000**

19829 **2000 Vince Carter Summer Olympics Game Worn Uniform.** Just two years removed from the Carolina Tarheel hardcourt at the time of the Sydney Games, this slam dunk afficionado was a key component in sealing the last Olympic Basketball Gold Medal performance for the United States. His 14.8 points and 3.6 rebounds per game were crucial in the team's eight victories, and his dunk over seven-foot two French center Frederic Weis in the Finals remains one of the most memorable moments in the tournament. Here we present a navy mesh jersey and matching shorts worn by the superstar guard during the last high-water mark for American basketball in international play, deriving from an impeccable source within the NBA league offices. The jersey features red and white tackle twill identifiers announcing "USA 9" upon the chest, with "Carter 9" taking up the rear. A "USA Basketball" patch is affixed at left shoulder. Dual "Champion" labeling in the tail features "2000 USA Olympic Team" exclusivity and size "50" tags, the latter marked with number "9" in red marker and trailing a "+2 Length" flap tag. An identical exclusivity label appears in the waistband, with a "Champion [size] 44" label to the right, which sprouts "+2 Inseam" and "+2 Rise" flaps at right. Light but certain wear is evident, proper for limited tournament play. Overall, an outstanding representation from the emergence of one of the NBA's most recognizable stars. *LOA from Lou Lampson.* Minimum Bid: $600

19830 **2000-01 Allen Iverson Game Worn Jersey.** Road blue Philadelphia 76'ers gamer dates to The Answer's incredible MVP season, one in which the future Hall of Fame guard posted a then-career high thirty-one points per game while leading his team all the way to the NBA Finals. Arguably the most desirable vintage of Iverson jerseys after the all-important rookie, this fifth-year style boasts a stylish "Sixers" patch upon the upper chest, with number "3" in two-tone tackle twill below. "Iverson 3" appears on verso. Extensive "Champion" brand tagging in the tail speaks to Sixers "Exclusivity" and size "42," with a "2000-2001" year flap tag underneath the former. Wear is minimal but acceptable for a superstar jersey, and surely good enough for a shirt with this level of historical appeal. *LOA from Lou Lampson.* Minimum Bid: $400

19831 **2002-03 Michael Jordan Game Worn Jersey.** Intense rarity, ironclad provenance and a spectacular late-career performance by the game's greatest figure makes the offered home white mesh gamer one of the most important Jordans to reach the market in recent memory. Our records show not a single instance of a final-season Michael Jordan jersey presented at auction to date, as MJ and the Wizards have kept tight wraps on the available specimens. This one does come directly from a team source, however, with a letter on Wizards/Mystics/MCI Center letterhead attesting that "this item was personally worn on December 18, 2002, by Michael Jordan and signed on March 10, 2003 by Michael Jordan." And what a game it was. After a recent two-point game had started the whispers that the Jordan magic was finally gone, the thirty-nine year old legend led the Wizards to a 118 to 100 victory over the Memphis Grizzlies, posting thirty-three points while going fourteen for twenty-three from the floor with three steals, five boards and two three-pointers. "I ain't seen nothing like that," Grizzlies rookie Drew Gooden said after the game. "I ain't seen nothing like that in I don't know how long, but he was on. It seemed like every time he shot it was going in."

The home white mesh shirt provides the distinctively fonted "Wizards" upon the chest with Jordan's immortal number "23," each applied in tri-color tackle twill. "Jordan 23" fills the verso. "Nike [size] 50" labeling in the tail features the logos of the Wizards and the NBA, and dangles a "Length +4" flap tag to match Jordan's preferred tailoring modifications. Wear is light but definite, appropriate for a single game of superstar use. A 10/10 silver sharpie signature on verso is joined by an Upper Deck serialized holographic authenticating sticker, and the corresponding certificate is present, as is UDA's high-tech "PenCam" DVD that further documents the signing. Not a single bell or whistle is missing from this package, which is certain to draw the interest of the most discerning of Jordan collectors. *LOA from the Washington Wizards (jersey & autograph). LOA from Lou Lampson (jersey). LOA from UDA (autograph). LOA from PSA/DNA (autograph). LOA from James Spence Authentication (autograph).* Minimum Bid: $3,000

19832 **2003-04 Carmelo Anthony Game Worn Rookie Jersey.** After his freshman heroics led the Syracuse Orangemen to the 2003 NCAA Championship, the tough kid from the Red Hook projects of Brooklyn was the third overall pick in the 2003 NBA draft at age nineteen, and would become the first rookie to lead his team in scoring since David Robinson accomplished the feat in 1989-90. Presented here is a home white jersey worn by this young phenom during that historic first season in which he helped transform the Denver Nuggets from a League-worst laughing stock to a playoff contender. "Nuggets 15" appears in solid block upon the chest, with "Anthony 15" applied to verso. "Reebok" labeling in tail features the logos of the NBA and the Nuggets, and holds triple flap tagging: "2003-2004, 2" L.B., 52." Light but certain wear is evident. Though he still has many years of play ahead of him, Anthony is currently well on pace for eventual Hall of Fame enshrinement, which would make this Nuggets jersey pure gold one day. *LOA from Lou Lampson.* **Minimum Bid: $400**

19833 **2003-04 Lebron James Game Worn Rookie Jersey.** Almost as if the basketball gods knew that we needed something to fill the void left by the final retirement of Michael Jordan, they delivered to the NBA the greatest high school basketball phenom in history, who seems destined to carve a similar legacy for himself in the professional ranks as well. This red mesh roadster exhibits definite but appropriately light wear for a superstar jersey, as do almost all Lebron representations that have escaped to the hobby. The jersey was sourced about the time of the All-Star break during this Rookie of the Year season that saw the eighteen-year old superstar average twenty-one points and six assists per game. "Cleveland 23" is applied in white tackle twill with golden edging to the chest, with "James 23" announced on verso. Proper "Reebok" labeling likewise holds the logos of the NBA and the Cavs, with a size "50 2LB" flap tag at right and a "2003-2004" tag below. With Michael Jordan rookies having realized as much as $45,000 at auction in recent years, the offered lot may well be the smartest investment piece in this Signature auction. *LOA from Lou Lampson.* **Minimum Bid: $1,000**

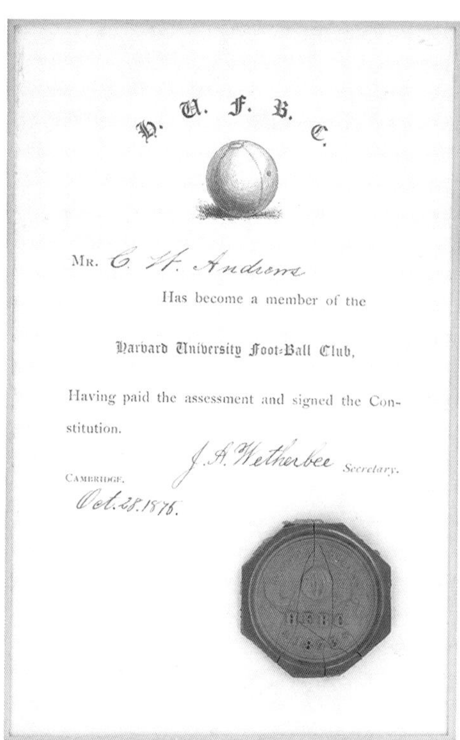

H. U. F. B. C.

Mr. C. W. Andrews

Has become a member of the

Harvard University Foot-Ball Club,

Having paid the assessment and signed the Constitution.

Cambridge, J. A. Wetherbee Secretary.

Oct. 28. 1876.

19834 **1875 Harvard University Football Club Membership Certificate.** Seminal document is among the very earliest American football pieces ever to be offered at public auction. Though most historians point to an 1869 contest between Rutgers and Princeton as the first ever football game in the United States, this match was played under rugby-style Association rules, which bore only passing resemblance to the sport as we know it. The first to utilize rules far more closely approximating those which are in place today found Harvard hosting Tufts University on June 4, 1875 at Cambridge, Massachusetts' Jarvis Field, just four months before this certificate was issued. This new style, featuring an egg-shaped ball, eleven men on a side, and the concept of tackling to impede the progress of the offense came to be known as "The Boston Game" due to its Harvard roots.

Elegant in its simplicity, this 5x7.5" certificate begins with the letters "H.U.F.B.C." arching over an early spherical football, and goes on to attest, "Mr. C.W. Andrews Has become a member of the Harvard University Foot-Ball Club, Having paid the assesment and signed the Constitution. (Signed) J.A. Wetherbee, Secretary, Cambridge, Oct. 28, 1876." A wax seal at lower right features another image of a spherical football with the latin phrase "Semper Surgens" (translation, "Forever Rising") and "H.F.B.C. 1873." Short of the lightest hints of foxing, the certificate remains in splendid, undamaged condition, free of any creases, tears or stains that are all but ensured with a paper artifact of this vintage. The certificate is tastefully matted and framed to final dimensions of 11.5x14". A marvelous piece with the scarcity and relevance to attract the most serious of football collectors. **Minimum Bid: $1,000**

19835 Jim Thorpe Memorabilia Archive Including 1912 Carlisle Indian School Game Worn Helmet & Cleats.

Born on May 28, 1887 to the daughter of the last great Sauk and Fox chief Black Hawk, a revered warrior and athlete, James Francis Thorpe was given the Indian name Wa-Tho-Huk, which translates to "Bright Path." It was a name that few would ever hear, but one that would prove to be perfectly fitting. The American political philosophy of Manifest Destiny had already decimated the population of Native Americans in our ever-expanding nation, and marginalized those who survived its brutality. Through this enforced segregation, Thorpe found his way to the Carlisle Industrial Indian School in rural Pennsylvania in 1904 at age sixteen. It was there that his phenomenal athletic career began, as a member of the school's track and football teams, and that he fell under the tutelage of gridiron legend Glenn "Pop" Warner during eight years on campus. The pieces that would construct Thorpe's immortality started to fall into place.

While the legend of Jim Thorpe began to grow within the collegiate football ranks during the later years of the twentieth century's first decade, it was 1912 that saw his conversion to international superstar. At the 1912 Stockholm Olympic Games, a twenty-four year old Thorpe dominated the pentathlon and decathlon, earning Gold in each and his proudest compliment from King Gustav of Sweden, who said to him, "Sir, you are the greatest athlete in the world. I would consider it an honor to shake your hand." Thorpe's reply: "Thanks, King."

The year 1912 also brings us to the premiere pieces that Heritage Auction Galleries is pleased and privileged to present to the collecting community. The incredible leather helmet and cleats stand as the only Jim Thorpe game used material ever to surface from his days with the Carlisle Indians. It was in 1912 that the tiny school shocked the collegiate football world by wresting the NCAA Championship from the death grip of the Ivy League. In twelve games, Thorpe scored twenty-five touchdowns and 198 points. While it is all but guaranteed that the offered game used helmet and cleats, worn in the months immediately following Thorpe's Olympic Gold, represent Thorpe's sole examples of such for the entirety of the season, we are certain of their use at the very least in the historic meeting with Army. In this twenty-seven to six victory, Thorpe saw a ninety-two yard touchdown run annulled due to a teammate's infraction. The next play he carried the ball ninety-seven yards to paydirt. Also during this game occurred a fateful meeting with history, as a young Army defender named Dwight David Eisenhower saw his football career ended as he badly injured his leg trying to bring down a rushing Thorpe.

The leather helmet exhibits terrific wear, but none of the damage one would expect for a piece fast approaching its centennial. The toning of the hide has deepened to an antique deep brown, and the interior webbing, so often damaged in helmets decades younger, is solid and complete. There are no apparent manufacturer's labels, though this is to be expected, as anything imprinted on the helmet's interior would have been lost long ago to age and wear. The pair of cleats also show tremendous wear, each sporting seven rounded studs on the sole applied with a trio of short nails. Ancient "Spalding" tags are found inside each tongue, stamped with the proper "8 ½" size. A portion of one shoelace keeps the pair joined, and minor tears in the ankle region of each shoe cause no concern. Together the helmet and cleats form a display that even Canton couldn't match, and one that the Hall of Fame would surely be overjoyed to present should the winning bidder feel charitable. Again, these are the only Jim Thorpe Carlisle Indian School game worn pieces known.

The massive Thorpe archive extends well beyond this helmet and cleats however, and while we would encourage serious bidders to visit our Dallas headquarters to examine the lot in person, we will endeavor to convey its magnitude here in print. While not one hundred percent comprehensive, the list is as follows:

1) Twelve Jim Thorpe signed photographs. Most are signed on the photos' verso with the notation "Property of Jim Thorpe," as is the case with the dozens of individually listed photographs in this auction. All are in 9/10 or better ink, with the exception of one in equally strong pencil. Two have vintage tape repairs to photos crossing the writing. One is signed on front, featuring an image of Thorpe in Canton football uniform. Another photo simply identifies "Carl Phillip Thorpe" on the photo's backside, an autograph of sorts-this is not included in the count of twelve. Photos are mostly 8x10", with a few exceptions. Except for tape-repaired photos mentioned, photos average VG-EX.

2) Incredibly important presentational plaque presented to Thorpe by the Associated Press naming him the "America's greatest athlete of the past 50 years." Plaque is signed by the Attorney General of the United States and the publisher of The Washington Post. The wooden laminated wall hanging measures 12.5x18" in size.

3) Presentational "Key to the City" of Philadelphia. Displayed in a shadow box measuring 12x13x2".

4) Three Holy Bibles. First is embossed in gold on the cover, "James Thorpe, Christmas 1904." Cover is almost entirely loose, but still technically attached. Second dates to 1940's, origin unknown, very worn. Third appears to have been used at Thorpe's funeral, with apparent inscription from his widow saying farewell on opening page. Best condition of the three.

5) Thorpe's personal copy of the script for the film, "Jim Thorpe-All-American." VG-EX. Dated August 3, 1950.

6) 1950 presentational certificate of lifetime achievement in leather binding from the Touchdown Club of Washington, D.C. Embossed gold lettering on cover. 7) Presentational certificate naming Patricia Thorpe an honorary citizen of the newly named Jim Thorpe, Pennsylvania.

8) 1946 Track & Field 2nd place presentational plaque, likely belonging to son of Thorpe.

9) Several chapters of the typed manuscript for Thorpe's biography, written by his widow Patricia.

10) Three hardcover football books once belonging to Thorpe. Two are inscribed to him by the authors.

11) Approximately fifty unmailed invitations to Thorpe's sixty-fourth birthday party. 12) Three reel-to-reel audiotapes holding interviews with Thorpe recounting the highlights of his athletic career (a terrific historian's tool!).

13) Oversized one-of-a-kind studio pressing record albums also holding Thorpe interviews (special turntable needed for these).

14) Vast array of unsigned photographs (including snapshot of Babe Ruth, small wire photo (PR-GD) of Thorpe in New York Giants uniform, etc.), newspaper clippings (many pasted within a scrapbook) recounting the many highlights of Thorpe's life, a letter signed by Chief Justice Warren of "Warren Commission" fame, two badges issued for the Dedication of the Jim Thorpe Memorial.

15) A few other odds and ends.

The winning bidder of this lot could certainly open a small museum using only the pieces offered here, and any researcher would find the vast amount of textual and audio documentation to be of tremendous service. Accompanying this historic offering is a letter of provenance from the widow of Charles Gorham, Thorpe's lawyer and close friend. She attests to the particulars of the collection, from the fact that it was all given to her husband by the Thorpe family, to the exact provenance of the game worn materials as dating to Carlisle Indian School, 1912. Furthermore, a 1967 letter from Thorpe's widow Patricia explicitly states that the helmet and cleats belonged to Jim. This is unquestionably the finest, largest and most historically relevant offering of Jim Thorpe material ever to be placed upon the auction block, with the most iron clad provenance imaginable. To call this a "once in a lifetime opportunity" is merely to state the obvious. **Minimum Bid: $60,000**

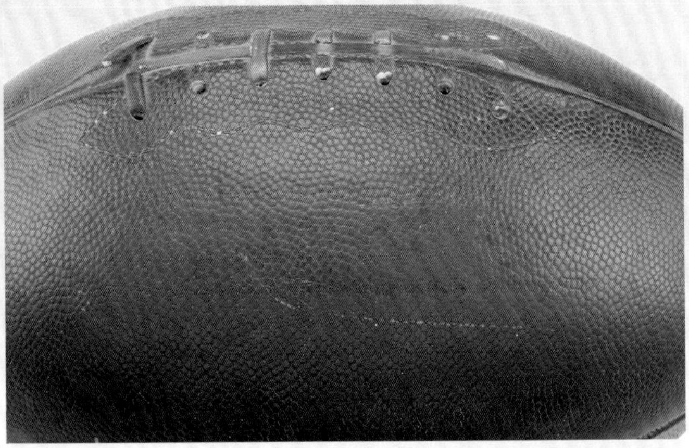

19836 **1925 Knute Rockne's Presentational Humidor Signed by Rockne, Pop Warner & Tad Jones.** It was back in May 2006 that Heritage auctioned a sister piece to the humidor we present here, clearly deriving from the same event and bearing the same trio of collegiate gridiron legends. Though we will admit that the earlier offering presented bolder signatures, as well as the addition of the great Jim Thorpe, this particular example has appeal that the former example couldn't possibly match. Applied to the wooden base of this unique keepsake is a brass plaque with the engraving, "Knute K. Rockne, Compliments of Christy Walsh." Our consignor, who lives just six miles from South Bend, Indiana, discovered this special piece at a local flea market, and realized the plaque denoted this humidor as Rockne's personal model. She was then able to track down an image of Rockne holding the humidor, locking down the provenance to the ultimate degree. The three signatures that are boldly visible in the image are quite a bit lighter now, perhaps 2/10, but are still legible and unmistakable, with each signer adding the school he represents—Notre Dame, Stanford and Yale respectively—after his autograph. A sticker affixed inside the humidor details the event that spawned the piece, reading, "Knute Rockne's Souvenir, All America Football Dinner, Appreciation to my Newspaper Friends, and in Honor of Knute Rockne, Tad Jones, Glenn Warner, Fielding Yost and my Other Associates, Christy Walsh, Hotel Commodore, New York, Nov. 30, 1925." A bit of the lacing at the exterior has been lost to the ravages of time, but otherwise the humidor has weathered the passing decades quite well, and would surely serve its intended purpose of cigar maintenance well. As one of the few personally owned pieces of Rockne memorabilia to reach the auction block, and an autographed piece besides, the appeal of the offered lot should be evident to all. *LOA from PSA/DNA. LOA from James Spence Authentication.* **Minimum Bid: $3,000**

19837 **1926 Dedication of Soldier Field Program, Ticket Stub, Usher's Armband and Panoramic Photograph.** Proving the popular maxim that war has no winners, two branches of the United States military battled to a twenty-one to twenty-one draw to christen the enormous new Chicago sporting palace on November 27, 1926. Offered here are several artifacts birthed by that historic draw. 1) Game program. Wear to covers and spine but complete and tightly bound, VG. 2) Ticket stub. Vertical crease near right edge, otherwise EX. 3) Usher's armband. Wear and some staining, VG. 4) Panoramic photograph. Measures 10.5x28". Tiny chip at right lower corner, and small tear at upper border, otherwise EX-MT. An impressive congregation of pieces from the debut of one of America's most esteemed sporting venues. **Minimum Bid: $400**

19838 **Circa 1930 Knute Rockne Signed Photograph.** The first major sports figure (followed by Rocky Marciano, Roberto Clemente and Thurman Munson) to perish in an airplane accident, Rockne presents a particular challenge to autograph collectors due to his sudden, untimely death in 1931. Here we present an especially desirable example of his tough signature, provided by the legendary Notre Dame coach to his personal physician upon a fine studio portrait photograph. Rockne inscribes upon the wide lower border of the image, "To my friend Dr. Clif Barborka, in deepest admiration, Knute Rockne." The black fountain pen ink maintains an impressive boldness of 9/10, and the photo itself is likewise in marvelous condition, with no noteworthy flaws. Including the simple wooden frame that houses it, the photo measures approximate 7.5x10" in size. A fine, dignified remembrance of this larger than life Golden Age figure. *LOA from PSA/DNA. LOA from James Spence Authentication.* **Minimum Bid: $1,000**

19839 **1931 Rose Bowl Program & Ticket Stub.** In just a few month's time, an eighteen year old kid named Paul Bryant, better known to history as "Bear," would arrive in Tuscaloosa to begin his football career. Surely he was playing close attention to this match between his future alma mater and the Washington State Cougars, who would fall to the Tide in a lopsided twenty-four to nothing rout. Here we offer a program and ticket stub from the early Pasadena contest, among the scant few examples to have survived the passing years. The program exhibits a vertical center fold and some paper loss along the bottom edge, but otherwise presents quite nicely in G-VG condition, remaining tightly bound by its original staples. Only typical edge and corner wear is to be noted in regard to the ticket stub. Also here is the front page of the January 2, 1931 Evening Express newspaper recounting the Alabama victory, and a letter responding to the fan's ticket request sent from the Business Manager of Athletics of the University of Alabama, complete with mailing envelope. **Minimum Bid: $300**

19840 **1932 Jim Thorpe Signed Photograph.** Former President Dwight D. Eisenhower, whose own leg was broken by the Native American sporting legend in a 1912 gridiron meeting between Army and the Carlisle Indian School, recalled Thorpe in a 1961 speech, saying, "Here and there, there are some people who are supremely endowed. My memory goes back to Jim Thorpe. He never practiced in his life, and he could do anything better than any other football player I ever saw." Here we present the finest photographic portrait we've encountered of this gifted superstar, printed with crystal clarity to a size of 8x10". At right, the subject signs in 9+/10 black ink, "Sincerely, Jim Thorpe, Oct. 17th, 1932." The photo is likewise in flawless condition, sporting a lengthy handwritten biography of Thorpe on verso, seemingly in the hand of the photographer. A majestic piece of the highest quality. *LOA from PSA/DNA. LOA from James Spence Authentication.* **Minimum Bid: $1,000**

19841 **1934 Rose Bowl Trophy.** The final Rose Bowl appearance by an Ivy League school on this 1934 New Year's Day was likewise the last time the Ivy League posted a Rose Bowl victory, with Columbia topping Stanford seven to nothing in what was considered one of the greatest gridiron upsets to that time. Though the Light Blue had recorded an impressive seven and one record for the season, the Stanford Indians had allowed just four scores during all the course of their campaign, and were heavily favored to take the victory. Upon the muddy Pasadena battlefield, however, the Columbia side was able to completely shut down the Stanford offense, and executed a trick play in the second quarter to post the deciding, single touchdown.

Recalling that momentous occasion is this marvelous art deco prize, consigned to Heritage by the grandson of the Secretary/Treasurer of the Tournament of Roses Association that year. With top notch aesthetics to match its historical appeal, the ten-inch tall trophy rests upon a polished wooden base fronted by an engraved decorative plaque which reads, "Rose Bowl, Stanford, Columbia, 1934." As our eyes travel upward, we encounter double football goal posts, which frame at front a map of the United States and a second engraved plaque reading, "Pasadena Tournament of Roses, East - West, Intercollegiate Rose Bowl Award." A figural football serves as the trophy's spire. A degree of oxidation is to be noted upon the brass fixtures, and an imperceptible degree of restoration has improved the look of the front goalpost, but otherwise the award appears to have suffered very little over its seventy-four years of life. Certainly one of the finest prewar collegiate football trophies to enter the hobby, and, to the best of our knowledge, the first of Rose Bowl pedigree ever to be offered publicly. **Minimum Bid: $5,000**

19842 **Mid-1940's College All-Star Game Worn Jersey with George Halas Signed Letter.** Arresting blue durene jersey is the true embodiment of the phrase, "They don't make them like that anymore." Surfing a wave of American nationalism in the years just following our victorious showing in the Second World War, this gamer pulls out all the patriotic stops, with star-studded shoulders and striped side paneling. Satin number "44" is applied to chest and back in a distinctive and unusual font, and the buttoned crotchpiece holds a great "May & Halas Inc, Chicago" manufacturer's label, complete with size "46" and "Dry Clean Only" flap tags. Light staining to the white numerals and minor moth damage to the felt stars are noted in the interest of full disclosure, but cause no major visual concern. The jersey was once the proud possession of U.S. Military Academy standout Hank Foldberg, who suited up in the shirt for the 1948 Chicago All-Star Classic at Soldier Field, where the All-Stars were beaten twenty-eight to nothing by the NFL Champion Chicago Cardinals in front of more than one hundred thousand fans. The jersey is joined by two signed typed letters sent to Foldberg by Charles F. Walsh of the Los Angeles Rams and Hall of Fame legend George Halas, each on team letterhead, inquiring about his availability in joining the professional ranks following graduation. The letters exhibit original mailing folds and minimal edge and corner wear, but otherwise present perfectly, with 10/10 closing signatures. *LOA from Lou Lampson (jersey). LOA from PSA/DNA (autographs). LOA from James Spence Authentication (autographs).* **Minimum Bid: $1,000**

19843 **1948 AAFC Most Valuable Player Trophy Presented to Frank Albert & Otto Graham.** Long before the WFL, the USFL and the absolutely dreadful XFL, there was the All-America Football Conference, perhaps the most formidable, but still ultimately unsuccessful, challenger to the gridiron dominance of the National Football League. Though its life ended almost sixty years ago in 1949, the three-year experiment did give birth to both the San Francisco 49'ers and the Cleveland Browns, who battle on to this day and whose quarterbacks were the joint recipients of the elegant prize presented here. The honorees, San Francisco's Frank Albert and Cleveland's Otto Graham, shared a unique proclivity toward rushing, often putting up similar yardage totals with both their arms and their legs. While Graham's name is immortalized at Canton, Albert was a worthy partner for this top prize, leading the 49'ers to an outrageous 3,138 yards on the ground for the 1948 season.

This fine trophy stands just over twenty-six inches tall and bursts with figurals of a rushing ball carrier, perched eagles and a laurel-bearing victory. An engraved brass plaque upon the substantial wooden base speaks to the specifics, exclaiming, "All-America Football Conference, Most Valuable Player Trophy, Awarded in 1948 to Frank C. Albert, San Francisco Forty-Niners and Otto E. Graham, Cleveland Browns." While a degree of wear consistent with sixty years of life is to be noted, this is confined almost entirely to rubbing at the wood edges, with a clipped eagle wing the only issue that could rightfully be characterized as "damage." One will quickly realize that these faults have very little bearing upon the tremendous aesthetics of the artful offering, and certainly none upon its immeasurable historic appeal. The twin attributions both to this short-lived professional football league and to the brilliance of one of the most iconic figures in the sport make it a priceless treasure to the cultured collector. **Minimum Bid: $2,000**

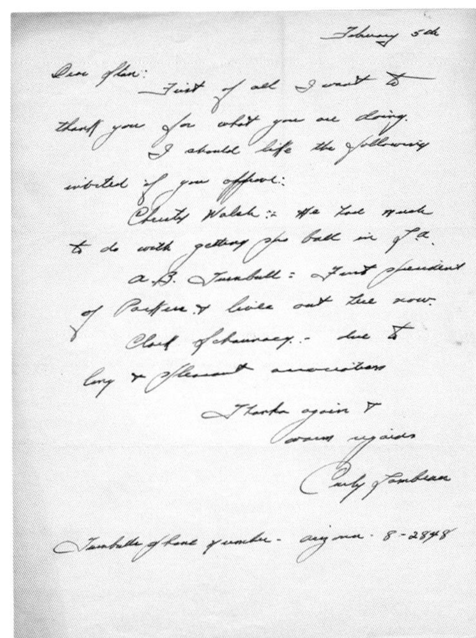

February 5th

Dear [illegible]:

First of all I want to thank you for what you are doing.

I should like the following invited if you approve:

Christy Walsh: He had much to do with getting pro ball in L.A.

A.B. Turnbull: First president of Packers & lives out here now.

Clark Shaughnessy: due to long & pleasant associations

Thanks again & warm regards

Curly Lambeau

Turnbull's phone number - [illegible] 8-2848

19844 **1952 Curly Lambeau Handwritten Signed Letter.** The heart and soul of the early Green Bay Packers, who provides his name to their "frozen tundra," suggests names of invitees to a banquet being held in his honor. Among the gentlemen whose presence he requests are pioneering sports agent Christy Walsh, who "had much to do with getting pro ball in L.A.," and A.B. Turnbull, "First president of Packers & lives out here now." Closing signature is in the desirable "Curly Lambeau" format. The single 8.5x11" page remains in terrific condition, with all ink continuing to register at a strength of 9+/10, and only original mailing folds and light toning to note. Lambeau is an essential to any early football autograph collection, and particularly those concentrating on Green Bay Packers history. Please also see the George Marshall signed letter to the same recipient that follows this lot. *LOA from PSA/DNA. LOA from James Spence Authentication.* **Minimum Bid: $1,000**

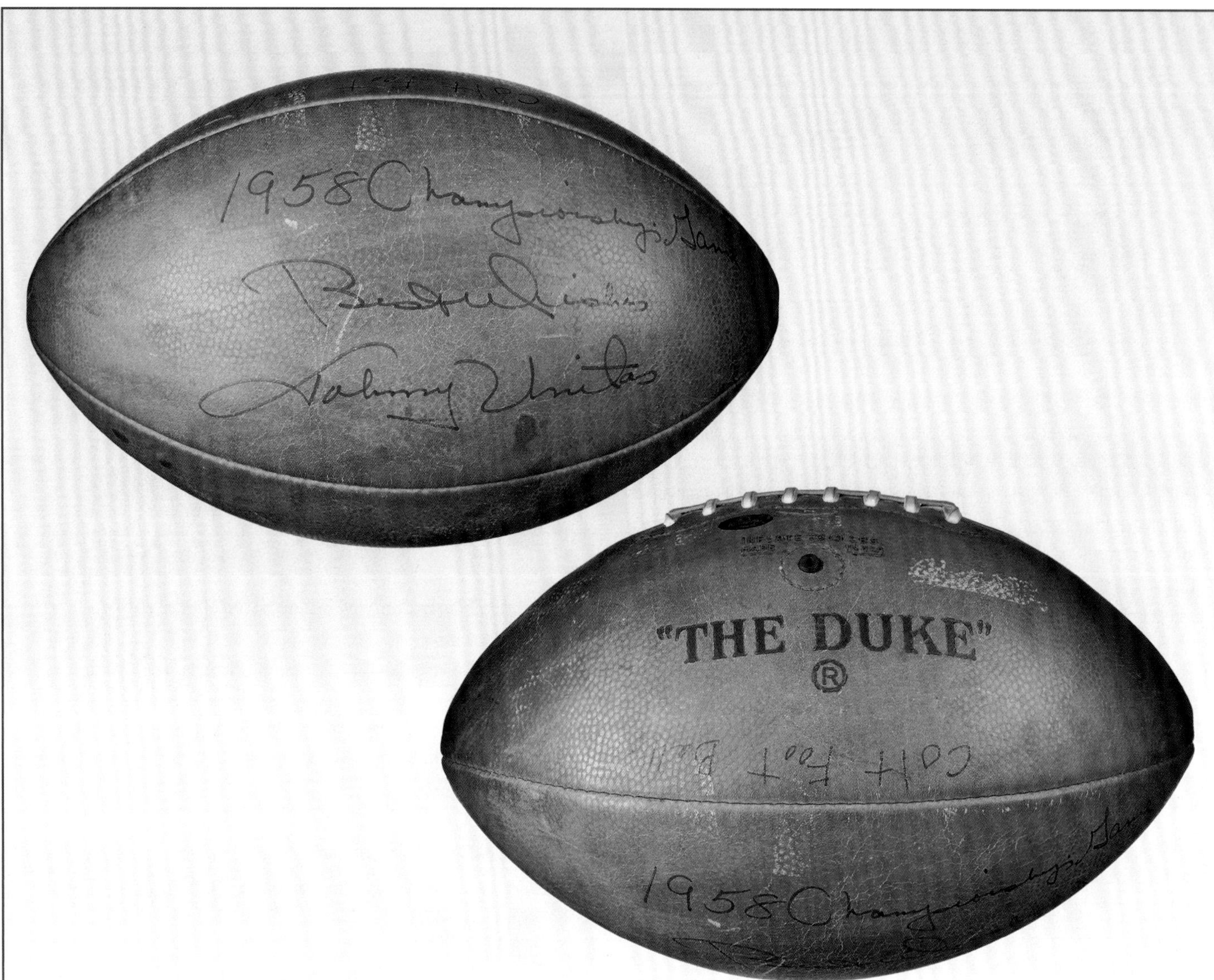

19845 **1958 N.F.L. Championship Game Used Football Signed by Unitas.** Known in the football world as simply "The Greatest Game Ever Played," the historic meeting of the Baltimore Colts and the New York Giants to establish N.F.L. supremacy in 1958 remains one of the noteworthy events in the annals of American athletics. Yankee Stadium, the site of so many unforgettable moments in baseball lore, served as the battlefield in a game that is credited with bringing professional football into prominence, essentially giving birth to the modern N.F.L. It was a game that had it all—lead changes, turnovers, a game-saving goal line stand, a game-tying last minute field goal. Every minute, it seemed, history was being made. "When the game ended in a tie," Colts quarterback Johnny Unitas remembered, "we were standing on the sidelines waiting to see what came next. All of a sudden, the officials came over and said, 'Send the captain out. We're going to flip a coin to see who will receive.' That was the first we heard of the overtime period."

Of course we all know how it ended, with a single-yard dive by Hall of Fame running back Alan Ameche to sentence the Giants to sudden death and clinch for the Baltimore Colts a piece of immortality. And now, as we approach the Golden Anniversary of this gridiron milestone event, Heritage is proud to present for the first time to the collecting community this Bert Bell "The Duke" football battled over on December 28, 1958 on the ground where Ruth and DiMaggio once plied their trade. But on this day, it was Unitas, Ameche, Berry and Gifford that hallowed the Bronx turf and turned Yankee Stadium once again into the center of the sporting world. And as if any football used on this day would not be appealing enough, this remarkable pigskin was carried home from the game by Johnny Unitas himself, who later gave the ball to a family friend. A notarized letter from the son of the recipient explains that his father worked for the local Coca-Cola distributorship and serviced the Colts' training camp, and how he himself used to babysit for the Unitas children. The letter goes on to attest that the ball was given to the man's father following the 1958 Championship Game.

The ball shows fine use from that day, and holds the words "Colt Foot Ball" written in the consignor's youthful vintage hand. Years later, the man tracked down Unitas, introducing himself and presenting the ball that his father had received as a gift after the sport's most noteworthy event. Unitas remembered well, and offered his 10/10 black ink blessing of the ball: "1958 Championship Game, Best Wishes, Johnny Unitas." Remarkably, the ball remains perfectly inflated and ready for action, though we would suggest that display in a glass case would be far more appropriate than a game of backyard catch. It's certainly one of the most important football artifacts to reach the auction block in recent memory. *LOA from PSA/DNA. LOA from James Spence Authentication.* **Minimum Bid: $4,000**

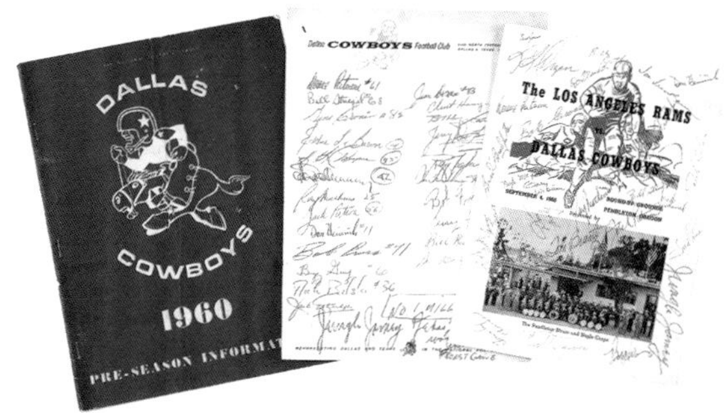

19846 **1960 Dallas Cowboys Team Signed Early Publication Collection.** The earliest days of "America's Team" are thrillingly recounted by this offering from a local Dallas man who was on hand to witness the birth of the 'boys. Perhaps most exciting is a September 4, 1960 preseason program for a meeting with the Los Angeles Rams, signed by close to thirty Cowboys including Meredith, Braatz, Tubbs and Cone. All blue ink is 9/10 or better, and the program itself remains in impressive EX condition. A second team signed piece comes in the form of a page of Cowboys letterhead, featuring LeBaron, Dupree and Cross among the twenty-four 9/10 and better signatures. The page shows some water staining and edge damage, though neither issue affects the autographs in the slightest. Finally, we have a forty-page rare publication introducing the team to the football world, entitled "Pre-Season Information." Though the condition is technically EX due to expected wear, the softcover volume remains tightly bound and entirely intact. For Dallas Cowboys afficionados and NFL historians, this is a "must bid" lot. *LOA from PSA/DNA. LOA from James Spence Authentication.* **Minimum Bid: $400**

MIGHTY MEN, MINK FOR THEIR LADIES

19847 **1962 Green Bay Packers Presentational Mink to Jerry Kramer's Wife.** Vince Lombardi believed that behind every great football player was a great woman. Evidence of his philosophy is provided by this gorgeous mink stole that the Packers Hall of Fame coach gave Barabara Kramer (now Jerry Kramer's ex wife) after one of the Packers' NFL Championship victories. The proper "Da Vinci" tag is affixed in the neckline, in addition to Barbara's initials, "BJK," in the lining. This rare piece is in very nice condition with minor wear in the lining. Also included in this offering is a 1962 issue of *Life Magazine* that features an article about Lombardi, showcasing a photo of the coach with the players' wives and girlfriends showing off their new gifts. An unusual artifact for the Packers collector who has everything. **Minimum Bid: $500**

19848 **1966 Green Bay Packers Game Worn Sideline Jacket Attributed to Jim Taylor.** Jim Taylor will always be renowned as the Packers gritty fullback who ran over defenders with ease, joining fellow Canton resident Bart Starr as the twin hearts of the Green Bay offense. Not only did the great Hall of Famer display extraordinary strength on the Lombardi dynasty teams of the 1960's, but he also exemplified the heart of a champion. Taylor would exit the game at the top, with his final contest a victory over the Kansas City Chiefs in Super Bowl I in 1966, the season he made use of the offered garment. As confirmed by numerous video images, Taylor wore this style warm up during home and road games. This example features the player identification "31," affixed to the base of the body in the same manner as "PACKERS," which arches across the back of the jacket in gold tackle twill lettering. The "Sand Knit [size] 50" tag in the neckline is consistent with apparel produced by the company in 1962, and proper for Taylor's build. The remnants of some form of tagging is apparent below, but we cannot determine what this may have been. Condition of the jacket is fantastic throughout, with none of the staining or moth damage one typically encounters from this era. This Canton-worthy artifact has been graded an A9 by MEARS and comes with their full Letter of Opinion, along with images used for style matching. *LOA from MEARS. LOA from Lou Lampson.* **Minimum Bid: $2,000**

19849 **1967 Green Bay Packers Team Signed Football.** The greatest dynasty in NFL history puts the finishing touch on their World Championship ways, claiming a victory in Super Bowl II, their last first place finish before the departure of iconic head coach Vince Lombardi. Though Lombardi fails to appear among the fifty autographs that decorate this specially stamped Rozelle NFL pigskin, there is no shortage of Canton-quality names, like Starr, Nitschke, Wood, Jordan, Kramer (4/10), Adderley (4/10). Unless otherwise noted, all signatures listed above present at a strength of 8/10 or better, as do all but six of the balance. A high-grade keepsake recalling the close of a special era on the gridiron. *LOA from PSA/DNA. LOA from James Spence Authentication.* **Minimum Bid: $500**

19850 **1968 New York Jets Team Signed Helmet.** The team that shocked the football world (and certainly the highly-favored Baltimore Colts) with a Super Bowl III victory reunite upon this ProLine helmet to celebrate their historic upset. Twenty-seven Champs are here in total, signing in flawless black sharpie. Chief among them are Namath, Snell, Boozer, Maynard, Philbin, Elliot, Mathis, Sauer, Hill, Rochester, Herman and Baker. If Namath's game worn Super Bowl helmet also offered within this auction is a bit too rich for your blood, this would make a fine consolation prize. *LOA from PSA/DNA. LOA from James Spence Authentication.* **Minimum Bid: $300**

19851 **Early 1970's Joe Namath Game Worn Jersey.** Paving the way for brash young gunslingers like Jim McMahon and Brett Favre, Joe Namath brought a dynamism and charisma to the quarterback position that was unlike any that had preceded him in the professional game. His flowing mane, fu manchu mustache and bold Super Bowl predictions endeared him to a new generation of football fans, and served as a very real catalyst in elevating the game of football to its current position as the number one spectator sport in America. Those growing up in the early 1970's will recognize this green mesh jersey as if it were a long-lost friend, its bold and simple aesthetics instantly recalling that exciting period in gridiron history. Namath's number "12" is screened in white to chest and back, with contrasting green numerals commanding each white sleeve. Two and a half inch tall white block lettering spells "Namath" across the shoulders. The simple "Champion Products Inc. [size] L" label in the tail appears to have been applied in error, as the jersey measures more closely to the proper 46-48 XL range. Namath's preferred four inches of extra length is likewise present and correct here. The wear is light, but appropriate for the quarterback position, and a 9/10 black sharpie signature upon the chest further serves to authenticate the piece. A definitive and unmistakable artifact of the early 1970's game. *LOA from Lou Lampson. LOA from PSA/DNA (autograph). LOA from James Spence Authentication (autograph).* **Minimum Bid: $2,000**

19852 **Early 1970's John Riggins Game Worn Jersey.** This superstar running back toppled Hall of Fame great Gale Sayers' collegiate career rushing record at Kansas, then stormed into the NFL where he twice earned the Jets MVP Award during his five seasons of service. Presented is a fantastic nylon durene gamer from the New York Jets' first pick (and sixth player overall) in the 1971 draft. In all probability, this shirt can be dated to the 1971-73 era, suggesting the very real possibility that this is a rookie model. Riggins' number "44" is applied in green tackle twill to the white body on chest and back, with the coloring reversed at the sleeves. "Riggins" stands in two and a half inch block across the shoulders. The heavy weight of the jersey would have made it appropriate only for cold weather games, and the moderate wear is further indication of its limited use. The original crotchpiece is in place, as are five of its six buttons, and the dual "Sand-Knit" tagging resides here, expressing "Jets Exclusivity" and the proper "Size 52." A moderate degree of staining throughout must be noted, and a six by nine inch area of excessive material wear that has given this area a translucent quality. These faults are just a small distraction, however, and the visual strength very successfully matches the considerable historical appeal. A marvelous early representation from the Hall of Famer and ultimate short-yardage workhorse. *LOA from Lou Lampson.* Minimum Bid: $3,000

19853 **1970 University of Texas Longhorns Team Signed Football.** Astoundingly Mint football was purchased by a student at the campus bookstore soon after the team secured its second consecutive National Championship and soon forgotten. The result is a ball literally unchanged by the passing of time, still in its original packaging. A comprehensive roster of over eighty have applied their 10/10 black ink signatures, most notably coach Darrell Royal and All-Americans Atessis, Feller, Henderson and Worster. While the ball holds air just fine, we've even got the inflation needle that came with the ball here. We cannot stress this enough—this is the finest example on earth, bar none. *LOA from PSA/DNA. LOA from James Spence Authentication.* Minimum Bid: $500

19854 **Early 1970's Bob Lilly Game Worn Jersey.** A number one draft choice of the new Cowboys' franchise during their second season in 1961, the TCU All-American went to play fourteen seasons in the Lone Star State, eleven of which were of Pro Bowl caliber. This late career representation exhibits solid wear from the Hall of Fame defensive lineman, particularly evident in the scuffing of the blue tackle twill identifiers and team repairs at the chest and shoulders. The unforgettable number "74" appears on chest, back and shoulders, where they straddle the line between mesh body and durene sleeves upon this tough "hybrid" style. "Lilly" is applied in blue tackle twill to a white satin twill plate across the shoulders. The Cowboys' local "Southland Athletic Mfg. Co." label appears inside collar, with size "48" flap tag affixed below. The package is tied up very neatly with the bow of a clearly vintage 7/10 blue marker inscription at the left end of the rear nameplate which reads, "To Bill from Bob Lilly #74 Cowboys." The player, the style, the wear and the first-person provenance delivered by the autograph conspire to make this a top-tier collectible for the cultured football jersey enthusiast. *LOA from Lou Lampson. LOA from PSA/DNA (autograph). LOA from James Spence Authentication (autograph).* **Minimum Bid: $2,000**

THE JOE MONTANA NOTRE DAME COLLECTION

The following lots were consigned to Heritage Auction Galleries by Joe Montana's first wife Kim, who had been his high school sweetheart and became Mrs. Montana during the future Hall of Famer's second semester at Notre Dame. The collection provides a first, intensely personal view of a young athlete quite different from the consummate field general who delivered four Super Bowl Championships to the people of San Francisco. Each lot will be accompanied by a letter of provenance from Kim Montana.

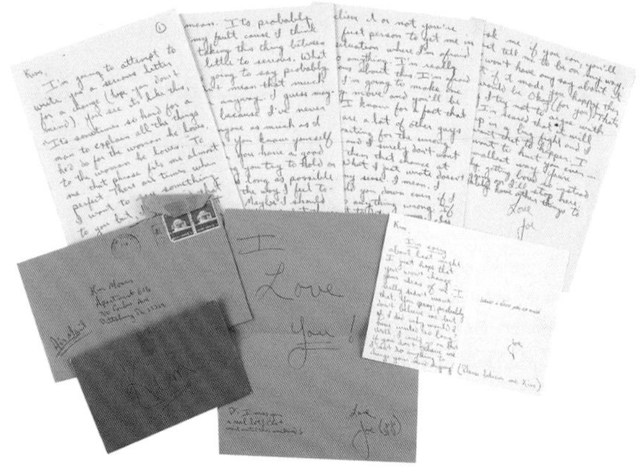

19855 **Early 1970's Joe Montana Handwritten Love Letters to Girlfriend Lot of 3.** Intensely personal handwritten correspondence from the Hall of Fame quarterback. 1) Brief note reads, "Guess What? I Love You! Love Joe (JoJo)." With mailing envelope. 2) Small card reads, in part, "I'm sorry about last night. I just hope that you won't change your ideas of me. I really don't want that..." Signed, "Joe." 3) Four-page letter reads, in part, "I guess maybe it's because I've never loved anyone as much as I love you. You know yourself that when you have a good thing going you try to hold on to it for as long as possible..." Signed, "Love, Joe." All ink is 10/10, and paper is likewise free of noteworthy flaws. **Minimum Bid: $500**

19856 **1973-74 Joe Montana Ringgold High School Memorabilia Collection.** The earliest Joe Montana sports collectibles known to exist, presented in one exciting lot. 1) Ringgold Rams football practice jersey. Tremendous wear, but fine, undamaged condition. Certainly the oldest Montana jersey ever to reach the hobby. 2) "Super Bowl of Prep Football Game" used quarterback towel. Notated in unknown hand, "Starting Q.B. Joe Mantana (sic), 'Big 33' Penn - 14 Ohio - 7, 8/10/74." 3) Program for this game at Hershey Stadium. EX-MT. 4) 1973 & 1974 prom photos (3) with future wife Kim. 4) Kim's prom purse. 5) Five personal snapshots of Joe, including one playing basketball, two playing baseball, and two horsing around in the snow. VG-EX. 6) Joe's official high school basketball portrait, with signed dedication to Kim on verso. 7) Various high school commencement paperwork including program, invitation. 8) Various newspaper clippings. 9) Photographic wooden die-cut of Joe posing in his high school basketball uniform. 13" tall. **Minimum Bid: $1,500**

THE UNIVERSITY OF NOTRE DAME
Awards to
JOSEPH C. MONTANA
A Grant-in-Aid covering
FULL - FOOTBALL

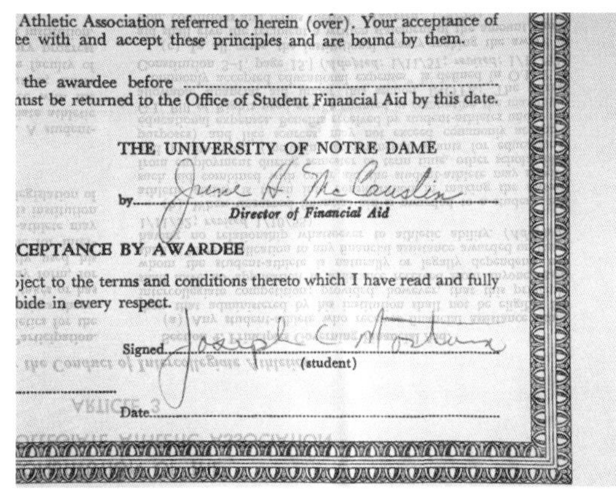

Athletic Association referred to herein (over). Your acceptance of
ee with and accept these principles and are bound by them.
the awardee before
must be returned to the Office of Student Financial Aid by this date.
THE UNIVERSITY OF NOTRE DAME
by *June H. McCauslin*
Director of Financial Aid
CEPTANCE BY AWARDEE
ject to the terms and conditions thereto which I have read and fully
bide in every respect.
Signed *Joseph C. Montana* (student)
Date

Montana going to Notre Dame

19857 **1974 Joe Montana Signed "Letter of Intent" to Attend Notre Dame University.** One of the most important documents in the long and glorious history of Notre Dame football is presented for the ultimate Fighting Irish fan, the paperwork that brought the future Hall of Fame quarterback Joe Montana to South Bend, Indiana. The standard 8.5x14" document begins with the earthshaking words "The University of Notre Dame Awards to Joseph C. Montana a Grant-in-Aid covering Full-Football for the Academic Year(s) 1975-76." The eighteen-year old phenom's full "Joseph C. Montana" autograph is a perfect 10/10 at the close. Included are several newspaper clippings with titles like "Notre Dame gets Montana of Ringgold" and "Montana Going to Notre Dame," each with photos of the long-haired youngster signing the paper we present here. Will one generous booster win this lot and donate it to the Notre Dame archives, earning their everlasting gratitude? Or will it end up in the private collection of the school's proudest alumnus? We'll have to wait for the gavel to fall for that answer. **Minimum Bid: $2,000**

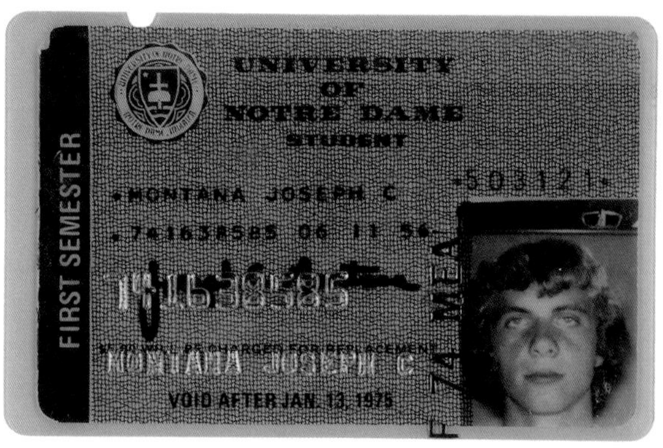

19858 **1974 Joe Montana Notre Dame Freshman Student I.D. Card.** We suspect that this top high school football prospect needed no introduction to most folks on the Notre Dame campus, but nonetheless he was issued this card just in case. His stamped name and reprinted signature join a small color photo of the curly-haired kid who would one day establish himself as one of the greatest quarterbacks in the history of the sport. Light wear from a "First Semester" in Joe's wallet, otherwise the card exhibits no flaws of note. **Minimum Bid: $400**

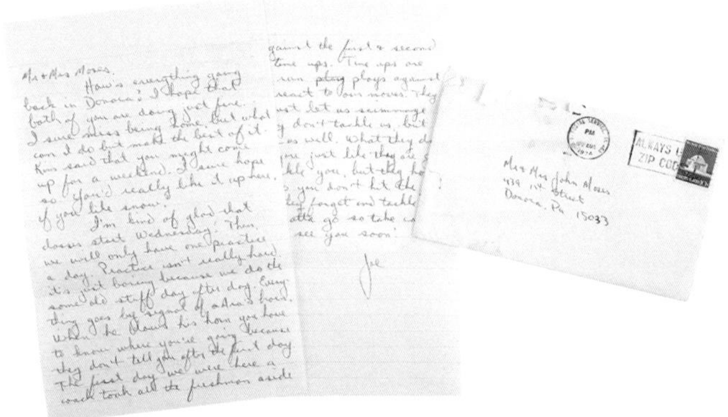

19859 **1974 Joe Montana Handwritten Signed Letter to Kim's Parents about First Notre Dame Football Experiences.** Fantastic three-page letter provides a fresh insight into the earliest days of this superstar's collegiate football career. He writes, in part, "...The first day we were here a coach took all the freshman aside and taught us how to do warm-up. Then he went through our daily work out. You have to memorize how it goes. Learning the plays was the hardest of all. The become a little confusing at first, but after a while everything falls into place. I'm doing pretty good now. We had two scrimmages and I did pretty good in both..." Closing is simply, "Joe." All ink is 10/10, and pages show original mailing folds but no other faults. Original mailing envelope, postmarked "26 Aug 1974," is included. *LOA from PSA/DNA. LOA from James Spence Authentication.* **Minimum Bid: $400**

19860 **1975 Joe Montana Wedding Artifacts Collection.** A rather sizeable collection of letters, cards, photographs and various other pieces saved by Joe's first bride, and offered here for the first time. 1) Joe's handwritten card to Kim hinting at his impending proposal. "...I did a lot of thinking today and I know for sure what I want to do..." Signed, "I love you, Joe." EX-MT. 2) Two-page handwritten letter from Joe discussing the preparations for the wedding. "...I think I want to have Clark as my best man and have Mark & J.J. as the other two. That's if Mark will be willing to leave Jeanie for awhile..." Signed, "I love you, Joe." EX-MT. 3) *What is Marriage?* book with many notations from Joe inside. The final page reads, "I just can't wait until everything is all over with and the day finally comes when I won't ever have to leave your side again, Love, Joe." EX-MT. 4) Wedding register with handwritten note from Joe and wedding napkins. 5) Marriage ceritificate. 6) Kim's bridal veil. 7) Dozens of photographs of the wedding, both snapshot and 8x10" size. 8) Three monogrammed handkerchiefs given to Kim by Joe. 9) Various wedding cards sent to the couple. 10) Newspaper clippings. **Minimum Bid: $500**

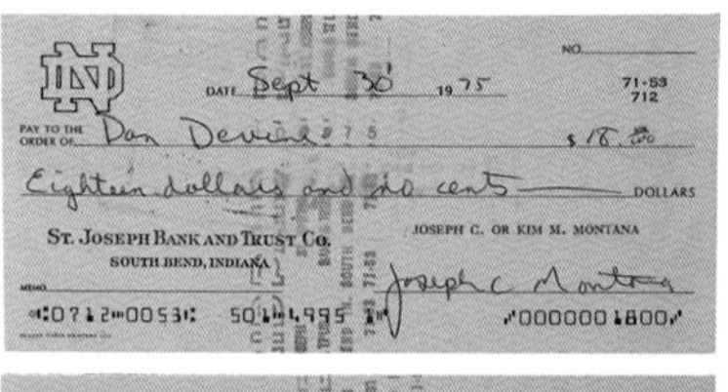

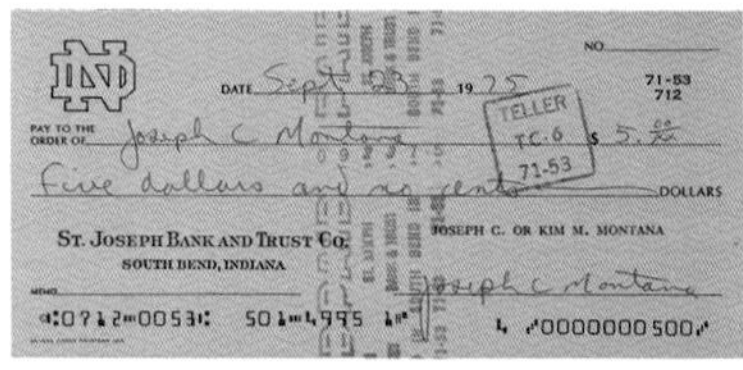

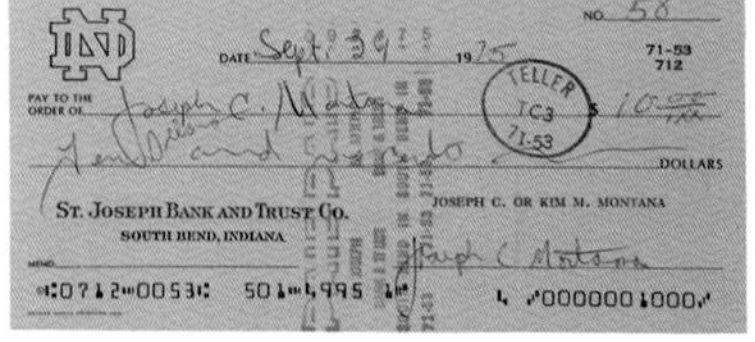

19861 **1975 Joe Montana Signed Checks Lot of 3.** Three checks drawn on Joe and Kim Montana's Notre Dame bank account are the most interesting from the collection. Two are triple-signed, used by Montana to draw cash from his account, and the third pays eighteen dollars to Notre Dame coach Dan Devine, who endorses the verso. Each is filled out entirely in the superstar quarterback's hand, and signed "Joseph C. Montana," seven such signatures in total. All are in flawless condition, with no folds, tears or other condition problems. One of several lots of checks offered within this auction. We are aware of no other Montana checks ever having surfaced in the hobby prior to this grouping. *LOA from PSA/DNA. LOA from James Spence Authentication.* **Minimum Bid: $400**

19862 **1975-76 Joe Montana Signed Checks/Deposit Slips Lot of 10.** Eight checks drawn on Joe and Kim Montana's Notre Dame bank account make payments to Thrifty Mart, the telephone company and the South Bend Medical Foundation. Each is filled out entirely in the superstar quarterback's hand, and signed "Joseph C. Montana" at the close. Two deposit slips for the same encount are similarly signed. All are in flawless condition, with no folds, tears or other condition problems. One of several lots of checks offered within this auction. We are aware of no other Montana checks ever having surfaced in the hobby prior to this grouping. *LOA from PSA/DNA. LOA from James Spence Authentication.* Minimum Bid: $750

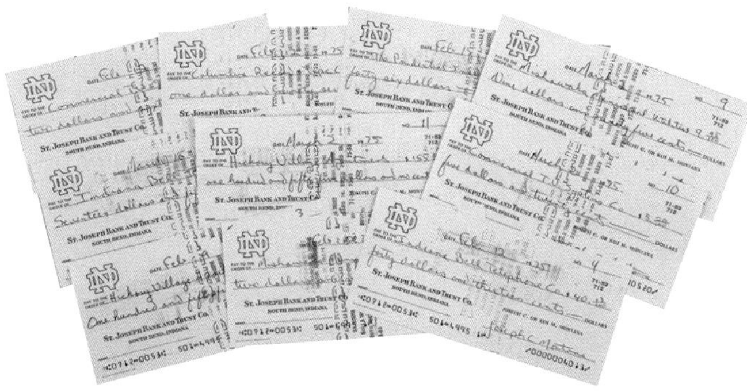

19863 **1975-76 Joe Montana Signed Checks Lot of 10.** Ten checks drawn on Joe and Kim Montana's Notre Dame bank account make payments to his apartment complex, Columbia Record & Tape Club, the telephone company and his apartment complex. Each is filled out entirely in the superstar quarterback's hand, and signed "Joseph C. Montana" at the close. All are in flawless condition, with no folds, tears or other condition problems. One of several lots of checks offered within this auction. We are aware of no other Montana checks ever having surfaced in the hobby prior to this grouping. *LOA from PSA/DNA. LOA from James Spence Authentication.* Minimum Bid: $750

19864 **1975-76 Joe Montana Signed Checks Lot of 10.** Ten checks drawn on Joe and Kim Montana's Notre Dame bank account make payments to his apartment complex, Columbia Record & Tape Club, the telephone company and a florist. Each is filled out entirely in the superstar quarterback's hand, and signed "Joseph C. Montana" at the close. All are in flawless condition, with no folds, tears or other condition problems. One of several lots of checks offered within this auction. We are aware of no other Montana checks ever having surfaced in the hobby prior to this grouping. *LOA from PSA/DNA. LOA from James Spence Authentication.* Minimum Bid: $750

19865 **1975-76 Joe Montana Signed Checks Lot of 10.** Ten checks drawn on Joe and Kim Montana's Notre Dame bank account make payments to his apartment complex, utilities and an animal hospital. Each is filled out entirely in the superstar quarterback's hand, and signed "Joseph C. Montana" at the close. All are in flawless condition, with no folds, tears or other condition problems. One of several lots of checks offered within this auction. We are aware of no other Montana checks ever having surfaced in the hobby prior to this grouping. *LOA from PSA/DNA. LOA from James Spence Authentication.* Minimum Bid: $750

19866 **Joe Montana Notre Dame Archive of Autographs, Programs, Etc.** Intriguing assortment of keepsakes and collectibles is comprised entirely of artifacts the young Montana felt compelled to save to recall personal gridiron highlights of his collegiate career. 1) High school helmet chinstrap. Fine wear. Notated "Joe 11/9/73," most likely in Kim's hand. 2) 1977 Cotton Bowl National Championship team signed football given to Kim by Joe. Panels are cracking but the 75+ autographs, including Joe's, remain strong. 3) Six (6) Notre Dame Football Guides (1967, 1969, 1971, 1972, 1973, 1978). Average EX-MT. 4) 1978 Notre Dame vs. Purdue program with Joe on cover, EX+. 5) 1977 Programs & Ticket Stubs for games vs. Michigan State & USC. EX average. 6) Joe's Notre Dame student laundry tag. 7) 1977 Notre Dame Football Review & 1978 Notre Dame Spring Football Prospectus. EX-MT average. 8) 1977 Notre Dame National Champ bumper sticker. EX-MT. 9) 1978 Cotton Bowl NCAA Championship ticket stub, VG-EX. 10) Three (3) "Kim Montana for Heiswoman" bumper stickers. EX. 11) Various other odds and ends. **Minimum Bid: $500**

19867 **Late 1970's Tony Hill Game Worn Jersey.** Blue durene beauty dates from the era of the first two of Hill's three Pro Bowl appearances, earned as one of Roger Staubach's favorite targets during some of the most productive years for the Dallas Cowboys franchise. Exhibiting fine wide receiver wear, with a large team repair at the chest, the classic gamer sports white tackle twill number "80" on chest, back and sleeves and local "Southland Athletic Mfg. Co." tagging inside the collar. Cloth flap tag has become disengaged, though the jersey measures out to the appropriate size 44 to 46. Name on back has been removed, a common occurrence for game jerseys reconditioned for a second life as a practice model. Our records show no other examples of Hill jerseys appearing in major auctions over the past eight years, so this should be seen as a rare opportunity for the Cowboy faithful. *LOA from Lou Lampson.* **Minimum Bid: $400**

19868 **1978-85 University of Nebraska Football Championship Rings Lot of 3.** Collection of three rings was awarded to a Cornhuskers staff member for the Big 8 powerhouse's winning ways. Featured are the following: 1) 1978 Big 8 Champions. "Walsh Coach" engraved on right shank. Engraved "Ursula Walsh" inside band. Size 7. 2) 1981 Big 8 Champions. "Walsh Staff" engraved on right shank. Size 7.5. 3) 1985 Sugar Bowl Champions. "Walsh" engraved on right shank. Size 6.5. Each is crafted by Balfour, and presents in fine, undamaged condition. An exciting find for the Husker alumni or enthusiast. **Minimum Bid: $750**

19869 **1982-83 University of Nebraska Football Championship Rings Lot of 3.** Trio of rings was awarded to a Cornhuskers staff member for the Big 8 juggernaut's winning ways. Featured are the following: 1) 1982 Big 8 Champions. "Walsh Staff" engraved on left shank. Size 8. 2) 1983 Orange Bowl Classic. No personalization. Size 7.5. 3) 1983 Big 8 Champions. "Walsh Staff" engraved on left shank. Size 6.5. Each is crafted by Balfour, and presents in fine, undamaged condition. An exciting find for the Husker alumni or enthusiast. **Minimum Bid: $750**

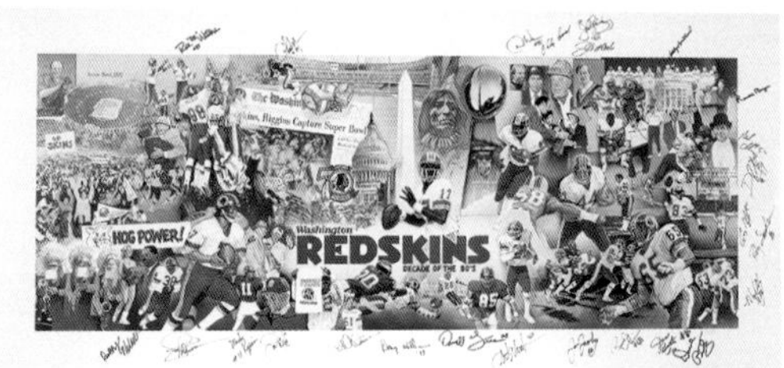

19870 **1980's Washington Redskins Signed Oversized Print with Ronald Reagan.** President Reagan fittingly highlights this impressive print celebrating football in the nation's capital during the Eighties, as there was surely no bigger name in that town than the Gipper. Joining him in 10/10 black sharpie are John Riggins, Jack Kent Cooke, Bobby Bethard, Ronald Reagan, Joe Jacoby, Russ Grimm, Art Monk, Darell Green, Joe Theisman, Bobby Mitchell, Joe Gibbs, Doug Williams and more. Twenty-five autographs are here in total, running the perimeter of the 28x61" print, which is mounted on a foam core backing for display. Massive and almost certainly one of a kind, this is a piece that should rise to the top of any true Redskins fan's want list. *LOA from PSA/DNA. LOA from James Spence Authentication.* **Minimum Bid: $600**

19871 **Mid-1980's Eric Dickerson Game Worn Jersey.** Early career gamer was worn by the standout running back from Southern Methodist University, the second overall pick in the 1983 NFL draft. Though wear is quite light for running back usage, it is certainly conceivable that the jersey saw some action during Dickerson's incredible 1984 season that shattered O.J. Simpson's 1973 rushing record of 2,003 yards by more than the length of a football field. The home blue mesh jersey provides classic Los Angeles Rams styling, with number "29" screened in bold yellow font to chest, sleeves and back, and "Dickerson" screened in white to rear nameplate. Huge yellow rams horns curl from rib cage to mid-sleeve, and Dickerson's customized "v" collar is present. Dual "Sand-Knit" labels express "Rams Exclusivity" and size "48" designations. An important rookie-era shirt from one of the most dynamic ball carriers in the history of the National Football League. *LOA from Lou Lampson.* **Minimum Bid: $1,000**

19872 **National Football League Alumni Ring.** Impressive for both its aesthetics and for the brotherhood it denotes, the offered ring was presented to quarterback Tom O'Malley, who saw a single game of action as Tobin Rote's back-up for the 1950 Green Bay Packers. Football imagery dominates the face, with a diamond-studded gold football set upon a blue stone, lined by the text, "National Football League Alumni." The left shank provides a chaotic action scene and the text "NFL Founded 1920," while the right offers a clever mode of identifying the ring as O'Malley's, with his name applied to the shoulders of a miniature player, and his number engraved on the back of that player's helmet. An "NFL Alumni" logo appears on the center of the jersey. Maker's mark "Jenkins 10K" appears inside the band, which measures out to a size twelve. An eye-catching keepsake, and a ring that rarely finds its way into the hobby. **Minimum Bid: $500**

19873 **Circa 1990 Joe Montana Game Worn Jersey.** Red mesh gamer dates from late in the Hall of Fame quarterback's tenure with the San Francisco 49'ers, which was likewise his most dominant age, as he closed out the 1989 season with a fifty-five to ten Super Bowl XXIV victory over the Denver Broncos, and cruised to a fourteen and two regular season record the following year. His unforgettable number "16" is applied in white tackle twill to chest, sleeves and verso, with "Montana" spelled in three-inch block across rear nameplate. Proper "Wilson [size] 46" tagging appears in left front tail. Wear is admittedly light, though this is the case for the vast majority of star jerseys (and particularly Montana's) emanating from the 49'ers franchise during this period, indicative of a single game's wear. Overall a perfectly acceptable representation of a gamer from the twilight of Montana's career by the Bay. *LOA from Lou Lampson.* **Minimum Bid: $750**

19874 **1998 Marshall Faulk Game Worn Jersey.** Road white mesh gamer is one of the last worn by this superstar running back in service to the Indianapolis Colts, as Faulk would be traded during the offseason for St. Louis Rams draft picks that the Colts would ultimately use to secure the services of Edgerrin James. This fantastic representation from one of the few players in NFL history to post both 10,000 rushing and 5,000 receiving yards illustrates the rough life of the professional ball carrier, with four team repairs, numeral scuffing and pilling of the spandex suffered in battle. Number "28" is applied to chest, back and sleeves in blue tackle twill, with "Faulk" in block across rear nameplate. "Logo Athletic NFL ProLine Authentic" label in tail finds "98" embroidered year swatch to the left and size "46" flap tag below. Faulk's March 2007 announcement of retirement has put collectors on notice that the supply of his gamers has ended, so now is the right time to invest in this seven-time Pro Bowler. *LOA from Lou Lampson.* **Minimum Bid: $500**

19875 **2000 Brett Favre Game Worn Jersey.** Though this guaranteed first ballot Hall of Famer has cried wolf in the past, few doubt that his retirement proclamations this time around are going to stick. So it's a very safe bet that the Packers won't be making any more of these, and there will never be a better time than the present to secure a Favre gamer in your collection. The offered green mesh representation dates to a campaign that saw the NFL career leader for completions, passing yards and passing touchdowns lead the Pack to a nine and seven record while adding 3,800+ yards and twenty touchdowns to his world-beating lifetime totals. Wear is light but definite, indicative of a single game of quarterback use. The soon-to-be-retired number "4" appears in white tackle twill on chest, back and shoulders, with "Favre" applied in three-inch block to rear nameplate. Wide-mouth sleeves are lightly elasticized to Favre's preferences. Collar holds year/size "00-48" tagging, and the "100% Nylon" tag at the interior side seam denotes local "Berlin, WI" manufacturing. A 10/10 black sharpie signature on the rear numeral wraps up the package, and bears a holographic authenticating sticker from Favre's personal marketing company. *LOA from Lou Lampson. LOA from PSA/DNA (autograph). LOA from James Spence Authentication (autograph).* Minimum Bid: $1,000

19876 **2000 Donovan McNabb Game Worn Jersey.** The Syracuse standout recorded a true "breakout" season in his second NFL season, passing for over 3,300 yards and rushing for over 600 more while leading his Philadelphia Eagles to an eleven and five wild card playoff berth. This white mesh gamer exhibits fantastic quarterback wear from the season that put the National Football League on notice, with some nice contact marks at the shoulders at chest. Number "5" is applied to chest, shoulders and back in green and black tackle twill, with "McNabb" spanning the rear dazzle cloth nameplate. Logo birds screech at each sleeve. The cuffed sleeves are unusual for a quarterback, but videotape does show that McNabb favored this style in 2000. Interior collar holds "00-50" year/size tagging, and the "Puma/NFL" label in the tail holds correct size "50" and "6" L.B." flap tags at right. A black sharpie signature on the rear numeral "5" does not contrast particularly well against the dark background but rates a technical 9+/10. One of the finest McNabb representations on the market today. *LOA from Lou Lampson. LOA from PSA/DNA (autograph). LOA from James Spence Authentication (autograph).* Minimum Bid: $600

19877 **2002 Steve McNair Game Worn Jersey.** The star quarterback for the Tennessee Titans led his team all the way to the AFC Championship Game this year, posting an impressive eleven and five regular season record en route to the playoffs. This white mesh gamer exhibits terrific wear from that campaign, remaining in its unlaundered state after seeing its hard-hitting NFL action. McNair's number "9" is applied in two tones of blue tackle twill to chest, back and shoulders, with the name on back appearing in navy block. Team logo patches are found at each sleeve above the wide uncuffed quarterback sleeve openings. Heavy customizations in the tail region feature elasticized hemming and velcro patches to keep the shirt tucked tight, sacrificing manufacturer's labelling in the process. Year/size tagging inside collar reads, "02-54." A fine, dirty specimen from a memorable season down south. *LOA from Lou Lampson.* **Minimum Bid: $600**

19878 **2003-04 Cedric Benson Game Worn Jersey.** Often compared to Ricky Williams for his running style, college choice and distinctive dreadlocks, Benson finds himself second only to Williams in the University of Texas rushing record books with 5,540 yards over his four seasons of Longhorns service. This classic white mesh gamer shows solid running back wear, with a nice assortment of team repairs criss-crossing the dazzle cloth shoulders. "Texas 32" is properly screened upon the chest, which likewise bears patches of the Big Twelve and Nike logo. "Benson 32" is screened upon verso, with the number "32" repeated upon each sleeve. The jersey features quality customization which further augments its authenticity. First, the side panels are custom hemmed from underarm seam to tail and provide a more snug fit. Secondly, the tail is hemmed to reduce extra length often noticeable in shots of Benson when his shirt tail hangs out. The inner collar has the correct "Nike [size] 48" label. In short, a fine representation from one of the most prolific ball carriers in Longhorns history. *LOA from Lou Lampson.* **Minimum Bid: $750**

19879 **2005 Texas Longhorns Game Used Football Signed by Vince Young.** Registering one of the most brilliant and heroic individual performances in NCAA history to lead the underdog Horns to the National Championship with a Rose Bowl victory over the heavily-favored USC Trojans, quarterback Vince Young joined the likes of Sam Houston and Davey Crockett as one of the Lone Star State's most adored immortals. Here we present a ball used during that glorious season, signed in 9/10 silver sharpie by Young, who adds the notation "Game Used." Acquired from a source within the UT athletic department. *LOA from PSA/DNA. LOA from James Spence Authentication.* Minimum Bid: $300

19880 **2005 Ramonce Taylor Game Worn Jersey.** Burnt orange gamer was worn by the Texas Longhorns star running back during the glorious NCAA Championship season, a fact assured by the number "11" screened on front, back and shoulders, as 2005 was the only year Taylor would sport the digits. "Texas" and "R. Taylor" balance the design on front and back. Big Twelve and Nike patches adorn the upper right and left chest respectively. Taylor's twelve rushing and three receiving touchdowns this season made him a key factor in the drive to destiny that culminated in the thrilling upset over the heavily favored USC Trojans in the 2006 Rose Bowl. The shoulder and sleeve areas show dings and minor turf paint remnants, speaking to the moderate but entirely acceptable wear. A special keepsake of a season no UT fan will soon forget. *LOA from Lou Lampson.* Minimum Bid: $300

19881 **2005 Vince Young Game Worn Cleats.** Size 13.5 black Nike cleats opened the glorious NCAA Championship season in a sixty to three nail-biter of a University of Texas victory over Louisiana-Lafayette at Darrel K. Royal-Texas Memorial Stadium. This first of thirteen consecutive victories culminating with the thrilling Rose Bowl upset over the heavily-favored USC Trojans saw Young toss three touchdowns and run for another in a first hint of great things to come this season. The cleats show appropriate single-game wear, with each signed in 10/10 silver sharpie at the toes with "Game Used 9-3-05" notations. Acquired from a source within the Longhorns football program. *LOA from Lou Lampson. LOA from PSA/DNA (autograph). LOA from James Spence Authentication (autograph).* Minimum Bid: $400

19882 **2005 Roy Williams Game Worn Jersey.** Considered one of the finest safeties in the National Football League, this number eight overall pick in the 2002 draft was able to prowl closer to the line of scrimmage in 2005 due to Anthony Henry's stabilization of the right cornerback position, allowing Williams to record two and a half sacks to go along with his three interceptions. This white mesh gamer from Williams' third Pro Bowl season exhibits great overall wear, with contact scrapes on the white dazzle cloth shoulders and dirt marks throughout. Number "31" is applied in royal blue tackle twill to chest, back and shoulders, with "R. Williams" spanning the rear nameplate in bold block lettering. "Reebok [size] 48" tagging is found at front left tail, with "05-48" year/size swatch joining Prova Group's authenticating serialized stickering below. Incidentally, Williams has announced he will switch to his old college number "38" for the 2008 season, making the offered jersey all the more appealing. *LOA from Lou Lampson.* Minimum Bid: $400

19883 **2006 Chris Canty Game Worn Throwback Uniform.** Tons of dirty, sweaty wear tells the story of fierce battles of the line of scrimmage for this star Dallas Cowboys defensive end. Canty's number "99" and surname are applied in bold tackle twill to the mesh and dazzle cloth jersey, which sports "05-48" label inside collar and "Reebok" label in left front tail with "6" L.B." and "48" flap tags at right. Matching pants have number "99" in marker on interior waistband, and "Reebok" label with "42" and "S. INS." flap tags affixed. "04" year label sewn in waistband. Unbeatable provenance is delivered in the form of "Game Exclusives" paperwork, signed by the vice president of the Cowboys' merchandising department. *LOA from Game Exclusives. LOA from Lou Lampson.* Minimum Bid: $300

19884 **2006 Limas Sweed Game Worn Jersey.** His size, strength and soft hands make him one of the most highly touted wide receiver prospects entering the 2008 NFL draft, and established him as the favorite target for Colt McCoy the season he wore this white mesh Texas Longhorns gamer. Classic burnt orange identifiers announcing "Texas 4" on the chest and "Sweed 4" on verso are properly screened in place, as are the number "4" and double striping at each sleeve. Big Twelve and Nike patches rest high at right and left chest respectively. Sweed's personal customizations are present in the side panel hemming that tightens the fit, and the hemming of the tail to reduce the length, each furthering the authenticity of the garment. Wear is light but acceptable for the wide receiver position. A high-quality "star" jersey from one of college footballs most storied programs. *LOA from Lou Lampson.* Minimum Bid: $500

End of Auction